MONETARY POLICY IN DEVELOPED ECONOMIES

Handbook of Comparative Economic Policies

1. National Economic Policies
   Dominick Salvatore, editor
2. National Trade Policies
   Dominick Salvatore, editor
3. Monetary Policy in Developed Economies
   Michele U. Fratianni and Dominick Salvatore, editors

MONETARY POLICY IN DEVELOPED ECONOMIES

EDITED BY
MICHELE U. FRATIANNI
AND
DOMINICK SALVATORE

HANDBOOK OF COMPARATIVE ECONOMIC POLICIES
VOLUME 3

GREENWOOD PRESS
Westport, Connecticut • London

Library of Congress Cataloging-in-Publication Data

Monetary policy in developed economies / edited by Michele U.
Fratianni and Dominick Salvatore.
    p.   cm.—(Handbook of comparative economic policies, ISSN
1054–7681 ; v. 3)
    Includes bibliographical references and indexes.
    ISBN 0–313–26869–X (alk. paper)
    1. Monetary policy.   I. Fratianni, Michele.   II. Salvatore,
Dominick.   III. Series.
HG230.3.M6375   1993
332.4'91722—dc20   92–4886

British Library Cataloguing in Publication Data is available.

Library of Congress Catalog Card Number: 92–4886
ISBN: 0–313–26869–X
ISSN: 1054–7681

First published in 1993

Publisher and sole distributor for the U.S.A. and Canada:
Greenwood Press, 88 Post Road West, Westport, CT 06881
An imprint of Greenwood Publishing Group, Inc.

Sole distributor outside the U.S.A. and Canada:
ELSEVIER SCIENCE PUBLISHERS, B.V.
P.O. Box 1991
1000 BZ Amsterdam
The Netherlands

Printed in the United States of America

The paper used in this book complies with the
Permanent Paper Standard issued by the National
Information Standards Organization (Z39.48–1984).

10   9   8   7   6   5   4   3   2   1

CONTENTS

Illustrations   vii

Preface   xiii

1. Introduction   1
   Michele U. Fratianni and *Dominick Salvatore*

Part I: Major Issues

2. Monetary Policy and the Money Supply Process   25
   Robert H. Rasche

3. Monetary Policy and Economic Activity   55
   Richard T. Froyen

4. Monetary Policy and Inflation   93
   Eduard J. Bomhoff

5. Monetary Policy and Reputation   125
   Keith Blackburn

6. Monetary Policy and Bank Regulation   165
   Anthony M. Santomero

Part II: U.S. Monetary Policy

7. The U.S. Central Banking Experience: A Historical
   Perspective   195
   Elmus Wicker

8. The Conduct of U.S. Monetary Policy   245
    Raymond E. Lombra

Part III: Monetary Policy in the Other G-7 Countries

9. Germany   299
    Manfred J. M. Neumann and *Jürgen von Hagen*

10. France   335
    Jacques Mélitz

11. Italy   371
    Franco Spinelli and *Patrizio Tirelli*

12. The United Kingdom   405
    Patrick Minford

13. Japan   433
    Shinichi Ichimura

14. Canada   459
    Peter W. Howitt

15. Monetary Policy Coordination in the European
    Monetary System   509
    Jürgen von Hagen

    Selected Bibliography   561

    Index   565

    About the Contributors   571

ILLUSTRATIONS

FIGURES

2.1   Growth Rate of Monetary Base Measures 59:2–90:3   36

6.1   The General Equilibrium of the Economy in $[r_E P]$ Space from Equations (21) and (22)   180

8.1   The Basics of the Policy Process   249

8.2   The Fed's View of the Transmission Mechanism for Monetary Policy   250

8.3   Economic Effects of an Increase in Money: Simulated Responses with the Fed's Version of the MPS Model of the United States   252

8.4   Stages and Linkages in the Formulation of Monetary Policy   256

8.5   Hypothetical Bluebook Menu of Longer Run (Year Ahead) Policy Options   259

8.6   The Skeletal Structure of the Fed Staff's Money Market Model   260

8.7   Hypothetical Bluebook Menu of Short-Run (Quarterly) Policy Options   261

8.8   1990 Monetary Policy Objectives: The Fed's July 18, 1990, Report to Congress   263

8.9   Formulating Monetary Policy: The Analytical Linkages   266

8.10   The Fed's Provision of Nonborrowed Reserves and "Reserve Conditions"   270

8.11   Fed Accommodation: How Does the Supply of Reserves and Money Come to Be Perfectly Elastic (at least in the short run)   273

8.12   Fed Flexibility and the Use of Information/Indicator Variables in the Actual Implementation of Monetary Policy   275

8.13   The Typical Fed Response to Deviations of Money Growth from Target Under the Federal Funds Rate Operating Procedure   276

8.14   The Automatic Response of the Federal Funds Rate to Deviations of Money Growth from Target Under the Nonborrowed Reserves Operating Procedures   279

9.1   Contributions of Excess Inflation and Changes in the External Value of the DM to Deviations from the Monetary Target, 1979–89   314

9.2   The Bundesbank's Net Dollar Reserves and Value of DM Against the U.S. Dollar, 1978–89   325

10.1   The Transmission Mechanism   356

10.2   Real Interest Rates on Government Bonds   361

11.1   Output Growth and Inflation   373

11.2   Wage Inflation and Unemployment   374

11.3   Monetary Base and the Money Supply   375

11.4   Nominal Exchange Rate Vis-à-Vis the U.S. Dollar, 1970–79   376

11.5   Nominal and Real Effective Exchange Rates, 1980–89   377

11.6   Public Deficits   378

11.7   Seigniorage   379

11.8   Public Debt, 1970–89   380

11.9   Nominal and Real Interest Rates   381

11.10 Domestic and Foreign Creation of the Monetary Base, 1980–89   388

12.1   RPI Inflation, All Items   406

12.2   PSBR/Nominal GDP   407

12.3   The Medium-Term Financial Strategy and Sterling M3   409

12.4   The Medium-Term Financial Strategy and the PSBR   410

12.5   M4 Growth   410

12.6	M0 Growth	411
12.7	Real GDP Growth	412
12.8	NRS, Treasury Bill Rate	413
12.9	NRL, Long-Term Government Bond Yield	414
12.10	Shock Tactics Simulation: Inflation	416
12.11	Shock Tactics Simulation: GDP Growth	417
12.12	Shock Tactics Simulation: Unemployment	417
12.13	Excess Money Supply Growth	420
12.14	Inflation of the United Kingdom and Industrialized Countries	421
12.15	Real Exchange Rate	422
12.16	Domestic Credit Expansion	423
13.1	The Japanese Financial System	437
13.2	Sectoral Excess or Shortage of Funds	447
13.3	Money Supply and GNP	453
14.1	90 Days Treasury Bill Rate, 1954–62	480
14.2	Exchange Rate (U.S. Cents/Canadian Dollar), 1954–62	480
14.3	Percentage Change in M1 from Four Quarters Earlier, 1954–62	481
14.4	Percentage Change in Money from Four Quarters Earlier, 1961–75	483
14.5	90 Days Treasury Bill Rate, 1961–75	484
14.6	Exchange Rate (U.S. Cents/Canadian Dollar), 1961–75	485
14.7	CPI/Inflation Rate (Percentage), 1961–75	486
14.8	Percentage Change in Money from Four Quarters Earlier, 1975–90	487
14.9	CPI/Inflation Rate (Percentage), 1975–90	488
14.10	Canadian Dollar Index Against G10 Currencies, 1975–90	489
14.11	90 Days Treasury Bill Rate, 1975–90	490

TABLES

1.1	The Rate of Inflation in Seven Industrialized Countries	3
1.2	Relative Contributions to the Growth of the Monetary Base, 1980–87	4

2.1	Typical Balance Sheet of a Central Bank	27
4.1	Forecast Errors of Velocity	116
7.1	Annualized Average Monthly Growth Rates of M1 and M2 at Six-Month Intervals During the 1923–24 and 1926–27 Recessions	207
7.2	Bond Purchase Fund Acquisitions at Par Value, April 4, 1918–January 31, 1919	215
7.3	Excess Reserves of Member Banks, Monetary Gold Stock, U.S. Government Securities Held in Special Open Market Investment Account, Annually, 1929–37	217
7.4	Liquidation of Government Securities, Direct and Guaranteed, by Select New York City Banks, July 1, 1936–April 7, 1937	221
9.1	CPI Inflation Rates in the Main Industrialized Countries	300
9.2	Monetary Targets, Inflation, and the External Value of the Deutsche Mark, 1979–89	312
9.3	Main Sources of Central Bank Money, 1978–89	315
9.4	Contributions to Monetary Base Growth and Variability, 1986–89	322
9.5	Estimates of the Bundesbank's Degree of Sterilization	328
10.1	Basic French Statistics	342
11.1	The Balance of Payments, 1950–69	382
11.2	The Balance of Payments, 1970–80	385
11.3	Total Domestic Credit Expansion, 1974–80	387
11.4	Credit and Monetary Aggregates, 1984–89	391
11.5	The Balance of Payments, 1980–89	391
13.1	Japan's Long-Term Capital Account	442
13.2	Net External Assets or Liabilities	443
13.3A	Major Markets of Foreign Exchange	444
13.3B	Market Size of the World Stock Exchanges, 1988	444
13.4	Assets of Financial Intermediaries, 1987–end	445
13.5	Foreign Currencies in Official Reserves	445
13.6	Financial Assets by Three Economic Sectors	448
13.7	Transition of Government Bonds Issued	449
14.1	Bank of Canada Balance Sheet as of December 31, 1989	473

14.2	Correlation Between Cyclical Movements in Real GNP in Quarter t and M2 in Quarter $t + k$, over the Period 1968:II to 1990:III	496
15.1	CPI Inflation Rates, EMS and Non-EMS Countries	519
15.2	Growth Rates of Real GDP	520
15.3	Unemployment Rates	521
15.4	Average DM—Exchange Rate Changes	523
15.5	A Model of Policymaking in the EMS	524
15.6	Results of German Dominance Tests	544
15.7	Responses to Unit Interest-Rate Innovations, 1979–83	548
15.8	Decomposition of Interest-Rate Changes	550

PREFACE

The present volume is the third in a series of comparative economic handbooks. It presents an overview and comparison of monetary policies in the United States and in the world's leading industrial countries. Volume 1 presented an overview of national economic policies, whereas Volume 2 presented an overview of national trade policies. Future volumes will deal with fiscal, economic development, tax, and environmental policies.

Monetary policy is one of the most powerful instruments at the disposal of the monetary authorities of a nation that can be used to avoid or overcome problems of inflation and unemployment, and to promote long-term economic growth. However, many questions and controversies regarding the theory and practice of monetary policy both in the United States and abroad remain unresolved.

This volume seeks to examine the theory and practice of monetary policy in the United States and in the world's leading industrial or G-7 countries (the United States, Germany, France, the United Kingdom, Italy, Japan, and Canada). A comparative study of monetary policies in the world's leading countries is extremely important, not only for the specific knowledge that it provides on monetary policies in each country, but also and more important because of the light it can shed on the practice and effectiveness of monetary policies under the different institutional arrangements existing in each country. Furthermore, in a world that is daily growing more and more interdependent, monetary policies in each of the leading countries have important repercussions on all other countries. No volume on the market today presents such an in-depth, up-to-date, and exhaustive comparative study.

After an introductory chapter by the editors, the volume is divided into three parts. Part I (chapters 2 to 6) presents the major issues in the theory and practice of monetary policy. It deals with monetary policy and the money supply process, economic activity, inflation, reputation, and bank regulation. Part II (chapters 7 and 8) deals with monetary policy in the United States. Specifically, Chapter 7 presents an historical perspective of monetary policy in the United States, whereas Chapter 8 examines the more recent experience in U.S. monetary policy during the 1980s and up to the very present. Part III (chapters 9 to 15) examines monetary policy in each of the other six G-7 countries (Germany, France, Italy, the United Kingdom, Japan, and Canada), as well as monetary policy coordination in the European Monetary System (EMS).

The chapters in this volume have been written by some of the world's most renowned experts in the field of monetary economics and presents the most comprehensive and current comparative study of such policies on the market today. Thus, the handbook can be of great use to students of monetary economics in general and to economists, policymakers, and the general informed public as a very useful source of reference and comparison. The references at the end of each chapter and the selected bibliography at the end of the volume identify the most important sources of additional information and detail about monetary policies in the world's leading industrial countries.

1

INTRODUCTION

Michele U. Fratianni and Dominick Salvatore

THE MAIN ISSUES

The history of monetary policy theory—or, more precisely, how monetary policy actions affect prices and output—has had ups and downs of its own. After World War II academic economists paid virtually no attention to the subject. The policy discussion reflected such a neglect: fiscal policy and fiscal measures were at center stage. Simply put, money did not matter. The orthodox Keynesian model had relegated monetary policy to a *curiosum*. The reawakening in monetary matters owes a great deal to the Chicago school led by Milton Friedman (Friedman, 1956, 1959; Friedman and Meiselman, 1963; Friedman and Schwartz, 1963). Once again monetary policy became a respectable subject—so much so that the pendulum of ideas moved drastically against fiscal policy and in favor of monetary policy. In other words, the issue among academic economists became whether money alone mattered for changes in nominal income.

Reflecting the mood of the times, Karl Brunner in 1968 coined the term *monetarism* in an article published in the Federal Reserve Bank of St. Louis *Review* (Brunner, 1968). In this work, drawing also from his own work with Allan Meltzer, Brunner set forth the monetarist thesis. The three basic propositions of the thesis are that (1) the actions of the monetary authority dominate the growth of the monetary base, (2) the growth of the monetary base dominates the growth of the money stock over the business cycle, and (3) accelerations and decelerations of the money stock are closely followed by cyclical expansions and contractions of output. To these three propositions Brunner and Meltzer (1989, Chap. 1) would add that (4) money growth tends to behave procyclically (at least for the United States), (5) velocity growth also tends to behave procyclically (at least for the United

States), (6) permanent money growth in excess of output growth is a sufficient condition for inflation, and (7) discretionary monetary policy aggravates the business cycle and, hence, is a source of additional uncertainty in the economic system.

In a world of rational expectations, discretionary monetary policy can be suboptimal. At any point in time, the monetary authority can rightfully consider that the growth rate of the money supply expected by the private sector is given. On the basis of this consideration, it can generate a monetary surprise that would alter the combination between inflation and unemployment. But this action does not go unnoticed by the private sector which will consider it, not an isolated event, but part of a policy process. Expectations will be revised upward and the system will settle with a higher inflation rate, without having altered the average output growth rate of the economy. This is the problem of time consistency brought out by Kydland and Prescott (1977). A rule, that is, a stable process, would do better in the sense that it would yield a higher expected utility to the private sector.

But rules, in the form of firm commitments to ex-ante low-inflation policies, cannot be enforced in the absence of a mechanism that would punish the central bank—or, better, the central banker—whenever it deviates from such a rule. The nonenforceability of policy commitments is at the root of the inflation bias (Barro and Gordon, 1983). In sum, (8) although rules are better than discretion, it is necessary to find an institutional mechanism to render rule-making feasible.

One way to remedy the noted institutional deficiency is for central banks with low credibility to delegate policymaking authority to central banks that have a high degree of credibility. This delegation can be executed by having the central bank that generates high inflation peg the rate of exchange to the currency issued by a central bank that generates low inflation. This is one interpretation of the European Monetary System (EMS). High-inflation Italy pegs the Italian lira to the Deutsche mark because the Bank of Italy wishes to borrow credibility from the Bundesbank. This argument raises two obvious questions. First, why can the Bank of Italy precommit itself to an exchange-rate rule and not to a money-growth rule? The second question is what does the high-credibility Bundesbank gain from the arrangement?

A more fundamental way to resolve the impasse that low credibility creates is to ask what institutional reform may be required to make the commitment to low inflation credible, for example, the formation of a central bank independent from government. The aspect of institution-building goes at the heart of what the European Community is doing these days in bringing about monetary union in Europe.

To put the credibility problem in a quantitative perspective, Table 1.1 reviews the inflation performance of the seven most industrialized coun-

Table 1.1
The Rate of Inflation in Seven Industrialized Countries

The seventies			The eighties		
Germany	5.0	(1.4)	Japan	1.7	(1.3)
US	7.3	(2.3)	Germany	2.6	(1.9)
Canada	7.5	(2.7)	US	4.6	(1.9)
Japan	8.7	(5.0)	Canada	5.5	(2.8)
France	9.9	(2.9)	UK	5.8	(2.3)
UK	12.6	(6.5)	France	6.2	(4.0)
Italy	14.7	(5.4)	Italy	9.8	(5.2)

Source: OECD, *Economic Outlook*, data diskettes no. 41 and no. 48.

Notes: The first numbers are annual percentage changes in the consumption deflator, while the numbers in parentheses refer to the sample standard deviation. The 1970s cover the period 1971–80 and the 1980s, 1981–90.

tries, whose monetary policy is analyzed in this handbook, during the 1970s and the 1980s. The data show a wide dispersion of outcomes, suggesting that the seven central banks had different abilities or inclinations to affect inflation. There is also an apparent positive correlation between institutional and personal independence and inflation performance. The country chapters of the book reveal that the banks in Italy, France, and the United Kingdom are institutions closely bound to the government, whereas German, U.S., and Japanese banks enjoy a high degree of independence. Canada, on the other hand, provides an interesting example of a central bank that, on paper, is totally dependent on government but in practice is not. This evidence is roughly in agreement with previous work in the area that has ranked the Bundesbank as the most independent central bank; the Federal Reserve System and the Bank of Japan a notch below; the Bank of Canada, the Bank of England, and the Banque de France a further notch below; and, finally, the Banca d'Italia the least independent central bank in the G-7 group (Alesina, 1989; Bade and Parkin, 1987).

Additional evidence on central bank independence can be gleaned from Table 1.2 which reports the relative contributions of the main source components of the monetary base to the growth of the monetary base over the period 1980–87. Column two of this table quantifies the ratio of the average growth of the monetary base attributable to direct government finance to the average growth of the total monetary base. Since this ratio reflects the direct or indirect recourse of the Treasury to the "printing press," it can be interpreted as an index of central bank independence. The very low independence ranking of the Banca d'Italia is confirmed by the data: the automatic access the Treasury had with the Banca d'Italia accounted for over 100 percent of the growth of the monetary base from 1980 to 1987. The data also confirm the discrepancy between form and practice insofar

Table 1.2

Relative Contributions to the Growth of the Monetary Base, 1980–87

Countries	(1) Foreign Component	(2) Govt Finance	(3) Market Operations	(4) Bank Lending	(5) Other sources
US	0.00	-0.04	0.93	0.00	0.11
Japan	0.22	0.49	0.42	0.20	-0.33
Germany	-0.11	0.07	0.49	-0.07	0.62
France	0.61	-0.13	0.42	-0.04	0.14
Italy	0.02	1.04	0.03	0.00	-0.09
UK	0.71	-2.57	2.08	0.00	0.77
Canada	0.01	-0.03	1.02	0.13	-0.13

Source: Kneeshaw and Van den Bergh (1989), p. 16.

as the Bank of Canada is concerned, namely, that this Bank is much more independent than the statutes indicate. Altogether four countries had negative growth in the government finance ratios—meaning that government served as net lender rather than net borrower. This is an indication of the size of the investment in central bank independence credibility achieved in the 1980s. What is surprising is that the highly regarded Bank of Japan heavily financed the Treasury.

The data roughly conform to the notion that a central bank that is removed from political pressure is better able to control inflation than one that takes instructions from government. The weak central banks—that is, the central banks with the highest degree of government dependence—display a higher trend inflation rate than the strong central banks. The data also reveal that inflation performance greatly improved in the 1980s relative to the 1970s; moreover, not only trend inflation but also its variability has fallen. It may well be that the economic conditions of the 1980s were easier for monetary policymakers than the shock-ridden 1970s. However, there is evidence that central bankers learned the lessons of the 1970s and became disenchanted with activist demand management that delivered high and variable inflation rates. In this sense, the seven central banks under review built credibility and were rewarded by falling rates of inflation. This result holds just as well for the three EMS central banks—Germany, France, and Italy—as for the four non-EMS central banks, suggesting that credibility is not a prerogative of fixed exchange rates.

The downward shift in trend inflation has been accompanied by a fairly uniform change in the way monetary policy has been conducted. In the 1980s all seven central banks used a monetary aggregate as an intermediate target, or at least announced adherence to the target. For example, in the 1989–90 period, the United Kingdom targeted the monetary base (officially called M0), Canada the narrow definition of money (M1), and the other five countries broader definitions of money (Federal Reserve Bank of St. Louis, 1990).

Another common feature among the seven central banks is the large reliance they place on money-market interest rates as operating targets. Given a stable demand for the monetary base, the monetary authority can obtain a desired level of the monetary base supply by setting an appropriate short-term interest rate. Changes in interest rates, in turn, are affected by specific policy actions such as open market or interbank operations, interventions in the foreign exchange market, bank lending, changes in reserve requirements ratios, and so on. It is clear from Table 1.2 that the preferred monetary policy instrument of the 1980s in the G-7 group has been open market or interbank operations (column 3), whereas the use of the "discount window" has declined (column 4). The table also indicates the relative importance of the foreign component (column 1), which reflects the exchange-rate regime adopted by the country. Not surprisingly, the United States and Canada show a zero contribution, whereas the EMS countries have sizable contributions. The United Kingdom, though not part of the exchange-rate mechanism of the EMS, turns out to have heavily intervened in the foreign exchange market.

An operating procedure centered on money-market interest rates has a bias in favor of interest-rate smoothing. The monetary authorities resist interest-rate volatility partly because they are pressured from the public and the government. Interest rates are continuously observed variables and directly influence investment and portfolio decisions; the money supply, calculated at fixed intervals, does not directly enter the individuals' maximization calculus. Hence, it is not surprising that individuals and groups react forcefully and negatively to interest-rate volatility. Yet, despite the aversion to large interest-rate volatility, the central bankers of the 1980s have permitted the interest rate to adjust to new market conditions more speedily than in the past (Batten et al., 1990, p. 31). These changes have been particularly pronounced for the Banque de France, the Banca d'Italia, and the Bank of Japan which had a tradition of employing quantitative credit controls of one type or another to determine the stock of the monetary base.

SUMMARY OF THE CHAPTERS

The first five chapters of the handbook deal with major issues of monetary policy, including standard models, reputational considerations, and the effect of the regulatory environment on the effectiveness of monetary policy. In Chapter 2, Robert H. Rasche surveys the process by which central bank actions affect the stock of money. By using the base money multiplier as a framework of analysis, he studies how portfolio decisions of depository institutions, private households, and nonfinancial firms influence the transmission of changes in base money to changes in the stock of transactions money. The structure of the reserve requirement system, the ratio of depository institutions' excess reserves to total assets, and the adjustments of currency and time deposit holdings relative to holdings of demand deposits affect the money multiplier. However, the principal force underlying money growth over the long run is base money growth. An important theme of this chapter is that money growth is controllable by the Fed. The sources of forecast errors of money growth can be traced either to factors influencing the monetary base, which are beyond the control of the Fed, or to imperfectly predictable movements of the money multiplier. The Fed can easily offset unwanted changes in the monetary base. As to the multiplier, Rasche concludes that relatively low forecast errors can be obtained either by forecasting the multiplier as a whole, using time-series models, or by forecasting each of the component ratios entering the multiplier. Available evidence from time series and studies of individual asset demand functions suggests that the interest and income elasticities of currency and time deposit holdings relative to demand deposit holdings are small, particularly in the short run. Thus, even with the large elasticities of the base multiplier to currency and time deposit components, policy-induced interest-rate and income changes will not be a significant source of variation in the money stock. In sum, income changes can be controlled to an acceptable degree.

In Chapter 3, Richard T. Froyen reviews the issue of the neutrality of money and its implications for the transmission mechanism of monetary policy. The neutrality of money in the classical model implies that policymakers should not attempt to control real variables but should aim to stabilize prices through steady money growth. The new classical model supports the control of nominal variables and asserts that neutrality depends on whether the policy action is anticipated or unanticipated. The Keynesian model advocates policies that target instability in private sector demand and encourage steady growth of aggregate demand. This approach is due to the belief that money affects real variables through the interest rate and nominal wage rigidities. The new Keynesian model explains nonneutrality through real rigidities and menu costs. In addition, the new Keynesians stress counteractive measures to negative shocks on output. Monetarists stress the short-run nonneutrality and long-run neutrality of money. They also stress the superiority of policy rules over policy discretion, a conclusion that stems from the fact that we have an imperfect knowledge of how the economy operates and that the lags between policy actions and ultimate effects are variable and uncertain. A more recent extension of the classical view is found in the real business cycle model, which ignores the money stock altogether but not its services. The link is between inside money and output due to the role of financial intermediaries in the production process; the positive correlation between money and output comes from real shocks to the financial system that affect both quantities. Causality runs from output to money. This theory also favors a slow, steady money growth rule.

In Chapter 4, Eduard J. Bomhoff critically examines the statistical modeling of inflation. This modeling is important for forecasting future inflation as well as for designing, implementing, and evaluating monetary policy. The monetary model favored by the literature regards inflation as a function of lagged money growth, income growth, interest rates, and other variables that influence money demand. This model is criticized for its difficulty in adjusting to trend changes in demand for real balances and in imposing cross-equation restrictions on coefficients associated with output and prices. The excess demand model favored by central bankers and professional forecasters hypothesizes a relationship between changes in the excess demand for goods and services and labor and changes in the inflation rate. Three measures of excess demand are commonly used in the regression equation: the difference between actual and natural unemployment rates; the difference between actual economic growth and long-run equilibrium growth; and capacity utilization. The monetary model implies that monetary aggregates, not interest rates, are appropriate targets for setting policies, whereas the excess demand model suggests the opposite.

Bomhoff argues that the terms of the old debate about the nature of inflation—namely, whether inflation comes from the demand or the cost side—have changed. Today, the relevant research agenda is between modeling inflation as responding to excess demand as well as monetary policy and modeling inflation by linking directly money growth to inflation. As Bomhoff puts it, "In either case the monetary authorities may try to precisely accommodate the expected rate of inflation when setting monetary policy."

Empirical work on inflation became less popular in academic journals by the late 1970s for two reasons: (1) the perceived instability in the demand for money schedule in the United States and (2) evidence of substantial lags between changes in money and changes in the inflation rate. The first made it harder to connect changes in inflation to earlier changes in money, and the second could not be explained on a sound theoretical basis. With the use of state-space modeling, a possible solution to these empirical problems is examined, taking into account the link between money growth and inflation, which depends on the stochastic trend in the income velocity of money. Even if it is often nonstationary, velocity can still be predicted with sufficient accuracy using a Kalman filter. This filter can then be used in the implementation of a monetary targeting rule.

In Chapter 5, Keith Blackburn reviews the literature on the game-theoretic aspects of monetary policy. There are three types of policy games:

those involving a single policymaker and the private sector; those involving more than one policymaker holding office at the same time; and, finally, those involving policymakers holding office at different times.

The literature has focused almost exclusively on the first of the three policy games to explain the issue of credibility. Policymakers are always subject to a credibility problem as long as the economic environment allows them to optimize their preferences more than once over a given time horizon. This ability suggests that the constraints acting on the policymaker are not binding. If policymakers could or were forced to precommit themselves to a specified plan, they could not get away by "changing their minds." Their behavior would be time consistent in the sense that ex-ante and ex-post outcomes would coincide. Hence, outcomes under commitment are expected to be generally superior to outcomes under discretion because of the imposition of incentive compatibility constraints in the latter.

Commitments come in different forms: commitment to pursue a specified path of money growth, commitment to honor debt, or commitment to maintain a fixed rate of exchange vis-à-vis a strong, noninflating currency. Alternatively, a credibility problem can be solved by altering the policy-maker's preferences, such as appointing a conservative central banker to offset the inherent inflationary bias of this institution. But the solution of a conservative central bank is not a panacea. To begin with, as long as there is value in stabilizing output around a target, a central bank cannot be too conservative to lose sight completely of the stabilization function of the central bank. It has to retain "sufficient" flexibility in its conduct of monetary policy. Beyond this, there is the public choice issue of why it is easier to appoint a conservative central banker than to change the inflationary bias of the institution itself.

The second policy game can be categorized further into games played at the domestic level and the international level. The domestic level refers to interdependent decision making on the part of independent fiscal and monetary authorities, whereas the international analyzes interdependent behavior between policymakers in different countries. One way of looking at economic policy is to see it as a product of political bargaining between groups, like central bank officials and government representatives. If monetary and fiscal policies are delegated to separate institutions, then the credibility of the overall macroeconomic program may suffer from a lack of cooperation between these institutions. The solvency condition on the government's lifetime budget constraint imposes restrictions on the set of feasible financial policies. A policy designed to avoid the monetization of fiscal deficits requires the issue of debt. In general, the degree of non-coordination between monetary and fiscal authorities is important for determining both the variance and dynamic behavior of government debt.

The literature on international policy games focuses on the potential inefficiencies of noncooperative policymaking by governments of interdependent economies. One arrangement that can alleviate credibility problems is for monetary policy to be supervised by an independent international authority such as the International Monetary Fund or the World Bank.

The third class of games is concerned with policymaking conducted by political agents alternating in office. Political business cycles refer to policy-induced fluctuations in economic activity which are synchronized with the dates of election. One view, the median voter theorem, asserts that these cycles reflect the vested interests of democratically elected policymakers in manipulating the economy for electoral gains. Under certain conditions in a two-party system, this results in policy convergence; as election looms, both parties offer the same policies reflected by the interests of the median voter (the moderate or "silent majority"). Another view looks at politicians as ideologically motivated, with power being a means to an end. Here, the only credible preelection announcement about a postelection policy is that which is consistent with the party's ideology, because once the party is in power, it will implement its most desired course of action.

The methodological approach in all these classes of games is to treat the policymaker like any other economic agent, facing a particular set of objectives and constraints while solving a well-defined optimization problem. This may be looked at as a positive theory of policymaking under alternative institutional arrangements, or as a normative theory of institutional reforms designed to improve policy outcomes.

In Chapter 6 Anthony M. Santomero analyzes the changes in the financial structure caused by changes in bank regulation as well as regulatory avoidance, and their effect on the viability and efficiency of monetary policy. The financial structure of the United States has undergone a deep transformation since the 1930s. In response to the events of the Great Depression, the Congress enacted the Glass-Steagall Act (1933), which categorically separated commercial bank from investment bank activity and imposed a blanket of regulations, including interest-rate fixing on bank liabilities. Regulations gave way to regulatory avoidance in the 1950s and eventually to deregulation after the inflationary climate of the 1970s spurred financial innovation that led to heavy bank disintermediation.

What is the link between the effectiveness of monetary policy and types of financial structures, where these structures depend critically on the prevailing regulations? Santomero reports that, in a comparative dynamic sense, changes in the monetary base have the same qualitative effect on interest rates, prices, and output for a wide range of financial structures. Some are better than others, in the sense that they generate a lower variance of nominal gross national product (GNP) around its expected value for certain types of macroeconomic disturbances. However, choosing an optimal structure requires knowledge of the exact nature and size of the disturbances. This is a very demanding task to say the least, and even if it were possible, the optimal regulatory framework could not be expected to be stable over time, unless the stochastic regime were also to remain stable.

The stability of the financial system depends on the form and substance of bank regulation. Hence, both the causes and effects of financial crises may be crucially related to the nature and extent of regulation. To put it differently, shocks to banking and financial activity are endogenous to the regulation regime. Thus, heavy reliance on bank deposit insurance, through the Federal Deposit Insurance Corporation, encourages risk on the part of banks and bank borrowers, in turn exacerbating the effect of random shocks, raising the probability of financial crises and leading to a suboptimal level of investment in society. On the other hand, less regulation leads to a smaller flow of risk capital to the real sector and leaves the single financial institution more exposed to the consequences of bank runs and panics. The search for an optimal regulatory structure must ultimately consider these two offsetting public policy concerns.

The next two chapters look at U.S. monetary policy since the creation of the Fed. The chapter by Elmus Wicker traces the historical development of the Fed's policymaking. When the Fed was created in 1914, interest-rate seasonality, which corresponded closely to times of financial panics, disappeared, but to what extent the Fed deserves credit is still a matter of dispute. It learned to avert impending crises in the central money market (as evidenced by its behavior in 1920 and 1929) but was unsuccessful in preventing three successive waves of bank failures in the early 1930s. At the start of the recession, the policymakers' response was the same as it had been in the 1923–24 and 1926–27 recessions, but the effect on the economy was different. Later, Fed officials had some difficulty understanding why the banks desired to hold excess reserves and thereby refrained from further purchases of securities. There is substantial and growing evidence that the Federal Reserve officials' knowledge of the monetary effects of open market operations was inadequate, leading in turn to the Fed's poor performance in the 1930s. Clearly, there is no evidence to suggest that the U.S. central bank understood how to use monetary policy in a countercyclical manner.

The literature interpreting the Fed's behavior has been completely dominated by a single paradigmatic model in which the monetary authority attempts to maximize the public interest. The newer bureaucratic models, where Federal Reserve officials are motivated, though not entirely, by their own self-interest do a better job of explaining certain aspects of Fed activity, for example, the propensity of central bankers to withhold information, but it is too early to tell whether they can explain Fed behavior before World War II. Of particular interest is the question how the Fed managed to survive the disaster of the 1930s. The fact that the Congress patched up the system by introducing central bank reforms and deposit insurance rather than abolish the Fed seems to suggest that the Congress saw ineptness rather than an entrenched bureaucracy as the source of the problems. Were Fed officials so clever to deflect public criticism and to convince legislators not to tamper with their institution?

The so-called independence of the Fed has also been questioned. In good economic climate, Congress and the President left the Fed virtually to its own devices. In a few instances, the president or the Treasury secretary asserted his political prerogative to intervene. In 1933 President Roosevelt, without specific authorization, assumed responsibility for the conduct of monetary policy. After the crisis, monetary management was returned to the Fed. This event served to remind Fed officials that their institution is a creature of Congress and that the independence of the monetary authority has no constitutional guarantee.

In Chapter 8, Raymond E. Lombra reviews in some detail the analytical and historical developments that have shaped the conduct of U.S. monetary policy since the late 1970s. It serves as a field guide to Federal Reserve policymaking rather than focusing on normative issues emphasized in the literature on the optimal policy design. The latter can lead to a misleading view of the policy process characterized by undue precision and rigor, unless it is tempered with an understanding of the uncertainties, complexities, and external pressures faced by monetary authorities.

Conceptually, monetary policy involves the setting and adjustment of policy instruments by the Fed to achieve the national economic goals, which are laid out in broad, general guidelines under various pieces of legislation. The Federal Open Market Committee (FOMC), which is the chief policymaking body within the Fed, debates and discusses the forecasts and implications of various alternatives and selects a monetary policy strategy for the coming year, which is then reported to Congress. Once the long-run policy stance is set, the focus shifts to the short run. Current economic conditions and strains in domestic and global financial systems and the political setting are some of the major factors that guide open market operations until the next FOMC meeting. The emphasis on current economic conditions tends to bias monetary policy toward the achievement of short-run goals.

During the 1970s the U.S. monetary authority relied on a procedure that essentially supplied nonborrowed reserves in such an amount to maintain the federal funds rate of interest at an appropriate level, and the targeted interest-rate level was altered infrequently. The outcome was a rising trend of money growth and procyclical movements of money growth around this trend. With the appointment of Paul Volcker to the chairmanship in 1979, the Fed switched to a radically different operating procedure: nonborrowed reserves were targeted at such a level to reestablish the Fed's credibility as an inflation fighter, and the rates of interest were allowed to seek their own level in the marketplace. The success of this policy can be measured, not only in terms of the substantial reductions in the U.S. inflation rate, but also in terms of the positive spillovers it created for other industrialized countries to embark on a much needed disinflationary path.

The Fed moved away from nonborrowed reserve targeting in 1982. The relationship between money, nominal income, and other macroeconomic variables had become less stable and less predictable; consequently, simple monetary targeting also had become a less reliable means to attain the Fed's goals. The deep recession of 1980–82, financial innovations, the debt problems of the less developed countries, and market globalization all contributed to the new way of conducting monetary policy.

Huge swings in real exchange rates, along with increasing interdependencies between the United States and other countries made it important for policymakers both in the United States and abroad to engage in some type of consultation, cooperation, and coordination. Naturally, there exists a reluctance to give up much sovereignty, as evidenced by considerable disagreement about the strength of cross-border relationships and the degree to which coordination can contain the effects of various shocks to the domestic and world economies. It is increasingly clear, however, that global considerations are now playing an ongoing role in the conduct of U.S. monetary policy. Against the background of German unification, "Europe 1992," and the still large U.S. current-account deficit, the prominence of international issues will only increase.

Part III deals with monetary policy in the other G-7 countries: Germany, France, Italy, the United Kingdom, Japan, and Canada. The study of actual monetary operations in these countries (as well as that of the United States) should serve to narrow the gap between theory and reality and suggest possible directions for future research. In Chapter 9, Manfred J. M. Neumann and Jürgen von Hagen describe the institutional framework of German monetary policy and the strategy and operating procedure of the Bundesbank. The international reputation acquired by the Bundesbank for its commitment to domestic price stability has made it more successful than others in fighting inflation. This performance is deeply anchored to a strict institutional and personal independence of the German monetary authority with respect to the political authority. In fact, the Bundesbank is not constrained to follow government instructions in the conduct of its policy. Furthermore, the central bank has no obligation to extend credit to government, except for a rather insignificant short-term overdraft facility. There is a limit, however, to the Bundesbank's autonomy in as much as the selection of the exchange-rate regime is a decision that falls under the jurisdiction of the Ministry of Finance. As a consequence, the central bank may not be completely free in determining the total size of the monetary base or its distribution between foreign and domestic components. For example, under the Bretton Woods Agreement of 1944, the Bundesbank could control the distribution but not the total monetary base. In the

1980s matters have been more complex because Germany enjoyed an adjustable peg system vis-à-vis the EMS countries but a flexible exchange-rate system vis-à-vis other countries, particularly the U.S. dollar. The issue of what the central bank can control depends on the commitment of the Bundesbank to pursue a "leaning-against-the-wind" policy with regard to the dollar and the relative strength of the mark in the EMS. For example, during 1985–87 the mark was appreciating with respect to the dollar and the EMS currencies. The Bundesbank purchased foreign-denominated assets in the exchange markets in order to dampen the fall of the dollar and to maintain its EMS commitment. Complete sterilization of these purchases—that is, sales of the domestic component of the monetary base—was achieved in the short run but not in the long run. The end result was an overshooting of the monetary target and a return to inflation in Germany.

In sum, the Bundesbank's monetary policy is best characterized as a regime of monetary targeting aimed at price stability under the dual exchange-rate constraints of the EMS and the desire to smooth fluctuations in the external value of the Deutsche mark. Thus, the obligation to honor exchange-rate agreements imposed by the federal government set an upward limit on the ability of the Bundesbank to fulfill monetary targets. Consequently, it embeds an inflation bias, though small, in German monetary policy.

Monetary targeting is implemented in two stages involving temporary and permanent changes in the monetary base. Daily operations are geared to targeting a short-term money market rate, an aggregate measure of the supply price of the monetary base. The Bank's approach to sterilizing foreign exchange market interventions is in line with this operating regime. Sterilization is the crucial link between monetary targeting and the dual external constraints facing the Bundesbank. The more completely interventions are sterilized, the less binding are the external constraints. In the short run, sterilization is generally complete, but in the long run, interventions affect monetary growth if both constraints require interventions in the same direction, as in the case of the 1985–87 episode.

The high reputation of the Bundesbank has led to the popular claim that Germany is the anchor of the European Monetary System (EMS). This issue is explored in more detail in Chapter 15. Here, suffice it to say that the evidence suggests that the Bundesbank is independent but not dominant. That is, it has been able to carry out monetary policy independently of the policies pursued in other EMS countries, but not to force its policy on other central banks.

Jacques Mélitz's chapter is devoted largely to French monetary policy prior to the recent reforms and tracks the fundamental changes leading to the present situation. Historically, France's monetary structure has been wrought with restrictions and controls. From the end of World War II until the mid-1960s, it had a highly administered system of money and credit, characterized by thin financial markets. With large reserve inflows and balanced budgets in the mid-1960s, interest-rate intervention lessened and bank profitability became a fundamental consideration. When monetary targets were introduced, the *encadrement* system, which defines ceilings on credit growth for individual banks, took on a more prominent role. With the Socialists' rise to power came the administrative complexities of reconciling money-growth targets with subsidized credits. In late 1984, the Socialist government unexpectedly announced a significant overhaul of the system; the *encadrement* system was scrapped, monetary authorities relied more heavily on interest-rate changes, and domestic and foreign financial liberalization took effect.

In France, the banks do not face any quantitative limit on the amount of central bank money they can obtain, and the interpretation of the ratio of the money stock to the monetary base as a multiplier is misleading because the money stock and the monetary base are determined simultaneously. The ratio of the money stock to the monetary base can only be properly seen as pertaining to the respective market shares of the government and the banks in the issue of money. There is no causality from either monetary base to money or from money to monetary base. It is the change in bank profitability that is essential for the monetary transmission. Instability of money demand has not been a problem in France as it has been in the United States or the United Kingdom, perhaps because France has enjoyed universal banking and interlocking ownership. These features help to explain the impressive record of monetary targeting in France and the decline in the effectiveness of monetary policy in the United States and the United Kingdom after financial liberalization. Membership in the EMS may have also helped to stabilize money demand by increasing the predictability of monetary policy and by reducing shifts in demand between partner currencies. More importantly, EMS membership has forced discipline on fiscal authorities and wage settlements.

Chapter 11 deals with Italian monetary policy. The authors, Franco Spinelli and Patrizio Tirelli, emphasize the long historical evolution that the Banca d'Italia has undergone concerning the objectives and strategy of monetary policy in the postwar period. During the 1950s the Bank aimed at providing sufficient monetary growth to accommodate economic growth in an environment of low rates of inflation. In the 1960s the Bank became Keynesian: its preference function gave substantial weight to output stabilization. The end product was a series of balance-of-payments crises and a monetary cycle that actually exacerbated rather than dampened the Italian business cycle. The 1970s stood out as the dark age of postwar Italian monetary policy. Burdened with the consequences of the oil shocks and an explosion of government expenditures, the Banca d'Italia could do no better than accommodate the rising borrowing requirements of the Italian Treasury. To facilitate this regime of "fiscal dominance" and maximize seigniorage, the Bank imposed a complex web of administrative controls on banks and an extensive network of capital and exchange controls. The network of capital and exchange controls insulated national money and financial markets from those abroad and permitted the country to finance the rising government debt at negative real rates of interest. High rates of inflation were the natural outcome. The Bank attempted to restore its credibility in fighting inflation in the 1980s. It is debatable whether the entry in the EMS marks a turnaround in Italian monetary policy. More important is the so-called divorce of 1981 when the central bank was no longer present at the Treasury auctions as a buyer of last resort of unsold government securities. There were achievements: monetary growth was much lower in the 1980s than in the 1970s; parity realignments in the EMS were frequent up to 1983 but less frequent afterward; and the last significant realignment dates back to January 1987. Despite these achievements, Italian inflation remains appreciably higher than the German inflation rate, and the large and rising government debt serves as a constant reminder of the constraints acting on monetary policy.

As the Bank's objectives changed over the years, so did monetary policy strategy. In the 1950s the nonactivist Bank compensated the growth of the foreign and Treasury components of the monetary base by compressing loans and rediscounts to banks. In the 1960s the activist Bank followed an interest-rate stabilization strategy and for a period of three years a complete pegging. The regime of fiscal dominance in the 1970s generated a new intermediate target, total domestic credit creation. This theoretically ambiguous concept, in practice, served to accommodate substantial monetary financing of government budget deficits. Finally, the more inflation-conscious Bank of the 1980s returned to target the monetary base.

In Chapter 12 Patrick Minford discusses monetary policy in the United Kingdom since 1979, when Margaret Thatcher came to power. In 1979 Mrs. Thatcher inherited a monetary disaster; inflation was rising, and the system of wage controls, put in place in 1978 to hold it down, disintegrated and ushered in the "winter of discontent." The key problem was absence of long-term credibility in counterinflationary policy. After thirty years in which monetary policy played at most a supporting role—whether to a fixed exchange rate, fiscal policy, or incomes and price controls—the 1980s witnessed a prolonged experiment in the use of monetarist policy to control inflation. The dominant official model of the 1980s was one in which the public formed rational expectations and carefully watched the government play a repeated game. Out of this experiment emerged a strategy for setting long-term monetary targets (the Medium-term Financial Strategy), backed up by targets for public sector borrowing requirements. As a result of these policies, the inflation rate fell to 5 percent from 1983–87. The rise in inflation since then reflects a loosening of monetary policy after the October 1987 stock market crash and the effect of the EMS.

A similar framework of analysis has also become influential outside of the United Kingdom, especially among central bankers. This has strengthened the tradition of constitutional restraint on monetary policy through an independent central bank. In some countries, it has prompted the switch to a hard exchange-rate link to the Deutsche mark to exploit the Bundesbank's great reputation for independence. There was a long debate in the United Kingdom as to whether the country should have adopted this link to the Deutsche mark or a common European currency. While the exchange-rate mechanism would deliver low inflation under certain arrangements, it would also remove a key policy instrument from British hands, besides implying a stronger political union than is acceptable to the British. One alternative is to continue with a loose currency relationship with the European Community (EC). The experience of the 1980s suggests that such policies can control inflation without interfering with supply-side reform programs.

Shinichi Ichimura, in Chapter 13, takes an historical approach in explaining the objectives, strategy, and operating procedures of the Bank of Japan. The Japanese economy has experienced a deep transformation in the postwar period: from capital-poor to capital-rich; from a regime heavily controlled and guided by a powerful bureaucracy to one where market forces dominate; from an insular economy to an economy that is increasingly integrated with that of the rest of the world. The banking and financial industry has followed the evolution that has taken place in the real sector of the economy. Thus, the segmentation and functional specialization of financial intermediaries are disappearing under the pressure of deregulation, domestic and international competition, and computerization. Regulation of bank deposit interest rates are long gone, and so are capital and foreign exchange controls. Interestingly enough, the government's rising borrowing needs after the mid-1970s have broadened the size of this market beyond the traditional outlets of financial intermediaries. The public is now a very important holder of government debt; as a consequence, other borrowers have had to issue competitively priced financial instruments. In sum, the "cozy" arrangement of price fixing has virtually disappeared.

The Bank of Japan conducts monetary policy in response to the evolution of the price level, economic growth, the external imbalance, and exchange rates. Price stability, however, appears to be the most important objective, and to achieve it the Bank has relied on the money supply as its intermediate variable. The policy has met with a high degree of success. The Bank's operating procedures now emphasize interventions in the money markets to determine the price and quantity of reserves made available to banks.

An interesting issue centers on how effective the monetary policy will be in the newer and freer environment. First, Ichimura reports the generalized concern of specialists and the public at large about the impact that a large and growing public debt might have on the conduct of monetary policy. The fact that the Bank, by statute, cannot buy government bonds appears to be a credible response to such a concern. Second, monetary policy can no longer count on interest rates being rigid. The impact of policy actions on quantities will necessarily pass through the complex web of portfolio substitution effects. Finally, the internationalization of money and capital markets has opened up the door of competitive regulatory environments. If the Japanese money and capital markets are relatively overburdened with regulation, Japanese financial producers will have an incentive to shift into easier regulatory regimes, such as the Euro-yen deposit market. Here the monetary policy and regulations become closely intertwined.

In Chapter 14 Peter W. Howitt discusses Canadian monetary policy. Fundamental in this discussion is the Bank of Canada's degree of independence. Here we have a good example of the large discrepancy that can arise between statutes and practice. According to the Bank of Canada Act, monetary policy falls under government jurisdiction. In fact, the governor of the Bank has to consult regularly with and submit an annual report to the minister of finance on the conduct of monetary policy. More importantly, in the event a disagreement arises between the governor and the government, the government has the final say. Furthermore, the government has the power to initiate proceedings to dismiss the governor. In sum, a strict reading of the statutes would place the Bank of Canada at the same level of independence of the Banque de France, the Bank of England, and the Banca d'Italia—that is, its independence would be virtually nonexistent.

In practice, the Bank of Canada has a high degree of independence. The reason is that the Bank and its governor count a lot in the political arena. A disagreement on the conduct of monetary policy between the Bank and the government cannot be settled simply, with the government issuing a directive compelling the governor to implement a prescribed course of action or by initiating a dismissal procedure. In a democracy, a dispute invites debate, and with debate comes the consequent assessment of the disputants' positions. Here lies the Bank's power and the source of its independence. This power rises the higher the governor's prestige, the more effective is the governor in representing the views of the Bank's bureaucracy and the interests of the financial community, and the broader is the public's support for the Bank's policy. The evidence seems to suggest that ideas are as important as vested interests in shaping the conduct of Canadian monetary policy.

The Bank of Canada's operating procedures require that the short-term interest rate is the proximate monetary policy instrument. In principle these operating procedures can achieve either a quantitative monetary target or an interest-rate target; in practice, however, they are better suited for an interest-rate target than for a quantitative money target. As is true of banks in other countries, the Bank of Canada has given substantial weight to maintaining orderly financial conditions, which is the code word for interest-rate smoothing.

Historically, interest-rate smoothing has been dominant. Yet, from 1975 to 1980 the Bank of Canada targeted the narrowly defined money stock M1; this achieved a trend reduction of M1 growth but failed to bring down the rate of inflation. The reason was a reduction in the M1 demand, induced partly by technology-driven financial innovations and partly by the banks that encouraged customers to move out of M1-type accounts. The targeting of a broadly defined money stock might have avoided both problems. In the late 1980s the Bank of Canada returned to monetarism by emphasizing the achievement of a low and stable price level. In sum, Peter Howitt concludes: "the Bank of Canada has shown a commendable willingness to learn from past mistakes."

The last chapter, by Jürgen von Hagen, presents an overview of policy coordination in the EMS. Exchange-rate fluctuations have long been regarded as a source of instability in the world economy since the breakdown of the Bretton Woods system. The EMS was created to prevent deleterious exchange-rate swings and to improve the performance of the international monetary system. It has succeeded in reducing nominal and real exchange-rate variability and, thus, has reduced overall macroeconomic uncertainty.

Despite the general acclaim of its success, however, there is little agreement on the nature of its achievements. There is little empirical support for the view that the EMS contributed significantly to European disinflation in the 1980s. Empirical evidence supports neither the view that EMS acts as a disciplinary device—the credibility hypothesis—nor the stronger view that there is a hierarchical structure in the EMS, with the Bundesbank, the German monetary authority, dominating policymaking in the system. Policymakers in the EMS may have found it easier to implement a stabilization program simply by pegging the relatively stable Deutsche mark, making the Bundesbank the focal point of policymaking in the region. But this is a much weaker role than the coercive one claimed by the credibility hypothesis.

The EMS seems best characterized as a framework for optional rather than automatic policy coordination, leaving its members considerable room for independent policymaking. Although there is some suggestive evidence of the merits of strategic policy coordination, the gains appear to be badly distributed and lack robustness to asymmetries in economic structures and fluctuations. Monetary independence stands in sharp contrast to the goal of complete exchange-rate stability in the European Community implied by the current push for a European and Monetary Union (EMU). Ultimately, however, the decision for or against EMU is a political one, and its prospects rest on the strength of the quest for political union in Europe.

The increasing interdependence of sovereign economies and the growing acclaim for international policy coordination suggest that future research will incorporate game—theoretic aspects (cf. Chapter 5 by Keith Blackburn). This literature has yielded many important insights; yet caution is needed. Further analysis should tackle a number of issues, including how the bargaining process will determine the distribution of any gains from cooperation; the signs and sizes of spillover effects between countries; and the sensitivity of results to certain features of the models employed.

UNRESOLVED ISSUES

Monetary policy theory and monetary policy practice is in much better shape now than a decade ago. Yet, a great deal remains to be done. As a departing note, we would like to suggest what we take to be the main unresolved issues and puzzles in this field. First, if commitment to a low-inflation strategy is so important to society, why do we not observe more of it? Is it a matter of the institutions not receiving clearly the message from the people; or the inability of "weak" central banks to acquire the necessary degree of independence from governments; or public apathy? Suppose it were apathy, can we blame the public? After all, the post–World War II record has not been that bad. Most democratic governments have presided over a period of sustained economic growth without experiencing hyperinflation. The worst performance among the G-7 countries was that of Italy in the 1970s, but it was contained to less than 15 percent per annum. It appears that the democracies of the industrial countries have been able to control trend inflation much better than countries besieged by social unrest and weak governments (Capie, 1986). Although the direction of causality is not always clear, inflation and weak governments are positively correlated. It may well be that the voters of the successful democracies do not perceive inflation to be serious enough to require radical institutional reform.

The second unresolved issue has to do with the movement of the inflation rate around a trend. Here again, it appears that the key to progress rests on a better understanding of the interaction between politics and monetary policy. A rapidly growing literature has investigated the link existing between the timing of election and monetary policy. The prevailing hypothesis, tested predominantly using U.S. data, is that politicians manipulate the economy to maximize their own reelection chances (Davidson et al., 1990; Woolley, 1984, Chap. 6). Even apart from the selfish interests of politicians, voters may not want a central bank that pursues low inflation without giving due weight to stabilizing business cycle fluctuations. The desire of wanting low inflation and yet flexibility may have been a reason why the public has not pushed for "stronger" central banks.

Finally, we point out the gulf that exists between the theory of policy cooperation and the practice. The theory tells us that in many instances countries ought to engage in monetary policy cooperation; the practice tells us that there are few successful instances of international cooperation. The discrepancy can possibly be explained by the fact that the theory of cooperation has not properly emphasized whether or not agreements to cooperate are incentive compatible. Incentives to cheat increase with the complexity of the agreement. Cooperative arrangements involving money supplies are bound to imbed more cheating than agreements involving exchange rates. The challenge for the future is to devise cooperative strategies for which the monitoring costs do not exceed the added benefit derived from cooperation. The EMS provides one such example, even though it is not a first best solution.

REFERENCES

Alesina, Alberto. 1989. "Politics and Business Cycles in Industrial Democracies." *Economic Policy*, no. 8 (April): 55–98.
Bade, Robin, and Parkin, Michael. 1987. "Central Bank Laws and Monetary Policy." University of Western Ontario. Mimeo.
Barro, Robert, and Gordon, David. 1983. "Rules, Discretion and Reputation in a Model of Monetary Policy." *Journal of Monetary Economics* 12: 101–22.
Batten, Dallas; Blackwell, Michael; Kim, In-Su; Nocera, Simon E.; and Ozeki, Yuruzu. 1990. "The Conduct of Monetary Policy in the Major Industrial Countries: Instruments and Operating Procedures." International Monetary Fund (IMF) Occasional Paper No. 70, July. Washington, D.C.: IMF.
Brunner, Karl. 1968. "The Role of Money and Monetary Policy." Federal Reserve Bank of St. Louis *Review* 50 (July): 9–24.
———, and Meltzer, Allan H. 1989. *Money and the Economy: Issues in Monetary Analysis*. The 1987 Raffaele Mattioli Lectures. Cambridge, England: Cambridge University Press.
Capie, Forrest. 1986. "Conditions in Which Very Rapid Inflation Has Appeared." *Carnegie-Rochester Conference Series on Public Policy* 24: 115–68.
Davidson, Lawrence S.; Fratianni, Michele; and von Hagen, Jürgen. 1990. "Testing for Political Business Cycles." *Journal of Policy Modeling* 12: 35–59.
Federal Reserve Bank of St. Louis. 1990. *International Economic Conditions*. St. Louis, Mo., December.
Friedman, Milton. 1959. *A Program for Monetary Stability*. New York: Fordham University Press.
———, ed. 1956. *Studies in the Quantity Theory of Money*. Chicago: University of Chicago Press.
———, and Meiselman, David. 1963. "The Relative Stability of Monetary Velocity and the Investment Multiplier in the United States, 1897–1958." In *Stabi-*

lization Policies. Englewood Cliffs, N.J.: Prentice-Hall for the Commission on Money and Credit, 167–268.

————, and Schwartz, Anna J. 1963. *A Monetary History of the United States, 1867–1960*. Princeton, N.J.: Princeton University Press for the National Bureau of Economic Research.

Kneeshaw, J. T., and Van den Bergh, P. 1989. "Changes in Central Bank Money Market Operating Procedures in the 1980s." BIS Economic Papers No. 23, January. Basle: Bank of International Settlements.

Kydland, F. E., and Prescott, E. C., 1977. "Rules Rather Than Discretion: The Inconsistency of Optimal Plans." *Journal of Political Economy* 85: 473–92.

Woolley, John T. 1984. *Monetary Politics: The Federal Reserve and the Politics of Monetary Policy*. Cambridge, England: Cambridge University Press.

PART I

MAJOR ISSUES

2

MONETARY POLICY AND THE MONEY SUPPLY PROCESS

Robert H. Rasche

This chapter surveys the process by which the monetary policy actions of central banks affect the stock of money. In section 1 the definition of transactions money and the framework within which a typical central bank operates are established. Section 2 discusses the mechanisms by which a central bank affects the supply of government money. In section 3, the economic forces that link changes in government money to changes in transactions money are investigated. Section 4 reviews the role of reserve requirements in the relationship between government money and transactions money. Particular attention is given to the controversy over contemporaneous versus lagged reserve requirements that was prominent in discussions of monetary policy in the United States in the early 1980s. Section 5 considers some peculiar problems of monetary control through nonborrowed reserves operating procedures. In section 6 the empirical evidence on the interest elasticity of various money multipliers is reviewed. Finally, section 7 summarizes conclusions.

1. DEFINITION OF MONEY AND THE ORGANIZATION OF THE MONEY SUPPLY PROCESS

Any discussion of the process by which money is supplied in any economy presupposes a definition of the commodity that is being supplied. The present discussion concentrates on the narrow definition of money as those commodities that function as a medium of exchange—that is, those commodities that are generally acceptable in exchange for goods and services.

In virtually all economies, governments have decreed a legal monopoly over the issue, or manufacture, of the money commodity. The details of the implementation of this monopoly vary from country to country, but an essential element is the organization of a monetary agency or authority within the government: a nationalized firm.[1] The government, acting either through its monetary authority or other agencies, typically chooses to franchise private firms (banks or, more generally, depository institutions) to participate in the process of supplying (or manufacturing) the medium of exchange. The rules of the franchise agreement (bank charter) specify restrictions that apply to the franchisees, and define the relationship between the franchisees and the government monetary authority.

The franchise arrangement is the source of the economic problem of the money supply process. The monetary authority can, if it chooses, exercise precise control over the amount of government money that is supplied to the economy. Although the amount of private money that is manufactured by depository institutions can be influenced by the government monetary authority, it is also affected by portfolio decisions of the depository institutions and private households and nonfinancial firms. If substantial portfolio reallocations occur in response to changes in economic activity or in rates of return that are available to various assets in the economy, the correlation between changes in the quantity of government money in the economy and changes in the total stock of money in the economy may be low. The mechanism and forces that influence the quantity of money available to the economy for a given quantity of government money is known as the money supply process.

2. THE GOVERNMENT MONETARY AUTHORITY AND THE SUPPLY OF GOVERNMENT MONEY

The government agency that is charged with implementing the monopoly powers that the government has expropriated over the money stock is the central bank. A principal authority of this agency is the power to print money. This power is in part literal, since paper money and coinage that circulate in the economy usually are manufactured on the authority of the central bank.[2] More frequently and more importantly, the central bank "prints" government money in a figurative sense. This is because the franchise agreement between the government and the private depository institutions provides the opportunity for the private institutions to maintain demand balances at the central bank. In many countries the franchise agreement now requires depository institutions to maintain certain amounts of demand balances at the central bank.

The central bank maintains a fixed exchange rate on these demand balances by agreeing to exchange them on a unit-for-unit basis for paper currency and/or coins. Coin, currency, and the demand balances of depository institutions maintained with the central bank compose the entire stock of government money available to the economy. This stock of gov-

Table 2.1
Typical Balance Sheet of a Central Bank

Assets	Liabilities
1. Government Securities	1. Coin and Currency
2. Foreign Exchange	2. Deposits due to private depository institutions.
3. Loans to Depository Institutions	3. Deposits due to Government
4. Misc. Assets	4. Misc. Liabilities and Net Worth

ernment money is variously known as outside money (Gurley and Shaw, 1960), high-powered money (Friedman and Schwartz, 1963), demand debt of the government (Tobin, 1963), or source base (Brunner, 1968). This high-powered money is the principal liability of the central bank as illustrated in Table 2.1.[3]

Central banks typically hold several major types of assets against these liabilities. The most important of these assets are (1) interest-bearing debt of the central government, (2) foreign exchange, and (3) loans to depository institutions.

Lending to depository institutions is frequently referred to as discount window operations, since, historically, following practices developed at the Bank of England, such loans were extended when the central bank purchased short-term private debt instruments that were sold from the asset portfolios of depository institutions. The common practice today is for central banks to make loans to depository institutions that are secured by assets in the portfolio of the borrowing institution rather than purchasing the assets outright.

The outstanding stock of high-powered money (government money) in an economy is affected when the central bank acquires or sells any of the various assets that it holds. Discount window lending affects the high-powered money holdings of depository institutions directly since the proceeds of the loan (or the private paper purchase) are credited to the transaction account of that institution at the central bank. In 1914, when the

Federal Reserve System was organized in the United States, this mechanism was conceived as the fundamental means by which a central bank could change the outstanding stock of government money and in turn influence the available money stock in the economy. This mechanism was viewed as the means by which the Federal Reserve would execute its chief responsibility of providing an "elastic currency" that would fluctuate positively with economic activity. During the first decade of the Federal Reserve System, rediscounting at the Federal Reserve Banks was the primary source of high-powered money for the U.S. banking system.

The interest rate that depository institutions are required to pay on outstanding borrowings from the central bank is the discount rate (or the rediscount rate if the central bank actually purchases private securities from the borrowing institution). The appropriate formula for establishing the discount rate is a longstanding controversy in monetary policy discussions, at least in the United States. One alternative practice, which has antecedents in the policies of the Bank of England, is to maintain a positive spread between the discount rate and short-term market interest rates. This practice is known as a penalty rate policy. Under such conditions, depository institutions are generally offered the *right* to borrow as much as they want at the established discount rate; that is, the supply curve for borrowed high-powered money is perfectly elastic at the prevailing penalty rate.

A second alternative emerged early in the development of Federal Reserve practices. In the United States the discount rate is not linked to market rates of interest in any precise fashion; it may be changed infrequently, and it can be below market rates, sometimes for many months. This practice is inconsistent with a perfectly elastic supply of borrowed high-powered money, since profit-maximizing institutions have the incentive to borrow unlimited amounts of high-powered money as long as a substantial negative spread is maintained between the discount rate and market interest rates. Federal Reserve practice recognizes this problem and holds that access to the discount window is a privilege, not a right, for depository institutions. Such privileges are available only to those institutions that conform to a more or less well-defined set of administrative guidelines.[4] Under this regime, the supply curve for borrowed high-powered money is not perfectly elastic, and the relationship between the discount rate, market interest rates, and the outstanding quantity of borrowed high-powered money can be difficult to predict (Kier, 1981). On several occasions proposals have advanced within the Federal Reserve System to modify or abandon the historical structure of the discount window in the United States, but major changes have not been implemented (Board of Governors, 1971; Kier, 1981).

Quantitatively, central bank lending to depository institutions is relatively unimportant, although it retains a pivotal role in the implementation of monetary policy, at least in the United States. Today borrowings by depository institutions in the United States typically are less than $1 billion, compared to a total stock of high-powered money in excess of $250 billion.[5] Such borrowing became quantitatively less important when central banks (in particular the Federal Reserve System) discovered that changes in the amount of high-powered money could be affected indirectly through purchases or sales of assets in organized secondary markets for securities or foreign exchange. Such purchases or sales of government debt and/or foreign exchange by central banks are known as open market operations.[6]

Open market operations affect changes in high-powered money when payment for the purchase or sale of securities/foreign exchange is accomplished. Such payments are made by debits or credits to the transaction account at a depository institution of the securities or foreign exchange dealer through which the sale or purchase is effected and a corresponding debit or credit to the account of that depository institution at the central bank.[7] Consequently, such open market operations sales or purchases produce a one for one decrease or increase in the quantity of high-powered money outstanding in the economy. The total stock of high-powered money supplied to an economy net of borrowing by depository institutions is known as nonborrowed high-powered money or net base money. A simple rearrangement of the central bank balance sheet in Table 2.1 by subtracting borrowing from both total assets and liabilities reveals that the major source of nonborrowed high-powered money is the acquisition of government securities or foreign exchange by the central bank through open market operations.

Open market operations have become the dominant source of supply for high-powered money to the economy because (1) they are initiated exclusively at the discretion of the central bank, (2) they can be adjusted to any size impact that the central bank desires to accomplish, and (3) they can be utilized to offset the impact on the outstanding stock of high-powered money of other forces that are beyond the control of the central bank. Open market operations undertaken for the third objective are classified as defensive as distinguished from dynamic open market operations that are undertaken for the purpose of altering the outstanding stock of high-powered money (Roosa, 1956). An example of a defensive operation is the purchase of government securities at the time that seasonal tax payments are made into the government treasury. Without such purchases, the stock of high-powered money would decline as Treasury cash balances accumulate at the central bank. A defensive open market operation that is frequently employed is a purchase or sale by the central bank in the government securities market on the occasion of a sale or purchase of foreign exchange. These defensive operations are said to "sterilize" the impact of the foreign exchange market intervention on the stock of outstanding high-powered money.

3. RELATIONS BETWEEN HIGH-POWERED MONEY AND THE TOTAL MONEY STOCK

The relationship between high-powered or base money and the total money stock in an economy frequently is summarized in terms of a base money multiplier. It is important to remember that there is no unique algebraic expression of this relationship, and different analysts use alternative representations (explicitly or implicitly) depending on their particular hypotheses about the behavior of depository institutions and nonfinancial economic units. A frequently used representation starts from the definitional identities for total high-powered money (B) and total transactions money ($M1$):[8]

(1) B = balances held by depository institutions at the central bank (R) + currency in circulation (C)

and

(2) $M1$ = transactions deposits held by the public at depository institutions (D) + currency holdings of the public (C).

The ratio of $M1$ to base money (B) is

(3) $$\frac{M1}{B} = \frac{D+C}{R+C}.$$

The right-hand side of this equation can be multiplied by D/D, and the resulting expression can be rearranged as

(4) $$\frac{M1}{B} = \frac{1+k}{r+k} = m,$$

where $k = C/D$ is the ratio of currency to transactions deposit holdings of the public and $r = R/D$ is the ratio of deposits held by depository institutions at the central bank to their transaction deposit liabilities. The "money multiplier" nomenclature for m is natural since $M1 = mB$. This representation is the form used by Brunner and Meltzer (1964, 1968).

The nonuniqueness of this expression is easily seen. Consider multiplying the right-hand side of equation (3) by $M1/M1$. The resulting expression can be manipulated to

(5) $$m = \frac{1}{r^* + k^*},$$

where $r^* = R/M1$ is the ratio of deposits at the central bank to total transactions money and $k^* = C/M1$ is the ratio of currency holdings of the public to total transactions money. The k^* ratio is analyzed by Cagan (1965).

Relations such as (4) and (5) are tautologies. Over an extended period of time, an economic theory of the behavior of individual depository institutions and the public developed, which hypothesizes that the *marginal impact* of a unit change in base money is measured by the size of the *average* money multiplier. The important elements of this theory are (1) individual depository institutions have optimal (or desired) fractions of transactions deposit liabilities that they wish to hold as deposits at the central bank, (2) individual nonfinancial economic agents have optimal (desired) currency-transactions deposits ratios, (3) all economic agents can maintain their actual portfolio shares equal to their desired portfolio shares, (4) changes in the stock of base money do not substantially affect the determinants of the optimal portfolio shares, and (5) the demand for loans from depository institutions is not perfectly inelastic. Under these assumptions, new loans are originated by depository institutions that are the recipients of additional central bank deposits, and multiple deposit expansion occurs in the aggregate as measured on the margin by the average money multiplier. This process is the classic geometric deposit expansion process detailed in money and banking textbooks.[9]

The appropriateness of the average money multiplier as a measure of the marginal effect of a change of base money on the outstanding stock of transactions money, and hence the usefulness of money multipliers in monetary analysis, has been, and to some extent continues to be, the source of considerable controversy. At one extreme there is a tradition that assumes the aggregate currency/deposit ratio and the aggregate reserves/deposit ratio can be treated as constants. Gurley and Shaw (1960) and Tobin (1963a) label this view the old view (or alternatively the traditional view) of monetary analysis. Taken literally, such analysis assumes that depository institutions possess a "widow's cruse" (Tobin, 1963a), which permits them in the aggregate to expand (or contract) transactions money in the economy to some multiple of changes in base money, regardless of the asset demand preferences of nonfinancial economic agents.

The countervailing or "new view" of monetary analysis is that k and r are not fixed parameters, either for individual agents or in the aggregate, but rather variables that assume different values depending on the economic decisions of individual agents. In particular, advocates of this new view hypothesize that agents choose optimal portfolios in response to observed rates of return on alternative asset forms, and adjust the composition of their portfolios in response to changes in relative rates of return. If such portfolio adjustments are rapid and substantial, then the new view analysts correctly emphasize that the assumption of equality of the average and marginal money multipliers is not appropriate, and depository institutions do not possess a "widow's cruse" in supplying transactions money to the economy.

New view analysts note that, if the demand for government securities is not perfectly interest elastic, then open market sales by the central bank will be accomplished only when the prices of government securities are reduced (interest rates are increased). Higher interest rates on government debt are transmitted to markets for other assets as agents adjust their asset portfolios. Specifically, higher market rates on securities and/or bank loans may induce profit-maximizing depository institutions to reduce the relative size of deposits at the central bank in their asset portfolios in favor of a larger portfolio share for securities and loans. Under these circumstances, the r ratio will decrease and the money multiplier will increase. Therefore, in the absence of any shift in the relative aggregate portfolio shares of currency and transactions deposits of the public, the assumption of a fixed money multiplier overstates the impact of a given change in high-powered money on total transactions money.

The principle that the algebraic components of the money multiplier, however formulated, vary in response to the economic decisions of both depository institutions and the public is now widely accepted among monetary analysts. However, within this theoretical framework wide differences of opinion continue. At one extreme are analysts who argue that the dominant source of change in the outstanding source of transactions money is a change in the stock of base money.[10] At the other extreme are analysts who argue that changes in base money are only one of several important sources of change in the stock of transactions money. Brunner (1968) explains why this wide range of opinion is consistent with the new view:

The New View as a program is a sensible response to a highly unsatisfactory state of monetary analysis inherited in the late 1950s. . . . The New View proposed a systematic application of economic analysis, in particular an application of relative price theory, to the array of financial intermediaries, their assets and liabilities.

This program is most admirable and incontestable, but it cannot explain the conflict revealed by critique and countercritique. . . .

It is important to understand, however, that neither research strategy nor specific empirical conjectures are logical implications of the general program. The explicit separation of the three aspects is crucial for a proper assessment of the New View . . . the New View . . . consist(s) of a program acceptable to all economists, a research strategy rejected by the Monetarist position, and an array of specific conjectures advanced without analytical or empirical substantiation. (P. 11)

The ultimate test of the proposition that changes in base money are the single most important source of changes in the stock of transactions money is a test of the elasticities of the multiplier components such as r and k with respect to the economic variables that are most likely to show large and immediate changes as a result of open market purchases or sales. The measurement of these elasticities is discussed in section 6 below.

4. THE ROLE OF REQUIRED RESERVES IN THE MONEY SUPPLY PROCESS

As noted above, the central bank or other government agencies that franchise private depository institutions to participate in the money manufacturing process impose restrictions on the admissible behavior of the depository institutions. Numerous restrictions have been imposed on different occasions and in different national economies. Included among such restrictions are minimum capital requirements, maximum permissible interest rates on deposits, and reserve requirements. Formal, effective reserve requirements probably have been more important in the U.S. financial system than in other countries. The legal reserve requirement states the minimum percentage of various liabilities that a depository institution must maintain in specific asset forms. The assets eligible to satisfy any reserve requirements include deposits at the central bank and may include other assets such as cash in the vaults of depository institutions.[11]

In such an institutional framework, the sum of all balances held in asset forms eligible to satisfy reserve requirements are known as total reserves (R); the minimum fraction of liabilities that must be held to meet the reserve requirement is known as required reserves (RR); and the difference between total reserves held by a depository institution and its required reserves is known as excess reserves (ER).

Following the usual U.S. practice, we assume that transactions deposit liabilities are subject to one reserve requirement and that time deposit liabilities are subject to a different reserve requirement. The fractions of these two types of deposit liabilities that must be held as reserves are designated r_D and r_T, respectively.[12] Under these assumptions:

$$(6) \quad R = RR + ER = r_D D + r_T T + ER,$$

and

$$(7) \quad r = \frac{R}{D} = \left[\frac{r_D D + r_T T + ER}{D + T}\right]\left[\frac{D + T}{D}\right] = (rr + e)(1 + t),$$

where $e = ER/(D + T)$ is conventionally known as the excess reserve ratio, $rr = (r_D D + r_T T)/(D + T)$ is a weighted average reserve requirement, and $t = T/D$ is the ratio of time deposits to transactions deposits held by the public.[13] These definitions can be applied in the money multiplier expression (5) to give

$$(8) \quad m = \left[\frac{1+k}{(rr+e)(1+t) + k} \right].$$

Again, it is important to remember that the multiplier representations such as (8) are not unique. Tobin (1969), for example, outlines a theory of depository institution asset portfolio allocation over total discretionary assets, $(1-rr)(D+T)$. He is concerned with the fraction of this total allocated to excess reserves, $e^* = ER/(1-rr)(D+T) = e/(1-rr)$. With this specification of depository institution portfolio behavior, the natural representation of the money multiplier is

$$(9) \quad m = \left[\frac{1+k}{(rr+e^*\{1+rr\})(1+t) + k} \right].$$

Both (8) and (9) reveal that there are four possible sources of changes in the stock of transactions money in addition to changes in base money. These are (1) changes in the weighted average reserve ratio either because of changes in legal reserve requirements or shifts in deposits, (2) changes in desired excess reserves holdings by depository institutions, (3) changes in desired currency-transactions deposit ratios by the public and (4) changes in desired time deposit-transactions deposit ratios by the public.

In some environments, such as the United States, the central bank or a government agency has the discretion to change the legal reserve ratios.[14] Such changes in legal reserve ratios are generally classified as a third tool of monetary policy, in addition to open market operations and discount window lending. The last two actions affect the stock of base money directly, whereas the first affects the money multiplier as formulated in (8) and (9). Many analysts desire a single summary measure of monetary policy that indicates the total effect of all three tools of monetary policy. This summary measure is desired since (infrequent) changes in legal reserve ratios are rarely initiated in isolation, but rather are accompanied by open market operations that offset the initial impact of the change in the ratios on the stock of transactions money. Subsequently, the simultaneous open market operation is reversed, so that the full impact of the change in reserve ratios is distributed over time.

Two types of summary measures are available. In the United States these are known as the monetary base, published by the Board of Governors of the Federal Reserve System, and the adjusted monetary base, published by the Federal Reserve Bank of St. Louis.[15] Both measures attempt to incorporate the impact of changes in legal reserve ratios into movements of the respective monetary base measures and purge the effect from the corresponding money multipliers. The technical differences in the construction of the two series result in different short-run (week-to-week or month-to-month) movements in the two series, but over longer periods of time the two measures grow at similar rates (see Figure 2.1).

A significant issue in the administration of legal reserve requirements is the base on which the requirements are imposed. Such requirements are never imposed instantaneously or continuously. Rather, depository institutions must meet the requirement on an average basis over fixed time intervals. Within this interval or reserve averaging period, the management of the depository institution can exercise discretion over the day-to-day fluctuations of its reserve balance. For depository institutions under the Federal Reserve System, the reserve averaging period has been one or two weeks at various times. Prior to September 1968, these institutions were required to maintain average reserve balances during the reserve averaging period greater than or equal to average required reserves for the same period. This system is known as the contemporaneous reserve requirement (CRR) system. From September 1968 to February 1984, the Fed utilized an alternative system. During that time required reserves were based on average deposits held two weeks prior to the current reserve accounting period, while total reserves were computed from contemporaneous average reserve balances. This system is known as the lagged reserve requirement (LRR).[16] In 1984 the Federal Reserve reverted to an almost contemporaneous system of reserve requirements.

Lagged reserve accounting became extremely controversial after October 1979, when the Federal Reserve announced that it would deemphasize its attention to the level and movements of the federal funds rate (Fed funds operating procedure) and place increased attention on controlling fluctuations of reserve aggregates. Some analysts, particularly monetarists, argued that the Fed should target either the monetary base or aggregate reserves of depository institutions. Other analysts argued that an operating procedure that targeted either the monetary base or total reserves was not feasible under a system of lagged reserve accounting (Judd and Scaddings, 1980; Leroy, 1979; Lindsey et al., 1984; Lombra and Kaufman, 1985). In reality, the Fed adopted a system (1979–82) that emphasized the growth of nonborrowed reserves (Thornton, 1982).

Control of total reserves (or the monetary base) was not a feasible operating procedure for monetary policy under LRR because during any reserve averaging period the Fed faced a minimum amount of required reserves that it was obliged to supply in the aggregate. This minimum is determined by deposits that were outstanding two weeks earlier, which predetermined aggregate required reserves for the current period. In effect the demand for aggregate total reserves is perfectly inelastic at some minimum (positive) level in every reserve period. If the Fed tried to reduce

Figure 2.1
Growth Rate of Monetary Base Measures 59:2–90:3

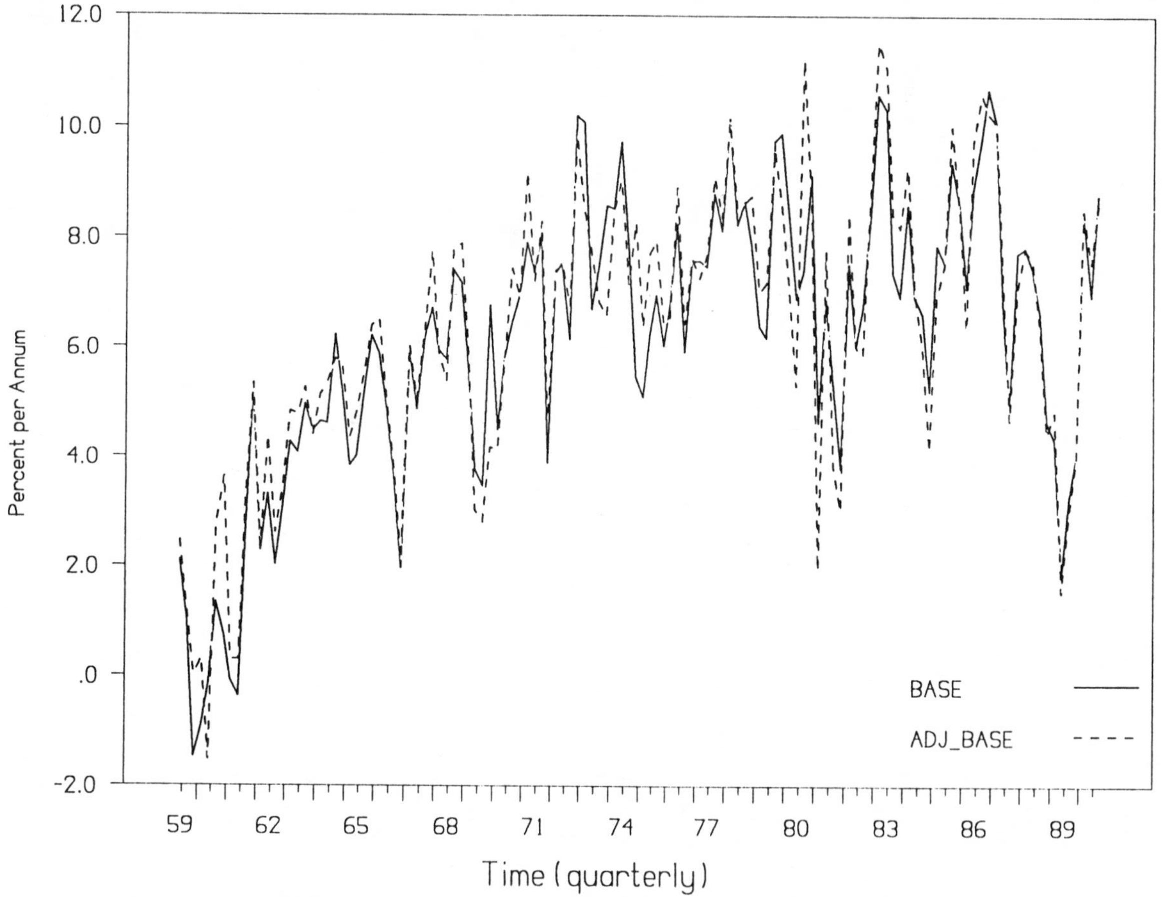

total reserves to (or toward) this minimum, the federal funds rate could jump sharply. Ultimately, the Fed would have to lend depository institutions sufficient reserves so that the minimum aggregate total reserve constraint would be met. All that open market operations aimed at reducing aggregate total reserves below the predetermined minimum can accomplish is the reallocation of reserves between nonborrowed and borrowed reserves.

In the aggregate, depository institutions hold almost no excess reserves during the LRR years; hence, it is inferred that it is difficult, if not impossible, for the Fed to reduce total reserves under these reserve requirement rules. Some analysts go beyond this position and argue that with lagged reserve requirements depository institutions can engage in a sophisticated game of "chicken" with the central bank. This argument asserts that there is no contemporaneous link between total reserves and deposits, so depository institutions can expand loans and deposits to any degree that they desire. Two weeks later, a predetermined level of aggregate total reserves that the central bank must accommodate through open market operations or discount window lending exists as a result of this lending behavior. The LRR system makes the central bank a passive supplier of the reserve demand generated by previous lending. Thus, during the reserve averaging period, an observed money multiplier for total reserves or the monetary base does not reflect a causal relationship from reserves or the base to money. Rather, the appropriate relationship is between deposits lagged two weeks and current reserves or base money, with causality running from deposits to reserves. This is exactly opposite from the causation suggested by the multiplier specification (Feige and McGee, 1977; Pierce, 1976).

This argument appears to have some merit as a characterization of the reserve supply process that existed in the United States during 1968–84. However, the assertion or implicit assumption that reserve supply *must* be passive in all lagged reserve accounting regimes is problematic. Models that generate this result typically specify that the aggregate demand for excess reserves is a function of the current short-term interest rate and that the demand for borrowed reserves is a function of the current spread of a market rate over the discount rate (for example, Lombra and Kaufman, 1984). Goodfriend (1983) shows that the administration of the Fed discount window rules generates a dynamic demand for borrowings that depends not only on the current rate spread, but also on expected future rate spreads. During much of the lagged reserve accounting period in the United States, it was well known that the Fed had a strong aversion to sharp fluctuations in interest rates. Under such conditions, the current short-term interest rate is a rational expectation of near future interest rates, and the current rate spread is a reasonable proxy for expected future rate spreads. Goodfriend argues that the use of different central bank practices with respect to interest-rate smoothing would cause the aggregate borrowings relationship to be different from that historically observed. This is an example of a "Lucas effect."

A similar argument applies to the demand for excess reserves. In a lagged reserve accounting environment, the opportunity cost for new lending in a particular reserve accounting period is the expected federal funds rate two or more weeks in the future. The higher the expected present value of future federal funds rates, the more a depository institution will expect to earn by foregoing lending at the present time, generating larger excess reserves two weeks in the future, and lending such excess reserves in the Fed funds market at that time. This dynamic aspect of bank behavior is not generally captured in models or empirical studies of excess reserve behavior under lagged reserve accounting. It is difficult to capture in empirical studies because historically the contemporaneous funds rate is a good measure of expected future funds rates.

Under alternative central bank procedures, which accept more short-run variability in interest rates, depository institutions in the aggregate would likely hold higher levels of excess reserves.[17] The larger excess reserves in turn provide a buffer that gives the central bank more flexibility in adjusting the outstanding stock of total reserves without encountering minimum limits imposed by exogenous required reserves.

Furthermore, models that hypothesize the absence of a relationship between contemporaneous deposits and reserves in a lagged reserve requirement regime generally ignore "adding up" constraints imposed on individual depository institutions by balance sheet constraints (Brainard and Tobin, 1968). Regardless of whether required reserves are predetermined for an institution, or whether they fluctuate with lending by that institution, the economic problem faced by that institution is to ascertain what fraction of discretionary assets (total assets net of required reserves) should be allocated to loans, securities, and excess reserves (see Tobin, 1969). This point is emphasized by Thornton (1983) who notes Pesek and Saving's (1968) analysis of depository institutions that face zero reserve requirements (and hence totally predetermined required reserves), but for which there is a relationship between excess reserves and current deposits as these institutions attempt to maintain profit-maximizing portfolio allocations.

When required reserves are totally predetermined, demand for total reserves is still related to contemporaneous deposits by the relationship:

(10) $R = (1 - e^*)\overline{RR} + e^*(D + T),$

for $e^* = ER/(D + T - RR)$. Equation (10) can be utilized to develop a money multiplier relationship for a lagged reserve requirement environment. Assume an n week discrete lag in reserve requirements. After some manipulation, it can be shown that

$$(11) \quad M1 = \left[\frac{1+k}{e^*(1+t)+k}\right]B - \left[\frac{1+k}{e^*(1+t)+k}\right]\left[\frac{rr(1+t_n)}{1+k_n}\right]M1_n,$$

where $M1$ is the stock of transactions money in the current reserve settlement period, B is the stock of base money in the same period, t_n is the t ratio lagged n weeks, k_n is the k ratio lagged n weeks, and $M1_n$ is the stock of transactions money lagged n weeks. Two points are apparent from equation (11). First, there is a contemporaneous relationship between $M1$ and B under the lagged reserve requirement regime (in addition to the common currency component), and, second, this is a dynamic relationship represented by a difference equation in $M1$. Thus, the impact on $M1$ of a change in B is distributed over time. In the absence of significant changes in e^*, t, or k, the initial (or impact) effect of a change in B on $M1$ is larger than the long-run effect. Under these same conditions, the long-run effect of a change in B is the money multiplier in equation (9).

The rationale for the introduction of lagged reserve requirements by the Fed was to facilitate reserve management for depository institutions. Under contemporaneous reserve requirements, a depository institution must adjust its portfolio of reserve assets while experiencing simultaneous fluctuations in its required reserve objective in response to contemporaneous deposit inflows and outflows. Such deposit flows are in part unpredictable. The advantage of lagged reserve accounting from the perspective of an individual depository institution is that its required reserve objective is known in advance of the reserve settlement period.

Apparently, the implications of lagged reserve accounting for a monetary policy that sought to influence outstanding transactions money by targeting base money or total reserves were not considered when reserve requirements were restructured in 1968. This is not surprising, since at that time the Federal Reserve was neither utilizing nor actively considering such monetary control procedures.

Subsequently, several analysts questioned the appropriateness of lagged reserve accounting for monetary control purposes (Laufenberg, 1979; Laurent, 1979; Poole, 1976), and proposed alternative reserve requirement schemes. In general, these proposals fall into a class of models in which required reserves are a distributed lag on deposits. A particularly interesting proposal is that of Poole (1976) who suggested a 100 percent reserve requirement on changes in deposits over the most recent two weeks and a fractional reserve requirement (rr) on deposits outstanding two weeks previously. Poole's formula is[18]

$$(12) \quad \begin{aligned} RR &= [(D+T) - (D+T)_{-2}] + rr(D+T)_{-2} \\ &= (D+T) - (1-rr)(D+T)_{-2}. \end{aligned}$$

After some tedious algebraic calculations similar to those used to obtain equation (11), it can be shown that the Poole 100 percent marginal reserve requirement implies

$$(13) \quad M1 = \left[\frac{1+k}{(1+e^*)(1+t) + k}\right]B$$

$$+ \left[\frac{1+k}{(1+e^*)(1+t) + k}\right]\left[\frac{(1-rr)\,(1+t_2)}{(1+k_2)}\right] M1_2.$$

Under this proposal, as with lagged reserve requirements, a dynamic response of $M1$ to B is implied. In the absence of significant changes in e^*, t, and k, the long-run implications of the two reserve requirement structures are identical. The difference between the reserve requirement regimes is in the initial effect of a change in B on transactions money. Under the Poole proposal, the initial effect is smaller than the ultimate effect, and the response of $M1$ to a change in B gradually increases over time. This regime contrasts with the lagged reserve requirement regime, where the initial effect overshoots the long-run effect.

None of the alternative proposals for distributed lags on reserve requirements has any particular advantage in a world in which the central bank can exert precise control over the outstanding stock of base money or total reserves and can predict the base or reserve multiplier without error. Under such conditions, the central bank can choose a path for the monetary base (or total reserves) that will produce any desired path of transactions money over time. In practice, central banks face two difficulties: (1) base money or total reserves can fluctuate because of factors beyond the control of the monetary authorities (for example, changes in Treasury cash balances and central bank float) and (2) the base money or reserve multipliers are not perfectly predictable. Under these circumstances, the size of unexpected changes in the stock of transactions balances depends on the size of the money multiplier and the elasticities of the multiplier with respect to its component ratios. The advantage of the Poole proposal for 100 percent reserve requirements on changes in deposits is that the impact money multiplier is smaller than the corresponding multiplier for other proposals in this general class of reserve requirements. It also has smaller elasticities with respect to the component ratios than the multipliers implied by other proposals. Consequently, the structure proposed by Poole minimizes short-run stochastic fluctuations of transactions balances outside the control of the central bank.

5. THE RELATION BETWEEN TRANSACTIONS MONEY AND NONBORROWED RESERVES

Nonborrowed reserves were the focus of the New Operating Procedures adopted by the Federal Reserve in October 1979 and subsequently abandoned in 1982. During this period, the Fed sought to maintain the growth of nonborrowed reserves stock along a path that it believed to be consistent with the established objective for the growth of transactions money. In practice, persistent deviations from the desired path of nonborrowed reserves were permitted. Specifically, when actual nonborrowed reserves rose above or fell short of the desired level, the Fed did not try to move back to the desired level immediately, but instead attempted to implement the adjustment gradually (see Lindsey et al., 1984; Tinsley et al., 1981). The desired path for nonborrowed reserves was constructed using an implicit nonborrowed reserves-transactions money multiplier, similar to the monetary base multipliers discussed above. The actual steps used by the Federal Reserve staff economists are discussed in Wallich (1980) and translated into the equivalent money multiplier framework in Rasche and Johannes (1987).

The average money multiplier implicit in this approach to monetary policy can be derived from the definition of nonborrowed reserves:

$$(14) \quad NBR = R - BOR = RR + ER - BOR,$$

where BOR = borrowings by depository institutions from the central bank. A borrowed reserves-total deposits ratio, $b = BOR/(D + T)$, can be defined, and the definitions of k, t, rr, and e established above can be used to obtain the average nonborrowed reserves-transactions money multiplier as:

$$(15) \quad \frac{M1}{NBR} = \frac{1 + k}{(rr + e - b)(1 + t) + k}.$$

The Federal Reserve determined the desired stock of nonborrowed reserves from (1) its target stock of $M1$ and (2) staff forecasts of the marginal component ratios: k, t, rr, e, and b. In practice, it proved difficult to obtain accurate forecasts of the marginal nonborrowed reserves multiplier, largely because of forecast errors for the marginal borrowings ratio.

Forecasts of the borrowings ratio were generated from models that assumed that the ratio responded (positively) to the spread of the federal funds rate over the discount rate. Kier (1981) discusses the instability of regression estimates of this model, and Goodfriend (1983) provides a theoretical analysis that demonstrates why such regression estimates can be expected to be unstable under the conditions that existed in the United

States in the early 1980s. Tinsley et al. (1982) propose a complicated non-linear specification of the borrowings ratio as a function of the interest-rate spread that attempts to deal with (1) switching from borrowing at the central bank to borrowing from other depository institutions when the rate spread becomes negative and (2) an asymptote for total aggregate central bank borrowing that arises when a high proportion of depository institutions cannot borrow as much as they desire because of administrative rationing of borrowing by Federal Reserve lending officers. Dutkowski and Foote (1985) constructed a "switching regression" model to deal with the same specification problems. However, neither of these specifications allows for the dynamic factors that Goodfriend shows to be the consequence of the administrative procedures of the Federal Reserve discount facility.

An additional problem that the literature has not recognized would arise in modeling the money supply process under conditions of lagged reserve accounting *and* a totally predetermined supply of nonborrowed reserves. All the models that address this environment specify demand functions for excess reserves and borrowing for an individual depository institution. All these models presume that the institution has sufficient freedom to establish the desired amounts of both excess reserves and borrowed reserves during a particular reserve settlement period (see, for example, Lombra and Kaufman, 1984). Typically, desired excess reserves are specified as a function of a market rate of interest such as the federal funds rate, and desired borrowings are specified as a function of a market rate–discount rate spread. At this point in the analysis, a representative firm assumption is invoked, explicitly or implicitly, to justify aggregate demand functions for excess reserves and borrowings of the same form as the hypothesized microeconomic relationships.

This approach overlooks a fundamental aggregation problem that occurs with lagged reserve requirements and predetermined aggregate nonborrowed reserves. Since

$$(16) \quad NBR = R - BOR = RR + ER - BOR,$$

then

$$(17) \quad ER - BOR = NBR - RR,$$

and in the aggregate actual excess reserves net of borrowings (free reserves) is totally predetermined under the assumed regime. Alternatively, in the aggregate, depository institutions do not have sufficient degrees of freedom to choose independently both their holdings of excess reserves and their borrowings from the central bank.

6. EMPIRICAL EVIDENCE

Two distinctly different approaches have been used in the empirical analysis of the money supply process. The first approach utilizes time-series econometric techniques to examine the predictability of the money multiplier for different reserve aggregates (including total reserves, nonborrowed reserves, the monetary base, and the net monetary base). The second approach undertakes estimation of demand function specifications for the various component ratios of the various multipliers.

The time-series analyses have been constructed on two different levels. Some studies (Bomhoff, 1977; Hafer et al., 1983; Hafer and Hein, 1984; Spindt, 1984) specify relatively simple time-series models for particular money multipliers. The general conclusion of these studies is that a simple time-series specification is capable of generating predictions of money multipliers that are quite accurate. Since predictions from time-series models are functions only of the history of the time series under consideration, one interpretation of these results is that economic forces such as changes in relative rates of return or changes in income have relatively little effect on the marginal money multiplier. The validity and accuracy of these time-series models have been challenged. Pierce (1976) and Feige and McGee (1977), for example, argue that conclusions drawn from such analyses are inappropriate, at least for the period of lagged reserve accounting. They find that causation in this regime goes from money to future reserves and not in the reverse direction as is assumed in the construction of a money multiplier. They present timing (Granger causality) analyses based on weekly data in support of this contention.

In addition, Lindsey et al. (1984) criticize the time-series analyses, independent of lagged or contemporaneous reserve requirement regimes. They argue that historically the Federal Reserve has never utilized a reserve aggregate to control any monetary aggregate (with the possible exception of the nonborrowed reserve operating policy during 1979–82). Instead, the Federal Reserve has attempted to implement its monetary policy objectives by manipulating interest rates (e.g., a federal funds rate operating procedure). Under these conditions, both transactions money and the monetary base (or reserves) should be viewed as jointly endogenous variables in the observed data. They argue that any analysis that both uses the historical data and assumes that the monetary base (or reserves) is exogenous suffers from statistical bias and underestimates the forecast errors that would be generated by such time-series models when applied in a regime in which the monetary base (or reserves) is truly set exogenously by the central bank. This criticism does not directly address the question of the influence of interest rates and/or income on marginal money multipliers. Rather, it suggests the possibility that such effects are potentially greater than implied by the time-series analyses. Rasche and Johannes

(1987) show that the size of the biases that concern Lindsey et al. (1984) is directly related to the interest elasticities of the component ratios of the money multipliers.

Johannes and Rasche (1979, 1981) and Rasche and Johannes (1987) employ a second type of time-series analysis. In these studies, time-series econometric techniques are applied in the analysis of the component ratios from which the various money multipliers are constructed. They show that highly accurate predictions of the various component ratios can be obtained from simple time-series models. Furthermore, they show that these time-series models are quite robust in the presence of the extensive financial innovation and deregulation that characterized the United States in the late 1970s and early 1980s and during the period of significantly greater interest rate volatility in 1979–80. These results also suggest relatively minor impacts of interest rates and income on marginal money multipliers. Anderson, Johannes, and Rasche (1983) demonstrate how this conclusion is consistent with the results of econometric studies of the demands for currency, time deposits, demand deposits, excess reserves, and borrowings.

Lindsey et al. (1984) also criticize the Johannes-Rasche conclusions as being subject to the endogeneity bias problem. In this context, the argument for endogeneity bias implies that the time-series characteristics of one or more of the component ratios of the various money multipliers change as the focus of the central bank's operating procedure is altered. Among the component ratios—k, t, rr, e, and b—the ratios for which this argument seems to be most plausible are e and b. As noted above, Kier (1981) argues that econometric specifications of the aggregate demand for borrowing from the Federal Reserve, estimated on the basis of data prior to the October 1979 implementation of the New Operating Procedure, do not appear to be stable during the 1979–80 period. Kaufman and Lombra (1980) contend that the demand for excess reserves changed with the implementation of lagged reserve accounting in 1968, at least to the extent that a small reduction took place in the average level of aggregate excess reserve demand. There do not appear to be any studies which argue that aggregate demand functions for currency, transactions deposits, or time deposits are sensitive to changes in central bank operating procedures.[19]

These critiques give rise to the following question: how sensitive is the money multiplier to changes in the several component ratios? As is apparent from equations (8) and (15), instability of the demand for borrowing has no impact on the multiplier for the monetary base (or total reserves), but it is a potential source of significant change in the multiplier for nonborrowed reserves (or the net monetary base). This question can be investigated by constructing a first-order Taylor series expansion of the log of the money multiplier around the logs of the component ratios. As an example, consider the monetary base multiplier in equation (8):

(18) $\Delta lnm = \epsilon(m,k) \, \Delta lnk + \epsilon(m,t) \, \Delta lnt + \epsilon(m,rr) \, \Delta lnrr$
$+ \, \epsilon(m,e) \, \Delta lne + R,$

where $\epsilon(m,\bullet)$ represents the elasticity of the multiplier with respect to the several component ratios and R is the residual of the expansion. Rasche and Johannes (1987) show that for the monetary base and total reserves the approximation residual is very small and has a small variance. Consequently, the log linear effects of changes in the component ratios are the most important source of changes in these multipliers.

Measures of the relevant elasticities can be derived using the formula provided in Rasche and Johannes (1987). The important point for this discussion is that the elasticity of the monetary base multiplier with respect to the excess reserve ratio, given levels of excess reserves that have been observed in the United States in the postwar period, is extremely low. Therefore, major instability of the excess reserve ratio, or a substantial interest-rate elasticity of this ratio, has only a minor impact on the monetary base multiplier in the United States. The same conclusion holds for the net monetary base multiplier. Elasticities of the total reserves and non-borrowed reserve multipliers with respect to the excess reserve ratio are larger than the base multiplier elasticities. Nonetheless, they are still too small for this ratio to be a major source of interest-rate elasticity of the marginal money multipliers.

In contrast, the multiplier elasticities with respect to the k and t component ratios, given the relative magnitudes of currency, transactions deposits, and time deposits observed for the U.S. economy, are quite large. Therefore, the most likely sources of changes in money multipliers are either unpredictable changes in the k or t ratios, or changes in these ratios that arise in response to interest-rate and/or income fluctuations, including those induced by central bank dynamic open market operations. Currency demand has been examined in several studies including Cagan (1965), Garcia and Pak (1979), Fry (1974), and Dotsey (1988). None of the results of these investigations suggests that the currency-deposit ratio is highly interest elastic.

The second approach to empirical analysis of the money supply process focuses on the estimation of demand functions for the component ratios of the multipliers.[20] A review and analysis of a number of such studies constructed prior to 1970 can be found in Rasche (1972). Rasche concludes that a wide range of analyses show that the interest elasticity of the monetary base multiplier is quite small. Since 1972, relatively few studies have focused directly on the question of the interest (or income) elasticity of the multiplier component ratios. The greatest proportion of such research has examined the aggregate demand function for borrowing (Dutkowsky and Foote, 1985; Kier, 1981; Resler et al., 1985; Tinsley et al., 1982). These analyses suggest that when the discount rate is maintained below the federal funds rate, and in the absence of severe rationing by Federal Reserve lending officers, the interest elasticity of aggregate borrowing can be substantial. Even though the elasticity of the net monetary base and nonborrowed reserve multipliers with respect to the borrowing ratio is small, this suggests that under some circumstances the net monetary base multiplier and the nonborrowed reserve multiplier can be substantially affected by changes in interest rates induced by open market operations. Unfortunately, the same studies also suggest that the specification of a robust aggregate borrowing demand function is extremely difficult.

Finally, a number of disaggregated demand for money studies have been done in the tradition of Goldfeld (1973). Anderson, Johannes, and Rasche (1983) show how implicit k and t ratio interest elasticities can be derived from such analyses. Based on the estimates that are reported in the Goldfeld study (which are representative of the estimates in the subsequent literature), the interest elasticities of the k and t ratios, particularly short-run elasticities, are very small.

Another type of econometric study that addresses these issues implicitly is the construction of econometric models of the money market. Examples of such analyses are found in Farr (1981), Judd and Scaddings (1981), and Thompson, Pierce, and Parry (1975). These models do not explicitly address the question of the interest elasticity of money multipliers or their component ratios. However, Anderson and Rasche (1982) demonstrate simulation techniques that can be applied to such models to generate estimates of the implied multiplier interest elasticity. These techniques, applied to the models constructed by Farr (1981) and Judd and Scaddings (1981), also reveal implicit interest elasticities for money multipliers that are quite small.

7. CONCLUSION

This chapter has examined the role of a central bank in affecting the stock of transactions money that is available in an economy. There is no doubt that a central bank can control the amount of government or base money in the economy with considerable precision. The desired changes in base money can be implemented either through open market operations or through active manipulation of the rate at which depository institutions are permitted to borrow from the central bank.

The most important question concerning the money supply process is the extent to which actions by private economic agents influence the transmission of changes in base money to changes in the stock of transactions money in the economy. A convenient framework for summarizing this question is a base money multiplier. In this framework, the critical question is the size of the marginal money multiplier relative to the average money multiplier. If, in response to monetary policy actions, the marginal multiplier is close to the average value of the multiplier, then changes in base money are the dominant source of changes in transactions money and are the most important aspect of the money supply process.

Institutional arrangements, such as the structure of the reserve requirement system are believed to be one important factor influencing the size of the marginal money multiplier. Lagged reserve requirements are generally believed to reduce substantially a central bank's ability to affect the stock of transaction money, although this conclusion is drawn primarily for regimes where the operating procedures of the central bank focused on smoothing interest rates rather than controlling the growth of base money. The projection of this experience to regimes in which much more interest-rate volatility is permitted is problematic.

Portfolio reallocations by private economic agents represent a potential important source of offsetting effects on the stock of transactions money in response to central bank monetary policy actions. Such reallocations can be generated by interest-rate changes provoked by monetary policy actions. Some adjustments, such as changes in excess reserve holdings of depository institutions, cannot play a significant role in the money supply process unless excess reserves achieve a substantial fraction of total assets. When excess reserves are only a small fraction of total assets, the elasticity of the money multiplier is so small that, even with very large percentage changes in excess reserves, only small changes in the money multiplier would result.

More important sources of induced responses in money multipliers are adjustments of currency and time deposit holdings relative to holdings of demand deposits. Available evidence from several different types of statistical analysis, including time-series analyses, econometric models, and studies of individual asset demand functions, suggests that the interest and income elasticities of currency-transactions deposits and time deposit-transaction deposits ratios are quite small, particularly in the short run. Therefore, even with the large elasticities of the base multiplier with respect to these components, policy-induced changes in interest rate and income are unlikely to be a significant source of variation in the stock of transactions money.

Unsystematic and unpredictable shocks to the currency–transactions deposit and the time deposit–transactions deposit ratio are significant sources of short-run changes in the base money multiplier that are outside the control of a central bank. Over the longer run, such random movements tend to average out, so that changes in base money are the most important source of changes in transactions money. However, in the short run considerable noise can be expected in the transmission of monetary policy actions through the money supply process.

NOTES

1. In several prominent cases, notably the Bank of England and the Bank of France, the monetary authority was historically a private firm that was explicitly nationalized. In other cases, such as the Federal Reserve System in the United

States, the regional Federal Reserve Banks still exist legally as private firms, but over time decision-making authority in the system has become centralized in the Board of Governors, an independent agency of the U.S. Congress.

2. In the United States a hybrid arrangement now exists where paper money is manufactured on the authority of the Federal Reserve System (Federal Reserve Notes), while coinage is manufactured on the authority of the U.S. Treasury and distributed by the Federal Reserve System on behalf of the Treasury.

3. A typical central bank also functions as the monetary agent for the central government. As such, it is the bank at which the government treasury holds its working cash account. Such deposits of the treasury are an additional liability of the central bank. However, they are not important for this discussion since they cancel out in a consolidation of all the financial accounts of the central government.

4. Such administrative guidelines are generally defined in Federal Reserve publications and regulations, although the precise implementation of the guidelines in the case of a particular depository institution is ultimately at the discretion of the lending officer of the individual Federal Reserve Bank.

5. On several occasions during the past twenty years, the Federal Reserve has extended large loans to a number of large banks that have experienced liquidity crises. Since 1980 such borrowing has been classified as extended credit borrowing. In the stated view of the Federal Reserve it is not a mechanism for affecting the supply of high-powered money to the economy as a whole (see footnote 4, Statistical Release H.3, Board of Governors of the Federal Reserve System).

6. In those countries where there is a large outstanding quantity of interest-bearing government debt and a well-developed secondary market for these debt instruments, open market operations are usually conducted in the government securities markets. In countries where there is only a small quantity of interest-bearing government debt outstanding, or where secondary markets for such securities are not highly developed, open market operations may be conducted in foreign exchange markets.

7. In principle, the central bank can undertake open market operations with any private economic agent. In practice, such transactions are limited to selected dealers in either government securities or foreign exchange, so-called primary dealers.

8. These equations assume that all currency is held by nonfinancial economic agents ("the public") and that none is held in depository institutions in the form of vault cash. This issue is discussed in more detail below in the discussion of reserve requirements.

9. For an excellent summary of the historical development of the theory of the role of individual depository institutions and the aggregate of all depository institutions in the expansion or contraction of transactions money under the assumption of fixed reserve- and currency-deposit ratios, see Humphrey (1987).

10. The most frequent advocates of this proposition are analysts of the monetarist persuasion.

11. Prior to 1959, member banks of the Federal Reserve System could only satisfy reserve requirements with deposits held in Federal Reserve Banks. Since then, vault cash, measured on one of several bases, has counted toward reserve requirements. Prior to the Monetary Control Act of 1980, state-chartered non-member banks in the United States frequently were able to utilize vault cash,

transactions balances held at correspondent banks, and government securities to meet any reserve requirement. Since 1980, all depository institutions in the United States with transaction deposit liabilities have been required to satisfy Federal Reserve requirements for reserves.

12. Other liabilities have been subjected to reserve requirements at various times. In particular, on several occasions reserve requirements have been implemented against borrowing by U.S. banks from their foreign branches (so-called Eurodollar borrowings). Under the Monetary Control Act of 1980, only transactions deposits and nonpersonal time deposits are subject to reserve requirements at U.S. institutions. In addition, demand deposits of the U.S. Treasury and foreign central banks and official institutions at depository institutions are subject to reserve requirements in the United States, even though these deposits are not considered to be part of transactions money.

13. Note that if eligible reserve assets include vault cash of depository institutions, then in equation (1) R should be interpreted as deposits at the central bank plus vault cash held by depository institutions and the identity holds, regardless of the amount of vault cash in the financial system. When vault cash (V) is present but is not eligible to meet required reserves, then equation (1) must be modified: $B = R + V + C$, where R is total reserves, and C is currency held by the public.

14. In the United States such authority was instituted in 1933.

15. For the technical details in the differences in construction of these two measures, see Burger and Rasche (1977), Gilbert (1980a, b, 1983, 1984), and Tatom (1980). The reader is cautioned that prior to the publication of the Board of Governors monetary base series, the St. Louis Federal Reserve Bank measure was known as the monetary base.

16. In practice the system of reserve requirements was more complicated during this period. The difference between required reserves based on deposits two weeks previously and average vault cash held two weeks previously had to be covered by average contemporaneous balances at the Federal Reserve Banks.

17. In fact, some evidence exists that aggregate excess reserves increased in the United States after October 1979 when the Fed permitted greater short-run variability of the funds rate (Kaufman and Lombra, 1986).

18. This clearly falls into a general class of reserve requirements of the form $RR = a_0(D+T) + a_1(D+T)_{-1} + a_2(D+T)_{-2} + \ldots$ In this proposal $a_0 = 1$, $a_1 = 0$, $a_2 = (rr-1)$ and $a_i = 0$, $i > 2$.

19. Numerous studies of U.S. data and data from several other countries report the instability of estimates of aggregate money demand (in particular transactions deposits) functions in the late 1970s and early 1980s. Although many theories have been advanced to account for the observed instability, differences in central bank operating procedures are not included in the list (principally because the major instabilities are noted during periods or in countries where there are no changes in central bank procedures). Lengthy bibliographies of these studies are found in Judd and Scaddings (1982) and Rasche and Johannes (1987).

20. Frequently, demand functions for such ratios are not estimated directly, but demand functions for separate assets such as currency and transactions deposits can be used to derive the implicit demand function for a component ratio (see Anderson, Johannes, and Rasche, 1983).

REFERENCES

Anderson, R. G.; Johannes, J. M.; and Rasche, R. H. 1983. "A New Look at the Relationship Between Time-Series and Structural Econometric Models." *Journal of Econometrics* 23: 235–51.

Anderson. R. G., and Rasche, R. H. 1982. "What Do Money Market Models Tell Us about How to Implement Monetary Policy?" *Journal of Money, Credit and Banking* 14 (November): Part 2, 796–828.

Baghestani, H., and Mott, T. 1988. "The Money Supply Process under Alternative Federal Reserve Operating Procedures: An Empirical Analysis." *Southern Economic Journal* 55 (October): 485–93.

Beek, D. C. 1981. "Excess Reserves and Reserve Targeting." Federal Reserve Bank of New York *Quarterly Review* (Autumn): 15–22.

Board of Governors of the Federal Reserve System. 1971. "Summary of the Proposed Redesign of the Discount Window." In *Reappraisal of the Federal Reserve Discount Mechanism*. Washington D.C.

Bomhoff, E. J. 1977. "Predicting the Money Multiplier: A Case Study for the U.S. and the Netherlands." *Journal of Monetary Economics* 3 (July): 325–45.

Brainard, W., and Tobin, J. 1968. "Pitfalls in Financial Model Building." *American Economic Review* 58 (May): 99–122.

Brunner, K. 1961. "A Schema for the Supply Theory of Money." *International Economic Review* 2 (January): 79–109.

———. 1968. "The Role of Money and Monetary Policy." Federal Reserve Bank of St. Louis *Review* 50 (July): 9–24.

———, and Meltzer, A. H. 1964. "Some Further Investigations of Demand and Supply Functions for Money." *Journal of Finance* 19: 240–83.

———. 1968. "Liquidity Traps for Money, Bank Credit and Interest Rates." *Journal of Political Economy* 76: 1–37.

Bryant, R. C. 1982. "Federal Reserve Control of the Money Stock." *Journal of Money, Credit and Banking* 14 (November): Part 2, 597–625.

Burger, A. E., and Rasche, R. H. 1977. "Revision of the Monetary Base." Federal Reserve Bank of St. Louis *Review* 59 (July): 13–27.

Cagan, P. 1965. *Determinants and Effects of Changes in the Stock of Money, 1875–1960*. New York: Columbia University Press.

Coats, W. L. 1976. "Lagged Reserve Accounting and the Money Supply Mechanism." *Journal of Money, Credit and Banking* 8 (June): 167–80.

Cosimano, T. F. 1987. "Reserve Accounting and Variability in the Fed Funds Market." *Journal of Money, Credit and Banking* 19 (May): 198–209.

Dotsey, M. 1988. "Demand for Currency in the United States." *Journal of Money, Credit and Banking* 20 (February): 22–40.

Dutkowsky, D., and Foote, W. 1985. "Switching, Aggregation and the Demand for Borrowed Reserves." *Review of Economics and Statistics* 67 (May): 331–35.

Farley, D. E., and Simpson, T. D. 1979. "Graduated Reserve Requirements and Monetary Control." *Journal of Finance* 34 (June): 999–1012.

Farr, H. T. 1981. "The Monthly Money Market Model." Washington D.C.: Board of Governors of the Federal Reserve System Mimeo.

Feige, E. L., and McGee, R. T. 1977. "Money Supply Control and Lagged Reserve Accounting." *Journal of Money, Credit and Banking* 9 (November): 536–51.

Friedman, M., and Schwartz, A. J. 1963. *A Monetary History of the United States 1867–1960*. Princeton, N.J.: Princeton University Press.

Froyen R. T., and Kopecky, K. J. 1983. "A Note on Reserve Requirements and Monetary Control with a Flexible Discount Rate." *Journal of Banking and Finance* 7 (March): 101–9.

Fry, C. L. 1974. "An Explanation of Short-run Fluctuations in the Ratio of Currency to Deposits." *Journal of Money, Credit and Banking* 6 (August): 403–12.

Garcia, G., and Pak, S. 1979. "The Ratio of Currency to Deposits in the U.S." *Journal of Finance* 34 (June): 703–15.

Gilbert, R. A. 1980a. "Lagged Reserve Requirements: Implications for Monetary Control and Bank Reserve Management." Federal Reserve Bank of St. Louis *Review* 62 (May), 7–20.

———. 1980b. "Revision of the St. Louis Federal Reserve's Adjusted Monetary Base." Federal Reserve Bank of St. Louis *Review* 62 (December): 3–10.

———. 1983. "Two Measures of Reserves: Why Are They Different?" Federal Reserve Bank of St. Louis *Review* 65 (June/July): 16–25.

———. 1984. "Calculating the Adjusted Monetary Base under Contemporaneous Reserve Requirements." Federal Reserve Bank of St. Louis *Review* 66 (February): 27–32.

———. 1985. "Operating Procedures for Conducting Monetary Policy." Federal Reserve Bank of St. Louis *Review* 67 (February): 31–46.

Goldfeld, S. M. 1973. "The Demand for Money Revisited." *Brookings Papers on Economic Activity* 3: 577–638.

———. 1976. "The Case of the Missing Money." *Brookings Papers on Economic Activity* 3: 683–730.

Goodfriend, M. 1983. "Discount Window Borrowing, Monetary Policy and the Post 10/6/79 Federal Reserve Operating Procedure." *Journal of Monetary Economics* 12 (September): 321–30.

———. 1984. "The Promises and Pitfalls of Contemporaneous Reserve Requirements for the Implementation of Monetary Policy." Federal Reserve Bank of Richmond *Economic Review* 70 (May/June): 3–12.

Gurley, J., and Shaw, E. S. 1960. *Money in a Theory of Finance*. Washington D.C.: Brookings Institution.

Hafer, R. W., et al. 1983. "Forecasting the Money Multiplier: Implications for Money Stock Control and Economic Activity." Federal Reserve Bank of St. Louis *Review* 65 (October): 22–33.

———, and Hein, S. E. 1984. "Predicting the Money Multiplier: Forecasts from Component and Aggregate Models." *Journal of Monetary Economics* 14 (November): 375–84.

Hamdani, K. 1984. "CRR and Excess Reserves: An Early Appraisal." Federal Reserve Bank of New York *Quarterly Review* 9 (Autumn): 16–23.

Humphrey, T. M. 1987. "The Theory of Multiple Deposit Expansion of Deposits: What It Is and Whence It Came From." Federal Reserve Bank of Richmond *Economic Review* 73 (March/April): 3–11.

Johannes, J. M., and Rasche, R. H. 1979. "Predicting the Money Multiplier." *Journal of Monetary Economics* 5 (July): 301–25.

———. 1981. "Can the Reserves Approach to Monetary Control Really Work?" *Journal of Money, Credit and Banking* 13 (August) 298–313.

Judd, J. P. 1977. "Dynamic Implications of Poole's Proposed Reserve Requirement Rule: A Note." *Journal of Money, Credit and Banking* 9 (November): 667–71.

———, and Scaddings, J. L. 1980. "Short-run Monetary Control under Alternative Reserve Accounting Rules." Federal Reserve Bank of San Francisco *Economic Review* (Summer): 3–21.

———. 1981. "Liability Management, Bank Loans, and 'Deposit Market' Disequilibrium." Federal Reserve Bank of San Francisco *Economic Review* (Summer): 22–44.

———. 1982. "The Search for a Stable Money Demand Function." *Journal of Economic Literature* 20 (September): 993–1023.

Kaminow, I. 1977. "Required Reserve Ratios, Policy Instruments and Monetary Control." *Journal of Monetary Economics* 3 (October): 389–408.

Kaufman, H. M., and Lombra, R. E. 1980. "The Demand for Excess Reserves, Liability Management, and the Money Supply Process." *Economic Inquiry* 18 (October): 555–66.

———. 1986. "The Effect of Changes in the Federal Reserve's Policy Rule on the Stochastic Structure Linking Reserves, Interest Rates and Money." *Southern Economic Journal* 53 (April): 1080–87.

Kier, P. 1981. "Impact of Discount Policy Procedures on the Effectiveness of Reserve Targeting." In *New Monetary Control Procedures I*. Washington, D.C.: Board of Governors of the Federal Reserve System.

Knobel, A. 1977. "The Demand for Reserves by Commercial Banks." *Journal of Money, Credit and Banking* 9 (February): Part I, 32–47.

Kopecky, K. J. 1984. "Monetary Control under Reverse Lag and Contemporaneous Reserve Accounting: A Comparison." *Journal of Money, Credit and Banking* 16 (February): 81–188.

———. 1988. "A Mean-Variance Framework for Analyzing Reserve Requirements and Monetary Control." *Journal of Banking and Finance*: 151–60.

———; Parke, D. W.; and Porter, R. D. 1983. "A Framework for Analyzing Money Stock Control under the Monetary Control Act." *Journal of Economics and Business* 35 (June): 139–57.

Lane, T. D. 1984. "Money Supply Control and Lagged Reserve Accounting: A Comment." *Journal of Money, Credit and Banking* 16 (November): Part I, 536–46.

Laufenberg, D. E. 1976a. "Reserve Measures as Operating Variables of Monetary Policy: An Empirical Analysis." *Journal of Finance* 31 (June): 853–64.

———. 1976b. "Contemporaneous vs Lagged Reserve Accounting: Comment." *Journal of Money, Credit and Banking* 8 (June): 239–45.

———. 1979. "Optimal Reserve Requirement Ratios Against Bank Deposits for Short-Run Monetary Control." *Journal of Money, Credit and Banking* 11 (February): 91–105.

Laurent, R. D. 1979. "Reserve Requirements: Are They Lagged in the Wrong Direction?" *Journal of Money, Credit and Banking* 11 (August): 301–10.

Leroy, S. F. 1979. "Monetary Control under Lagged Reserve Accounting." *Southern Economic Journal* 46 (October): 460–70.

———, and Lindsey, D. E. 1978. "Determining the Monetary Instrument: A Diagrammic Exposition," *American Economic Review* 68 (December): 801–12.

Lindsey, D. E., et al. 1984. "Short-Run Monetary Control: Evidence under a Nonborrowed Reserve Operating Procedure." *Journal of Monetary Economics* 13 (January): 87–111.

Lombra, R. E., and Kaufman, H. M. 1984. "The Money Supply Process: Identification, Stability and Estimation." *Southern Economic Journal* 50 (April): 1147–59.

———. 1985. "The Money Supply Process: Reply." *Southern Economic Journal* 52 (October): 527–31.

Mengle, D. L. 1986. "The Discount Window." Federal Reserve Bank of Richmond *Economic Review* 72 (May/June): 2–10.

Pesek, B., and Saving, T. R. 1968. *The Foundations of Money and Banking*. New York: Macmillan.

Pierce, D. A. 1976. "Money Supply Control: Reserves as the Instrument under Lagged Reserve Accounting." *Journal of Finance* 31 (June): 845–52.

Poole, W. 1976. "A Proposal for Reforming Bank Reserve Requirements in the United States." *Journal of Money, Credit and Banking* 8 (May): 137–47.

Rasche, R. H. 1972. "A Review of Empirical Studies of the Money Supply Mechanism." Federal Reserve Bank of St. Louis *Review* 54 (July): 11–19.

———, and Johannes, J. M. 1987. *Controlling the Growth of Monetary Aggregates*. Boston: Kluwer Academic Publishers.

Resler, D. H., et al. 1985. "Detecting and Estimating Changing Economic Relationships: The Case of Discount Window Borrowing." *Applied Economics* 37 (June): 509–27.

Roosa, R. V. 1956. *Federal Reserve Operations in the Money and Government Securities Markets*. New York: Federal Reserve Bank of New York.

Santomero, A. M. 1983. "Controlling Monetary Aggregates: The Discount Window." *Journal of Finance* 38 (June): 827–43.

Saving, T. R. 1977. "A Theory of the Money Supply with Competitive Banking." *Journal of Monetary Economics* 3 (July): 289–303.

———. 1979. "Money Supply Theory with Competitively Determined Deposit Rates and Activity Charges." *Journal of Money, Credit and Banking* 11 (February): 22–31.

Selgin, G. A. 1989. "Commercial Banks as Pure Intermediaries: Between "Old" and "New" Views." *Southern Economic Journal* 56 (July): 80–86.

Spindt, P. A. 1984. "Modeling the Money Multiplier and the Controllability of the Divisa Monetary Quantity Aggregates." *Review of Economics and Statistics* 66 (May): 314–19.

Steindl, F. G. 1985. "The Money Supply Process: Comment." *Southern Economic Journal* 52 (October): 523–26.

Tatom, J. A. 1980. "Issues in Measuring an Adjusted Monetary Base." Federal Reserve Bank of St. Louis *Review* 62 (December): 11–29.

Thistle, P. D., et al. 1989. "Interest Rates and Bank Portfolio Adjustments." *Journal of Banking and Finance* (March): 151–61.

Thompson, T. D.; Pierce, J. L.; and Parry, R. T. 1975. "A Monthly Money Market Model." *Journal of Money, Credit and Banking* 7 (November): 411–31.

Thornton, D. J. 1982. "Simple Analytics of the Money Supply Process and Monetary Control." Federal Reserve Bank of St. Louis *Review* 64 (December): 22–39.

————. 1983. "Lagged and Contemporaneous Reserve Accounting: An Alternative View." Federal Reserve Bank of St. Louis *Review* 65 (November): 22–33.

————. 1988. "Borrowed Reserves Operating Procedures: Theory and Evidence." Federal Reserve Bank of St. Louis *Review* (January/February): 30–54.

Tinsley, P. A., et al. 1981. "Money Market Impacts of Alternative Operating Procedures." In *New Monetary Control Procedures II*. Washington D.C.: Board of Governors of the Federal Reserve System.

————. 1982. "Policy Robustness: Specification and Simulation of a Monthly Money Market Model." *Journal of Money, Credit and Banking* 14 (November): Part II, 829–56.

Tobin, J. 1963a. "Commercial Banks as Creators of Money." In *Banking and Monetary Studies*, edited by D. Carson. Homewood, Ill: Richard D. Irwin, 408–19.

————. 1963b. "An Essay on the Principles of Debt Management." In Commission on Money and Credit, *Fiscal and Debt Management Policies*. Englewood Cliffs, N.J.: Prentice-Hall.

————. 1969. "A General Equilibrium Approach to Monetary Theory." *Journal of Money, Credit and Banking* 1 (February) 15–29.

Van Hoose, D. D. 1987. "A Note on Discount Rate Policy and the Variability of Discount Window Borrowing." *Journal of Banking and Finance* (December): 563–70.

————. 1988. "Discount Rate Policy and Alternative Federal Reserve Operating Procedures in a Rational Expectations Setting." *Journal of Economics and Business* (November): 285–94.

Wallich, H. C. 1980. "Techniques of Monetary Control." Remarks before the Missouri Valley Economics Association, Memphis (March 1). Mimeo.

3

MONETARY POLICY AND ECONOMIC ACTIVITY

Richard T. Froyen

An observer at a conference once asked, "If money is neutral, why are so few people neutral about monetary policy?" The *neutrality of money* is the proposition that changes in the quantity of money will affect only nominal variables. Real variables, including output and employment, will be unaffected by such changes. Whether monetary policy is neutral in its effects, especially in the short run, has been the focus of the most important controversy in monetary economics during the past sixty years. This chapter examines this controversy and its roots in earlier theories of the role of money. The focus is not just on whether money is neutral, but more broadly on the *transmission mechanism* for monetary policy. Via what channels does money affect output? Or if monetary policy is neutral, what features of the economy cushion output from the effect of changes in the money supply?

We begin in Section 1 with an examination of the quantity theory of money, a part of what is called classical economics. Then we consider John Maynard Keynes's attack on the quantity theory, which was part of his broader attack on classical economics (Section 2). Not all economists found Keynes's critique of the quantity theory convincing. Milton Friedman and other monetarists constructed a modernized version of the classical quantity theory. The monetarist view, discussed in Section 3, leads to different conclusions about the role of money in the economy and the proper conduct of monetary policy. The new classical economics is a second attack on the Keynesian theory. The relationship between money and output posited by new classical economists is also fundamentally different from the Keynesian view. The new classical view is discussed in Section 4. Sections 5 and 6 consider two recent directions in research on the relationship between money and economic activity: real business cycle models and new Keynesian models. Section 7 contains concluding comments.

1. THE QUANTITY THEORY OF MONEY

During the sixteenth century the price level more than tripled in Spain and more than doubled in England, France, and northern Italy. This was a period of huge flows of gold and silver from America to Spain and then into the rest of Europe. Jean Bodin, a French writer, used data to demonstrate the connection between this price explosion and the influx of money into Europe. This is the origin of the classical quantity theory of money.

From the Equation of Exchange to the Quantity Theory

The quantity theory of money states that the aggregate price level is proportionate to the quantity of money in circulation. An increase in the quantity of money leads to a proportionate change in the price level. To understand the quantity theory, a useful starting point is the equation of exchange which can be written as

(1) $MV_T \equiv P_T T,$

where M is the quantity of money, V_T is the transactions velocity of money, P_T is a price index for the items traded, and T is the volume of transactions.

The equation of exchange is an identity relating the volume of transactions at current prices $(P_T T)$ to the stock of money multiplied by the turnover rate for money (MV_T). The turnover rate for money measures the number of times the average dollar is used in transactions during each period and is called the *velocity* of money. The equation of exchange is an identity because velocity is defined ex post. If, for example, in a given year the value of transactions in $(P_T T)$ was \$6,400 billion and the money supply (M) was \$800 billion, we would define the transactions velocity of money to be

(2) $V_T \equiv P_T T/M = 6400/800 = 8.$

The version of the equation of exchange in equation (1) is the transactions version developed by Irving Fisher (1922). But overall transactions include transactions involving financial assets as well as newly produced and previously produced goods—a difficult concept to measure. Another version of Fisher's equation of exchange focuses only on current national income (GNP) transactions. This income version is

(3) $MV \equiv Py,$

where M is the quantity of money. V is now the *income velocity* of money, the number of times the average dollar is used in national income transactions. The price index is the GNP deflator and y is real income. Again the relationship is an identity, with V defined residually ($V \equiv Py/M$).

The equation of exchange, because it is an identity, cannot explain the variables it contains. To convert this identity to the quantity theory, classical economists posited that the equilibrium values of V and y were determined by other forces. If this is the case, the equation of exchange defines a proportionate relationship between P and M, with M taken to be set exogenously by the monetary authority

(4) $P = (\overline{V}/\overline{y})M$,

where the bars (–) over V and y indicate that their values are fixed by other factors. This is the quantity theory of money.

But what other factors determine y and V? In the case of V, quantity theorists argued that the other factors were institutional ones. In the short run, the equilibrium value of velocity (the turnover rate of money) was determined by the payments habits and payments mechanisms in a society. To give some examples, the prevalence of trade credit among firms and the use of credit cards are institutional factors that affect velocity. The more widespread the used trade credit or credit cards, the higher would be velocity. This follows because money would need to be used only at intervals to settle outstanding balances. There would then be more income transactions per dollar of the money supply, which is to say the average dollar would have a higher turnover rate. Because such institutional features change only slowly over time, classical economists believed that velocity could be taken as a constant for analysis of the short run.

Output and Employment in the Classical Model

Even if V is taken to be a constant, the equation of exchange tells us only that Py will be proportionate to M. A given exchange in M will cause a proportionate change in nominal income. It is because classical economists believed that real income (y) was determined by real supply-side factors—not monetary ones—that they thought the whole adjustment would come in the price level. A simple mathematical representation of the classical view of output determination is as follows:

(5) $y = A(t)\, F(\overline{K},N)$ $F_K, F_N > 0,\ F_{NN} < 0,$

(6) $N^d = h\left(\dfrac{w}{p}\right)$ $h_{\frac{w}{p}} < 0,$

(7) $N^s = g\left(\dfrac{w}{p}\right)$ $g_{\frac{w}{p}} > 0.$

Equation (5) is an aggregate production function that specifies the amount of real output produced by given quantities of capital ($\overline{K}$) and labor (N) inputs. The $A(t)$ term reflects the influence of technological change that is assumed to occur over time (t). The amount of output will increase as K or N is increased ($F_K, F_N > 0$).[1] Output will also increase with technological progress ($A(t)$ rises).

The bar ($-$) over the capital stock (K) indicates that we are considering the short run and taking the existing stock of capital as given. Moreover, in the short run we can also take the state of technology as given, thereby fixing the $A(t)$ term. Given these assumptions, the level of output varies only as employment changes.

Firms in this setup have only to decide on how much labor to demand which, in turn, will determine how much output they produce. The aggregate (summed over all firms) demand for labor function is given in equation (6). Labor demand depends negatively on the real wage ($h_{\frac{w}{p}} < 0$). Firms will hire labor to the point where the contribution of the marginal unit of labor to output, the marginal product of labor, is equal to the cost of the unit of labor, which is equal to the real wage. The marginal product of labor declines as more labor is employed with a given amount of capital and for a given state of technology ($F_{NN} < 0$). The higher is the real wage, the fewer workers will be employed before the marginal product has declined to the level of the real wage.

Equation (7) is the labor supply function. The quantity of labor supplied by households is assumed to depend positively on the real wage. To workers, the real wage is the command over goods and services they receive in return for giving up leisure and supplying labor. As this return increases, classical economists assumed that workers would supply more labor.

Taken together with the equilibrium condition, $N^s = N^d$, equations (5) through (7) form a system of three equations in three unknowns: output (y), employment (N), and the real wage (W/P). The factors that determine output and employment in the classical system are those that enter these three equations. Notice that all of these equations are from the supply side of the output market. Equation (5) determines the output level firms will *supply* once they determine employment, which is in turn determined by equilibrium in the labor market. Supply-side factors such as technological change, capital formation, changes in labor-leisure preferences, and population growth will cause output to vary over the long run. In the short run, however, output will be fixed at a level determined by the fixed level of the supply-side factors. This is the justification for setting $y = \bar{y}$ in the quantity theory equation (4).

Aggregate demand for output plays no role in determining output and employment in the classical system. Thus, the quantity of money cannot affect output and employment in the classical system. This follows because the role of money in the classical system is to determine aggregate demand, as we see presently.

The Classical Monetary Transmission Mechanism

Thus far, we have said little about the economic process that causes the aggregate price level to be proportionate to the money supply. How do changes in the money supply cause changes in the price level? The nature of this process, the monetary (policy) transmission mechanism, is better understood after considering an alternative formulation of the quantity theory, the *Cambridge approach*. The Cambridge approach was developed by Alfred Marshall and A. C. Pigou. Their version of the quantity theory arrives at the same result as Irving Fisher's but via a somewhat different route. In Pigou's words, "He [Fisher] has painted his picture on one plan, and I paint mine on another. But the pictures we paint are of the same thing" (1917–18, p. 39).

The *plan* of Marshall and Pigou's picture begins with the question of the optimal amount of money to hold—the demand for money. Pigou and Marshall believed that "everybody is anxious to hold enough of his resources in the form of titles to legal tender [money] both to enable him to effect the ordinary transactions of life without trouble and to secure himself against unexpected demands" (1917–18, p. 40). According to the Cambridge formulation, the demand for money was taken to be proportional to income

(8) $M^d = kPy,$

where Py is nominal income and k, which is called the Cambridge k, is the fraction of income individuals desire to hold in the form of money. This fraction was assumed to be relatively stable in the short run, depending, as in Fisher's formulation, on the payment habits and technology of the society. Because the usefulness of money in the classical system derives from its role in effecting transactions, the demand for money depends on the volume of transactions. Nominal income is assumed to be a good measure of the volume of transactions.

We assume that the central bank sets the supply of money exogenously. In equilibrium, the exogenous money supply must equal money demand

(9) $M = M^d = kPy.$

If k is treated as fixed and real output y is assumed to be determined by supply factors, as explained in the previous subsection, the Cambridge equation also reduces to a proportionate relationship between the quantity of money and the price level

(10) $(1/\bar{k}\bar{y})M = P$,

where the bars (–) over k and y indicate that they are taken as fixed.

The formal equivalence of the Cambridge and Fisherian approach can be seen from equation (10), which is the equivalent of the Fisherian equation (4) with $k = 1/V$. This relationship between velocity (V) and the Cambridge k has the simple interpretation that, for example, if individuals want on average to hold one eighth ($k = \frac{1}{8}$) of their income in the form of money, then the turnover rate of the average dollar, which is velocity, will be 8.

Although the Cambridge and Fisherian versions are formally equivalent, the Cambridge equation leads more naturally to an understanding of the economics of the quantity theory. Consider, for example, the effect of doubling the quantity of money using the Cambridge formulation.

Initially, there would be an excess of money supply over money demand. According to the classical quantity theorists, this excess supply of money would spill over into the goods market as an excess demand; individuals would demand more goods. But there are no more goods to be had since output is fixed by supply factors ($y = \bar{y}$). There would then be "too much money chasing too few goods." Consequently, prices rise. Prices will continue to rise until the excess supply of money is eliminated. This will happen when the price level has doubled because at that point the volume of transactions (Py) and therefore demand for money will have doubled.

Implications for Monetary Policy

Money is neutral in the classical model; money and the real level of economic activity are not related. Money, as Pigou called it, is a *veil* that determines the nominal value in which we measure the level of economic activity, but it has no effect on real quantities. Monetary policy should not therefore be geared to control of real variables such as output and employment. In another sense money is very important; the quantity of money determines the aggregate price level. The goal for monetary policy suggested by the classical quantity theory is, therefore, price stability.[2] This implies that the monetary authority should seek stability of money growth.

2. MONEY IN THE KEYNESIAN MODEL

The title of Keynes's major work, *The General Theory of Employment, Interest and Money*, reflects his view that money is linked to employment (and therefore real economic activity), the link being the interest rate.

Keynes had already analyzed this linkage in his earlier *Treatise on Money* in 1930.

Since the injection of an increased quantity of cash (using the word to include central bank reserves) into the monetary system will increase the reserve-resources of member banks, it will for reasons already explained, render the latter more willing lenders on easier terms; that is to say the new money stimulates the banks to put resources at the disposal of those borrowers who are ready to employ them, if they are offered satisfactory terms. (Keynes, 1930, pp. 262–63)

In the next step in the process, "The lower rate of interest will stimulate the production of capital goods" (Keynes, 1930, p. 263), that is, *investment.*

When we examine the relationship between money and economic activity, we must consider two links: the relationship between money and the interest rate and the relationship between the interest rate and investment, as well as other components of aggregate demand. We consider each linkage in turn.

Money and the Interest Rate

Keynes structured his theory of interest to highlight the relationship between the money supply and the interest rate.

To begin, let us first consider the case of an individual with a given amount of wealth (Wh). For simplicity (following Keynes) assume that there are only two assets in which wealth can be held: money and bonds. Money (M) can be thought of as currency plus checkable bank deposits.[3] The bond asset (B) represents nonmoney assets such as corporate equities and actual bonds (corporate and government). The important distinction between the two types of assets is that money is a short-term asset, whereas bonds are a long-term asset. Because there are only two assets, we have

(11) $Wh \equiv B + M.$

All wealth must be held in one asset or the other.

The identity (11) will hold for each individual and therefore in the aggregate as well. From this it follows that if the bond market is in equilibrium, in that there is neither an excess demand for or supply of bonds, it must be true that the money market is in equilibrium and vice versa. If in the aggregate individuals are in equilibrium with respect to their bond holdings, they must also be satisfied with their holdings of money—for they could only change money holdings by changing bond holdings. We can therefore define the equilibrium interest rate on bonds as the rate that equates supply and demand in the bond market or in the money market. Keynes chose the money market to emphasize the role of the money supply.

If we take the money supply as set exogenously by the central bank, we can define the equilibrium interest rate as the rate at which the public's demand for money is just equal to the existing money supply. The level of the money supply will then be one factor that determines the level of the interest rate. The factors that determine the demand for money will be the others.

The Keynesian Theory of Money Demand

Keynes considered three motives for money demand: the transactions motive, the precautionary motive, and the speculative motive. Considering all three motives, Keynes postulated a money demand function (he called it liquidity preference) of the form

$$(12) \quad \left(\frac{M}{P}\right)^d = L(y,r) \qquad L_y > 0; L_r < 0,$$

where P is the aggregate price level, y is real income and r is the nominal interest rate.

The presence of income in the money demand function comes as a result of Keynes's transactions and precautionary motives. Money is held for use in transactions, and some additional money balances are held as a precaution against unpredictable expenses (e.g., car repair bills). This is much in the spirit of the classical analysis.

The novel feature of equation (12) is that money demand is postulated to depend negatively on the interest rate ($L_r < 0$). This is an important feature because if the amount of money demanded for a given level of income varies inversely with the interest rate, there is no proportionate relationship between money and income. Keynes and later economists working within the Keynesian framework have advanced several reasons for the negative relationship between money demand and the rate of interest.

Speculative Demand for Money

Keynes's explanation was his speculative motive for holding money. Some money was held as an asset to speculate on future movements in bond prices. Bonds are the long-term asset. As such, their price will move inversely with their yield, which is the interest rate. If an investor believes that a rise in interest rates will occur in the future, with a resulting capital loss (fall in price) for the bond, he or she may want to hold the fixed price asset, money—even if money paid no interest. The expected capital loss on bonds would simply have to be large enough to outweigh the interest earned on the bond.

Keynes then argued that the lower the level of the interest rate relative to what an investor believed was a *normal* level, the more likely such an interest rate rise (back toward the normal level) would be. Thus, as we consider progressively lower levels of the interest rate, more investors will come to expect large capital losses on bonds and the speculative demand for money will rise.

Money Demand as Behavior Toward Risk

James Tobin (1958) extended Keynes's theory of the demand for money as an asset. Tobin's theory explains why some money might be held as an asset even if there is no expected capital loss on bonds. In Tobin's model the individual maximizes utility from wealth, which depends positively on the expected return from his or her portfolio of assets and negatively on the riskiness of the portfolio (measured as the standard deviation of returns).[4] Suppose that the interest rate was expected to remain constant in the future. Thus, neither a capital gain nor a loss is expected. As an investor considers portfolios with more bonds and less money, the riskiness of the portfolio increases as does the expected return. This follows because bonds are the risky (variable price) asset while money is the riskless asset, and because bonds pay interest while money does not. An individual will hold some money as long as a diversified portfolio provides higher utility than one with 100 percent bonds. This will happen if at some point the addition to utility from the higher expected return as more bonds are added to the portfolio is exceeded by the loss in utility from the additional risk undertaken. The demand for money as an asset is *behavior toward risk*.

Within Tobin's framework, the interest rate on bonds is a payment to the investor for taking on risk. Tobin's analysis can be used to show that as the interest rate rises—as the payment for undertaking risk increases—investors will respond by buying more of the risky asset, bonds.[5] They will hold less money. Thus, Tobin's model also implies a negative relationship between money demand and the interest rate.

The Baumol-Tobin Inventory Theoretical Approach

The final rationale we consider for the negative relationship between the interest rate and money demand concerns the transactions demand. Keynes did not believe that the interest rate was an important determinant of the transactions demand, but later Keynesian economists have come to the opposite conclusion. The models of Baumol (1952) and Tobin (1956) take an inventory theoretical approach to the transactions demand for money.

An individual (household) receives income payments at discrete intervals (e.g., monthly) but makes outlays with greater frequency (e.g., many times a day).[6] A stock (inventory) of cash is held to make these outlays much as a firm holds an inventory of raw materials. It would not be economical to have to sell bonds each time an outlay must be made.

But just as firms consider the carrying cost of inventories, households (or firms) consider the opportunity cost of holding an inventory of money. In our two-asset model, that opportunity cost is the interest foregone by not buying bonds. This suggests that the higher the interest rate, the more households (and firms) will economize on their holdings of money. The inventory theoretical approach suggests an additional rationale for the negative relationship between the interest rate and demand for money.

The Keynesian Monetary Policy Transmission Mechanism: Part One

If the money supply were increased by a government transfer payment, the transmission mechanism from the money supply to the interest rate would be quite simple. If at a given rate of interest and given level of income the money holdings of individuals increase, there is initially an excess supply of money counterbalanced by an excess demand for bonds. The excess demand for bonds pushes bond prices up and the interest rate down.

The quote presented earlier in this section clearly indicates that Keynes was considering an increase in the money supply via an injection of reserves into the banking system. In the United States this increase would be accomplished by a Federal Reserve purchase of government securities in the open market in New York. As Keynes explained, as a result of the increase in reserves, banks would try to expand lending by offering lower interest rates. Banks might also be willing to lend to some marginal borrowers that were unable to get loans previously. Bank purchases of government and private bonds would increase. The other side of this process of bank asset expansion is an expansion of deposits on the liability side. This is the textbook deposit expansion process where one bank's loans or security purchases generate deposits at other banks.

A new equilibrium is reached (considering just a short period before the output market has time to adjust) when the interest rate falls by enough so that two adjustments have occurred: the fall in the interest rate is just sufficient to leave the public in equilibrium holding the larger money supply, and the increase in deposits is just sufficient to leave the banking sector in equilibrium holding the higher level of reserves.

The Interest Rate and Aggregate Demand: The Keynesian Transmission Mechanism: Part Two

The next link in the Keynesian monetary policy transmission mechanism is that from the interest rate to aggregate demand. Keynesian economists have found it convenient to consider several elements in this second linkage.

The Portfolio Effect. The portfolio effect consists of the direct effect that a change in the interest rate induced by a monetary policy has on the level of aggregate demand. Suppose we consider the effects of a fall in the interest rate as a result of an increase in the money supply. Warren Smith explained the Keynesian view of this process as follows:

> With the expected yield on a unit of real capital initially unchanged, the decline in the yields on financial assets, and the more favorable terms on which new debt can be issued, the balance sheets of households and businesses will be thrown out of equilibrium. The adjustment toward a new equilibrium will take the form of a sale of existing financial assets and issuance of new debt to acquire real capital and claims thereto. This will raise the price of existing units of real capital—or equity claims against these units—relative to the (initially unchanged) cost of producing new units, thereby opening up a gap between desired and actual stocks of capital, a gap that will gradually be closed by production of new capital goods. (Smith, 1969, p. 107)

The fall in the interest rate, through the process of portfolio adjustment as described by Smith, stimulates investment. The term *investment*, however, should be broadly defined to include "the demands for a wide variety of both business and consumer capital—including plant and equipment, inventories, residential construction, and consumer durable goods" (Smith, 1969, p. 107).

Wealth Effects. An increase in the money supply that comes through a government transfer will directly increase wealth. This effect is called the real balance or Pigou effect (after A. C. Pigou).

If the increase in the money supply comes through an open market purchase, there will be a decline of equal magnitude in the public's holding of government bonds. Whether there is a direct effect on the public's total wealth depends on whether government bonds are net wealth. This in turn depends on whether the public views the future tax payments that will have to be made to finance interest payments on these bonds as a liability.[7] The Pigou effect is not, however, the central wealth effect for monetary policy in the Keynesian system. Again, in Keynes's view it was the change in the interest rate that was important. In the case of an expansion in the money supply, the resulting decline in the interest rate represents a rise in the price of existing bonds. As bond yields fall and bond prices rise, investors switch to equities and equity prices also rise. These changes represent increases in the net wealth of households. As household wealth rises, so does consumption demand, especially the demand for consumer durable goods.

Credit Availability Effects. The idea that monetary policy affects aggregate demand via an effect on the availability of credit as well as the interest rate has long been a part of the Keynesian view of the monetary policy process (Scott, 1957). The general presumption has been that a significant amount of credit rationing takes place in financial markets. When the central bank reduces the money supply and banks must reduce the amount of credit they extend, more borrowers are rationed out of the market. During monetary policy expansions marginal borrowers get loans, which in other periods they would not.

Recent research has focused both on why credit rationing exists and its implications for the monetary policy transmission mechanism. Stiglitz and Weiss (1981) explain credit rationing as a response to imperfect information about borrowers and consequent adverse selection problems. Banks can only imperfectly screen potential borrowers with regard to the risk of their projects. If banks raise interest rates to the point where the market is cleared, they will attract more borrowers with higher risk projects (the adverse selection) and cause their current borrowers to move into riskier projects to try to earn a higher return. It is instead profit maximizing to ration credit. Blinder and Stiglitz (1983) argue that it is by increasing the severity of credit constraints that restrictive monetary policies have their greatest impact.

The Exchange-Rate Effect. In an open economy if exchange rates are flexible, changes in the money supply will also affect aggregate demand via an effect on the exchange rate. An expansionary monetary policy in the United States, for example, will cause the exchange rate, measured as the price of foreign currency in domestic currency units (e.g., 1 pound = $1.67), to rise. This follows because the increase in the money supply causes the U.S. interest rate to fall, which makes U.S. financial assets less attractive relative to foreign financial assets. Both domestic and foreign investors will, to some extent, switch from U.S. to foreign assets, reducing the demand for the domestic currency and increasing the demand for foreign currencies. If exchange rates are flexible, the U.S. exchange rate will rise; the dollar will depreciate.

A rise in the U.S. exchange rate will make U.S. exports cheaper to foreigners (dollars cost less) and imports more expensive for U.S. residents. Consequently, aggregate demand in the United States will increase as foreigners buy more of our exports and U.S. residents substitute domestic goods for now more expensive imports.

Monetary Policy and Real Output

The preceding two sections have shown that in the Keynesian system an increase in the money supply leads to a fall in the interest rate which, in turn, increases aggregate demand via a number of channels. But an increase in the money supply leads to an increase in aggregate demand in the classical model as well, albeit through a different channel. In the classical model this increase in demand results only in a higher aggregate price level with all real variables unchanged; money is neutral. Why is money not neutral in the Keynesian system?

In the classical system wages and prices were perfectly flexible. If the money supply went up by 20 percent, for example, both the price level and the money wage would rise by 20 percent. The real wage would be unchanged, and therefore in the labor market equilibrium employment would be unchanged. With employment unchanged, output would also remain the same. Money is not neutral in the Keynesian system because prices and wages do not make these equilibrating changes. Thus, quantities, that is, output and employment, must change. Traditional Keynesian analysis has focused on factors that cause rigidity in the money wage. Our discussion here follows this approach. A number of recent studies have explored possible reasons for price rigidity. These will be considered in Section 6.

Keynesians have been critical of the classical approach where the labor market functions as an auction market, much like a stock market. The money wage moves instantaneously to clear the market. In contrast, in the Keynesian view

wages are not set to clear markets in the short run, but rather are strongly conditioned by longer-term considerations involving . . . employer-worker relations. These factors insulate wages . . . to a significant degree from the impact of shifts in demand so that the adjustment must be made in employment and output. (Okun, 1981, p. 233)

Rather than an auction market, Keynesians see the labor market as contractual. In the unionized sector, the money wage is often set in an explicit contract of two or three years' duration. Money wages in the nonunionized sector are influenced by the union wage. Moreover, in the nonunionized sector implicit contracts often fix the wage for some period.

Another aspect of the classical auction market characterization of the labor market is that workers are assumed to know the real wage at the time they make their labor supply decision. If, however, the workers are entering contracts for future labor supply, they will know the money wage, as set by the contract, but they must base their decision on an expectation of the price level. In the Keynesian view, workers' expectations about future prices are formed in a mostly backward-looking manner, depending for the most part on the past behavior of the price level. Even when contracts are renegotiated, the money wage demands of workers will therefore depend heavily on the behavior of the price level in past periods and respond only slowly to economic conditions.

For these two reasons—labor contracts and backward-looking price expectations—money wage rates will be somewhat rigid. Firms will respond to changes in demand by changing output and employment. An increase in the money supply will, for example, increase aggregate demand. The price firms receive for their product will rise, since at the initial price level there is now an excess demand. Since the rigid money wage will not rise proportionately, the higher price will cause firms to expand output and employment.

Endogenous Money

In much macroeconomic analysis, especially textbook treatments, it is convenient to assume (as we have above) that the money supply is exogenous. The money supply is assumed to be the monetary policy instrument. Keynesians, however, believe that when confronting real world monetary policy, this assumption is misleading. Rather than setting the money stock exogenously, Keynesian economists believe "that the central bank controls some short-term money-market interest rate and/or reserve aggregates and that these variables simultaneously affect other interest rates and financial quantities, GNP expenditures, *and* monetary aggregates" (Tobin, 1978, p. 421).

If the central bank is using a short-term interest rate or reserve aggregate to closely control the money supply and if we consider an interval over which such close control is feasible (e.g., six months to one year), then the money supply will be exogenous or nearly so. If the central bank is not following this procedure, which is called intermediate targeting on money, then the money supply will be partly endogenous, responding to the state of the economy. This will especially be the case if the central bank follows a procedure of targeting the interest rate. In the extreme, if the central bank concentrates on pegging an interest rate at a particular level (as was done in the United States from 1942 to 1951), the money supply will become completely endogenous; the central bank will have to supply whatever amount of money the public demands at the pegged rate.

An interest-rate peg is a special case. More generally, if we consider the type of monetary policy strategies the Federal Reserve has followed over the past three decades, Keynesians would expect changes in the money supply to reflect in part exogenous central bank policy actions and in part endogenous responses to the state of the economy.

Implications for Monetary Policy

In the Keynesian system, monetary policy has the ability to affect real variables. How should this power be used? Keynesians accept what economist Franco Modigliani has called the "fundamental practical message" of Keynes's *General Theory*, namely, that "a private enterprise economy using an intangible money *needs* to be stabilized, *can* be stabilized, and, therefore, *should* be stabilized by appropriate monetary and fiscal policies" (Modigliani, 1977, p. 1).

As a result of rigidity in the money wage, swings in aggregate demand will cause fluctuations in output and employment. Keynesian economists believe that private sector demand is subject to considerable instability, especially components such as business investment, residential construction, and consumer durable purchases. They believe that monetary along with fiscal policy should be used to counteract this instability and keep aggregate demand growing steadily. Keynesians therefore advocate an activist role for monetary policy. This requires allowing a good deal of discretion to the central bank. Keynesians oppose binding monetary policy to simple rules.

MONETARISM: THE MODERN QUANTITY THEORY OF MONEY

The quantity theory of money, along with the rest of the classical economics, was thrown into disrepute by the Great Depression of the 1930s. The sustained massive unemployment in industrialized countries during this period was inconsistent with the full-employment nature of the classical system. By the later 1940s Keynesian economics had become the new orthodoxy. Not all economists, however, welcomed the Keynesian revolution. In the early 1950s a group of economists led by Milton Friedman began to reformulate the quantity theory and lay the foundation for the theory called monetarism.

The Quantity of Money and Level of Economic Activity

Monetarists believe that changes in the money supply are a very important determinant of changes in the level of economic activity, in both real and nominal terms. As Karl Brunner (1968, p. 16) states their position (in the first article to use the term *monetarism*), monetarists believe that "pronounced accelerations in monetary forces are followed subsequently by accelerations in the pace of economic activity, and that pronounced decelerations in monetary forces are followed later by retardations in economic activity." Milton Friedman (1970, p. 27) states a strong form of the monetarist view as follows: "I regard the description of our position as 'money is all that matters for changes in nominal income and for *short-run* changes in real income' as an exaggeration but one that gives the right flavor to our conclusions." Friedman and other monetarists believe that money is the dominant influence on nominal income and on real income in the short run.

This strong monetarist view is controversial. In the Keynesian system, monetary policy is one of a number of important influences on aggregate demand and therefore on nominal and real income. Other influences include fiscal policy variables such as government spending and tax rates, autonomous shocks to investment demand, and, in the open economy, exports and shocks to imports. To understand the basis for the monetarist position, we begin by considering the monetarist reformulation of the classical quantity theory of money.

Friedman on the Demand for Money

Friedman returned to the Cambridge version as the starting point for his restatement of the quantity theory. His first observation was that the Cambridge quantity theory was essentially a theory of money demand. It became a theory of the price level only with two ancillary assumptions: that income was completely supply determined at a full-employment level and that the Cambridge k (the inverse of velocity) was fixed. With these assumptions the Cambridge quantity theory implied a proportionate relationship between the price level and the money supply ($M = \bar{k}P\bar{y}$). Friedman believed that the depression of the 1930s had discredited the classical supply-determined theory of output and employment. If output was not fixed, however, the Cambridge quantity theory with k still assumed constant would imply a proportionate relationship between nominal income (Py) and the money supply. Changes in nominal income would be proportionate to changes in the money supply. Consistent with the monetarist position stated previously, changes in the money supply would result in changes in both real income (in the short run) and the price level. Consistent with Friedman's statement of the strong form of monetarism, the money supply would be the dominant (in fact, the only) determinant of nominal income.

But is k a constant, or close to it? The Cambridge k is the inverse of the velocity of money (Py/M). So here we are really asking whether the ratio of nominal income to money is highly stable in the short run. Keynesians would not expect this ratio to be stable. The Keynesian theory of money demand postulates that for a given level of income the demand for money depends negatively on the interest rate. In equilibrium, then, the ratio of money to income, the Cambridge k, will depend negatively on the interest rate, and velocity will depend positively on the interest rate.

Friedman's own theory looks at the demand for money as "formally identical with that of a consumption service" (Friedman, 1956, p. 4). Therefore,

as in the usual theory of consumer choice, the demand for money . . . depends on three major sets of factors: (a) the total wealth to be held in various forms—the analogue of the budget restraint; (b) the price of and return on this form of wealth and alternative forms; and (c) the tastes and preferences of wealth owning units. (Friedman, 1956, p. 4)

This view of money having value for the services it yields follows the classical perspective. But, following Keynes, rates of return on competing assets are given explicit consideration.

Developing this general perspective, Friedman (1956, 1989) arrives at the following demand for money function:

$$(13) \quad \frac{Md}{P} = L(y, r_M^*, r_B^*, r_E^*, r_D^*, \omega, \nu),$$

with

$$L_y, L_{r_M^*}, L_\omega, L_\nu > 0; L_{r_B^*}, L_{r_E^*}, L_{r_D^*} < 0,$$

where y, M, P are as previously defined and r_M^* = expected nominal return on money; r_B^*, r_E^* = expected nominal rates of return on bonds and equities, respectively, inclusive of expected changes in their prices; r_D^* = expected nominal return of physical assets (land, consumer durables, etc.); ω = ratio of nonhuman to human wealth; ν = parameter to reflect other variables that affect the utility attached to the services of money.

The variables in equation (13) reflect the set of influences in (a), (b), and (c) above: relative rates of return, tastes, and a broad income measure (y) to proxy for wealth. The ω variable is included to take account of the fact that households with large amounts of nonhuman wealth (financial assets and property) are likely to hold more money than those (e.g., graduate students) whose wealth is largely in the form of human capital. Finally, the shift variable (ν) captures any other influences.[8]

The Friedman money demand function implies that the Cambridge equation be rewritten as

$$(14) \quad M^d = k(r_M^*, r_B^*, r_E^*, r_D^*, \omega, \nu)Py.$$

Rather than being a constant, Friedman's theory implies that the Cambridge k depends on all the variables other than income that affect the demand for real balances.

Recognizing that k is the inverse of the income velocity of money and assuming that we are in equilibrium ($M = M^d$), equation (14) can be rewritten as

$$(15) \quad M \cdot V(r_M^*, r_B^*, r_E^*, r_D^*, \omega, \nu) = Py.$$

Since velocity is a function of several economic variables, equation (15) no longer implies a proportionate relationship between nominal income (Py) and the money supply; neither does (15) imply that the money supply is the dominant influence on nominal income.

Friedman notes two conditions under which equation (15) will be a theory of nominal income: (1) if the demand for money and therefore velocity is highly inelastic with respect to variables other than y, or (2) if all these variables are fixed. If one and/or the other of these conditions hold, at least approximately, then fluctuations in V can be ignored as being of second-order in magnitude and it will be fluctuations in M that dominate movements in nominal income. In Friedman's view, if such is the case, "appreciable changes in the rate of growth of the stock of money are a necessary and sufficient condition for appreciable changes in the rate of growth of money income" (Friedman and Schwartz, 1963).[9]

Prices or Output

In the monetarist view, a change in the growth rate in the money supply will cause the growth rate in nominal income to change by approximately the same amount. But will the change come mostly in the form of higher growth in real output or a higher inflation rate? Friedman's view on this issue, which is representative of that of other monetarists, is as follows:

In the short run, which may be as long as three to ten years, monetary changes affect primarily output. Over decades . . . the rate of monetary growth affects primarily prices. What happens to output depends on real factors: the enterprise, ingenuity and industry of the people; the extent of thrift; the structure of industry and government; the relationships among nations and so on. (Friedman, 1989, p. 32)

Money is not neutral in the short run but is neutral in the long run. In the long run, this view of output determination coincides with that of the classical economists; output and employment are determined by real supply-side factors. Friedman characterizes this with the concept of natural rates of output and employment (and therefore unemployment) to which these variables tend in long-run equilibrium. Changes in money growth can displace output and employment from their natural rates in the short run, but they cannot alter the natural rates. The reasons why changes in money-growth rates affect output and employment in the short run are not substantively different from those in the Keynesian analysis: rigidity in money wages and backward-looking price expectations.

Consider the effects of an increase in the money-growth rate after a period of stable prices. To begin, monetarists would expect the effect to come mostly in increased output and employment. At first there would be little inflationary pressure because "People have been expecting prices to be stable, and prices and wages have been set for some time in the future on that basis. It takes time for people to adjust to a new state of demand" (Friedman, 1968, p. 10). In the longer run, however, as contracts expire and expectations adjust, prices and wages rise and output and employment fall back to their natural rates. As long as the higher money-growth rate is maintained, there will be a higher inflation rate and a higher growth rate in the money wage.

The Monetarist Transmission Process

Contracts and backward-looking price expectations explain why output and employment increase following a rise in the money growth rate as people "take time to adjust to a new state of demand." But what is the process in the monetarist model by which a change in monetary policy affects aggregate demand? What is the monetarist monetary policy transmission mechanism?

In the Keynesian model, monetary policy actions affect aggregate demand indirectly via changes in interest rates on financial assets. Monetarists have argued that this view of the transmission mechanism is too narrow. In addition to an effect via the interest rate on financial assets, monetarists believe that changes in the quantity of money directly affect spending on goods, including residential construction and consumer durables. This is consistent with the classical view that stressed the spending effects of money supply changes. As interest rates and relative prices change in response to increased spending as well as changes in interest rates, monetarists believe there are further effects on the balance sheets of firms and households. These in turn lead to additional effects on aggregate demand.

In response, Keynesians argue that the monetarist criticisms pertain only to the simpler versions of the Keynesian system, particularly to the Hicksian IS-LM curve model. They argue that the more complex theoretical and econometric Keynesian models (e.g., de Leeuw and Gramlich, 1969; Tobin, 1969, 1982) allow for the same channels as the monetarist model (e.g., Brunner and Meltzer, 1972, 1976).[10]

Implications for Monetary Policy

In the monetarist view stability of money growth is crucial to economic stability. How best should monetary policy be conducted to assure stable growth in the money supply? The answer to this question given by Milton Friedman is that monetary policy should be governed by a simple rule for money growth and not be left to the discretion of policymakers. Friedman has long advocated a constant money-growth rate rule to prevent instability in the money-growth rate with resulting instability in prices and output.

Monetarists recognize that institutional changes may alter the money-income relationship. In the United States in the 1980s, institutional changes in the deposit market caused a high degree of instability in M1 velocity. Monetarists accept that this instability would call for either a change in the target money-growth rate (Laidler, 1982, p. 162) or tying the target money-growth rate to past observed changes in velocity (Meltzer, 1987). The key point is that the target rate would not be changed in response to general economic conditions; there would be no discretionary monetary stabilization policy.

In theory, monetary authorities could improve on the economic performance that will result from a constant money-growth rate rule by making adjustments in the money-growth rate to offset any shocks that do affect private sector demand. In practice, monetarists do not believe this to be feasible. Friedman and other monetarists maintain that changes in money-growth cause changes in the income growth rate in income with a significant lag. To cancel out the effect of shocks, the monetary policy authority would have to be able to predict those shocks well in advance. Monetarists argue that "forecasts of main economic aggregates are so inaccurate—so wide of the mark on average—that discretionary policies based on forecasts are unlikely to stabilize the economy" (Meltzer, 1987, p. 1).

The monetarist view of monetary policy is at odds with the Keynesian view that the economy needs to be stabilized by active monetary and fiscal policies. Activist stabilization policies require that discretion be left to policymakers. For this reason, Keynesians oppose fixed rules for policy, such as the constant money-growth rate rule. They do not believe that velocity is stable; thus, stable money growth does not guarantee stable growth in income. They do not see Friedman's theory of the natural rate of output as relevant for short-run stabilization policy, which is aimed at reducing the cyclical variance in output and employment.[11]

THE NEW CLASSICAL VIEW

The monetarists and Keynesians disagree on many issues, but a common feature of their models is the short-run nonneutrality of money. In the new classical view, which as the name suggests has its origins in the classical model, whether or not monetary policy actions are neutral depends on whether they are anticipated or unanticipated. Anticipated monetary policy actions will be neutral, whereas unanticipated actions will be nonneutral. Moreover, the new classical economists believe that rational economic agents will come to anticipate any systematic patterns in monetary policy actions. Such systematic policy actions—for example, a pattern of responses to past changes in the level of economic activity—will therefore not affect real output and employment. Only nonsystematic monetary surprises will have real effects.

The new classical view of the effects of monetary policy is one aspect of a broader policy ineffectiveness proposition which can be stated as follows: systematic aggregate demand management policies will have no effect on the distribution of real output and employment. This proposition is broader because it pertains to other policies, such as fiscal policy, which work via aggregate demand.

The policy ineffectiveness proposition concerns the effect of aggregate demand on the distribution of real variables. New classical models characterize macroeconomic variables as being generated by stochastic processes. These macroeconomic aggregates (e.g., output) will therefore be random variables that have probability distributions. The policy ineffectiveness postulate states that the whole distribution of the real variables is unaffected by systematic aggregate demand policies. This implies that the means and variances (as well as other moments) will be unaffected.

To understand the basis for the new classical view of the money-output relationship, we begin by explaining the concept of rational expectations, which is a central element in the new classical view.

Rational Expectations

The concept of rational expectations is attributable to John Muth (1961), who explains his view as follows. "I should like to suggest that expectations, since they are informed predictions are essentially the same as the predictions of the relevant theory" (Muth, 1961, p. 316). More precisely, Muth proposed that "expectations . . . (or more generally, the subjective probability distribution of outcomes) tend to be distributed, for the same information set, about the prediction of the theory (or the objective probability distribution of outcomes)" (Muth, 1961, p. 316).

New classical economists assume that economic agents will form rational expectations of policy variables such as the rate of growth in the money supply. The expected values of these policy variables will be used in formulating labor suppliers' expectations of inflation. Being rational, these expectations of policy variables will employ all relevant available information, including any systematic patterns in past policy behavior.

The rational expectations assumption is in sharp contrast to the assumption of backward-looking expectations of inflation in the Keynesian and monetarist models. In those models, the labor suppliers' expected rate of inflation was assumed to change only slowly over time, responding mostly to past rates of inflation. Rational expectations of inflation are instead forward-looking predictions, adjusting quickly to any new information that has implications for future inflation rates.

The Policy Ineffectiveness Proposition

To illustrate the new classical policy ineffectiveness proposition and its relationship to the rational expectations assumption, we consider the following simple stochastic model.[12]

(16) $y_t = a_0 + a_1(m_t - E_{t-1}m_t) + a_2 y_{t-1} + u_t,$

(17) $m_t = m_0 + m_1 y_{t-1} + \epsilon_t,$

where y = real output, m = money growth rate, u and ϵ are white noise (zero mean and serially uncorrelated) random terms, and E_{t-1} indicates the expected value of a variable as of $t-1$.

Equation (16) expresses real output as a function of a constant term, the deviation of the money-growth rate from its expected value, the lagged level of output, and a random element. Lagged output enters because we assume that some factors have effects on output that persist for more than one period. The random term represents nonsystematic factors that affect output. Equation (17) is a monetary policy feedback rule. If m_t is zero, we have the monetarist constant money-growth rate, except for random disturbances represented by the ϵ term. A nonzero value for m_t represents an active stabilization policy.

The assumption that expectations are rational implies that any systematic monetary stabilization pattern will be anticipated. This enables us to write

$$(18) \quad E_{t-1}m_t = m_0 + m_1 y_{t-1}.$$

But because the systematic component of monetary policy is anticipated, it will not affect real output. To see this we substitute equations (17) and (18) into (16) to yield

$$(19) \quad y_t = a_0 + a_1 \epsilon_t + a_2 y_{t-1} + u_t.$$

Real output depends on nonsystematic (and therefore unanticipated) money growth, ϵ_t, not on m_0 or m_1.

In the monetarist or Keynesian view, where expectations are backward-looking, equation (16) would be replaced by

$$(16') \quad y_t = a_0 + a_1 m_t + a_2 y_{t-1} + u_t.$$

Monetary policy actions, whether or not they are anticipated, have real effects. In this case an active monetary policy would be called for to prevent shocks from previous periods from affecting current output via y_{t-1}. This could be done by an appropriate setting of m_1.[13]

Implications for Monetary Policy

The policy ineffectiveness proposition implies that monetary policy should not be geared to stabilize output and employment. Instead, it should be geared to control nominal magnitudes. Important here is the fact that even anticipated monetary policy actions *do* affect nominal variables such as the price level and money wage. An anticipated increase in money growth, for example, causes labor suppliers to expect a rise in the inflation rate. Money wage demands increase. The inflation rate and rate of money wage growth rise proportionately. Consequently, the real wage is unchanged, as are real output and employment. As long as higher money growth is maintained, the higher inflation rate is also maintained.

A sensible monetary policy goal is then to keep the money-growth rate and hence the inflation rate low and stable. Although this can be accomplished in a number of ways, one is Milton Friedman's constant money-growth rate rule, with a low constant rate.

In the new classical view, Friedman's rule would have two additional advantages. First, if the monetary policy authority focuses its attention on achieving a constant growth rate for a monetary aggregate, monetary surprises—the ϵ shocks in (19)—will be minimized. This is desirable since such surprises have no stabilization value; they simply make output more variable. Second, if the monetary authority commits to a constant growth rate rule, it gains credibility. As it sets a rate and achieves it, economic agents forming rational expectations will come to believe that the rule will be followed and a climate of low inflationary expectations will result.[14]

Doubts About the Policy Ineffectiveness Proposition

The new classical policy ineffectiveness proposition has been the source of an extended controversy. Many economists, especially Keynesians, have expressed doubts about the relevance of the proposition to the actual economy.

One criticism has been the failure of the new classical model to incorporate labor contracts, which Keynesians believe make money wages sticky. If money wages are fixed by labor contracts, then, for example, increases in the money supply even if they are anticipated will not simply result in proportionately higher prices and money wages. Quantity variables, including output and employment, will have to adjust. Fischer (1977) and Taylor (1979) have constructed models in which expectations are rational and anticipated monetary policy actions still affect real output owing to the existence of fixed money wage contracts.

Objections have also been raised to the "extreme informational assumptions" (Friedman, 1979) implicit in the rational expectations concept. Given the cost of gathering and processing information, many economic agents might find it "economically rational" to employ much less than all available relevant information in making forecasts. In this case the monetary authority, which may be assumed to use all available information, can employ systematic monetary policy actions to insulate real output from changes in aggregate demand that are unanticipated by the public. This is true even within new classical models such as Barro (1976), where there are no nominal rigidities such as fixed money wage contracts.

Finally, Keynesians question whether new classical models can explain the size and persistence of deviations from potential output over the business cycle. In new classical models, unanticipated declines in aggregate demand that result either from monetary surprises or other shocks will cause output and employment to fall. But Keynesians (e.g., Modigliani, 1977) question whether such misperceptions can explain real-world business cycles. Once economic agents perceive the shock to aggregate demand, the money wage adjustment should take place and output should quickly return to the level of potential output. New classical economists have developed rationales for the persistence of output movements even if misperceptions are short-lived. These rationales include structural lags attributable to costs of adjustment (Sargent, 1987, Chap. 18) and information lags (Lucas, 1975). Keynesians find these rationales less plausible than explanations of persistence based on nominal rigidities and backward-looking expectations.

REAL BUSINESS CYCLE THEORY

Two new lines of research on the money-income relationship developed out of the controversy between new classical and Keynesian economists during the 1970s. One, strongly rooted in the classical tradition, is the real business cycle theory. The other, the new Keynesian theory, is in the Keynesian tradition. The real business cycle theory is examined in this section, and new Keynesian models are the subject of section 6.

Equilibrium Business Cycles

One important aspect of the new classical approach is the view of the business cycle as an equilibrium phenomenon. This is in contrast to the Keynesian approach where labor contracts and other possible rigidities prevent the money wage from moving to clear the labor market. In contrast to the original classical model, the equilibrium in the new classical model is a stochastic one. Output and employment do move in response to random shocks to aggregate demand.

The real business cycle theory is also an equilibrium approach. Real business cycle theorists, however, accept the Keynesian view that the misperceptions approach cannot explain the size and persistence of real-world business cycles. Still, they do not accept the Keynesians' own explanation of business cycles. Rather, they return to the classical view that real variables are determined by real supply-side factors. This view pertains to cyclical movements as well as long-run growth in output and employment.[15] As King and Plosser (1984, p. 363) explain, business cycles "are seen as arising from variations in the real opportunities of the private economy, which may include government purchases or tax rates as well as technical and environmental conditions." Changes in government purchases or tax rates affect the real interest rate and therefore firms' demand for capital.

This in turn affects output. Shocks to technology or the environment (e.g., a drought) affect the amount of output that can be produced with given factor inputs.

Real business cycle models must also provide an explanation of the persistence that characterizes the cyclical behavior of output and employment. One possibility is that the real shocks that affect output are themselves autocorrelated; technological advances may "bunch up." Another possibility is that there are structural lags in economic process. In the Kydland and Prescott (1982) model, for example, the structural lag is the "time to build" phenomenon. Shocks to technology affect investment, but actual capital goods come on line only after a number of periods pass. Persistence of the effects of shocks may also result from confusion between permanent and transitory shocks. Firms may wish to respond only to permanent shocks that affect productivity; they respond gradually then as they try to sort out which shocks are permanent.

Money in Real Business Cycle Models

By definition, real business cycle theory denies that money is important for business cycles. Real business cycle models such as Long and Plosser (1983) and Kydland and Prescott (1982) do not even include money as a variable.

Although there is no role for money per se in real business cycle models, there is a role for financial services. Such services are an input into the productive process. Here by financial services we can think of the activities of financial intermediaries. They process business transactions and provide credit to firms. Since the deposit liabilities of these financial intermediaries are included in the money supply, there is a link between output and *inside* money, the portion of the money supply that is the liability of private (depository) institutions.

This link is important in real business cycle models in two ways. First, since financial services are an input into the production process, we would expect the quantity of the demand for these services to vary directly with the output. The quantity of money would then be positively correlated with output, but the causality would run from output to money. Correlation between money and output is "reverse causation."[16]

Second, if financial services are a productive input, then shocks to the financial intermediation industry will have real effects. A negative shock, like the widespread U.S. bank failures of the early 1930s, would adversely affect output. The bank failures would be accompanied by a drop in the money supply, so there would be a positive correlation between the quantity of money and the level of output. Still, the real shock, the bank failures, not the decline in the money supply, would be the cause of the fall in output.[17]

Implications for Monetary Policy

The role of outside money (liabilities of the monetary authority) in a real business cycle model is to determine the price level. Money is neutral in real business cycle models. The monetary authority should then focus on control of the price level rather than on output or employment, which it cannot control. This leads to the conclusion that a desirable monetary policy would be one that resulted in slow, steady growth in the money supply (at least outside money). A money-growth rate rule, or a rule for growth in the monetary base (outside money), would be a sensible way to achieve this. This conclusion agrees with that of the other equilibrium theories (classical and new classical) as well as with the monetarist view.

6. NEW KEYNESIAN MODELS

Another active research area in recent years has been the attempt to develop models that are Keynesian in spirit but are derived from sound microeconomic foundations. The models that are emerging from this research are called new Keynesian models. They are Keynesian in that they attempt to explain why prices and wages do not fully adjust to changes in nominal demand and therefore output and employment must adjust. New Keynesian models are in part a response to the new classical attack on older Keynesian models as inconsistent with the optimizing behavior of economic agents. The new classical economists argued that useful macroeconomic models must have the properties that agents optimize and markets clear. New Keynesian models are models in which agents optimize but markets do not always clear. Keynesian involuntary unemployment occurs.

The new Keynesian literature is characterized by what Blanchard and Fischer (1989) call a "dizzying diversity" of approaches, but it possesses several common elements.[18]

1. In new Keynesian models, some form of imperfect competition is assumed for the product market, in contrast to the assumption of perfect competition in earlier Keynesian models.

2. In earlier Keynesian models, the key nominal rigidity is that of the money wage. In new Keynesian models, the key nominal rigidity pertains to the price level. Consequently, new Keynesian models are often called sticky price models.

3. In addition to nominal rigidities many new Keynesian models introduce real rigidities—factors that cause the real wage or firm's desired relative price to be rigid in the face of changes in aggregate demand.

Sources of Aggregate Price Rigidity in New Keynesian Models

Keynesian models of the 1960s and 1970s relied on the rigidity in the money wage as the central explanation of the nonneutrality of money. The product market in those models was characterized by perfect competition. Keynesians did not believe that most real-world product markets were perfectly competitive. The assumption of perfect competition was made for simplicity and also reflected the Keynesian view at the time that money wage rigidity was the "root of all evil" (Mankiw, 1987, p. 105).

But the assumption of perfect competition and price flexibility in Keynesian models has a drawback. With price flexibility, as nominal aggregate demand rises and falls over the business cycle, the price level will adjust quickly upward or downward, respectively, but the money wage will not. Therefore, real wages will fall in expansions and rise in contractions; the real wage will be countercyclical. This poses no problem in theory, but at least in the U.S. economy there is no clear countercyclical pattern to movements in the real wage.[19] If there was also rigidity in product prices, this could explain the absence of a countercyclical pattern of real wages.

With perfect competition, prices are simply set by the forces of supply and demand. Individual firms have no power over their product price; they face horizontal demand schedules. If in the face of a fall in nominal demand, a perfectly competitive firm maintained its original product price it would sell no output. New Keynesian models have substituted the assumption that product markets are characterized by monopoly (Mankiw, 1985) or monopolistic competition (Akerlof and Yellin, 1985; Blanchard and Kiyotaki, 1987) for that of perfect competition. With these alternative market structures, it makes sense to think of firms as price setters. Let us take the case of monopolistic competition and examine the reaction of firms to a fall in nominal demand.

Consider first the equilibrium prior to the fall in demand. Each firm sets its price along its demand curve at the output level where marginal cost equals marginal revenue. Because the monopolistically competitive firm faces a downward-sloping demand curve, the output level at this point is below the intersection of the marginal cost curve and demand schedule. Output is therefore below that of the level in perfect competition and price is higher.

Now consider the effect of an economy-wide fall in nominal demand as the result of a decline in the nominal money supply. We assume that the position of the demand curve facing each firm depends on the level of real money balances (M/P), which is a proxy for aggregate demand.[20] The demand curve facing each of n firms is thus of the form

$$(20) \quad d_i = d_i\left(\frac{P_i}{P}, \frac{M}{P}\right) \qquad i = 1, n,$$

where P_i is the ith firm's price. Each firm's demand depends negatively on its relative price and positively on the aggregate level of real money balances. A fall in the money supply will shift the demand curve (and marginal revenue schedule) facing each firm to the left, causing each firm to lower product price. As they do, the aggregate price level will fall, raising the level of real money balances and reversing the shift. The new equilibrium will come when real balances have been restored to their original level. Output, employment, and relative prices will also be back at their initial level. Imperfect competition by itself does not make money nonneutral.

But now assume that the firm incurs a cost when it changes its price, or what the literature calls a *menu cost*. The name stems from the fact that if restaurants change prices they must print new menus, but the term should be more broadly interpreted as any cost of making a price change. A key insight of new Keynesian models is that even small menu costs can make prices sticky in the face of changes in nominal demand. The reason is that the cost to the individual firm of *not* changing price is small, being in the neighborhood of the initial equilibrium. This follows because, as Akerlof and Yellin observe, "The error in prices . . . caused by inertial behavior will result in losses to the agent that are second order in terms of the policy shock, since at the equilibrium prior to the shock, the agent chooses prices so that the marginal benefit of higher prices was just offset by marginal costs" (Akerlof and Yellin, 1985, p. 826). In other words, at the initial equilibrium the profit function is flat plotted against price; therefore, divergences of actual price from optimal price in the neighborhood of this equilibrium point result in negligible costs.

Notice that the situation is different for the perfectly competitive firm. Should the firm fail to lower price when the industry-wide equilibrium price falls, its sales and therefore total revenue fall to zero. It is the combination of imperfect competition and menu costs that results in price rigidity. If all firms maintain their prices as the money supply falls, then the aggregate price level will be unchanged; output and employment will fall. Money will be nonneutral.

The argument so far, however, pertains only to the neighborhood of the original equilibrium price, where the divergence of actual price from optimal price is small (the flat portion of the profit function). For shocks that cause larger displacements from the original optimum, whether or not product prices will be rigid depends on the size of menu cost relative to the cost a firm incurs if it fails to change its price. The firm is more likely to leave its price unchanged if (1) its marginal cost curve is relatively flat, so that unit costs do not change much as output varies; (2) there is a low degree of substitutability among the outputs of the individual firms that is, there is a large deviation from perfect competition; and (3) the menu cost is high.[21]

The Role of Real Rigidities

The previous section explains how a combination of menu costs and imperfect competition can generate nonneutrality of money. This is a nominal rigidity (a menu cost), as is the money wage rigidity of earlier Keynesian models. A number of new Keynesian models also incorporate factors that cause real rigidities. A real rigidity is a stickiness in a real variable—the real wage (W/P) or a firm's relative price (P_i/P). Ball and Romer (1990) show that large, persistent nonneutral effects from changes in the money supply (and other shocks to aggregate demand) are more likely to result if there is a combination of a nominal rigidity, such as a menu cost, and a real rigidity in either the labor or product market.[22] New Keynesian economists have suggested a number of factors that lead to real rigidities, namely,

Models of Efficiency Wages

The central feature of efficiency wage models is that the productivity of workers depends positively on the real wage they are paid. This being the case, the real wage which firms pay is set on efficiency grounds and will not respond to shocks to nominal demand.[23]

The efficiency wage concept can be formalized by writing the aggregate production function as

(21) $y = af(e(w)N)$,

where a is a parameter, y is real output, N is the number of workers, w is the real wage (W/P), and $e(w)$ is an index of the effort level (and therefore productivity level) of each worker. This effort level is assumed to be an increasing function of the real wage ($e_w > 0$).

The firm is assumed to maximize profit (in real terms) given by $af(e(w)N) - wN$. It can be shown that the firm will choose the optimal w to satisfy the following first order condition:

(22) $e_w W/e(w) = 1$.

The condition in equation (22) states that the real wage will be set so that the elasticity of the index of worker effort with respect to the real wage equals one. Notice that equation (22) contains only the real wage (not N) and therefore pins down the optimum real wage. This is what is meant by saying that the real wage is set on efficiency grounds.

A number of rationales have been offered to explain why worker effort depends on the real wage. Each has the property that firms find it optimal on efficiency grounds to pay a wage higher than the market clearing wage, with resulting unemployment. In Shapiro and Stiglitz (1984), by setting the wage above market-clearing levels, a firm gives the worker an incentive not to shirk on the job. If the worker does, he or she may be fired and forced to seek a job at a lower wage. If firms can monitor job performance only imperfectly and at some cost, such an efficiency wage strategy may be optimal. In Salop (1979), firms pay a real wage in excess of the market-clearing level to reduce labor turnover which lowers productivity. In Akerlof (1982), they pay high wages to improve worker morale and therefore work effort.

Whatever the underlying rationale, if firms set wages on efficiency grounds, the real wage will not respond to changes in demand; instead, employment will adjust. Payment of efficiency wages does not in itself imply the nonneutrality of money. If a fall in the money supply causes nominal demand to fall, the firm can respond by lowering the price level and money wage but maintaining the real wage and employment. Together with a menu cost, or nominal rigidity, however, the efficiency wage hypothesis implies that the price level will not adjust (due to menu costs); both the money wage and real wage will also be rigid. Following a fall in nominal demand, the level of involuntary unemployment will rise as output falls and layoffs result.[24]

Other Real Rigidities

New Keynesian economists have explored a number of other possible causes of real rigidities in addition to the efficiency wage hypothesis. Each of these rigidities together with nominal price rigidity may contribute to the nonneutral effect of money supply changes.

Explicit or implicit contracts that represent insurance schemes between risk-neutral employers and risk-averse employees (e.g., Azariadis, 1975) may result in real wage rigidity, with effects similar to the real wage rigidity in the efficiency wage case.

A source of a relative price rigidity is the "kinked" demand curve analyzed by Stiglitz (1979) and Woglom (1982).[25] Suppose that after a period of searching for the best prices all customers have settled as buyers from particular firms in a setting of monopolistic competition. After an equilibrium is reached, all firms end up with the same price.

The kink in the demand curve arises at this equilibrium price, where in the Stiglitz (1979) framework the demand curve will be quite flat above the equilibrium price but steeper below it. If the firm raises its price above the initial equilibrium level, many customers will go to other firms believing they can get a lower price. If the firm lowers its price, however, it will attract few new customers because search is costly and only a fraction of the customers of other firms will observe the price decline.

Because of the kink, the firm may not want to vary its relative price even with a change in nominal demand. All firms may then leave their prices unchanged, which means the aggregate price level will be rigid. As can be seen from Woglom (1982), this is not the only equilibrium. All firms could change price by the same amount, leaving relative prices unchanged. Nominal price rigidity, owing to menu costs, may make the fixed price equilibrium more likely. If the price level is fixed, money will be nonneutral.

Implications for Monetary Policy

The new Keynesian literature examines a number of reasons why monetary policy might not be neutral. This suggests a possible role for monetary policy in stabilizing output and employment. In this sense the policy conclusion of the new Keynesian models conforms to the older Keynesian analysis. There are some differences, however.

In new Keynesian models with monopolistic competition, equilibrium output is too low in a welfare sense. If output rose to the level that would exist with perfect competition, consumer surplus would increase. With monopolistic competition there exists the externality discussed in Blanchard and Kiyotaki. When all the firms in a monopolistically competitive equilibrium have set their prices optimally, they have no incentive to lower prices. "Suppose however that all price setters decrease their prices simultaneously; this increases real money balances and aggregate demand. The increase in output reduces the initial distortion of underproduction and underemployment and increases social welfare" (Blanchard and Kiyotaki, 1987, p. 653).

Consider the implication that this externality has for optimal monetary policy in a world where there are both positive and negative shocks to private sector aggregate demand. As pointed out by Ball and Romer (1989) (under certain assumptions), the welfare losses from negative shocks are counterbalanced by welfare gains from positive shocks that move output toward the competitive level. The argument for stabilizing output around the monopolistically competitive equilibrium would have to be made in terms of the costs resulting from higher variance in output. However, there would also be an argument for using monetary policy to offset any negative shocks to output.

7. CONCLUSION

The question of the neutrality of money is a central one in macroeconomics. Classical economists and real business cycle theorists have developed models in which money is neutral. In new classical models, all systematic monetary policy actions are neutral in their effects; only monetary surprises affect real variables. Keynesians, new Keynesians, and monetarists have constructed models in which money is nonneutral (at least in the short run). The neutrality of money is not only central to macroeconomics, but it is also important to the real economy. Whether or not money is neutral has implications of the most fundamental nature for the proper conduct of monetary policy. Macroeconomics does not answer the question definitively. It does, however, define the issues. Central bankers are left to choose operating procedures depending on their view of how the real economy functions.

NOTES

1. Here and below we use the letter indicating a function with the letter(s) indicating an argument of the function as a subscript to denote the partial derivative of the function with respect to that argument.

2. We have dealt here with the equilibrium version of the classical system. There was also a classical analysis of the transition from one equilibrium to another. Within this transition period, classical economists as far back as David Hume considered the possible real effects of money supply changes. On this disequilibrium classical analysis, see Patinkin (1972).

3. We neglect explicit consideration of interest paid on bank deposits. Incorporating a deposit rate into the analysis would not lead to fundamental changes.

4. This is the case of a risk-averse investor. Tobin (1958) also considers other possibilities.

5. This requires certain assumptions about the investor's utility function; see Tobin (1958, pp. 48–50) or Froyen (1990, pp. 443–48) for more details.

6. For the firm, the story is a little different, because both receipts and outlays occur almost continuously. It is the uncertainty of the level of outlays that is crucial to the firm (see Miller and Orr, 1966). Uncertainty of outlays is also of importance to households. Waud (1975) uses net outlay uncertainty to develop a rationale for the precautionary demand for money.

7. This is the question of whether what is called *Ricardian equivalence* holds. On this issue, see Barro (1974), Bernheim (1987), and Tobin and Buiter (1979).

8. Although not explicitly included in equation (13), the expected inflation rate does influence the demand for money. As Friedman (1989) notes, "arbitrage between real and nominal assets introduces an allowance for anticipated inflation in the nominal interest rate."

9. Friedman's theory is not the only monetarist framework. An alternative version of a monetarist model is contained in a series of influential papers by Karl Brunner and Allan Meltzer (1972, 1973, and 1976).

10. On these issues, see the papers in Stein (1976) and Mayer (1978).

11. Moreover, in the 1980s a number of Keynesian economists challenged the notion that there were natural rates of output and employment. On this issue, see Blanchard and Summers (1986) and Solow (1986).

12. More complete, important new classical models are Lucas (1973, 1975), Sargent and Wallace (1975), and Barro (1976).

13. Equations (16') and (17) imply the following reduced form for output

$$(19') \quad y_t = a_0 + a_1 m_0 + (a_1 m_1 + a_2)y_{t-1} + u_t + a_1 \epsilon_t.$$

The optimal setting for m_t is $(-a_2/a_1)$, which eliminates y_{t-1} from (19′).

14. In fact, more direct support for a monetary policy rule in models with rational expectations is provided in some of the literature on monetary policy credibility surveyed in Chapter 5 of this volume.

15. Early influential real business cycle models are Long and Plosser (1983), Kydland and Prescott (1982), and King and Plosser (1984). Surveys of the real business cycle literature include McCallum (1989), Rush (1987), Stockman (1988), and Mankiw (1989).

16. This linkage implies that the inside money to output correlation would be stronger than the outside money to output correlation, where outside money is the part of the money supply that is the liability of the monetary authority. King and Plosser (1984) present some evidence that this is the case.

17. Bernanke (1983) finds evidence of such nonmonetary effects of bank failures in the 1929–33 period. His estimates imply, however, that these effects augment the direct effects that the fall in the money supply had on output.

18. Surveys of this literature are provided by Blanchard (1990), Blanchard and Fischer (1989, Chaps. 8–9), Gordon (1990), and Rotemberg (1987).

19. Mankiw points out another difficulty with the Keynesian reliance on money (nominal) wage rigidity: "if nominal wage contracts are responsible for large and inefficient fluctuations in employment, then rational workers should not agree to them. . . . Ultimately, assuming such nominal wage rigidity is tantamount to assuming substantial departures from rationality" (Mankiw, 1987, p. 105).

20. Factors other than real balances may affect aggregate demand. New Keynesian models adopt a quantity theory view only for simplicity. Other factors can be modeled as velocity shocks.

21. The discussion here has focused only on the comparative static effects of a change in the money supply. There are a number of dynamic new Keynesian models. These are able to deal with questions such as the persistence of the real effects of shocks to nominal demand. Blanchard and Fischer (1989, pp. 376–414) survey this literature.

22. A difficulty in generating large output fluctuations with just a nominal rigidity has to do with the role of a flat marginal cost curve mentioned in the previous section. If there is a substantial shock to nominal aggregate demand, firms will make a large change in output while not adjusting price only if marginal cost does not change very much. This is in turn likely only if the money wage does not change much. For employment to vary substantially (which it must for output to vary substantially) while the money wage changes vary little requires an implausibly high elasticity of labor supply.

23. A number of important contributions to the efficiency wage literature are collected in Akerlof and Yellin (1986). See also Katz (1986) and Weiss (1990).

24. Notice that here changes in employment take place as workers join or leave the pool of the involuntarily employed. Employment changes are not movements along a labor supply function. This eliminates the difficulty explained in note 22.

25. The kinked demand curve idea has a long history going back to Hall and Hitch (1939) and Sweezy (1939). The rationale for the kink given in the recent literature is different, however.

REFERENCES

Akerlof, George A. 1982. "Labor Contracts as a Partial Gift Exchange." *Quarterly Journal of Economics* 97 (November): 543–69.

———, and Yellin, Janet. 1985. "A Near-Rational of the Business Cycle with Wage and Price Inertia." *Quarterly Journal of Economics* 100, Supplement, 823–38.

———. 1986. *Efficiency Wage Model of the Labor Market.* Cambridge, England: Cambridge University Press.

Azariadis, Costas. 1975. "Implicit Contracts and Underemployment Equilibria." *Journal of Political Economy* 83 (December): 1183–1202.

Ball, Laurence, and Romer, David. 1990. "Real Rigidities and the Non-Neutrality of Money." *Review of Economic Studies* 57 (April): 183–203.

———. 1989. "Are Prices Too Sticky?" *Quarterly Journal of Economics* 104 (August): 507–24.

Barro, Robert J. 1974. "Are Government Bonds Net Wealth?" *Journal of Political Economy* 81 (November/December): 1095–1117.

———. 1976. "Rational Expectations and the Role of Monetary Policy." *Journal of Monetary Economics* 2 (January): 1–32.

Baumol, William. 1952. "The Transactions Demand for Cash: An Inventory-Theoretic Approach." *Quarterly Journal of Economics* 66 (November): 545–56.

Bernanke, Ben S. 1983. "Nonmonetary Effects of the Financial Crisis in the Propagation of the Great Depression," *American Economic Review* 73 (June): 257–76.

Bernheim, B. Douglass. 1987. "Ricardian Equivalence: An Evaluation of Theory and Evidence." *NBER Macroeconomics Annual* 2: 263–304.

Blanchard, Olivier V. 1990. "Why Does Money Affect Output?" In *Handbook of Monetary Economics,* edited by B. Friedman and F. Hahn. Amsterdam: North-Holland.

———, and Fischer, Stanley. 1989. *Lectures on Macroeconomics.* Cambridge, Mass.: MIT Press.

———, and Kiyotaki, Nobuhiro. 1987. "Monopolistic Competition and Aggregate Demand," *American Economic Review* 77 (September): 647–66.

———, and Summers, Lawrence. 1986. "Hysteresis and the European Unemployment Problem." *NBER Macroeconomics Annual* 1: 15–78.

Blinder, Alan S., and Stiglitz, Joseph E. 1983. "Money, Credit Constraints, and Economic Activity." *American Economic Review* 73 (May): 297–302.

Brunner, Karl. 1968. "The Role of Money and Monetary Policy." Federal Reserve Bank of St. Louis *Review* 50 (July): 9–24.

———, and Meltzer, Allan H. 1972. "Money, Debt, and Economic Activity." *Journal of Political Economy* 80 (September/October): 951–77.

———. 1973. "Mr. Hicks and the Monetarists." *Economica* 40 (February): 44–59.

———. 1976. "An Aggregative Theory for a Closed Economy." In *Monetarism.* edited by Jerome Stein. Amsterdam: North-Holland.

de Leeuw, Frank, and Gramlich, Edward. 1969. "The Channels of Monetary Policy:

A Further Report on the Federal Reserve—MIT Econometric Model."
Journal of Finance 24 (May): 265–90.

Fischer, Stanley. 1977. "Long-Term Contracts, Rational Expectations and the Optimal Money Supply Rule." *Journal of Political Economy* 85 (February): 191–206.

Fisher, Irving. 1922. *The Purchasing Power of Money*. New York: Macmillan.

Friedman, Benjamin M. 1979. "Optimal Expectations and the Extreme Informational Assumption of 'Rational Expectations' Macromodels." *Journal of Monetary Economics* 5 (January): 23–41.

Friedman, Milton. 1956. "The Quantity Theory of Money: A Restatement." In *Studies in the Quantity Theory of Money*, edited by Milton Friedman. Chicago: University of Chicago Press.

———. 1968. "The Role of Monetary Policy." *American Economic Review* 58 (March): 1–17.

———. 1970. "A Theoretical Framework for Monetary Analysis." *Journal of Political Economy* 78 (March/April): 193–238.

———. 1989. "Quantity Theory of Money." In *The New Palgrave: Money*, edited by J. Eatwell, M. Milgate, and P. Newman. New York: W. W. Norton.

———, and Schwartz, Anna. 1963. "Money and Business Cycles." *Review of Economics and Statistics* 45 (February): 32–64.

Froyen, Richard T. 1990. *Macroeconomics: Theories and Policies*. 3rd ed. New York: Macmillan.

Gordon, Robert J. 1990. "What Is New-Keynesian Economics?" *Journal of Economic Literature* 28 (September): 1115–71.

Hall, R. L., and Hitch, C. J. 1939. "Price Theory and Business Behavior." *Oxford Economic Papers* 2 (May): 12–45.

Katz, Lawrence F. 1986. "Efficiency Wage Theories: A Partial Evaluation," *NBER Macroeconomics Annual* 1: 235–76.

Keynes, J. M. 1930. *Treatise on Money*. New York: Harcourt Brace.

King, Robert G., and Plosser, Charles. 1984. "Money, Credit, and Prices in a Real Business Cycle." *American Economic Review* 74 (June): 363–80.

Kydland, Fynn, and Prescott, Edward. 1982. "Time to Build and Aggregate Fluctuations." *Econometrica* 50 (November): 1345–70.

Laidler, David. 1982. *Monetarist Perspectives*. Oxford: Philip Allan.

Long, John, and Plosser, Charles. 1983. "Real Business Cycles." *Journal of Political Economy* 91 (February): 39–69.

Lucas, Robert E., Jr. 1973. "Some International Evidence on Output-Inflation Tradeoffs." *American Economic Review* 63 (June): 326–34.

———. 1975. "An Equilibrium Model of the Business Cycle." *Journal of Political Economy* 83 (December): 1113–44.

Mankiw, Gregory N. 1985. "Small Menu Costs and Large Business Cycles." *Quarterly Journal of Economics* 100 (May): 529–39.

———. 1987. "Comment." *NBER Macroeconomics Annual* 2: 105–10.

———. 1989. "Real Business Cycles: A New Keynesian Perspective." *Journal of Economic Perspectives* 3 (Summer): 79–90.

Mayer, Thomas. 1978. *The Structure of Monetarism*. New York: W. W. Norton.

McCallum, Bennett T. 1989. "Real Business Cycle Models." In *Modern Business*

Cycle Theory, edited by R. J. Barro. Cambridge, Mass.: Harvard University Press.

Meltzer, Allan. 1987. "Limits of Short-run Stabilization Policy." *Economic Inquiry* 25 (January): 1–14.

Miller, Merton H., and Orr, Daniel. 1966. "A Model of the Demand for Money by Firms." *Quarterly Journal of Economics* 80 (August): 413–35.

Modigliani, Franco. 1977. "The Monetarist Controversy or, Should We Forsake Stabilization Policies." *American Economic Review* 67 (March): 1–19.

Muth, John. 1961. "Rational Expectations and the Theory of Price Movements." *Econometrica* 29 (July): 315–35.

Okun, Arthur. 1981. *Prices and Quantities*. Washington, D.C.: Brookings Institution.

Patinkin, Don. 1972. "On the Short-Run Non-Neutrality of Money in the Quantity Theory." Banca Nationale del Lavora *Quarterly Review* 25 (March): 3–22.

Pigou, A. C. 1917–18. "The Value of Money." *Quarterly Journal of Economics* 32: 38–65.

Rotemberg, Julio. 1987. "The New Keynesian Microfoundations." *NBER Macroeconomics Annual* 2: 69–104.

Rush, Mark. 1987. "Real Business Cycles." Federal Reserve Bank of Kansas City *Review* 72 (February): 20–32.

Salop, Steven C. 1979. "A Model of the Natural Rate of Unemployment." *American Economic Review* 69 (March): 117–25.

Sargent, Thomas J. 1987. *Macroeconomic Theory*. 2d ed. New York: Academic Press.

———, and Wallace, Neil. 1975. "Rational Expectations, the Optimal Monetary Instrument and the Optimal Money Supply Rule." *Journal of Political Economy* 83 (April): 241–54.

Scott, Ira O. 1957. "The Availability Doctrine: Theoretical Underpinnings." *Review of Economic Studies* 25 (October): 41–48.

Shapiro, Carl, and Stiglitz, Joseph E. 1984. "Equilibrium Unemployment as a Worker Discipline Device." *American Economic Review* 74 (June): 533–44.

Smith, Warren. 1969. "A Neo-keynesian View of Monetary Policy." In *Controlling Monetary Aggregates*. Boston: Federal Reserve Bank of Boston.

Solow, Robert M. 1986. "Unemployment: Getting the Questions Right." *Economica* 53, Supplement, S.23–S.34.

Stein, Jerome L. 1976. *Monetarism*. Amsterdam: North-Holland, 1976.

Stiglitz, Joseph E. 1979. "Equilibrium in Product Markets with Imperfect Information." *American Economic Review* 69 (May): 339–45.

———, and Weiss, Andrew. 1981. "Credit Rationing in Markets with Imperfect Information." *American Economic Review* 71 (June): 393–410.

Stockman, Alan C. 1988. "Real Business Cycles." Federal Reserve Bank of Cleveland *Economic Review* 24 (Quarter 4): 24–47.

Sweezy, Paul M. 1939. "Demand under Conditions of Monopoly." *Journal of Political Economy* 47 (August): 568–73.

Taylor, John. 1979. "Staggered Wage Setting in a Macro Model." *American Economic Review* 69 (May): 108–13.

Tobin, James. 1956. "The Interest-Elasticity of Transactions Demand for Cash." *Review of Economics and Statistics* 38 (August): 241–47.

————. 1958. "Liquidity Preference as Behavior Towards Risk." *Review of Economic Studies* 25 (February): 65–86.

————. 1969. "A General Equilibrium Approach to Monetary Theory." *Journal of Money, Credit and Banking* 1 (February): 15–29.

————. 1978. "Monetary Policies and the Economy: The Transmission Mechanism." *Southern Economic Journal* 44 (January): 421–31.

————. 1982. "Money and Finance in the Macroeconomic Process." *Journal of Money, Credit and Banking* 14 (May): 171–204.

————, and Buiter, William. 1979. "Fiscal and Monetary Policies, Capital Formation, and Economic Activity." In *The Government and Capital Formation*, edited by G. Von Furstenberg. New York: American Council of Life Insurance.

Waud, Roger N. 1975. "Net Outlay Uncertainty and Liquidity Preference as Behavior Towards Risk." *Journal of Money, Credit and Banking* 7 (November): 799–806.

Weiss, Andrew. 1990. *Efficiency Wages*. Princeton, N.J.: Princeton University Press.

Woglom, Geoffrey. 1982. "Underemployment with Rational Expectations." *Quarterly Journal of Economics* 97 (February): 89–108.

4

MONETARY POLICY AND INFLATION

Eduard J. Bomhoff

INTRODUCTION

This chapter critically discusses the statistical modeling of inflation, which is defined here as the rate of change of a deflator for gross domestic product (GDP) or gross national product (GNP).[1] The importance of this topic goes beyond the obvious point that producers, wage earners, and consumers want to make informed guesses about the rate of price change in the future, and that holders of assets know that inflationary expectations are important for the valuation of stocks, bonds, foreign exchange, and all tangible assets.

Statistical work on inflation is important not only for forecasting future inflation, but also for designing, implementing, and evaluating monetary policy. In a closed economy, or an open economy on floating exchange rates, the rate of growth of the money supply is correlated with the rate of inflation, but usually with a long and variable lag. Estimation of this relationship is therefore difficult but essential for policy purposes. In a forecasting context, however, regressions of inflation on current or immediate past rates of change in prices, wages, and other cost factors, together with measures of demand in the goods or labor markets, will likely produce more explanatory power than regressions on monetary variables only. This explains why professional forecasters tend to emphasize cost factors and the state of excess demand rather than monetary developments. At the same time, academic researchers criticize such work for being ad hoc and not based on optimizing behavior; for data-mining, especially as far as lags are concerned; and for causing confusion between changes in relative prices and changes in the absolute price level.

The next two sections of this chapter summarize both the monetarist

and the excess demand model of inflation and discuss the practical difficulties with the monetarist and the theoretical problems with the excess
demand model.[2] Section 4 contains a historical overview of important statistical studies of inflation performed over the past twenty years. Representative examples of the different approaches implemented for the
postwar period have been selected. Regrettably, the discussion is limited
to inflation in the industrial countries. The link between monetary policy
and inflation in developing countries is an important topic, but falls outside
the scope of this chapter.[3]

If we accept the monetarist view of inflation, we end up with a forecasting
equation for inflation that looks like an inversion of the demand for money
schedule. In fact, many such equations were estimated in the 1970s, with
the rate of inflation a function of lagged money growth, income growth,
and other variables that temporarily affected the demand for money. But
one crucial set of variables in the demand for money function tended to
be omitted in work on inflation: the rate of return on money and the rates
of return on its substitutes. The issue was investigated by Sims (1980) who
found that it makes a lot of difference for inverted demand for money
schedules whether one includes or excludes interest rates as explanatory
variables.

During the 1980s statistical research on the link between money and
prices continued both in the form of inverted money demand schedules,
with the rate of price change as the dependent variable and in the form of
money demand equations. However, academic activity was far less than it
had been during the late 1960s and 1970s. Of course, inflation in the major
industrial countries declined on average during the 1980s, thus reducing
the demand for such work. In addition, both policymakers and public
opinion in general became more comfortable with the monetarist notion
that inflation is primarily a monetary phenomenon. Hence, it became less
necessary to provide statistical ammunition for now superseded disputes
between monetarist and so-called Keynesian economists. Finally, monetary
theorists became more interested in a range of issues that were far removed
from the estimation of reduced forms: much effort was devoted to further
refinement of the cash-in-advance model and the overlapping generations
model, as well as to attempts to develop a quantitative theory of the real
business cycle hypothesis. The more or less unrestricted reduced-form estimates of the connection between money and prices that were popular
during the previous period did not fit well with these theoretical efforts.

In recent years, the strengthening of the exchange-rate mechanism in
the European Community area and the prospects of a future European
Central Bank have stimulated a new wavelet of empirical research in the
money demand area. At the end of Section 4 a representative example,
the Kremers and Lane (1990) study of money demand in the European
Community, is reviewed. Specific criticisms of this and related work lead

to a further statistical discussion in the final section of the chapter. This section shows how new developments in Kalman filtering and smoothing make it possible for the first time to take into account that the link between money growth and inflation depends on the stochastic trend in the income velocity of money. First, important research by Bordo and Jonung (1987), which has documented the importance of changes over time in the trend of the income velocity of money, is summarized. Regressions of inflation on past money growth—and past income growth—fail in part because of oversimplifying assumptions regarding the trend in velocity: the work of Bordo and Jonung has shown that velocity over the longer term cannot be modeled correctly as a function of time. Next we introduce a particular Kalman filter algorithm as a more flexible and realistic way to statistically model the links between money and inflation. The filter and smoother are applied to data sets for the United States, Japan, and Germany in the final section.

1. THE EXCESS DEMAND MODEL OF INFLATION

A now discarded tradition in Keynesian macroeconomics held that "excess demand"[4] in the goods and labor markets was connected to the rate of inflation. Milton Friedman (1968) pointed out that there was no theoretical justification for such a connection: no possible model of rational price and wage setting by firms could result in such dynamics for inflation and excess demand. Equilibrium in the goods and labor markets requires that agents incorporate expectations about future excess demand in their current behavior, and it would be inconsistent for practitioners of the science of rational behavior to assume that such expectations would be irrational.

Empirically, it was obvious that a cross-section of countries provided no support for the hypothesis of the old Phillips curve: economic growth was no higher on average in inflationary economies, nor did low inflation appear to require permanent sacrifices in the form of sluggish economic growth.

Friedman's (1968) paper and the work by Phelps and others (1971) helped to shift the relationship between inflation and economic growth into the next higher gear: changes in excess demand might be related to changes in the rate of inflation. The connection can be seen in either of two ways:

(1) Δ excess demand $\rightarrow$ Δ inflation

or

(2) Δ money growth $\begin{array}{l} \nearrow \Delta \text{ excess demand} \\ \searrow \Delta \text{ inflation.} \end{array}$

In the case of equation (1), we try to measure excess demand in the labor market by using the difference between actual unemployment and its natural rate, or in the output market, by comparing actual economic growth to long-run equilibrium real growth or using numbers for capacity utilization, and we regress changes in inflation on such measures. The macroeconomic background to the changes in a variety of measures of excess demand may be provided with the analysis, but this is not necessary.

In the case of equation (2), we assume a link between growth in the money supply and inflation as well as a connection between (unanticipated) changes in money and changes in excess demand. The model in equation (2) leaves open the possibility that other macroeconomic forces have temporary effects on excess demand, but it does stipulate the trend in the rate of growth of the money supply as the prime cause of sustained inflation.

The first equation is implemented in all excess demand models of inflation. Here follows a model that summarizes the modeling behind many of the empirical studies of inflation in the past twenty years:

(3) $\Delta p_t = \Delta p_{t-1} + \alpha \, gap_t + v_t,$

(4) $gap_t = y - y^e + \Delta p_t - \Delta p_{t-1},$

(5) $\Delta M_t - \Delta p_t = m + \Delta y_t - \epsilon \, \Delta i_t + w_t,$

(6) $\Delta Y = \Delta p + \Delta y,$

where

p = price level
gap = gap between normal and actual nominal GDP
Y = nominal GDP
y = real GDP
M = nominal money supply
m = average rate of growth of the demand for real balances
i = representative opportunity cost of money
ϵ = semi-interest-rate elasticity of the demand for money

All variables apart from the opportunity cost variable are natural logarithms. The superscript e represents an expectation; Δ stands for the first difference of a variable; and v and w are error terms with zero means and constant variances.

Equation (3) shows how changes in the rate of inflation are related to the variable gap that represents the state of excess demand. Equation (6) shows the breakdown of the rate of growth of nominal GDP into real growth and inflation. Equation (4) contains the definition of *gap* as well as two implicit assumptions about the dynamics of *y* and *p*. It is assumed that the rate of growth of output can be regarded as a stationary variable for the purposes of this model, so that discrepancies between the actual and expected levels of output can be proxied by the differences between the actual rate of economic growth and its longer term average. The dynamics of inflation are different. The simplifying assumption has been made here that the rate of inflation is a pure random walk, which is to say that changes in the rate of inflation are unpredictable.[5] Because of the random walk assumption, the last period's rate of inflation is the best predictor of the current and all future rates of inflation as long as the forecaster does not possess extraneous sources of information about future changes in inflation.[6]

Equation (5) is a simple demand for money schedule. The rate of growth of the demand for real balances is assumed to be equal to a constant, *m*, on average, with short-term disturbances represented by the error w_t. More appropriate dynamics for the rate of growth of the demand for money will be discussed extensively later in this chapter. Equation (5) does not contain the own rate of return on money, but is limited to a single opportunity cost variable. In practice, if the researcher has available a time series that indicates how much utility the holding of money balances delivers to the owner per unit of time, he or she will want to include such a series on the own rate of return in the model. In addition, advanced empirical work on the demand for money sometimes introduces more than a single rate of return on substitutes for money holdings: two or more rates of interest, or a rate of interest as well as the rate of inflation indicating the substitution margin between money balances and goods.

Solving this model leads to

$$(7) \quad \Delta\Delta p_t = \frac{\alpha}{1-\alpha}(\Delta y_t - \Delta y_t^e) + \frac{v_t}{1-\alpha},$$

$$(8) \quad \Delta M_t - \Delta M_t^e = \Delta\Delta p_t + \Delta y_t - \Delta y_t^e - \epsilon \, \Delta i_t + w_t.$$

Equation (7) indicates that changes in the rate of inflation will depend on the forecast error in the rate of growth of real GDP, but this error is equal, of course, to the forecast error in the *level* of the rate of GDP.

Equation (8) may be developed further if we make assumptions about the dynamics of nominal interest rates.[7] For example, if the real rate is constant, we can replace Δi by $\Delta\Delta p$ and obtain

$$(9) \quad \Delta M_t - \Delta M_t^e = (1-\epsilon) \Delta\Delta p_t + \Delta y_t - \Delta y_t^e + w_t.$$

It follows from this model that the monetary authorities will try to keep the absolute size of *gap* small if they are satisfied with the most recent rate of inflation. Hence, the planned rate of money growth will be such that little change will occur in the actual rate of price change. In that case most changes in the observed rate of price change will be temporary, caused by shocks v_t. It will be hard to determine whether inflation is a sluggish process governed by sticky prices that can be best predicted using a long distributed lag of past rates of price change, or whether inflation is a monetary phenomenon, to be explained by past rates of money growth. The polar case would be that of relatively unimportant temporary shocks to the price level v_t but important permanent changes in the rate of nominal money growth. Such changes would be part of the expected rate of money growth for all future periods once they had been observed and hence would be incorporated in expected rates of inflation for the complete future. In that case, inflationary expectations would not be based on a long distributed lag of past rates of price change, but would depend on the dynamics of monetary growth.

Formalizing these notions, in the first case we would add to equations (7) and (8) an expression for the expected rate of money growth that should be called a reaction function for the monetary authorities. They aim at maintaining the (variance of the) *gap* variable or a similar expression at a minimum. Deviations between actual and expected money growth are basically a random variable. With that additional assumption, equations (7) and (8) may be solved for the actual rate of price change and the actual rate of economic growth. In the other case we would add to equations (7) and (8) another equation describing the dynamics of money growth that is now exogenous. The expected rate of money growth would be derived from the model for actual money growth, and equations (7) and (8) would then again determine the rate of inflation and the rate of economic growth.

In both cases, inflation remains a monetary phenomenon in the strict sense that changes in money are a necessary and sufficient condition for persistent inflation. Whether the data will show this in a reduced-form regression of inflation on past rates of inflation and past rates of money growth will depend on the size of the disturbances to equations (7) and (8), on the size of the coefficient α, on the dynamics of money growth, and on the behavior of the monetary authorities. Do they follow a reaction function trying to minimize *gap*, or do they follow a more or less exogenously determined monetary policy?[8]

A well-known criticism of the so-called Lucas (1972) short-term supply curve applies with full force to the model above. Surprises in output according to these models should coincide with surprises in inflation. But empirical research has shown conclusively that there is no reliable positive correlation between short-term fluctuations in output and contemporaneous changes in inflation. The finding is robust against different assumptions about the formation of expectations for future output and prices.

The empirical finding that money does not affect inflation at the same time that it affects output should not surprise readers of Friedman (1968) or Brunner and Meltzer (1976, 1989). It does not invalidate the view that inflation is a monetary phenomenon, but it shows the limitations of models that relate the dynamics of inflation to measurements of excess demand in the goods market.

Can this problem be solved by allowing for lags in equation (3)? The answer is yes, using the ideas of Fisher (1977) and Taylor (1979, 1980) about staggered contracts in the goods or labor markets.[9] But it will be hard to determine the correct coefficients, because they will always be a function of the characteristics of the noises in equations (3) and (5), as Lucas (1972) has explained. The optimal forecast formula will depend on the dynamics of the money supply, on the relative importance of the noise terms in all equations, as well as on the specified lags in the effects of changes in money on changes in economic growth and inflation.[10]

2. THE MONETARIST MODEL OF INFLATION

An example of a monetarist model is as follows:

$$(10) \quad \Delta M_t = \Delta M_{t-1} + a_{1,t}; \qquad \Delta M_t^e = \Delta M_{t-1},$$

$$(11) \quad \Delta M_t = \Delta p_t + \Delta y_t - \epsilon \Delta i_t + a_{2,t},$$

$$(12) \quad \Delta y_t^e = c,$$

$$(13) \quad (\Delta y - \Delta y^e)_t = -\beta_2 (\Delta p - \Delta p^e)_t + \beta_3 (\Delta g - \Delta g^e)_t + a_{4,t},$$

$$(14) \quad (\Delta y - \Delta y^e)_t = \alpha_1 (\Delta p - \Delta p^e)_t + a_{5,t},$$

$$(15) \quad r_t = i_t - \Delta p_{t+1}^e,$$

where

g = government expenditure on goods and services
c = constant
a_t = vector of serially uncorrelated error terms

The first equation, (10), indicates the dynamics for the money supply. In this monetarist type of model, the money supply is assumed to be exogenous in the sense that it does not depend on the other variables in the model according to a well-recognized reaction function. This is not to say that the money supply is determined by random behavior, but that its economic determinants are sufficiently far removed from the variables in equations

(11) through (14) for the simplifying assumption of equation (10) to be acceptable. Equation (11) is a demand-for-money schedule, expressed in relative rates of growth. Once again, the own rate of return on money has been omitted, and a single interest rate represents the opportunity cost of holding money. More extensive models might include a measure of the return on money balances as well as other rates of return, including the rate of return on the holding of goods (the negative of the rate of inflation). Equation (12) stipulates that the expected rate of growth of output and real demand is a constant. This simplifying assumption may be justified with an argument formally similar to the reasoning behind equation (10): economic determinants of the expected rate of economic growth may be demographic variables, (changes in) the tax system, various other supply-side factors, the real exchange rate, and a host of other variables, but as long as the expected rate of economic growth does not depend significantly on the short-term dynamics of the other variables, g, p, and M in the system, the simplifying assumption that the expected rate of growth of output is a constant could be acceptable. Both equation (13) for short-term movements in aggregate demand and equation (14), a Lucas-type aggregate supply curve, could well be modified, for instance, through incorporation of a term describing changes in the relative price of oil in the supply equation or through inclusion of different fiscal variables in the demand equation. Finally, equation (15) defines the real rate of interest as the difference between the nominal rate and the expected rate of inflation.

There are two principal problems with this model. First, just as for the gap model, it imposes a constraint on the coefficients in the reduced forms for output and prices: any factors that affect aggregate demand—equation (13)—should have consequences for output and prices that are dictated by the movement of a short-term demand curve that traces out supply-side responses. Hence, the effects should be simultaneous, and the ratio of the price and output effects should be identical for all impulses to aggregate demand. These so-called cross-equation constraints on the reduced forms for output and prices have been rejected in all applications of the model.

Second, it is difficult to accommodate changes in the trend in the demand for real balances. In equation (11) above, the trend in the equation for real balances is put at zero; a constant term in this equation would represent a constant linear trend. If any changes in the trend in velocity cannot be modeled exactly with measurable economic variables, it will be necessary to difference the system of equations once more. In particular, the relationship between expected money growth and expected inflation will have to be estimated as a relationship between changes in expected money growth and changes in expected inflation. However, this will reduce the signal-to-noise ratio in the estimated equations and make the testing of hypotheses harder, especially if there are long and variable lags between changes in money and changes in prices.

3. REPRESENTATIVE EMPIRICAL STUDIES

Trevithick and Mulvey (1975) accurately convey the flavor of research in the early 1970s.

In our opinion the monetarist explanation of inflation is superior to the "institutionalist" or cost-push explanations of inflation for it explains in very simple terms two phenomena:

(i) it explains why [prices have] accelerated in the United Kingdom, the United States, Japan and many other advanced economies since around 1967—there is no evidence of substantial changes in the structure of the economies around this time;

(ii) it explains why, despite ripples of relatively minor magnitude, inflation under a system of fixed exchange rates is essentially a worldwide phenomenon. (P. 6)

Despite this advocacy of a monetarist view of inflation, Trevithick and Mulvey retain analyses that concentrate on short-term price dynamics and attempt to connect inflation to cost developments. After a historical introduction, chapters follow about theories of cost inflation, wage inflation and excess demand, wage and price inflation, trade unions and inflation, and expectations and inflation. Much of their book relates to different cost-setting schemes in firms, to the markup of prices over costs, and to the particulars of the wage-setting process. The emphasis is on various extensions of the gap model described in Section 1 of this chapter.

If we assume that a reasonable indicator of the pressure of demand is the unemployment rate, the income-expenditure and monetarist models produce the identical prediction that a fall in the unemployment rate produced by expansive monetary/fiscal policies should be correlated with a rise in the rate of inflation. The same is true . . . for a rise in the unemployment rate produced by a contractionary monetary/fiscal policy.

This consideration led Samuelson and Solow (1960) to propose the following experiment in an attempt to distinguish demand from cost inflation:

If a small relaxation of demand were followed by great moderations . . . wages and other costs . . . then the demand-pull hypothesis would have received its most important confirmation. On the other hand, if mild demand repression checked cost and price increases not at all or only mildly . . . then the cost-push hypothesis would have received its most important confirmation.

The methodology of this approach is to examine whether the demand-pull prediction stands up to empirical scrutiny and, should it fail to do so, to deduce, faute de mieux, that cost-push factors were responsible for inflation.

Nor would the situation be much improved if monetarists were to produce a series of statistical equations to demonstrate the dependence of the rate of inflation upon the rate of monetary expansion. The more sophisticated among cost-push theorists . . . would simply reverse the direction of causation. . . .

It should be clear by now that, at a high level of aggregation, a number of insuperable hurdles are encountered in testing the cost-push theses. This is due principally to the immeasurability of most of the cost-push variables, such as the degree of social conflict. . . . No immediate test of the cost-push diagnosis is readily forthcoming. (Pp. 37–38)

As discussed in Section 1, the terms of the debate changed soon after publication of this volume. In empirical research, the main distinction became that between models that view (changes in) inflation as a function of (changes in) excess demand with monetary policy an important determinant of changes in excess demand, and models that allow for direct links between money growth and inflation. In either case, the monetary authorities may try to precisely accommodate the expected rate of inflation when setting monetary policy, so that the past rate of inflation is a good predictor of the future rate of inflation (a "sluggish" inflation process). Alternatively, the monetary authorities may try to influence expectations and accept responsibility for steering the rate of inflation.

The debate as to whether excess demand is a useful element in the analysis of inflation continues. The old distinction between cost-push or demand-pull inflation has disappeared because the term *cost-push* became associated with approaches to inflation that either neglected the distinction between relative price changes and changes in the absolute price level or that did not incorporate the assumption of a stable longer term demand for money. Nevertheless, we could continue to use the term *cost-push* for specific instances where exogenous political events, for instance, important union activity that results in major increases in economy-wide wages, forced the central bank to expand the money supply in order to prevent pressure on profit margins. In such cases the change in the rate of inflation, whether temporary or permanent, derives not from a deliberate change in the rate of growth of nominal demand, but from changes in nominal labor costs.

Meiselman and Laffer (1975) published their survey *The Phenomenon of Worldwide Inflation* in the same year. Allan Meltzer (1975) commented on the enterprise as follows:

We have represented here monetarist, fiscalist, international, European, and Phillips-curve views, plus some other views and even overviews. I am grateful to have been spared the oil-energy view, the beef-shortage view and other examples that I lump together as the worm's-eye view, or perhaps views, on inflation. The first fact to note is that neither economic theory nor evidence sustains anything like the number of separate and independent views of inflation represented on the program.

More than two hundred years ago economists had learned that prices rise whenever the quantity of nominal money increases relative to real output if money is maintained at the new level. This proposition was tested at the beginning of the eighteenth century, during the last ten years, and on many occasions in between. No exact correspondence exists between the growth of money and the rate of inflation in the eighteenth century, at present, or in most inflations that have been studied, so there is room for supplementary explanations. I find the integration of the dominant monetary explanation of inflation with other explanations more appealing than an attempt to pose the issue as a conflict of "views." To me, the notion that there are five or six "views" of the causes of inflation smacks of the politician, or the economist turned politician, who finds a new explanation of inflation each time he changes anti-inflation policy—about every six months in recent years. (P. 53)

Meiselman (1975) usefully pointed out that the growth rates of the money supply in most industrial countries moved very similarly from 1966 through 1970, but that the correlations were broken in 1971. He emphasized the rapid growth of dollar-denominated reserves outside of the United States, supplied through investment of the U.S. current-account deficits in dollar paper, and the introduction of the Special Drawing Rights by the International Monetary Fund in 1970, which provided another source of supply of international reserves and hence of money in the world economy.

Although the Trevithick-Mulvey and the Meiselman-Laffer books were eclectic, as noted by Meltzer, the work by Parkin, Zis, and their co-workers exhibited a systematic preference for monetary models of inflation. In the two final collections of papers (1976a, b) that resulted from the research project supervised by Parkin and Laidler at Manchester University, they presented a number of attempts to empirically connect money growth to inflation, both for national economies and for world aggregates.[11]

Spinelli's paper (1976) on inflation in Italy, for instance, begins by testing whether the wage-price nexus has its own dynamics that derives from negotiations in the labor market, so that central bank attempts to steer inflation through changing aggregate demand become very costly: the old debate between cost-push and demand-pull inflation, subsumed now under the more sophisticated question of whether the central bank validates whatever happens or is likely to happen in the labor market, or whether the central bank is responsible for inflationary expectations.

Spinelli tests the dynamics of the wage-setting process by regressing the rate of change of earnings on (a function of) unemployment and on various measures of strike activity by the Italian trade unions. He finds no effect for union activity and concludes that wages reflect a time-varying equilibrium in the labor market: "the evidence strongly denies any usefulness in augmenting the Phillips curve with some measure of strike activity."[12] The issue is important in Spinelli's analysis because he deduces that "some sort of incomes policy as the *major* anti-inflationary weapon cannot be justified" (pp. 218–19).

Spinelli then adds the lagged rate of world inflation for this period of fixed exchange rates to his regressions for inflation in Italy. We observe in his paper:

1. Autonomous events in the labor market may have one-time effects on the rate of inflation because the monetary authorities feel obliged to accommodate, but these are the exception. The rule is that wage setting is an equilibrium process and that wages do not cause inflation.
2. The inflation equation does not incorporate specific notions about price setting behaviour by firms, but is simply a distributed lag of past inflation and excess demand.
3. International factors have a place in the model for inflationary expectations in the fixed-rate period.

The international monetarist approach could provide a systematic story about the general increase in inflation throughout the Organization for Economic Cooperation and Development (OECD) area during the final years of the Bretton Woods period. Parkin (1977), for instance, offered a model that is very similar to equations (3)–(6) above. His paper shows how the richer dynamics in equation (3)—connecting changes in inflation to excess demand—and in equation (5)—the demand for money schedule—together with a richer but ad hoc formula for inflationary expectations result in a much more complicated reduced-form equation for the rate of inflation. The latter is now a function of lagged rates of inflation and lagged rates of money growth. As in most other papers of this period, Parkin accepts a constant term as sufficient for modeling all changes in the demand for real money balances that are not explained by changes in income.

The 1977 Brookings volume *Worldwide Inflation, Theory and Recent Experience*, edited by Krause and Salant, shows the rapid progress in the theoretical debate about inflation, particularly by providing international channels for the transmission of inflation. The two introductory papers by Swoboda and Branson emphasize the international transmission of inflation through the goods and asset markets. Branson's paper is entitled "A 'Keynesian' Approach to Worldwide Inflation," but he only fleetingly refers to wage setting. Instead, he concentrates on the interaction between the goods and asset markets in a spirit very similar to that of Brunner and Meltzer's earlier work. The main interest in both opening papers is on the endogeneity of the central bank's international reserves under fixed exchange rates.

The conference volume *The Problem of Inflation*, edited by Brunner and Meltzer (1978), contains a number of country studies that apply versions of the monetary model of equations (10)–(15) above. The crucial expectations of future money growth, as well as growth in other exogenous variables, are computed using Box-Jenkins time-series models. Typically, the different papers follow a two-step procedure. First, the econometrician computes expected values for all his exogenous variables and subtracts the expectations from the realizations to obtain a time series for the unexpected changes. In the second step, the expected and unexpected parts are used in the model equations. The reduced-form equations for inflation in this volume are generally similar to "St. Louis equations" but with two important differences:

1. The dependent variable is the rate of inflation rather than the rate of growth of nominal GDP.

2. Sharp distinctions are made between expected and unexpected changes in all explanatory variables, and allowance is made for the possibility that expected changes in money have a proportional effect on the rate of inflation, whereas unexpected changes in money have a less than proportional effect on the price level. Similarly, expected trends in fiscal policy may not affect inflation at all, whereas unexpected changes in fiscal policy have effects on the rate of price change. The same applies to expected and unexpected changes in the world trade, import prices, and other explanatory variables.

The papers are similar in spirit and execution to the well-known paper by Barro (1977) on the effects of unanticipated money on unemployment in the United States. Barro's discussion of the so-called observational equivalence problem also applies to the papers in the Brunner-Meltzer volume: if inflation is claimed to be a function of (lagged) expected money and (lagged) unexpected changes in money, it is hard to reject the possibility that inflation is correlated with a distributed lag of past rates of money growth, without any need to distinguish between expected and unexpected changes in money. In fact, one needs either a richer model (as in Barro, 1977) or data from another period in which the dynamics of money were different in order to settle the issue.

The Carnegie-Rochester conference volume (Brunner and Meltzer, 1978) and the Barro papers represent the peak of activity in applying either of the two theoretical models above to the analysis of inflation. After 1978, we observe a rapid shift of interest away from this type of applied work. The principal reason was a perceived instability in the demand for money schedule in the United States that made it harder to connect changes in inflation to earlier changes in money. The case that the demand for money had become less predictable was made very effectively by Goldfeld (1976). It is important for the discussion in Section 4 to note that Goldfeld and many other researchers tested specifications for the change in real money balances that allowed for only the following two causes of a trend in the income velocity of money:

1. a significant interest-rate elasticity, together with a secular increase or decline in that interest rate; and

2. an income (or wealth) elasticity that was different from cause one.

The majority view became that these two assumptions were not sufficient to explain the behavior of money demand in the United States. Certain trends in velocity could not be modeled as a function of changes in interest rates and growth in income.[13]

A second reason why empirical research on inflation became much less popular in academic journals was the conflict between the evidence of substantial lags between changes in money and changes in the rate of inflation and the theoretical difficulties in developing a well-founded story to account for such lags. Theoretical research in monetary macroeconomics shifted to deriving a demand for money from a bequest motive in the so-called overlapping generations model or from the need to accumulate money before making purchases, the cash-in-advance model. Whatever the merits of these theories,[14] they did not lead to useful testable hypotheses in the area of inflation.

Empirical work on inflation continued to be published in the Brookings Papers on Economic Activity and in the Carnegie-Rochester conference series. Bomhoff (1982) derived a statistical model for inflation using Kalman filtering techniques that allowed for both permanent and temporary shocks to the income velocity of money. A representative example of the papers published by Brookings is Robert Gordon's (1985) paper. Gordon makes assumptions about the labor market to derive a series for "natural real GNP."[15] The ratio of real to natural real GNP represents the output ratio and appears (with lags of up to eight quarters) as the most significant cause of changes in the rate of inflation. Differences between trend and actual movements in productivity play a similar role.

In a later section of his paper, Gordon adds a monetary variable that is computed as the quarterly difference between money growth and the rate of growth of natural real GNP. By itself this variable does not add to the explanation of changes in U.S. inflation, given the other causal factors. However, if it is included together with the rate of change of the income velocity of money, the two variables are jointly significant in a single equation for the period 1954:2–1984:4. Gordon experiments in this and earlier papers with several international variables, but he finds no significance for import prices or the exchange rate of the dollar. Gordon does not address the question of whether the limited influence of money in his model is caused by problems with lags and measurement errors, or whether it derives from a persistent lack of stability in the demand for money schedule.

A later analysis by Gordon (1990) confirms that for U.S. inflation past rates of change in wages are not required once the regression includes past rates of price change and some measure of excess demand and/or the cyclical position of productivity: "inflation depends on past inflation, not past wage changes." Gordon concludes that the dynamics of wages are important for the distribution of income, but not for explaining changes in the aggregate price level.

The *Economic Review* of the Federal Reserve Bank of San Francisco is a good source of empirical work on inflation in the 1980s that specifically takes into account a variety of open economy effects.[16] Here is a representative example from a paper by Rose McElhattan. Table 6 of her paper shows a reduced-form equation for inflation, with the following coefficients, which may be interpreted as elasticities (p. 51).

$$(16) \quad \Delta p_t - \Delta p_{t-1} = -12.090 + 0.148\, CU_t - 1.44\, WPON_t$$
$$\phantom{(16) \quad \Delta p_t - \Delta p_{t-1} = } (-4.2) \qquad (4.3) \qquad (-1.9)$$
$$+ 0.95\, WPOFF_t + 0.039\, DDIPE_t + 0.058\, DDIPE_{t-1}$$
$$(1.4) \qquad\qquad (3.6) \qquad\qquad (5.4)$$
$$+ 0.059\, DDEX_t + 0.107\, DDEX_{t-1},$$
$$(1.2) \qquad\qquad (2.4)$$

$$R^2 = 0.80$$
$$D.W. = 2.24$$
$$S.E.E. = 0.69$$

Period: 1979:1–1983:4 (quarterly data)

where

CU = capacity utilization rate
$WPON$ = wage/price controls "on"
$WPOFF$ = wage/price controls "off"
$DDIPE$ = acceleration in relative price of oil
$DDEX$ = acceleration in exchange rate of U.S. dollar

Once again, we observe that quarterly analyses of the change in the rate of price change require a measure of excess demand—and in this case also an important relative price, the acceleration in the relative price of oil— but not a monetary variable. The long and variable lag between changes in money growth and changes in inflation, as well as the incorporation of other variables such as capacity utilization and the exchange rate, which are influenced by past money growth, imply that there is little place for a monetary variable by itself in this type of regression.

In the late 1980s the dearth of empirical studies of inflation continued, but there was a modest revival of empirical work on the demand for money. Papers by Poole (1988) and Lucas (1988) had helped to re-ignite the debate, but were not sufficiently sophisticated econometrically to convince those who maintained that no stable demand for money schedule existed in the United States. The apparent success of the Swiss and German central banks in producing low and stable inflation after the shock of the first oil crisis (a few years around 1980 excepted) using targets for the money supply or for the monetary base should already have suggested that the problem of lack of stability in the demand for money schedule might be to some extent specific to the United States. The even more impressive performance of the Bank of Japan in delivering low and stable inflation as a consequence of low and stable money growth for an even longer period after the inflationary episode of the early 1970s suggests that monetary targeting becomes easier once the markets are accustomed to a stable and predictable monetary policy that is not subject to continuously changing degrees of political pressure or frequent changes in the regulatory and tax environment.

Very little comparative research was done, however, on the relative stability of the demand for money in different countries until the political movement toward a European central bank stimulated fresh research on the demand for money in Europe. Kremers and Lane (1990), for example, collected evidence about the stability of the demand for money and produced their own estimate of a money demand schedule for aggregate data relating to the European Community. Their preferred equation is reproduced here because it is representative of the most recent output on the demand for money.[17]

$$(17) \quad (m-p-y)_t = -5.92 - 0.67\ i_{s,t} - 1.40\ \Delta p_{t-1}$$
$$ (0.01)\quad (0.15)\qquad (0.53)$$
$$ + 0.079\ ecu_t,$$
$$ (0.007)$$

$$R^2 = 0.91$$
$$\sigma = 1\ \text{percent}$$

Quarterly data 1978:4–1987:4

where

m = logarithm of narrow money, taken from the International Financial Statistics
p = four-quarter moving geometric average of the ERM-wide Consumer Price Index
y = real GNP converted to Deutsche mark at ppp rates
i_s = short-term interest rate
Δp = rate of price change, used as indicator of the opportunity cost of money
ecu = nominal exchange rate of the ECU in terms of U.S. dollars

$$(18) \quad \Delta(m-p)_t = 0.002 + 0.67\ \Delta y_t - 0.86\ \Delta i_{l,t}$$
$$ (0.002)\quad (0.32)\qquad (0.31)$$
$$ - 0.46\ \Delta i_{s,t-3} - 0.95\ EC_{t-1},$$
$$ (0.29)\qquad\qquad (0.18)$$

$$R^2 = 0.66$$
$$\sigma = 0.82 \text{ percent}$$

Quarterly data 1979:1–1987:4

where

i_l = long-term interest rate
EC = residuals of equation (17)

Equation (17) is the first part of a so-called co-integration model. It stipulates that velocity is a function of an average short-term interest rate, i_s.[18] In addition, the opportunity cost of money is modeled by the rate of inflation, lagged one quarter, and Kremers-Lane also introduce the exchange rate of the ECU. Equation (18) is the second part of the co-integration model. This equation shows how changes in real balances depend on yet another opportunity cost variable, the long-term interest rate in the community, changes in real income, lagged changes in the short-term interest rate, and particularly on the one-quarter lagged residual EC from the first equation.

Before the arrival of co-integration, severe serial correlation of the residuals in an equation such as equation (17) was taken as a sign of an omitted variable. This technique, however, tells the user not to worry about serial correlation because the second step—the error-correction model—will offer a chance to eliminate it. The only diagnostic test on serial correlation of the residuals that really matters is the test on the residuals of equation (18). As a consequence of this procedure, the issue of a variable trend in the income velocity of money is swept under the carpet: the residuals of equation (17) quite possibly exhibit nonstationary behavior, but all the explanatory variables in equation (18) can contribute to produce well-behaved second-stage residuals.

Equation (17) has two strongly nonstationary variables on the right-hand side (the past rate of inflation and the nominal exchange rate of the ECU) and a third variable (the short-term interest rate) that may also be regarded as nonstationary. This set of nonstationary variables is used in the first stage of the co-integration to produce the best possible fit in a linear model for the level of velocity, but the question of whether there are trends in velocity related to the introduction of new substitutes for money, changes in payments techniques, or other developments in the financial services industry cannot be addressed in this framework. Nor will the co-integration technique show up diagnostics that point to a nonconstant trend in velocity.

The residuals in the Kremers-Lane analysis are small, as indicated by the standard error of estimate of approximately 1 percent per quarter. This would suggest a demand for money function on the European scale that is sufficiently stable to be exploited for monetary targeting by the future European System of Central Banks. Equations such as (17) and (18) contain a rather large number of explanatory variables and are the selected outcomes of an extensive search over different lags. (This description also applies to the other studies cited in note 18.) Because it is not clear on the basis of such historical studies how robust the estimated standard errors would be once we move to the forecasting context, the next and final section of this chapter approaches the same relationship between money and the price level from a technically different perspective, that of the Kalman filter.

4. DYNAMIC MODELING OF THE INCOME VELOCITY OF MONEY

The analysis in this section is based on annual data for the United States, Japan, and Germany over the postwar period. Use of a long period and emphasis on annual rather than quarterly data allow us to focus on the connections between money growth, velocity, and inflation without having to specify lag structures that are very unlikely to be time-invariant.[19] The single equation to be estimated is as follows:

$$(19) \quad p_t + y_t - M_t = V_t = c + \alpha tr_t + \theta i_t + u_t.$$

In equation (19), p_t represents the natural logarithm of the price level in an economy, y_t the log of a measure of income appropriate to the demand for money, M_t the log of the money supply, and hence V_t the log of the income velocity of money. c represents a shift term in the regression, tr_t a linear trend for the log of V, i_t the log of some relevant interest rate, and u_t the residual in the regression. α and θ are regression coefficients to be estimated by linear least squares.

The economic model is the simplest possible one. The income elasticity of money demand is fixed at unity, and a single interest rate is used to represent the opportunity cost of money, using the simplifying assumption that the own rate of return on money in each country is constant over time at the margin. With such simple assumptions, the resulting models will not be the optimal forecasting tools for velocity. However, the results from these minimal specifications may contribute more convincingly to the debate about the predictability of velocity, because uniform and simple models for six different countries are less subject to the suspicion of being based on data mining than multiparameter models with extensive lag structures and many free parameters that are tuned to the actual data in each country.

More sophisticated versions of equation (19) have been used to make the point that velocity has become highly unstable and unpredictable, at least in the United States since 1979. Here, however, with little loss of generality we will focus on the simple equation (19).[20]

Should this rock-bottom model for velocity be estimated in terms of levels, first differences, or second differences? Harvey (1980) discusses whether one can use some goodness-of-fit criterion to decide the issue. He concludes that this is likely to work in long data sets, but that in shorter sets big losses are bound to be incurred from time to time by wrongly failing to differentiate nonstationary data. Many subsequent papers on variance ratio tests, co-integration, or error-correction models have made the point that in nonexperimental data sets of limited length there is no test with strong discriminating power to decide whether or not differencing the data is called for.[21]

Bordo and Jonung (1987) contributed to the empirical literature on money demand and velocity in the longer term by documenting trends in velocity in five different countries over a hundred-year period. Their research convincingly shows that over the longer term velocity is non-stationary. They test a number of hypotheses about the changes in the trend in velocity and prefer an institutional approach that emphasizes the secular decline in velocity as an economy makes more and more use of money for transactions, followed by a secular rise in velocity as agents devise ways to economize on money, and as the technology of making payments and shifting money from transaction balances to inter-est-bearing savings accounts improves. Eventually, velocity may also in-crease more slowly or not at all if advances in technology and competitive pressures force banks to offer market-determined rates of return on money balances.[22]

The variable trend in velocity poses severe problems for empirical re-search on the demand for money, in both its normal and inverted forms, beginning with the problem mentioned before: whether to work with (nat-ural logarithms of) levels or with differenced data. Some researchers do not reject the hypothesis that the levels (of the natural logarithms) of money, income, and possibly a relevant interest rate are co-integrated, meaning that a regression of the level of real balances on the level of income (and the opportunity cost variable) is permissible. (See Boughton and Tavlas, 1990, who use data from five of the G-7 countries; see also Hendry and Ericsson, 1991, for the United Kingdom only, and Hoffman and Rasche, 1989, for the United States.) Others prefer to work in terms of first differences of money, income, and interest rates without reliance on a long-term relationship in terms of the levels (see, for example, Hetzel and Mehra, 1989; Mehra, 1989; and Rasche, 1987; for the United States). Unless explanatory variables can explain all changes in the rate of growth of velocity (and the work by Bordo and Jonung, 1987, suggests that neither income nor institutional variables that represent monetization or economic development can provide more than a partial explanation), it follows that even regressions in first differences are misspecified: one would have to difference at least twice.[23]

It is hard to resolve the dispute with least squares regression techniques. Recall that the natural context for any least squares model is that of stationary variables, because least squares regressions for nonstationary variables have to work with a system matrix $X'X$ that is a function of the number of data points. Such regressions do not satisfy ergodicity. Thus, it is not plausible that a single collection of historical data can be used for the estimation of coefficients with distributions that relate to repeated sampling.[24]

Of course, each differencing operation increases the probability that the transformed series are stationary. But if the relationship when specified in terms of levels is subject to both temporary and permanent disturbances, differencing results in a deterioration of the signal-to-noise ratio and less well-determined coefficients.

By contrast to linear regression techniques, Kalman filters and smoothers are designed to work with nonstationary data, because the filters and smoothers produce distributions of the so-called state variables that are conditional on the previous realization of the states. For that reason, nonstationarity in itself presents no problem, and ergodicity can be satisfied, implying that the distributions of the coefficients have a meaningful interpretation. The only reason why Kalman filtering has not yet become the natural way to model multivariate time series has been the technical difficulty of combining estimation of the states with estimation of other parameters required to run the filter successfully.

This chapter presents a method for estimating states and parameters jointly, using smoothing algorithms developed by Maybeck (1979, 1982), together with an estimation technique developed by Dempster, Laird, and Rubin (1977) and adapted to the Kalman filter case by Shumway and Stoffer (1982).[25]

The Kalman filter model will be estimated in terms of levels, with allowance for three types of shocks to velocity (V):

1. temporary shocks to the level of V;
2. permanent shocks to the level of V; and
3. permanent changes in the trend of V.

Note that the second type, permanent shocks to the level, can also be described as representing temporary disturbances to the rate of growth.

The variances of the different types of shocks, and hence their relative importance, will be estimated on the basis of the data. In this way the methodological difficulties associated with indirect tests for nonstationarity or co-integration are avoided: the data will tell us whether or not it is useful to account for stochastic changes in the trend.[26]

The general state-space notation is as follows:

(20)
$$V_t = (1 \ 0 \ i_t) \begin{pmatrix} c_t \\ tr_t \\ \vartheta_t \end{pmatrix} + u_t,$$

$$var \ (u) = R$$

(21)
$$\begin{pmatrix} c \\ tr \\ \vartheta \end{pmatrix}_{t+1} = \begin{pmatrix} 1 & 1 & 0 \\ 0 & 1 & 0 \\ 0 & 0 & 1 \end{pmatrix} \begin{pmatrix} c \\ tr \\ \vartheta \end{pmatrix}_t + \begin{pmatrix} 1 & 1 & 0 \\ 0 & 1 & 0 \\ 0 & 0 & 0 \end{pmatrix} \begin{pmatrix} w_1 \\ w_2 \\ w_3 \end{pmatrix}_t$$

$$var \begin{pmatrix} w_1 \\ w_2 \\ w_3 \end{pmatrix} = \begin{pmatrix} Q_1 & 0 & 0 \\ 0 & Q_2 & 0 \\ 0 & 0 & 1 \end{pmatrix}.$$

Equivalently:

(22) $V_t = m_t + \vartheta i_t + u_t.$

In equation (5), m_t is no longer a fixed intercept, but a dynamic stochastic trend, subject to both permanent shifts in its level and a time-varying rate of growth. Analysis of equations (3) and (4) will show that they can be summarized in the more easily recognized equation (5) which differs from standard reduced forms for the demand for money only by a much more flexible intercept term.

Equation (3) is the observation equation. It states that the level of the log of velocity, V, equals the sum of a shift parameter, the product of the interest-rate elasticity, θ, and the long-term interest rate, i_t, and a residual term u_t. This observation equation is identical to an ordinary regression equation. The column vector in equation (3) contains the three so-called state variables of the Kalman filter model. These three variables together provide sufficient information about the current level of the natural logarithm of velocity. In each year, velocity is a linear function of the three state variables together with the residual term of equation (3) which is assumed to be serially uncorrelated.

To model the dynamics of velocity, the Kalman filter methodology adds equation (4), the so-called state update equation. It shows how three state variables change from period to period. The equation has a predetermined part and a stochastic part. In the predetermined part, the shift parameter is adjusted upward in each period by the amount, tr_t, which represents a trend. In the stochastic part of equation (4), the trend term, tr_t, is subject to a stochastic shock, w_2, and the shift parameter is subject to permanent stochastic shocks, w_1. The interest-rate elasticity is not subject to stochastic shocks over time.

The two stochastic shocks w_1 and w_2 are not observed, and forecasts of velocity have to be made before these shocks are realized in each period. Obviously, the residuals u_t in equation (3) also are only observed after the fact. The Kalman filter will be used to generate forecasts that are produced online: starting in the first year of the period of estimation, the filter moves forward and generates a forecast for each period that uses the long-term interest rate for that year but does not use knowledge of any of the three shock terms that will effect velocity in the forecast year. However, the Kalman filter requires estimates of the average relative importance of the three different types of shock over time. In other words, the user needs to specify estimates of the variances Q_1, Q_2, and R. These estimates are obtained with the use of Kalman filters and smoothers in combination with the expectation maximization algorithm, described by Dempster et al. (1977) and Watson and Engle (1983) and adapted to our case by Shumway and Stoffer (1982).[27] The variance terms $Q1$ and $Q2$ as well as the residual variance R indicate the relative importance of the three types of different shocks that impact velocity. With different values for $Q1$ and $Q2$, the Kalman filter can include both a least squares specification for the level of log velocity and a specification for its rate of growth. The level specification is obtained by putting both $Q1$ and $Q2$ equal to zero; a least squares specification for the rate of growth of velocity inclusive of a constant deterministic trend is obtained by allowing for nonzero $Q1$ but keeping $Q2$ equal to zero. The Kalman filter includes both specifications as particular cases, so that comparisons between a least squares model in terms of levels and a least squares model in terms of rates of growth can be made within the context of a single encompassing Kalman filter model. Other statistical techniques for comparing levels and first-difference specifications suffer from the disadvantage that the two competing hypotheses are nonnested.[28] Note that the regression coefficients in the least squares model become state variables in the Kalman filter.

The crucial advantage of the state-space formulation is that it allows for estimation in terms of levels while at the same time incorporating all three different types of shocks to the logarithm of velocity: temporary shocks to the level (u_t), permanent shocks to the level (w_1), and permanent changes to the rate of growth of velocity (w_2). The Kalman filter approach allows for analysis of nonstationary series such as the logarithm of the income velocity of money, because all variances that are computed with the Kalman filter refer to conditional second moments, which are conditional on the complete history up to the present time of all the observable variables in the system. By contrast, ordinary least squares estimation is meant to compute unconditional variances for the computed least squares coefficients, including the constant term.

The only free parameters in the models are the interest elasticity, which is assumed to be constant over time, and two variance terms: the variance of the permanent shocks to the level of the series and the variance of the permanent shocks to the trend in velocity.[29]

The income elasticity of money is not a free parameter in this Kalman filter model. It is hypothesized here that financial innovations lead to changes in velocity trends that are spuriously picked up by nonunitary income elasticities in the traditional money demand specifications. The principal attraction of this hypothesis is that it is not troubled by the substantial differences between the income elasticities in different countries over identical time periods in traditional models that do not allow for stochastic trends but include the income elasticity as a free parameter.

The exogenous explanatory variable is the domestic yield on long-term government bonds. No experiments were undertaken with other rates of return or with lag structures, and the same specification was imposed for all countries. We have tested this interest-rate elasticity for stability by allowing for a different value before and after 1980. The hypothesis that the interest-rate elasticity did not differ between these two subperiods was not rejected.

Table 4.1 shows the results for Germany, the United States, and Japan. For each country the interest-rate elasticity is shown for M1 velocity and M2 velocity, together with the estimated standard error of the coefficient. For M1 all interest-rate elasticities are significant at the 0.05 level. In the case of M2, statistical significance is reached for Japan and Germany. In both countries, the interest-rate elasticity of M2 is smaller than that of M1.

Table 4.1 also shows the size of the forecast errors. These are conditional on the realized value of the long-term domestic bond yield and the estimated interest-rate elasticity and on the optimal estimates of the relative importance of the three different types of shocks that affect velocity. As far as the intercept and the trend in velocity are concerned, the forecasts are purely ex ante and are computed recursively without any smoothing. The stochastic trend does change over time, but the filter does not utilize future observations to fit a trend to the complete period. Instead, it moves through the data and from the data learns how to adjust the trend as time proceeds.

There are two reasons for computing the forecasts conditional on the interest rate for the current year. First, the outcomes are directly comparable to results from studies of the demand for money. Second, interest rates are observed without lag and without measurement error, so that policymakers can always adjust any targets for a monetary aggregate if interest rates during the planning period deviate from their predicted values

Table 4.1
Forecast Errors of Velocity

A:

	M1 Semi-interest Elasticity (S.E.)	R.M.S.E. (robust estimate)	M2 Semi-interest Elasticity (S.E.)	R.M.S.E. (robust estimate)
Country				
United States 1956 - 90	0.23 (0.036)	2.45 % (1.80 %)	0.24 (0.36)	2.28 % (2.45 %)
Japan 1968 - 90	0.20 (0.058)	5.35 % (4.84 %)	0.13 (0.049)	4.37 % (2.27 %)
Germany 1958 - 90	0.20 (0.036)	3.45 % (3.15 %)	0.16 (0.032)	2.93 % (2.36 %)

Forecast Errors of Velocity Before 1980 vs. 1980–90

B:

Country	M1 R.M.S.E. before 1980	M1 R.M.S.E. 1980 - 90	M2 R.M.S.E. before 1980	M2 R.M.S.E. 1980 - 90
United States	2.18 %	2.94 %	2.04 %	2.72 %
Japan	6.74 %	3.20 %	5.69 %	2.14 %
Germany	3.62 %	3.08 %	3.46 %	1.36 %

when the targets were set. Hence, forecasts conditional on interest-rate realizations produce more useful evidence about the forecastability of velocity than forecasts that are conditional only on past values of velocity, income, and interest rates.

For each velocity model, Table 4.1 presents two indicators of the forecast accuracy. The first number of each pair is the root mean square error (rmse) of the forecasts produced by the Kalman filter, expressed in percent. The second number of each pair is an estimate of the same rmse, but is computed using a robustified procedure. The mean of the absolute values of all forecast errors is computed and is divided by the correction factor 0.6745. This results in a robust estimate of the rmse, which is less sensitive to single outliers in the residuals.

The bottom part of Table 4.1 compares root mean square errors before and after 1980. The velocity of M1 became harder to predict according to the Kalman filter for M1 in the model in the United States, but easier to forecast in the other two countries. Forecast errors in M2 velocity in the United States also became substantially larger after 1980 according to this statistical model, but once again M2 velocity became easier to predict in Japan and Germany. The data, therefore, show the dangers of generalizing on the basis of experience in a single country.

The results of this Kalman filter exercise suggest that given a proper forecasting model that allows for learning about any possible changes in the stochastic trend in velocity, it is possible to produce forecasts of the velocity of money that are sufficiently accurate to be used in setting up a monetary rule. Hence, this chapter can end on a positive note. Both the Kremers and Lane analysis for a European monetary aggregate using quarterly data and the Kalman filter analysis for the United States, Japan, and Germany suggest that velocity, even though often nonstationary, can still be predicted with sufficient accuracy to be used in implementing a monetary targeting rule. As we have seen, this finding is not contradicted by the observation that short-term forecasts of inflation are often made without recourse to lagged rates of growth in the money supply. Other macroeconomic variables such as changes in the rate of capacity utilization, are available that, together with lagged actual rates of price change and possibly lagged rates of change in the price of energy, can help to produce accurate short-term forecasts of inflation. Sluggishness in the actual rate of price change means that multivariate autoregressions are the proper practical way to produce optimal short-term inflation forecasts. The fundamental dependence of inflation on lagged money growth is confirmed by recent work on the stability of the demand for money and serves as a basis for setting monetary policy.

NOTES

I am grateful to Camiel de Koning, and Tom van Veen for their assistance with this research, and to Ivo Arnold for useful discussions. Jolande Quik, Erna Zwaanswijk-ten Cate, and Peter Gerbrands helped to prepare the manuscript.

1. See Carlson (1989) for a comparison of different price indices in the United States.
2. There has been some interest in attempts to predict inflation using indices for commodity prices. Research by von zur Muehlen (1990) has demonstrated that the relative price effects in indices of raw materials dominate any information they might contain about future trends in the general price level.
3. See, for example, the May 1990 issue of the *World Economic Outlook* by the International Monetary Fund for a useful recent analysis of inflation and inflationary uncertainty in developing countries.
4. The term "excess demand" is ill defined. It is used from here on without the quotation marks.
5. We call a time series a "random walk" if its change between measurements has an expected value of zero and a constant variance. The term "martingale" is

used for a series that also has period-to-period changes that are unforecastable and have a mean of zero but about whose variance nothing is known.

6. Statisticians call random walks and martingales "memory-less" processes: knowledge of the most recent value of the series is useful for making forecasts, but it makes no sense to use a collection of previous values to construct some type of moving average for predictive purposes: old values can be discarded.

7. If we prefer to stipulate that changes in the real rate are related to fluctuations in economic growth and/or to accelerations in money growth, we will have to be precise about the horizon to which the expected rate of inflation applies, before being able to eliminate changes in the real rate of interest and changes in the expected rate of inflation from the model.

8. See Leamer (1986) for a sophisticated statistical analysis of the relative importance of excess demand versus monetary factors, which unsurprisingly does not lead to a clear-cut answer. See also Perry (1980) for a less sophisticated analysis with a comparable outcome.

9. See Ball, Mankiw, and Romer (1988) for an extensive recent analysis of "sluggishness" and lags in the new Keynesian economics.

10. See Gordon (1984) for an empirical analysis of U.S. money demand that emphasizes this interpretation of why such equations are so often unstable.

11. A very similar analysis of inflation in a number of industrial countries was performed by Keran (1975).

12. Smyth (1978) notes correctly in a markedly hostile review of "Inflation in open economies" that strike activity has costs that depend on employer attitudes and that if these change over time it is no longer correct to map union behavior on strike activity.

13. But see Judd and Motley (1984) for a defense of the continued stability of M1 in the United States. These authors assert that allowance for some change in the interest-rate elasticity of U.S. M2 is sufficient also to retain the usefulness of that aggregate.

14. See Gavin (1991) for a series of articles on these theories, together with critical comments by Howitt, Summers, and others.

15. A series of earlier papers in the Brookings Papers used much more detailed assumptions about wage formation in the United States. See, for instance, Perry (1980) for one of the more recent examples of an analysis that emphasizes differences in wage formation between the unionized and nonunionized sectors.

16. See also Koch, Rosensweig, and Whitt (1988) for an analysis using causality tests of the bivariate relationship between the exchange rate of the dollar and a variety of domestic U.S. price indices. In their bivariate context, a permanent 10 percent decline in the dollar leads to a 5 percent rise in U.S. price level.

17. See Boughton (1991) and Hendry and Ericsson (1991) for very similar studies of money demand, all using the co-integration technique.

18. See Kremers and Lane (1990) for details about the aggregation procedures for income, prices, and money to get European totals in terms of the Deutsche mark. They reject aggregation at current nominal exchange rates and prefer to use purchasing power parity exchange rates.

19. See Boughton and Tavlas (1990b) and Cuthbertson and Taylor (1990) for useful surveys of econometric estimates of money demand using quarterly data.

They concentrate on various implementations of the so-called buffer stock approach.

20. The simple specification in this chapter does not separate the changes in V into changes in money, M, and changes in gross national product, y. It has been argued that such a disaggregation of the changes in V is useful, since the dynamic impact of a change in M on velocity will differ from the dynamic impact of a change in y. Gains in forecasting accuracy that are based on this disaggregation may be particularly valuable in longer term forecasts, and/or in multi-equation models. In this chapter I limit the discussion to the single-equation analysis of V, with one interest rate as the only explanatory variable.

21. Diebold and Nerlove (1988) provide a selective survey of the literature on unit roots.

22. Bordo and Jonung (1987) test whether empirical proxies can be found to represent some longer term dynamics of the demand for money. They are careful not to claim that inclusion of such variables captures all permanent changes in level or growth rate of velocity. Kenny (1991) has additional tests of institutional and demographic variables in an extensive cross-country analysis.

23. See Nelson and Plosser (1982) for discussion of traditional econometric tests of the levels versus first-differences specification. Such tests have low power. More recent work on co-integration allows one to work with levels, but only if some linear combination of the series in the analysis is exactly stationary. That condition is unlikely to be met in the context of the demand for money where there are likely to be permanent shocks to the level of velocity that cannot be modeled by causal economic variables.

24. Durlauf and Phillips (1988) provide an excellent theoretical analysis of the difficulties that arise when ordinary least squares are applied to nonstationary time series, with the possibility that the errors are also nonstationary and nonergodic. See also Plosser and Schwert (1979) and Nelson and Plosser (1982). This line of research originated with Paul Newbold; see Granger and Newbold (1974).

25. This section is based in part on my 1991 paper. The models are similar to those in Harvey (1980, 1989) who, however, uses a different estimation technique.

26. See Swamy, Von zur Muehlen, and Mehta (1989) for a very critical methodological discussion of co-integration tests.

27. See Nelson (1988) for evidence from his univariate research of U.S. GNP that optimization with respect to the unknown variances of the different shocks to the level and the shocks to the trend of a nonstationary time series may be a delicate matter. This is a topic for additional research.

28. See Nelson and Plosser (1980) for discussion of traditional econometric tests of the levels versus first- differences specification. Such tests have low power. More recent work on co-integration allows us to work with levels, but only if some linear combination of the series in the analysis is exactly stationary. That condition is unlikely to be met in the context of the demand for money where there are likely to be permanent shocks to the level of velocity that cannot be modeled by causal economic variables.

29. The variance of the temporary shocks to the level of velocity could be seen as a third variance parameter, but the models are homogeneous of the first degree in all the variance and covariance terms. Hence, this variance is best viewed as computed ex-post from the results of the Kalman filter.

REFERENCES

Ball, L. and Cecchetti, S. G. 1990. "Inflation and Uncertainty at Short and Long Horizons." *Brookings Papers on Economic Activity* 1: 215–54.

———; Mankiw, N. G.; and Romer, D. 1988. "The New Keynesian Economics and the Output-Inflation Trade-off." *Brookings Papers on Economic Activity* 1: 1–82.

Barro, R. J. 1977. "Unanticipated Money Growth and Unemployment in the United States." *American Economic Review* 67: 101–15.

Bomhoff, E. J. 1982. "Predicting the Price Level in a World That Changes All the Time." In K. Brunner and A. H. Meltzer, eds., *Carnegie-Rochester Conference Series on Public Policy*, 17: 7–56.

———. 1991. "Stability of Velocity in the Major Industrial Countries." *IMF Staff Papers* 38, no. 3 (September): 626–42.

Bordo, M. D., and Jonung, L. 1987. *The Long-run Behavior of the Velocity of Circulation: The International Evidence.* Cambridge, England: Cambridge University Press.

Boughton, J. M. 1991. "Long-run Money Demand in Large Industrial Countries." *IMF Staff Papers* 38, no. 1 (March): 1–32.

———, and Tavlas, G. S. 1990a. "Demand for Money in Major Industrial Countries: A Comparison of Error Correction and Buffer Stock Models." Washington, D.C.: International Monetary Fund.

———. 1990b. "Modeling Money Demand in Large Industrial Countries: Buffer Stock and Error Correction Approaches." *Journal of Policy Modeling* 12 no. 2: 433–61.

Branson, W. H. 1977. "A "Keynesian" Approach to Worldwide Inflation." In *Worldwide Inflation*, edited by L. B. Krause, and W. S. Salant. Washington, D.C.: Brookings Institution.

Brunner, K., and Meltzer, A. H. 1976. "An Aggregative Theory for a Closed Economy." In Monetarism, edited by J. L. Stein, Amsterdam: North-Holland.

———. 1978. "The Problem of Inflation." *Carnegie-Rochester Conference Series on Public Policy* 8.

———. 1989. *Monetary Economics.* Oxford: Basil Blackwell.

Carlson, K. M. 1989. "Do Price Indexes Tell Us About Inflation? A Review of the Issues." *Review Federal Reserve Bank of St. Louis* 71, no. 6 (November/December): 12–30.

Chopra, A. 1985. "The Speed of Adjustment of the Inflation Rate in Developing Countries: A Study of Inertia." *IMF Staff Papers* 32 (December): 693–733.

Cooley, T. F., and Leroy, S. F. 1981. "Identification and Estimation of Money Demand." *American Economic Review* 71 (December): 825–44.

Cuthbertson, K., and Taylor, M. P. 1990. "Money Demand, Expectations, and the Forward-Looking Model." *Journal of Policy Modeling* 12, no. 2: 289–315.

Dempster, A. P.; Laird, N. N.; and Rubin, D. B. 1977. "Maximum Likelihood from Incomplete Data via the EM-Algorithm." *Journal of the Royal Statistical Society*, Series B, 39: 1–22.

Diebold, F. X., and Nerlove, M. 1988. "Unit Roots in Economic Time Series: A Selective Survey." *Finance and Economics Discussion Series*, no. 49. Washington, D.C.: Division of Research and Statistics, Federal Reserve Board.

Durlauf, S. N., and Philips, P. C. 1988. "Trends Versus Random Walks in Time Series Analysis." *Econometrica* 56 (November): 1333–54.

Fisher, D. 1989. *Money Demand and Monetary Policy*. Ann Arbor: University of Michigan Press.

Fisher, S. 1977. "Long Term Contracts, Rational Expectations and the Optimal Money Supply Rule." *Journal of Political Economy* 85 (February): 191–205.

Friedman, M. 1968. "The Role of Monetary Policy." *American Economic Review* 58: 1–17.

Gavin, W. T. 1991. "Price Stability, A Conference Sponsored by the Federal Reserve Bank of Cleveland." *Journal of Money, Credit and Banking* 23, no. 3, part 2 (August): 433–631.

Goldfeld, S. M. 1976. "The Case of the Missing Money." *Brookings Papers on Economic Activity* 3: 683–730.

Goodhart, C.A.E. 1989. *Money, Information and Uncertainty*. 2d ed. Hong Kong: MIT Press.

Gordon, R. J. 1984. "The Short-run Demand for Money: A Reconsideration." *Journal of Money, Credit and Banking* 16, no. 4 (November): 403–34.

———. 1985. "Understanding Inflation in the 1980's." *Brookings Papers on Economic Activity* 1: 263–302.

———. 1990. "U.S. Inflation, Labor's Share, and the Natural Rate of Unemployment." In *Economics of Wage Determination* edited by H. Koning. New York: Springer Verlag, 1–34.

Granger, C.W.J., and Newbold, P. 1974. "Spurious Regressions in Econometrics." *Journal of Econometrics* 2: 111–20.

Harvey, A. C. 1980. "On Comparing Regression Models in Levels and First Differences." *International Economic Review* 21 (October): 707–20.

———. 1989. "Forecasting, Structural Time Series Models and the Kalman Filter." New York: Cambridge University Press.

Hendry, D. F., and Ericsson, N. R. 1991. "An Econometric Analysis of UK Money Demand in Monetary Trends in the United States and the United Kingdom by Milton Friedman and Anna J. Schwartz." *American Economic Review* 81 (March): 8–38.

———. 1991. "Modeling the Demand for Narrow Money in the United Kingdom and the United States." *European Economic Review* 35: 833–86.

Hetzel, R. L., and Mehra, Yash P. 1989. "The Behavior of Money Demand in the 1980s." *Journal of Money, Credit and Banking* 21: 455–63.

Hoffman, Dennis, and Robert H. Rasche. 1989. Long-Run Income and Interest Elasticity of Money Demand in the United States. Mimeo.

International Monetary Fund. 1990. *World Economic Outlook*. Washington, D.C. (May).

Judd, J. P., and Motley, B. 1984. "The 'Great Velocity Decline' of 1982–83: A Comparative Analysis of M1 and M2." *Economic Review Federal Reserve Bank of San Francisco* 3 (Summer): 56–74.

Kenny, L. W. 1991. "Cross County Estimates of the Demand for Money and Its Components." *Economic Inquiry* 29: 695–705.

Keran, M. W. 1975. "Towards an Explanation of Simultaneous Inflation-Recession." *Business Review Federal Reserve Bank of San Francisco* (Spring): 18–30.

Koch, P. D.; Rosensweig, J. A.; and Whitt, J. A., Jr. 1988. "The Dynamic Relationship Between the Dollar and U.S. Prices: An Intensive Empirical Investigation." *Journal of International Money and Finance* 7, no. 2 (June): 181–204.

———. 1988. "The Dynamic Relations Between the Dollar and U.S. Prices: An Intensive Empirical Investigation." *Journal of International Money and Finance* 7 (June): 181–204.

Krause, L. B., and Salant W. S. eds. 1977. *Worldwide Inflation, Theory and Recent Experience*. Washington, D.C.: Brookings Institution.

Kremers, J.J.M., and Lane, T. D. 1990. "Economic and Monetary Integration and the Aggregate Demand for Money in the EMS. *IMF Staff Papers* 37, no. 4 (December): 677–705.

Laidler, D. 1990. "Understanding Velocity: New Approaches and Their Policy Relevance-Introduction." *Journal of Policy Modeling* 12, no. 2: 141–63.

Leamer, E. E. 1986. "A Bayesian Analysis of the Determinants of Inflation." In *Model Reliability*, edited by P. A. Belsley and E. Kuh. Cambridge, Mass.: MIT Press, 62–89. Reprinted in C.W.J. Granger, ed. 1990. *Modelling Economic Series*. Oxford: Clarendon Press, 235–59.

Levy, M. D. 1981. "Factors Affecting Monetary Policy in an Era of Inflation." *Journal of Monetary Economics* 8, no. 3 (November): 351–73.

Ljung, L., and Söderström, T. 1983. *Theory and Practice of Recursive Identification*. Cambridge, Mass.: MIT Press.

Lucas, R. E., Jr. 1972. "Expectations and the Neutrality of Money." *Journal of Economic Theory* 4 (April): 103–24.

———. 1983. "Understanding Business Cycles." In *Theory, Policy, Institutions: Papers from the Carnegie-Rochester Conferences on Public Policy*, edited by K. Brunner and A. H. Meltzer. Amsterdam: Elsevier Science Publishers, 1–24. Reprinted from "Stabilization of the Domestic and International Economy. 1977. *Carnegie-Rochester Series on Public Policy* 5: 7–30.

———. 1988. "Money Demand in the United States: A Quantitative Review." *Carnegie-Rochester Conference Series on Public Policy* 29: 137–68.

Mackinnon, J. G., and Milbourne, R. D. 1988. "Are Price Equations Really Money Demand Equations on Their Heads?" *Journal of Applied Econometrics* 3: 295–305.

Maybeck, P. S. 1979. "Stochastic Models, Estimation and Control." *Mathematics in Science and Engineering*. Vol. 1. New York: Academic Press.

———. 1982. "Stochastic Models, Estimation and Control." *Mathematics in Science and Engineering*. Vol. 2. New York: Academic Press, 141–42.

McCallum, B. T. 1981. "Price Level Determinacy with an Interest Rate Policy Rule and Rational Expectations." *Journal of Monetary Economics* 8, no. 3 (November): 319–29.

———. 1983. "The Role of Overlapping-Generations Models in Monetary Economics." *Carnegie-Rochester Conference Series on Public Policy* 18 (Spring): 9–44.

McElhattan, R. 1985. "Inflation, Supply Shocks and the Stable Inflation Rate of

Capacity Utilization." *Economic Review Federal Reserve Bank of San Francisco* 1 (Winter): 45–63.

Mehra, Y. P. 1989. "Some Further Results on the Source of Shift in M1 Demand in the 1980s." *Economic Review Federal Reserve Bank of Richmond* 75, no. 5 (September/October): 3–13.

Meiselman, D. I. 1975. "Worldwide Inflation: A Monetarist View." In *The Phenomenon of Worldwide Inflation*, edited by D. I. Meiselman and A. B. Laffer. Washington, D.C.: American Enterprise Institute for Public Policy Research.

Meltzer, A. H. 1975. "Comment." In *The Phenomenon of Worldwide Inflation*, edited by D. I. Meiselman and A. B. Laffer. Washington, D.C.: American Enterprise Institute for Public Policy Research, 53–56.

Meiselman, D. I. and Laffer, A. B., eds. 1975. *The Phenomenon of Worldwide Inflation*. Washington, D.C.: American Enterprise Institute for Public Policy Research.

Muehlen, Peter von zur. 1990. "Predicting Inflation with Commodity Prices." *Finance and Economics Discussion Paper Series* 118. Washington, D.C.: Board of Governors of the Federal Reserve System (March).

Nelson, C. R. 1988. "Spurious Trend and Cycle in the State Space Decomposition of a Time Series with a Unit Root." *Journal of Economic Dynamics and Control* 12: 475–88.

———, and Plosser, C. I. 1982. "Trends and Random Walks in Macroeconomic Time Series: Some Evidence and Implications." *Journal of Monetary Economics* 10: 139–62.

Pagan, A. 1980. "Some Identification and Estimation Results for Regression Models with Stochastically Varying Coefficients." *Journal of Econometrics* 13: 341–63.

Parkin, M. 1977. "A 'Monetarist' Analysis of the Generation and Transmission of World Inflation 1958–1971." *American Economic Review* 67 (February): 164–71.

———, and Zis, G. eds. 1976a. *Inflation in Open Economies*. Manchester: Manchester University Press.

———. 1976b. *Inflation in the World Economy*. Manchester: Manchester University Press.

Perry, G. L. 1980. "Inflation in Theory and Practice." *Brookings Papers on Economic Activity*. 1: 207–60.

Phelps, E. S., et al. 1971. *Microeconomic Foundations of Employment and Inflation Theory*. London: Macmillan and Co.

Plosser, C. I., and Schwert, W. G. 1979. "Money, Income and Sunspots: Measuring Economic Relationships and the Effects of Differencing." *Journal of Monetary Economics* 4 (November): 637–60.

Poole, W. 1988. "Monetary Policy Lessons of Recent Inflation and Disinflation." *Journal of Economic Perspectives* 2 (Summer): 73–100.

Rasche, Robert H. 1987. "M1-Velocity and Money Demand Functions: Do Stable Relationships Exist?" *Carnegie-Rochester Conference Series on Public Policy* 27 (Autumn): 9–88.

Samuelson, P. A., and Solow, R. M. 1960. "Analytical Aspects of Anti-inflation Policy." *American Economic Review* 50 (May): 177–94.

Sargent, T. J. 1987. *Dynamic Macroeconomic Theory*. Cambridge, Mass.: Harvard University Press.

——, and Wallace, N. 1975. "Rational Expectations, the Optimal Monetary Instrument, and the Optimal Money Supply Rule." *Journal of Political Economy* 83 (April): 241–54.

Shumway, R. H., and Stoffer, D. S. 1982. "An Approach to Time Series Smoothing and Forecasting Using the EM Algorithm." *Journal of Time Series Analysis* 3: 253–64.

Sims, C. A. 1980. "Comparison of Interwar and Postwar Business Cycles: Monetarism Reconsidered." *American Economic Review* 70, no. 2: 250–57.

Spinelli, F. 1976. "The Determinants of Price and Wage Inflation, the Case of Italy." In *Inflation in Open Economies*, edited by M. Parkin and G. Zis. Manchester University Press, 201–36.

Stokey, N. L., and Lucas, R. E. Jr. 1989. *Recursive Methods in Economic Dynamics*. Cambridge, Mass.: Harvard University Press.

Swamy, Peter A.V.B.; P. von zur Muehlen; and J. S. Mehta. 1989. Board of governors of the Federal Reserve System, Finance and Economics Discussion Series, no. 96, November.

Swoboda, A. K. 1977. "Monetary Approaches to Worldwide Inflation." In *Worldwide Inflation*, edited by L. B. Krause and W. S. Salant. Washington, D.C.: Brookings Institution.

Taylor, J. B. 1979. "Staggered Wage Setting in a Macro-model." *American Economic Review Papers and Proceedings* 69 (May): 108–13.

——. 1980. "Aggregate Dynamics and Staggered Contracts." *Journal of Political Economy* 88 (February): 1–23.

Trevithick, J. A., and Mulvey, C. 1975. *The Economics of Inflation*. London: Martin Robinson.

Watson, M. W., and Engle, R. F. 1983. "Alternative Algorithms for the Estimation of Dynamic Factor, Mimic and Varying Coefficient Regression Models." *Journal of Econometrics* 23: 385–400.

5

MONETARY POLICY AND REPUTATION

Keith Blackburn

INTRODUCTION

Two decades have now past since the rational expectations hypothesis
began to establish a new methodology in macroeconomics. Of all its contributions, the insight due to Lucas (1976) remains the most enduring. Put
generally, this hypothesis states that the decision rules (e.g., consumption,
money demand, and investment functions) of optimizing agents are non-
invariant with respect to changes in the decision rules of policymakers.
Equivalently, there is an interdependence between private equilibrium
behavior and centralized decision making. This interdependence invites
comparison with game situations. A game is defined as any activity with
a certain set of prescribed characteristics.[1] Game theory is the study of
games: it is a methodological branch of mathematics devoted to the analysis
of conflict and cooperation. My intention in this chapter is to provide a
broad, but selective, survey of the application of game theory to the study
of monetary policy.[2]

If there is one issue that dominates the literature, it is the role of credibility in determining equilibrium policy. Early thoughts on this issue were
expressed by Fellner (1976, 1979) who coined the term *credibility hypothesis*. This hypothesis makes two assertions: (1) policies work better when
they are more credible; and (2) policies become more credible the longer
they are adhered to. Many factors can influence credibility, but one has
received the most notice. This is the extent to which an optimal policy
does not remain optimal with the passage of time. Under such circumstances, a policymaker has an incentive to renege on announced plans.
Thus, given that the public understands this incentive, there is a threat to

credibility. In short, a policy announced ex ante may not be credible simply because it may not be optimal to implement ex post.

The distinction between ex-ante and ex-post optimality is known as the time inconsistency phenomenon (Kydland and Prescott, 1977).[3] This phenomenon arises whenever the following conditions are satisfied: first, there is some form of conflict between the policymaker and public; and second, there is an insufficient number of policy instruments to enable the first-best outcome to be achieved. Under the first condition, if no conflict existed, then the policymaker and public could effectively form a team and nothing would be gained by engineering policy surprises. A conflict may exist due to a difference in objectives or a difference in constraints. Notice, therefore, that even a benevolent policymaker may be tempted to renege because of a divergence between private and social optimality: while it is individually rational for agents to ignore the effects of their own behavior on aggregate outcomes, it is rational for a policymaker to internalize these externalities. With regard to the second condition, this can be understood as follows. If the policymaker had enough instruments to reach the first-best outcome, then nothing could be gained by unexpectedly resetting these instruments. If not, then policy surprises offer a means of approaching this outcome by acting as additional policy instruments.

The conditions noted above are extremely weak, so that time inconsistency is likely to be the rule rather than the exception. But whether there is a problem of credibility depends on whether policymaking is conducted under commitment or discretion. If policymakers could precommit themselves to announced plans, then no problem would arise. Typically, however, policymakers enjoy the freedom to reoptimize. Now, equilibrium policies must be both optimal and credible. The requirement of credibility imposes a binding incentive compatibility constraint that rules out surprises in equilibrium. In the case of precommitment, this constraint is automatically satisfied. In the case of discretion, it represents an additional restriction. Intuitively, therefore, we would expect outcomes under commitment to be generally superior to outcomes under discretion.

Monetary policy games can be usefully classified under three broad headings: games involving a single policymaker and private sector; games involving multiple policymakers holding office at the same time; and games involving multiple policymakers holding office at different times. The first of these has occupied the discussion so far. The second can be categorized further into games played at the domestic level and games played at the international level. The domestic level refers to interdependent decision making on the part of independent fiscal and monetary authorities. The international level gives notice to interdependent behavior between policymakers of different countries. Together, these make up the research on domestic and international policy coordination. The third class of games concerns politico-economic models of monetary policy. In these models, policymaking is conducted by political agents alternating in office. This is the area of research on politics and credibility.

The methodological approach of the literature is to treat the policymaker like any other economic agent—namely, as facing a particular set of objectives and a particular set of constraints and solving a well-defined optimization problem. This approach may be considered in two ways: first, as a positive theory of policymaking under alternative institutional arrangements; and, second, as a normative theory of institutional reforms designed to improve policy outcomes. The literature is striking for the questions it asks and the standards it sets for answering these questions. Not only has it dealt with many important issues, but also it has done so with a remarkable degree of precision and completeness. By confronting what micro-foundations are less ambiguous to interpret and offer more meaningful welfare comparisons. On the other hand, they are less easy to manipulate, especially when the game scenarios are more complicated.

Dynamic Optimal Taxation

In this example, drawn from Calvo (1978), the policymaker has an incentive to create surprise inflation. By doing so, he or she imposes a lump-sum tax on previously accumulated money balances and reduces the need for distortionary taxation. This is a generic example of time inconsistency in optimal taxation which arises when the elasticities of tax bases change over time.[4]

Consider a two-period economy populated by many identical agents and a benevolent government. Each agent derives utility from consumption of a single commodity (c), leisure (l), and real money balances ($m = M/P$, where M denotes nominal balances and P the price level). Leisure is consumed only in the second period. Intertemporal utility is given by $U = U(c_1,c_2,l_2,m_2)$, where $t = 1,2$ is the time index and

(1) $U(c_1,c_2,l_2,m_2) = u(c_1) + c_2 + v(l_2) + w(m_2).$

The functions $u(\bullet)$, $v(\bullet)$ and $w(\bullet)$ are assumed to be strictly increasing and concave.[5] In the first period, each agent receives an exogenous endowment (e) that is allocated between consumption and saving. The only form of saving is money. In the second period, each agent has access to the linear production technology $y_2 = \alpha n_2$, where y denotes output and n labor effort. Labor is taxed at the rate τ and satisfies the time constraint $1 = l_2 + n_2$, where total time has been normalized to unity. The real value of money holdings accumulated in the first period is M_1/P_2. Hence, the budget constraints facing an agent are

(2) $c_1 + m_1 = e,$

(3) $c_2 + m_2 = (1 - \pi)m_1 + (1 - \tau)\alpha n_2,$

where $\pi = 1 - P_1/P_2$ is a measure of the rate of inflation. It is clear from equation (3) how inflation acts like a tax on previously accumulated money.

Maximizing the expected value of (1) subject to (2), (3), $1 = l_2 + n_2$ and $m_1 \geq 0$ defines the individual's optimization problem. The first-order conditions are

(4) $u_c(c_1) \geq 1 - E\pi$

(5) $Ev_l(1 - n_2) = (1 - E\tau)\alpha,$

(6) $Ew_m(m_2) = 1,$

where E denotes the expectations operator. The inequality in equation (4) reflects the nonnegativity constraint on m_1. Strict inequality is associated with $m_1 = 0$. Otherwise, both (4) and (5) show the usual effects of distortionary taxes as driving a wedge between marginal rates of substitution and marginal rates of transformation.[6] The condition in (6) states that real balances are constant in the second period. These first-order conditions and (2) imply the following decision rules for consumption, saving, and planned labor supply:

(7) $c_1 = c(E\pi),$

(8) $m_1 = m(E\pi),$

(9) $En_2 = n(E\tau),$

where $c_\pi(\bullet) > 0$, $m_\pi(\bullet) < 0$ and $n_\tau(\bullet) < 0$.[7]

The government in this economy behaves as follows. Goods purchased in the first period are stored for the second period at a zero rate of interest.[8] This storage (s), the proceeds from taxes ($\tau\alpha n_2$), and the issue of new currency (m_2) are used to meet private sector claims and exogenous expenditures (g). The government's budget constraints read

(10) $s_1 = m_1,$

(11) $g_2 + (1 - \pi)m_1 = m_2 + \tau\alpha n_2 + s_1.$

It is assumed that $(g_2 - m_2)/m_1 > 1$, in which case an equilibrium will always involve taxes on labor. The problem for the government is to choose taxes so as to maximize the welfare of the representative agent subject to the private sector first-order conditions, the private sector budget constraints, the government's own budget constraints, and the technology for making commitments. Equivalently, the problem is to choose π and τ so as to maximize (1) subject to (3), (6)–(11) and the "rules of the game."[9]

Consider, first, the case of precommitment. The government precommits itself to announcements about taxes, π^A and τ^A say, made prior to any private decisions being made. Hence, $\pi = \pi^A = E\pi$ and $\tau = \tau^A = E\tau$. Appropriate substitution in (1), using (3) and (7)–(9), gives the indirect utility function

(12) $V(\pi,\tau) = u(c(\pi)) + (1 - \pi)m(\pi) + (1 - \tau)\alpha n(\tau) - m_2 +$
$v(1 - n(\tau)) + w(m_2).$

Consolidating (10) and (11) delivers

(13) $g_2 = m_2 + \tau\alpha n(\tau) + \pi m(\pi).$

The optimization problem has been transformed into one of maximizing (12) subject to (13). The first-order conditions can be reduced to

(14) $\dfrac{(1 - \tau)/\tau}{(1 - \pi)/\pi} = \dfrac{\xi^n}{\xi^m},$

where $\xi^n = -v_l(\bullet)/n_2 v_{ll}(\bullet)$ and $\xi^m = -u_c(\bullet)/m_1 u_{cc}(\bullet)$ are the elasticities of labor supply and money demand, respectively.[10] The expression in (14) is an example of the well-known Ramsey (1927) rule for optimal taxation. This states that an optimal tax rule is one that equates the marginal distortion of the last unit of tax revenue across different tax bases. It implies the taxation of relatively inelastic tax bases at relatively high rates to minimize distortions. Let us denote by $\bar{\pi}$ and $\bar{\tau}$ *the equilibrium tax rates implied by (14).*[11] Then $\bar{c}_1 = c(\bar{\pi})$, $\bar{m}_1 = m(\bar{\pi})$, $\bar{n}_2 = n(\bar{\tau})$ and $\bar{c}_2 = (1 - \bar{\pi})m_1 + (1 - \bar{\tau})\bar{n}_2 - m_2$. Equilibrium welfare follows as $\bar{U} = u(\bar{c}_1) + \bar{c}_2 + v(1 - \bar{n}_2) + w(m_2) = V(\bar{\pi},\bar{\tau})$. This equilibrium is formally identical to the game-theoretic notion of open-loop Stackelberg equilibrium.[12] It is a second-best equilibrium owing to the presence of distortionary taxes.

Now let us turn to the case of discretion. Here, the government has the freedom to re-optimize at the beginning of the second period. This makes the tax rule (14) non-credible: $\bar{\pi}$ and $\bar{\tau}$, while optimal ex ante, are not optimal ex post. The tax rule is time inconsistent. To see this, observe the following. *Ex ante*—in the first period—the demand for money is elastic $(0 < \xi^m < \infty)$; but *ex post*—in the second period—it is perfectly inelastic $(\xi^m = 0)$. Since nominal balances are given in this period, it is optimal to tax them to the largest possible extent $(\pi = 1)$. A discretionary equilibrium is constructed on the principle that agents understand the incentive to renege. According to game theory, the equilibrium to look for is a sequentially rational Nash equilibrium (sometimes referred to as a closed-loop Nash equilibrium).[13] Anticipating the full expropriation of money balances, agents set $E\pi = 1$. From (4), this implies $m_1 = 0$. Hence, the government is forced to rely exclusively on the labor tax, defined implicitly by $g_2 = m_2 + \hat{\tau}\alpha n(\hat{\tau})$. *It follows that equilibrium consumption and labor supply are* $\hat{c}_1 = e$, $\hat{n}_2 = n(\hat{\tau})$ and $\hat{c}_2 = (1 - \hat{\tau})\alpha\hat{n}_2 - m_2$, implying a level of welfare $\hat{U} = u(\hat{c}_1) + \hat{c}_2 + v(1 - \hat{n}_2) + w(m_2) = V(\hat{\pi},\hat{\tau})$. This equilibrium involves an overtaxation of labor and zero saving. It is clearly inferior to the equilibrium under commitment.

Optimal Demand Management

This second example has been popularized by Barro and Gordon (1983a). As above, the policymaker has an incentive to create surprise inflation. In this case, however, the intention is to stimulate the economy by moving it along the Phillips curve.

The policymaker is concerned about two outcomes: inflation (π) and output (y). His preferences are summarized by the quadratic objective function $u_t = u(\pi_t, y_t)$, where

(15) $u(\pi_t, y_t) = -(\Lambda_1/2)(\pi_t - \Lambda_\pi)^2 - (\Lambda_2/2)(y_t - \Lambda_y)^2.$

According to this expression, deviations of inflation and output from target values (Λ_π and Λ_y) yield convex costs.[14] The quantities Λ_1 and Λ_2 represent weights assigned to the two objectives. The ratio of these, Λ_2/Λ_1, may be interpreted as the relative weight given to economic stimulation versus inflation prevention. The most important assumption of the model is that the policymaker is dissatisfied with the natural rate of output (y_n). This may be justified by appealing to the existence of various labor market distortions (e.g., income taxation and unemployment insurance) which bias the natural rate downward. Formally, the assumption is that $\Lambda_y = \kappa y_n$, where $\kappa > 1$. Output and inflation are related through the Phillips curve

(16) $y_t = y_n + \beta(\pi_t - E\pi_t),$

where $E\pi_t$ is the private sector's expected rate of inflation.[15]

Substituting $\Lambda_y = \kappa y_n$ and (16) into (15) gives

(17) $v(\pi_t, E\pi_t) = -(\Lambda_1/2)(\pi_t - \Lambda_\pi)^2 - (\Lambda_2/2)(\beta(\pi_t - E\pi_t) - \Lambda_y')^2,$

where $\Lambda_y' = (\kappa - 1)\Lambda_y$. The policymaker's optimizing criterion is the intertemporal objective function $U = E\Sigma_{t=0}^{T}\lambda^t u(\pi_t, y_t) = E\Sigma_{t=0}^{T}\lambda^t v(\pi_t, E\pi_t)$, where $0 < \lambda < 1$ is a discount factor. His or her problem is to maximize this subject to the "rules of the game." As it stands, the model contains no intertemporal linkages so that the problem reduces to period-by-period maximization of (17). For the moment, and as before, the policymaker's choice variable is taken to be inflation.

In the case of precommitment, the policymaker announces and precommits him or herself to an inflation rate π_t^A ($= \pi_t = E\pi_t$). The optimal inflation rate is $\bar{\pi} = \Lambda_\pi$, implying an equilibrium payoff $\bar{u} = v(\bar{\pi}, \bar{\pi}) = -\Lambda_2\Lambda_y'^2/2$. *Hence, equilibrium inflation is target inflation, and equilibrium output is the natural rate.*

In the case of discretion, $\bar{\pi}$ is not credible because it is not optimal ex post. Rather, given that $E\pi_t = \bar{\pi}$, it is optimal to set $\tilde{\pi} = \Lambda_\pi + \beta\Lambda_2\Lambda_y'/(\Lambda_1 + \beta^2\Lambda_2)$. This creates a surprise inflation and increases output above its natural rate. The payoff for this is $\tilde{u} = v(\tilde{\pi}, \bar{\pi}) = -\Lambda_1\Lambda_2\Lambda_y'^2/2(\Lambda_1 + \beta^2\Lambda_2) > \bar{u}$. Imposing the credibility constraint leads to a Nash equilibrium where the incentive to create surprises vanishes. This equilibrium is constructed as follows. From equation (17), the optimal rate of inflation for any given expected inflation is

$$(18) \qquad \pi_t = \frac{\beta^2\Lambda_2 E\pi_t + \Lambda_1\Lambda_\pi + \beta\Lambda_2\Lambda_y'}{\Lambda_1 + \beta^2\Lambda_2}.$$

Agents understand this relationship and use it to form expectations. Hence, $E\pi_t = \Lambda_\pi + \beta\Lambda_2 \Lambda_y'/\Lambda_1$. This is, indeed, a rational expectation since substituting it back into (18) reveals equilibrium actual inflation to be $\hat{\pi} = \Lambda_\pi + \beta\Lambda_2\Lambda_y'/\Lambda_1$ also. The payoff to the policymaker follows as $\hat{u} = v(\hat{\pi}, \hat{\pi}) = -(\Lambda_1 + \beta^2\Lambda_2)\Lambda_2\Lambda_y'^2/2\Lambda_1$ which is inferior to the payoff under commitment. The discretionary equilibrium is characterized by an inflationary bias with no gain in output: inflation is high but not surprisingly high.

The lesson to be learned from this section can be stated as follows: in the absence of a commitment technology, a policymaker's incentive to reach the first-best equilibrium drives the economy away from the second-best equilibrium and into a third-best equilibrium. The pervasiveness of this problem makes it both profound and disturbing. Indeed, its very obviousness and incontrovertibility are the aspects that have excited such widespread attention.

RESTRICTIONS, REPETITION, AND INSTITUTIONAL REFORMS

In this section we examine ways of either resolving or alleviating credibility problems. Two broad approaches may be identified in the literature. The first involves changing the constraints in policymakers' optimization problems, and the second involves changing the very objectives of policymakers. An alternative distinction is between formal restrictions and informal incentive schemes. The formal draw attention to the possible restructuring of social institutions, while the informal give notice to ideas from repeated game theory.

Partial Commitment

Suppose that a policymaker is able to make at least some commitments: this policymaker is *partially* committed. Then, the constraints imposed by these commitments may be such as to enforce other policies as if these were commitments as well. To be sure about this, consider the following.

A government trades debt with the private sector. This debt is a linkage between periods (a state variable) which the government can exploit to influence its future optimization problem. In particular, by manipulating debt, the government is able to manipulate its future constraints. In this way, it may be able to reduce the difference between ex-ante and ex-post optimality. This is the idea of strategic debt management. The crucial assumption is that the government fully honors its outstanding debt obligations. It is in this sense that the government is partially committed.

Manipulating debt means manipulating the composition of debt. Two cases have been studied in the literature. The first involves the distinction between real (indexed) and nominal (nonindexed) debt (Persson, Persson, and Svensson 1987). The second is concerned with debt of different maturities (Lucas and Stokey, 1983; Persson and Svensson, 1984). To illustrate the first case, go back to the model of optimal taxation and modify it in the following way. Let b and B denote the real value of indexed and nonindexed debt, respectively. Let r and R denote the real and nominal rates of interest, respectively. Finally, abstract from storage and let government expenditure take place in the first period. The government's budget constraints (10) and (11) become[16]

$$(19) \quad g_1 = b_1 + B_1 + m_1$$

$$(20) \quad rb_1 + R(1 - \pi)B_1 + (1 - \pi)m_1 = m_2 + \tau\alpha n_2.$$

Surprise inflation now erodes the real value of both money and nonindexed debt. But suppose that this debt represents claims by the government on the private sector. Suppose also that the value of these claims in the second period is equal to the value of the private sector's claims on the government in this period (i.e., assume $-R(1 - \pi) B_1 = (1 - \pi)m_1$ or $-RB_1 = m_1$). Then the government enters this period with a net nominal liability position of zero towards agents. This eliminates the incentive to create surprise inflation because no revenue is gained from it. In a similar way, a government may be able to move the third-best equilibrium closer to the second-best equilibrium by suitably choosing the maturity structure of its debt. Aside from qualifying credibility problems, these results are suggestive of how policymaking might be influenced by political considerations. We return to this subject later.

Perhaps the most obvious example of partial commitment is that of a fixed exchange-rate regime. There is a strong presumption that such a regime imposes a discipline on monetary policy which limits the scope for discretionary opportunism. This is because of the drain on foreign exchange reserves resulting from excessive monetary growth. If monetary growth was to remain unchecked, then reserves would be exhausted and the fixed exchange rate would collapse.[17] An interesting dimension of this matter concerns the prospect of speculative currency attacks or balance-of-payments crises (Blackburn, 1988; Flood and Garber, 1984; Obstfeld, 1986a, b). These situations occur when speculators, anticipating a collapse, suddenly take part in a run on the unsafe currency. Now, these crises in confidence may be purely self-fulfilling. If so, then the survival of a fixed exchange-rate regime would appear to be rather tenuous. Indeed, a regime may collapse because of the very problem that it was supposed to resolve in the first place—namely, the lack of credibility of noninflationary monetary policy.

The foregoing discussion leaves an important question unanswered: why might it be the case that some commitments are easier to make than others? At the present level of abstraction, there is nothing significantly different between a commitment to monetary policy, a commitment to honoring debt obligations, and a commitment to a fixed exchange-rate regime. In practice, however, there does seem to be a difference. Monetary policy can be changed at relatively short notice, and inflationary surprises are not always obvious. By contrast, the taxation of debt and currency realignments may well require constitutional decisions in the glare of publicity. An interesting challenge for future research would be to model these differences explicitly.

Conservatism

The difference between ex-ante and ex-post optimality will depend on a policymaker's objectives. Therefore, this difference could be reduced by changing these objectives. This is the idea of appointing a conservative policymaker—a policymaker for whom the incentive to create surprises is relatively weak. The initial insight is attributable to Rogoff (1985a). The idea may be illustrated for both the optimal tax problem and the optimal demand management problem. Each is considered in turn.

Suppose that the two-period economy is populated by two groups of agents—capitalists and workers.[18] The capitalists allocate their first-period endowment between consumption and saving; they consume all their saving in the second period. The workers receive income from working in both periods, where income is taxed only in the second period; they consume all their income within each period. A capitalist's decision problem is to maximize (the expected value of)

(21) $U(c_1^k, c_2^k, m_2) = u(c_1^k) + c_2^k + w(m_2)$,

subject to

(22) $c_1^k + m_1 = e$

(23) $c_2^k + m_2 = (1 - \pi)m_1$,

while a worker's decision problem is to maximize (the expected value of)

(24) $V(c_1^w, c_2^w, l_1, l_2) = c_1^w + v(l_1) + c_2^w + v(l_2)$,

subject to

(25) $c_1^w = \alpha n_1$,

(26) $c_2^w = (1 - \tau)\alpha n_2$,

and $1 = l_t + n_t$ $(t = 1,2)$. The first-order conditions yield the decision rules (7)–(9), where c_t is replaced by c_t^k, together with the properties that both m_2 and n_1 are constant. The policymaker still faces the budget constraints (10) and (11). But although he or she is still benevolent, his or her optimizing criterion is no longer the utility function of the representative agent since agents are now heterogeneous. Rather, it is the Pigovian welfare function

(27) $W = \Lambda U(c_1^k, c_2^k, m_2) + (1 - \Lambda)V(c_1^w, c_2^w, l_1, l_2)$,

where $\Lambda/(1 - \Lambda)$ is the relative weight assigned to capitalists $(0 < \Lambda < 1)$. This weight is taken to reflect society's true preference for trading off the capitalist's welfare for the worker's welfare.

The optimal tax rule ex ante is

(28) $\left(\dfrac{\Lambda}{1 - \Lambda}\right)\left[1 - \left(\dfrac{\tau}{1 - \tau}\right)\xi^n\right] = \left[1 - \left(\dfrac{\pi}{1 - \pi}\right)\xi^m\right]$,

which is a modified version of (14). The optimal tax rule ex post is

(29) $\left(\dfrac{\Lambda}{1 - \Lambda}\right)\left[1 - \left(\dfrac{\tau}{1 - \tau}\right)\xi^n\right] = 1$,

which is obtained from (28) with $\xi^m = 0$. The question is how, if at all, can (28) be made credible under discretion? The answer is simple: society should appoint a policymaker who assigns a relative weight to capitalists' welfare equal to $(\Lambda/(1 - \Lambda))' = (\Lambda/(1 - \Lambda))/[1 - (\pi/(1 - \pi))\xi_m]$. This ensures coincidence of (28) and (29). Notice that $(\Lambda/(1 - \Lambda))' > \Lambda/(1 - \Lambda)$: the appointed policymaker should value capitalists' welfare more than society itself does. In other words, delegating policy to an authority with "distorted" preferences may be welfare improving.[19]

Obtaining a similar result in the second of our examples is relatively more straightforward. Recall that the discretionary equilibrium is characterized by the rate of inflation $\hat{\pi} = \Lambda_\pi + \beta\Lambda_2\Lambda_y'/\Lambda_1$ and the payoff to the policymaker $\hat{u} = -(\Lambda_1 + \beta^2\Lambda_2)\Lambda_2\Lambda_y' /2\Lambda_1$. Evidently, increasing Λ_1 reduces both the inflationary bias and the policymaker's loss. Hence, the discretionary equilibrium moves closer to the commitment equilibrium the more weight is given to inflation prevention relative to economic stimulation.

The idea of conservatism is deceptively simple. By focusing on the objectives of policymakers, it raises the question of how these objectives are chosen. This leads naturally to a discussion of policymaking within a broader context of political economy. This discussion is presented later in this chapter, as is the discussion of how the results obtained above may be qualified in a stochastic environment.

Repeated Policy Games

Agents are unlikely to forget how a policymaker has behaved in the past. On the contrary, they are liable to use this information as a guide to what may happen in the future. In turn, the policymaker must respect this when making his or her decisions in the first place. To this point, we have ignored such considerations by focusing on one-shot games. But interactions between a policymaker and public occur repeatedly over time. This is to say that monetary policy is more appropriately viewed as a *repeated game* or *supergame*. Such games can blur the distinction between commitment and discretion because the equilibrium under commitment in a one-shot game can almost always be sustained as a discretionary equilibrium in a repeated game. This works through a system of rewards and penalties in the form of trigger mechanisms that threaten any disobedient behavior with retaliatory action. Barro and Gordon (1983b) were the first to apply this idea to monetary policy in the context of the Phillips curve example.

Consider the case in which agents revise their expectations according to the following rule:

(30) $$E\pi_t = \begin{cases} \bar{\pi} & \text{if } \pi_{t-s} = \bar{\pi} \text{ for all } s \geq 1 \\ \hat{\pi} & \text{otherwise.} \end{cases}$$

Inflationary expectations are held down provided that actual inflation has been held down in the past, and inflationary expectations are raised if actual inflation has ever been raised. This is an example of an expectations trigger mechanism. Sequential rationality implies that, given this mechanism, the policymaker finds it optimal to confirm expectations. Let us suppose that the game is repeated an infinite number times.[20] Let us further suppose that the game is currently located at the outcome $\pi_t = E\pi_t = \bar{\pi}$. Policymakers are faced with two choices. On the one hand, they can continue to play low inflation. By virtue of (30), this means that agents continue to expect low inflation. This yields the discounted payoff $\bar{U} = \sum_{t=0}^{\infty} \lambda^t \bar{u}$, where $\bar{u} = v(\bar{\pi},\bar{\pi})$ was defined previously as the payoff in the second-best equilibrium. On the other hand, policymakers can raise inflation to $\hat{\pi}$, which was also defined previously. Doing so yields the contemporaneous payoff $\tilde{u} = v(\hat{\pi},\bar{\pi})$. But then, according to (30), inflationary expectations are raised for all subsequent periods. Given that $E\pi_t = \hat{\pi}$, it is optimal for policymakers to set $\pi_t = \hat{\pi}$ as well. In this case, therefore, the discounted payoff is $\tilde{U} = \tilde{u} + \sum_{t=1}^{\infty} \lambda^t \hat{u}$, where $\hat{u} = v(\hat{\pi},\hat{\pi})$ is the payoff in the one-shot Nash equilibrium. Thus, the punishment for cheating in any period is reversion to the third-best equilibrium for the rest of game. Is this punishment severe enough to sustain the second-best equilibrium? The answer is yes if $\bar{U} \geq \hat{U}$, a condition that may be expressed as

$$(31) \quad \frac{\lambda}{1 - \lambda} \geq \frac{\tilde{u} - \bar{u}}{\bar{u} - \hat{u}}.$$

This has a very strong intuition. We may interpret the numerator and denominator on the right-hand-side as, respectively, the temptation to cheat and the cost of cheating. Thus, the greater the temptation, the smaller the cost, and the higher the discount rate, the less likely it is that equation (31) will be satisfied. The influence of the discount rate is explained by the fact that the cost of cheating is incurred in the future. Provided that (31) is satisfied, then the second-best equilibrium is an equilibrium of the repeated game.

What we have just shown is an example of the folk theorem of repeated game theory. The implication is that informal incentive schemes can substitute for formal commitments in enforcing the second-best equilibrium. Appealing though this may appear, it is as well to look a gift-horse in the mouth. The fact of the matter is that (30) is not the only scheme imaginable. It is possible to conjure up a multiplicity of others and to sustain any equilibrium between the second- and third-best. Without any systematic criterion for discriminating between these schemes, the theory is devoid of any predictive value.[21] This problem of multiple equilibria is common in game theory. One response to it has been to look for equilibrium refinements—stronger concepts of equilibrium that limit the number of possibilities. The notion of sequential rationality is a prime example, as is the related concept of subgame perfection. But the problem still remains of how a decentralized economy is supposed to coordinate upon one particular outcome. Studying this problem is another potentially rewarding avenue for future research.

INFORMATION AND REPUTATION

To this point, we have assumed that the policymaker and public share the same information. In many ways, this makes the game trivial by ruling out any scope for the policymaker to influence the public's beliefs. In turn, this tends to contradict what we usually have in mind when we think about credibility. The discussion that follows is concerned with the idea that a policymaker with private information may be able to use this information strategically. That is, he or she may be able to manipulate beliefs by revealing, concealing, or misrepresenting what he or she knows. It is here that we appeal to the concept of reputation. From a policymaker's point of view, reputation is like an asset that can be built up, maintained, or run down depending on what policies are chosen. Formally, it is a probabilistic state variable measuring the public's perception about a particular characteristic (e.g., the preferences or commitment technology) of the policymaker. The relevant equilibrium concept is a reputational equilibrium, the computation of which involves a complicated chain of reasoning. To begin with, agents will not be ignorant about everything. They will understand at least the policymaker's incentives relating to information disclosure. As such, they will interpret his or her actions with care when forming their beliefs. In turn, the policymaker will have to respect this when choosing his or her actions in the first place. And the whole process is dynamic, with agents updating their beliefs on the basis of new information and the policymaker having to optimize a complex intertemporal tradeoff. Backus and Driffill (1985a, b), Barro (1986), and Vickers (1986) have made the seminal contributions in this area. These contributions are based on the Phillips curve example and may be outlined as follows.

Mimicking and Signaling

In general, a reputational equilibrium may be either a separating equilibrium or a pooling equilibrium. In the first, the actions of a policymaker are sufficient to reveal his or her private information. In the second, the converse is true. To study these, let us simplify matters by rewriting (15) as

(32) $u_i(\pi_t, y_t) = - (\Lambda_1/2)\pi_t^2 + \Lambda_{2i}(y_t - y_n).$

The policymaker has a zero target rate of inflation and prefers any level of output greater than the natural rate. The index $i = 1,2$ will be commented on shortly. Combining (32) with (16) gives the analogue to (17) as

$$(33) \quad v_i(\pi_t, E\pi_t) = -(\Lambda_1/2)\pi_t^2 + \Lambda_{2i}\beta(\pi_t - E\pi_t).$$

The reader may verify that $\bar{\pi}_i = 0$ and $\bar{u}_i = (\bar{\pi}, \bar{\pi}) = 0$ characterize the equilibrium under commitment and that $\hat{\pi}_i = \Lambda_{2i}/\Lambda_1$ and $\hat{u}_i = v(\hat{\pi},\hat{\pi}) = -\Lambda_{2i}^2/2\Lambda_1$ characterize the equilibrium under discretion. Notice that $\hat{\pi}_i$ is the dominant strategy of the policymaker: it is the strategy that is optimal against any given expected inflation.[22]

There are two types of policymaker in this model: a low-inflation type (type 1) and a high-inflation type (type 2). The index $i = 1,2$ is used to distinguish between them. Hence, $\Lambda_{21} < \Lambda_{22}$, implying $\hat{\pi}_1 < \hat{\pi}_2$. Agents know about these types but are unsure of which type they are actually facing. They assign a probability, $0 < \vartheta < 1$, that the policymaker is of type 1. This is the reputation of the policymaker. Now, both types have an incentive to invest in a reputation: by doing so, inflationary expectations are reduced. In the case of a type 1, this implies a less severe recession and the prospect of a low-inflation equilibrium. In the case of a type 2, it means greater potential gains from inflationary surprises and avoidance of a high-inflation equilibrium. The corollary of this is the following: while a low-inflation type wants its identity to be known, a high-inflation type wants to conceal its identity. Hence, each type is motivated to act very differently. *Signaling* behavior is a means for the type 1 to try to distinguish itself from the type 2. *Mimicking*, on the other hand, is the way that the type 2 can try to make itself look like the type 1. For signaling to be successful, the type 1 must be able to set a rate of inflation which the type 2 has no incentive to copy. Under such circumstances, we end up in a separating equilibrium. Otherwise, pooling is obtained, and agents must figure out whether the low inflation they observe is nothing more than the dissembling actions of an imposter.

To make matters more precise, we may proceed as follows. Let us simplify the problem further by pretending that the game lasts for only two periods ($T = 2$). In the first period, inflationary expectations are given by the probability weighted average

$$(34) \quad E\pi_t = \vartheta_t\pi_{1t} + (1 - \vartheta_t)\pi_{2t},$$

where π_{it} is the inflationary strategy chosen by the policymaker of type i ($i = 1,2$). The actual inflation observed in this period determines the outcome in the next period. Since the game ends at this point, each type of policymaker is sure to set second-period inflation equal to his or her dominant strategy, $\pi_{it+1} = \hat{\pi}_i$ $(i = 1,2)$.

A separating equilibrium is based in the following expectations rule:

$$(35) \qquad E\pi_{t+1} = \begin{cases} \hat{\pi}_1 & \text{if } \pi_t \le \pi^s \\ \\ \hat{\pi}_2 & \text{otherwise,} \end{cases}$$

where π^s is some rate of inflation determined below. Thus, by playing this inflation, it may be possible for type 1 policymakers to signal their identities. Define $v_i(\pi^s, E\pi_t)$ as the first period payoff to a type i policymaker when this policymaker sets $\pi_{it} = \pi^s$. Similarly, define $v_i(\hat{\pi}_i, \hat{\pi}_1)$ as the policymaker's second-period payoff associated with playing his or her dominant strategy, having previously played $\pi_{it} = \pi^s$. Finally, let $v_i(\hat{\pi}_i, E\pi_t)$ and $v_i(\hat{\pi}_i, \hat{\pi}_2)$ be the first- and second-period payoffs when the policymaker chooses his or her dominant strategy in the first period. The (two-period) discounted loss associated with each of these cases is

$$(36) \quad U_i^s = v_i(\pi^s, E\pi_t) + \lambda v_i(\hat{\pi}_i, \hat{\pi}_1)$$

$$(37) \quad \hat{U}_i = v_i(\hat{\pi}_i, E\pi_t) + \lambda v_i(\hat{\pi}_i, \hat{\pi}_2)$$

which the reader may wish to compute using (33) and the expressions for $\hat{\pi}_i$ given earlier. A type 1 policymaker will choose $\pi_{1t} = \pi^s$ in preference to his or her dominant strategy, $\pi_{1t} = \hat{\pi}_1$, if $U_1^s \ge \hat{U}_1$. Separation will then occur provided that the type 2 does not find it profitable to play $\pi_{2t} = \pi^s$ also: the condition for this is $U_2^s \ge \hat{U}_2$. Given that both conditions are satisfied, the separating equilibrium is characterized by the following: $\pi_{1t} = \pi^s$, $\pi_{2t} = \hat{\pi}_2$ and $E\pi_t = \vartheta_t \pi^s + (1 - \vartheta_t)\hat{\pi}_2$; $\pi_{it+1} = \hat{\pi}_i$ and $E\pi_{t+1}$ from (35).[23] Hence, there is a first-period recession if the policymaker is a type 1 and a first-period boom if the policymaker is a type 2.

For a pooling equilibrium, inflationary expectations are assumed to satisfy

$$(38) \qquad E\pi_{t+1} = \begin{cases} \vartheta_t \hat{\pi}_1 + (1 - \vartheta_t)\hat{\pi}_2 & \text{if } \pi_t \le \pi^P \\ \\ \hat{\pi}_2 & \text{otherwise,} \end{cases}$$

for some inflation rate π^P.[24] As before, we may define $v_i(\pi^P, E\pi_t)$ and $v_i(\hat{\pi}_i, \vartheta_t \hat{\pi}_1 + (1 - \vartheta_t)\hat{\pi}_2)$ as the first- and second-period payoffs to each policymaker associated with playing $\pi_{it} = \pi^P$. The discounted payoff is

$$(39) \quad U_i^p = v_i(\pi^P, E\pi_t) + \lambda v_i(\hat{\pi}_i, \vartheta_t \hat{\pi}_1 + (1 - \vartheta_t)\hat{\pi}_2).$$

Pooling occurs if both types of policymaker find it optimal to play $\pi_{it} = \pi^P$ (i.e., if $U_i^p \geq \hat{U}_i$). The pooling equilibrium is then characterized as follows: $\pi_{it} = \pi^P$ and $E\pi_t = \pi^P$; $\pi_{it+1} = \hat{\pi}_i$ and $E\pi_{t+1} = \vartheta_t\hat{\pi}_1 + (1 - \vartheta_t)\hat{\pi}_2$. In this case, therefore, there is a second-period recession (boom) if the policymaker is of type 1 (type 2).

As the reader may verify, whichever type of equilibrium is obtained depends on the extent to which the preferences of different policymaker types diverge. In particular, pooling is more likely for relatively dissimilar types. The reason for this is that a greater divergence between preferences implies greater potential gains for a high-inflation type if this type can successfully masquerade as a low-inflation type. Consequently, it is more difficult for the low-inflation type to set a rate of inflation that would not be copied. Pooling is also more likely the higher is the initial reputation of the policymaker: from the perspective of a type 2, there is a greater incentive to mimic because the cost of losing a high reputation is large; from the perspective of a type 1, there is less incentive to signal because the benefits of increasing reputation further are small.

Randomization

In the above equilibria, each policymaker chooses a particular rate of inflation with certainty. Equilibria of this sort are referred to as equilibria in pure strategies. By extending the analysis, it is possible to construct an equilibrium in randomizing or mixed strategies. A randomizing strategy is a probability mixture of pure strategies. If policymakers randomize, they leave it to chance whether inflation will be high or low.[25] Clearly, only a type 2 would want to do this since only he or she wants to disguise his or her intentions. Extending the game in this way adds a further dimension as well. This is the public's updating of the probability ϑ_t according to an optimal learning rule. The precise form of this rule is given below.

Consider the case in which $\pi^s < 0$: to successfully identify themselves, type 1 policymakers have to set a negative rate of inflation.[26] It is straightforward to verify that, under such circumstances, such policymakers will always choose $\pi_{1t} = \pi^P = 0$. The choice for the type 2 is whether to play $\pi_{2t} = 0$ as well or $\pi_{2t} = \hat{\pi}_2$. Let ϕ_t be the probability of choosing $\pi_{2t} = 0$ (so that $1 - \phi_t$ is the probability of choosing $\pi_{2t} = \hat{\pi}_2$) and define ϕ_t' as the public's perception of ϕ_t. Inflationary expectations in the first period are given by

$$(40) \quad E\pi_t = (1 - \vartheta_t)(1 - \phi_t')\hat{\pi}_2,$$

and in the second period by

(41) $E\pi_{t+1} = \begin{cases} \vartheta_{t+1}\hat{\pi}_1 + (1 - \vartheta_{t+1})\hat{\pi}_2 & \text{if } \pi_t = 0 \\ \hat{\pi}_2 & \text{otherwise.} \end{cases}$

Observe that $\phi'_{t+1} = 0$: in the second period, the type 2 policymaker is known to play his or her dominant strategy, $\pi_{2t+1} = \hat{\pi}_2$. The process for updating reputation is given by Bayes' rule:

(42) $\vartheta_{t+1} = \dfrac{\vartheta_t}{\vartheta_t + (1 - \vartheta_t)\phi'_t}.$

Now, with probability ϕ_t, the type 2 chooses $\pi_{2t} = 0$, enhances his or her reputation, and receives the discounted payoff $v_2(0, E\pi_t) + \lambda v_2(\hat{\pi}_2, \vartheta_{t+1}$ $\hat{\pi}_1 + (1 - \vartheta_{t+1})\ \hat{\pi}_2)$, where ϑ_{t+1} follows from (42). Conversely, with probability $(1 - \phi_t)$, he or she chooses $\pi_{2t} = \hat{\pi}_2$, blows his or her reputation, +and receives $v_2(\hat{\pi}_2, E\pi_t) + \lambda v_2(\hat{\pi}_2, \hat{\pi}_2)$. A comparison between these payoffs will determine which choice is made. If the payoffs are identical, then the type 2 is indifferent between masquerading as a type 1 and blowing his or her disguise. It is in this case that the policymaker randomizes, setting $0 < \phi_t < 1$.

In the seminal contributions by Backus and Driffill (1985a,b) and Barro (1986), a $T > 2$ period version of this game was considered for the case in which $\Lambda_{2t} = 0$ (so that the type 1 policymaker always plays zero inflation). The equilibrium properties of such a game look something like the following. For some period at the start, the type 2 plays zero inflation with certainty. This establishes an outcome identical to the second-best equilibrium. This period lasts until the type 2 becomes indifferent between continuing to invest in a reputation and raising inflation. This is the start of randomization where inflationary expectations are raised and a recession emerges if actual inflation continues to turn out zero. Sooner or later, the type 2 inflates with certainty as the net benefits from doing so outweigh any further gains from building up goodwill.[27]

We have now spent some time in looking at reputational models of monetary policy. What is one to make of such models? Clearly, they are much richer in content than the models we have previously looked at, and in many respects, they mark a significant improvement on those models. By focusing on the role of information, they offer many new insights and pay more than lip-service to the notion that information may be used strategically. In particular, they are able to account for business cycle

phenomena (fluctuations in output and inflation) and to explain why policymakers may have a natural desire for secrecy. This last observation, in
particular, is worth noting for much of the discussion that lies ahead. On
the other hand, the models leave unexplained what determines the public's
initial beliefs. These beliefs are fundamental to the evolution of the game.
In addition, the modeling of signaling behavior may be regarded as being
somewhat naive. The only way that a policymaker can signal is through
his or her actual inflationary policy. But what of public debate, confrontation with opponents, and any stand that is taken on other issues? And
what of a policymaker's ideological commitment? As before, these considerations invite us to think of politico-economic models of monetary
policy.

STABILIZATION

It is now time to depart from the fiction of a deterministic environment
and consider the issues raised within a stochastic context. The most important of these issues concerns the use of countercyclical monetary policy
as a means of stabilizing the economy in the face of exogenous shocks.
This issue lies at the center of one of the most longstanding controversies
in macroeconomics. Although the arguments involved have changed over
the years, the debate remains as lively today as it was in the past. Some
of the more recent contributions can be allied to the game-theoretic literature.

Conservatism Versus Flexibility

The idea developed in this section is based on Rogoff (1985a). Consider
introducing a stochastic perturbation (a supply shock) into the Phillips
curve (16). Specifically, let

$$(43) \quad y_t = y_n + \beta(\pi_t - E\pi_t) + \epsilon_t,$$

where ϵ_t is an independently distributed random normal variate with mean
zero and variance σ_ϵ^2. Together with (15), we have

$$(44) \quad v(\pi_t, E\pi_t) = -(\Lambda_1/2)(\pi_t - \Lambda_\pi)^2 - (\Lambda_2/2)(\beta(\pi_t - E\pi_t) + \epsilon_t - \Lambda_y')^2.$$

Suppose that the policymaker is able to observe ϵ_t (but that $E\epsilon_t = 0$). The
equilibrium policy rule under discretion follows as $\hat{\pi}_t = \hat{\pi} - \beta\Lambda_2\epsilon_t/(\Lambda_1 + \beta^2\Lambda_2)$, where $\hat{\pi}$ is defined as before. The second term in this rule represents
the stabilization component of policy. It is a countercyclical feedback on

the supply shock which reduces the impact of this shock on output. The (expected) payoff to the policymaker is $E\hat{u} = \hat{u} - \Lambda_1\Lambda_2\sigma_\epsilon^2/ 2(\Lambda_1 + \beta^2\Lambda_2)$, where $\hat{u}$ is also defined as before.

In this setup, the appointment of a conservative policymaker does not necessarily result in an improved outcome. While an increase in Λ_1 continues to reduce the inflationary bias (the term $\beta\Lambda_2\Lambda_y'/\Lambda_1$ in $\hat{\pi}$), it also reduces the feedback coefficient on the supply shock (the term $\beta\Lambda_2/(\Lambda_1 + \beta^2\Lambda_2)$). The net effect on welfare is ambiguous. This is the so-called tradeoff between conservatism and flexibility. The more conservative the policymaker is, the more willing he or she is to stabilize inflation but the less willing to stabilize output. The implication is that the policymaker ought not to be "too" conservative. This is a qualification to our earlier arguments about conservatism.

Private Information

Canzoneri (1985) raised an issue in connection with a policymaker's alleged superior information about monetary shocks. Go back to the case in which $\epsilon_t = 0$ but assume that inflation is no longer perfectly controllable. Rather, suppose that $\pi_t = \mu_t - v_t$, where μ_t is monetary growth and v_t is an independently and normally distributed random variate with mean zero and variance σ_v^2. This may be interpreted as a velocity shock or a control error in the setting of monetary policy. The policymaker is assumed to possess private information about this shock. His forecast of it is $Fv_t = v_t + \zeta_t$, where ζ is a white noise forecast error with variance σ_ζ^2. From the public's point of view, $Ev_t = 0$, so that $E\pi_t = E\mu_t$.

The analogue to (44) is

$$(45) \qquad v(\mu_t, E\mu_t) = -(\Lambda_1/2)(\mu_t - v_t - \Lambda_\pi)^2$$
$$- (\Lambda_2/2)(\beta(\mu_t - v_t - E\mu_t) - \Lambda_y')^2.$$

It is straightforward to show that an equilibrium policy and an equilibrium (expected) payoff may each be decomposed into two parts: a deterministic component (d) and a stochastic component (s). Formally, $\mu_t = \mu_d + \mu_s$ and $Eu_t = u_d + u_s$. The deterministic components are given by either $\mu_d = \bar{\mu}$ and $u_d = \bar{u}$ (in the second-best equilibrium) or $\mu_d = \hat{\mu}$ and $u_d = \hat{u}$ (in the third-best equilibrium), where all terms are defined as before with π replaced by μ. The stochastic components are the same in each case, being $\mu_s = Fv_t$ and $u_s = -(\Lambda_1 + \beta^2\Lambda_2)\sigma_\zeta^2/2$.

Now, agents cannot distinguish between the two components of policy. All they observe is the joint signal $\mu_t = \mu_d + \mu_s$. But this suggests the following possibility: by misrepresenting their private information, policymakers could disguise a strategic ride on the Phillips curve as an attempt to stabilize the economy. To be sure, observe that a strategy of cheating involves setting $\mu_d = \bar{\mu}$, where $\bar{\mu}$ was derived previously as $\bar{\mu} = \tilde{\mu} + \beta \Lambda_2 \Lambda_y'/(\Lambda_1 + \beta^2 \Lambda_2)$. If policymakers were to announce a forecast $(Fv_t)^A = Fv_t + \beta \Lambda_2 \Lambda_y'/(\Lambda_1 + \beta^2 \Lambda_2)$, then they could make this cheating strategy observationally equivalent to the second-best rule: from the viewpoint of agents, monetary policy would look like $\mu_t = \tilde{\mu} + (Fv_t)^A$.

In this setting, therefore, an apparent adherence to the second-best policy is not verification that this policy is actually being followed. Moreover, even a nonopportunistic policymaker could suffer a crisis in confidence if agents were to misinterpret a genuine act of stabilization as an attempt to cheat. These considerations have a bearing on some of our previous results. Clearly, they question the suitability of the sorts of trigger mechanism discussed earlier under Repeated Policy Games. These mechanisms are far too simple to be of much use in the present context: rather, it is necessary to think of other schemes that respect the private information aspects of the problem.[28] Another point worth noting relates to the reputational models of monetary policy. Driffill (1987) has extended those models to include a random element in the setting of monetary policy. In this case, observation of high inflation is consistent with the policymaker being of a type 1. This has the effect of weakening the reputational forces that motivate a type 2 to set low inflation: it is now possible for this policymaker to inflate the economy without blowing his or her disguise since there is always a probability that the inflation is due to a control error on the part of a type 1.

This seems as good a point as any to inject a note of caution into proceedings. The assumption maintained above is that policymakers have quicker access to data than the public does. Perhaps central banks do indeed enjoy a temporary informational advantage as regards monetary statistics (e.g., data on bank deposits). But, typically, these statistics become available for public consumption with a fairly trivial delay, and once they are available, the public could figure out the reason for any past change in policy. Moreover, if a policymaker was suspected of systematically exploiting his or her informational advantage, then agents would presumably have an incentive to eliminate this advantage. Thus, the importance to be attached to the issues raised above is somewhat debatable.

We have now reached the end of our discussion on monetary policy in a stochastic environment. There is just one final matter that ought to be attended to. In general, the full optimal state-contingent policy rule will be a complicated function of many of the variables in a system. This complexity may be damaging to the rule if it frustrates the public from fully understanding it. Simpler feedback-type rules, though weaker in their powers of stabilization, may well command greater respect. This suggests a tradeoff between credibility and flexibility in a similar way as the following, more trivial, observation: greater scope for discretion, though exacerbating credibility problems, enables a more flexible response to unforeseen contingencies. This tradeoff can be used as an argument for simplicity in policy design. What form might this simplicity take? One possibility is the design of policy rules with explicit escape clauses. Such rules would tie down policy for most of the time while allowing scope for discretion in the case of "abnormal" events. The postwar system of fixed exchange rates is a nice example of this: the rule required countries to maintain fixed parities with the dollar but allowed changes in parities in cases of "fundamental disequilibria." Another possibility is to implement a feedback on only a subset of variables in the system. A rule for adjusting the money supply in response to interest-rate fluctuations is an example that comes to mind here. More generally, the need to strike a balance between credibility and flexibility suggests that attention be devoted to simple policy rules that display good operating characteristics.

MONETARY POLITICS

The fiction of a benevolent policymaker maximizing the welfare of a representative agent may be useful in some circumstances but wholly misleading in others. In the real world, individuals differ and governments face important distributional considerations. Decisions about monetary policy are reached through political institutions, the task of which is to aggregate the diversity of individual interests into collective government action. In a representative democracy, this process of aggregation takes place via the electoral system: citizens indicate their preferences by voting for political candidates in regular periodic elections. In this section we review some recent politico-economic models of monetary policy. In doing so, we reveal another potential source of credibility problems—namely, the difference between a policymaker's preelection and postelection opportunities.

Political Business Cycles I: Office-Motivated Politicians

The term *political business cycles* is used to refer to policy-induced fluctuations in economic activity which are synchronized with the dates of election. According to one view, these cycles reflect the vested interests of democratically elected policymakers in manipulating the economy for electoral gains. This view is based on the median voter theorem, a central tenet of which is that politicians seek power for power's own sake and not because it enables them to pursue other objectives. Thus, the overriding concern of politicians is seen to be the maximization of their chances of election by the maximization of the number of votes cast for them. To achieve this, they are led into tailoring their policies to those voters in the middle of the ideological spectrum who are open to capture by all political parties. In a two-party system and under certain conditions, this results in policy convergence: as an election draws near, both parties offer the same policies so that the interests of the median voter (the moderate majority) are realized.

Traditional models of political business cycles combined the above with the assumption of an irrational electorate (Nordhaus, 1975). These models predicted that a government could engineer a preelection boom and fool voters into believing that the good times were there to stay: being entirely backward-looking, voters would fail to realize the postelection U-turn called forth by the mounting inflationary pressures. Moreover, there was nothing to stop the government from fooling the electorate systematically by repeating its strategy at every election. Needless to say, this story is not very convincing. One task of the new generation of politico-economic models has been to generate electoral cycles on the assumption that voters are rational and forward-looking. As we will see, this has been achieved by replacing irrationality with imperfect information.

The following example is based on the work of Rogoff (1990) and Rogoff and Sibert (1988). It is closely related to the two-period signaling model studied earlier. A policymaker (a political candidate or party) is in office in the first period. An election takes place at the end of this period when voters decide whether to reelect the incumbent or appoint an opponent. Both candidates share the same objectives for output and inflation. In addition, each one values holding office. Let us write the instantaneous payoff to candidate j ($j = I$ for incumbent and $j = O$ for opponent) as

$$(46) \quad u(\pi_t, y_t, D_{jt}) = -(\Lambda_1/2)\pi_t^2 + \Lambda_2 y_t + \Lambda_3 D_{jt},$$

where D_{jt} is a dummy variable that takes the value of 1 (0) when party j is in (out of) office.

Each candidate may be either of two types: a competent type or an incompetent type. By competency is meant the ability of a candidate to improve the natural rate of output.[29] To model this, rewrite the Phillips curve as

$$(47) \quad y_t = y_{nt} + \beta(\pi_t - E\pi_t),$$

where $y_{nt} = \eta_{jt}$ and $\eta_{jt} = \chi_{jt} + \chi_{jt-1}$. The quantity η_{jt} measures the competency of candidate j. This is given as a moving average of a random variable, χ_{jt}. That competency is random reflects the idea that it depends on the particular policy problem to be solved. That it is influenced by both current and past shocks implies that it is partially lasting. The distribution of χ_{jt} is summarized by the following: $\chi_{jt-1} = 0$; $\chi_{jt+s} = \chi^+ > 0$; with probability p_{t+s} $(s = 0,1)$; $\chi_{jt+s} = \chi^- < 0$ with probability $1 - p_{t+s}$ $(s =$

$0,1)$; and $E\chi_{jt} = p_t\chi^+ + (1 - p_t)\chi^- = 0$. Thus, χ^+ is associated with a competent type and χ^- is associated with an incompetent type.

The aim of voters is to elect the most competent candidate. But post-election competency, $\eta_{jt+1} = \chi_{jt+1} + \chi_{jt}$, is unknown at the time of election. Hence, voters look at the current competency of each party, $\eta_{jt} = \chi_{jt}$. Clearly, the competency of the opponent is unobservable, so that $E\eta_{Ot} = E\chi_{Ot} = 0$. In addition, for the model to be interesting, we must also assume that the competency of the incumbent is unknown: if not, then the outcome would be obvious—the incumbent would win (lose) if $\chi_{It} = \chi^+ (\chi_{It} = \chi^-)$. In what follows, χ_{It} is taken to be purely private information, so that $E\eta_{It} = E\chi_{It} = 0$.

The game revolves around the idea that the level of output observed in the first period may act as a signal of the incumbent's competency. In particular, the incumbent may be tempted to engineer a preelection boom so as to create a good impression. He may be able to do so by engineering surprise inflation. Notice that both types of incumbent (the competent and incompetent) may be motivated to act in this way. The benefits from doing so must be traded off against the higher-than-otherwise inflation.

Consider the outcome in the second period. Since the game ends in this period, a policymaker has no incentive either to signal or mimic. Hence, $\pi_{t+1} = E\pi_{t+1} = \hat{\pi}$, where $\hat{\pi} = \beta\Lambda_2/\Lambda_1$ is the discretionary rate of inflation. The expected payoff to the incumbent if he is reelected is $Eu(\hat{\pi},y_{t+1},1) = u(\hat{\pi},\chi_{It},1)$. The expected payoff to him if he is not reelected is $E(\hat{\pi},y_{t+1},0) = u(\hat{\pi},0,0)$.[30] It is straightforward to verify that the value of being reelected is greater for a competent type than for an incompetent type.

Moving to the first period, suppose that the incumbent wants to generate a particular level of output, y_t. To do so, he must set inflation at the rate $\pi_t = \pi(y_t,\chi_{It})$, where

(48) $\pi(y_t,\chi_{It}) = E\pi_t + (y_t - \chi_{It})/\beta.$

This yields the first-period payoff, $u(\pi(y_t,\chi_{It}), y_t,1)$. The alternative is to set $\pi_t = \hat{\pi}$ and receive $u(\hat{\pi},\chi_{It}+\beta(\hat{\pi}- E\pi_t),1)$. We may now gather our results together and define

(49) $U(y_t,\chi_{It}) = u(\pi(y_t,\chi_{It}),y_t,1) + \lambda[\rho u(\hat{\pi},\chi_{It},1) + (1 - \rho)u(\hat{\pi},0,0)],$

as the incumbent's discounted payoff associated with signaling and the probability, ρ, of reelection, and

(50) $V(\chi_{It}) = u(\hat{\pi},\chi_{It}+\beta(\hat{\pi}-E\pi_t),1) + \lambda u(\hat{\pi},0,0),$

as the discounted payoff in the opposite case.

In a separating equilibrium, voters can correctly infer the competency of the government from the observed level of output in the first period. The rule for updating beliefs is given by

$$
(51) \qquad p_{t+1} = \begin{cases} 0 & \text{if } y_t < y^s \\ 1 & \text{otherwise,} \end{cases}
$$

for some appropriately chosen y^s. For separation to occur, the competent (incompetent) type must (not) find it profitable to set a rate of inflation that generates y^s. Formally, $U(y^s, \chi^+) > V(\chi^+)$ and $U(y^s, \chi^-) < V(\chi^-)$ with $\rho = 1$. If these conditions are satisfied, then the rationally expected rate of inflation is $E\pi_t = p_t \pi(y^s, \chi^+) + (1 - p_t)\hat\pi.$[31] In the first period, therefore, either $\pi_t = E\pi_t + (y^s - \chi^+)/\beta$ or $\pi_t = \hat\pi$, where $E\pi_t = \hat\pi + p_t(y^s - \chi^+)/\beta(1 - p_t)$; and in the second period, $\pi_{t+1} = E\pi_{t+1} = \hat\pi$. Thus, if the incumbent is competent (incompetent), there is a preelection boom (recession) and the incumbent stays in (moves out of) office. We have just generated a political business cycle.

In pooling equilibrium, both types of incumbent choose the same level of output, and voters remain ignorant of the incumbent's competency. In this case, voters' beliefs satisfy

$$
(52) \qquad p_{t+1} = \begin{cases} p_t & \text{if } y_t > y^p \\ 0 & \text{otherwise,} \end{cases}
$$

for some appropriately chosen value of y^p. Given these beliefs, a competent incumbent can do nothing to raise his chances of reelection. Thus, he sets $\pi_t = \hat\pi$, yielding a level of output, $y^p = \chi^+ + \beta(\hat\pi - E\pi_t)$. An incompetent type will aim to generate the same level of output by setting $\pi_t = \pi(y^p \cdot \chi^-)$ if $U(y^p, \chi^-) > V(\chi^-)$ with $\rho = 1/2.$[32] Under such circumstances, $E\pi_t = p_t\hat\pi + (1 - p_t)\pi(y^p, \chi^-)$. Thus, the pooling equilibrium is characterized by the following: either $\pi_t = \hat\pi$ or $\pi_t = E\pi_t + (y^p - \chi^-)/\beta$ with $E\pi_t = \hat\pi + (1 - p_t)(y^p - \chi^-)/\beta p_t$; and $\pi_{t+1} = E\pi_{t+1} = \hat\pi$. Prior to the election, output is the same for both types of incumbent, although inflation is unexpectedly negative (positive) for a competent (incompetent) type.

We have now seen how the political incentives of a government can give rise to distorted policies and the synchronization of economic fluctuations with the dates of elections. We have obtained these results without having to resort to voter irrationality. A questionable maintained hypothesis, however, is that politicians are office-motivated. In another branch of the literature, this assumption is replaced by an alternative which is discussed below.

Political Business Cycles II: Partisan Politicians

The presumption maintained here is that different political candidates have different objectives that reflect the interests of a core set of voters to whom each party appeals.[33] Achieving these objectives is the reason why a candidate wants to gain office: politicians are now ideologically motivated, with power being a means to an end rather than an end in itself. In general, this implies a tradeoff between that policy which is closest to a party's ideology and that policy which maximizes the party's chances of election. It also implies that the only credible preelection announcement about a postelection policy is that which is consistent with the party's ideology—for once the party is in office, it is sure to implement its most desired course of action. The discussion that follows draws from the work of Alesina (1987, 1988) and Alesina and Cukierman (1988).

Go back to the case in which a policymaker of type i ($i = 1,2$) has the objective function in (33). But now, think of this policymaker as a political party—the type 1 (type 2) as a Conservative or Republican (Socialist or Democrat) perhaps. Assume that voters know each party's objectives and consider an election period. Voters understand that, after the election, party i will set the discretionary rate of inflation, $\hat{\pi}_i = \beta\Lambda_{2i}/\Lambda_1$. Hence, all voters whose preferred rate of inflation is less (greater) than $(\hat{\pi}_1 + \hat{\pi}_2)/2$ will vote for party 1 (party 2). Let π_M be the preferred rate of inflation of the median voter. Then party 1 wins if $\pi_M < (\hat{\pi}_1 + \hat{\pi}_2)/2$, and party 2 wins if $\pi_M > (\hat{\pi}_1 + \hat{\pi}_2)/2$. If the turnout of the electorate is random, then π_M will be a random variable. Denoting by $P(\pi_M)$ the cumulative distribution of this variable, we find that the probability of party 1 winning is given by $\rho = P((\hat{\pi}_1 + \hat{\pi}_2)/2)$.

Now let us consider some implications of this setup. Voters expect a postelection inflation rate equal to $E\pi_t = \rho\hat{\pi}_1 + (1 - \rho)\hat{\pi}_2$. Hence, there is a recession (boom) if party 1 (party 2) is elected, and we have generated a political business cycle again. Clearly, however, this is quite different from the cycle studied above: it occurs after, rather than before, the election and does not come about because of the desire to gain office. In addition, the magnitude of the fluctuations is allied to the degree of political polarization: the greater the divergence between parties' ideologies, the more extreme are the booms or recessions.

Evidently, this model is incapable of explaining policy convergence—or is it? A trivial extension suggests otherwise. If the electoral cycles are damaging to the economy, then each party would presumably have an incentive to eliminate them by coordinating on a common policy with the other. True enough, there would be a standing temptation to deviate from this policy once elected. But the fact that elections are repeated could remove this temptation: on the one hand, each party could threaten its rival with noncooperation at the next election; and on the other, each party could be threatened with being voted out of office by the electorate. In contrast to traditional theory, policy convergence is seen as a response to, not a cause of, electoral cycles.

The literature on political business cycles has developed at a staggering pace in recent years. What distinguishes the new from the old generation of models is the old generation's respect for the principle of rationality. Not only has this led to new insights into old issues, but it has also drawn attention to new issues altogether. Nevertheless, the research is still very much in its infancy. One idea worth pursuing is whether delegating monetary policy to an independent central bank would mitigate the sorts of pre- and postelection inflation volatility identified in the foregoing analysis.[34] Another is the extent to which outcomes could be improved by various types of electoral reform. These and other matters represent an exciting challenge for future research.

Policy Bargains

One way of looking at economic policy is to see it as a product of political bargaining—a consequence of the pressures exerted by individuals and groups with conflicts of interests that are only partly reconciled by the existing system of power relationships.[35] Among those groups that influence monetary policy, the two most obvious are central bank officials and government representatives. Conflicts between these may arise for a number of reasons, the most notable being allied to inflation. Thus, it is commonly alleged that governments, in particular, have a natural propensity to resort to monetary expansion. This may reflect such motives as the pursuit of short-run electoral gains, the desire to reduce debt service payments, and the incentive to raise revenue through the inflation tax. Central bankers, on the other hand, are typically regarded as being more conservative, having greater respect for long-run considerations even if these require policies that are politically unpopular in the short run.[36] Our earlier arguments about the merits of appointing a conservative policymaker may be seen in this light. In general, it is possible to view decisions about monetary policy as reflecting a compromise between advocates of economic stimulation and advocates of inflation prevention. Moreover, it is easy to think of this compromise as changing over time as changes take place in the political composition of each group and the power relationships between them.

The foregoing observations do more than merely illustrate why agents may be imperfectly informed about monetary objectives. They also suggest that a monetary authority itself could be uncertain of what these might be in the future. Cukierman and Meltzer (1985) have studied the implications of this by modeling the tradeoff between economic stimulation and inflation prevention (the ratio Λ_2/Λ_1) as a serially correlated stochastic process.

Agents are never sure of this tradeoff and, instead, draw inferences about it from observations of past inflation. These inferences are noisy because inflation fluctuations reflect transitory control errors as well as persistent shifts in preferences. This, in turn, means that it is optimal for agents to only partly adjust their expected inflation in response to changes in actual inflation. Meanwhile, the monetary authority is aware of its current objectives but is unsure of those in the future. It must predict these, however, because what it does currently affects what it can do in the future by affecting future inflationary expectations.

One prediction of this framework is that when policymakers become less concerned with inflation prevention (e.g., during the 1960s and the early 1970s) the sluggishness in expectations adjustment offers scope for increasing output. Conversely, periods characterized by more conservative policymakers (e.g., the 1980s) are likely to display recessions. Credibility is now defined as the speed with which the public realizes that a shift in preferences has occurred. This turns out to be a decreasing function of the variance of monetary control errors. Hence, the greater the precision of control procedures, the less are the costs of disinflation while a noisier control technology tends to complement a shift toward economic stimulation by slowing down agents' recognition of this shift. Here, then, lies another explanation for why monetary objectives may be shrouded in secrecy: by keeping them ambiguous, the policymaker enjoys greater flexibility in the timing of inflationary surprises.

Several other results emerge from this analysis, but let us turn, instead, to a few issues that are left outstanding. All of these concern the shifts in objectives. The first point to note is that such shifts are often associated with other notable developments, not the least of which are changes in the operating procedures of monetary policy. Consider, for instance, the predominant concern with full employment during the 1960s and the use of interest rates at that time as the main instrument of monetary policy; compare this with growing concern over inflation throughout the 1970s and the eventual adoption of monetary targets. A second observation is that changes in objectives are unlikely to arise from pressures exerted by any single individual or group, but rather are likely to reflect a widespread shift of opinion throughout the policymaking hierarchy. If so, however, then surely these changes would be more apparent to the public than the foregoing analysis implies. Third, and finally, it is reasonable to believe that changes in objectives, rather than occurring exogenously, are the natural responses to changes in economic conditions. Consider, again, the rising inflation during the 1970s and the subsequent shift towards anti-inflation objectives.

All of the above suggests considerable scope for further research. This would involve specifying more fully both the channels of influence on monetary policy and the bargaining process that is used to solve the problem of whose interests to satisfy and to what extent. As for the link between politics and secrecy, one approach might be to borrow from the literature on bureaucracy in central banking.[37] According to this, central bank behavior is best understood by regarding central banks as political institutions that are concerned mainly with their own self-esteem and self-preservation. To achieve these objectives, they are motivated to find ways of protecting themselves from outside interference and critical investigation. By securing such immunity, they are able to publish selective information that magnifies their successes and obscures their failures.

Debt, Deficits, and Democracy

A final class of politico-economic models is directed towards a theme introduced earlier in the chapter. This concerns the role of government debt as an intertemporal linkage in policymakers' optimization problems. One issue here is that of domestic policy coordination (Alesina and Tabellini, 1987a,b; Persson and Svensson, 1987; Tabellini, 1986).[38] If monetary and fiscal policies are delegated to separate institutions, then the credibility of the overall macroeconomic program may founder on a lack of cooperation between these institutions. To see this, write the government's budget constraint as

$$(53) \quad g_t + (1 - \pi_{t-1})m_{t-1} + r_{t-1}b_{t-1} = m_t + b_t + h_t,$$

where h_t denotes tax revenue and all other terms are defined as before.[39] Solving (53) forward in time yields

$$(54) \quad b_{t-1} = \sum_{s=0}^{\infty} R_s[(h_{t+s} - g_{t+s}) + m_{t+s} - (1 - \pi_{t+s-1})m_{t+s-1}],$$

where $R_s = \Pi_{\tau=0}^{s} r_{t+s-1}^{-1}$. Equation (54) has been derived using the *no-Ponzi game* condition, $\lim_{T \to \infty} R_T b_{t+T} = 0$. This ensures that the government remains solvent over its lifetime without having to repudiate its debt. Thus, according to (54), the initial level of debt must equal the present discounted value of primary surpluses as well as the present discounted value of revenue from money creation. Now, the effect of the solvency condition is to impose restrictions on the set of feasible financial policies. A policy designed to avoid the monetization of fiscal deficits requires the issue of debt which stores up future outlays in the form of interest payments. If the government is to remain solvent under such a policy, it must eventually run an appropriate stream of budget surpluses. In the absence of such a fiscal correction, agents are sent a clear signal of the inflationary consequences of debt financing: for the only way to ensure a nonexplosive path for debt is to resort to seigniorage.

Given the above, it is easy to see how the separation of monetary and fiscal management can lead to credibility problems. Suppose, for the reasons discussed earlier, that the central bank wishes to pursue a tight monetary policy but the government wants to implement an expansionary fiscal policy. We have a "game of chicken" between two powerful decision makers, each of whom is struggling to gain dominance over the other. By sticking to its policy, each one invests in a reputation for being tough and continually tests the nerve of its rival to do likewise. The composite macroeconomic program is not credible simply because it is not feasible. One of the players has to give way, and it matters for inflation which of them does so: if concessions are made on the fiscal side, then the economy is kept under a tight monetary rein; otherwise, the prospect of persistent fiscal deficits must be met by monetization. Such coordination problems create uncertainty for agents and invite speculation over when the game will end and who will win it. More generally, the degree of noncoordination between monetary and fiscal authorities is important for determining both the variance and dynamic behavior of government debt.

Another issue worth mentioning is the following. Recall the earlier discussion on strategic debt management. Think of relating that discussion to the case in which there is a sequence of policymakers (political administrations) alternating in office. The implication is that, even if these policymakers have different objectives, the government of the day may be able to saddle its successor with a set of constraints which makes the process of changing policies difficult. In this way, political parties can leave their opponents with an ideological legacy and minimize the costs of being out of office. This is, indeed, an intriguing idea. Preliminary investigations into it have been conducted by Alesina and Tabellini (1987b), Cukierman and Meltzer (1990) and Persson and Svensson (1989).

INTERNATIONAL POLICY COORDINATION

Beginning with the work of Hamada (1976), there is now a vast literature on monetary policy games played at the international level. The focus of this literature is on the potential inefficiencies of noncooperative policymaking by governments of interdependent economies. These inefficiencies reflect certain externalities ignored under noncooperation. By internalizing these externalities, cooperation between governments offers a means of improving policy outcomes.

Methodologically, the literature adopts two broad approaches. The first involves the use of small analytical models for which tractable solutions can be found (Blackburn, 1987; Canzoneri and Gray, 1985; Canzoneri and Henderson, 1988, 1991; Rogoff, 1985b). The second is based on more complicated systems that require the application of numerical simulation (Hughes-Hallet, 1986, 1987; Levine and Currie, 1987; Miller and Salmon,

1984; Oudiz and Sachs, 1984; Sachs, 1983). We may illustrate some of the issues raised in the literature by suitably modifying our two generic examples of equilibrium monetary policy. The simplest way of doing so is to extend each example to an open economy and to replicate this economy abroad. This gives us a world of two symmetric countries which we may label domestic (d) and foreign (f).

Optimal Demand Management

Consider the following representation of a world economy, adapted from Canzoneri and Henderson (1988):

(55) $y_t^i = y_n + \beta(\pi_t^i - E\pi_t^i),$

(56) $y_t^d - y_t^f = \delta(\pi_t^f + \sigma_t - \pi_t^d),$

(57) $\Pi_t^d = (1 - \gamma)\,\pi_t^d + \gamma(\pi_t^f + \sigma_t),$

(58) $\Pi_t^f = (1 - \gamma)\,\pi_t^f + \gamma(\pi_t^d - \sigma_t),$

(59) $u(\Pi_t^i, y_t^i) = -(\Lambda_1/2)\Pi_t^{i2} + \Lambda_2(y_t^i - y_n),$

where $i = d, f$ and all variables are expressed in either levels or rates of change. Equation (55) is the Phillips curve for each country, where π_t^i is the price of goods produced in country i. Equation (56) states that the relative demand for goods in each country depends on the real exchange rate, where σ_t is the nominal exchange rate. Equations (57) and (58) define the consumer price indeces, Π_t^i, as weighted averages of the prices of home-produced goods and the exchange-rate-adjusted prices of overseas produced goods. Equation (59) gives the objective function for each government. As before, it is assumed that π_t^i can be perfectly controlled through monetary policy.

Reducing the system in the usual way, we may write country i's payoff as $u_t^i = v(\pi_t^i, \pi_t^j, E\pi_t^i, E\pi_t^j)$, where

(60) $v(\pi_t^i, \pi_t^j, E\pi_t^i, E\pi_t^j) = -(\Lambda_1/2)(\pi_t^i + \Gamma[\pi_t^i - E\pi_t^i) - (\pi_t^j - E\pi_t^j)])^2$
$+ \beta\Lambda_2(\pi_t^i - E\pi_t^i),$

and $\Gamma = \gamma\beta/\delta$. It is evident from (60) that the welfare of each country depends on events at both home and abroad. In particular, each country's inflation rate, Π_t^i, is a function of relative monetary policies, $\pi_t^i - \pi_t^j$. *Ceteris paribus*, an increase in π_t^i causes a real depreciation in country i's currency, which adds to the effect on inflation. Conversely, an increase in π_t^j causes country i's currency to appreciate, which reduces inflation in that country. This latter effect is the externality in the model. Notice that both effects vanish when $\gamma = 0$, which returns us to the framework of previous sections.

It is instructive to begin our analysis of international policy coordination by abstracting from the interactions between governments and agents. These interactions, which have occupied our attention up to now, will be reintroduced shortly. For a moment, let us simply set $E\pi_t^i = 0$. Considering, first, the case in which governments do not cooperate, the relevant equilibrium concept is the Nash equilibrium. In this, each government chooses its monetary policy so as to maximize its own welfare, treating as given the monetary policy of its rival. Doing this yields the reaction function for each government

$$(61) \qquad \pi_t^i = \frac{\Lambda_I \Gamma (1 + \Gamma) \pi_t^j + \beta \Lambda_2}{\Lambda_I (1 + \Gamma)^2}.$$

The noncooperative Nash equilibrium is obtained by solving the two simultaneous equations in (61). This gives $\pi_t^i = \pi^{NC} = \beta \Lambda_2 / \Lambda_I (1 + \Gamma)$ which, in turn, delivers $u_t^i = u^{NC} = v(\pi^{NC}, \pi^{NC}, 0, 0) = -\beta^2 \Lambda_2^2 (1 + 2\Gamma) / 2\Lambda_I (1 + \Gamma)^2$. In the case of cooperation, both governments choose monetary policy so as to maximize a weighted average of their payoffs, $\Lambda u_t^d + (1 - \Lambda) u_t^f$. For simplicity, assume that both countries are weighted equally so that $\Lambda = 1/2$. The analogue to (61) is

$$(62) \qquad \pi_t^i = \frac{2\Lambda_I \Gamma (1 + \Gamma) \pi_t^j + \beta \Lambda_2}{\Lambda_I ((1 + \Gamma)^2 + \Gamma^2)},$$

implying $\pi_t^i = \pi^C = \beta \Lambda_2 / \Lambda_I$ and $u_t^i = u^C = v(\pi^C, \pi^C, 0, 0) = -\beta^2 \Lambda_2^2 / 2\Lambda_I$.

It is evident that $\pi^{NC} < \pi^C$ and $u^{NC} < u^C$: monetary policy under noncooperation is less expansionary than monetary policy under cooperation, and welfare under noncooperation is lower than welfare under cooperation. These results are explained as follows. When governments act noncooperatively, each one is tempted to reduce inflation by surprising its rival with an unexpected monetary contraction. This generates a real exchange-rate appreciation and exports inflation abroad. When both governments attempt to do this, the equilibrium is characterized by a deflationary bias. Another interpretation is to note that a unilateral monetary expansion, while raising output, increases inflation both directly and indirectly through a real exchange-rate depreciation. The latter effect, which tempers the incentive to pursue such a policy, is removed when governments cooperate.

Now, the question to be asked is how might cooperation be enforced? As the reader may verify, each government has an incentive to unilaterally defect from cooperation. An answer to the question is suggested by repeated game considerations. Each government could threaten its rival with reversion to its Nash policy should the rival ever deviate from cooperative behavior. This sort of simple 'tit-for-tat' strategy may well do the trick. There is, still, of course, the problem of multiple equilibria, however.

It is now time to reintroduce private sector rationality into the story. The importance of doing so is that the welfare rankings observed above may be overturned: international policy coordination might actually be counterproductive. Notice that the policies we have derived are equivalent to the policies under discretion. Rational expectations imply $E\pi_t = \pi^{NC}$ and $E\pi_t = \pi^C$ in the two cases. Hence, equilibrium welfare in each case becomes $\hat{u}^{NC} = v(\pi^{NC},\pi^{NC}, \pi^{NC},\pi^{NC}) = -\beta^2\Lambda_2^2/2\Lambda_1 (1 + \Gamma)^2$ and $\hat{u}^C = v(\pi^C,\pi^C,\pi^C, \pi^C) = -\beta^2\Lambda_2^2/2\Lambda_1$. Certainly, therefore, $\hat{u}^{NC} > \hat{u}^C$. In general, noncooperation exerts a discipline on governments and reduces each one's individual incentive to cheat the public. Cooperation removes this discipline and makes credibility problems more acute.

Dynamic Optimal Taxation

The analysis in this section is drawn from Blackburn and Christensen (1990). It is based on a two-country version of our previous optimal tax model. Consider a world of currency substitution where residents of each country are free to hold both the currency issued at home and the currency issued abroad. Focusing on the domestic economy, let m_t^{dd} and m_t^{fd} be the real values of domestic and foreign cash balances held by domestic residents. These are defined by $m_t^{dd} = M_t^{dd}/P_t^d$ and $m_t^{fd} = S_t M_t^{fd}/ P_t^d$, where M_t^{dd} and M_t^{fd} denote nominal balances, P_t^d the domestic price level and S_t the nominal exchange rate. Total real balances are $m_t^d = m_t^{dd} + m_t^{fd}$. The representative domestic agent maximizes

(63) $U(c_1^d,c_2^d, l_2^d,m_2^d) = u(c_1^d) + c_2^d + v(l_2^d) + w(m_2^d),$

subject to

(64) $c_1^d + m_1^{dd} + m_1^{fd} = e$

(65) $c_2^d + m_2^{dd} + m_2^{fd} = (1 - \pi^d)m_1^{dd}$
$+ (1 - \sigma)(1 - \pi^d)m_1^{fd} + (1 - \tau^d)\alpha n_2^d,$

plus $m_t^{id} \geq 0$ and $1 = l_2^d + n_2^d$, where $1 - \sigma = S_2/S_1$ is the gross rate of domestic currency depreciation. The first-order conditions are

(66) $u_c(c_1^d) \geq 1 - \pi^d,$

(67) $u_c(c_1^d) \geq (1 - \sigma)(1 - \pi^d),$

(68) $v_l(1 - n_2^d) = (1 - \tau^d)\alpha,$

(69) $w(m_2^d) = 1.$

From (66) and (67), we observe the following: a monetary equilibrium in which both monies are valued requires $\sigma = 0$ (a fixed exchange rate); a monetary equilibrium in which only domestic money is valued is associated with $\sigma > 0$ (domestic currency appreciation); and a monetary equilibrium in which only foreign money is valued is associated with $\sigma < 0$ (domestic currency depreciation). We may state these results in a different way if we assume the goods market arbitrage condition, $P_t^d = S_t P_t^f$ or $(1 - \pi^d) = (1 - \sigma)(1 - \pi^f)$: for both currencies to be valued, the rates of inflation at home and abroad must be equalized ($\pi^d = \pi^f$); if domestic inflation is lower than foreign inflation ($\pi^d < \pi^f$), then only domestic currency is valued; and if domestic inflation is higher than foreign inflation ($\pi^d > \pi^f$), then only foreign currency is valued.

The (domestic) governments' budget constraints read

$$(70) \quad s_1^d = m_1^{dd} + m_1^{df},$$

$$(71) \quad g_2 + (1 - \pi^d)(m_1^{dd} + m_1^{df}) = m_2^{dd} + m_2^{df} + \tau^d \alpha n_2^d + s_1^d,$$

where m_1^{df} denotes real domestic currency balances held by foreigners. When governments act noncooperatively, each one chooses tax policy so as to maximize the welfare of its own citizens, taking as given the tax policy of its rival. When governments cooperate, tax policy is chosen so as to maximize some joint welfare function. What do the noncooperative and cooperative equilibria look like?

We already know that $\pi^d = \pi^f$ for both monies to be held. In a non-cooperative Nash equilibrium, $\pi^{dNC} = \pi^{fNC} = 0$. The proof of this is as follows. If $\pi^d = \pi^f > 0$, then each government would have an incentive to undercut the other by slightly reducing its own rate of inflation. By doing so, it would be able to attract all the world's savings and make itself strictly better off. At the same time, neither government would want to subsidize savings by setting negative inflation. Hence, $\pi^{dNC} = \pi^{fNC} = 0$ is, indeed, the Nash equilibrium.

The cooperative equilibrium is obvious: assuming equal weights for both countries, it is the discretionary equilibrium of the closed economy. The optimal tax rule ex ante is of the form (14) but the optimal tax rule ex post involves setting $\pi = 1$. Compared to the noncooperative equilibrium, taxes on labor are the same, but money is no longer valued. Again, therefore, international policy coordination is counterproductive. By removing the competition between currencies, which exists under noncooperation, it invites back exactly the same credibility problems as those encountered in the closed economy context.

This analysis may be extended in the following way. Suppose that instead of there being two tradeable currencies there is a common currency issued by both governments. This is the case of monetary unification, with which is associated a different externality: welfare in each country depends on the world inflation rate that is determined by the joint actions of both governments. The implication is that each government has an incentive to shift part of the burden of the inflation tax onto the other. In this case, noncooperation has none of the effects reported above.

It is evident from the foregoing discussion that, in general, equilibrium international monetary policies will depend on the particular type of international monetary arrangement. In addition to those policies above, one other such arrangement might be for monetary policy to be supervised by an independent international authority—a world central bank created by consensus among sovereign states. As was true before, it is possible to view this as a means of alleviating credibility problems. In Europe, in particular, the issue of international monetary reform continues to excite widespread debate.

The literature on international policy coordination has yielded many important insights. A general conclusion is that the gains from coordination tend to be small (and may even be negative). There are reasons, however, why one may wish to treat the results obtained so far with some caution. First, there is still no firm evidence on the signs and sizes of the spillover effects between countries. Second, very little attention has been given to the bargaining process which determines the distribution of any gains from cooperation. Third, the results may well be sensitive to certain features of the models employed. Fourth, it is not clear that a comparison between optimal cooperative and optimal noncooperative policies can be generalized to the more relevant comparison between suboptimal cooperative and suboptimal noncooperative policies. Fifth, some of the gains from cooperation may well be unobservable, while the scope for cooperation may be checked by technical factors not accounted for so far. These and other issues are no doubt on the agenda for future research.

CONCLUSION

The application of game theory to the study of monetary policy may at first seem a little odd. Yet any difficulties in understanding this must be attributed to preconceived misguided notions, based on traditional analysis, of what policymaking is about. It is hoped that this chapter convinced the reader that the game elements in monetary policy are far more real than apparent. Respecting these elements is to confront what was fatally ignored in the past and to invite a radically different view of equilibrium policy. The intention here has been to provide a broad but selective, intuitive but rigorous, survey of the literature. The aim has been to summarize its main insights, point out some unresolved issues, and offer a few useful suggestions for further research.

NOTES

1. The most important characteristic is the interdependence between two or more decision makers (players), each of whom is concerned about an outcome that depends on the actions of everyone.

2. Other useful surveys include Alesina and Tabellini (1988), Blackburn and Christensen (1989), Cukierman (1985), Driffill (1988), Fischer (1986a,b), Persson (1988), and Persson and Tabellini (1991).

3. Earlier insights into this can be found in Phelps (1967) and Phelps and Pollack (1968).

4. Other examples include capital taxation (Fischer, 1980) and debt repudiation (Calvo, 1988).

5. In particular, $u_c(\bullet)$, $v_t(\bullet)$, $w_m(\bullet) > 0$ and $u_{cc}(\bullet)$, $v_{tt}(\bullet)$, $w_{mm}(\bullet) < 0$. The Inada conditions, $lim._{c \to 0} u_c(\bullet) = lim._{t \to 0} v_t(\bullet) = \infty$ and $lim._{c \to \infty} u_c(\bullet) = lim._{t \to \infty} v_t(\bullet) = 0$, are also assumed to hold. It is possible to consider more general utility functions, though at the cost of tractability. The inclusion of real balances in the utility function is made for simplicity and allows us to ignore the well-known unraveling problem. It may be rationalized by appealing to an underlying trans-actions technology.

6. Since the marginal utility of second-period consumption is unity, the marginal rates of substitution are just $u_c(\bullet)$ and $v_t(\bullet)$.

7. Specifically, $c(\pi) = u_c^{-1}(1 - \pi)$, $m(\pi) = e - u_c^{-1}(1 - \pi)$ and $n(\tau) = 1 - v_t^{-1}((1 - \tau)\alpha)$. Hence, $c_\pi(\bullet) = -1/u_{cc}(\bullet)$, $m_\pi(\bullet) = 1/u_{cc}(\bullet)$ and $n_\tau(\bullet) = \alpha/v_{tt}(\bullet)$.

8. Only the government has access to this storage technology. Its effect is to create an intertemporal linkage of the sort that could be equally motivated, by the assumption of government bonds.

9. Strictly speaking, of course, π is not a choice variable of the government. In this model, however, there is a unique relationship between inflation and mon-etary growth so that choosing monetary growth is equivalent to choosing the former.

10. Optimizing the Lagrangian with respect to π and τ delivers $u_c(\bullet)c_\pi(\bullet) + m_\pi(\bullet) = (1 + \lambda)(\pi m_\pi(\bullet) + m_t)$ and $n_\tau(\bullet)(\alpha - v_t(\bullet)) = \alpha(1 + \lambda)(\tau n_\tau(\bullet) + n_2)$ where λ is the Lagrange multiplier associated with the constraint (13). Combining these expressions, using the relationships in (4) and (5), and recalling from note 7 the definitions of $c_\pi(\bullet)$, $m_\pi(\bullet)$ and $n_\tau(\bullet)$, we have $(1 - u_c(\bullet))/(1 - u_c(\bullet) + m_t u_{cc}(\bullet)) = (\alpha - v_t(\bullet))/(\alpha - v_t(\bullet) + n_2 v_{tt}(\bullet))$ which simplifies to $(1 - u_c(\bullet))/m_t u_{cc}(\bullet) = (\alpha - v_t(\bullet))/n_2 v_{tt}(\bullet)$. Multiplying the left-hand-side by $u_c(\bullet)/u_c(\bullet) = u_c(\bullet)/(1 - \pi)$ and the right-hand-side by $v_t(\bullet)/v_t(\bullet) = v_t(\bullet)/\alpha(1 - \tau)$ gives (14).

11. Throughout the analysis, we assume that the equilibrium is unique.

12. An open-loop equilibrium is one in which strategies are based on the infor-mation set at the start of the game. The Stackelberg terminology is used to refer to the presence of a dominant player (here, the government) who takes into account the effect of his own behavior on the behavior of his rivals (in this case, private agents).

13. A closed-loop equilibrium is supported by strategies based on current in-formation. The Nash equilibrium concept means that each player chooses his or her best course of action, taking other players' actions as given.

14. There is still much debate about why inflation per se should be regarded as

costly. Plausible candidates include the costs of making more trips to the bank (the so-called shoe-leather effects of inflation), the costs of adjusting prices (menu costs), and the costs of keeping the tax system inflation neutral. A recent survey of the debate is provided by Driffill, Mizon, and Ulph (1989). The quantity Λ_π may be interpreted as the optimal rate of taxation on cash balances.

15. In the present context, (16) is most appropriately motivated by appealing to a model of long-term nominal wage contracts.

16. The private sector's budget constraints, (2) and (3), become $c_1 + b_1 + B_1 + m_1 = e$ and $c_2 + m_2 = rb_1 + R(1 - \pi)B_1 + (1 - \pi)m_1 + (1 - \tau)\alpha n_2$. If we were to repeat the earlier analysis, it would be necessary to include m_1 in the utility function as well as m_2.

17. This is to abstract from capital controls and the like which increase the feasibility of running independent monetary and exchange-rate policies.

18. Related analyses are conducted by Hillier and Malcolmson (1984) and Rogers (1986).

19. Notice also that $[\Lambda/(1 - \Lambda)]'$ is increasing in ξ_m: a higher ex-ante elasticity of saving, by motivating a lower ex-ante optimal inflation tax, implies larger cash balance holdings and a greater incentive to raise inflation ex post, which is offset by a larger bias in favor of capitalists.

20. This assumption is not innocuous. Without it, we would encounter the chain store paradox where in the solution of the game unravels backwards, yielding the one-shot discretionary equilibrium in all periods.

21. Rogoff (1987) discusses this point at length.

22. The cheating strategy is $\tilde{\pi}_i = \hat{\pi}_i$, yielding the payoff $\bar{u}_i = v(\tilde{\pi},\tilde{\pi}) = -\hat{u}_i$.

23. The value of π^s is determined from the equality conditions $U_i^s = \hat{U}_i$ ($i = 1,2$). These deliver two values, $\pi^{s'}$ for $i = 1$ and π^s for $i = 2$. The reader may verify that $\pi^{s'} < \pi^s < \hat{\pi}_1$ so that π^s is preferred signal.

24. It will be noted that the probability ϑ_i is unchanged between periods. An extension of the game to include an updating rule for ϑ_i is considered shortly.

25. Although this may seem an implausible characterization of policymaking, it is a feature that is specific to the structure of the model and can be removed by suitable respecification without altering the broad conclusions of the analysis.

26. This is the case for a sufficiently small value of Λ_{2l}.

27. The particular evolution of the game depends on the particular values of certain parameters. For example, a higher initial reputation, a lower rate of discount, and a longer time horizon make the zero inflation outcome more likely and last longer.

28. The scheme studied by Canzoneri (1985) involves the public assigning confidence intervals to monetary policy, raising expectations if inflation is observed to lie outside of these intervals.

29. For example, one candidate may be more able than another in instituting trade union legislation or tax reform.

30. These payoffs are computed using $E\eta_{lt+1} = \chi_{lt}$ and $E\eta_{Ot+1} = 0$. Hence, $u(\hat{\pi},\chi_{lt},1) = -(\Lambda_1/2)\hat{\pi}^2 + \Lambda_2\chi_{lt} + \Lambda_3$ and $u(\hat{\pi},0,0) = -(\Lambda_1/2)\hat{\pi}^2$.

31. The quantity y^s is determined from the condition $U(y^s, \chi^-) = V(\chi^-)$. This is the least costly signal.

32. In a pooling equilibrium, both the incumbent and opponent look alike so that each one has the same probability of being elected.

33. Evidence to support this view can be found in Alesina and Sachs (1988), Beck (1982a), and Havrilesky (1987).

34. The reasons why this might be so are taken up shortly.

35. Useful accounts of this view are given by Beck (1982b), Hetzel (1985), and Woolley (1984).

36. On the relationship between central banks and governments, see Beck (1982b), Havrilesky (1988), Hetzel (1985), Kane (1980, 1982), Weintraub (1978), and Woolley (1984).

37. See, for example, Acheson and Chant (1972, 1973).

38. This has its roots in the seminal contribution by Sargent and Wallace (1981).

39. Hence, g_t is government expenditure, $m_t = M_t/P_t$ is real money balances, $b_t = B_t/P_t$ is real government debt, $1 - \pi_t = P_t/P_{t+1}$ is the gross rate of deflation, $r_t = R_t(1 - \pi_t)$ is the real gross rate of interest, and R_t is the gross nominal rate of interest.

REFERENCES

Acheson, Keith, and Chant, John F. 1972. "The Choice of Monetary Instrument and the Theory of Bureaucracy." *Public Choice* 12: 13–33.

———. 1973. "Bureaucratic Theory and the Choice of Central Bank Goals." *Journal of Money, Credit and Banking* 5: 637–55.

Alesina, Alberto. 1987. "Macroeconomic Policy in a Two Party System as a Repeated Game." *Quarterly Journal of Economics* 102: 651–78.

———. 1988. "Credibility and Policy Convergence in a Two Party System with Rational Voters." *American Economic Review* 78: 796–805.

———, and Cukierman, Alex. 1988. "The Politics of Ambiguity." NBER Working Paper No. 2468.

———, and Tabellini, Guido. 1987a. "Rules and Discretion with Non-coordinated Monetary and Fiscal Policy." *Economic Inquiry* 25: 619–30.

———. 1987b. "A Political Theory of Fiscal Deficits and Government Debt in a Democracy." NBER Working Paper No. 2308.

———. 1988. "Credibility and Politics." *European Economic Review* 32: 542–50.

———, and Sachs, Jeffrey. 1988. "Political Parties and the Business Cycle in the United States, 1948–1984." *Journal of Money, Credit and Banking* 20: 63–82.

Backus, David, and Driffill, E. John. 1985a. "Inflation and Reputation." *American Economic Review* 75: 530–38.

———. 1985b. "Rational Expectations and Policy Credibility Following a Change in Regime." *Review of Economic Studies* 52: 211–22.

Barro, Robert J. 1986. "Reputation in a Model of Monetary Policy with Incomplete Information." *Journal of Monetary Economics* 17: 3–20.

———, and Gordon, David B. 1983a. "A Positive Theory of Monetary Policy in a Natural Rate Model." *Journal of Political Economy* 91: 589–610.

———. 1983b. "Rules, Discretion and Reputation in a Model of Monetary Policy." *Journal of Monetary Economics* 12: 101–22.

Beck, Nathaniel. 1982a. "Parties, Administrations and American Macroeconomic Outcomes." *American Political Science Review* 26: 83–93.

———. 1982b. "Presidential Influence on the Federal Reserve." *American Journal of Political Science* 26: 83–93.

Blackburn, Keith. 1987. "International Policy Games in a Simple Macroeconomic Model with Incomplete Information: Some Problems of Credibility, Secrecy and Cooperation." In *Game Theory and Policy Coordination in Open Economies*, edited by C. Carrero and F. Giavazzi. Venice, Italy: University of Venice.

———. 1988. "Collapsing Exchange Rate Regimes and Exchange Rate Dynamics: Some Further Examples." *Journal of International Money and Finance* 7: 373–85.

———, and Christensen, Michael. 1989. "Monetary Policy and Policy Credibility— Theories and Evidence." *Journal of Economic Literature* 17: 1–45.

———. 1990. "Equilibrium Policies in Interdependent Monetary Economies." University of Southampton. Mimeo.

Calvo, Guillermo. 1978. "On the Time Consistency of Optimal Policy in a Monetary Economy." *Econometrica* 46: 1411–28.

———. 1988. "Servicing the Public Debt: The Role of Expectations." *American Economic Review* 78: 647–61.

Canzoneri, Matthew B. 1985. "Monetary Policy Games and the Role of Private Information." *American Economic Review* 75: 1056–70.

———, and Gray, Jo Anne. 1985. "Monetary Policy Games and the Consequences of Non-cooperative Behaviour." *International Economic Review* 26: 547–64.

———, and Henderson, Dale. 1988. "Is Sovereign Policy Making Bad?" *Carnegie-Rochester Conference Series on Public Policy* 28: 93–140.

———. 1991. *Monetary Policy in Interdependent Economies: A Game Theoretic Approach.* Cambridge, Mass.: MIT Press.

Cukierman, Alex. 1985. "Central Bank Behaviour and Credibility—Some Recent Developments." Federal Reserve Bank of St. Louis. Mimeo.

———, and Meltzer, Allan H. 1985. "A Theory of Ambiguity, Credibility and Inflation under Discretion and Asymmetric Information." *Econometrica* 54: 1099–1128.

———. 1989. "A Political Theory of Government Debt and Deficits in a Neo-Ricardian Framework." *American Economic Review* 79, 713–32.

Driffill, E. John. 1988. "Macroeconomic Policy Games with Incomplete Information: A Survey." *European Economic Review* 32: 533–41.

———. 1987. "Macroeconomic Policy Games with Incomplete Information: Extensions and Generalisations." University of Southampton. Mimeo.

———, Mizon, Graham E., and Ulph, Alistair. 1989. "The Costs of Inflation." In *Handbook of Monetary Economics*, edited by B. M. Friedman and F. H. Hahn. Amsterdam: North-Holland.

Fellner, William. 1976. "Towards a Reconstruction of Macroeconomics—Problems of Theory and Policy." American Enterprise Institute.

———. 1979. "The Credibility Hypothesis and Rational Expectations: Implications of the Gramlich Study." *Brookings Papers on Economic Activity* 1: 167–89.

Fischer, Stanley. 1986a. "Time Consistent Monetary and Fiscal Policy: A Survey." Cambridge, Mass.: Massachusetts Institute of Technology. Mimeo.

————. 1986b. "International Macroeconomic Policy Coordination." NBER Working Paper No. 2244.

————. 1980. "Dynamic Inconsistency, Cooperation and the Benevolent Dissembling Government." *Journal of Economic Dynamics and Control* 2: 93–107.

Flood, Robert P., and Garber, Peter M. 1984. "Collapsing Exchange Rate Regimes: Some Linear Examples." *Journal of International Economics* 17: 1–13.

Hamada, Koichi. 1976. "A Strategic Analysis of Monetary Interdependence." *Journal of Political Economy* 84: 677–700.

Havrilesky, Thomas. 1987. "A Partisan Theory of Fiscal and Monetary Regimes." *Journal of Money, Credit and Banking* 19: 308–25.

————. 1988. "Monetary Policy Signalling from the Administration to the Federal Reserve." *Journal of Money, Credit and Banking* 20: 83–101.

Hetzel, Robert L. 1985. "The Formulation of Monetary Policy." Federal Reserve Bank of Richmond. Mimeo.

Hillier, Brian, and Malcolmson, James M. 1984. "Dynamic Inconsistency, Rational Expectations and Optimal Government Policy." *Econometrica* 52: 1437–51.

Hughes-Hallett, Andrew J. 1986. "International Policy Design and the Sustainability of Policy Bargains." *Journal of Economic Dynamics and Control* 10: 469–94.

————. 1987. "The Impact of Interdependence on Economic Policy Design: The Case of the US, EEC, and Japan." *Economic Modelling* 4: 377–96.

Kane, Edward J. 1980. "Politics and Fed. Policy Making: The More Things Change, the More They Remain the Same." *Journal of Monetary Economics* 6: 199–212.

————. 1982. "External Pressure and the Operation of the Fed." In *Political Economy of International and Domestic Monetary Relations*, edited by R. E. Lombra and W. E. Witte. Iowa City: Iowa State University Press.

Kydland, Finn, and Prescott, Edward C. 1977. "Rules Rather Than Discretion: The Inconsistency of Optimal Plans." 1977. *Journal of Political Economy* 85: 473–93.

Levine, Paul, and Currie, David A. 1987. "Does International Macroeconomic Policy Coordination Pay and Is It Sustainable? A Two Country Analysis." *Oxford Economic Papers* 39: 38–74.

Lucas, Robert E. 1976. "Econometric Policy Evaluation: A Critique." *Carnegie-Rochester Conference Series on Public Policy* 1: 19–46.

————, and Stokey, Nancy L. 1983. "Optimal Fiscal and Monetary Policy in an Economy Without Capital." *Journal of Monetary Economics* 12: 55–93.

Miller, Marcus, and Salmon, Mark. 1984. "Policy Coordination and the Time Inconsistency of Optimal Policy in Open Economies." *Economic Journal* (supplement): 124–35.

Nordhaus, William. 1975. "The Political Business Cycle." *Review of Economic Studies* 42: 169–90.

Obstfeld, Maurice. 1986a. "Speculative Attack and the External Constraint in a Maximising Model of the Balance of Payments." *Canadian Journal of Economics* 19: 1–22.

————. 1986b. "Rational and Self-fulfilling Balance of Payments of Payments Crises." *American Economic Review* 76: 72–81.

Oudiz, Gilles, and Sachs, Jeffrey. 1984. "Policy Coordination in Industrialised Countries." *Brookings Papers on Economic Activity* 1: 1–77.

Persson, Mats, Persson, Torsten, and Svensson, Lars. 1987. "Time Consistency of Fiscal and Monetary Policy." *Econometrica* 55: 1419–32.

———, and Svensson, Lars. 1984. "Time Consistent Fiscal Policy and Government Cash Flow." *Journal of Monetary Economics* 14: 365–74.

———. 1989. "Why a Stubborn Conservative Would Run a Deficit: Policy with Time Inconsistent Preferences." *Quarterly Journal of Economics* 104: 230–45.

———, and Tabellini, Guido. 1991. *Macroeconomic Policy, Credibility and Politics.* London: Harwood Academic Publishers.

Persson, Torsten. 1988. "Credibility of Macroeconomic Policy: A Broad Survey." *European Economic Review* 32: 524–32.

Phelps, Edmund S. 1967. "Phillips Curves, Expectations of Inflation and Optimal Employment over Time." *Economica* 34: 254–81.

———, and Pollack, Robert A. 1968. "Second Best National Saving and Game Equilibrium Growth." *Review of Economic Studies* 2: 185–99.

Ramsey, Frank P. 1927. "A Contribution to the Theory of Taxation." *Economic Journal* 37: 47–61.

Rogers, Carol A. 1986. "The Effects of Distributive Goals on the Time Inconsistency of Optimal Taxes." *Journal of Monetary Economics* 17: 251–70.

Rogoff, Kenneth. 1985a. "The Optimal Degree of Commitment to an Intermediate Monetary Target." *Quarterly Journal of Economics* 100: 1169–89.

———. 1985b. "Can International Monetary Policy Cooperation Be Counterproductive?" *Journal of International Economics* 25: 1–23.

———. 1987. "Reputational Constraints on Monetary Policy." Carnegie-Rochester Conference Series on Public Policy, Vol. 26, 141–82.

———. 1990. "Equilibrium Political Business Cycles." *American Economic Review* 80: 21–36.

———, and Sibert, Anne. 1988. "Elections and Macroeconomic Policy Cycles." *Review of Economic Studies* 55: 1–16.

Sachs, Jeffrey. 1983. "International Policy Coordination in a Dynamic Macroeconomic Model." NBER Working Paper No. 1166.

Sargent, Thomas J., and Wallace, Neil. 1981. "Some Unpleasant Monetarist Arithmetic." *Federal Reserve Bank of Minneapolis Quarterly Review* 5: 1–17.

Tabellini, Guido. 1986. "Money, Debt and Deficits in a Dynamic Game." *Journal of Economic Dynamics and Control* 8: 427–42.

Vickers, John. 1986. "Signalling in a Model of Monetary Policy with Incomplete Information." *Oxford Economic Papers* 38: 443–55.

Weintraub, Robert. 1978. "Congressional Supervision of Monetary Policy." *Journal of Monetary Economics* 4: 341–62.

Woolley, John. 1984. *Monetary Politics—the Federal Reserve and the Politics of Monetary Policy.* Cambridge, England: Cambridge University Press.

6

MONETARY POLICY AND
BANK REGULATION

Anthony M. Santomero

The second half of the twentieth century has seen dramatic changes in the financial structure of the United States. In a period of two decades, a combination of deregulation and financial innovation has substantially altered the landscape of the financial service industry. As a result, many have begun to question the macroeconomic effects of the changing financial structure. (See, for example, Wojnilower, 1980; Hester, 1982; and Kaufman, 1976.) It has been contended, for example, that the changing financial structure has led to a breakdown in domestic policy conducted by the government itself and the Federal Reserve. In addition, some have claimed that such changes substantially reduce the efficiency of monetary policy specifically.

These questions surrounding the effectiveness of government stabilization policy, and most notably monetary policy, in light of the changing financial structure are reminiscent of a debate in the literature that occurred some thirty years ago. Contributions by Gurley and Shaw (1956) and Pesek and Saving (1969) explored the effect of financial structure on the economy's efficiency. In addition, the significant contributions of Brunner and Meltzer (1968) and Tobin and Brainard (1963) addressed themselves to monetary policy. Although the first set of contributions centered on the effect of changes in the financial structure on macroeconomic equilibrium, the second focused on the transmission mechanism of monetary policy in a financial environment with an advanced intermediary sector.

In light of the dramatic changes that have occurred recently in the U.S. financial environment, these same issues are being raised again and seem to warrant additional attention. Accordingly, this chapter addresses the changes in the financial structure, caused by both changes in bank regulation and regulatory avoidance by the financial sector, and their effect on the viability and efficiency of monetary policy.

It will be argued here that, in a comparative dynamic sense, variations in the quantity of base money by the monetary authority will have the same qualitative effect for a wide range of financial intermediary structures. Bank regulation may indeed alter the value of impact multipliers of monetary policy, but not their signs. In addition, variations in the financial structure precipitated by regulation will alter the variance around the expected value of any monetary equilibrium. Specifically, some financial structures are better than others, in the sense that they reduce the variance of nominal gross national product (GNP) around its expected value for certain types of macroeconomic disturbances. Unfortunately, choosing an optimal structure requires knowledge of the exact nature of disturbances in the economy, for not all financial structures are preferred for all disturbances.

Beyond these results, the present chapter also argues that the underlying stability of the financial structure itself is conditional on the form and substance of bank regulation. Therefore, both the causes and effects of financial crises may be importantly related to the nature and extent of financial regulation. Accordingly, even though the expected sign of monetary policy may be immune from the effects of regulatory change, and the dynamics of the real economy may even be helped by the dampening of the variability of prices for some financial disturbances, some financial structures are more prone to disturbance than others. In the end, micro regulation of the intermediary sector may have wide-reaching effects because of what it achieves at the financial market and institutional level, even more than its effect on macroeconomic transmission coefficients.

The chapter develops these themes in four steps. Section 1 reviews the changing financial structure precipitated by changes in the regulatory environment. It also attempts to address the reasons for this dynamic alteration in the intermediation system. Section 2 attempts to analyze the first-order effects of the variations in the financial system. It begins with necessary conditions for monetary policy to be effective in its impact on nominal GNP. Next it develops a stylized general equilibrium model which indicates that, as long as a stable medium of exchange exists, monetary policy will have the same qualitative effect, that is, the same sign, independent of the intermediation structure that results from bank regulation. Section 3 analyzes the effect of such regulation on the variability of nominal GNP by examining the effect of regulatory change on the variance surrounding the expected nominal GNP target of monetary policy. Here, it demonstrates that the variance of nominal GNP around its expected value is, in general, a function of the financial structure. It also reviews which type of structure is preferred for each type of disturbance on these grounds. Section 4 looks at the issue in another way. Rather than centering on the macroeconomic financial structure issues, it examines the effect of bank regulation on the likelihood of micro level financial disruption requiring policy response. Here, recent work on intermediation theory suggests that this effect of regulation may be far more important than the usual transmission discussions. Section 5 closes with a summary of the discussion and its conclusions.

1. THE RECENT EFFECT OF REGULATION ON THE FINANCIAL SYSTEM

The U.S. financial services industry in general and its depository institutions specifically have gone through a period of transition from a highly regulated structure to one with fewer constraints on both product offerings of depository institutions and their pricing flexibility. This section briefly reviews this evolution using a historical perspective, and proceeds to examine the economic forces motivating such changes.[1]

The Dynamics of Change in the Financial System

The midtwentieth-century U.S. banking structure, which included both substantial product market restrictions on commercial banks and price regulation for all depository institutions, can be traced back to the Glass-Steagall Act of 1933. This law, more properly titled the Banking Act of 1933, separated both commercial and investment banking and is the root of product-price regulation in the United States. In terms of products, the act effectively established product market barriers to entry in the commercial and investment banking businesses by separating deposit-taking activity from securities and underwriting. It also introduced the notion of price legislation by prohibiting interest on demand deposits, a custom that was common prior to the time of enactment. It divided a once integrated industry by severely restricting both the prices and the product lines that commercial banks could offer and by forbidding banking activity within their investment banking counterparts. After much discussion, the commercial banking sector retained trust activity, which was also subject to divestiture.

In the 1940s little was done to challenge this division of the product lines of the banking industry, as the economy of the 1930s and the following war period did not lend itself to experimentation. Thus, it was not until the late 1950s that banking firms tried to broaden their markets through product expansion and limited innovation within the bank itself. Once begun, the process accelerated but always within the severe restrictions of banking regulation on allowable activity. The advent of the widespread use of the holding company form, however, made substantive regulatory avoidance of product line restriction possible. Then, banks wishing to expand their activity could do so through the establishment of a holding company which transcended the bank-specific restrictions and regulations that were relevant to their wholly owned banking subsidiaries.

In 1956 the passage of the Bank Holding Company Act gave the Federal Reserve Board the authority to determine the permissible activities of these multibank holding companies. To some, this was seen as the first step in the regulators' attempt to control the expansion of this form of financial firm. However, to avoid the restrictions imposed on multibank holding companies, many banks exploited a loophole in the law and maintained a one-bank holding company structure that allowed continued expansion of its nonbanking activities without regard to national regulatory approval. The 1970 amendment closed this loophole by requiring that one-bank holding companies adhere to all provisions of the 1956 Bank Holding Company Act. This new law enabled the Federal Reserve Board to maintain closer control over the activities of all commercial bank holding companies, which were, in turn, restricted to those product areas that were consistent with or equivalent to the business of banking. Yet, to a large extent, the law sanctioned the use of a holding company structure to broaden bank activity. It eliminated the incentives to maintain a one-bank holding company structure, and it prompted several banks to expand by acquiring additional banks both domestically, where possible, and internationally.

At the same time, interpretation of federal regulation during the 1970s and 1980s tended to reduce the prohibitions on activity in the banking industry and ratified the ongoing product development within the banking firms. During this time, private placements, mortgage banking, off-balance sheet guarantees, and increasing security market activity were added to the allowable activity of banking organizations. Accordingly, the post–1970 amendment period was one of rapid expansion for major U.S. banking firms with at least tacit regulatory approval.

Product innovation was not the only area of change. The economic environment of the period was one in which price regulation could not survive. From the credit crunch of 1966 to the subsequent period of double-digit inflation, price regulation enforced through Federal Reserve Regulation Q became increasingly bothersome and anachronistic.

Originally passed as a protection device to maintain conservative bank portfolios, the restriction of allowable interest-rate payments to depositors dates back to the same Glass-Steagall Act of 1933 referred to above. At that time, Congress prohibited interest on demand deposits, and the seeds of price regulation were sown. Yet, the importance of price controls of bank activity was minimal until the inflation of the 1970s. At that time, restrictions on savings deposit interest payments, under Regulation Q, and the prohibition of interest on demand deposits by statute lead to disintermediation at both commercial banks and the thrift industry.

Through the use of offshore deposits such as the Eurodollar market, the impact of price constraints was substantially blunted, at least for large banks and corporations. However, small depositors had no recourse. In addition, within the banking industry itself, regional and community banks felt the effects of price restriction rather severely. The use of NOW accounts, a negotiable order of withdrawal from an alleged savings deposit account, proved to be a convenient initial regulatory loophole, first for New England banks and then for the other institutions along the East Coast. But the allowable interest rate on NOW deposits could not keep pace with the ever-rising nominal interest rates available in the financial markets. Aware of this situation, the securities industry quickly moved in by supplying depository substitutes. For the consumers of financial services, the entry of these firms, through the introduction of money market mutual funds and cash management accounts, proved to be an effective mechanism to avoid onerous rate limits in a time of double-digit inflation. For them, money market mutual funds proved to be an efficient deposit substitute with many of the benefits of depository products but a far better return. For the suppliers in this market it meant substantial disintermediation.

Recognizing the futility of the regulation of price in a dynamic financial market, the Depository Institution Deregulation and Monetary Control Act of 1980 initiated steps to eliminate rate ceilings within the industry. Immediately, consumer NOW accounts were made legal on a nationwide basis. In addition, the act established a board to phase in the total deregulation of all liability prices. This became a reality in 1986, whereupon the committee freed all savings deposit prices and ceased to exist. As a result, for the first time in post-depression U.S. history the banking sector is completely free of price restrictions of any kind.[2]

Spurred on by these newfound freedoms, banking firms, particularly those located in major financial centers, increased their presence on the national scene. This very fact attracted the attention of out-of-state legislators who sought to bring the increased employment potential of money center bank activity to their economically stagnant markets. Accordingly, some states welcomed out-of-state banking institutions in the 1980s to the extent that they provided employment opportunities. The key elements that such locations offered large banking institutions were attractive regulation and low operating costs in terms of land, labor, and taxation. By design, legislation was passed aimed at expanding the permissible activities of banking firms and entry by out-of-state institutions, frequently requiring that their activities be conducted only with out-of-state clients.

In addition, the boundary between the commercial and investment banking industries more or less dissolved. The product lines of each part of the financial service industry have become even more intertwined. Investment banks have expanded into a relatively large segment of the retail banking market with the introduction of the mass market distribution of various types of mutual funds, CMA accounts, and most recently their own, fixed-rate liabilities. Similarly, commercial banks have expanded their corporate banking activities in private placements, corporate finance, and commercial paper. The main recipients of this expansion have been money center banks, but major regional firms have also garnered an appreciable market share.

At the beginning of this decade, then, the U.S. industry was quite different than it had been only fifty years earlier. Banks had expanded into a substantially larger product area than the writers of post-depression legislation had envisioned. They now offer a wider array of corporate banking services and have attracted a larger set of retail customers. The former services, offered through a subsidiary of the bank or holding company, include the de facto underwriting of commercial paper and private placement. These activities are increasingly beginning to resemble investment banking. At the consumer level, trust and investment activity has expanded, and the industry is fully competitive in the area of fixed-rate liability offerings. In this regard the expanded liability products were aimed at a broader segment of household savings.

The industry's evolution continues. Banks are still pushing the boundaries of Glass-Steagall in the move to become full-service institutions. Recently, this objective received a substantial boost by interpretations of the 1933 act which would allow the major banks to engage in limited security underwriting through affiliates. The Supreme Court let stand the Federal Reserve Board's approval for commercial bank affiliates to underwrite commercial paper, municipal revenue bonds, and securities backed by mortgages and consumer debt under the condition that a bank affiliate's underwriting be limited. The industry therefore has increased ability to sell financial assets into the marketplace after origination, rather than hold them to be financed by savings deposits. Accordingly, the very foundation of the industry, as one in which credit is supported by deposit gathering, has been shaken.[3]

As the above review shows, the American banking scene has changed a great deal. Price regulation is a thing of the past. The old lines dividing commercial from investment banking are quickly eroding. State boundaries, too, have fallen to regional banking trends and the quick evolution to interstate banking. This history is a fairly idiosyncratic one created by the historical structure and regulation of American banking. Yet, the forces that led to the decline in the regulation of both product and price are universal. Understanding them is a prerequisite to understanding the institutional evolution reported. Accordingly, next we attempt to discuss the forces that produced the changes.

The Forces of Change in U.S. Financial Markets

The motive forces behind the evolution of the U.S. banking system appear to center around two fundamental issues that financial service reg-

ulators did not appreciate. First, prices cannot be arbitrarily set in a competitive financial market. To do so leads either to regulatory avoidance or
disintermediation. In the last two decades we have seen both occur. Second,
the product line offered to the industry's natural constituents, firms and
households, cannot be arbitrarily segmented across industry lines. The
attempts to do so were inherently inefficient and opened the way for economic forces consistent with an expansion in the product line offered by
various financial entities. Ultimately, technology made both geography and
product definition less meaningful as a constraint on the delivery system
of financial services. In most cases, this has resulted in an environment
with increased competition, more efficient pricing, and a reduction in the
number of competitors in the industry as a whole.

It should have been apparent that price regulation could not have worked
in an open and competitive market such as that which exists for financial
services. Such regulation requires monopoly positions by the regulated
firms. To the extent that substitute products are available, either in other
locales or across industry boundaries, price regulation is doomed to failure.
This was seen quite early in the development of the Eurodollar market for
large corporate customers. It was also evident in the explosion of money
market mutual fund deposits and the resultant turnaround of the mutual
fund industry that it caused. Forced by such innovations, it was but a matter
of time until price regulation was abandoned on the liability side of the
bank's balance sheet.

In the area of product restrictions, too, it should have been evident as
early as 1933 that the arbitrary division of products offered to the banking
industry's natural constituents was doomed to failure. In any case, as the
previous section recounts, banks sought to expand their product menu to
satisfy customer needs. This was done first by an expansion into corporate
banking services with longer maturity instruments in areas such as the
private placement of middle market lending and the use of venture pools.
This expansion was followed by a realization that a substantial portion of
investment banking activity was essentially a substitute for the lending
function, even at the short end of the maturity spectrum. Commercial paper
facilitation and Euromarket syndication are clear cases of loan alternatives
into which commercial banks have sought entrance.

At the consumer level the same process was at work. Increasingly, household portfolio choice was viewed as hampered by arbitrary restrictions
along industry activity lines. The simple savings account gave way to a
complex array of portfolio options, only a few of which were previously
viewed as allowable activities for commercial banks. Institutions that refused to innovate found themselves losing household market shares to a
securities industry that adapted well to the consumer's desire for participation in a wider array of debt instruments and access to the equity market.
Mutual funds, money market funds, and tax-deferred or tax-exempt in-

struments all developed as an alternative to the previously rather staid and increasingly obsolete bank savings vehicles. Banks had little choice but to pattern their evolution on their customers' needs for greater savings vehicle flexibility.

2. THE EFFECT OF FINANCIAL STRUCTURE ON THE EXPECTED IMPACT OF MONETARY POLICY

As the above makes clear, the financial structure has undergone substantial change in the post-depression U.S. economy. Many analysts have therefore begun to conclude that monetary policy is slowly but surely losing its ability to control the economy. To see if this is indeed the case, here we will attempt to evaluate the feasibility and effectiveness of monetary policy in several steps. First, we review the necessary conditions for monetary policy to have an effect on a macroeconomy of whatever type. Next, we try to sketch a simple model in which to evaluate the impact of these recent changes on the viability and efficiency of monetary policy. Third and finally, we use this model to address the question of whether financial structure matters in the ability of the monetary policy to affect the aggregate economy.

The Necessary Conditions for Effective Monetary Policy

To analyze the effect of financial structure on monetary policy, we must begin with a fundamental understanding of the necessary conditions that must exist in any economy to allow a central bank to affect nominal GNP. In this regard a recent paper by Fama (1983) is an effective starting point. Drawing on earlier work by Patinkin (1961) and Black (1981), Fama argues that there are three necessary conditions for the central bank to be effective in changing the real value of a unit of account through manipulation of the reserve base.

1. The unit of account must have no perfect substitutes.
2. The unit of account must pay a fixed rate of interest.
3. The unit of account must be dominated by alternative financial assets.

These three conditions are essentially the same as those stated by Tobin (1969), in which he argued that the existence of a demand function for money in real terms is a sufficient condition for open market operations to have an effect. In essence, the central bank must have control of a nominal asset with a fixed rate of return, which is exchanged at face value in terms of the unit of accounts. Such an asset will generally serve as the medium of exchange in transactions because of its features. Satisfying the

Patinkin, Tobin, Fama conditions implies that the central bank, through the control of the supply of the unit of account, can control nominal GNP.[4]

It would appear that all forms of the U.S. financial structure that have existed over this century can be characterized by these three conditions. There is a unit of account, without substitute. For some transactions both this unit of account and representative substitutes, such as deposit balances, can be used but not for all. In any case, households have real demand for currency for transactions purposes that cannot be perfectly substituted for by deposit liabilities. In addition, the financial intermediary sector has a real demand function for high-powered money, driven by the stochastic demand for deposit conversion, and to satisfy legal reserve requirements.[5] For a number of technical reasons,[6] this currency or high-powered money pays a fixed, zero, rate of interest. Although many have speculated on the nature of a system with positive and variable interest-rate payments on reserve, the zero interest rate paid on the quantity of both reserves and currency in circulation clearly satisfies condition three above. It, therefore, seems reasonable to accept the view that the current system is one in which monetary policy can be effective in determining the value of nominal GNP.[7]

Note that nominal GNP is assumed to be the relevant variable to be controlled. As this is the product of the nominal price level and real GNP, the ability to control this quantity is not a sufficient description of the dynamics of the economy. However, to be more precise requires knowledge of the division between the real and monetary effects of high-powered money variation. In a full-employment general equilibrium model, output is constant and the nominal price level changes. In the pure Keynesian framework, the reverse is true. Since we know little about the underlying dynamics of this mix, euphemistically known as the Phillips curve relationship,[8] the goal of policy will be taken to be the stabilization of nominal GNP. In the model below, this is captured by looking at the comparative static effects of regulation on price-level variability, under the assumption of constant real output. Any combination of price and output variability could have been chosen with no loss in generality.

If we accept the fact that monetary policy is viable in general, the next question we must ask is how various types of financial intermediaries impact on the transmission mechanism. This query can be addressed in several ways, each of which is discussed below. At the first level of analysis, this section investigates whether the sign of the transmission mechanism between high-powered money stock and the expected value of nominal GNP is independent of the exact nature of the financial intermediary structure. That is to say, can it be shown that variations in high-powered money will alter the nominal price level, in a full-employment model, in the same direction independent of the financial structure and conditional only on the absence of subsequent disturbances?

The work of Santomero and Siegel (1982) directly addressed this issue and is drawn on here. Building on the work of Brainard and Tobin (1963) and Brunner and Meltzer (1972), their approach was to look at the implications of a variation in high-powered money within a rather small, general equilibrium model. To see the nature of this framework and its insights, the next section develops the general equilibrium model.

A General Equilibrium Framework for Financial Analysis

Assume a financial environment in which there are $\eta + 2$ asset markets: one market each for high-powered (base money); $\eta - 1$ types of intermediary product markets and markets for bonds and equity. There are, therefore, $\eta + 2$ markets, numbered as follows.

- The high-powered money (H) market is market 0.
- The intermediary product or deposit markets (D_i) are markets $1 \ldots \eta - 1$.[9]
- The bond (B) market is market η.
- The equity (E) market is market $\eta + 1$.

There are four types of economic agents in the economy: households, financial institutions, firms, and the government. The household is assumed to have demand functions for all assets subject to the aggregate budget constraint for the sector. Members of the intermediary sector may hold high-powered money, other depository institutions' products or deposits, and direct asset claims, defined here as bonds. These market demand and supply functions will be a function of regulation and regulatory avoidance, as outlined above. In addition, the number of financial products and markets are a result of a given regulatory regime. All that is necessary here is that the resultant derived demand functions can be written in general form as below. Within this framework, firms issue equity to support capital ownership, and because of the Modigliani-Miller Theorem their bond issuances (if any) are suppressed. Finally, the government is the sole net supplier of bonds and high-powered money, which are viewed as net wealth.[10]

In essence, each financial regulation regime should be viewed as possessing a different set of equations that are unique to the form and substance of regulation. This view of the financial sector can be characterized as a set of equilibrium conditions for each of the above assets which are conditional on the regulatory regime and the nature of the intermediary structure.

In all the equations that follow, all demands and supplies (except the supply of high-powered money), income, and wealth are expressed in real terms. For the high-powered money market, H, the market equilibrium condition is

$$(1) \quad H_h^d(r_{D_i}, r_b, r_E, Y, W) + \sum_{i=1}^{n-1} H_{F_i}^d(r_{D_i}, r_b) = H^s/P,$$

where subscript h denotes household demand functions, r_{D_i} is the vector of i deposit rates, r_b is the bond rate, r_E is the equity rate, Y is real income, W is real wealth, $H_{F_i}^d$ is the demand of the ith financial institution (assumed, for simplicity, to issue the ith product) for high-powered money (reserves) under a given regulatory regime, H^s is the nominal supply of base money, and P is the price level. The equilibrium condition for the market for each internal financial asset, D_i, is

$$(2) \quad D_{ih}^d(r_{D_i}, r_b, r_E, Y, W) + \sum_{\substack{j=1 \\ j \neq 1}}^{n-1} D_{iFj}^d(r_{D_i}, r_b) = D_i^s(r_{D_i}, r_b); \; i = 1 \ldots n - 1,$$

where D_{iFj}^d is the demand of the jth financial institution for the ith deposit product, conditional on the regulatory structure relevant to the economy in question. The equilibrium condition for the bond market is

$$(3) \quad B_h^d(r_{D_i}, r_b, r_E, Y, W) + \sum_{i=1}^{n-1} B_{F_i}^d(r_{D_i}, r_b) = B_g^s,$$

where $B_{F_i}^d$ is the demand of the ith financial institution for bonds and B_g^s is the real supply of government bonds.[11] Similarly, the equilibrium condition for the equity market is

$$(4) \quad E_h^d(r_{D_i}, r_b, r_E, Y, W) = E^s,$$

where E^s is the fixed capital stock K.

The budget constraints for the household, any specific depository institution structure, and firm sectors are

$$(5) \quad H_h^d + \sum_{i=1}^{n-1} D_{ih}^d + B_h^d + E_h^d = W = B_g^s + H/P + K,$$

$$(6) \quad H_{F_i}^d + \sum_{j=1}^{n-1} D_{jF_i}^d + B_{F_i}^d = D_i^s; \; i = 1 \ldots n - 1,$$

$$(7) \quad E^d = E^s = K.$$

As is readily apparent, the differential effect of bank regulation alters the size and sensitivity of equation (6) but may not violate the budget constraint that pertains to a specific regulatory structure.[12] For example, if we were to compare two regimes with differential reserve requirements on specific institutions, the $H_{F_i}^d$ would be different for each institution, as would its demands for bonds, $B_{F_i}^d$, and other financial institutions products, $D_{jF_i}^d$. In either case, however, the institution would still be subject to its appropriate budget constraint.

Simplification of the System

The view of depository and nondepository financial institutions and markets in the general equilibrium framework of equations (1)–(4) is most general and as such suffers from some difficulty of manipulation. To lend substance and to simplify the subsequent analysis, more specific assumptions about the determination of asset rates are in order. In considering the nature of financial institutions' products and deposit liabilities, two distinct types emerge. First, the rates of some deposits are set primarily by the traditional price regulation outlined above, at some fixed level. This was the case historically for such liabilities as bank demand deposits and passbook savings accounts. Second, for some products yields move closely with open-market rates. Money Market Mutual Fund balances fall into this category, as do other bank products and liabilities tied to general money market rates. For such products, the institution pays the depositor a market-based return less some average transactions account fee, average cost, or spread that reflects the bank's monopoly position.[13] Because the observable financial structures appear to exhibit such pricing schemes, the current analysis takes these as an institutional reality.

These pricing schemes make the quantity supplied of these products dependent solely on the demand for them at the given vector of rates. The size of these depository markets, therefore, is demand determined, so that $D_i^s \equiv D_h^d$. Hence, the budget constraint for each institution and/or product may be written as

$$(8) \quad H_{F_i}^d + \sum_{j=1}^{n-1} D_{jF_i}^d + B_{F_i}^d, = D_{ih}^d, \quad i = 1, \ldots n - 1,$$

where D_{ih}^d is evaluated at the fixed r_{Di} or at the deterministic relationship between r_{Di} and r_b (denoted $r_{Di} = \psi_i(r_b)$). In either case the number of equations in the system is reduced from $n + 2$ to 3.

Next, we define the ratio of high-powered money demanded to each product or deposit supplied from each financial institution as $\hat{k}_i (\hat{k}_i \geq 0)$. In any regulatory framework, this will be a function of the bond rate, that is, the opportunity cost of reserves, and the promised yield on the product,

$$(9) \quad \hat{k}_i \equiv \frac{H^d_{F_i}}{D^s_i} = \hat{k}_i(r_b;r_{D_i}).$$

The vector of rates r_{D_i} can be parameterized on the degree of government regulation and the bond rate. Similarly, we define the ratio of the jth deposit demanded by the ith institution $D^d_{jF_i}$ to the ith supplied as d_{ji}, which can be denoted as

$$(10) \quad d_{ji} \equiv \frac{D^d_{jF_i}}{D^s_{F_i}} = d_{ji}(r_b;r_{D_i}).$$

From the budget constraint in equation (8), we have

$$(11) \quad \hat{k}_i + \sum_{j=1}^{n-1} d_{ji} + b_i = 1 \text{ for } i = 1, \ldots n - 1,$$

where $b_i \equiv B^d_{F_i}/D^s_{F_i}$ is the ratio of bonds demanded by the ith institution to deposits supplied.

The system of equations (2)–(4) can now be written as

$$(12) \quad H^d_h(r_b,r_E,Y,W; r_{D_i}) + \sum_{i=1}^{n-1} \hat{k}_i(r_b; r_{D_i}) D^d_{ih}(r_b,r_E,Y,W; r_{D_i})$$

$$+ \sum_{i=1}^{n-1} \sum_{\substack{j=1 \\ j \neq 1}}^{n-1} \hat{k}_j(r_b; r_{D_i})d_{ji} (r_b; r_{D_i})D^d_{ih} (r_b,r_E,Y,W; r_{D_i}) = H^s/P,$$

$$(13) \quad B^d_h(r_b,r_E,Y,W; r_{D_i}) + \sum_{\substack{i=1 \\ j \neq i}}^{n-1} \sum_{\substack{j=1 \\ j \neq 1}}^{n-1} (1 - \hat{k}_i(r_b; r_{D_i})$$

$$- \hat{k}_j(r_b; r_{D_i})d_{ji} (r_b; r_{D_i}))D^d_{ih} (r_b,r_E,Y,W;r_{D_i}) = B^s_g,$$

$$(14) \quad E^d_h(r_b,r_E,Y,W; r_{D_i}) = K.$$

The third term in equation (12) includes the derived demand for high-powered money owing to the intradepositing within the financial institution sector.[14]

It is convenient to define a reduced-form reserve ratio, which includes both the reserves supporting the household sector's deposits and the reserves supporting a financial institution's deposits at other institutions. We denote this general reserve ratio as k_i, where

(15) $k_i(r_b; r_{D_i}) = \hat{k}_i + \sum\limits_{\substack{j=1 \\ j \neq i}}^{n-1} \hat{k}_j d_{ji}.$

Further, we define D_o as currency so that k_o equals unity, and D_n as bonds with k_n equal to 0. Therefore, equations (12)–(14) can be written compactly as

(16) $\sum\limits_{i=0}^{n} k_i(r_b; r_{D_i}) \, D_{ih}^d(r_b, r_E, Y, W; r_{D_i}) = H^s/P,$

(17) $\sum\limits_{i=0}^{n} (1 - k_i(r_b; r_{D_i})) \, D_{ih}^d(r_b, r_E, Y, W; r_{D_i}) = B_g^s,$

(18) $E_h^d(r_b, r_E, Y, W; r_{D_i}) = K.$

Equations (16)–(18) are the financial market equilibrium conditions in an overall macrofinancial model. The endogenous variables are Y, r_b, P, and r_E. Assume that the real sector determines Y and r_E. In this case, the financial structure determines the price level, P, and the rate of interest r_b.[15] By Walras' Law only two of the three equations in system (16)–(18) are independent; we can therefore write the system as equations (16) and (17), with (18) determined by the system's budget constraint. The work of Santomero and Siegel (1981, 1982) suggests that the two equilibrium conditions have more intuitive appeal if they are written as the excess demand for high-powered money, equation (16), and the excess demand for all liquid financial assets, defined as all financial assets less equity, equations (16) plus (17). This is represented by

(19) $H^d \equiv \sum\limits_{i=0}^{n} k_i D_{ih}^d = H^s/P,$

(20) $A^d \equiv \sum\limits_{i=0}^{n} D_{ih}^d = H^s/P + B_g^s.$

Equilibrium in the economy exists when the total demand for liquid assets, denoted A^d (currency, all deposits, plus bonds), equals the supply (high-powered money plus government bonds) and the reserve weighted demand for these liquid assets, denoted H^d, equals the supply of high-powered money.

Implications for the Expected Effect of Monetary Policy

As can be seen from the above, independent of the exact nature of the regulatory structure, the financial system can be characterized by a small set of equilibrium conditions, equations (19) and (20). As long as we can define a set of demand functions that result from the banks' optimizing behavior within a given regulatory structure, we can derive such excess demand functions for financial assets, including the high-powered money. These reduced-form equations can be shown to be sufficient to assure the potency of monetary policy. In any such system, variations in H^s in equations (19) and (20) will alter the equilibrium value of the endogenous variables P and r_b, for a given r_E and Y. A sufficient condition for the potency of standard monetary policy in this deterministic monetary model is that the k_i functions are well behaved and exhibit standard demand function conditions.[16]

Beyond this, it can also be shown that such potency remains even when the real sector is added to this analysis. Consider the interaction of the above financial system with a flow real sector. The flow real sector is assumed to be characterized by equilibrium of real output supply, Y^s, and the aggregate demand for such output. In this full-employment version of such a model, we define Y^s as real potential output supply, and we assume that demand may be captured by a simple commodity expenditure function, which is determined by the real rate of return on capital. Evaluating the return on capital at equilibrium, we may write this underlying real sector equilibrium condition as

(21) $Y^s = C(r_E)$.

Equation (21) can be seen as a reduced form of IS curve of the real sector equilibrium. This flow equation is the counterpart of the standard macroequilibrium typical of a general equilibrium, full-employment model or Keynesian "vertical cross."

The real sector may be joined with the financial sector of equations (19) and (20) by converting these equations into equilibrium conditions in the same $[r_E P]$ space. In these two dimensions, the financial equilibrium condition that results from the financial sector has an upward slope, as contrasted with the horizontal real sector condition:

(22) $\log P = F_E r_E$,

where $F_E = \dfrac{H_B A_E - A_B H_E}{H_p A_B - H_B A_p} > 0$, with subscripts denoting partial deriv-

Figure 6.1
**The General Equilibrium of the Economy in $[r_E P]$ Space from Equations (21)
and (22)**

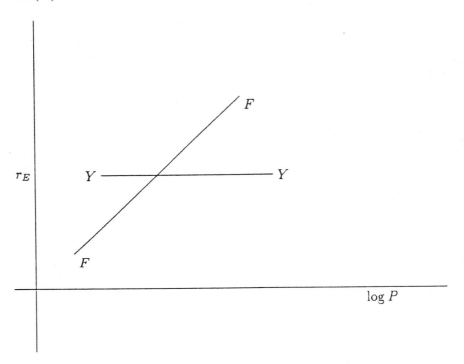

atives of the demand functions with respect to the two endogenous interest rates and (the log of) the aggregate price level. This equilibrium of the economy may be seen in two-dimensional space as Figure 6–1.[17]

As is evident from the above, variations in high-powered money, H^s, will alter the financial equilibrium locus and the resultant consumption-savings division, producing a variation in capital intensity and the aggregate price level. These results are consistent with the seminal work of Metzler (1951), and the standard results of the impact of open market operations in macro texts; see Sargent (1979).

To be sure, the impact effect or "bang per buck" of monetary policy will change, dependent on the financial structure and its effect on the exact k_i functional form. Nonetheless, policy has never been gauged by this criterion. To the extent that policy concern centers on feasibility of policy, the above demonstrates that policy remains potent for all reasonable sets of regulatory structures. The above suggests, therefore, that variations in the reserve base will alter the nominal price level along the qualitative lines consistent with traditional theory. One only needs to view the real and financial sector as driven by such general underlying equilibrium condition contained above.

3. MACROECONOMIC STABILITY ISSUES

The previous section illustrates that the qualitative impact of monetary policy is not reversed by a variation in financial structure as long as the monetary authority can be assured of a stable exchange system in which it controls the fixed-rate medium of exchange and unit of account. This result is substantive, for it should allay the fears of those concerned about policy viability.[18]

Assuring a positive effect of open market operations does not, however, indicate any rank ordering of financial systems and their associated regulatory structure. "Bang per buck" is clearly not an appropriate criterion. As noted above, it has long been recognized that the desirability of a financial structure should not be based on impact multipliers as the monetary authority can costlessly alter the size of its policy variables in a nonstochastic system so as to compensate for any change in the response of the financial system to autonomous shifts. Accordingly, all we can conclude from the above is that monetary policy is still viable in such a deterministic world.

When we move to a stochastic environment, however, the situation changes. To the extent that stochastic disturbances alter the underlying aggregate sectoral demand functions, the responsiveness of the system to such shocks becomes important. If it can be shown that one regulatory framework results in less variation in the economy when it is subject to random disturbances, then one may be able to define one financial structure and associated regulatory framework as preferred to another.

The work of William Poole (1970) is useful here. More than twenty years ago, Poole had pointed out that the failure of the monetary authority to assess accurately the current values of all endogenous variables in an uncertain environment leads one to rank financial strategies. If it can be shown that the output effects of variations that are the result of stochastic disturbances can be mitigated by the choice of financial structure, such alterations may have important and beneficial effects on the real economy. Even if stochastic disturbances in the underlying demand function of the macroeconomy have zero means, the existence of such disturbances causes variations in the economic environment which have detrimental effects on output and social welfare. To the extent that regulatory structure alters the underlying financial excess demand functions above, some regulatory structures may be preferred to others.

The work of Santomero and Siegel (1981) is directly applicable here. As an illustration, consider a situation in which there exists mean zero error terms in the underlying excess demand equations contained in the financial sector, equations (19) and (20), as well as the real sector, equation (21). Linearizing the equilibrium conditions around r_E and $log\ P$, and taking the first and second moments, results in

$$(23) \quad \bar{p} = -\frac{F_E}{C_E}\bar{\epsilon}_R + \bar{\epsilon}_F,$$

$$(24) \quad \sigma_p^2 = (F_E/C_E)^2\sigma_R^2 - 2(F_E/C_E)\sigma_{RF} + \sigma_F^2,$$

where ($\bar{\epsilon}_R$) captures the mean zero real sector disturbances and ($\bar{\epsilon}_F$) represents the composite financial market disturbances. These terms affect the variance around the equilibrium, as shown in equation (24). Unlike the real sector disturbance, however, financial disturbances affect the system through the financial system, and only after relative prices in those markets adjust accordingly. Therefore, the financial sector disturbance term above is a composite error term that includes the random, mean zero, disturbances contained in the $n + 2$ financial market equilibrium conditions and adjustments in the financial sector to such disturbances.[19]

The effect of all disturbances on price variability is a function of the underlying demand elasticities contained in F_E in equation (24).[20] This equation illustrates the relationship between the variance of (the log of) P which is detrimental to social welfare and the underlying stochastic disturbances of the economy. The variance of the price level depends not only on the stochastic disturbances, but also on the sensitivity of the price level to such disturbances.

It should be clear from inspection that the effect of disturbances on the variability of prices depends directly on the elasticities of the system to such disturbances. Accordingly, different bank regulation schemes will result in a different time series of prices for any economy, because such regulation affects the underlying elasticities of the economy to stochastic disturbances. We cannot be more explicit without specific reference to the underlying disturbance, however. It can be shown, for example, that one specific form of regulation is preferred for some stochastic disturbances but exacerbates others. Without specific knowledge of these disturbances, little more can be said.

It might be suggested, however, that, relatively speaking, the more regulated financial environment of the 1950s, in which a limited set of options existed in the financial market, would seem to imply larger impact multipliers for financial disturbances. This is because the vector of rates contained within the financial markets was more severely regulated in those years than in the more deregulated environment of the last two decades. Therefore, endogenous interest rates were not permitted to adjust to demand disturbances to dampen their effects. This result, first pointed out by Santomero and Siegel (1982), suggests that the financial sector should be more stable in the current deregulated environment.

Deregulation, however, implies innovation and close substitutes within the financial sector, which in turn may imply less stability in the underlying financial sector. Accordingly, the financial equilibrium locus contained above may have a larger variance in today's less regulated financial market than in the past. This conclusion is impressionistic, for little is known about such disturbances by definition. All the same, the matter warrants consideration, for it may at least partially offset the beneficial effects on financial sector disturbance propagation.

In terms of the impact of real disturbances, the ratio of F_E/C_E determines the effect on the price variance. A larger absolute value of this ratio will result in a larger utility cost to real sector disturbances. Langohr and Santomero (1984) have shown that increasing deregulation of financial portfolios has just such an effect. Therefore, unlike the previous result, a less regulated financial sector tends to increase the impact of real sector disturbances, and on these grounds it may be viewed as detrimental to the overall economy.

Taken as a whole, the results suggest that the main effect of financial deregulation on the economy may center more on the effect on price dynamics, owing to various disturbances, than on policy viability itself. Financial regulation clearly affects the dynamic behavior of the economy but differentially across different types of stochastic disturbances. In this regard the results mirror the work of Poole (1970) in that regulation is shown to change the economy's reaction to stochastic disturbances, and optimal financial structure can only be defined after full knowledge of the stochastic disturbances affecting the economy.

4. FINANCIAL STABILITY AND FINANCIAL STRUCTURE

Section 2 above suggested that the existence of a financial system in which monetary authorities have control of the fixed-rate medium of exchange is sufficient to assure their capability to control the expected value of nominal GNP. However, the last section indicated that the variation in price around this expected value could be affected by the intermediary structure brought about by regulation. Therefore, such regulation cannot be arbitrarily chosen. Yet, in order to select a preferred regulatory structure, monetary authorities must possess full knowledge of the underlying disturbances to both the real and financial sector and the likelihood of occurrence. As one financial structure does not clearly dominate all others for all disturbances, a single regulatory mechanism cannot be defined unambiguously as preferred to all others for any set of disturbances. Unfortunately, the kind of information that would be required to select regulatory regimes on the basis of their ability to stabilize the macroeconomy is unlikely to be forthcoming. Furthermore, because demand functions change through time, as a result of the forces outlined in Section 1, any regulatory regime that is optimal at one point in time will not necessarily be optimal at a later date. Accordingly, it seems unlikely that an ordinal ranking of regulatory structures can be achieved in this way.

The above notwithstanding, many analysts have suggested that a greater underlying uncertainty is likely to be associated with demand functions in a deregulated environment, in which many substitute products are allowed to flourish, than in a more tightly controlled system. This has led some (Wojnilower, 1980, and Hester, 1982, for example) to the conclusion that a deregulated environment may be destabilizing. However, this argument should not be taken as a sufficient rationale for limiting financial innovation by regulatory fiat. Inasmuch as it can be argued that social welfare has individual utilities and financial efficiency, as well as price variation, a more rigid financial system cannot be shown to improve utility. The rigid system may indeed reduce price variation but only at the expense of output efficiency and private sector welfare.

Indeed, a recent perspective in the financial intermediation literature centers on the importance of the financial structure to individual economic agents and its associated gains to the aggregate economy. Rather than the earlier work on intermediation theory, which concentrated on the role of banks as transaction agents, more recent contributions center on the importance of the financial structure in providing funds for real investment. According to this literature, the real value of these institutions to society is overcoming information problems and facilitating the flow of capital to the real sector. In the modern theory of intermediation, spearheaded by works such as Leland and Pyle (1977), Campbell and Kracaw (1980), and Diamond (1984), the functions performed by intermediaries for agents in the financial markets are essential.

Institutions are viewed as primarily performing two distinct functions. The first of these functions is to evaluate investment opportunities available in the marketplace. Their job is to determine a project proposal's expected return and risk from the data presented by the demander of funds. From this exercise the bank obtains a clearer, more objective view of the proposal presented, owing to its specific capital or information processing capability. In so doing, the bank provides needed funds to the entrepreneur seeking to exploit private and public welfare-improving opportunities. Once investment decisions are made, ongoing monitoring is conducted by the same institutions. In this second role intermediaries insure the maximum probability of efficiency and lender repayment by continually reviewing project data and performance.

The financial structure is, therefore, an essential part of efficiently providing funds for risky investments in a world of imperfect information and cash-starved entrepreneurs. Regulations that enhance its ability to provide this function increase efficiencies, potential output, and long-term capital intensity as well. In fact, a growing portion of the literature centers around the substantial effect disruptions in this channeling of funds can have on an economy. Work by Bernanke (1983) and Bernanke and Gertler (1989) argue, rather convincingly, that one explanation for the severity of the depression was the disruption in the financial structure and the demise of valuable financial intermediaries.[21] Entrepreneurs lost both their own personal wealth that served as a source of funds and the needed intermediary sector that could credibly represent them to investors for additional borrowed funds.

This newer strand of literature suggests that, at the micro level, financial institutions provide an important, indeed critical, function. The economy's well-being depends on their efficiency and their health. Accordingly, the underlying demand functions of the real sector critically depend on the ability of the entrepreneur to obtain funds to gain the positive rate of return on equity.

In the present context, this literature implies that regulation has an enormously important role in the economy. The intermediation process, or more generally the financing process, converts viable investment projects to real sector flow investment demand and future capital stock. By structuring incentives at the micro level, both to provide needed capital to the real sector and to allocate that capital across projects, the regulatory structure is a crucial linkage between savers and investors. The efficiency of the financial sector determines the extent to which economically viable projects can and will be undertaken in a market characterized by imperfect and asymmetric information. A regulatory structure that supports this process aids the economy as a whole and facilitates aggregate investment demand. To the extent that regulation hinders the flow of funds to the entrepreneurial sector, the underlying demand for real goods will decline and capital growth will be slower than in a more efficient system. In essence, the implicit function of equation (21), which leads directly to the variance expression, (24), is conditional on a financial structure.

To state this perspective on regulation in a somewhat more recognizable way, regulatory policy affects the underlying functions of the real sector economy, and any policy analysis must recognize this endogeneity. This is the fundamental insight of the Lucas critique of all policymaking.[22] It is true at the microeconomic structure level as well as the macroeconomic policy level.

Beyond this, regulatory structure also affects the stability of the system itself. To the extent that financial regulation affects the preference for risk taking by the intermediation sector, it determines the underlying character of the stochastic disturbances captured in equation (24) above. The recent work by Diamond and Dybvig (1983) and Gorton (1988) suggest that the severity of the portfolio disturbances outlined above is critically dependent on regulation, allowable activity, and the safety nets in place.

Regulation, therefore, will not only determine the extent of the flow of new capital to the real sector, but also its nature will determine what types of projects will be approved. To the extent that it discourages risks, only relatively conservative projects will be funded through this sector.[23] On the other hand, if regulation encourages risk, it reduces its price and encourages this activity in the economy.[24]

To the extent that regulation fosters risk, it may precipitate financial crises and suboptimal investment decision making. These, in turn, may destroy the very institutions that regulation is designed to protect and cause unintended financial disruption. In essence, then, regulation itself may cause the disturbances to both the real and the financial sector captured above, or at least increase their severity.

This is the basic line of reasoning used by those who have protested the blanket use of deposit insurance and the relatively low regulatory capital standards for insured institutions.[25] They argue, rather convincingly, that current regulation fosters risk by underpricing it. Deposit insurance is priced independently of the risk in the bank's portfolio, and depositors are assured of full payment independent of the outcome. Owners and managers, therefore, skew their investments to high-risk projects, where gains accrue to the risk taker but losses are borne by the government insurance agency. Benston et al. (1986) argue that capital standards must be increased and improved to offset this risk-seeking behavior. However, current regulatory design suggests that little is likely to be done in this direction. Indeed, recent capital standards, heralded as risk related, have little to do with risk weighting as others have reported (Kim and Santomero (1988). However, without such an increase in capital, Herring and Vankudre (1987) have shown that risk-taking behavior will continue.

This tendency toward risk-taking behavior, which is fostered by some regulation, has two distinct effects. First, as noted above, the underlying portfolio of projects approved and funded at the intermediary tends to be riskier than it would be in the absence of such regulation. Second, this portfolio bias leads to potential institutional instabilities that make the system which supplies capital to the real sector more vulnerable to random economic disturbances. Diamond and Dybvig (1983) and Jacklin and Bhattacharya (1988) have recently raised this issue as it relates to institutional liquidity. They make the point that investments in illiquid assets, coupled with the fixed price of liabilities at financial institutions, makes the intermediary sector inherently unstable. They argue that this instability requires regulation and deposit insurance to prevent runs that would otherwise occur at even solvent institutions. Gorton (1988) extends this idea further. He shows that, in a world of imperfect information, bank panics result from concerns about the general economy. Institutions are vulnerable, not only because of their own actions, but also because of the aggregate state of the economy. Once panics and bank runs begin, only a regulatory umbrella, or complete suspension, will suffice to stop them.

The upshot of this newer literature is the recognition of the important role micro bank regulation has on the financial sector, its stability and its ability to channel needed funds into the real sector. Financial disturbances and their impact on the real sector are seen as endogenous to the regulatory structure that determines institutional vulnerability. Once disturbances occur, regulation determines the depth and breadth of the financial disturbance and its real sector impact. It is as if the disturbances in the previous section were at least partially endogenous, and the magnitudes of the impact effects, contained in both the real and financial sector elasticities, were also endogenously determined by the regulatory structure.[26]

Bank regulation, therefore, ought to be selected with full knowledge of both its impact on the aggregate transmission mechanism and its effect on the microeconomic decision processes within the financial sector. Optimal regulation should be of a form that recognizes these interrelationships and evaluates both the micro and macro implications of regulatory form. All too frequently, optimal regulation discussions are narrowly focused on either micro or macro optimality concerns. In truth, regulation affects the financial sector at both levels.

Therefore, as the current debates about the structure of deposit insurance continue, it is crucial to recognize that altering this system will affect both the financial sector's risk-taking behavior and the macrodynamics for the economy as a whole. This suggests that the optimal policy discussion debate should go beyond market-pricing proposals (Merton, 1977, 1978 and Sharpe, 1978) to the macroeconomic changes resulting from such policy recommendations.[27] The same can be said for the debate over appropriate standards for bank capital (Benston et al., 1986) and financial conglomerate structure (Herring and Santomero, 1990). Let us hope that the next phase of the micro policy discussion will incorporate these additional issues in the debate.

5. SUMMARY AND CONCLUSIONS

The financial structure of the United States has changed substantially over the past half century. From the depression, the U.S. financial system has seen regulation initially increase in response to the rather dramatic events of the 1930s. Then, fostered by changes in the economic environment, regulation gave way to regulatory avoidance and, finally, deregulation. There are clear reasons for this economic history. Nonetheless, the changes that this variation in regulatory structure precipitated have led many to question the impact of deregulation on the feasibility and efficiency of monetary policy.

In this chapter, it has been argued that monetary policy remains potent in spite of all these changes. Its impact multipliers have no doubt changed, as specific regimes have differential multiplier effects for the same open market operation, but this is of little concern. More substantively, it is also argued that the dynamics of the economy are also affected by the nature of the financial intermediary sector. Unfortunately, without full knowledge of the underlying stochastic disturbances in the economy, we cannot define an optimal structure or conclude whether recent changes have been beneficial. Finally, it is suggested that both the disturbances and the systemic responses to them may be the direct result of the bank regulatory environment. Current regulation tends to increase the underlying instability of the financial sector by mispricing risk and insuring that depositors will be insulated from any subsequent loss owing to an economic disturbance.

Such regulation was put in place to prevent the disruption of the intermediation sector and the financial channels that are essential for a developed economy. Yet, this rationalization of previous regulation leaves the question of optimal regulatory form very much unanswered. This much is known: Regulation aimed at insuring the channels of finance increases the probability of financial instability and exacerbates the effect of random disturbances. On the other hand, less regulation and more market-based solutions lead to a smaller flow of risk capital to the real sector and may be followed by more disruptions in the financial system. To arrive at an appropriate financial structure, optimal regulation must weigh these two offsetting public policy concerns. The latter will have a well-defined effect of monetary policy, a unique stochastic disturbance structure, and an associated degree of financial structure stability. Unfortunately, we are a long way from being able to define such a structure.

NOTES

1. This section draws on some material in Santomero (1990).

2. Usury ceilings continue to apply on the asset side, however.

3. See Santomero (1988) for the reasons why depository institutions have moved so quickly into this area of activity.

4. See Fama (1983) for a clear discussion of why these conditions assure monetary policy potency.

5. Currency plus reserve base is equal to the total monetary base or high-powered money.

6. See, for example, Johnson (1967) and Friedman (1969) for a discussion of why reserves have not paid interest, as well as the effect of this institutional reality.

7. Kareken (1984) questions this position by arguing that the above conditions need not be satisfied for all economies. Although this may be true in general, it appears to be beyond our current interest.

8. See Santomero and Seater (1978) and Gordon (1985) for an extensive review of this debate.

9. Assume, for example, demand deposits are market 1, time deposits at commercial banks are market 2, and so on. More will be said below about this ordering system.

10. If government bonds are not considered net wealth, the analysis proceeds with open market operations equivalent to high-powered money issuance.

11. If the household or public sector is a net borrower from the financial institution sector, household bond demand will be negative. B_g^s need not be positive for any of the analysis.

12. The existence of bank capital is suppressed in these models as can be seen in equation (6). The importance of capital in this analysis is mentioned below and treated in some detail in Langohr and Santomero (1984).

13. See Black (1975) for a discussion of the competitive equilibrium nature of such a pricing scheme in an unregulated environment.

14. Inasmuch as required reserves are held in pass-through balances at a correspondent bank and institutions continue to hold deposit liabilities of other institutions, interinstitutional deposit ratios remain relevant in any realistic characterization of the financial markets.

15. The Keynesian counterpart of this model appears in Santomero and Siegel (1981).

16. See Tobin (1969) for a general treatment of this point.

17. The equilibrium rate of return for any specific financial asset can be derived from this equilibrium condition.

18. In subsequent work by Santomero and Siegel (1986) the robustness of this issue is examined. There it is indicated that demand functions would have to be quite peculiar to reverse the clear message of section 2 above.

19. The exact value of ϵ_F in equations (23) and (24), using the same partial derivative notation, is

$$\epsilon_F = -\frac{A_B \epsilon_H - H_B \epsilon_A}{H_p A_B - B_B A_p}.$$

20. See Santomero and Siegel (1981) for an exact treatment of this issue.

21. See Gertler (1988) for a fine review of this growing area of the literature.

22. The rational expectations literature which resulted from the Lucas critique is quite large. Interested readers should refer to Lucas (1976) for his initial insight and to Barro (1985) for a review of subsequent work.

23. To the extent that a nonregulated financial sector exists, this regulatory constraint may be significantly, if not totally, offset.

24. For the beneficial side of this, see Goodman and Santomero (1986).

25. See Kane (1985) and Benston et al. (1986) for a vivid presentation of this view.

26. Some years ago, Brainard (1969) considered optimal policy with multiple uncertainty, and his work is applicable here.

27. Goodman and Santomero (1986) try to take this approach with substantially different results.

REFERENCES

Barro, R. J. 1985. "Recent Developments in the Theory of Rules Versus Discretion." *Economic Journal* 95, Supplement: 23–37.

Benston, G.; Eisenbeis, R.; Horvitz, P.; Kane, E.; and Kaufman, G. 1986. *Perspectives on Safe and Sound Banking: Past, Present and Future.* Cambridge, Mass.: MIT Press.

Bernanke, Ben S. 1983. "Non-Monetary Effects of the Financial Crisis in the Propagation of the Great Depression." *American Economic Review* 73 (June): 257–76.

———, and Gertler, Mark. 1989. "Agency Costs, Net Worth, and Business Fluctuations." *American Economic Review* 79 (March): 14–31.

Black, Fisher. 1975. "The Bank Fund's Management in an Efficient Market." *Journal of Financial Economics* 2 (December): 325–39.

———. 1981. "A Gold Standard with Double Feedback and Near-Zero Reserves." Working Paper, Sloan School of Management, MIT, December.

Brainard, W. C. 1969. "Uncertainty and the Theory of Policy." In *Targets and Indicators of Monetary Policy*, edited by K. Brunner. San Francisco: Chandler Publishing.

———, and Tobin, J. 1963. "Financial Intermediaries and the Effectiveness of Monetary Controls." *American Economic Review Proceedings* 53 (May): 383–400.

Brunner, K., and Meltzer, A. 1972. "Money, Debt and Economic Activity." *Journal of Political Economy* 80 (May): 951–77.

———. 1968. "Liquidity Traps for Money, Bank Credit and Interest Rates." *Journal of Political Economy* (January): 1–37.

Campbell, T., and Kracaw, W. 1980. "Information Production, Market Signalling, and the Theory of Financial Intermediation." *Journal of Finance* 35 (September): 863–82.

Diamond, Douglas. 1984. "Financial Intermediation and Delegated Monitoring." *Review of Economic Studies* 51 (July): 393–414.

———, and Dybvig, Philip. 1983. "Bank Runs, Deposit Insurance, and Liquidity." *Journal of Political Economy* 91: 401–19.

Fama, E. 1983. "Financial Intermediation and Price Level Concern." *Journal of Monetary Economics* 12: 7–28.

———. 1985. "What's Different about Banks?" *Journal of Monetary Economics* 15 (January): 29–40.

Friedman, Milton. 1969. *The Optimum Quantity of Money and Other Essays.* Chicago: Aldine.

Gertler, Mark. 1988. "Financial Structure and Aggregate Economic Activity: An Overview." *Journal of Money, Credit and Banking* 20 (August): 569–84.

Goodman, L. and Santomero, A. M. 1986. "Variable-Rate Deposit Insurance: A Re-examination." *Journal of Banking and Finance* (May): 257–76.

Gordon, Robert J. 1985. "Understanding Inflation in the 1980s." *Brookings Papers on Economic Activity* 1: 263–300.

Gorton, Gary. 1985. "Bank Suspension of Convertibility." *Journal of Monetary Economics* 15 (March): 177–93.

————. 1988. "Banking Panics and Business Cycles." *Oxford Economic Papers*.

Gurley, John G., and Shaw, Edward S. 1956. "Financial Intermediaries and the Savings-Investment Process." *Journal of Banking and Finance* (May): 257–76.

Guttentag, J., and Lindsay, R. 1968. "The Uniqueness of Commercial Banks." *Journal of Political Economy* 76, no. 5 (October): 991–1014.

Herring, Richard, and Santomero, Anthony. 1990. "The Corporate Structure of Financial Conglomerates." *Journal of Financial Services Research* 4, no. 4: 471–98.

————, and Vankudre, Prashant, 1987. "Growth Opportunities and Risk Taking by Financial Intermediaries." *Journal of Finance* 42 (July): 583–99.

Hester, D. 1982. "The Effect of Eurodollar and Domestic Money Market Innovations on the Interpretation and Control of Monetary Aggregates." In *Political Economy of International and Domestic Relations*, edited by R. Lombra and W. Witte. Ames: Iowa State University Press.

Jacklin, C., and Bhattacharya, S. 1988. "Distinguishing Panics and Information-based Bank Runs: Welfare and Policy Implications." *Journal of Political Economy* 96, no. 3 (June): 568–92.

Johnson, Harry G. 1967. *Essays in Monetary Economics*. Cambridge, Mass.: Harvard University Press.

Kane, E. 1985. *The Gathering Crisis in Federal Deposit Insurance*. Cambridge, Mass: MIT Press.

Kareken, John H. 1984. "Bank Regulation and the Effectiveness of Open Market Operations." *Brookings Paper on Economic Activity* 2: 405–44.

Kaufman, Henry. 1976. "Banks May Be All the Better for a Few Restrictions." *Euromoney* (June): 70–75.

Kim, Daesik, and Santomero, A. M. 1988. "Risk in Banking and Capital Regulation." *Journal of Finance* (December).

Langohr, Herwig, and Santomero, A. M. 1984. "The Impact of Equity in Bank Portfolios." *Proceedings of a Conference on Bank Structure and Competition*. Federal Reserve Bank of Chicago, April.

Leland, Hayne, and Pyle, David. 1977. "Informational Asymmetries, Financial Structure and Financial Intermediation." *Journal of Finance* 32 (May): 371–87.

Lucas, R. E. 1976. "Econometric Policy Evaluation: A Critique." In *The Phillips Curve and Labor Markets*, edited by K. Brunner and A. Meltzer. Amsterdam: North-Holland.

Merrick, J. J., and Saunders, A. 1985. "Bank Regulation and Monetary Policy." *Journal of Money, Credit and Banking* 17 (November): 691–717.

Merton, Robert C. 1977. "An Analytic Derivation of the Cost of Deposit Insurance and Loan Guarantees: An Application of Modern Pricing Theory." *Journal of Banking and Finance* 1 (June): 3–11.

————. 1978. "On the Cost of Deposit Insurance When There Are Surveillance Costs." *Journal of Business* 51 (July): 439–52.

Metzler, L. 1951. "Wealth, Savings and the Rate of Interest." *Journal of Political Economy* 59: 93–116.

Patinkin, D. 1961. "Financial Intermediaries and the Logical Structure of Monetary Theory." *American Economic Review* 51: 95–116.

Pesek, B., and T. Saving. 1969. *Money, Wealth and Economic Theory*. New York: Macmillan.

Poole, William. 1970. "Optimal Choice of Monetary Policy Instruments in a Simple Stochastic Macro Model." *Quarterly Journal of Economics* 84 (May).

Santomero, Anthony M. 1988. "The Intermediation Process and the Future of the Thrifts." *Expanding Competitive Markets and the Thrift Industry*. 13th Annual Conference of the Federal Home Loan Bank of San Francisco.

———. 1990. "European Banking in Post 1992: Lessons from the United States." In *European Banking in the 1990s*, edited by Jean Dermine. London: Basil Blackwell Publishing, February.

———, and Seater, J. J. 1978. "The Inflation-Unemployment Tradeoff: A Critique of the Literature." *Journal of Economic Literature* (June).

———, and Siegel, J. J. 1981. "Bank Regulation and Macroeconomic Stability." *American Economic Review* 71, no. 1 (March): 39–53.

———. 1982. "A General Equilibrium Banking Paradigm." *Journal of Finance, Papers and Proceedings* 37, no. 2 (May): 357–69.

———. 1986. "Deposit Deregulation and Monetary Policy." *Carnegie Rochester Conference Series on Public Policy* 24, Supplement to the *Journal of Monetary Economics*.

Sargent, Thomas J. 1979. *Macroeconomic Theory*. London: Academic Press.

Sharpe, William F. 1978. "Bank Capital Adequacy, Deposit Insurance and Security Values." *Journal of Financial and Quantitative Analysis Proceedings Issue* (November).

Tobin, J. 1969. "A General Equilibrium Approach to Monetary Theory." *Journal of Money, Credit and Banking* 1 (February): 15–29.

———, and Brainard, W. C. 1963. "Financial Intermediaries and the Effectiveness of Monetary Controls." *American Economic Review* 53 (May): 383–400.

Wojnilower, A. M. 1980. "The Central Role of Credit Crunches in Recent Financial History." *Brookings Papers on Economic Activity* 2: 277–326.

PART II

U.S. MONETARY POLICY

7

THE U.S. CENTRAL BANKING EXPERIENCE: A HISTORICAL PERSPECTIVE

Elmus Wicker

The Fed opened its doors on November 16, 1914, three months after the onset of World War I—certainly not the most propitious time for inaugurating a new central banking system in the United States. The Fed had been established to prevent financial crises in the central money market. Presumably, the Federal Reserve would be guided by the behavior of the gold reserve ratio—the ratio of gold held by the Fed to Federal Reserve Notes and Deposit liabilities—in making adjustments to the domestic money stock following the alleged practice of central banks under the international gold standard. With the collapse of the international monetary order in 1914, the gold reserve ratio as a policy guide became obsolete. The Fed adopted an interest-rate smoothing objective during World War I, and after 1922 it began to experiment with output and employment smoothing objectives while awaiting the reconstruction of the international gold standard. Its success in achieving these goals in the 1920s is still controversial. Chandler (1958) and Friedman and Schwartz (1963) have argued that Fed policymakers learned how to use open market operations to stabilize economic activity in the 1920s, whereas Wicker (1969), Brunner and Meltzer (1964), Wheelock (1989b), and Toma (1989) maintain that they did not. The explanation for their failure to have smoothed output and employment is the central problem in assessing Federal Reserve performance during the Great Depression. What did Fed officials know about how monetary policy was supposed to work and what had they learned, if anything, from their experience in the 1920s? These issues will be addressed in Sections 2 and 3 of this chapter.

The incidence and timing of financial panics in the United States were closely associated with strong seasonality in nominal interest rates, and the remedy allegedly resided in the removal of the seasonals. The interest-rate seasonals vanished in 1914. But the following questions remain unanswered: Can the disappearance of the seasonals in interest rates be attributed solely to action taken by the Fed? Is there any evidence that the seasonals may have been removed earlier? We will examine this issue more closely and also attempt to identify the channels through which the seasonals were supposedly removed in Section 4. Interest-rate smoothing during both world wars also will be examined in Section 4. Section 5 deals with the reserve requirement increases in 1936 and 1937. No single policy episode has generated as much controversy. It goes to the very crux of our understanding of what Reserve officials knew or did not know about how instrument changes could affect interest rates and the money stock.

Our knowledge of Fed behavior is affected not only by changing perceptions of policymakers' understanding of how monetary policy is supposed to work, but also by our perceptions of the economy's past performance and the incentive system motivating the monetary decision makers. Perceptions of how the economy behaves condition our understanding of Fed performance. Measures of output and employment provide the descriptive framework within which Fed policy can be interpreted. Revisions of the conventional measures may require not only a reinterpretation of the economy's cyclical performance, but also the Fed's performance. Christine Romer (1986a, b, 1989) has challenged the reliability of historical GNP and unemployment data. Her revised estimates reveal little or no damping of the business cycle between the period 1893–1927 and the post–World War II economy. Moreover, her estimates downgrade the 1920–21 depression to a serious recession and suggest that unemployment in the two interwar recessions may not have increased by more than one percentage point! We review the literature generated by Romer's critique of the conventional estimates in Section 1.

Perhaps no more significant change is taking place than in our understanding of what motivates Fed policymakers' behavior. The literature on central banking has been thoroughly imbued with the idea that central bankers, quite unlike ordinary commercial bankers, are motivated by considerations of public interest rather than self-interest. They attach top priority to certain desirable social goals such as stable exchange rates, stable prices, and high output and low unemployment. More recently, central banks have been viewed as bureaus similar to other government bureaus with central banker motives similar to those of other bureaucrats: for example, self-interest, inertia, secrecy, and self-preservation. The newer bureaucratic models presume to explain certain alleged characteristics of central bankers' behavior, for example, secrecy and inertia, that have managed to elude the understanding of those who have pursued the traditional public interest approach. Although little or no work has been done in applying bureaucratic models to Fed behavior before World War II, Section

6 will see what sense can be made of that behavior within this newer framework.

Section 7 is an all too brief excursion into the realm of monetary politics. We will attempt to show what the historical evidence tells us about presidential influence and how it was exerted before World War II. Monetary historians have not yet begun to mine this potentially rich vein opened up by the initial inquiries of political scientists.

1. NEW MEASURES OF EMPLOYMENT AND OUTPUT

Our perceptions of how the Fed has behaved in the past are irrevocably linked to our knowledge of the economy's performance. Output and unemployment estimates are essential if we are to assess the effects of policymakers' actions. And revisions of these estimates may require a reconsideration of Fed behavior. In this section we review recent revisions of the historical data on unemployment and GNP and examine the implications, if any, for interpreting monetary policy.

Conventional measures of output and employment reveal a record of pronounced economic disruption before World War II; three serious depressions in 1920–21, 1929–33, and 1937–38 and two mild recessions in 1923–24 and 1926–27. This record contrasts sharply with the economy's performance after World War II, which was blemished by seven mild recessions and only one near-depression when unemployment rose to 10 percent of the labor force. From casual inspection we might correctly infer that there was greater output and employment stability after World War II than during the 1920s and 1930s.

If there was greater economic stability after World War II, it does not necessarily follow that the Fed's behavior was solely responsible for the observed output and employment smoothing. Conceivably, increased stability could have been due to fiscal measures, including automatic stabilizers, which was perhaps a fortuitous event or some combination thereof. Nevertheless, we may conclude that the available historical evidence is not inconsistent with the interpretation that the Fed may have played an important stabilizing role in the post–World War II economy.

In a series of papers, Christine Romer (1986, 1989) has challenged the reliability of the historical GNP and unemployment data. She has created a new time series that presumably portrays pre–World War II cyclical movements more accurately. Official estimates of GNP, Romer maintains, probably exaggerate cyclical fluctuations because estimates of noncommodity output were constructed from data on commodity output, and commodity output allegedly is far more cyclically sensitive than GNP. She regressed percentage deviations from trend GNP on deviations from trend of aggregate commodity output from 1909 to 1928. The estimated coefficients provide new estimates of GNP for 1872–1918, the key assumption being that the relationship between GNP and commodity output remained stable between the prewar and the interwar years.

Romer's revised estimates reveal that the period 1893–1927 was only slightly more volatile than the post–World War II economy—1951–80. The depression years of the 1930s were excluded because there was no disagreement about their high volatility. She concluded that there was little or no dampening of the amplitude of the business cycle between the two periods. This conclusion is not implausible inasmuch as the new estimates downgrade the 1920–21 depression to a serious recession and almost, but not quite, eliminate the two interwar recessions. Moreover, the Great Depression is excluded.

Romer has also revised Lebergott's (1957) estimates of unemployment. She argues that the dampening of the post–1948 business cycle is an error that has arisen from the use of inconsistent unemployment estimates. When the post–1948 estimates of unemployment are derived using the same procedures that were utilized to obtain the prewar estimates, Romer concludes that the dampening disappeared.

Romer's estimates have not gone unchallenged, however. Weir (1986) reevaluated her estimates and concluded that there is evidence of increased stability after World War II. By stabilization Weir meant a fall in unemployment volatility from the prewar to the postwar periods. Weir performed a series of tests to measure the sensitivity of Lebergott's estimates to variations in his assumptions. He could find no foundation for Romer's inference that Lebergott's unemployment estimates contain excess volatility of employment by more than 50 percent. By his own estimates, excess volatility was probably no more than one third or more than one half of the difference between the two periods.

Balke and Gordon (1989) have constructed new estimates of prewar nominal and real GNP from previously unused data sources for the periods 1869–1908 and 1869–1928. They concluded, contrary to Romer, that the U.S. economy exhibited postwar stabilization of real output, and they reaffirmed the earlier view that real GNP was more volatile before 1929 than since 1946.

De Long and Summers (1988) also rejected the Romer hypothesis. They advanced three reasons explaining why macroeconomic policy performance has improved since World War II: changes in the output gap, skewness of unemployment, and the persistence of real GNP. In their judgment GNP gap-based measures are superior to volatility measures utilized by Romer. The mean output gap, De Long and Summers (1988, p. 461) estimated, was at least 50 percent greater before the Great Depression than after World War II: "The difference in mean output gaps suggests that the United States has on average come 1 percent of production closer to potential output since World War II than it did before the Depression." They surmised that automatic stabilizers played a much more important role than discretionary fiscal or monetary policy in contributing to output stability after World War II.

Revisions of the historical data series on unemployment and GNP by Romer and Balke and Gordon may require reconsideration of some episodes of business cycle history, notably the amplitude of the 1920–21 depression and the 1923–24 and 1926–27 recessions. Cycle amplitude is one of relevant dimensions in assessing the effectiveness of monetary policy. These revisions are significant in that our perception of how the Fed has behaved is conditioned by what we know about the performance of the economy. Using available information, the National Bureau of Economic Research (NBER) has attempted to identify and to date cyclical peaks and troughs in U.S. economic activity since 1854. Until quite recently, no serious doubts were raised either about cycle chronology or the standard estimates of GNP and unemployment for the interwar period. The Fed's performance has been evaluated within this standard framework.

Romer's (1988) downward revision of Lebergott's unemployment percentage in 1921 from 11.7 to 8.7 percent is significant inasmuch as it removes the 1920–21 contraction from the depression to the recession category following the NBER rule that an unemployment percentage above 10 percent warrants a classification of a cycle episode as a depression. The reclassification simply reduces the magnitude of the Fed's alleged negligence in failing to reduce the discount rate during the downturn. Balke and Gordon's real GNP estimates show an even more moderate decline than Romer's estimates. From a peak in 1919 to a trough in 1921, real GNP declined by only 5.6 percent—even less if we consider only the change between 1920 and 1921. The 1920–21 depression is downgraded to a serious recession.

But the revision of the unemployment and GNP estimates for the two recession episodes may have important implications for interpreting Fed behavior in the 1920s. According to Romer's revised annual estimates of real GNP, output increased in both recessions: 3 percent in the first recession (1923–24) and 1 percent in the second (1926–27). Balke and Gordon (1989) also show a 2.6 percent increase in 1923–24 and a 0.5 percent increase in 1926–27. Department of Commerce annual estimates of real GNP indicate that GNP increased 1 percent between 1923 and 1924 and decreased by a fractional 0.2 percent between 1926 and 1927.

The annual real GNP estimates of both Romer and Balke and Gordon may not be credible guides to what happened during the two recessions because both have a duration of fourteen and thirteen months, respectively, and include a significant portion of both years of the recession, a little more than one half in 1923 and one half in 1924—less so in 1926–27 (the last quarter of 1926 and the first three quarters of 1927). Since quarterly estimates are not available, a note of caution must suffice in interpreting the behavior of the annual estimates as a reliable measure of amplitude during these two recessions.

The standard (Lebergott) unemployment estimates show that unemployment increased from 2.41 percent in 1923 to 4.95 percent in 1924, a 2.54 percentage point increase. The percentage point increase in 1924 underestimates recession unemployment inasmuch as the recovery, as we have already indicated, began in the middle of the year. Romer's unemployment estimates show that unemployment increased by only one percentage point (from 4.8 to 5.8) in 1924 and by 1.3 percentage points between 1926 and 1927.

2. INTERPRETATIONS OF PRE-GREAT DEPRESSION MONETARY POLICY

The importance of the 1922–29 era in Federal Reserve history cannot be underestimated. What policymakers learned or did not learn is critical to our interpretation of monetary policy during the depression episode of the 1930s. According to Chandler (1958) and Friedman and Schwartz (1963), the Fed learned how to use open market operations successfully to counteract cyclical downturns in economic activity. The new evidence of Romer and Balke and Gordon tends to confirm the mildness of both recession downturns. If they were so successful in the 1920s, how then do we account for their alleged failures in the 1930s?

Friedman and Schwartz advance what they have labeled the shift-of-power hypothesis. Until 1928, they argued, the New York Fed and its head Benjamin Strong provided the leadership and initiative that explain the Fed's policy successes. After Strong's death in October 1928, a leadership vacuum was created that was not filled either by the Federal Reserve Board in Washington or Strong's successor George Harrison at the New York Federal Reserve Bank. Power began to shift away from the New York Bank to the Board in Washington, culminating in 1930 in the complete reorganization of the Open Market Investment Committee to include all twelve Federal Reserve Bank governors.

Chandler (1958, pp. 188–89) argued that during the period 1922–28 the Federal Reserve hammered out the goals of economic stabilization and refined the art of monetary management by which Governor Strong singlehandedly steered the country successfully through the relatively mild 1923–24 and 1926–27 recessions. Presumably, Fed policymakers learned how to use open market operations to attain stabilization objectives.

Like Friedman and Schwartz, Trescott (1982) also concluded that there had been a sharp break in the conduct of monetary policy between the 1920s and the 1930s. But in lieu of an historical interpretation of the alleged policy hiatus, he proposed an empirical test of the Friedman and Schwartz hypothesis. He estimated a regression equation to explain security purchases/sales for the 1924–29 period. Using the same regression coefficients that he obtained in the 1924–29 equations, Trescott estimated the amount of open market operations that would have been necessary to have achieved the same results each month between 1930 and 1933. The difference between the estimated amount of open market operations and the actual amount represented "shortfall," which he calculated to be $220 million for 1930, $420 million in 1931, and $870 million in 1932. From these counterfactual calculations, Trescott concluded that there had been a significant change in monetary policy between the two periods. But he made no attempt to identify the cause for a regime change.

Trescott's explanation of security purchases and sales relies heavily on the relevance of Roosa's (1956) famous classification of open market operations as defensive and dynamic to monetary policy in the 1920s. Roosa maintained that anticipated changes in the principal determinants of bank reserves due, for example, to seasonal demands that are completely offset by open market operations can best be labeled defensive, that is, concerned with keeping a given volume of reserves in existence. Dynamic open market operations refer to purchases and sales of government securities that add to or subtract from the total quantity of reserves in existence. When open market operations are defensive, changes in the gold stock, currency in circulation, or borrowing from the Fed are offset presumably one-to-one by open market operations and are entered in the regression equations as independent variables on the right-hand side with the expected sign of -1. To represent dynamic considerations, Trescott introduced a discount rate and a time trend. He found that the estimated coefficients for the period 1924–29 had the necessary signs and were approximately equal to 1, thus confirming the significance of defensive operations.

Part of Trescott's error resides in incorrectly modeling Federal Reserve monetary strategy in the 1920s. Policymakers in the 1920s, as we will attempt to show, rejected the implicit Roosa assumption that the Fed could control the amount of bank reserves. Reserve officials observed that reserves remained invariant with respect to open market operations as long as borrowing was greater than zero. Borrowing varied inversely with purchases and sales of securities. When the Fed purchased securities, banks reduced their indebtedness to the Fed. Trescott has the causation reversed; that is, open market operations were not responding to changes in borrowing, and bank borrowing was responding to changes in open market operations. Reserves were not the target of monetary policy; rather, borrowing was. The negative coefficient on the borrowing term in Trescott's regressions can equally be construed as confirming reserve position theory, as we will explain further in the next section.

Roosa acknowledged that seasonal demands for reserves were not always automatically accommodated by defensive open market operations. Roosa never implied that they were. Seasonal demands when met through the discount window could be of some importance in implementing dynamic policy.

Trescott concluded that few Fed critics have recognized the extent to which the Fed conducted defensive operations. But that inference does not follow necessarily from Trescott's regression results. The Fed was genuinely surprised to discover that borrowing was responding passively to open market operations. Their initial intent had clearly been to increase reserves as part of a dynamic policy, but to their chagrin they discovered that open market operations were offset by decreases in the amount of borrowing. Trescott misleadingly labeled such operations as defensive.

Wicker (1969) explained why Federal Reserve officials failed to mimic their 1923–24 and 1926–27 behavior in 1930, that is, to purchase government securities to moderate the contraction. They were guided by what Wicker (1969, pp. 319–20) refers to as the "Strong Rule"; at a Governors' Conference in March 1926, Benjamin Strong stated:

As a guide to the timing and extent of any purchases which might appear desirable, one of our best guides would be the amount of borrowing by member banks in principal centers, and particularly in New York and Chicago. Our experience has shown that when New York City banks are borrowing in the neighborhood of 100 million dollars or more, there is then some real pressure for reducing loans, and money rates tend to be markedly higher than the discount rate. On the other hand, when borrowings of these banks are negligible, as in 1924, the money situation tends to be less elastic and if gold imports take place, there is liable to be some credit inflation. . . . When member banks are owing us about 50 million dollars or less the situation appears to be comfortable, with no marked pressure for liquidation and with the requisite elasticity. . . . In the event of business liquidation now appearing it would seem advisable to keep the New York City banks out of debt beyond something in the neighborhood of 50 million dollars. It would probably be well if some similar rule could be applied to the Chicago banks, although the amount would, of course, be smaller and the difficulties greater because of the influence of the New York market.

The Strong Rule was applied not only in 1924 and 1927, but also in 1930 (Wicker, 1965, pp. 330–31):

Although the amount of securities in the Open Market Investment Account increased by only $46 million between January and March, 1930, the volume of member-bank indebtedness decreased from $700 million during the first week in January to $230 million in the first week of March. This reduction in borrowing, amounting to $470 million within three months, compared favorably with Federal Reserve behavior in 1924 and 1927. There had been no comparable sharp decrease in member-bank indebtedness since 1922. Member-bank borrowing stood at $54 million at the New York Federal Reserve Bank and $36 million at the Chicago Bank, well within the permissible range described by Governor Strong in his remarks to the Governors' Conference. . . . The amount of indebtedness of the banks in the Chicago and the New York Federal Reserve Districts was only slightly above the corresponding figures for 1924 but substantially below the amount during the 1927 recession. Total member-bank indebtedness never dropped below $400 million during the 1927 recession and never amounted to less than $370 million even as late as June, 1924.

What policymakers presumably learned in 1923–24 and 1926–27 was that eliminating the indebtedness of the banks in New York and Chicago Federal Reserve Districts was adequate to induce recovery. But no open market operations were required in the first three months of 1930 to achieve their objective. The large seasonal decreases in currency in circulation supplied reserves. There was no dramatic shift in the quality of Federal Reserve performance. The behavior of Federal Reserve officials remained consistent throughout.

Overemphasis on purely domestic considerations by Friedman and Schwartz (1963) and Brunner and Meltzer (1968) has tended to foster the interpretation that output and employment smoothing objectives were paramount in the behavior of Reserve officials in the 1920s. Wicker (1965) attempted to show that international considerations were at least as important as domestic considerations and to explain the timing of open market operations. The timing of the action taken in 1924 was perhaps more closely related to aiding Great Britain in restoring the gold standard by establishing a differential between rates in London and New York to reverse the gold flow. The timing of the monetary action in 1927 coincided so closely with the now-famous meeting in New York in July 1927 between Governor Strong, Governor Norman of the Bank of England, Hjalmar Schacht of the Reichsbank, and Charles Rist of the Bank of France that there can be little doubt that the international monetary situation was a major reason for the action undertaken. Following the July meeting, the Federal Reserve Bank of Kansas City reduced the discount rate from 4 to 3.5 percent. Purchase of securities followed to make the new rates effective. The interest rate differential widened between New York and London, accelerated the outflow of funds, and improved the sterling exchange rate.

The action taken in 1923–24 and 1926–27 can be attributed to a mixture of motives. Since no single motive explains completely the magnitude and timing of Federal Reserve action, it cannot be inferred that the lesson the Fed learned from this experience was how to use open market operations to smooth output and employment. The accidental juxtaposition of a set of motives that just happened to be consistent provides a more plausible interpretation of Fed policy action.

3. FED PERCEPTIONS OF OPEN MARKET OPERATIONS

The key to understanding monetary policy in the 1920s and 1930s is the perception of Fed policymakers about how open market operations were supposed to affect economic activity. In 1922 officials of the New York Federal Reserve Bank discovered much to their chagrin that reserves injected by open market operations tended to be offset by changes in borrowed reserves, thereby leaving total reserves unchanged. This struck the policymakers as anomalous. If an attempt to inject total reserves was unsuccessful, how then was monetary policy supposed to work? How could the Fed exert an influence on the economy if attempts to change the money stock were thwarted? The solution to this anomaly could not be found in the conventional wisdom of central banking. So reserve officials did what they were to do on so many occasions in the future: they devised their own interpretation of the observed behavior of borrowed reserves and open market operations. Central banking theory was as much, if not more, the product of central bank practice as interpreted by its own agents than the product of monetary theorists detached from actual operating experience of the central bank.

The interpretation carries the name of the authors: the Riefler-Burgess—Strong doctrine, or, sometimes, just reserve position theory. The first stage in constructing an explanation of the observed inverse relationship between open market operations and borrowed reserves was to ask why the member banks borrowed from the Fed. Conceivably, banks could borrow for purely profit considerations, that is, to take advantage of unexploited profit opportunities when there was a discrepancy between the Fed's discount rate and open market rates. But Riefler (1930, pp. 19–36) rejected the profit theory because open market rates did not move in tandem with the discount rate, as indeed we might expect if profit considerations were paramount. In the bank acceptance market where the Fed set the rate at which it would be willing to acquire acceptances, the two rates did not diverge. Officers of the New York Fed asked why, if banks did not borrow for profit, they did not then borrow? Burgess (1936, pp. 219ff.) revived a view prevalent in the nineteenth century that commercial banks were reluctant to reveal evidence of borrowing from other banks on their balance sheets because it might be construed as a sign of weakness. They took elaborate precautions through so-called window dressing to conceal borrowing. Burgess suggested that member banks would likewise be reluctant to borrow from the Fed, and when they did, it would be for considerations of need; banks would place the highest priority on the repayment of their indebtedness to the Fed. Consequently, when banks had positive net indebtedness to the Fed, they would be reluctant to expand earning assets, thereby contracting the supply of loanable funds and raising interest rates. The New York Fed thought it had discovered a key link in the monetary policy transmission chain: a sale of securities induced an increase in banks' indebtedness to the Fed, which, in turn, exerted increased pressure in the money market, raising interest rates and ultimately moderating spending. It did not matter, or so they thought, that total reserves and the money stock remained unchanged. The effects of monetary policy were transmitted through changes in interest rates, not through changes in the money stock.

The two explanations for discount rate borrowing, the profit theory and the need theory, are alike inasmuch as both predict a positive relationship between borrowed reserves and open market rates. But they differ in their predictions about the direction of causation. According to the profit theory, a change in rates causes a change in borrowed reserves. When the Fed purchases securities, open market rates tend to decrease relative to the discount rate, which causes a decrease in borrowed reserves. According to the need theory, a change in borrowed reserves causes a change in open market rates. When the Fed purchases securities, banks reduce their indebtedness to the Fed; borrowed reserves decrease, which causes a decrease in open market rates. Both theories predict an inverse relationship between open market operations and borrowed reserves. A strong interpretation of reserve position theory suggests that a one-to-one inverse relationship exists—that is, if borrowing is completely unresponsive to changes in interest rates. According to the profit theory, the extent to which borrowing changes depends on the elasticity of borrowing with respect to the profit spread. Only when that elasticity is infinite will the relationship be one to one. Generally, the profit theory predicts that induced borrowing will offset only a part of the change in reserves owing to open market operations; total reserves will increase, and the money stock will expand. Consequently, even when open market operations are completely offset by changes in borrowing, a change in interest rates induced by open market operations may affect the money multiplier if the reserve-deposit and currency-deposit ratios are interest sensitive, and thereby increase the money stock.

Both Wheelock (1989b) and Toma (1989) have attempted to breathe new life into this ancient controversy by proposing empirical tests of the reserve position hypothesis in its strong form: open market operations did not directly affect the money stock because total reserves remained unchanged. Wheelock regressed the change in borrowed reserves on four independent variables: profit spread, unborrowed reserves, lagged borrowing, and bank debits (to capture the influence of economic activity on the demand for borrowed reserves). He obtained two sets of estimates. The first set covered the period extending from January 1924 to September 1929, and the second extended to August 1931. Wheelock concluded from the first set that the strong and significant coefficients on changes in unborrowed reserves support the Fed's interpretation of why member banks borrow. About 85 percent of the change in unborrowed reserves was offset by opposite changes in borrowed reserves. The estimates for the more extended period through 1931 only confirmed the earlier findings.

Toma (1989) proposed a different test of the hypothesis that open market operations left the money stock unchanged. He maintained that a decisive test involved establishing the direction of causality. Do open market operations cause changes in borrowing, or does borrowing cause changes in open market operations? Toma conducted bivariate Granger (1969) causality tests by running monthly changes in the Fed's government security portfolio on a lagged value of itself and on changes in member bank borrowing for the 1924–29 episode. These tests could not reject the strong hypothesis of reserve position theory—that is, an injection of reserves in the current month leads to a decrease in borrowing, which offsets the original injection exactly! A $1.00 security purchase in the current month implies a $0.97 cent decrease in borrowing after five months. Similar tests and similar findings using weekly data did not significantly alter the findings from the monthly data set.

To eliminate the possibility that open market operations could have affected interest rates and indirectly the money multiplier and the money stock, Toma conducted Granger causality tests between changes in government security holdings and changes in the call rates of interest and changes in M2. He found that no causality could be inferred between open market operations and interest rates. Furthermore, open market operations did not Granger-cause money, nor did money Granger-cause open market operations during the 1924–29 period. On this basis he concluded that serious doubt is cast on the hypothesis that open market operations may have indirectly affected the money stock through the money multiplier.

Toma's evidence led him to reject the Friedman and Schwartz view that the Fed used its open market powers to control the money stock in the 1920s. We can go further than Toma's evidence—and that of Wheelock— strictly warrant: that there was no radical change in policy, that is, no change in monetary regime, between the 1920s and 1930s!

Perhaps a more decisive test of the two theories of borrowing would be bivariate, Granger causality tests to show whether or not borrowing causes changes in interest rates, or vice versa. The distinguishing property of the two theories is not so much the inverse relationship as it is whether borrowing responds endogenously to changes in interest rates or whether interest rates respond endogenously to the amount of borrowing.

Both Wheelock and Toma therefore concluded that Fed open market operations did not directly affect the money stock because total reserves remained unchanged. Toma questioned whether or not the Fed had pursued countercyclical monetary policies during the 1920s. Their findings are in direct conflict with the Friedman-Schwartz and Chandler views that the Fed learned how to use open market operations for the explicit purpose of moderating downturns in economic activity in the 1923–24 and 1926–27 recessions.

Nor does the evidence of the behavior of the monetary aggregates—M1 and M2—provide strong support for the Friedman-Schwartz and Chandler

Table 7.1
Annualized Average Monthly Growth Rates of M1 and M2 at Six-Month Intervals During the 1923–24 and 1926–27 Recessions

	(%)		
1923-1924	Pre-Recession 6 Months	Recession First Six Months	Recession Second Six Months
M 1	7.44	1.10	.84
M 2	9.24	5.36	3.64
1926-1927			
M 1	-1.34	-2.48	1.88
M 2	1.98	1.28	5.

Source: Banking and Monetary Statistics (Washington, D.C.: Board of Governors of the Federal Reserve system, 1976).

hypothesis. Friedman concluded that for minor depression cycles since 1867 the money stock (M2) tended to rise in both the recession and recovery phases of the cycle primarily because of the strong trend element present in the M2 time series. To remove the effects of trend, he calculated rates of change by logarithmic first differencing. Friedman (1969, pp. 202–3) then estimated the relationship between the variability of the money stock and the variability of income as measured by net national product. From this relationship he inferred that "There is a close relation between the variability of money and of net national product." Levels of the money stock, he thought, were less useful than rates of change as a monetarist measure of the thrust of Federal Reserve monetary policy during minor depression cycles.

Annualized average monthly growth rates of M1 and M2 at six-month intervals are shown in Table 7.1 during the 1923–24 and 1926–27 recessions. Each recession is dated according to National Bureau of Economic Research chronology and divided into six-month stages, with a carryover of three months in the first recession and two months in the second. The division of each recession into six-month stages is consistent with the assumption that six months is the minimum lag length time that it would take for the two monetary aggregates to exert some influence on real output. Most estimates of response time fall somewhere between six and eighteen months. Few estimates, if any, show any immediate response of output to a change in either M1 or M2.

The data in Table 7.1 show monetary deceleration during the first six months of each recession, whether or not we employ M1 or M2. Both aggregates behaved procyclically during the second six months of the 1923–24 recession and countercyclically during the second six months of the 1926–27 recession, but this would have been too late to have exerted any influence on output before the very end of the 1926–27 recession. The evidence from the behavior of the monetary aggregates alone during the 1923–24 and 1926–27 recessions does not warrant any strong inference about the role the Fed played in moderating the two downturns in the 1920s. The evidence, however, is consistent with Toma's conclusion that the Fed did not pursue countercyclical policies.

The balance of the historical and statistical evidence fails to confirm the Friedman/Schwartz and Chandler hypothesis that Reserve officials learned how to use open market operations for countercyclical purposes during the 1920s. Or better, their understanding was incomplete. By Friedman's own criterion for measuring the thrust of monetary policy, M1 and M2 decelerated; that is, they behaved procyclically in both six-month phases of the 1923–24 recession. During the 1926–27 recession, both monetary aggregates behaved procyclically in the first phase and countercyclically in the second, probably too late to have exerted a strong influence on output until after the recovery was underway.

Romer's revised output and unemployment estimates reveal how mild these two recessions really were: a change in real GNP of one percentage point or less and an increase of one percentage point or more in the unemployment percentage. It is unlikely, therefore, that the mildness of the recessions can be attributed to the favorable effects of Fed monetary policy.

Wheelock and Toma showed convincingly that there was no connection between the money stock and open market operations in the 1920s. And Wicker explained why policymakers were reluctant to acquire securities at the beginning of 1930. The indebtedness of the New York and Chicago banks to the Fed had been practically eliminated through currency inflows at the beginning of the year. That had been the policymakers' guide during both interwar recessions. Power may have shifted away from the New York Fed after the death of Governor Strong, but there is no evidence that Reserve officials had abandoned the Strong Rule as the appropriate guide to policy during an economic downturn. That is, the elimination of the indebtedness of the banks in the New York and Chicago Federal Reserve Districts is sufficient to induce economic recovery.

4. INTEREST-RATE SMOOTHING

Interest-rate smoothing in one of its various guises has exerted a strong and persistent influence on Federal Reserve policymakers. At the very outset, Fed officials considered the removal of interest-rate seasonals as a precondition for eliminating financial panics. During both world wars and their immediate aftermath, interest-rate movements were circumscribed by the priorities of war finance. After the famous Federal Reserve–Treasury Accord in 1951 when support for a fixed pattern of rates was abandoned, interest-rate smoothing reemerged, but this time in the guise of maintaining money market stability. Any effort to interpret and to appraise Federal Reserve conduct requires some understanding of these monetary policy episodes when interest-rate smoothing objectives were paramount. We will discuss the first two objectives in turn. The last falls outside of our reference period.

Whatever merits are ultimately assigned to the various kinds of interest-rate smoothing, there has been at least one variant that, until quite recently, was widely acclaimed as a major achievement of Fed policy—the elimination of seasonal variations of interest rates. The nonrecurrence of financial panics was the overriding consideration in the foundation of the Federal Reserve System; the last of these panics struck in 1907. Contemporaries associated crises with large seasonal swings in interest rates owing mainly to currency outflows from the banks induced by requirements of the crop-moving season. Presumably, currency outflows induced decreases in the banks' reserve-deposit ratios. When reserve-deposit ratios were low (in the autumn) owing to an increase in currency held by the public, the banking system was especially vulnerable to panic. High interest rates coupled with low reserve deposit ratios invited trouble—either a financial or a real shock could easily provoke a liquidity crisis. Therefore, the association of seasonal fluctuations in interest rates with financial crises was the initial motivation for interest-rate smoothing by the Fed. The advocates of banking reform unanimously believed that the removal of interest-rate seasonals would substantially reduce the likelihood of financial panics.

Both Schiller (1980) and Miron (1986) produced evidence that the Fed had been successful in bringing about a pronounced decline in seasonality in nominal interest rates before the Great Depression. They concluded, however, that the seasonal was not completely eliminated during World War I. Before the Fed's inadvertent discovery of open market operations in 1922, the principal policy instrument for supplying reserves was the discount mechanism. It could be argued that some rise in interest rates was necessary to induce borrowing from the Fed, unless the discount rate was lowered. A seasonal outflow of currency in the hands of the public reduced bank reserves, thereby pushing short-term interest rates up relative to the discount rate and evoking bank borrowing from the Fed. Interest rates rose but not by as much as they would have if currency held by the public and bank reserves moved one to one; an increase in currency held by the public reduces reserves by the same amount. But two considerations reduced the importance of the discount mechanism: the large inflows of gold from Europe, and the reductions in reserve requirements when the system went into operation. After 1922, Reserve officials injected reserves through open market operations without any necessity for a rise in interest rates to induce borrowing.

Schiller (1980) has pointed out that apparently it never occurred to Fed policymakers to ask whether eliminating the seasonal in nominal rates meant necessarily the elimination of the seasonal in real interest rates. Schiller (1980, p. 137) concluded "that we can't say with any confidence whether a policy of eliminating the seasonal pattern of nominal rates reduced the seasonal pattern of real rates." No concern had ever been expressed about the economic effects of a seasonal in real rates. It was the alleged relationship between the seasonal in nominal rates and bank panics that mattered most to the founders of the Fed.

Holland and Toma (1989) have suggested an alternative explanation for the decline in the seasonality of interest rates. The Fed's role of lender of last resort reduced the seasonal in interest rates by reducing the seasonality of the expected availability of credit to the banks. By reducing the seasonal fluctuations in the probability of bank failures and financial panics, the Fed reduced the seasonal fluctuations in interest rates. Only the expected line of credit from the Fed, not the actual amount of credit supplied, influenced the interest rate.

According to Holland and Toma, the creation of the Fed in 1914 constituted a significant regime change by altering permanently the expectation of agents (banks) about the resources available to them through the Fed for avoiding financial disturbances. Contrary to Miron's interpretation, there was no need for open market intervention to smooth interest rates. Nor was there any need to invoke a seasonal in Federal Reserve Credit as the necessary concomitant to seasonal open market operations (defensive). Bankers' expectations of a seasonal supply of funds was alone adequate. According to their account, there was no need to use actively the instruments of monetary control, namely, open market operations and the discount rate.

Holland and Toma do not conclude that the creation of the Fed necessarily caused a reduction in the seasonality of interest rates. They admit that World War I financing techniques and the suspension of the gold standard may have been important determinants of the reduction in the seasonality of interest rates.

The Miron model requiring open market operations for interest-rate smoothing has a testable implication. That is, seasonality of interest rates and seasonality of Federal Reserve Credit will tend to be negatively related. In other words, a reduction in interest-rate seasonality will increase the seasonality of Federal Reserve Credit, whereas in the Holland–Toma model, they will be positively related. A reduction in seasonal fluctuations in expected lines of credit will reduce the seasonal interest rates without the necessity for seasonal fluctuations in Federal Reserve Credit.

Holland and Toma use monthly data to test the two hypotheses about the relationship between seasonals in Federal Reserve Credit and interest rates over various subperiods between 1890 and 1933. For the period 1915–21, they concluded that the reduction in the seasonal fluctuations of the call rate was not accompanied by any significant seasonal fluctuations in Federal Reserve Credit. For the period 1922–28 the seasonal patterns in Fed Credit and the call rate were similar. When fluctuations in Fed credit became highly seasonal in the 1920s, there was an increase, not a decrease as called for by Miron's hypothesis, in the call rate. During the Great Depression of 1929–33, Holland and Toma did not discover seasonals in either Fed credit or the call rate. They rejected Miron's interpretation that open market operations were required to induce a reduction in interest-rate seasonals.

Clark (1986) does not dispute Miron's and Schiller's conclusions that seasonal variations in nominal interest rates vanished with the advent of the Fed. But he questioned whether that change was the direct result of Federal Reserve action. Clark argued that interest-rate seasonals disappeared three years before any monetary policy was undertaken to eliminate them. Moreover, he showed that interest-rate seasonals were eliminated in Britain as well about the same time. Clark concluded that the disappearance of interest-rate seasonals was a worldwide phenomenon attributable to common causes. Nevertheless, he could not identify what these common causes were.

Clark performed a series of statistical tests that demonstrated that interest-rate seasonals vanished in both Britain and the United States at the end of 1914. The disappearance of seasonals in interest rates should have been coterminous with the introduction of seasonals in the monetary base and currency, but according to Clark seasonals in both did not begin until the autumn of 1917. He suggested that the disappearance might be attributed to the breakdown of the international gold standard; it might also have been related to the effects of World War I. But the effects war had on the seasonal in interest rates requires further exploration.

Canova (1987) has found that a seasonal in high-powered money was present before the passage of the Aldrich-Vreeland Act in 1908, owing almost entirely to seasonal gold flows and National Bank Note issues. Moreover, he demonstrated that in some cases the Aldrich-Vreeland Act accounted for the shift in the seasonal patterns better than the creation of the Fed. International credit flows and capital market integration reduced the rigidities imposed by the gold standard and the National Banking Act, but also induced an international transmission of seasonal fluctuations in interest rates.

Canova was critical of the traditional evidence on the grounds that it restricts seasonality to be deterministic and independent of other features of the time series. He provided a more general definition of seasonality to include stochastic seasonality. Canova maintained that capital movements, National Bank note issues, and central bank-type actions undertaken by New York banks provided some seasonal elasticity before the advent of the Fed. The birth of the Fed may have had only a minor influence on the seasonal patterns of many changes in interest rates that he attributed to the Aldrich-Vreeland Act and to structural changes in the economy. For example, the share of agriculture in GNP dropped from 24 percent in 1900 to 12 percent in 1922. Canova (1987, p. 22) concluded: "the effects of the Federal Reserve Act on the seasonal pattern of U.S. variables have been overemphasized and the traditional perception of the Fed as responsible for the elimination of interest rate seasonals is inadequate."

No consensus has emerged about the role of the Federal Reserve in smoothing interest-rate seasonals. Schiller, Miron, Clark, and Holland–Toma agree that there was a significant reduction in the seasonal about the time the Fed came into existence. But Clark and Canova attempted to show that the disappearance of the seasonal could not be attributed to Federal Reserve behavior. Canova thought that the elimination of the seasonal had occurred earlier, whereas Clark attributed the reduction of the interest-rate seasonal to unidentifiable forces operating both in Europe and the United States. More work remains to be done in explaining why the interest-rate seasonal may have been simultaneously eliminated in England and other countries as well. Moreover, the connection between World War I financial policies and the elimination of interest-rate seasonals requires further study. Fishe (1990) has attempted to show that the smoothing of interest-rate seasonals between 1914 and 1917 was not due to the founding of the Federal Reserve System but to trade-related gold flow and the special financial events caused by World War I. One of these events was a 1917 amendment to the Federal Reserve Act that reduced the collateral requirements for notes issued and was passed for the primary purpose of assisting war-related financing.

One remaining question about interest-rate seasonals still remains unanswered: Can the significant decline in the interest-rate seasonal explain the absence of financial panics between 1914 and 1929? Perhaps we will never know, at least not until some way is found to test the counterfactual. That is, how many panics might there have been in the absence of the Fed? Nevertheless, we can identify two historical episodes in which deliberate Fed action contributed to the avoidance of serious economic disturbances.

After the collapse of the boom in May 1920, the immediate goal of Federal Reserve policy was to prevent a widespread banking crisis by maintaining the liquidity of the banking system. This the Fed did by making funds freely available at relatively high discount rates. Neither was there a liquidation of bank credit, nor a decline in the money stock during the first six months of the 1920–21 depression. Loans at commercial banks continued to increase, and member bank borrowing continued to rise. Bank credit failed to decline because the 1919 speculative orgy was aggravated by a series of transportation bottlenecks caused in part by threats of strikes. Large quantities of goods awaited removal from production centers. This delay in shipment put pressure on local banks for accommodation. As a result, there was little or no liquidation of inventories, at least before October 1920. Unfortunately, the policy, though successful in preventing a banking crisis, was inimical to a quick recovery of business activity because of the Fed's reluctance to reduce the discount rate.

The second dramatic episode in which the Fed stayed a potentially dangerous financial crisis took place immediately following the 1929 stock market crash. On the morning of October 29, the day of the deluge, the Federal Reserve Bank of New York purchased $132 million of government securities without the prior approval of the Board in Washington and outside the System's regular Open Market Investment Committee's (OMIC) account. This was due partly to psychological reasons and partly to the goal of preventing the tightening of the money market while stock exchange loans were transferred to many New York banks. Between October 30 and November 20, the OMIC acquired securities at the rate of $25 million a week. Again on November 25 authorization was given to purchase an additional $200 million of securities. The New York Federal Reserve Bank reduced its discount rate from 6 percent on November 1 to 4.5 percent on November 15. The Fed's immediate and effective response avoided a banking panic by endorsing a liberal discount policy combined with open market operations to ensure an orderly liquidation of stock market credit.

In neither of these two cases can the avoidance of financial panic be attributed to the removal of seasonal variations of interest rates. Both required action that was not directly related to seasonal considerations. That is not to say that there would not have been some panics in the absence of interest-rate smoothing by the Fed. But interest-rate smoothing by itself was not sufficient to avoid a potential threat to financial stability.

Miron (1986) attributed the reemergence of financial crises in the 1930s to the alleged fact that the Fed accommodated seasonal demands to a lesser extent between 1929 and 1937 than during the period 1922–28. There is no evidence that the first banking crisis in November and December 1930 was related in any way to the behavior of interest rates. As Wicker (1982) demonstrated, a comparison of customers' loan rates for the months of October, November, and December 1930 by member banks in leading cities reveals no effects on local loan rates of the banking crisis. Moreover, the failure in December of the Bank of United States in New York City with more than $180 million in deposits left no discernible trace on interest rates in the central money market.

Nor were the banking crises in 1931 and 1933 closely related to seasonal interest note considerations. The banking crisis in 1931 was the direct consequence of the Fed's policy of increasing the discount rate after Great Britain had departed from the gold standard—an error of commission, not omission. The final collapse in February and March 1933 had little or nothing to do with interest-rate smoothing or nonsmoothing by the Fed. The failure of the incumbent President Herbert Hoover, and the incoming President, Franklin Roosevelt, to agree to any joint action led directly to the collapse of the banking system.

Interest-rate smoothing is also a key consideration in understanding financial and monetary policy in both world wars. The reluctance to terminate those policies at the wars' end was the main source of monetary instability in the immediate postwar periods. Both Treasury and Federal Reserve officials firmly rejected the view that war borrowing could or should be financed on a purely commercial basis. Moreover, they maintained that it was politically infeasible to allow increases in interest rates on government securities to benefit a favored few due to the accident of war.

Secretary William Gibbs McAdoo decided to finance World War I at rates below those prevailing on the open market. He also recognized that the prices of newly issued government securities might fall below par and thereby discourage the public from making further purchases. At first, he relied solely on the patriotic motive to absorb the new issues. Later, he obtained congressional approval to support the market price of Liberty bonds. A clause was inserted in the Third Liberty Loan Act creating a Bond Purchase Fund that gave the U.S. Treasury the authority to purchase bonds for the explicit purpose of stabilizing bond prices during the intervals immediately following a new issue of government securities. The object of the Fund was not to peg the prices of Liberty bonds at par but to keep their prices "measurably around par." Interest rates increased in four successive Liberty Bond campaigns from 3.5 to 4.5 percent. The secretary of the Treasury was authorized to purchase at market prices not more than 5 percent of each outstanding issue. Proceeds from the sale of certificates of indebtedness would be used to buy bonds on the New York Stock Exchange. Total purchases are set out in Table 7.2. The sale of these certificates, mainly to commercial banks, was encouraged by permitting the banks to borrow from the Fed at a preferential discount rate. The success of the program is evidenced by the fact that the prices of government securities remained around par until the final Victory Loan in 1919.

It is of considerable interest that the mandate to stabilize the prices of long-term government securities originated with the Congress at the behest of the Treasury secretary and was administered by the Treasury. The Federal Reserve played no direct role in long-term interest-rate smoothing during World War I. Therefore, any attempt by the Fed to remove preferential discount rates to discourage inflation after World War I meant

Table 7.2

Bond Purchase Fund Acquisitions at Par Value, April 4, 1918–January 31, 1919

(\$000)

Liberty Loan	To November 15, 1918	To January 31, 1919
1st	656	656
2nd	190,345	195,345
3rd	70,936	115,936
4th		35,000

Source: Report Operations of the War Finance Corporation, 65th Cong., 3d Sess., House Document No. 1513, December 3, 1918; *Bond Purchases,* Letter from the Secretary of the Treasury, December 1, 1919, House of Representatives, 66th Congress, 2d Sess., House Document No. 393, pp. 2–3.

conflict with a congressional mandate to stabilize bond prices; it was not, as is sometimes suggested, simply a tiff between the Treasury and the Federal Reserve.

Interest-rate smoothing became interest-rate pegging during World War II and for a substantial period thereafter (until 1951). What is not so well understood is that the Federal Reserve initiated the policy of establishing a pattern of rates and the Treasury accepted it only after much argument and considerable delay. Both the Treasury and the Federal Reserve argued that an increase in interest rates could not forestall wartime inflation and that the rate on long-term government bonds should not rise above 2.5 percent. Disagreement existed, however, about the most effective technique for maintaining the fixed long-term rate. The Treasury's position was that the 2.5 percent rate could be maintained only if the Fed made provision for a large quantity of excess reserves. Treasury officials had little confidence that the Fed had the will to establish and to support a pattern of interest rates by discretionary purchases and sales of government securities. At first, neither the Fed nor the Treasury endorsed a policy of pegging short-term rates. Short-term rates were to remain completely flexible so as to be consistent with the fixed long-term rate. Only when it became apparent to Treasury officials that the Fed was adamantly opposed to increasing excess reserves did the Treasury demand that the bill rate be posted at 0.37 percent.

The official record simply does not support the hypothesis that the Fed relinquished its independence by acquiescing to the Treasury's desire to establish and to perpetuate a pattern of interest rates. What ultimately emerged was an uneasy and fragile compromise between two widely divergent views about how to maintain a pegged long-term rate.

The Treasury's initial view about how to finance the war was sent out in a memorandum dated February 1942 in response to the Fed's earlier recommendations: (1) The Treasury does not intend to issue bonds at a higher rate than 2.5 percent, (2) no attempt should be made to maintain any preconceived pattern of rates; short-term rates should be as low as necessary to maintain the desired level of long-term rates, (3) the Federal Reserve should make available a more adequate supply of excess reserves, and (4) no assurance should be given the market that any particular government security will be pegged at any price. What the memo demonstrates is the Treasury's opposition to the establishment of a pattern of rates. Treasury officials attributed the low bill rate to the large quantity of excess reserves and did not believe that the low rates could be maintained in any other way. Within two months, however, the Treasury had completely reversed its position. It agreed to the maintenance of a pattern of rates and demanded that the bill rate be pegged. The Treasury had retreated from its position on excess reserves.

A tentative agreement reached on March 20, 1942, defined the Treasury/Federal Reserve policy of war finance, with the Fed supporting the bill market at a bill rate approaching 0.37 percent. The secretary was unwilling to make a public announcement about the decision to maintain a 2.5 percent long-term rate. The market would have to form its expectations of the long-term rate on the basis of observing Fed/Treasury behavior. The learning process was not completed until the second half of 1943 when the commercial banks began in earnest to switch into longer term securities. As the share of the banks' holdings of short-term securities decreased, the Fed's share increased.

Interest-rate smoothing was probably one of the exigencies of war finance in a political environment presumably necessitated by a high proportion of borrowed funds to tax receipts. The ratio was determined by the president and the Congress. There was not much the Fed could do other than recognize its responsibilities for insuring the success of the Treasury's large-scale borrowing plans.

In wartime, the responsibility for monetary policy is not so clearly defined. Whatever the merits of dichotomizing the administration of fiscal policy in the Treasury and of monetary policy in the Federal Reserve during peacetime, the wisdom of such an arrangement in wartime is open to serious dispute. The principle of Federal Reserve independence may simply become inapplicable because in war the priority of goals is altered, as is the margin of tolerance for their nonattainment. Since the major aim of financial policy in wartime is to contribute to the successful conduct of the war, ultimately responsibility for financial policy (including monetary policy) must rest with the president and the Congress. More direct intervention during war can be expected. Fed opposition to

Table 7.3
Excess Reserves of Member Banks, Monetary Gold Stock, U.S. Government
Securities Held in Special Open Market Investment Account, Annually, 1929–37[a]

(\$ Million)

Year	Excess Reserves	Monetary Gold Stock	U.S. Government Securities
1929	43	3,996	208
1930	55	4,173	564
1931	89	4,417	669
1932	256	3,952	1,461
1933	528	4,059	2,052
1934	1,564	7,512	2,432
1935	2,469	9,059	2,431
1936	2,512	10,578	2,431
1937	1,220	12,162	2,504

Source: Board of Governors of the Federal Reserve System, *Twenty-Fourth Annual Report*,
    Washington, 1938, p. 42.

[a]Annual averages of daily figures.

financial policy was confined to the inner councils of war finance and
was not carried to the point of recalcitrance.

5. THE INCREASE IN RESERVE REQUIREMENTS, 1936–37

The Federal Reserve Board's understanding of how monetary policy was
supposed to work was put to a severe test in 1936 and 1937. Reserve
requirements were doubled in an effort to eliminate the huge accumulation
of excess reserves between 1933 and 1936, presumably as a purely precautionary measure to prevent future inflation. Table 7.3 shows the behavior
of excess reserves, the monetary gold stock, and the amount of government
securities held in the System Open Market Account annually from 1929
through 1937. The table clearly reveals that the increase in the supply of
excess reserves in 1932 and 1933 can be attributed to large purchases of
government securities for the System account. After 1933 the increase can
be attributed primarily to changes in the monetary gold stock.

The 1932 program of massive purchases of government securities is interesting in its own right. Why, for example, were the purchases delayed

so long? But this episode does reveal that System officials had encountered difficulties in interpreting the role of excess reserves prior to the doubling of reserve requirements in 1936–37. A program of purchases was initiated in March 1932—$100 million a week for ten weeks—and was terminated abruptly in May because of the completely unanticipated buildup of excess reserves in New York and Chicago. Reserve position theory could not explain why the indebtedness of the banks outside New York and Chicago remained at unacceptably high levels. Instead, interbank deposits increased by $830 million. Country banks were depositing their surplus funds in big city banks rather than taking down their indebtedness. Epstein and Ferguson (1984) summarize the fears among Reserve Bank governors that additional purchases would only expand further excess reserves, drive down short-term interest rates, reduce bank earnings, and thereby impair the solvency of the banking system. Furthermore, additional excess reserves might force bankers to suspend interest payment on demand deposits and encourage hoarding. This episode raises the same questions as does that of the reserve requirement increase. Did Fed officials view the presence of excess reserves as redundant?

More consideration has been given to testing purely speculative hypotheses about the buildup of excess reserves by the banks in the early and mid-1930s than to a careful analysis of the Fed's behavior as revealed by the Board's official records. These records contain detailed analyses by the Board's staff of the anticipated effects of the reserve requirement increases on interest rates, both short and long-term, portfolio composition of the large New York City banks, bank credit, and the money stock. Nothing in these records suggests that Reserve officials considered excess reserves in 1936 to be redundant. There is nothing to suggest that the Fed expected no change in the money stock or short-term interest rates in 1937.

According to the conventional wisdom, the Board took action as a precautionary measure to prevent future inflation, presumably with no immediately observable monetary effects. However, the Board's official records have a different story to tell. Policymakers hoped to "stiffen" short-term rates and to decelerate the growth of the money stock. But herein lies the paradox: they did not interpret their actions as a reversal of the policy of monetary ease. What they did not anticipate was huge bank sales of government bonds and a rise in long-term rates.

The significance of this episode resides primarily in what it can tell us about policymakers' understanding of how monetary policy is supposed to work. Were Fed officials guided by a misperception that banks regarded excess reserves as purely redundant, as argued by Friedman and Schwartz (1963) and Brunner and Meltzer (1964)? Or did Fed officials anticipate correctly most of the monetary effects of the reserve requirement increase? If they did assess correctly the monetary effects, why did they persist in going ahead with the increase in required reserves? Did they fail to see the connection between the monetary effects and the potential effects on output? Answers to these questions should throw some light on how well System officials understood the modus operandi of monetary policy.

The increase in excess reserves did not engage the serious attention of Reserve officials as a matter requiring immediate remedial action until the final months of 1935. Prior to 1932, excess reserves were negligible. Payment of interest on demand balances probably explains why banks in the interior of the country let their surplus funds accumulate in correspondent balances in reserve city and central reserve city banks rather than as excess reserves at Federal Reserve Banks. The level of correspondent balances increased from $4 billion in 1929 to $6 billion in 1936, despite the fact that banks were compelled in 1933 to discontinue interest payments on demand deposits. During 1932 open market policy was deliberately geared to creating a target level of excess reserves, with a view to encouraging the expansion of bank credit.

The $2 billion increase in excess reserves in 1934 and 1935 was viewed as a necessary condition for bringing down long-term interest rates and facilitating new financing in the capital market. Government bond yields responded favorably by declining from 3.5 percent in January 1934 to 2.7 percent in December 1935. All the increased activity in the new issues market was restricted to refunding previously existing obligations. Demand deposits expanded by $7 billion, which brought the level of deposits above the 1929 maximum for member banks, though not for all commercial banks. The sizable increase in demand deposit resulted partly from the gold inflow, but to an even greater extent from direct sales of new securities by the Treasury to the member banks. None of the increase can be accounted for by the expansion of loans, for total loans declined further in 1934 and only began to level off in 1935. Member banks increased their holdings of U.S. government securities and securities fully guaranteed by the government during this period by $5 billion. Of the $22.6 billion increase in public marketable securities between June 1933 and June 1941, no fewer than $18.3 billion were bonds in the ten- to twenty-year range—about 80 percent of the total. Treasury notes outstanding increased from $4.5 to $11.3 billion between June 1933 and June 1936.

Action to increase reserve requirements was not forthcoming before the passage of the Banking Act of 1935 in August when the Board obtained the authority to vary reserve requirements within specified limits. The Board had been given the power to raise reserve requirements in the Thomas amendment to the Agricultural Adjustment Act in March 1933, but it could do so only during an emergency declared as such by at least five members of the Federal Reserve Board and with the approval of the president. A memorandum prepared for the directors of the New York

Federal Reserve Bank in March 1935 took the position that the responsibility and power over excess reserves rested principally with the administration.

Discussions were held continually throughout 1934 and 1935 about introducing some flexibility into the Open Market Account by sales of securities. Since there had been no change in the Open Market Account since November 1933, there was widespread fear that sales would trigger a wave of selling and might be interpreted as a major reversal of System policy. Although a number of Federal Reserve Bank governors expressed a desire to increase reserve requirements in late October 1935, the majority did not favor an increase. Both Chairman Eccles and Governor Harrison, on the other hand, were anxious to take action because they thought other considerations would force a postponement for perhaps another year—at least until after the presidential election. These considerations included the reorganization of the Board of Governors on February 1, 1936, Treasury financial operations in December 1936 and the following March, and the political conventions in the summer.

There is no substance to the claims that Fed officials failed to consider carefully the monetary effects of the reserve requirement increase. System officials at both the Board in Washington and the Federal Reserve Bank of New York gave careful consideration to the impact of such action on (1) the money stock, (2) short- and long-term interest rates, (3) the amount of correspondent balances to be withdrawn from New York city banks, and (4) the bond market and the action to take if the increase created disorderly conditions. Not one of these considerations was neglected.

Nevertheless, a distinction should be drawn between the anticipated effects of the first reserve requirement increase in August 1936 and those of the second which took place in two installments, one half on March 1, 1937, and the other half on May 1. Reserve officials expected a deceleration of the money stock to follow the reserve requirement increases in both 1936 and 1937. George Harrison (September 19, 1935, p. 61), governor of the Federal Reserve Bank of New York, had told his directors what the monetary effects of the proposed increase might be: member banks in New York City would have to borrow heavily, and country banks would be forced to withdraw their balances from New York. Moreover, New York banks would not feel as free to subscribe to new Treasury issues, the effect of which would be smaller sales of new securities to the banking system and a slowing down in the rate of expansion of the money stock. He did not expect changes in either short- or long-term interest rates as a result of the first reserve requirement increase in 1936. Nor were the banks expected to dispose of long-term assets. There was clear recognition that an additional 50 percent increase in reserve requirements in 1937 would necessitate an increase in short-term rates but no change in long-term rates. The record is very straightforward. Monetary effects would attend a reserve

Table 7.4

Liquidation of Government Securities, Direct and Guaranteed, by Select New York City Banks, July 1, 1936–April 7, 1937

($ million)

Banks	July 1, 1936 – Feb. 24, 1937	Feb. 24, 1937 – April 7, 1937	Whole Period
Guaranty Trust	−219	− 32	−251
Bankers Trust	−142	− 88	−230
National City	−126	− 79	−205
Chase National	− 32	− 49	− 81
Central Hanover	− 16	− 34	− 50
New York Trust	− 14	− 21	− 35
First National	+ 26	+ 11	+ 37
Other Reporting			
Member Banks	−142	− 29	−171
Total:	−665	−321	−986

Source: Federal Reserve Board Records.

requirement increase in 1937. Nevertheless, Federal Reserve policymakers refused to acknowledge that either a deceleration of the money stock or a "stiffening" of short-term interest rates constituted a shift from a policy of monetary ease to monetary restraint. The market, as we will attempt to show, thought otherwise. Long-term interest-rate expectations changed, which led to panic-like conditions in the bond markets. But that is to run ahead of the story.

A survey of the reserve position of member banks made by the Federal Reserve Board's staff (1936) on May 25, 1936, concluded:

Practically all of the shortage of surplus funds below an amount sufficient to meet an increase of 50% in reserve requirements was in 18 New York City Banks (4 of which are the largest in New York City). In the event these banks would have needed an additional $87,000,000 of reserve balances. . . . On the average these 15 banks would have to reduce their secondary reserves by 5½%. Most of the 15 banks had ample street loans, acceptances and commercial paper, and Treasury bills, the most liquid types of secondary reserves, and would not have had to reduce their holding of longer-term assets.

The subsequent sale of over $600 million of long-term securities by New York City banks between July 1, 1936, and February 24, 1937, came as a complete surprise to Board officials. The extent of security sales by select New York City banks is shown in Table 7.4. At least 70 percent of the sales can be accounted for by three banks: Guarantee Trust, Bankers Trust, and National City. It was cheaper to liquidate long-term securities because of the substantial profits to be obtained. At the annual meetings of stockholders, the presidents of the leading New York City banks noted the large profits derived from the sale of securities in 1936. Bankers Trust showed a $2 million profit on the sale of securities; Manufacturers Trust announced a $5.7 million profit. Winthrop Aldrich (1937, p. 371) of Chase National Bank declared that "profits from the sale of securities again represented a considerably larger proportion of net earnings than is usual during years when interest rates and investment yields are on a more normal basis." The average yield on government bonds had declined from 2.68 percent in January 1936 to 2.27 percent in December. The reserve requirement increase altered long-term interest-rate expectations, and New York City banks responded by selling long-term securities contrary to the prediction of the Board's staff.

Fed policymakers did not oppose the idea of a reduction in the rate of expansion of bank credit and the money stock, because they thought that the volume of idle deposits was more than adequate to meet any sizable increase in the demand for bank credit. The rate of deposit turnover had been fifteen times per annum since 1933 compared with a deposit turnover rate of twenty between 1922 and 1926. They concluded that an expansion of bank credit was not a necessary condition to finance further recovery. Reserve officials did not err by concluding there would be no money stock effects of the first reserve requirement increase, although they were mistaken in their prediction that New York City banks would not sell long-term government securities.

The increase in reserve requirements that became effective in August 1936 reduced excess reserves to $1.8 billion, down from $3 billion reached in the earlier part of the year. By the end of December, however, excess reserves had increased by an additional $400 million because of gold imports. This meant that approximately one third of the $1.2 billion decrease in excess reserves in August had been regained within the short interval of four months. The continuation of the large gold inflow was responsible for directing the attention of System officials in November 1936 to the question of whether or not reserve requirements should again be increased. The Treasury, quite independently, was also considering whether or not to sterilize gold imports. The members of the Board of Governors and the presidents of the twelve Federal Reserve Banks preferred a policy of an additional increase in reserve requirements to the sale of securities on the grounds that sales might easily be interpreted as a reversal of their easy money policy.

Sometime in December 1936, the professional staff of the Board prepared a series of important and highly significant memoranda in an attempt to evaluate the expected effects of an additional reserve requirement increase. Perhaps the most influential and comprehensive memorandum was prepared by Woodlief Thomas (1937) who maintained that a 33.3 percent increase would necessitate the sale of a "not inconsiderable amount of marketable assets as well as some borrowing on the part of New York City banks." The increase in short-term rates would not be very large because of the large amount of idle funds of corporations awaiting profitable use. He estimated that the rate on open market commercial paper might rise from 0.75 percent to 1 or 1.25 percent, and he doubted whether the rate on Treasury bills having a maturity of nine months would rise above 0.75 percent. Two considerations, he said, set limits on the probable rise in rates: (1) the level of rates at which idle funds would be attracted from banks outside New York and from nonbank lenders, and (2) the bill-buying rate of the Federal Reserve Bank of New York. Thomas (1937) did not think that long-term rates would be very much affected:

The long-term bond market might be somewhat affected by the readjustment of the reserve position of a few banks, but this effect would probably be temporary. A change in reserve requirements by itself should not have a lasting effect upon the bond market, since the large supply of available investment funds outside banks is an important factor in this market.

He concluded by saying that if the authorities wished to maintain the extremely low short-term rates, they could reduce both the rediscount rate and the bill-buying rates. Although the reduction might not stimulate borrowing from the Federal Reserve Banks, it would probably increase interbank borrowing.

There was clear recognition that an additional 50 percent increase in reserve requirements would necessitate an increase in short-term rates and might exert a retarding influence on the growth of bank credit. No further increase in bank deposits was deemed desirable, for further expansion of credit might carry a danger of inflation. Nor did they think a "stiffening" of short-term rates would be undesirable. An increase might bring them more into line with long-term rates. Most Reserve officials believed that short-term rates were abnormally low relative to long-term rates. System officials did not regard such action as a reversal of the policy of monetary ease.

On January 30, 1937, the Board announced an increase in reserve requirements to take effect in two installments: one half on March 1 and one half on May 1.

In December 1936, the Board's staff estimated that an additional 50 percent increase in reserve requirements would lead to a withdrawal of as much as $200 million from New York City banks. They concluded that the banks would purchase Fed funds, borrow from the Fed, or liquidate short-term assets—Treasury bills, banker acceptances, and call loans. They were right inasmuch as $23 million of interbank deposits were withdrawn during the six-week period beginning February 24, 1937, and ending April 7. They were wrong about how the banks would make the adjustment. The New York City banks sold $321 million of government securities, approximately one half of the total amount of security sales by the banks during the preceding eight months. Five New York City banks account for approximately 90 percent of the sales within the city. Banks in the interior of the country followed the lead of the large New York banks and sold bonds to realize profits and avoid future losses as interest rates rose, but the amount of these sales can easily be exaggerated. Data for reporting member banks show that between December 31, 1936, and June 1937, New York and Chicago reduced their holdings of government securities by about $160 million. However, country banks had added $150 million to their total holdings during the same period.

Early in March there was a sharp and serious collapse of government bond prices. Large New York City banks again began to liquidate government bonds but not on a scale commensurate with the sales between July 1936 and February 24, 1937 (Table 7.4). On March 8, the Treasury announced the issue of 2.5 percent bonds in exchange for notes maturing April 15, 1937. Subscriptions were closed on March 10, at which time only $484 million of notes had been exchanged. The situation had deteriorated to the point that on March 9 and 10 the Federal Reserve made purchases of government securities for the Treasury account to prevent a disorderly market. On March 12, Secretary of Treasury Morgenthau described the condition of the bond market as one of "panic." George Harrison disagreed. He said that there had been no forced sales or real disorder in the bond market. Nevertheless, the effect was to move long-term rates upward. The market had been able to absorb the much larger sale of government bonds by the New York City banks between July 1, 1936, and February 24, 1937, without interrupting the continued decline in long-term rates. This did happen in March 1937. Interest-rate expectations were revised upward.

There are alternative interpretations of Federal Reserve Board behavior during this critical episode of monetary history: a Keynesian liquidity trap interpretation and a Friedman and Brunner/Meltzer interpretation, which maintains that Reserve officials failed to recognize the banks' desired relationship of excess reserves to deposits.

According to the liquidity trap version, interest rates and the demand for bank credit had fallen so low that banks had no choice but to accumulate excess reserves. But this liquidity trap is quite different from the one Keynes had in mind. Keynes was referring to uncertainty about future long-term interest rates, not short-term rates. When applied to the banks' demand for excess reserves, the referent is the short-term rate. And it is not uncertainty about short-term rates that is relevant but the level of the rate. Allegedly, the short-term rate had fallen so low as not to cover the transactions costs of asset switching. Federal Reserve officials were not guilty of the alleged offense. They expected a contraction of excess reserves, especially the second installment in 1937, to raise the short-term rate of interest and to reduce the rate of expansion of bank credit and the money stock.

Morrison (1966), Brunner and Meltzer (1964), and Peter Frost (1971) have all rejected the liquidity trap explanation for the accumulation of excess reserves in the early and mid–1930s. Morrison (1966) argued that the liquidity trap hypothesis could not explain why the excess-reserves-deposit ratios of Canadian banks did not increase in a manner similar to that in the United States. Moreover, he found no evidence that the interest elasticity of the demand for excess reserves as a percentage of deposits increases as the interest rate declines. Brunner and Meltzer (1964) rejected the liquidity trap interpretation on the basis of three kinds of evidence: (1) the deceleration of the money stock from May 1936 to December 1937, (2) the continued decline in long- and short-term interest rates, and (3) the expansion of the government portfolios of the banks. Long-term rates *increased* from 2.51 percent in December 1936 to 2.8 percent in April 1937. And short-term rates moved up from 1.2 percent to 1.65 percent between February and April 1937. The short-term data are inconsistent with a liquidity trap notion that government securities were dumped unwillingly on the banking system. Frost (1971) tested the hypothesis that the demand curve for excess reserves is kinked at some low rate of interest. Whenever the short-term rate falls below some critical value, all the parameters of the model increase in absolute value. His estimates strongly contradicted the view that the banks' demand for excess reserves became very elastic at some low level of the interest rate during the 1930s.

The alternative to the liquidity trap interpretation is the demand shift hypothesis associated primarily with Friedman and Schwartz (1963). The banks' demand for excess reserves was shocked by the widespread bank failures of the early 1930s and the abrupt increases in reserve requirements in 1936 and 1937. Morrison (1966) distinguished between a "shock" effect and an "inertia" effect. The shock effect produces an immediate and abrupt shift to a much higher desired cash ratio at the crisis point but a slow adjustment of the actual to the desired ratio. The inertia effect implies that a sudden unexpected increase of excess reserves will not lead to a sudden increase in the demand for earning assets. Banks will move cautiously. Morrison's regression evidence leads to a rejection of the shock effect interpretation in favor of the inertia effect. James Wilcox (1984) attempted to test the shock hypothesis. He found that such shocks to demand did exert a detectable influence on the demand for excess reserves. His estimates can account for the rise in excess reserves in the early 1930s, but they cannot explain the continued rise after 1935 or 1937. The statistical tests decisively rejected the hypothesis that the demand for excess reserves remained steep. He found that it became extremely flat at low rates.

The historical record tells quite a different story. The effects of increases in reserve requirements in 1936 and 1937 depended in an important way on the distribution of excess reserves as well as on the total amount. The increase fell disproportionately on a small number of very large New York City banks whose excess reserves were insufficient to meet the reserve requirement increase. Revised expectations about future long-term rates may explain why these banks unloaded bonds rather than shorter term securities, the ultimate effect of which was deceleration of the money stock and a rise in long-term rates. The failure of the Board's staff to have anticipated correctly the revision of long-term interest-rate expectations was the consequence of at least two factual errors: (1) they did not judge correctly the effect of the buildup of a speculative position in government bonds by certain banks, and (2) they also probably overestimated the amount of idle investment funds awaiting placement by corporations, trusts, and insurance companies that would respond to a slight increase in the yield on government bonds.

What requires further exploration is the connection, if any, between the setback in the government bond market in Great Britain about the same time as the bond market upheaval in the United States. In the six weeks preceding, the yield on gilt-edged securities had risen from 3 to 3.5 percent. Whether this was a mere coincidence or the result of broader forces at work yet unidentified in the United States and the United Kingdom is a matter that needs additional investigation.

6. INTERPRETING THE FED: THE NEWER BUREAUCRATIC APPROACH

The literature interpreting Fed behavior, which we have attempted to survey in the preceding pages, has been completely dominated by a single paradigmatic model. That model is based on the unexamined assumption that monetary policymakers attempt to maximize the public interest by identifying and pursuing desirable social goals with apparent disregard for the self-interest of the individual policymakers. A reaction function literature evolved in an effort to estimate the weights policymakers attached to the different social objectives of Federal Reserve monetary policy such as maximizing employment and minimizing inflation. Optimal control theory became the preferred analytical apparatus for understanding how monetary policy ought to be conducted. This so-called public interest approach has vitiated almost all the critical evaluations of central bank behavior in the United States as well as abroad.

Walter Bagehot (1887) was clearly one of the first persuasive and articulate spokesmen for the view that central bankers must place the public interest above the pursuit of private gain in responding to financial crises. The central bank was not like all other profit-maximizing commercial banks as Mr. Hankey, one of the Bank of England's directors, had maintained. Bagehot thought that the bank had a higher duty to maintain financial stability and that in certain circumstances profit maximizing should be a secondary consideration. Goodhart (1988, p. 9) claimed that the transition to a noncompetitive, nonprofit-maximizing role was the distinguishing feature of "proper" central banking. This process, he believed, was probably completed in Britain and Germany well before 1900. And it was at least implicit in the Federal Reserve Act of 1913.

The newer bureaucratic models differ from the older public interest models inasmuch as Federal Reserve officials are assumed to behave like all other agents in society: namely, they are motivated, though not entirely, by their own self-interest. The essence of these models can be summed up quite succinctly: the Fed, like any other central bank for that matter, is a bureaucratic organization whose agents maximize utility by the pursuit of such personal goals as power, prestige, and self-preservation. Bureaucratic behavior is characterized by a distinctive set of properties: inertia, secrecy, and an unwillingness or inability to learn from past experience, behaviors that are not easily accounted for by the public interest approach. The origins of the newer models are to be found in the theory of public choice as well as in the political and economic theories of bureaucracy.

Theorists of public choice are especially adamant in their rejection of the conventional approach. Buchanan (1986, p. 251), for example, has stated: "The whole Keynesian edifice was constructed on the preposterous supposition that economic advice is offered to a genuinely benevolent despot, and entirely devoid of its own interest, and presumably willing and able to implement without resistance, the advice offered to it." With less rhetorical flourish, Wagner (1986, p. 526) has written: "support for central banking seems more likely to be explained by the economic theory of rent-seeking than by the theories of market failure and public goods." Rent-seeking by bureaucrats refers to a wealth redistribution process whereby agents devise ways to transfer wealth to themselves from others. Some advocates of the bureaucratic models make more sweeping claims than others. Acheson and Chant (1986, p. 130) declare that "A large part of central banking can best be explained by the simple theory of bureaucracy." Others are more circumspect and claim merely that the bureaucratic model provides useful insights into specific forms of Fed behavior, most notably Fed secrecy and Fed inertia that may lack convincing explanations in the conventional public interest approach.

The newer bureaucratic models have been used extensively to interpret central bank behavior since World War II. But little or no effort has been made to use the bureaucratic model as the basis for organizing and interpreting pre–World War II Federal Reserve history. Select historical episodes may reveal what content, if any, can be given to interpreting Fed behavior in terms of bureaucratic motivation.

The public choice version of the bureaucratic model reduces the various motives—power, prestige, self-preservation—to a measurable quantity, the maximization of the bureau's budget with testable implications. Both Shuggart and Tollison (1986) and Toma (1986) have performed tests of such a model. Shuggart and Tollison concluded that there is a positive and statistically significant relationship between the monetary base and Fed size as measured by the number of employees over the period 1916–1981, and that the causation runs from the number of employees to the monetary base. They inferred that at least one motive for the expansion of the base and indirectly the money stock was to finance the growth of the Fed's bureaucracy. Nowhere in conventional money stock theory do we find growth of Fed employees as a fundamental determinant of the money stock.

Toma (1986) assumed that Fed officials maximized discretionary profits in the form of net operating revenues and that there is a causal relationship between Fed current revenues and Fed expenditures. Fed revenues induce Fed expenditures. Bureaucrats will use discretionary profits to expand expenditures on perks, larger salaries, and so on. He regressed a change in expenditures on a change in Federal Open Market Committee wealth as measured by the size of the government security portfolio and several other variables and found a statistically significant relationship for the period 1947–79. But that same relationship may not hold for the pre-World War II period. A casual inspection of the data on changes in current expenditures and current receipts for the earlier period 1914–40 reveals that in sixteen of the twenty-five pre–1940 years changes in expenditures do not move synchronously with earnings and are inconsistent with Toma's hypothesis.

Earnings considerations may, however, have been an important determinant, though not the only determinant, of open market operations as late as 1924, but not afterward. Since the twelve Federal Reserve Banks were expected to meet current expenses from current revenue to pay a maximum dividend to the member banks of 6 percent, and to revert any excess to the Treasury as a franchise tax, it was to be expected that earnings considerations would loom large, especially during the Fed's formative years. At the outset the Fed's principal source of revenue was interest earned on discounts and advances to the member banks. Net earnings were not sufficient to pay all accrued dividends in 1915 and 1916. Only six Reserve Banks paid dividends in 1917. However, in 1918 all the banks paid dividends and the franchise tax to the Treasury. Federal Reserve Banks were able to supplement their earnings by interest obtained on government security holdings during World War I. Afterward, the runoff of government security holdings and discounts at Federal Reserve Banks left Cleveland and Kansas City with insufficient earnings to cover current expenses, depreciation, and dividends in 1924. Boston, New York, Chicago, and San Francisco had earnings sufficient to cover current expenses but inadequate to meet full dividend requirements.

Large government security purchases by Federal Reserve Banks to restore earnings were made between November 1921 and May 1922, and again in 1924, but on this occasion the motives were mixed. Some Reserve Bank officials favored increased purchases for earnings considerations. So did C. S. Hamlin of the Federal Reserve Board. Nevertheless, Governor Strong of the Federal Reserve Bank of New York was urging purchases to moderate the recession and to proffer help to enable Britain to return to the gold standard. After 1924 earnings no longer were a factor in determining open market policy, and no mention was ever made again in Board minutes or the minutes of the Open Market Investment Committee to earnings considerations. There is absolutely no reason why earnings considerations should have been concealed in the official record.

A salient characteristic of bureaucratic administration is inertia—that is, a reluctance to act when the occasion warrants, to learn from previous experience and to innovate. Central banks in particular may be hesitant to change the direction of monetary policy. Milton Friedman (1986, p. 16) has pressed the charge of bureaucratic inertia the farthest:

My examination of that experience impresses me with the unbelievable strength of bureaucratic inertia in preventing the system from learning from experience. The inertia has prevailed not only since 1960, but for the whole sixty-seven years of the Federal Reserve existence. With perhaps a few minor exceptions, the system has repeatedly been unable or unwilling to change its methods of operation in order to benefit from its own experience. . . . I believe that the fundamental explanation for the persistence and importance of bureaucratic inertia in the Federal Reserve is the absence of a bottom line. The Fed is not subject to an effective budget constraint.

The evidence from the 1920s is difficult to reconcile with Friedman's claim that the Fed failed to learn from previous experience. Presumably the Fed learned how to respond to a financial crisis initiated in the central money market. By a liberal extension of Reserve Bank Credit through the discount window, the Fed prevented a widespread collapse of the banking system in 1920 after the collapse of prices in May. When the stock market crashed in October 1929, the Fed injected reserves immediately and on a scale to have warded off a financial panic. What the Fed perhaps did not learn in the 1920s was how to respond to accelerated bank failures that originated *outside* the central money market. In 1930 and 1931 responsibility for preventing bank failures passed to the Reconstruction Finance Corporation, of which the head of the Federal Reserve Board was also its chairman. The confusion over who had responsibility for bank failures was understandable.

Neither was inertia a cause of the Fed's failure to purchase securities in the early months of 1930. Both Chandler (1958) and Friedman and Schwartz (1963) have maintained that the Fed learned how to use open market operations for the purpose of moderating business fluctuations in the 1920s. Earlier we have shown why the Fed's behavior was perfectly consistent with its performance in 1923–24 and 1926–27. The Fed refrained from purchases in 1930 because the indebtedness of the Chicago and New York banks had been eliminated by return flows of currency at the beginning of the year. The Fed did not forget in 1930 what it had learned in the two previous recessions; it had behaved in a similar manner without similar results.

The Fed's failure to have raised the discount rate in 1919, which would halt inflation, and its resistance to lower rates once the downturn had begun cannot be attributed to inertia. Treasury pressure, not bureaucratic inertia, delayed the increase in rates in 1919. Lack of understanding of the relationship between interest rates and economic activity explains the delayed response of the discount rate. Never again has the Fed allowed the discount rate to remain unchanged during a recession in economic activity. What they learned left an indelible mark on the policymakers. Nor can the Fed's delayed discount rate response in 1928 and 1929 to stock market speculation be attributed to inertia. The majority of the Federal Reserve Board preferred moral suasion to a rate increase because of a fear that an increase in rates would precipitate a downturn.

Nor can bureaucratic inertia be used to explain the alleged procyclical behavior of the money stock. Not only was there a slow recognition of the turning points, but also there was imperfect understanding on the part of policymakers about how removing the indebtedness of the New York and Chicago banks to the Fed would initiate recovery.

The historical evidence does not favor the inertia principle as a guide to understanding Fed policymaking before World War II. Nor is the evidence convincing that the Fed failed to learn from previous experience during the interwar period.

Survival is another recognizable trait of the bureaucrat. The Fed's survival during the first thirty years is an achievement that requires some explaining. The alleged failures of the Fed between 1928 and 1938 are impressive: Reserve officials were unsuccessful in their efforts to prevent the stock market boom or the crash in 1928–29; they refrained from substantial purchases of government securities during the first six months of 1930; they raised the discount rate in October 1931 to stem the gold exodus and the domestic currency drain; and they failed to halt widespread bank suspensions in November and December 1930, the autumn of 1931, and again in the early months of 1933. How could the central bank survive in the face of these allegations of ineptness?

We might reasonably infer that the Fed's survival represented a bureaucratic triumph. By successfully evading responsibility for the worst of its alleged mistakes, the Fed managed to deflect criticism and thereby insure its survival. The Fed not only survived but emerged eventually and surprisingly with more power and effectiveness. The Congress did not attribute the Fed's relatively weak performance to personal ineptness. Bank failures, for example, were attributed to disruptive interest-rate competition between the banks and to certain illegal and questionable banking practices by investment bankers. The remedy was central bank reform, not the abolition of the Fed. The Banking Act of 1933 liberalized access of member banks to the discount window and abolished interest payments on demand deposits. The Banking Act of 1935 completely reorganized the Fed. Open market operations became the responsibility of a twelve-person Federal Open Market Committee. Power was more clearly centralized in Washington, D.C., with less influence for the Federal Reserve Bank of New York. The Federal Deposit Insurance Corporation (FDIC) was created as Title 3 of the 1935 Banking Act in an attempt to remedy widespread bank failures.

As a result of the Fed's poor performance during the Great Depression, Congress saw fit to intervene directly and on a scale never known either before or since. The Fed's survival was due less to a deliberative strategy and more to the sometimes faulty diagnosis of the banking system's ills by Congress. The theory of bureaucracy has so far made little contribution to our understanding of why and how the Fed avoided annihilation in the 1930s.

Secrecy has been another notorious characteristic of central bank behavior, and it is here that the newer bureaucratic theories have contributed the most to our understanding of why the policymakers are so stingy in the release of information. Presumably, they ration the information available so as to avoid or obfuscate public accountability. Secrecy forms part of the bureaucrat's defense to protect him or her from the prying eyes of the public. Too much central bank publicity may (or so it is alleged) impair the credibility of the monetary authority, especially in matters where political considerations are known to have influenced the course of policy or where the Fed's action would have significant political implications.

The Fed's large purchases of government securities during the 1923–24 recession is a good example of the use of secrecy to attain desirable ends. International considerations were a key factor in explaining the timing and the magnitude of the security purchases in 1924. Governor Strong's desire to aid Britain in returning to the gold standard was a potent force determining the extent of the action undertaken. Domestic considerations were also important. Nevertheless, too much publicity could not be given to the foreign factor because such considerations were not politically popular— either within the Open Market Investment Committee or the country as a whole. Similarly, in 1927 purchases were made presumably for domestic reasons—to moderate the recession. However, unlike 1924, purchases were made in 1927 to keep Britain on the gold standard. A conference was held in the summer of 1927 on Long Island whose participants included Montagu Norman, governor of the Bank of England, Charles Rist of the Bank of

France, and Hjalmar Schacht of the Reichsbank. The decision was made at this meeting to offer some support to Britain. The meeting was clouded in secrecy from beginning to end without the full proceedings even being reported to the Board in Washington.

Acheson and Chant (1986), in an early attempt to apply bureaucratic theory to explain central bank performance, hypothesized that central banks are concerned with being covert and that moral suasion as a monetary instrument is a covert instrument. They attempted to show how the Bank of Canada employed moral suasion to avoid public scrutiny. Since moral suasion is likely to be more effective in oligopolistic banking markets similar to banking markets in Canada, it is uncertain how applicable their argument is to explaining central banking practice in the United States.

Moral suasion was the main guide of the monetary policymakers in only one major episode in pre–World War II Fed history: that is, during 1928–29 when the Federal Reserve Board pursued a policy of "direct pressure" to reduce the amount of bank credit flowing to the stock market. Reserve officials were reluctant to use either the discount rate or open market operations for two reasons: a rise in rates might cause a serious recession, and the rise in rates would not deter speculation. There was nothing covert about the Board's policy. A letter was sent to all member banks requesting that banks exercise caution in making loans for purely speculative purposes. There was certainly no desire to avoid responsibility for the outcome. The policy of direct pressure did not qualify as a covert instrument.

We may now ask: How specifically do the bureaucratic models differ from the public interest models in predicting central bank responses to recession, inflation, and financial crises? Bureaucratic inertia and secrecy may explain the procyclical behavior of both M1 and M2 during the first six months of the 1923–24 and 1926–27 recessions, although both aggregates accelerated sharply during the residual three months of each recession—too late, however, to have had significant output effects. Public interest models predict a strong countercyclical response in both phases of recession.

At least one interpretation of the bureaucratic model, the political business cycle (PBC) (Nordhaus, 1989) with top priority being given to a desired political outcome, shows how the central bank may become a source of instability. The PBC approach, if valid, reveals the futility of countercyclical policy and the sterility of the public interest approach. So far, no attempt has been made to show the relevance of the PBC model to pre–World War II experience.

The bureaucratic model has had little to contribute to our understanding of the Fed's quick response to the threat of financial panic in 1920 and again in 1929. Apparently, the bureaucratic approach in terms of self-interest, prestige, and self-preservation produced the same response as the public interest approach. Nor has it contributed to our understanding of open market operations after 1924.

To date, therefore, the bureaucratic model remains largely a hypothesis about central banker behavior before World War II and raises as many questions as it answers, though with some exceptions. If the aim of the bureaucracy was survival, then a bureaucratic Fed succeeded; if the aims were also prestige and power, then the bureaucratic model failed. The Fed survived the depression upheaval but not without a serious loss of prestige, power, and credibility. Its reputation had been seriously compromised.

7. MONETARY POLICIES: THE ROLE OF PRESIDENT

In the period between the two world wars, presidential and legislative intervention in the affairs of the Fed was minimal except immediately following the inauguration of Franklin Roosevelt, when the president assumed full responsibility for monetary policy. Nevertheless, there are several isolated instances during the Harding and Hoover administrations when presidential influence was exerted on Federal Reserve officials. Probably the most significant from the standpoint of the conduct of monetary policy was the change in the discount rate in 1921 which came at the initiative of the new secretary of the Treasury, Andrew Mellon, who was an ex officio member of the five-man Federal Reserve Board. The discount rate had remained unchanged at its pre-depression high throughout most of the depression of 1920–21. At Mellon's first meeting with the Board on April 4, 1921, he recommended a one percentage point reduction in the discount rate from 7 to 6 percent. Governor Harding of the Federal Reserve Board—not to be confused with President Warren Harding—told his fellow Board member C. S. Hamlin that action should be taken before Congress convened to avoid the appearance of having acted under pressure. Chandler (1958, p. 174) quoted from Governor Strong's letter to Norman, governor of the Bank of England, to the effect that political pressures had built up for a change in the discount rate:

With this situation [price declines in agriculture and livestock] widespread in the West and South, economic pressure has been felt in Washington from the agricultural sectors of the country that measures be taken to ease up credit conditions. So far as I can discover the demand comes from no other class than those engaged in agriculture. They made an impressive showing and their complaints reached all classes of congressmen and executive officers of government right up to the President.

In another letter to Norman on July 5 that Chandler (1958, p. 176) quoted, he explained the reasons for the rate reduction, as follows:

The only other considerations entering into our policy are (1) general considerations of public policy where, under present conditions classical methods are not always the wisest, and (2) strictly political considerations brought about by the change in administration. . . . Considerations of general welfare lead me to believe that the process of deflation has gone dangerously far here and abroad. . . . As to political considerations, those are quite perplexing. Our new administration is determined to make business good, if means can be found to do so.

Strong would have preferred to have delayed the decrease in the discount rate by a few weeks, but he concluded (Chandler, p. 125):

A bullheaded resistance in this situation is always liable to invite political retaliation, and I frankly concluded that the wisest course was to meet, in part at least, the demand for lower rates. . . . This was all put to me most earnestly by my friends and associates in Washington and the feeling generally prevailed that the New York Bank was causing the deadlock.

This particular episode is made even more interesting inasmuch as there is apparently no other single incident in Fed history where the Fed acknowledged so candidly the role of political considerations in affecting policy. Presidential intervention occurred through the secretary of the Treasury as an ex officio member of the Federal Reserve Board with a change in administration. Moreover, it is obvious that the timing of the intervention was the direct result of political pressures that agricultural interests were able to exert on the incoming administration.

President Harding also intervened for purely partisan political purposes to have one of his political cronies appointed to a Class C directorship of the Cleveland Federal Reserve Bank. A Class C director who also held the job of Federal Reserve Agent was a full-time paying job. The Board refused the president's request. According to both C. S. Hamlin and Governor Strong, as a consequence the president failed to reappoint Governor Harding as head of the Federal Reserve Board. Hamlin (1924, p. 90) concluded two years later that the Fed "has been changed by President Harding's appointments into a purely political system." Perhaps Hamlin overreacted, but his response does reveal that Board members were very sensitive to even the hint of political interference on the part of the president.

On one other occasion during the Harding administration, the Treasury exerted its influence successfully to get the Federal Reserve Banks to reduce their holdings of U.S. government securities. Each Bank exercised initiative as to when and how much to buy or sell. The Treasury expressed concern that uncoordinated purchases and sales could interfere with debt management policy. The individual Federal Reserve Banks were mainly concerned about having adequate earnings to meet expenses and to pay dividends. Nevertheless, at the insistence of the Treasury, the Federal Reserve Banks reduced their holdings of government securities by approximately $500 million between May 1922 and June 1923. This rundown—not entirely voluntary—was another reason why substantial purchases were approved in 1924.

There is no evidence that President Coolidge ever used his influence to affect monetary policy. Hamlin (1926, pp. 91–92) wrote: "Coolidge never, directly or indirectly, had sought to influence policies." Moreover, Chandler (1958, p. 255) stated that when Hoover protested the easing of money in 1927, Coolidge refused to be drawn into the matter.

At the end of August 1930, Roy Young resigned as governor of the Federal Reserve Board to accept an appointment as governor of the Federal Reserve Bank of Boston allegedly because of the higher salary. President Hoover appointed Eugene Meyer governor on September 16. Vice Governor Platt had resigned the previous day to accept a position in private business. Since no more than one Board member may come from a single Federal Reserve District, Platt had to resign if Meyer was to be appointed. President Hoover had assumed by his appointive power some responsibility for providing the Board with new and more effective leadership.

But there may have been more to it than that. Both Hamlin and Congressman McFadden alleged that Hoover conspired to remove Governor Young and Vice Governor Platt from the Federal Reserve Board in order to appoint Eugene Meyer. Hamlin (1930, pp. 63–64) has described a conversation with Platt in which the subject of his resignation came up:

Had long talk with Platt as to his interview with Sec Mellon. Platt said that Mellon began by saying he had heard that Platt had had an offer from a group of banks— that they were all first class men and that he hoped Platt would accept it. Later he would have Platt to understand not directly but by necessary implication that Hoover hoped he would accept as he had someone he wanted to put in his place.

Hamlin thought that the president was attempting to inject politics into the Federal Reserve Board.

Congressman McFadden's allegation that Young and Platt had been ousted to make room for Meyer was examined in the Senate Hearings (1931) dealing with Meyer's nomination to the Federal Reserve Board. Meyer's biographer Merlo Pusey (1974, p. 204) maintained that there was no evidence to support McFadden's claim:

Young testified that Meyer had nothing whatever to do with his retirement; he had simply left a $12,000 job for one paying $30,000. Platt, too, had simply taken a more lucrative job. The two resignations were not connected, and Meyer had no advance knowledge of either of them. No doubt Hoover welcomed Platt's decision, as he was a New Yorker and the law forbade the appointment of two members from a single state, but there was no evidence that anyone had urged Platt to leave.

The evidence from the congressional hearings, however, does not dispose of the matter in a completely satisfactory manner. We cannot have expected Platt and Young to have testified otherwise, and we do not know the circumstances that led to the attractive offers to both Young and Platt. It is not inconceivable that all of this could have been engineered cunningly from the White House without fuss or publicity, or so the White House might have wished. Of course, the resignations of Platt and Young and the appointment of Meyer could have been an accident of timing, but that is not likely. Hamlin's conjecture has some credibility; that is, Ogden Mills, undersecretary of the Treasury, encouraged President Hoover to reorganize the Federal Reserve Board in the interest of increasing the influence of the New York Federal Reserve Bank.

Hoover also tried in vain during the last days of his administration to get the Federal Reserve Board to act to stave off the impending wave of bank failures. But a lameduck president's influence is minimal, even in an emergency, and the Board ignored his solemn entreaties for advice and assistance in warding off an impending banking crisis. It is quite clear that Hoover did not get the kind of monetary policy he wanted, but, again, it was not always clear what he wanted.

When Roosevelt was inaugurated president on March 4, 1933, the economy was at a low ebb; banking holidays had been declared in a half dozen states, and despair had replaced hope. The Fed had been completely discredited, having failed to stop bank suspensions or induce economic recovery. The policy vacuum created by the Fed's inaction was quickly filled by new monetary initiatives of Congress and the president. The president with the full approval of Congress assumed responsibility for monetary policy. He declared in unequivocal terms that the main goal of economic policy was to raise prices by restoring their 1926 level, presumably to ease debt burdens and to stimulate economic activity. His strategy was implemented by specific programs for raising the prices of agricultural commodities by crop restriction schemes (AAA), for increasing wages and prices in individual sectors of the economy (NRA), and for declaring a gold embargo and suspending the gold standard. Although the objective was clearly articulated, its rationale was not. The 1933 episode is unique in the annals of Fed policy. Congress intervened and transferred some responsibility for monetary policy from the Federal Reserve to the president.

This has been the only occasion since 1914 when Congress threatened to intervene directly in the management of money. Congress was dissatisfied with what the administration and the Fed were doing to promote business recovery in 1933. Inflation sentiment was growing for the issue of paper money. The Senate had just defeated by a vote of 43 to 33 the Wheeler amendment providing for the free coinage of silver at the ratio of 16 to 1. In April Senator Elmer Thomas of Oklahoma introduced an amendment to the Farm Relief bill that would have required the president to pursue a policy of inflation through the issue of paper money. Federal Reserve officials, orthodox monetary theorists, as well as the president himself, viewed the strategy of the inflationists in Congress as totally irresponsible. To curb the reckless instincts of Congress, Roosevelt intervened directly to revise the impending legislation. He feared that the Congress would override a presidential veto of the Thomas amendment. So he insisted that the power entrusted to him be discretionary rather than mandatory. Governor Harrison (1933, p. 162) of the Federal Reserve Bank of New York approved Roosevelt's suggested changes and said: "There seems to be no question that we were right on the edge of the precipice of wild legislation and that something had to be done to prevent Congressional excesses." Adolph Miller, the only economist member of the Board, was inclined to agree with the president.

The Thomas amendment authorized the president to direct the secretary of the Treasury to enter into an agreement with the Federal Reserve to expand the money stock by ordinary open market operations and by direct purchases of government securities from the Treasury in an amount not to exceed $3 billion. If, however, the Federal Reserve refused to enter into such an agreement, the president could issue $3 billion of greenbacks for the specific purpose of retiring government interest-bearing obligations. The Thomas amendment gave the president the initiative, if he wished to exercise it, to recommend purchases and sales of government securities, a radical shift in the powers of the Open Market Committee.

Reserve officials grasped fully the significance of the Thomas amendment and acted accordingly to ward off what they regarded as an unwarranted intrusion by the Congress and the president in monetary affairs. On April 22, 1933, the minutes (1933) of the Open Market Investment Committee stated that it would be advisable "to cooperate with the treasury with a view to facilitating any necessary issue of government securities or to support the market for government securities in order to make such public issue possible." The Committee was authorized to purchase up to $1 billion of government securities to meet Treasury requirements, thereby assuring Congress, the president, and the secretary of the Treasury of their willingness to cooperate with the administration and to avoid the possible threat of the issue of greenbacks. Between May 24 and October 25 purchases amounted to approximately $305 million. Before the program was initiated, excess reserves and member bank borrowing each averaged a little over $800 million, and member bank indebtedness had been reduced to the lowest levels since August 1917.

The president, in effect, seized control of monetary policy in 1933. He successfully curbed the monetary interventionists' appetite of the Congress but only by reducing the influence of the Federal Reserve. Reserve officials abdicated their responsibilities to the president. They assumed the role of the loyal opposition. Their dissent was vigorous; they rejected the president's goal of inflation; they rejected the policy of exchange depreciation; they deplored the failure of the World Monetary and Economic Conference in July; they opposed the gold purchase program; and they protested— this time successfully—against Roosevelt's initial suggestion to take over the gold of the Federal Reserve Banks without congressional approval. The Fed's behavior demonstrates that it was totally out of sympathy with the domestic and international monetary policies of the administration. But there was no dramatic confrontation, no embarrassing public conflict. When the president's monetary policy was so out of tune with that of the Federal Reserve policymakers, they reluctantly yielded responsibility to the president and conducted their operations in a manner that would not obstruct the president's initiatives.

The relationship between the Fed, the Congress, and the president cannot be defined a priori, that is, without specific reference to the economic and political circumstances existing at the time. The so-called independence of the Fed is always a relative matter. Our understanding of Fed behavior is not strengthened by undue attachment to a concept unhitched from what is historically relevant. The Fed's failure to act effectively in grave emergencies may provoke responses from the Congress and the president, as indeed it did in 1933 and again in 1935. Political pressures brought to bear on Congress and the president may simply have been too great to have been ignored. Prolonged unemployment and output contraction during the Great Depression created economic burdens whose consequences were communicated to the public's elected representatives. The political outcry was vocal and articulate. The Congress and the president were forced to intervene reluctantly to deflect damaging political criticism. That is essentially what happened in 1933 on a grand scale and also in 1921 on a smaller scale. It did not last long in 1933. When the political crisis had passed, Congress and the president allowed the Fed to manage money without their interference.

8. SUMMARY AND CONCLUSIONS

The first thirty-five years of Fed history were hectic years: only eight of these years were relatively free from either war and its aftermath or serious depression. Yet, during that time the Fed learned how to avert impending crises in the central money market as evidenced by its behavior in both 1920 and again in 1929. The Fed had been established to prevent crises in the central money market, and in that endeavor it had been successful. Interest-rate seasonals disappeared, but to what extent the Fed deserves credit for removing the threat of widespread bank suspensions by eliminating interest-rate seasonals is still a matter of dispute. It was unsuccessful in preventing three successive waves of bank failures in the early 1930s, but these bank suspensions did not create panic in the central money market.

Through the 1920–21 depression experience, the Fed learned the devastating effects of leaving the discount rate at a high and unchanged level throughout the economic downturn. That policy has never been repeated.

The Fed began to experiment with output and employment smoothing objectives before the principal European powers had returned to a modified prewar gold standard, France being one of the last in 1928. But there is a substantial and a growing body of evidence that Reserve officials never learned in the 1920s how to use open market operations to prevent cyclical instability. Their understanding of the monetary effects of purchases and sales of government securities was inadequate. Their response to the onset of the recession in the early 1930s had been similar to their response to the recessions of 1923–24 and 1926–27. With an incomplete understanding of how open market operations were supposed to work, the policymakers were reluctant to engage in substantial purchases after the member banks in New York and Chicago had eliminated their indebtedness to the Fed. Even after they had decided to go ahead with a $1 billion program of purchases in 1932, they took the large buildup of excess reserves to be evidence of the futility of further purchases. It is clear that Reserves officials were having some difficulty understanding why the banks desired to hold excess reserves. The problem surfaced again in 1936 and 1937 when Fed policymakers were concerned about the large increase of excess reserves resulting from gold imports. But this time the problem was not acting as if excess reserves were redundant. The Board's staff simply incorrectly concluded that certain large New York City banks with a reserve deficiency would not adjust their long-term government bond portfolios. They thought that these banks had an adequate stock of short-term assets and that no long-term security sales would be required. They did not predict that the Board's action raising reserve requirements may have changed long-term interest rate expectations. Actually, the long-term rate increased and the money stock declined. An imperfect understanding of how the instruments of monetary policy are supposed to work is an important part of the explanation for the Fed's poor performance in the 1930s.

It is too early to render a verdict on what the newer bureaucratic models will be able eventually to tell us about Fed behavior before World War II. These models may do a better job of explaining certain aspects of Fed activity than others, for example, the well-known propensities of central bankers to withhold information and to delay altering the course of policy. However, a brief review of Fed history as revealed in the official records does not indicate that the bureaucratic model will have very much to teach us about policymakers' behavior.

What the experience of the mid-1930s teaches is the fragility of the Fed's so-called independence. Roosevelt seized control of monetary policy from the Fed in 1933 after the Fed had lost all credibility. Congress reacted by initiating legislation in the form of the Banking Acts of 1933 and 1935 which brought far-reaching and innovative changes to the organization and administration of the Federal Reserve System. In fair weather, Congress and the president left the Fed pretty much to its own devices, but in periods of national emergency, such as war or economic malaise, the president and the Congress reasserted their political prerogative to intervene.

REFERENCES

Acheson, Keith, and Chant, John. 1986. "Bureaucratic Theory and the Choice of Central Bank Goals: The Case of the Bank of Canada." *Central Bankers, Bureaucratic Incentives and Monetary Policy*, edited by Eugenia Toma and Mark Toma. Dordrecht: Kluwer, 129–50.

Aldrich, Winthrop. 1937. *Commercial and Financial Chronicle*. January 12, 371.

Bagehot, Walter. 1987. *Lombard Street*. New York: Charles Sonders' Sons.

Balke, Nathan S., and Gordon, Robert J. 1989. "The Estimation of Prewar Gross National Product: Methodology and New Evidence." *Journal of Political Economy* 97 (February): 38–92.

Balke, Nathan S., and Gordon, Robert J. 1989. "The Estimation of Prewar Gross National Product: Methodology and New Evidence." *Journal of Political Economy* 97 (February): 38–92.

Brunner, Karl, and Meltzer, Allan H. 1968. "What Did We Learn from the Monetary Experience of the United States in the Great Depression?" *Canadian Journal of Economics* 1 (May): 334–48.

———. 1964. *The Federal Reserve's Attachment to the Free Reserve Concept*. Subcommittee on Domestic Finance Committee on Banking and Currency, House of Representatives, 88th Cong., 2d Sess., U.S. Government Printing Office: Washington, D.C.

Buchanan, James. 1986. "Ideas, Institutions, and Political Economy: A Plea for Disestablishment." Carnegie-Rochester Conference Series, *Real Business Cycles, Real Exchange Rates and Actual Policies* 25 (Autumn): 245–57.

Burgess, W. Randolph. 1936. *The Reserve Banks and the Money Market*. Rev. Ed. New York: Harper & Brothers.

Canova, Fabio. 1987. "Seasonality and the Creation of the Federal Reserve System." Manuscript, Providence, R.I., Brown University, September.

Chandler, Lester. 1958. *Benjamin Strong*. Washington, D.C.: Brookings Institution.

Clark, Truman A. 1986. "Interest Rate Seasonals and the Federal Reserve." *Journal of Political Economy* 94 (February): 76–125.

DeLong, Bradford J., and Summers, Lawrence H. 1988. "How Does Macroeconomic Policy Affect Output." *Brookings Papers on Economic Activity* 2: 433–80.

Epstein, Gerald, and Ferguson, Thomas. 1984. "Monetary Policy, Loan Liquidation, and Industrial Conflict: The Federal Reserve and the Open Market Operations of 1932." *Journal of Economic History* 44 (December): 957–83.

Federal Reserve Board Records. 1936. Board Files "Reserve Member Banks (1936).

Memorandum from V. Longstreet to Mr. Thomas. "Condition of 18 New York City Banks with Relatively Small Reserve Balances." May 25.

Fishe, Raymond P.H. 1990. "The Federal Reserve Amendments of 1917: The Beginning of a Seasonal Note Issue Policy." University of Miami, September. Mimeo.

Friedman, Milton. 1969. *The Optimum Quantity of Money*. Chicago: Aldine.

———. 1986. "Monetary Policy: Theory and Practice." *Central Bankers, Bureaucratic Inertia and Monetary Policy*, edited by Eugenia Toma and Mark Toma. Dordrecht: Kluwer, 11–35.

———, and Schwartz, Anna. 1963. *A Monetary History of the United States 1867–1960*. Princeton, N.J.: Princeton University Press.

Frost, Peter. 1971. "Banks' Demand for Excess Reserves." *Journal of Political Economy* (July/August): 805–25.

Goodhart, Charles. 1988. *The Evolution of Central Banks*. Cambridge, Mass.: MIT Press.

Gordon, Robert J. 1983. "Using Monetary Control to Dampen the Business Cycle: A New Set of First Principles." National Bureau of Economic Research, Working Paper Series No. 1210, October.

Granger, C.W.J. 1969. "Investigating Causal Relations in Econometric Models and Cross-Spectral Methods." *Econometrica* 37 (April): 424–38.

Guttentog, Jack. 1966. "The Strategy of Open Market Operations." *Quarterly Journal of Economics* 80 (February): 1–30.

Hamlin, C. S. 1923. *Diaries*. Washington, D.C.: Library of Congress, April 28.

———. 1924. *Diaries*. Washington, D.C.: Library of Congress, March 26.

———. 1926. *Diaries*. Washington, D.C.: Library of Congress, December 10.

———. 1930. *Diaries*. Washington, D.C.: Library of Congress, September 2.

Harrison, George L. 1933. *Harrison Papers*. Discussion Notes Bender 50. Butler Library, Columbia University, April 24.

———. 1936. *Harrison Papers*. Board of Directors, Butler Library, Columbia University, September 19.

Hearings, U.S. Senate. 1931. "Nomination of Eugene Meyer to be a member of the Federal Reserve Board, Hearings Before a Subcommittee of the Committee on Banking and Currency." U.S. Senate, 71st Cong. 3d Sess.

Holland, Steven, and Toma, Mark, 1989. "The Role of the Federal Reserve as 'Lender of Last Resort' and the Seasonal Fluctuations in Interest Rates." Manuscript, University of Kentucky.

Lebergott, Stanley. 1957. "Annual Estimates of Unemployment in the United States, 1900–1954." *The Measurement and Behavior of Unemployment*. Conference of the Universities-National Bureau Committee for Economic Research. Princeton, N.J.: Princeton University Press.

Lombra, Raymond. 1980. "Monetary Control: Consensus or Confusion." *Controlling Monetary Aggregates III*. Boston: Federal Reserve Bank of Boston, October, 270–305.

———, and Tonto, Raymond. 1973. "Federal Reserve Defensive Behavior and the Reverse Causation Argument." *Southern Economic Journal* 40 (July): 47–55.

Meigs, James. 1962. *Free Reserves and the Money Supply*. Chicago: University of Chicago Press.

Meltzer, Allan. 1984. "Comment on Federal Reserve Control of the Money Stock." *Journal of Money, Credit, and Banking* 14 (November): 632–40.

Miron, Jeffrey A. 1986. "Financial Power, the Seasonality of the Nominal Interest Rate, and the Founding of the Fed." *American Economic Review* 76 (March): 125–40.

Morrison, George R. 1966. *Liquidity Preference of Commercial Banks.* Chicago: University of Chicago Press.

Nordhaus, William D. 1989. "Alternative Approaches to the Political Business Cycle." *Brookings Papers on Economic Activity* 2: 1–56.

Pusey, Merlo. 1974. *Eugene Meyer.* New York: Alfred Knopf.

Riefler, Winfield. 1930. *Money Rates and Money Market in the United States.* New York: Harper & Brother.

Romer, Christine. 1986a. "Spurious Volatility in Historical Unemployment Data." *Journal of Political Economy* 94 (February): 1–37.

———. 1986b. "Is the Stabilization of the Postwar Economy a Figment of the Data?" *American Economic Review* 76 (June): 314–34.

———. 1988. "World War I and the Postwar Depression: A Reinterpretation Based on Alternative Estimates of GNP." *Journal of Monetary Economics* 22 (July): 91–115.

———. 1989. "The Prewar Business Cycle Reconsidered: New Estimates of Gross National Product, 1869–1908." *Journal of Political Economy* 97 (February): 1–37.

Roosa, Robert V. 1956. *Federal Reserve Operations in the Money and Government Securities Market.* Federal Reserve Bank of New York, July.

Shiller, Robert. 1980. "Can the Fed Control Real Interest Rates?" In *Rational Expectations and Economic Policy*, edited by Stanley Fischer. Chicago: University of Chicago Press, 117–68.

Shughart, William, II, and Tollison, Robert D. 1986. "Preliminary Evidence on the Use of Inputs by the Federal Reserve System." In *Central Bankers, Bureaucratic Incentives, and Monetary Policy*, edited by Eugenia Toma and Mark Toma. Dordrecht: Kluwer, 67–90.

Thomas, Woodlief. 1937. "Probable Effect of an Increase in Reserve Requirements on Money Rates." *Federal Reserve Board Records.* Board Files: Reserves-Member Banks, Federal Reserve Board Archive, Washington, D.C., January-May.

Trescott, Paul B. 1982. "Federal Reserve Policy in the Great Depression: A Counterfactual Assessment." *Explorations in Economic History* 19 (July): 211–20.

Toma, Mark. 1986. "Inflationary Bias of the Federal Reserve System." In *Central Bankers, Bureaucratic Initiatives, and Monetary Policy*, edited by Eugenia Toma and Mark Toma. Dordrecht: Kluwer, 37–66.

———. 1989. "The Policy Effectiveness of Open Market Operations in the 1920's." *Explorations in Economic History* 26 (October): 99–116.

Wagner, Richard. 1986. "Central Banking and the Fed: A Public Choice Perspective." *Cato Journal* 6 (Fall): 519–38.

Weir, David R. 1986. "Unemployment Volatility, 1890–1984: A Sensitivity Analysis." Manuscript, New Haven, Conn., Yale University.

Wheelock, David C. 1989a. "Member Bank Borrowing and the Fed's Contractionary Monetary Policy During the Great Depression." Manuscript, Austin, Tex., University of Texas-Austin, March.

———. 1989b "The Strategy, Effectiveness, and Consistency of Federal Reserve Monetary Policy 1924–1933." *Explorations in Economic History* 26 (October): 453–76.

Wicker, Elmus R. 1965. "Federal Reserve Monetary Policy, 1922–33: A Reinterpretation." *Journal of Political Economy* 73 (August): 325–43.

———. 1966. *"Federal Reserve Monetary Policy 1917–1933.* New York: Random House.

———. 1969. "Brunner and Meltzer on Federal Reserve Monetary Policy During the Great Depression." *Canadian Journal of Economics* 2 (May): 318–21.

———. 1990. "The Behavior of Nominal M1, Real M1, and the Adjusted Monetary Base in Four Recessions and Three Recoveries: 1948–1961." *Public Budgeting and Financial Management*, no. 3, 447–506.

Wilcox, James A. 1984. "Excess Reserves in the Great Depression." Manuscript, Berkeley, Calif., University of California, January.

8

THE CONDUCT OF
U.S. MONETARY POLICY

Raymond E. Lombra

The chief policymaking body within the Federal Reserve System, the Federal Open Market Committee (FOMC), meets on a Tuesday in February. It reviews recent economic and financial developments in the United States and around the world, staff forecasts, and a set of policy options for the coming year. Several weeks later the chairman of the Federal Reserve presents a formal report to the U.S. Congress on the particular policy adopted at the FOMC meeting and the resulting outlook for the U.S. economy. As the chairman testifies, financial market participants around the world listen carefully, poised to rearrange their portfolios at a moment's notice so as to maximize their profits or minimize their losses. Experience has taught them that shifts in the stance of monetary policy can have profound effects on interest rates, stock prices, and exchange rates. Between the periodic FOMC meetings, the person charged with carrying out the FOMC's policy instructions, the manager of the Federal Reserve's portfolio of securities who is located at the Federal Reserve Bank of New York, is busy each day buying or selling securities—called open market operations. The objective is to influence the prevailing supply of reserves, money, and credit in the financial system in a manner consistent with the desired policy stance.

This description accurately portrays the most general features of the process governing the conduct of U.S. monetary policy in recent decades. Not surprisingly, however, such a generality has a price: it glosses over the analytical and historical details that comprise the nuts and bolts of monetary policy and the theoretical and practical developments that shape it. For example, in 1980 the inflation rate was about 13 percent, the economy was in a recession, "new classical economics" (see Chapter 3) was sweeping the profession, and the Federal Reserve (the Fed hereafter) was in the early months of a new policy procedure adopted in late 1979. Designed to improve the Fed's control over the growth of the so-called monetary aggregates—a move long advocated by monetarists—the primary objective was to bring down the inflation rate. By the fall of 1982, with the inflation rate having fallen sharply, the velocity of money behaving in a seemingly aberrant fashion, and the economy mired in yet another recession, the Fed changed its policy procedures again, deemphasizing control over monetary aggregate growth. As the 1990s began, real business cycle theorists had raised important questions about the causal role of money in the economy, and many inside and outside the Fed were concerned about the lack of a specific and reliable guide or "anchor" for monetary policy. Yet, as of mid-1990 the economy had been in a continuous expansion for a record eight years and the underlying inflation rate seemed to have stabilized for several years in the 4 to 5 percent area. (Of course, the U.S. economy subsequently slipped into a recession lasting at least into 1992.)

Whether such outcomes reflect good or bad luck, good or bad policy-making, or a little of each, there is little doubt that the nuts and bolts of Fed policy, like economics itself, have changed in numerous ways over the years. Against this background, and mindful of the fact that discussions of various aspects of monetary policy are seldom in short supply, this chapter reviews in some detail the analytical and historical developments that have shaped the conduct of U.S. monetary policy since the late 1970s. Accordingly, the review focuses on what happens and why, and not on normative issues emphasized in the large and important literature on the "optimal" design of policy. This work is neither an exercise in "Fedbashing" nor an apologia for beleaguered policymakers; rather, the goal is to bring coherence and continuity to a vast literature while at the same time guarding against the tendency of economists to overly formalize their descriptions and analysis of the policy process. Typically, equations and graphs help us focus on the essential features of a problem. However, in this setting such tools, if not tempered with an understanding of the uncertainties, complexities, and external pressures present, can lead to a misleading view of the policy process characterized by undue precision and rigor. The making of U.S. monetary policy has been as much "art" as "science," and the attempt by economists here and elsewhere to define the structure and contours of policy should be interpreted as allegorical and metaphorical. Words like "flexible," "pragmatic," and "eclectic" fit the policy process better than the notion that policy involves the mechanical application of a well-understood set of theories and models (see Chapter 7). This is presumably what Gerald Corrigan, president of the Federal Reserve Bank of New York, is trying to tell us:

The first lesson of the 1980s could probably apply to almost any decade but may be especially relevant for the 1980s and that is the utmost need to be cautious about the extremes of economic doctrine and theory. Indeed, whether we are speaking of the Keynesian, the monetarist, the supply side, the rational expectationist, or any other school of thought, single-minded approaches to public policy can be very misleading if not dangerous (1989, p. 10).

1. A BRIEF INSTITUTIONAL OVERVIEW

The policymaking apparatus within the Fed comprises the twelve Federal Reserve Banks, the seven-member Board of Governors, and, most importantly, the Federal Open Market Committee (FOMC).[1] The Federal Reserve System divides the nation into twelve districts. In a major city within each district, there is a Federal Reserve Bank. The Reserve Banks play a major role in the nation's check-clearing and payments mechanism, the Board of Directors of each Reserve Bank may request changes in the discount rate (the rate the Reserve Banks charge depository institutions for borrowing reserves directly from the Fed through the so-called discount facility), and the president of each Reserve Bank (who is selected by the Bank's Board of Directors) participates in the formulation of monetary policy at FOMC meetings.

The Board of Governors consists of seven members appointed by the president and confirmed by the Senate; one is designated chairman and another vice chairman by the president, with both designations also subject to Senate confirmation. The Board considers requests for discount rate changes from the Reserve Banks and sets *reserve requirements* for depository institutions (the portion of each dollar of deposits received by a depository institution which must be held as required reserves). In practice, the reserve requirement instrument has not been actively used over the past twenty years, and the Board has usually approved Reserve Bank requests for changes in the discount rate *only* after the broader monetary policy stance directed by the FOMC has been decided and begun to be implemented.[2] In other words, unlike the situation in many foreign countries, *changes in the discount rate in the United States have usually followed and confirmed a change in the stance in monetary policy rather than initiated a change.*

The FOMC has twelve members—the seven members of the Board of Governors and five of the twelve Reserve Bank presidents. Since the president of the New York Federal Reserve Bank is a permanent member of the FOMC, the four remaining slots on the FOMC rotate yearly among the other eleven Reserve Bank presidents. The FOMC meets in Washington approximately eight times per year (about every six weeks). The major objective of each meeting—which is conducted behind closed doors—is to lay out a course for monetary policy, in general, and, more specifically to vote on a Directive (in effect, a set of operating instructions) to the Trading Desk and manager of the System Open Market Account at the Federal

Reserve Bank of New York. This Directive, which is released to the public approximately forty-five days after an FOMC meeting, provides guidelines for the day-to-day implementation of monetary policy through open market operations, which is by far the most important policy instrument in the United States. These open market operations (mainly the buying or selling of Treasury securities) affect the reserve base of the banking system and thus the cost and availability of funds in the economy. (The reader should refer to the previous chapter for an appreciation of how the various policy instruments have evolved over the history of the Fed.)

2. THE FORMULATION OF MONETARY POLICY: BACKGROUND

Conceptually, the conduct of monetary policy involves the setting and adjustment of policy instruments by the Fed so as to achieve the nation's economic goals. Figure 8.1, and the accompanying caption, lay out the basics. This conceptualization immediately raises two questions: (1) What are the goals? (2) How are the policy instruments and goal variables related?

Simply put, the goals are not spelled out anywhere with any degree of specificity. Instead, various pieces of legislation lay out broad, general guidelines for fiscal *and* monetary policymakers. For example, the Employment Act of 1946 requires the government to pursue "maximum employment, production, and purchasing power"; the Full Employment and Balanced Growth Act of 1978, also known as the Humphrey-Hawkins Act, calls for "full employment and production, increased real income, balanced growth, a balanced federal budget, adequate productivity growth . . . an improved trade balance . . . and reasonable price stability." It is important to note that these pieces of legislation do not spell out what methods should be used to achieve the various goals and, in effect, allow the Federal Reserve to choose which among the multiplicity of goals it will give priority to at any particular moment. The Humphrey-Hawkins Act does, however, require the Fed to report to the Congress semiannually (by February 20 and July 20) regarding its plans for monetary policy, its outlook for the economy, and how its plans relate to the president's announced economic goals. Not surprisingly, this report, and the accompanying testimony before the Congress by the Fed chairman, is often a focal point for discussions about the appropriateness of recent monetary policy actions.[3]

Against the background and guidance provided by current law, the Fed has tried to strike a balance among the employment, price, and growth objectives. In practice, this has usually meant assigning priority to the employment and real GNP goals when a recession appears, for example, and focusing on price stability when inflation accelerates. Although such "flexibility," as argued by Hoskins (1990) and Lombra (1988), is not with-

Figure 8.1
The Basics of the Policy Process

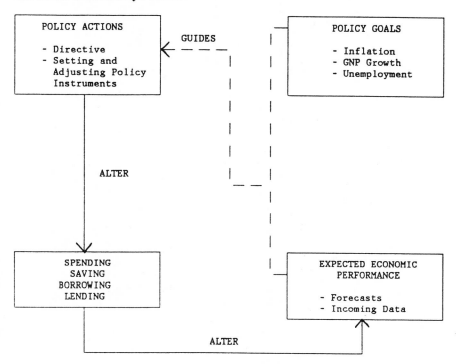

Note: The Fed has a set of goals it is aiming for. Given the flow of incoming data and the
forecasts produced by its staff, policymakers will decide on a set of policy actions at an
FOMC meeting, which they believe will be most likely to minimize the gap between the
policy goals and the performance of the economy. Of course, conditions can change,
and forecasts can be wide of the mark. Accordingly, between meetings the Fed monitors
incoming data, focusing in particular on whether or not the data are consistent with the
economic outlook they anticipated when policy was last adjusted. If not, a new set of
policy actions designed to alter spending, saving, borrowing, and lending in the economy—that is, the aggregate demand for goods and services—may be required.

out its own problems (examined further below), the discussion to this point
is sufficient to allow us to move on to the second question raised above in
conjunction with the depiction in Figure 8.2—namely, how, in the Fed's
view and in its procedures, are the policy instruments and goal variables
linked? As we will see, this is really a two-part question. The first part
pertains to the Fed's view of the transmission mechanism—that is, the set
of structural relationships linking a policy-induced change in the supply of
reserves, money, and credit to subsequent changes in the economy's performance, as reflected in the real GNP, price, and employment data. The

Figure 8.2
The Fed's View of the Transmission Mechanism for Monetary Policy

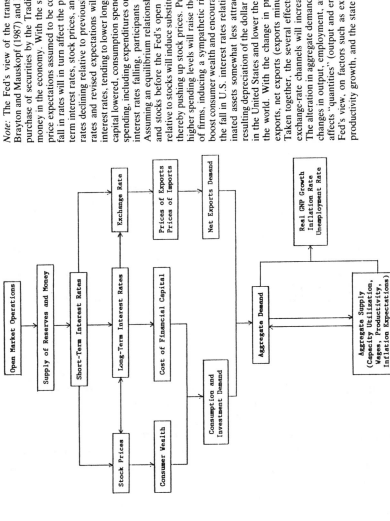

Note: The Fed's view of the transmission mechanism is laid out in some detail in Brayton and Mauskopf (1987) and Meulendyke (1989). For example, an open market purchase of securities by the Trading Desk will augment the supply of reserves and money in the economy. With the supply of funds expanding relative to demand, and price expectations assumed to be constant, short-term real interest rates will fall. This fall in rates will in turn affect the prices of other financial assets—most notably, long-term interest rates, stock prices, and the exchange rate. First, with short-term interest rates declining relative to previously held expectations, the lower level of short-term rates and revised expectations will work themselves through the term structure of interest rates, tending to lower longer term interest rates. With the real cost of financial capital lowered, consumption spending particularly on durable goods, and investment spending, including expenditures on housing, will be boosted somewhat. Second, with interest rates falling, participants in financial markets will be attracted to equities. Assuming an equilibrium relationship existed between the expected returns on bonds and stocks before the Fed's open market operation, the fall in the return on bonds relative to stocks will induce substitution in the direction of the higher yielding equities, thereby pushing up stock prices. Put a bit more formally, the fall in interest rates and higher spending levels will raise the discounted present value of the earnings streams of firms, inducing a sympathetic rise in stock prices. The resulting capital gains will boost consumer wealth and encourage an additional rise in household spending. Third, the fall in U.S. interest rates relative to world interest rates will make dollar-denominated assets somewhat less attractive than foreign assets to global investors. The resulting depreciation of the dollar will tend to raise the dollar price of imported goods in the United States and lower the foreign currency price of U.S. goods in the rest of the world. With the change in prices tending to discourage imports and stimulate exports, net exports (exports minus imports) demand in the United States will rise. Taken together, the several effects working through the cost of capital, wealth, and exchange-rate channels will increase the aggregate demand for goods and services. The alteration in aggregate demand will then interact with aggregate supply to produce changes in output, employment, and prices. The degree to which the rise in demand affects "quantities" (output and employment) as compared to prices, depends, in the Fed's view, on factors such as existing capacity utilization, the flexibility of wages, productivity growth, and the state of inflationary expectations.

second part pertains to the strategy and tactics that comprise the process and procedures linking the instruments and goal variables within the actual formulation of monetary policy.

The Transmission Mechanism

Simply put, the Fed believes the relationship between its primary policy instrument, open market operations, and GNP is complex and is characterized by significant time lags.[4] To be more specific, assume the Fed decides to "ease"—that is, pursue a policy that will increase (stimulate) aggregate demand. It will buy a substantial amount of government securities, thereby augmenting the supply of reserves and money in the financial system. The immediate impact of the Fed's action is that "money market conditions" are altered; in the Fed's lexicon, this typically means that short-term interest rates—most prominently, the Federal funds rate—fall. This policy action (or impulse) is then thought to be "transmitted" to the economy through a variety of channels that combine to boost the aggregate demand for goods and services. The rise in aggregate demand, as shown in Figure 8.2, then interacts with aggregate supply, and over a period of six to twelve months spending and thus GNP are expected to be noticeably affected. This initial impact, as shown in Figure 8.3, is thought to be mostly "real"—that is, real output rises and the unemployment rate falls. However, as time passes, and assuming the stimulative policy actions are not reversed, the initial real effects fade and the inflationary effects build.

Cast in terms of the analysis laid out by Froyen in Chapter 3, the Fed's view of the transmission mechanism implies that, by and large, it accepts the natural rate hypothesis and thus the *long-run* neutrality of money. However, the Fed does not accept the new classical, rational expectations, equilibrium business cycle framework and thus the accompanying notion that anticipated changes in money are neutral—that is, the changes have no *short-run* effects on output and employment. Brayton and Mauskopf (1987, pp. 94–95), for example, point to computational difficulties associated with operationalizing rational expectations models. Furthermore, they appeal to findings such as those presented by Blanchard (1984), suggesting there is little empirical evidence that autoregressive (adaptive) expectations mechanisms—such as those that appear prominently in the Fed's version of the MPS model—exhibit major weaknesses in practice.[5] Put a bit differently, as long as the Fed believes prices and price expectations adjust gradually (Gordon, 1981), then monetary policy actions can affect real interest rates and thus real economic activity over the short-run time horizons that encompass the planning horizons of policymakers.

The economy is sufficiently complex that economic agents are likely to understand it only imperfectly. Moreover, once sluggish adjustments owing to sources other

Figure 8.3
Economic Effects of an Increase in Money: Simulated Responses with the Fed's Version of the MPS Model of the United States

Economic Variable	Quarter(s) Following Increase in Money			
	1	4	8	12
Short-term Interest Rate (basis points)	-229	- 15	53	89
Long-term Interest Rate (basis points)	- 82	- 20	34	34
Exchange Rate (percent)	-2.9	-2.4	-2.8	- .3
Real GNP (percent)	0.3	1.2	1.1	0.5
Unemployment Rate (percentage points)	-0.1	-0.4	-0.5	-0.4
GNP Deflator (percent)	0	0.1	0.6	1.4

Brayton and Mauskopf (1987), p. 105, table 2.

Notes: The level of M1 is permanently increased by 1 percent in the simulations.

As sketched out schematically in Figure 8.2, the initial effect of the increase in money is lower interest rates and a depreciation of the dollar; in the first quarter following the policy action, short-term rates have fallen 229 basis points and the dollar has depreciated by nearly 3 percent. As these changes in asset prices work themselves through the financial system, they affect the spending, saving, borrowing, and lending behavior of households and firms through the so-called cost-of-capital, wealth, and exchange-rate channels. By the time four quarters have passed, the resulting rise in aggregate demand has boosted real GNP by 1.2 percent and lowered the unemployment rate by nearly 0.5 percentage point; the effect on inflation is barely perceptible at this point at 0.1 percent. As time passes, the rising demand for funds which accompanies the pickup in economic activity, and the buildup of price pressures and inflationary expectations, reverses the initial decline in interest rates. By the time three years have passed, the net stimulus to real economic activity has begun to fade—real GNP is now only 0.5 percent above its initial level—but inflationary pressures have continued to build.

than expectational lags (such as long-term contracts) are introduced into economic behavior, strong rational expectations models show characteristics similar to those with autoregressive expectations: both types of models generate business cycles and permit (expected) policy actions to affect real outcomes. (Brayton and Mauskopf, 1987, pp. 94–95)

Although the Fed's general view of the transmission mechanism appears to have changed remarkably little over the past decade or so, it is important to note that the Fed staff does not believe that the *details* of the transmission mechanism are immutable over time (Mauskopf, 1990). For example, many have noted both the decreased role of the credit-rationing channel following deregulation in the early 1980s and the increasing integration of the mortgage market into the national capital markets, *and* the increased role of the exchange rate as the financial and goods-producing sectors of the U.S. economy have become more "globalized"—that is, integrated with their foreign counterparts.[6]

Needless to say, such "structural changes" probably add to policymaker uncertainty concerning the *precise* nature of the transmission mechanism. "Qualitative knowledge," such as that captured schematically in Figure 8.2, is helpful, but "quantitative knowledge" of the magnitude of certain cause-effect relationships, such as that depicted in Figure 8.3, is what is really needed to make policy. As Bryant (1989, pp. 123–24) has noted, however, "notwithstanding the progress in research achieved during recent years, the economics profession has miles and miles to go before it will be possible to place much narrower confidence intervals around the quantitative estimates of the effects of policy actions."[7]

In other words, different models produce estimates that differ markedly from those shown in Figure 8.3. Given the implied limits to the power and illumination of the theoretical and statistical analysis provided by the economics profession, it is not surprising that policymakers agonize continually about the complexity of the transmission mechanism, the "long and variable" lags between policy actions and effects, and ongoing structural changes affecting both the strength of various channels of effects, and perhaps their dynamics (that is, the pattern of effects over time). In light of these concerns, policymakers have adopted a process and set of procedures governing the formulation of monetary policy that links their ultimate goals to their instruments. They believe this policy is sensitive to both the uncertain economic environment ("Where is the economy headed now?") and the uncertain state of knowledge about the effects of policy actions ("Will a 1 percent increase in reserve and monetary growth be sufficient to attain the near-term goals for inflation and economic growth, or is a 2, 3, or 4 percent increase required?").[8]

Fed Strategy and Tactics: The Role of Intermediate Targets and Operating Guides

Armed with a view of the transmission mechanism and the associated uncertainties, Donald Kohn, a senior Fed staffer, helps to refocus our discussion back on the policy process depicted in Figure 8.1: "The practical question a monetary policymaker must ask continually is, how do I judge whether the instruments at my disposal are at the right settings to foster national economic objectives?" (1989b, p. 53). Within the formulation phase of the conduct of monetary policy, policymakers approach the answer to this question through a highly stylized and structured set of procedures.[9] (An important issue examined later is the extent to which the process and procedures comprising the formulation of policy can be linked to and conform with the actions comprising the implementation of policy.) More specifically, the Fed has long utilized an *intermediate target approach* to the conduct of policy. The basic idea is that the Fed selects a variable—such as a monetary aggregate or an interest rate—which is in some sense midway between its instruments and the ultimate goals (sometimes called the "final" targets of policy). Achieving the target setting for this "intermediate" variable is then the focus of day-to-day open market operations. The rationale is that if the Fed hits the intermediate target, it will come reasonably close to achieving its economic objectives.

How does the Fed select a particular intermediate target variable (say, M1 or M2) and a particular targeted value (say, 5 percent growth) for such a variable? The basic criteria for selecting an intermediate target variable fall out of the preceding discussion. First, the variable should be reliably and thus predictably related to the goal variables; if a variable were not so related, hitting the intermediate target would not necessarily help to achieve the goals, and selecting a targeted value for the intermediate variable consistent with the economic objectives would be virtually impossible. To illustrate, a sailor traveling between point A and point B will often find it useful to guide his ship by initially aiming for a firmly anchored buoy (navigational aid) located midway between the two points. However, if such a buoy was not anchored, but instead floated aimlessly, it would not be a very useful guide.

Put a bit more analytically, we know from a simple version of the equation of exchange that

(1) $\dot{M} + \dot{V} = \dot{Y},$

where $\dot{M}$ = the growth rate of some monetary aggregate (say, M2), $\dot{V}$ = the growth rate of the "velocity" of that monetary aggregate, and $\dot{Y}$ = the growth rate of nominal GNP. Assuming the central bank has a particular growth rate goal for nominal GNP ($\dot{Y}^*$), we can rearrange equation (1) to derive that growth rate for the monetary aggregate—the intermediate target. The Fed should aim for ($\dot{M}^*$) as a means of achieving its ultimate goal. That is,

(2) $\dot{M}^* = \dot{Y}^* - \hat{V},$

where $\hat{V}$ = the Fed's estimate of the growth of velocity. As is immediately obvious, if the Fed's estimate of velocity is close to the mark, which is just another way of saying that the relationship between the intermediate target and final target is reliable and thus predictable, the intermediate target will prove very helpful as the Fed pursues its ultimate goals. On the other hand, if velocity growth is difficult to predict, monetary aggregates become analogous to our aimlessly floating buoy and, therefore, are less attractive candidates as intermediate targets.

The second criterion for an intermediate target variable is that policy-makers should be able to observe it regularly and be able to hit the targeted value of the intermediate variable—that is, control it—with its policy instruments, chiefly open market operations, with a reasonable degree of precision. As is perhaps obvious, limited observability and controllability mean that a particular variable would be of little practical use to policy-makers. Our intrepid sailor, for example, would find a navigation buoy of little use without a working compass, a nautical chart, good visibility, and the requisite knowledge about how to use the available tools, adjust for wind and current, and so on. In the Fed's lexicon, policymakers need "operating guides/procedures" that explicitly link their policy instruments to the intermediate target and foster the desired degree of control over the intermediate target variable.

Figure 8.4, and the accompanying caption, illustrate and describe the central features of the process comprising the formulation of monetary policy in the United States over the past twenty years or so, with particular emphasis on how intermediate targets and operating guides link policy instruments and policy goals. Given this general background, and the obvious importance for the efficacy of monetary policy, it is not surprising that there is a voluminous literature, both analytical and empirical, on the various issues governing intermediate target selection and control.[10] The Fed has drawn at least one relatively simple and straightforward conclusion from the literature on the choice of intermediate targets: pay relatively more attention to monetary aggregates as intermediate targets when "spending shocks" are large relative to "portfolio (money demand) shocks" and pay relatively more attention to interest rates (especially long-term interest rates) and less attention to monetary aggregates when portfolio shocks are large relative to spending shocks.[11]

Taken by itself, this Fed perspective goes a long way toward explaining why the Fed gave increased emphasis to monetary targets in the late 1970s and early 1980s as spending and thus inflation surged in the United States, and deemphasized monetary targets somewhat after 1982 as financial innovation and deregulation produced changes in the public's portfolio (money demand) behavior, which reduced the predictability of velocity. The details surrounding this evolution in the Fed's procedures will be examined further later in this chapter. Given the above overview of the various issues involved in formulating monetary policy, the evolution in the Fed's procedures will emerge naturally from a detailed review of the "nuts and bolts" of the actual formulation of monetary policy.

3. THE FORMULATION OF MONETARY POLICY: WHAT HAPPENS BEFORE AND DURING AN FOMC MEETING?

The Fed's staff is charged with developing an overall, integrated assessment of past, present, and future economic and financial developments,

Figure 8.4
Stages and Linkages in the Formulation of Monetary Policy

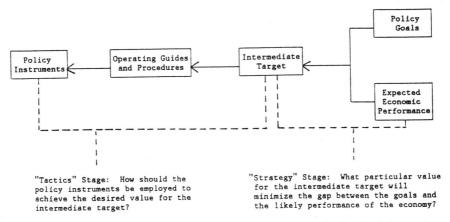

Note: The formulation of monetary policy involves devising a "battle plan" designed to achieve policymaker objectives. In the so-called strategy stage, assuming the Fed has already selected an intermediate target variable, the FOMC will examine staff analyses of incoming data and an array of staff forecasts for the economy over the next year or so, with each individual forecast based on a different monetary policy assumption—that is, a different value for the intermediate target variable. After the FOMC reaches a consensus on which particular value for the intermediate target variable it believes will minimize the gap between its goals and the likely performance of the economy over the next six to twelve months, policymakers shift their focus from longer run strategic issues to shorter run "tactics"—namely, how should the Fed maneuver (i.e., manipulate its instruments) between FOMC meetings so as to hit the intermediate target, on average, over time. Succinctly put, the formulation of monetary policy involves working from the goals backward to the policy instruments (right to left in the diagram), taking as a given estimates of the set of relationships linking the policy instruments to economic activity— that is, the transmission mechanism running from the left to the right of the schematic diagram.

laying out feasible policy alternatives for consideration by policymakers and making specific policy recommendations to the FOMC. Against this background, let's assume policymakers initially decide to adopt the growth of the monetary aggregates (say, M1 and/or M2) as their intermediate target, believing such growth has a reasonably reliable and predictable relationship with real GNP growth and inflation, and is observable and controllable. The next step is to pick particular "dial settings"—that is, particular targeted *yearly* growth rates—for the monetary aggregates. The information used by the FOMC in discussing and selecting the longer run yearly monetary targets is contained in a set of documents prepared by the staff for the FOMC.[12]

The Greenbook

A document called "Current Economic and Financial Conditions," or the Greenbook for short (because of its green cover), lays out the staff's analysis of recent and prospective economic developments. More specifically, it summarizes recently released economic and financial data, provides any historical perspectives or comparisons that may have some bearing on the outlook, lays out the key assumptions underlying the nonfinancial forecast (e.g., assumptions about fiscal policy and oil prices), and presents the forecast for GNP, inflation, and unemployment over the next year or so. The economic forecast is accompanied by a full explanation of any significant changes in the staff's outlook, given the prevailing (or likely) stance of monetary policy, as indexed by the existing set of targets for the various monetary aggregates (more on this below).

The process leading to the development of this document begins several weeks before each scheduled FOMC meeting. The main task before the staff is to develop a revised nonfinancial forecast. Staff experts on various sectors of the economy first assess the information that has become available since the last FOMC meeting (in recent years the FOMC has been meeting about eight times a year—about every six weeks or so), including recently released data and, for example, changes in the fiscal policy outlook. This information is then used as an input by the staff's "judgmental" forecasters, who develop projections with the aid of surveys of consumer sentiment and capital equipment spending plans, leading and lagging indicators, and other economic measures and by the staff's "econometric" forecasters, who develop projections with the staff's version of the MPS model.[13] Senior staff blend the MPS model projections and judgmental projections into a "consensus forecast" which is then presented in the Greenbook. Even a casual reading of the document, which is available to the public from the Fed after five years, clearly indicates that the staff's analysis is based on the model (as opposed to ad hoc) and falls well within the mainstream of economic analysis prevailing at the time it was written.

A Greenbook, containing a revised economic forecast, is prepared for each FOMC meeting. However, twice a year, typically in February and July, in conjunction with the preparation of its report on monetary policy to the Congress in accordance with the provisions of the Humphrey-Hawkins Act, the FOMC formally reconsiders its longer term policy stance as indexed by its yearly monetary targets. To assist the FOMC, the staff prepares a set of nonfinancial forecasts. More specifically, the staff's baseline or "no change in policy" forecast, which appears in the Greenbook, is supplemented with additional nonfinancial forecasts (usually two) based on alternative monetary policy assumptions. These alternatives, along with the staff's financial analysis, appear in the Bluebook.

The Bluebook

This document (so named for its blue cover) was entitled "Monetary Aggregates and Money Market Conditions" through the 1970s and early 1980s and retitled "Monetary Policy Alternatives" in early 1982. The first section of the typical bluebook reviews recent developments; analyzes deviations of monetary growth from projections; summarizes changes in short- and long-term interest rates; reports noteworthy developments in other sectors of the credit markets; and reviews the conduct of open market operations since the last FOMC meeting.

The second section (which typically appears twice a year, in February and July) presents the alternative longer run policy options described above (usually for a six- to eight-quarter horizon), and discusses the implications of each alternative for economic and financial developments. Figure 8.5 presents a hypothetical Bluebook menu of longer run policy options.

The third section (which appears in each Bluebook) presents alternative short-run (usually quarterly) policy options for the FOMC's consideration. The relationship between each short-run alternative and the longer run monetary targets is developed, along with the ramifications of each alternative for market expectations about policy, stock prices, interest-rate differentials and exchange rates, mortgage market activity, and so forth. (More details on the connection between the short-run decisions and longer run targets are given later in this chapter.) As is true in the preparation of the nonfinancial forecasts, econometric and judgmental inputs are used in deriving the staff's financial forecasts.

To understand how the staff derives the near-term financial forecasts contained in the Bluebook and the analysis underlying the forecasts, it will be useful to begin by laying out the general model that has long guided the econometric and judgmental inputs that go into preparing the staff's short-run financial projections. Fortunately, we do not have to guess what the general model looks like; it is readily available in a number of staff papers. Figure 8.6, adapted from Tinsley et al. (1982), provides the essential features of the staff's money market model.[14]

Equation (1) is a standard demand for money function, with the public's demand an increasing function of income and a decreasing function of the market interest rate (more specifically, the opportunity cost—the spread between the market rate and the rate paid on deposits). Income is taken as predetermined, based on the reasonable assumption that any change in money or interest rates this period will not affect income this period. In other words, there is a lag in the effect of monetary policy actions on the economy.[15]

Equations (2)–(7) comprise the supply side of the model. Equation (2) depicts the demand for borrowed reserves from the Fed's discount facility on the part of depository institutions ("banks" hereafter) as an increasing

Figure 8.5
Hypothetical Bluebook Menu of Longer Run (Year Ahead) Policy Options

	Strategy 1 (Easier policy)	Strategy 2 (Baseline)	Strategy 3 (Tighter policy)
M1 (Percent Change)	6	5	4
M2 (Percent Change)	$8\frac{1}{4}$	$7\frac{1}{2}$	$6\frac{1}{4}$
M3 (Percent Change)	9	8	7
Real GNP (Percent Change)	3	$2\frac{1}{4}$	$1\frac{1}{2}$
Inflation (Percent Change)	$4\frac{1}{4}$	$3\frac{1}{2}$	3
Unemployment Rate (Year End)	$5\frac{3}{4}$	6	$6\frac{1}{4}$

Note: In conjunction with the periodic review of longer run policy options by policymakers, the Fed staff produces a menu of policy alternatives. More specifically, the "baseline," no change in policy scenario, is compared and contrasted with an "easier" (that is, more stimulative) stance, wherein the growth of the various monetary aggregates will be higher than the baseline and a "tighter" (that is, more restrictive) stance wherein monetary aggregate growth will be lower than the baseline strategy. The expected economic implications of these alternative strategies, as depicted in Figures 8.2 and 8.3, include lower interest rates, higher aggregate demand, faster growth of real GNP, lower unemployment, and more inflation under the "easier" policy, and higher interest rates, lower aggregate demand, slower growth of real GNP, higher unemployment, and somewhat less inflation under the "tighter" policy. The monetary policy alternatives are usually expressed as ranges of growth for the various monetary aggregates, rather than as single figures; for example, M1 and M2 growth under Strategy 1 might appear as 5–7 percent and 7.5–9.5 percent, respectively. Since the staff and policymakers often think in terms of the midpoints of the various ranges in the design of the alternatives and in the decisions to be made, we utilize single figures throughout. (It should also be noted that M1 has been largely ignored in recent years as its relationship with economic activity became more unpredictable; of course, this too can change in the years ahead. Until such a development, the implication for this menu is that M1 would not typically appear.)

function of the spread between the funds rate and the discount rate. Simply put, as the funds rate rises above the discount rate, the "price" of reserves acquired by banks in the open market—that is, the funds rate—rises relative to the price of reserves borrowed through the discount facility. Accordingly, an increase in the spread will raise the demand for borrowed reserves. The demand for excess reserves by banks is shown in equation (3): as the funds rate rises, the opportunity cost associated with holding noninterest-bearing reserves rises. In response, banks may expand their earning assets and reduce their holdings of excess reserves. Hence, the demand for excess reserves is a decreasing function of the interest rate.[16]

Equations (4)–(6) are identities. To "close" the model—that is, solve for the equilibrium values for the model's endogenous variables—the Fed's operating procedure needs to be specified. As discussed briefly above, and in considerable detail below, the term *operating procedure* refers to how

Figure 8.6
The Skeletal Structure of the Fed Staff's Money Market Model

	Equation	Description
(1)	$M = a_0 + a_1\bar{Y} - a_2 i$	"Money" Demand
(2)	$BR = b_0 + b_1(i-DR)$	Borrowed Reserve Demand
(3)	$ER = c_0 - c_1 i$	Excess Reserves Demand
(4)	$RR = \gamma m$	Required Reserves
(5)	$TR = RR + ER$	Total Reserves (Uses)
(6)	$TR = BR + NBR$	Total Reserves (Sources)
(7a)	$i = i*$	Federal funds rate operating procedure (1970-79)
(7b)	$NBR = NBR*$	Nonborrowed reserves operating procedure (1979-82)
(7c)	$BR = BR*$	Borrowed reserves operating procedure (1982-)

Variable Definitions[1]

M = monetary aggregate (M1 = currency + checkable deposits, M2 = M1 + savings and "small" time deposits)

i = short-term interest rate, such as, the Federal funds rate (more precisely, the opportunity cost -- that is, the spread between the market rate and a weighted average of the rates paid on deposits included in the monetary aggregate)

$\bar{Y}$ = nominal income (assumed to be predetermined)

BR = borrowed reserves

DR = discount rate

ER = excess reserves

RR = required reserves

γ = reserve requirement

TR = total reserves

NBR = nonborrowed reserves

[1]All coefficients are nonnegative.

the FOMC goes about guiding its day-to-day open market operations to achieve its intermediate monetary targets and longer run economic objectives. Put more analytically, the operating procedure specifies how the Trading Desk at the Federal Reserve Bank of New York will employ open market operations so as to manage the supply of reserves relative to the demand for reserves.[17]

Figure 8.7 illustrates a typical menu of short-run policy options that the staff develops with the aid of full-blown statistical versions of the barebones model depicted in Figure 8.6 and that are presented in the third section

Figure 8.7
Hypothetical Bluebook Menu of Short-Run (Quarterly) Policy Options

	Alternative A	Alternative B	Alternative C
M1 Growth	5	4	3
M2 Growth	8½	8	7½
Federal Funds Rate	7½	8¼	9
Nonborrowed Reserve Growth	7	6	5
Discount Window Borrowing	$300 million	$600 million	$900 million

Note: Each alternative is designed with the aid of statistical models akin to the simple model presented in Figure 8.6. More specifically, the fundamental building blocks for each alternative are staff representations of functions describing the supply and demand for reserves and money. Simply put, higher (lower) money growth will require the Fed to engineer a rise (fall) in the supply of reserves and money relative to the demand for reserves and money, resulting in a fall (rise) in interest rates. For example, comparing alternatives A and C, note that A is the "easier" alternative. More specifically, A calls for a higher rate of monetary and reserve growth, and thus a lower funds rate and level of borrowings from the discount facility than alternative C. The logic is straightforward: the larger the supply of reserves provided through open market operations (i.e., nonborrowed reserves), the lower the funds rate, given the demand for reserves; the lower the funds rate, given the discount rate, the narrower the spread between the funds rate and the discount rate, and the lower is borrowing at the discount facility; the larger the supply of reserves and the lower the funds rate, the higher is monetary growth. As discussed in the text, each short-run alternative is tied to the prevailing longer run monetary targets.

of the Bluebook—that is, the section connecting the longer run (yearly) monetary targets with the shorter run (monthly and quarterly) targets guiding policy actions between FOMC meetings and "money market conditions" (that is, the level of the funds rate and the reserve positions of banks).

The need for an explicit connection between the short- and long-run monetary targets arises because, when the FOMC meets, the monetary aggregates are seldom growing at rates that exactly coincide with the midpoints of the longer run target ranges or sometimes even the ranges themselves (see Figure 8.5). Accordingly, each short-run alternative in the Bluebook is tied explicitly to the existing long-run monetary targets. Implicitly then, each alternative provides information to policymakers about the actions necessary to return actual monetary growth to the target range or the midpoint of the range. For example, suppose the FOMC is meeting in April and over the first quarter both M1 and M2 have grown at a 10 percent annual rate, compared to their respective 4 to 6 percent and 6 to 9 percent yearly target ranges. How quickly, if at all, should money growth be brought back down into the desired range? This is a crucial issue because, unless the surge in money growth was a random development, soon to be reversed without any action by the Fed, then, in general, *the faster the desired "reentry," the larger the required change in short-term interest rates and financial conditions.*

To illustrate, alternative A in Figure 8.7 might envision a slow return to the target range, say, by September, and thus the funds rate might only need to rise to 7.5 percent from the 7 percent level currently prevailing. In contrast, alternative C is expected to produce a much faster reentry, say, by July, and thus requires a more dramatic rise in the funds rate to 9 percent. Faced with the menus in Figures 8.5 and 8.7, what does the FOMC do?

FOMC Decisions

Most students of Federal Reserve policy would agree that the major factors influencing the FOMC's longer run, strategic policy decisions at any point in time include recent and prospective inflationary pressures, the current and prospective pace of economic growth, especially with reference to the economy's growth potential and degree of capacity utilization, the recent and prospective movements in the unemployment rate, and, perhaps to some extent, the recent behavior of the dollar in foreign exchange markets. Against this background, and within the context of the monetary policy alternatives prepared by the staff, the FOMC debates and discusses the forecasts and implications of the various alternatives and eventually selects a monetary policy strategy for the coming year. The strategy, which is reported to the Congress, includes target growth rates for the monetary aggregates and the economic conditions that FOMC members believe are consistent with policy and thus likely to emerge over the coming year. For example, the FOMC might adopt a strategy calling for 4–6 percent M1 growth and 6–9 percent M2 growth, in the belief that this implies 2–2.5 percent real GNP growth, and 3–4 percent inflation. Figure 8.8 shows the actual figures reported to the Congress on July 18, 1990. (As mentioned above, note that the Fed did not set a target for M1.)

Once the longer run policy stance is set, the focus of the FOMC shifts to the short run. The major factors influencing the selection of the short-run specifications that will guide open market operations until the next FOMC meeting include current economic and financial conditions—for example, recent data on inflation, real growth, the monetary aggregates, the exchange rate, and prevailing expectations, including those about policy—strains, if any, in the domestic and global financial systems, the political setting, and perceptions regarding the reliability and predictability of the relationship between monetary aggregate growth and the growth of the economy. Current conditions are important because much of the economic and political advice and pressure received and felt by the Fed is

Figure 8.8
1990 Monetary Policy Objectives: The Fed's July 18, 1990, Report to Congress

A. Ranges for Growth of the Monetary Aggregates[1]
(Percent Change, Fourth Quarter to Fourth Quarter)

	1989	1990	1991
M2	3-7	3-7	2½-6½
M3	3½-7½	1-5	1-5

B. Economic Projections[2]
(Percent Change, Fourth Quarter to Fourth Quarter;
unemployment rate is average fourth quarter level)

	1990	1991
Nominal GNP	5½-6¼	5¼-6½
Real GNP	1½-2	1¾-2½
Consumer Price Index	4½-5	3¾-4½
Unemployment Rate	5½-5¾	5½-6

[1]The FOMC did not set a target range for M1 because of its belief that the relationship between M1 and economic activity had become very uncertain and thus difficult to predict.

[2]These figures, which are the central tendency of the expectations of FOMC members and other Reserve Bank presidents, were prepared and presented *before* Iraq's invasion of Kuwait and the subsequent jump in oil prices.

generated by the latest data releases and prevailing expectations. In addition, policymakers distrust the forecasts, believing (correctly) that they are often quite wide of the mark (Karamouzis and Lombra, 1989). Operationally, this means the Fed would be unlikely to adopt a "tight" alternative if forecasts suggested rapid future growth and inflation, but current data on the economy were weak.

Concern over strains in the financial system emanates from the Fed's role as a lender of last resort and, more generally, its responsibility as a guardian of the safety and soundness of the financial system (Brimmer,

1989). Thus, the policy pursued in the face of the October 1987 stock market crash, for example, was much easier than otherwise might have been the case.

Lastly, and importantly, we have the reliability of the monetary aggregates as intermediate targets. The Fed believes the relationship between money growth and, say, GNP growth—as summarized by the growth of velocity—is often quite unreliable and unpredictable. The often aberrant behavior of velocity—itself a reflection of ongoing changes in the public's demand for money and other assets—poses a dilemma for the Fed which has a direct bearing on policy decisions and actions. When actual money growth is, say, above targeted money growth, should the Fed adjust its open market operations, reserve growth and money market conditions, more generally, so as to lower actual money growth back to the target, *or* should it do nothing in response—in effect accepting the excess money growth in the belief that velocity is growing more slowly (and money demand more quickly) than anticipated when the monetary target was adopted. (Note that *if* velocity is in fact growing more slowly, then money must grow by more than the original target if the GNP objective is to be achieved.)

The issue here is, of course, fundamental. Are the monetary aggregate variables to be targeted and controlled, or are they to be used "flexibly," along with other "information variables" in guiding the conduct of policy?[18] Suffice to say here, and as discussed further below, that the Fed has usually opted for flexibility, pragmatism, and eclecticism. In the formulation stage of policy this means that some members of the FOMC can vote for, say, alternative A in Figure 8.7 because they prefer the path for the monetary aggregates embedded therein, whereas other FOMC members, distrustful of the target and/or information value of the monetary aggregates, may also vote for alternative A because they prefer the funds rate and money market conditions it calls for. By not forcing agreement on the relationship between means and ends, the process does help breed a consensus that emerges in the form of a Directive issued to the Trading Desk at the Federal Reserve Bank of New York. However, to the extent that the aggregates are distrusted, as surely has been the case since the early 1980s, then, in effect, *the funds rate and money market conditions, more generally, are the intermediate targets of policy.*[19]

Against the background laid out above, the FOMC meets and debates the various alternatives presented by the staff. Eventually, it selects a short-run policy plan embracing growth rates for the monetary aggregates, and associated specifications for borrowed reserves and the funds rate. It then issues the Directive that will guide the conduct of open market operations until the next FOMC meeting.

Figure 8.9 summarizes the various decisions reached in the formulation phase of monetary policymaking and emphasizes the analytical linkages in the policy process.[20] With a plan in place, the next step is implementation.

4. THE IMPLEMENTATION OF MONETARY POLICY: WHAT HAPPENS AFTER AN FOMC MEETING

To focus on the nuts and bolts guiding Trading Desk activity between FOMC meetings, it will be helpful to begin by examining a synopsis of the operative portion of a Directive agreed on at a typical FOMC meeting. Simply put, the Directive is the link between the decisions comprising the formulation of policy and the actions comprising the implementation of policy. The following synopsis is from the Directive of the December 1987 FOMC meeting:

In the implementation of policy for the immediate future, the Committee seeks to maintain the existing degree of pressure on reserve positions. Taking account of conditions in financial markets, somewhat lesser reserve restraint or somewhat greater reserve restraint would be acceptable depending on the strength of the business expansion, indications of inflationary pressures, developments in foreign exchange markets, as well as the behavior of the monetary aggregates. The contemplated reserve conditions are expected to be consistent with growth in M2 and M3 over the period from November through March at annual rates of about 5 percent and 6 percent, respectively, while M1 growth is expected to remain relatively limited and the Federal funds rate is expected to trade in a range of 4 to 8 percent.

So what does this mean? The first sentence tells us that "the Committee seeks to maintain the existing degree of pressure on reserve positions." That is, no change in policy is planned for the period immediately following the FOMC meeting. More specifically, the FOMC does not plan to alter the current balance between the supply of reserves and the demand for reserves. This, of course, is just another way of saying that the Federal funds rate should remain relatively stable (more on this later). The second sentence might be called the triggering sentence; it tells us what might induce a change in policy during the intermediary period. The first phrase— "taking account of conditions in financial markets"—tells us that the Fed is still concerned about possible aftershocks associated with the October 1987 stock market crash.[21] More specifically, a noticeable tightening of policy is unlikely as long as financial market conditions are still viewed as fragile.

The next phrase—"somewhat lesser reserve restraint or somewhat greater reserve restraint would be acceptable"—is often referred to as a symmetrical Directive. This usually means that the FOMC believes there is no immediate need to adjust policy and that the direction of the next

Figure 8.9
Formulating Monetary Policy: The Analytical Linkages

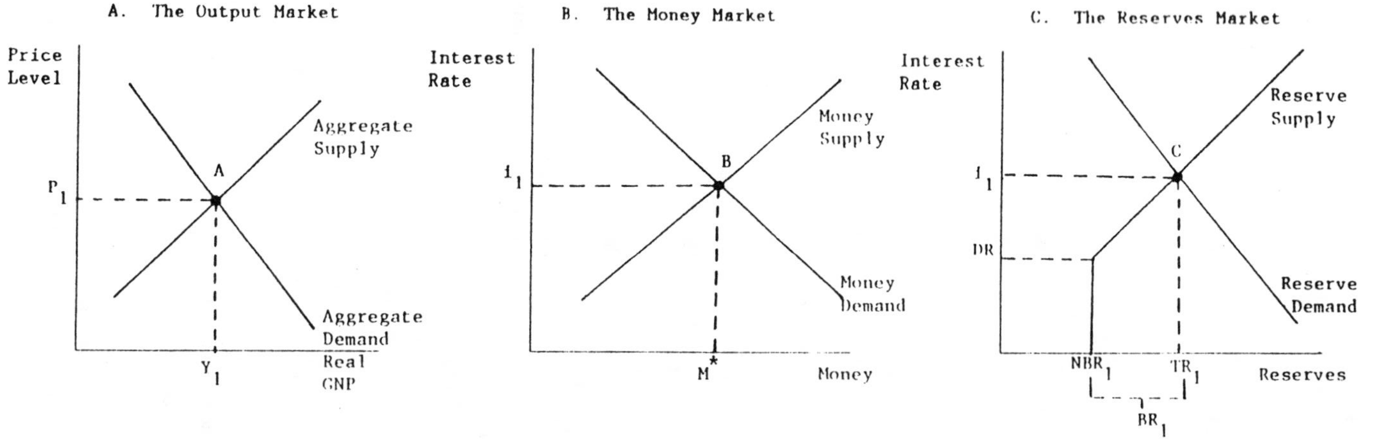
A. The Output Market
Price Level
Aggregate Supply
A
P1
Aggregate Demand
Y1
Real GNP
B. The Money Market
Interest Rate
Money Supply
B
i1
Money Demand
M*
Money
C. The Reserves Market
Interest Rate
Reserve Supply
C
i1
DR
Reserve Demand
NBR1
TR1
Reserves
BR1

Note: This exhibit pulls together the wide-ranging discussion and various exhibits in section 3 of the chapter. Given the prevailing state of the economy, the Fed's longer run policy goals, and the staff's menu of longer run policy options, the FOMC selects a particular growth rate (actually a range of growth) for its intermediate monetary target (M^*) which it believes will produce outcomes for prices and real output (P_1 and Y_1) which are "best"—that is, minimize, to the extent possible, the gap between the goals and the actual performance of the economy. In other words, the Fed attempts to manage aggregate demand appropriately. Given the longer run monetary target, the staff then presents the FOMC with a menu of short-run alternatives summarizing conditions in the money market and reserve market which, over time, are expected to be consistent with achieving the longer run monetary and economic objectives. When the FOMC selects a particular alternative—that is, a constellation of money market and reserve conditions (i_1, NBR_1 and BR_1)—it then issues a Directive to the Trading Desk which instructs the account manager with regard to the conduct of open market operations. In the process of undertaking these operations, the Fed is, in essence, attempting to manage the supply of reserves and money relative to demand so as to foster a set of financial conditions consistent with the longer run economic objectives. The equilibrium points in each market (A, B, and C) represent the hypothetical set of outcomes the Fed envisions as it completes the formulation phase of monetary policy.

267

policy move is just as likely to be an easing as a tightening. In this case, the FOMC was meeting in an environment characterized by considerable uncertainty about the economic outlook. With FOMC members referring to conflicting signs regarding the prospective strength of the economy, it is not surprising that the majority of FOMC members preferred to leave policy unchanged for the time being.[22] The list that follows in the Directive—strength of the expansion, inflationary pressures, exchange market developments, and the monetary aggregates—tells us what is currently guiding policy, with the order in which the items appear providing some information about the priority assigned to each (Heller, 1988, p. 428). More specifically, the FOMC was at this time rather skeptical about the wisdom of giving too much weight to its monetary aggregate targets, believing that the velocities of the aggregates and thus their correlation (or co-movement) with GNP and prices had become rather unreliable. Put another way, policymakers doubted that a deviation of monetary aggregate growth from target necessarily provided much information about the economy's performance relative to policymakers' objectives (see note 18). It will be helpful to keep all this in mind for the discussion below.

The rest of the Directive lays out in a general way the financial conditions expected to be consistent with the near-term economic outlook and thus expected to prevail over the first quarter of 1988. The key phrase—"contemplated reserve conditions"—is left completely undefined, however. Fortunately, through various insiders such as Heller (1988, p. 426) and Gilbert (1985, p. 19), we know this phrase actually refers to the level of borrowings at the discount facility and the Federal funds rate associated with the Bluebook alternatives the staff prepared for FOMC consideration (refer back to the discussion of Figure 8.7). Clearly, getting at the specifics here, which revolve around the supply of and demand for reserves, is the key to understanding the Fed's operating procedure—that is, how the manager of the Trading Desk comes to buy or sell securities, thereby adding or draining reserves from the banking system.

The Fed's Operating Procedure: The Use of Open Market Operations to Manage Reserve Conditions

The total demand for reserves is equal to the demand for required reserves plus the demand for excess reserves. The total supply of reserves is equal to borrowed reserves plus nonborrowed reserves, where nonborrowed reserves are, in turn, equal to the Fed's portfolio plus other reserve factors (see notes 17 and 20).

As every beginning student in economics would expect, the quantity of reserves demanded will equal the quantity of reserves supplied. But how does this come about? Suppose we fix the total demand for reserves in the weeks following an FOMC meeting at $40 billion. Assume further that the volume of borrowed reserves is initially zero and the supply of nonborrowed reserves is only $39.5 billion. Obviously, total quantity demanded exceeds total quantity supplied. What will happen? Simply put, the excess demand will show up in the Federal funds market—the market where bank reserves are bought and sold—and the funds rate will begin to rise. As it rises relative to the discount rate, depository institutions demanding reserves will be induced to borrow reserves at the increasingly cheaper discount facility. The data clearly indicate that the volume of borrowing is related to the spread between the funds rate and discount rate.[23] Thus, the excess demand for reserves will be satisfied by an increase in borrowed reserves induced by the rise in the funds rate relative to the discount rate. This is how the demand for reserves will come to equal the supply (wherein the supply, *or* sources of reserves, include borrowed reserves and nonborrowed reserves).

Since the FOMC adopted the borrowed reserves operating procedure in late 1982, the key variables in terms of policy implementation have been the level of borrowed reserves and the funds rate. In particular, these "reserve conditions," as illustrated in Figure 8.10, are the result of the Desk's open market operations.

To see how the Trading Desk decides whether to buy or sell securities— that is, decides whether to be more or less generous in providing reserves— given its focus on reserve conditions, suppose the Desk begins the period immediately following an FOMC meeting, such as the December 1987 meeting, with a Directive calling for "maintaining the existing degree of pressure on reserve positions." Translation: keep the level of borrowings around $250 million and the funds rate around 6.87 percent—the levels *prevailing* at the time of the December meeting.

Analytically, this is how the Desk executes its charge:

1. Estimate the demand for reserves—required reserves plus excess reserves— developed from the FOMC's monetary aggregates objectives (say, $40 billion).[24]
2. Subtract the prevailing level of borrowing (remember the Directive is calling for unchanged "reserve positions")—called the borrowings assumption or the borrowings target (say, $250 million).
3. Thereby deriving the nonborrowed reserves path, the Desk should aim at ($40 billion − $250 million = $39.75 billion).
4. Project what nonborrowed reserves will be, given the Fed's existing portfolio and the other reserve factors (say, $39 billion).
5. Supply $750 million reserves—that is, buy securities—if, as in this case, the path figure ($39.75 billion) is above the actual figure ($39 billion). [Alternatively, absorb reserves—that is, sell securities—if the actual figure for nonborrowed reserves is above the path].

In effect, the Desk derives the "reserve need," if any, which the projections suggest must be met with open market operations in order to maintain the

Figure 8.10
The Fed's Provision of Nonborrowed Reserves and "Reserve Conditions"

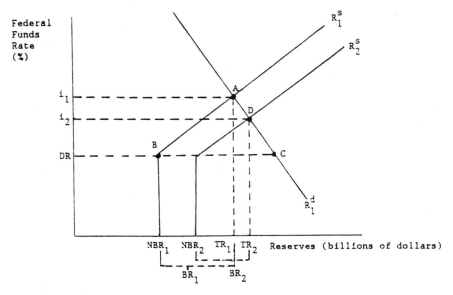

Note: Given the demand for total reserves (R_1^d), the volume of borrowed reserves and the equilibrium Federal funds rate will depend directly on the supply of nonborrowed reserves, which, in turn, depends directly on the Fed's open market operations. The equilibrium is reached in the following manner: The Fed supplies, say, NBR_1, through open market operations (and the other reserve factors) and borrowed reserves are initially zero (point B); but at this point reserve demand is greater than reserve supply (compare points C and B). As a result, the funds rate begins to rise; the rise in the funds rate in turn, leads banks to reduce their reserve demands somewhat (movement along R_1^d from point C toward A), and, at the same time, banks are induced to borrow reserves at the Fed's discount facility (movement along R_1^s from B toward A). The adjustments on the demand and supply side will result in an elimination of the disequilibrium (excess demand) and the establishment of equilibrium in the reserves market at point A. To drive home the central point regarding the Fed's role in establishing the equilibrium, in general, and the level of borrowed reserves and the funds rate, in particular, note that the *more* generous the Trading Desk is in providing nonborrowed reserves through open market operations (say NBR_2 instead of NBR_1), *given* the demand for reserves, the less the need for borrowed reserves and the lower is the funds rate and thus the spread between the funds rate and prevailing discount rate (compare BR_1 and BR_2, and i_1 and i_2). This is the equilibrium depicted by point D. Conversely, the *less* generous is the Desk's provision of nonborrowed reserves, given the demand for reserves, the more upward pressure there will be on the funds rate and thus the spread. The higher level of borrowings which would result would, therefore, be a direct consequence of the Desk's less generous provision of nonborrowed reserves.

existing levels of borrowings and the funds rate. Put another way, if all the projections are correct, and the Desk supplies more (less) than $750 million of additional reserves, reserve conditions will change. More specifically, the funds rate will fall (rise), inducing an undesired fall (rise) in borrowed reserves.

Operationally, the manager of the Trading Desk begins the period following the FOMC meeting with a view that he needs to supply about $750 million of reserves on average over the two-week reserve-accounting period. These so-called dynamic open market operations—that is, operations directed at hitting the nonborrowed reserve path thought consistent with maintaining the existing reserve conditions specified in the FOMC's Directive—are seldom executed immediately. The reason is that the manager knows that the weekly projection of "other reserve factors" used in calculating the expected level of nonborrowed reserves (step 4 above) is often in error by as much as $500 million to $1 billion. To illustrate, an unexpected rise in float, such as often occurs during winter storms when airports close and the clearing of checks is slowed, or an unanticipated drop in Treasury deposits at the Fed, will add additional reserves to the banking system. The resulting increase in the actual supply of nonborrowed reserves means that the "reserve need"—that is, the volume of dynamic open market operations—would be reduced accordingly.

Armed with his reserve projections and the knowledge that discretion is called for in the face of projections that are often considerably wide of the mark, the manager looks to the funds market itself for indications that reserves are in ample supply (funds trading around the recently prevailing 6.87 percent rate expected), in short supply (funds trading well above 6.87 percent), or overly abundant (funds trading well below 6.87 percent). If the projections suggest a need to provide $750 million of reserves, but funds are trading at, say 6.75 percent, the manager may infer the supply of reserves is ample for the time being and postpone any reserve-supplying operations. On the other hand, if funds are trading at, say 6.37 percent, the manager may infer that there is a substantial error in the reserve projections. The market is indicating a need to absorb reserves in order to maintain existing reserve conditions rather than the $750 million add job suggested by the projections. As suggested above, perhaps float or the Treasury balance is supplying more reserves than anticipated in the projections. Given these indications and the sensitivity of market participants to the prevailing funds rate and what it suggests about the stance of monetary policy, the manager will in all likelihood respond by absorbing reserves on that day. In effect, the manager conducts defensive open market operations—that is, operations designed to offset or neutralize the effect of actual or suspected changes in the other factors affecting reserves.

In practice, the overwhelming majority of Desk operations can be classified as defensive. They are designed to offset unexpected swings in the supply of reserves due to a variety of "other factors" which, if not offset, would induce an undesired change in "reserve conditions"—that is, the funds rate and the level of borrowings.

Changes in Reserve Management and Open Market Operations as Data Flow In

As the period between FOMC meetings progresses, various pieces of data accumulate. Each day the Fed updates its estimates of the supply of nonborrowed reserves, given yesterday's change in the Fed's portfolio, if any, and new information on the "other reserve factors." This continuous updating (step 4 above) will lead to revisions in the manager's estimate of the reserves he needs to supply or absorb to maintain existing reserve conditions.

Each week the Fed receives new data on the monetary aggregates. If the weekly data on the aggregates are, for example, coming in higher than estimated by the staff, then the demand for required reserves and thus total reserves estimated by the staff (step 1 above) are likely to rise. Such a rise in demand will, in the absence of any Desk action, lead to a rise in the funds rate and borrowed reserves—that is, a change in reserve conditions. Here is where the Directive summarized above comes in. Recall that in the sentence listing the items that might trigger more or less reserve restraint, the behavior of the monetary aggregates was listed last, suggesting that a moderate deviation of monetary growth from target would not, by itself, be sufficient to trigger a policy-induced change in reserve conditions.

As noted above, the relatively low priority assigned to the monetary aggregates at this time was the result of overriding concerns about the possibility of the October 1987 stock market crash leading to a recession *and*, more generally, a feeling by policymakers that the relationship between the monetary aggregates and their ultimate economic objectives had become somewhat less reliable and predictable. In other words, although the monetary aggregates were the de jure announced intermediate targets, de facto the Fed was using "reserve conditions" as the intermediate target.

Assuming, in light of the Directive, that no change in policy was forthcoming in response to higher than expected money growth, the staff would simply recalculate the "reserve need" (steps 1–4 above), utilizing the now higher estimate of the demand for reserves. The net result would be that the Desk would "accommodate" the rise in reserve demand by supplying more reserves through open market operations so as to maintain existing reserve conditions. This example, which is shown in Figure 8.11, illustrates a key feature of any operating procedure focusing on the Federal funds rate and borrowed reserves: in the absence of a decision by policymakers to change reserve conditions, any change in reserve and money demand

Figure 8.11

Fed Accommodation: How Does the Supply of Reserves and Money Come to Be Perfectly Elastic (at least in the short run)

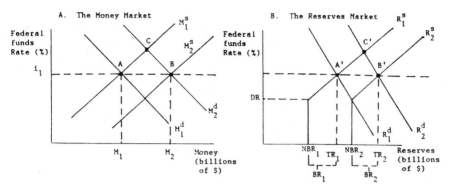

Note: Suppose we begin at an initial equilibrium, such as that depicted in Figures 8.9 and 8.10, and shown here as points A and A′ in the money and reserves markets, respectively. An unexpected rise in money demand (M_1^d to M_2^d) would, in the absence of any Fed response, increase the demand for reserves (R_1^d to R_2^d) and interest rates, thereby widening the spread between the funds rate and discount rate, and lead to an increase in borrowed reserves (points C and C′). If the Fed did not desire this change in "reserve conditions," the Trading Desk would conduct open market operations—more specifically, buy government securities—leading to an increase in the supply of nonborrowed reserves (NBR_1 to NBR_2) which matched precisely the rise in reserve demand. With the rise in reserve supply allowing banks to expand the supply of money to meet demand, "reserve conditions"—the funds rate and borrowed reserves—remain unchanged (points B and B′ where $BR_1 = BR_2$). In effect, the Fed's operating procedure, in the absence of a conscious policy decision to alter reserve conditions, produces a perfectly elastic supply of reserves and money (connect points A and B in the money market and points A′ and B′ in the reserves market), implying that the quantity of reserves and money, at least in the short run, are largely determined by movements in demand.

will be accommodated—that is, matched by a movement in the supply of reserves and money in the same direction. This has the effect of producing a perfectly elastic supply of reserves and money, resulting in the quantity of money and reserves being largely determined by demand.

Lastly, and in addition to the daily reserves data and the weekly monetary data, new monthly data on economic growth and inflation—such as the unemployment rate, retail sales, industrial production, and the consumer and producer price indices—are released during the intermeeting period. To see how such information can affect Desk activity, in particular, and the stance of monetary policy, more generally, we simply quote from the Fed's Record of Policy Actions (released with the Directive about forty-five days after an FOMC meeting) for the February 1988 FOMC meeting—the meeting following the December 1987 meeting referred to earlier: "In late January and early February, with incoming data suggesting some weakening in the economic expansion and in the context of a more stable dollar in foreign exchange markets, some easing was sought in the degree of pressure on reserve positions."[25] Recall the reference to the "strength of the business expansion" in the first part of the triggering sentence in the December Directive. Operationally, the Desk responded to incoming "information variables" providing data on the strength of the economy by increasing its provision of nonborrowed reserves through open market operations so as to "lessen reserve restraint." As a result, money market conditions eased. The funds rate fell from 6.87 percent to about 6.5 percent and borrowings at the discount facility declined, on average, by about $100 million from the prevailing $250 million to $150 million.[26]

To sum up, the Fed's reactions to incoming data illustrate the flexibility, focus on current economic conditions, downplaying of monetary aggregate targets, and other characteristics of policymaking present in the late 1980s and early 1990s and discussed to this point. Figure 8.12 provides a conceptual benchmark that facilitates a comparison of the actual implementation of policy depicted in this section with the more stylized conceptualization of the formulation of policy shown in Figure 8.4. An important and natural issue to examine more systematically is: how and why did the Fed drift away from intermediate monetary targeting during the 1980s?

5. HOW U.S. MONETARY POLICY EVOLVED THROUGH THE 1980S[27]

As the 1970s came to a close, U.S. monetary policy was in crisis. Between 1976 and 1979 the annual rate of inflation, as measured by the Consumer Price Index, rose from just under 5 percent to over 13 percent. The deterioration in monetary control and discipline was accompanied by a cumulative depreciation of the dollar exchange rate (on a trade-weighted basis) of over 16 percent. With the internal (domestic) and external (international) situations further aggravated by another OPEC-engineered hike in oil prices, existing policy procedures and strategies appeared ill equipped to stem the accelerating inflation.

For most of the 1970–79 period, the Fed employed a Federal funds rate operating procedure designed, at least in part, to control monetary aggregate growth (chiefly M1). Analytically, the formulation and implementation of policy followed the details of the borrowed reserves procedure discussed above. More specifically, the Fed, in effect, solved the money demand function (Figure 8.6, equation 1) for the level of the Federal funds rate it thought consistent with the targeted growth rate for M1 (M^*).[28] The Trading Desk then supplied nonborrowed reserves elastically so as to peg the funds rate at the appropriate level. As the actual data on

Figure 8.12
Fed Flexibility and the Use of Information/Indicator Variables in the Actual Implementation of Monetary Policy

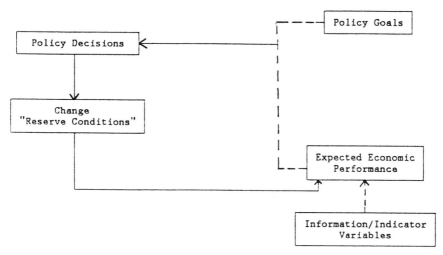

Note: In practice, during the late 1980s and early 1990s, the Fed monitored a host of variables it believed provided information about the future course of the economy. These information/indicator variables (see n. 18) include the monetary aggregates, commodity prices, the yield curve, the exchange rate, and various other pieces of data on the nonfinancial economy, such as employment, production, and price data. The key point is that the monetary aggregates are not the only or even the primary sources of information consulted when considering an alteration in "reserve conditions"—that is, borrowed reserves and the Federal funds rate. In effect, reserve conditions have become both the operating guide and the intermediate target (see Figure 8.4). Operationally, if the information variables suggest the economy's performance is likely to deviate markedly from that expected at the time of the FOMC meeting, then an appropriate change in reserve conditions is decided upon and open market operations are used to bring about the desired change in reserve conditions and the economy's performance.

the monetary aggregates (M) became available between FOMC meetings, policymakers might observe $M > M^*$. With the demand for money growing faster than expected, given the perfectly elastic supply of reserves and money, policymakers had to decide whether or not to raise the funds rate target, and by how much, so as to reduce the gap between M and M^*. As shown in Figure 8.13, the Fed often chose a rather modest response, based to some degree on the presumption that most short-run fluctuations in money growth were a reflection of short-run fluctuations in money demand unrelated to spending—that is, a reflection of portfolio shocks. As spelled out by Poole (1970) and Sellon and Teigen (1981) (see note 15), if such a presumption were usually correct, then little adjustment in the

Figure 8.13

The Typical Fed Response to Deviations of Money Growth from Target Under the Federal Funds Rate Operating Procedure

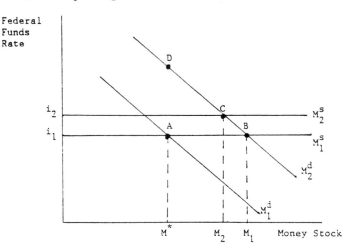

Note: In the formulation phase, policymakers chose the level of the Federal funds rate (i_1) it thought consistent with its M1 target (M^*). As policy was implemented, the Trading Desk supplied reserves and thus money elastically (M_1^s), anticipating an equilibrium in the money market illustrated by point A. In subsequent weeks, as new data on the monetary aggregates flowed in, the Fed might observe a larger level of M1 (and thus higher growth rate from the previous month's base) than anticipated (M_1). The implication was that money demand had increased (M_1^d to M_2^d). Given the implied equilibrium at point B, the Fed then had to decide how much to raise the Federal funds rate. In principle, policymakers could have raised the funds rate by enough to produce a new equilibrium at point D, thus pushing the actual money stock back to its target (M^*). In practice, the Fed often chooses a rather modest response (represented by M_2^s, i_2, and equilibrium point C), resulting in the money stock exceeding its target ($M_2 > M^*$).

funds rate would indeed constitute the appropriate response. However, to the extent that spending shocks and various associated expectational influences are behind the jump in money demand, then accommodation is not appropriate.

As the 1970s unfolded, many students of monetary policy noted that the trend growth of money was positive and increasing, and the deviations around the trend were often unduly procyclical. These "stylized facts," along with the gradual acceleration of inflation, led many inside and outside the Fed to question the bias towards accommodation and gradualism embedded in the Fed's employment of the Federal funds rate operating procedure.[29] Two Fed staffers put it this way: "This procedure presupposed both the ability of the Federal Reserve to assess correctly the appropriate level for the Federal funds rate and its willingness to adjust the rate sufficiently when conditions warranted" (Madigan and Trepeta, 1985, p. 2). Confirming that these potential problems were important in practice, Robert Heller, a former member of the FOMC observed: "One of the problems of the Federal funds operating procedure was that the FOMC did not always alter the funds rate promptly enough or sufficiently to keep monetary growth within the target ranges and consistent with long-term price stability" (1988, p. 425).[30]

With the need for drastic action increasingly obvious, President Carter appointed Paul Volcker to the Fed chairmanship in August 1979, and in October 1979 the Fed announced a fundamental change in the conduct of monetary policy.

The Nonborrowed Reserves Operating Procedure: October 1979–Summer 1982

It is important to recognize several features of the October 1979 alteration in policy procedures. First, the change was designed to improve the Fed's control over M1 growth. Second, the desire to improve control reflected the fact that "at the outset of this decade (1980s) there was a considerable degree of concordance between (most) policymakers and (most) academic economists. Monetary policy should be based on the achievement of monetary targets predicated on an assumed long-term stable relationship between the money stock and nominal incomes" (Goodhart, 1989, p. 296).[31] Third, with inflation accelerating in the United States, the Fed believed that reducing the fluctuations of monetary growth around the existing target would be insufficient to break the inflationary spiral and restore the Fed's credibility; the average pace of monetary growth, not just the deviations from the average, had to be reduced. Thus, the change in operating procedure was accompanied by an equally significant change in the overall stance of monetary policy.

Against this background, the Fed believed that a substantial rise in interest rates would be the most visible near-term effect of its effort to slow down monetary growth and to reduce inflationary pressures and inflation expectations. Given this belief, the newly adopted operating procedure was expected to have an attractive side benefit; by disavowing the Federal funds rate procedure and adopting the reserves-oriented procedure, the Fed hoped to alter the popular perception that it was the sole arbiter of interest rates. Rather, it could argue that, although policy actions affected the supply of reserves, interest rates were determined by the supply *and* demand for reserves. Putting some distance between their actions and the financial, economic, and political repercussions—that is, finding "political shelter" or "a better place to stand"—was thought increasingly es-

sential by the Fed so as to more effectively fend off the expansionary/
inflationary pressures it often felt.[32]

Analytically, the formulation of policy proceeded in a manner little
changed from that described in Section 3. The target path for nonborrowed
reserves was determined by solving equation (1) in Figure 8.6 for the funds
rate consistent with the target setting for M1. The derived funds rate,
deposit levels, and recent trends were then used to solve for the demand
for excess reserves (equation 3). Adding the latter to the demand for
required reserves consistent with the monetary target (essentially the reserve requirement multiplied by the volume of deposits) yielded the demand for total reserves. The last step involved computing the spread
between the funds rate and discount rate, given the level of the funds rate
solved for in the first step and assuming an unchanged discount rate, estimating the demand for borrowed reserves (equation 2), and subtracting
this estimate ($\hat{B}R$) from the demand for total reserves (TR^d). The resulting
nonborrowed reserve path ($NBR^* = TR^d - \hat{B}R$) became the primary
guide for daily open market operations.[33]

In implementing policy, the perfectly elastic short-run supply of reserves
and money which had been a key feature of the funds rate procedure
disappeared. In particular, instead of deliberating about the "appropriate"
change in the funds rate whenever the money stock deviated from its target
as shocks hit the system, adhering to the nonborrowed reserves path in
the face of such disturbances led to an *automatic* adjustment in the funds
rate. Simply put, and as illustrated in Figure 8.14, if money and thus reserve
demands rose, for example, the funds rate would have to rise to produce
a large enough spread of the funds rate over the discount rate to induce
enough borrowing at the discount window to equilibrate the supply of
reserves (nonborrowed plus borrowed) with the enlarged demand for reserves (required plus excess). In contrast, during the 1970s, the supply of
reserves and money was usually adjusted elastically to moderate or eliminate the near-term effects of a shift in money demand on the funds rate
(compare Figures 8.13 and 8.14). The automatic adjustment of the funds
rate in response to disturbances within the nonborrowed reserves operating
procedure was, in turn, expected to lead to a quicker return of the actual
money stock to its target path by inducing appropriate changes in the
quantity of money demanded.[34]

In effect, the nonborrowed reserve procedure represented a middle
ground between the perfectly interest-elastic (horizontal) short-run supply
of reserves under the old funds rate procedure and a completely interest-
inelastic (vertical) short-run supply of reserves (or the monetary base) often
advocated by those embracing the well-known multiplier approach to
money stock control.[35] The resulting positively sloped supply of reserves
(and money), which flowed mainly from the interest elasticity of the borrowed reserves demand function, was viewed by the Fed as a sensible

Figure 8.14
The Automatic Response of the Federal Funds Rate to Deviations of Money Growth from Target Under the Nonborrowed Reserves Operating Procedures

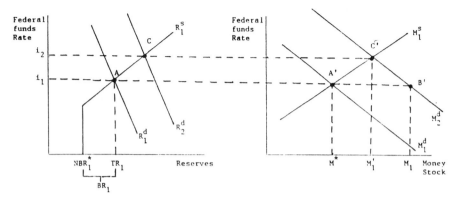

Note: In the formulation phase, policymakers chose the level of nonborrowed reserves (NBR_1^*) they thought consistent with their M1 target (M^*). In implementing policy, the Trading Desk conducted open market operations so as to achieve NBR_1^*, anticipating equilibriums in the reserve and money markets illustrated by points A and A', respectively. If in subsequent weeks the demand for money (and thus reserves) rose (from M_1^d to M_2^d and from R_1^d to R_2^d), the funds rate would rise *automatically* from i_1 to i_2: the rise in reserve and money demand relative to supply would induce a rise in the funds rate, and thus the funds rate-discount rate spread; the increase in the spread would induce banks to borrow more reserves from the discount facility (a component of the total supply of reserves), producing equilibrium at point C and C'. In contrast, to the "shock-absorbing" property of the funds rate operating procedure, note carefully that the difference between the actual level of the money stock and the target is much smaller, at least initially, under the nonborrowed reserves procedure ($M'_1 - M^*$) than under the funds rate procedure ($M_1 - M^*$) and the perfectly elastic supply of money embedded therein (point B'). To further close the gap between actual M1 and the target, the Fed could and did reduce NBR^*, thereby shifting the entire supply of reserves and money functions to the left and producing new equilibriums to the northwest along R_2^d and M_2^d.

hedge. The degree of accommodation, and thus procyclical impulses, delivered by policy in the face of systematic changes in the demands for money and credit related to spending shocks would be reduced. At the same time, the instability of money demand, and portfolio shocks, more generally, would still be partially accommodated, thereby moderating interest-rate volatility to a degree.

In a very important sense, the new procedure and the associated commitment to monetary control worked; the Fed did pursue a sustained disinflationary policy. The growth rate of M1, measured on a fourth-quarter to fourth-quarter basis, had been 8.2 percent in 1978 and about 9 percent per annum over the first three quarters of 1979. Over the next two years monetary growth decelerated significantly, registering 7.3 percent in 1980 and 5.1 percent in 1981. On the inflation front, the annual rate of change in the CPI peaked in early 1980 at around 13 percent and then fell sharply into the 4 to 5 percent area by the last half of 1982.

Viewed from a global perspective, Goodhart is surely correct: "This single step [the October 1979 change in Fed policy and procedures] transformed monetary conditions around the world, and was quite largely responsible, along with concurrent shifts to more deflationary policies in other major countries, for the shift from the generally inflationary conditions of the 1970s to the generally deflationary conditions of the 1980s" (1989, p. 301).[36] To illustrate the point, the average inflation rate in the other G–7 countries (the United Kingdom, West Germany, Japan, France, Canada, and Italy) was about 11.25 percent in 1980 and fell to about 5 percent by the end of 1983.

The Abandonment of the Nonborrowed Reserves Procedure and the Deemphasis of Monetary Targeting

Thus, by the summer of 1982 inflation had declined sharply in the United States and around the world, and, as a result, the Volcker-led Fed had regained much of the credibility it had lost during the 1970s. However, as Benjamin Friedman notes:

By the summer of 1982 the slowdown in U.S. business activity had developed into what was, by many measures, the most severe recession since the great depression of the 1930s. Unemployed labor, idle industrial capacity and business bankruptcies were all at post-war record levels. At the same time, bank failures had also reached record levels, and there were increasing signs of fragility throughout the financial structure. In August 1982 an impasse over Mexico's ability to meet its dollar-denominated external obligations called widespread attention for the first time to the debt problems not just of Mexico but of developing countries throughout Latin America and sub-Saharan Africa. (1988, p. 56)

With concerns over the deepening recession in the United States and the international debt problem growing, policymakers might normally be expected to increase the growth of nonborrowed reserves and thereby encourage a fall in short-term interest rates and a pickup in monetary growth. In this instance, however, policymakers faced a dilemma; incoming data on the monetary aggregates, particularly M1, were already running well above the target range. If the Fed was going to remain faithful to the nonborrowed reserves procedure, it had to allow the accompanying rise in reserve demand relative to the nonborrowed reserve path to push up the Federal funds rate. Alternatively, it had to raise the monetary target significantly.

With the incoming data on the nonfinancial economy and the monetary data yielding conflicting signals, the Fed, in effect, decided to give more weight to the nonfinancial data and less weight to the monetary data in guiding its actions. In August 1982, for example, the Fed encouraged a nearly 3 percentage point drop in the Federal funds rate, despite the fact that M1 growth for August was about 10 percent. In effect, the Fed signaled its willingness to let money grow much more quickly than called for by its previously announced targets.

Put more analytically, the Fed decided progressively over the summer and fall of 1982 that the linkages among money, income interest rates, and prices had become much more unstable and unpredictable. More specifically, financial innovation and deregulation appeared to have altered significantly the interest elasticity of the demand for money and thus the determinants of velocity growth. To illustrate, after having risen at about a 3 percent annual rate over the 1953–79 period, M1 velocity growth deviated significantly from this trend, declining by 4.5 percent in 1982.[37]

Against this general background, and given the analytical foundations laid in Section 3, the deemphasis of intermediate monetary targeting since the summer of 1982 and the accompanying change from the nonborrowed reserves operating procedure to the borrowed reserves procedure presented in Section 4 is readily understandable. Former FOMC member Heller (1988) summarizes the Fed view and actions succinctly:

In the 1980s, the relationship between money, nominal income, and other macroeconomic variables has become less stable and less predictable. Consequently, simple monetary targeting also became a less reliable means to attain the ultimate objectives. (P. 420)

An operating procedure based on nonborrowed reserves is . . . not advisable when the relationship of money to income is open to question. To achieve ultimate price and income objectives, shifts in the schedule of money demand unrelated to income movements have to be accommodated. (P. 426)

Since late 1982 . . . in recognition of the looser connection [between money and income] that has come to prevail, the FOMC has used an operating procedure that eliminates the automatic responsiveness of conditions in reserve markets and interest rates more generally to divergences of the monetary aggregates from targets. This procedure relies more heavily on judgments about the strength of spending tendencies and inflationary pressures. (P. 422)[38]

With pragmatism in and automaticity out, many wondered if the conduct of monetary policy had "come full circle since the 1950s" (Friedman, 1988, p. 70; Meulendyke, 1988, p. 6). In assessing the change in policy strategy and tactics over the decade of the 1980s, Goodhart (1989, p. 334) notes that "supporters would describe it as sensible pragmatism; detractors as a reversion to a muddled discretion, which, once again, allows the authorities more rope than is good for them, or us."[39]

Whatever the appropriate characterization of the policy process as the 1980s ended, several relatively incontrovertible and interconnected observations could be made: (1) the key relationships that had underpinned the move to monetary targeting at the beginning of the decade—the stability of money demand, and thus predictability of velocity, and the related notion that nominal exchange rates would be largely determined by price-level relationships (that is, purchasing power parity)—"appeared far more fragile than expected" (Goodhart, 1989, pp. 296–97); (2) despite the collapse of the analytical foundations, the performance of the U.S. economy from 1982 on suggests "U.S. monetary policy was a distinct success during these years" (Friedman, 1988, p. 51); (3) whatever the benefits of the Fed's willingness to modify its procedures in the face of emerging developments, it is also clear that such flexibility has resulted in an approach to policy-making that is not firmly grounded, or "anchored"—that is, policy discussions and actions appear to be loosely rather than tightly tied to a specific, tangible objective or set of objectives;[40] (4) huge fluctuations in real exchange rates, along with evidence of increased interdependencies between the United States and foreign economies (Fieleke, 1988), led many Fed policymakers to the view that the conduct of monetary policy was further complicated by such considerations. Therefore, it was increasingly important for U.S. monetary policymakers to engage in some type of consultation/cooperation/coordination with policymakers from the other major countries.

As the 1990s commenced, the latter issue—against the background of the reunification of Germany, "Europe 1992," yet another oil shock in 1990, the still large current-account deficit in the United States, and regular meetings of the finance ministers and central bankers of the major countries—promised to play a more prominent role in policy discussions, if not policy actions.

Increased Concern About International Issues in the Conduct of Monetary Policy

During the 1970s, the U.S. economy had to absorb two significant jumps in the price of oil. The shocks, along with the growing proportion of U.S. firms' sales and profits accounted for by their international operations, contributed to a heightened awareness of the fact that the United States was becoming an "open economy." Nonetheless, as the United States entered the 1980s, it is also clear that the cross-border linkages were not yet large enough to alter the firmly embedded "closed economy" approach to monetary *and* fiscal policymaking. To illustrate the point, it is sufficient to note that the U.S. current account registered a surplus of $2 billion in

1980—a barely perceptible proportion of the nation's $2.7 trillion of overall GNP.

As the 1980s unfolded, reality and perceptions changed dramatically. Fueled by an expansionary fiscal policy and a restrictive monetary policy mix in the United States, especially in relation to the monetary-fiscal policy mixes in the other major countries, the dollar appreciated by nearly 75 percent between late 1980 and early 1985.[41] The massive shift in the terms of trade was associated with a move of the current account from the small surplus in 1980 to a huge $141 billion deficit (3.3 percent of GNP) by 1986. With GNP growth obviously affected by this massive swing, the exchange-rate channel of the transmission mechanism for monetary and fiscal policy could no longer be ignored.

Viewing the first half of the 1980s from the financial side rather than the trade side is also illuminating. The basics of balance-of-payments accounting tell us that within a system of flexible exchange rates a current-account deficit must be matched by (and, in effect, financed by) net inflows of foreign capital. In other words, a deficit country must borrow from abroad. And borrow the United States did; the massive swing in the U.S. current account toward chronic deficits was matched by a move by the United States from the world's largest creditor (that is, net lending) nation to the largest debtor (that is, net borrowing) nation by 1985.

One need not look far to find some tangible evidence of how the situation in the United States changed. As the nation moved through the 1980s and the U.S. Treasury issued record amounts of new debt to finance the burgeoning federal budget deficit, it became increasingly clear that the interest rates set in the auctions of the new securities were not determined solely by economic and financial conditions in the United States. With advances in computer and telecommunications technology improving the flow of information around the world, relatively high real interest rates (and real returns, more generally) in the United States attracting the attention of foreigners, and domestic saving inadequate to finance the widening current account and budget deficits, it is not surprising that economic and financial conditions abroad, including the stance of monetary policy in Japan and Germany, the pace of inflation and economic growth in all the major countries, and the expected movement in exchange rates, all came to have increasingly important effects on the supplies and demands for securities, and thus security prices and interest rates in the United States.

The increased substitutability among securities denominated in different currencies—what some refer to as the globalization of securities markets—and the accompanying net demand for funds in the United States contributed to tighter linkages between foreign and domestic economic and financial conditions. But these developments had another somewhat more subtle and far-reaching effect: "the net result of these developments amounts to an erosion of sovereignty over U.S. monetary policy . . . Losing control over one's affairs is part of what a mounting debt level is all about, no less for a borrowing nation than for businesses or individual borrowers" (Friedman, 1988, p. 68).

Once the interconnectedness among countries is recognized, it is clear that the possibility exists for policies pursued in one country to affect economic conditions in another country. Given such possible interdependencies, it is not surprising that many have suggested that countries should consider coordinating their policies for their mutual benefit. Although the focus of this chapter is on the actual conduct of policy, and space limitations do not allow an in-depth examination of the burgeoning literature surrounding this topic,[42] it will be useful to review briefly the current situation regarding policy cooperation/coordination.

In theory, we can envision the possible relationships among domestic and foreign policymakers as falling somewhere along the following spectrum: autonomy → consultation → cooperation → coordination. Autonomous policymakers would largely ignore any interdependences that exist between countries. Consultation might include the periodic exchange of information on the domestic and world economies and discussions of likely policy actions and their effects within countries. The basic idea is that by sharing information uncertainty would be reduced. At the same time, however, each country would still be free to set its economic objectives and policies independently. In contrast, cooperation envisions some degree of interaction—formal or informal, regular or irregular. More specifically, the policy actions of other countries might be allowed from time to time to influence the actions of domestic policymakers to some degree. Coordination extends this interaction to its logical limit. Countries would relinquish their sovereignty and agree to centralized decision making wherein macroeconomic policy would be jointly determined by the coordinating countries and directed at a common and collective set of goals.[43]

Although the United States has moved some distance from the "benign neglect" regarding international linkages that it practiced in the 1970s, it is also clear that formal policy coordination between the Fed and other central banks is not yet on the horizon. Over the last half of the 1980s, however, there was much more consultation than previously, and occasionally policymakers found a degree of cooperation in their collective best interests. For example, in September 1985 the finance ministers of the leading countries met at the Plaza Hotel in New York City. Agreeing that the dollar was "overvalued" and that the budget and current-account deficits in the United States were unduly large and not consistent with stable, noninflationary growth in the world economy, Japan and Germany agreed to enact more stimulative fiscal policies, the United States agreed to bring down its budget deficit, and all countries agreed to intervene in the foreign exchange markets to encourage an orderly depreciation of the dollar. Although there is some disagreement about how much of the subsequent depreciation of the dollar can be directly attributed to the Plaza Agreement, it is a fact that between early 1985 and mid-1988 the trade-weighted value of the dollar vis-à-vis the major foreign currencies fell back to its 1980 level, completely reversing the huge appreciation over the 1980–85 period.

Continuing discussions among world policymakers, including the Louvre Accord reached in February 1987,[44] now routinely include the exchange of a wide range of relevant information. Beyond this, Gerald Corrigan, president of the Federal Reserve Bank of New York and vice chairman of the FOMC, argues:

In the 1980s we witnessed several extraordinary examples of international coop-eration at its best, including the initial efforts to contain and stabilize the problems growing out of the LDC debt crisis, the emergence of internationally accepted bank capital standards, the extraordinary speed and relative ease with which the European economic integration has proceeded, and the close collaboration among financial authorities in the time frame of the October 1987 stock market break. (1989, p. 13)

As the Fed entered the 1990s, it and the other major central banks increasingly understood that complete policy autonomy was no longer an option; interdependence could not be avoided. However, it must also be recognized that there exists a natural reluctance to give up much sover-eignty, and considerable disagreement prevails about the strength of cross-border relationships and the degree to which coordination can effectively contain the several effects of various shocks to the domestic and world economies. Given such uncertainty about the benefits, it is not surprising that little in the way of formal policy coordination has emerged. None-theless, it is also clear that global considerations are now playing an on-going, albeit subtle and difficult-to-quantify role in the conduct of U.S. monetary policy.

6. CONCLUDING THOUGHTS AND OBSERVATIONS

The conduct of monetary policy by the Federal Reserve over the past ten to fifteen years has undergone many significant changes in form and substance and in strategy and tactics. Given such alterations, the primary purpose of this chapter has been to trace the evolution in procedures and process, paying particular attention to the analytical roots, economic en-vironment, and perceptions that have helped shape the formulation and implementation of policy over time.

Looking ahead, senior Fed staffer Donald Kohn (1989, p. 141) argues that "as the 1990s begin, the challenge to policy is to strengthen the ele-ments that supply long-run discipline, without sacrificing the flexibility to adapt policy to changing conditions and to consider the consequences of policy actions for output and employment."[45] Such a view, along with the ever present uncertainties and complexities that confront policymakers, suggests that flexibility, pragmatism, eclecticism, and gradualism will continue to characterize the conduct of policy. Thus, David Romer (1989, pp. 118–19) is no doubt correct: the nuts and bolts of policy aside, Fed policymakers will in essence approach the conduct of policy the way they always have, "using a mix of formal models, rules of thumb, shrewd observation, instinct, guesswork, and prayer."

NOTES

My thanks to the editors, Brian Madigan, and my students and colleagues at Penn State for helpful comments on earlier drafts.

1. Given space limitations, many institutional details have been omitted. The interested reader is referred to a number of good money and banking texts, such as Mayer, Duesenberry, and Aliber (1990) and Mishkin (1992), for elaboration.

2. There are exceptions, of course. In December 1990, the Fed moved aggressively, cutting reserve requirements and the discount rate, in response to ongoing weakness in the economy, evidence suggesting banks had become more cautious in extending credit, and anemic growth in the monetary aggregates.

3. The Federal Reserve Reform Act of 1977, in contrast to the two other pieces of legislation, does assign some specific goals to the Fed—"to promote effectively the goals of maximum employment, stable prices, and moderate long-term interest rates." Here again, however, the decision on how best to pursue these goals is left to the Fed.

4. The phrase "the Fed believes," when used here and elsewhere, should be understood to mean the consensus view distilled from various writings by key staff members and FOMC members. Wherever possible, relevant references are provided. Please note, however, that the Fed is not a monolithic institution. A spectrum of views exists at any moment in time, and the consensus does shift over time as the knowledge base provided by the Fed staff and the economics profession, more generally, expands, and as actual experience suggests the need for modifications to the prevailing orthodoxy.

5. Laidler (1978, pp. 173–74), in an insightful essay on the transmission mechanism, argued that endogenous and forward-looking rational expectations, in contrast to backward-looking, exogenous, adaptive expectations, "short-circuited" the transmission mechanism built into the MPS model and, to a degree, had destructive implications for much of the empirical evidence on the transmission mechanism derived from such a model.

6. In addition to brief discussions in Brayton and Mauskopf (1987) and Meulendyke (1989), see also the informative papers by Akhtar and Harris (1987), Bosworth (1989), and Friedman (1989). The credit-rationing channel refers mainly to the nonprice rationing that occurred in the mortgage market as interest rates in the open market rose above both Regulation Q deposit rate ceilings, leading to disintermediation, and rose above usury ceilings. The Depository Institutions Deregulation and Monetary Control Act of 1980 suspended all usury ceilings and

began a six-year phase-out of the Regulation Q ceilings. These developments, along with integration of the mortgage market into the national capital markets, through such devices as collateralized mortgage obligations and other types of mortgage-backed bonds, have led researchers to the view that the influence of this type of credit rationing has declined significantly over the past ten to fifteen years. It should be noted, however, that as financial regulators required banks to raise their capital ratios, some evidence of credit rationing appeared in 1990. As of this writing, little in the way of hard evidence (aside from Fed surveys) is available to quantify and evaluate the significance of this development for the transmission mechanism.

7. Bryant's (1989) graphical illustration makes this point very neatly and convincingly.

8. It must also be said that the procedures adopted are also sensitive to the political environment within which policy is formulated and implemented; see Lombra (1988), and the references cited therein, for an extensive discussion of this aspect of policymaking. Simply put, we cannot abstract from "the political economy of policymaking" and hope to understand what policymakers do or fail to do. Nevertheless, an in-depth examination of this aspect of policymaking would take us too far away from the analytical and empirical focus of this chapter and volume. (See also note 39.)

9. Some, such as Bryant (1989, p. 113), view discussions of intermediate targets, rules versus discretion, operating guides, credibility, and policy coordination as "old chestnuts," that is, old, worn out, and, perhaps, very familiar. The implication is that everybody who needs to know, knows what we know, what we don't know, and knows what we need to know—so let's move on and not waste time "replowing" old ground. Although there is something to this perspective, even a casual glance at contemporary theoretical and empirical work in macroeconomics and monetary economics (including open economy work) suggests to me that the nuts and bolts of monetary policy *and* their importance for contemporary work are in fact not well understood.

10. See the seminal contribution by Poole (1970) and the recent superb survey by Friedman (1991).

11. Evidence supporting this inference is widely available: see, for example, a paper by a Federal Reserve Bank president and FOMC member (Boehne, 1987, p. 6), a paper by a senior FOMC and Board of Governors staffer (Kohn, 1989a, pp. 132–38), and papers by several Reserve Bank staffers (Carlson, 1988; Meulendyke, 1988). The basic results, following Poole's seminal work (1970), can be derived within the simplest of models (with all variables, except the interest rate, expressed in logs):

(a) $y = -\alpha_1 i + u$ IS curve; with y = real output, i = "the" interest rate, u
                = spending shock

(b) $m = \beta_1 y - \beta_2 i + v$ LM curve (with m "exogenous"); with m = the money
                stock, v = portfolio shock.

Prices and price expectations are assumed to be fixed, and the central bank's loss function is of the form:

(c) $L = (y - y^*)^2$ with y^* = the output target (presumably, the natural level of
                output).

Identifying the "optimal" intermediate target involves deriving the appropriate reduced forms for both an interest rate and a monetary target, computing the expected variances for output implied by each, and for given values of the relevant parameters, variances, and covariances, selecting the target variable expected to yield the smallest variance for output. The reduced form for output with an interest-rate intermediate target is simply equation (a), since the Fed will, in effect, supply enough reserves and money to produce an LM curve horizontal at the interest rate necessary to produce y^* when $u = 0$. Accordingly, $E(\sigma_y^2) = \sigma_u^2$, with an interest-rate intermediate target. Alternatively, with a monetary target, equation (b) is solved for i and substituted into equation (a) to get the relevant reduced form. Recomputing $E(\sigma_y^2)$ yields:

(d) $$E(\sigma_y^2) = \frac{\beta_2^2\,\sigma_u^2 + \alpha_1^2\,\sigma_v^2 - 2\alpha_1\beta_2\,\sigma_{uv}}{(\alpha_1\beta_1 + \beta_2)^2}.$$

While equation (d) involves all the model's parameters $(\alpha_1, \beta_1, \beta_2)$, the variances (σ_u^2, σ_v^2), and the covariance (σ_{uv}), it can be seen that as the variance of portfolio shocks (σ_v^2) and the interest elasticity of money demand (β_2) approach zero, so too does the expected variance of output with an intermediate monetary target. More generally, as σ_u^2 increases relative to σ_v^2, for given values of the relevant parameters, money comes to dominate the interest rate as an intermediate target. It should be noted that this entire approach to policymaking presupposes that money is non-neutral, even in the short run, that policymakers should in fact try to actively stabilize aggregate demand, and that policymakers can detect the sources and duration of shocks in a timely fashion. See Dotsey (1989) for elaboration and extensions.

12. This section draws heavily from Karamouzis and Lombra (1989); synopses of the documents are included there.

13. The words "judgmental" and "econometric" are shown in quotes to make the point that judgmental projectors do utilize empirical models in the process of analyzing data, and econometric forecasters routinely adjust their models (the so-called add factors) in response to their judgment about the recent tracking of the model and the perceived reasonableness of the pure model-based forecast. See Brayton and Mauskopf (1987) where the staff's version of the MIT-PENN-SSRC model and its role in the policy process is described in detail.

14. See also Farr and Porter (1982). Needless to say, the details of the model itself—parameter estimates, functional form, prior restrictions, measurement of key variables, sample period, specific equations, focus on M1 or M2, and so on— are under continual review and have been revised numerous times. In fact, we doubt if anyone has fit more versions of the equations in Figure 8.6 than the Fed's staff. Such "empiricism" does, of course, raise questions about overfitting and residual degrees of freedom. Periodic updates of various aspects of the staff's financial sector modeling efforts are typically available in working paper form from the Fed staff. See, for example, the interesting work reported by Small and Porter (1989).

15. It should be noted that in the post–1980 world, wherein deposit rates have been deregulated, the relationship between money demand and the interest rate depends in a possibly complicated way on (1) the deposit-rate setting behavior of

depository institutions, and (2) the response of the public to changes in the opportunity cost associated with holding deposits (that is, changes in the spread between the market interest rate and the rate on deposits). See Small and Porter (1989) for elaboration. These details (and others, such as the move from lagged to contemporaneous reserve accounting in 1984 and whether the Fed is focusing on M1 or M2), important though they may be for short-run monetary control, are not essential for our purposes and are ignored in the stripped-down model in Figure 8.6.

16. In practice, the existing literature suggests that the interest elasticity of the demand for excess reserves is very close to zero.

17. The sources or supply of total reserves can be derived by rearranging the Fed's balance sheet. More specifically, the asset items on the Fed's balance sheet are the Fed's portfolio (P), float (F), discount facility borrowings (BR), and other assets (OA). The liability items are reserve balances of depository institutions (TR), currency (C), Treasury deposits (T), and other liabilities (OL). (Vault cash, a relatively small component of total reserves, is ignored for simplicity.) Since assets must equal liabilities (ignoring net worth), we know

$$P + F + BR + OA = TR + C + T + OL.$$

Solving for TR yields the so-called bank reserves equation:

$$TR = P + F + BR + OA - C - T - OL.$$

Thus, the total supply of reserves is equal to the Fed's portfolio (P), plus borrowings (BR), plus other factors affecting reserves $(F + OA - C - T - OL)$. See John Partlan et al. (1986) for further details. It is perhaps worth mentioning here that an increase in any of the items entering the bank reserve equation with a plus sign $(P, F, BR,$ and $OA)$ will raise the supply of reserves, whereas an increase in any of the items entering with a negative sign $(C, T,$ and $OL)$ will reduce the supply of reserves (i.e., drain or absorb reserves).

Furthermore, note that nonborrowed reserves (NBRs) can be expressed as

$$NBR = TR - BR = P + F + OA - C - T - OL.$$

In view of the fact that the Fed has reasonably good daily data on the "other factors affecting reserves" $(F + OA - C - T - OL)$ with a one-day lag, and that its portfolio of securities (P) is by far the largest item on the balance sheet and thus in the "bank reserves equation," it follows that open market operations— that is, changes in the Fed's portfolio—enable the Fed to exercise close control over the supply of reserves in the financial system. If, for example, float (F) rises, the Fed can offset the effect of the rise on reserves by selling securities (i.e., reducing P).

18. Simply put, an information or indicator variable is a variable that policymakers can observe and that is correlated with another variable that they cannot yet observe. Accordingly, by observing information/indicator variables, such as the monetary aggregates, interest rates, exchange rates, and commodity prices, it is argued that policymakers can become better informed about the current and near-

term movements in real GNP and prices and adjust policy appropriately. Two simple equations summarize the point:

a. ΔPolicy $= f(G - G^*)$ where $(G - G^*)$ is the gap between policymaker goals
(G^*) and the actual movement in the goal variables (G = real GNP, prices, and employment)

b. $(G - G^*) = h$(information/indicator variables).

By observing the information variables, and knowing their typical relation (correlation) with the G variables, policymakers can draw inferences about $G - G^*$ and then adjust policy accordingly. In contrast to the use of intermediate monetary targets, there is no presumption or requirement that the Fed use its policy instruments (chiefly, open market operations) to achieve a particular value for an information/indicator variable. Rather, the Fed monitors and "filters" a number of such variables and then reacts if and when it appears necessary. Put a bit differently, it is argued that by focusing only on, say, an intermediate monetary target, the Fed ignores potentially useful information contained in the movement of other variables. The alleged inefficiencies of intermediate targeting and the usefulness of information/indicator variables are carefully presented in Bryant (1980) and Friedman (1990). Put in terms of recent econometric advances, an information variable might well be "co-integrated" with the goal variable.

19. The de facto, if not de jure, abandonment of monetary targets has been noted by many keen students of monetary policy. McCallum, for example, states: "It has become increasingly evident that the Federal Reserve's official strategy of the past decade, involving adherence to target paths for monetary aggregates ... , is not actually being utilized to any significant extent" (1989, p. 1). See also Hetzel (1986). This issue, which involves the form versus substance of monetary policy in the 1970s and 1980s, is discussed below.

20. The analytical details are available in Sellon and Teigen (1981), Gilbert (1985), and the references cited therein. Noteworthy features worth summarizing here are as follows: the positively sloped short-run aggregate supply function reflects the Fed's belief in the short run, nonneutrality of even expected policy actions flowing from the gradual rather than instantaneous adjustment of wages, prices, and expectations; the negatively sloped demand for total reserves emanates from banks' demand for required reserves, which is, in turn, derived from the public's negatively sloped (with respect to the interest rate) demand for money, and banks' demand for excess reserves, which may also be negatively related to the interest rate (see equation 3 in Figure 8.6); the total supply of reserves (see note 17) consists of the supply of nonborrowed reserves (NBR_1) provided by the Fed through open market operations and the reserves borrowed by banks through the Fed's discount facility (BR_1). The positively sloped section of the total supply of reserves schedule reflects the fact that borrowed reserves rise as the Federal funds rate rises above the discount rate (DR), which is assumed fixed (see equation 2 in Figure 8.6); the positively sloped money supply function (which can be derived by solving equations 2–6 in Figure 8.6 simultaneously for M, given a volume of nonborrowed reserves) results from the hypothesis that as the interest rate rises, for example, banks will reduce their holdings of excess reserves and increase their borrowed reserves so as to expand the earning assets and deposits on their balance sheets.

21. On October 19, 1987, the Dow Jones Industrial Index fell a record 508 points.

22. The FOMC Directive can also be asymmetrical. For example: "greater reserve restraint *would* be acceptable, while somewhat lesser restraint *might* be acceptable." This implies the Fed is more prepared to "tighten" than "ease."

23. For later reference, please note that the relationship between the volume of
borrowing and the spread is not extremely tight, suggesting that the demand for
borrowed reserves has shifted around considerably, especially in recent years.

24. The manager and Fed staff translate the FOMC's quarterly monetary growth
objectives into monthly objectives. Next, the staff deseasonalizes the data and
develops weekly, not seasonally adjusted paths for the monetary aggregates. Then
the staff computes the required reserves that depository institutions will have to
hold between FOMC meetings. These projected required reserves are the product
of the monetary paths developed and the reserve ratios that apply to the various
components of the aggregates. For example, required reserves against transaction
accounts (i.e., demand deposits plus other checkable deposits) will equal the transactions balances embedded in the staff's estimate of the M1 path multiplied by the
reserve requirement ratio on such deposits (currently 12 percent). By adding an
allowance for excess reserves based on recent experience and any seasonal patterns,
the staff produces an estimate for the demand for total reserves (required reserves
plus excess reserves), which it believes is consistent with the Directive voted by
the FOMC.

25. The Record of Policy Actions, along with the Directive, appears regularly
in the *Federal Reserve Bulletin*.

26. A rough, but useful, rule of thumb is that a 25-basis point change in the
funds rate, and thus the spread between the funds rate and discount rate, translates
into about a $100 million change in borrowing in the same direction. In other
words, 0.25 is a decent estimate of the coefficient b_1 in Figure 8.6 and thus the
slope of both the borrowed reserves demand function and the upward-sloping
portion of the total reserves supply function shown in various other exhibits.

27. This characterization follows the excellent survey by Goodhart (1989).

28. That is, $i = (a_0 + a_1\overline{Y} - M^*) \div a_2$.

29. See Heller (1988), Meulendyke (1988), Gilbert (1985), Bryant (1983), and
various references cited therein for details.

30. As Goodhart (1989) and others have noted, the Japanese and Germans have
been able to achieve more stable monetary and economic growth than the United
States utilizing an interest-rate operating procedure. This "suggests that it has not
been operating procedures that have distinguished the differing macroeconomic
outcomes of monetary policy" (Goodhart, 1989, p. 326). See Batten et al. (1990)
for an in-depth review of this and related issues.

31. Goodhart (1989, p. 334) emphasizes that this concordance was, more generally, based on several long-run considerations—namely, the natural levels of
output and unemployment, a stable money demand function, and thus predictable
velocity of money, and purchasing power parity—the relationship between domestic
and foreign inflation rates and changes in exchange rates.

32. For details, see the papers by Bouey (1982), Hetzel (1986), and Lombra
(1988).

33. It is worth repeating that, to this point at least, the steps outlined in deriving

the reserve path mirror rather closely those discussed at some length in section 4 above.

34. See Heller (1988, pp. 425–26) for elaboration on this and related points.

35. I have tried to avoid using labels in this chapter and thus hesitate to characterize this period as the "High Watermark of Monetarism," as in Goodhart (1989). Poole (1982) and Brunner and Meltzer (1983), for example, reject this characterization.

36. "Disinflationary" is probably a more accurate term than "deflationary."

37. See Goldfeld and Sichel (1991) for elaboration.

38. For other useful accounts and analyses by Fed insiders, see Madigan and Trepeta (1985), Meulendyke (1988), Carlson (1988, especially p. 8), and Kohn (1989a, especially pp. 132–33).

39. Fed senior staffer Kohn (1989a) spells out the problems that plagued the money market conditions strategy of the 1950s and 1960s and the Federal funds rate operating procedure of the 1970s. He notes the potential for similar problems under the borrowed reserves strategy. Nonetheless, Kohn concludes that policymakers are aware of the dangers and pitfalls, and given their earlier experience and attention to various "indicators," they are much less likely to make the same mistakes again. For some "deeper excavation" on what drives policymaking and the outcomes—both "successes" and "failures"—it helps produce, see Cukierman (1986), Mayer (1990); and the references cited therein. Unfortunately, space limitations do not allow me to pursue this topic in any detail here. Suffice to say that to fully understand what policymakers do or fail to do and why requires that discussions of technical considerations, emphasized by Kohn and others (innovation, deregulation, globalization, etc.), which may have well contributed to various problems in the formulation and implementation of policy, be supplemented by careful consideration of the objectives, incentive structures, institutional arrangements, and constraints that comprise the policymaking process, broadly defined.

40. Friedman notes that "it is difficult to escape the conclusion that there is now a conceptual vacuum at the center of the U.S. monetary policy-making process" (1988, p. 69); see also Judd, Motley, and Trehan (1986, p. 31). For an attempt to fill this void, see the discussion of so-called P^* in Hallman, Porter, and Small (1991).

41. Even after adjusting for inflation differentials, the real appreciation was still huge, amounting to more than 60 percent.

42. See Kahn (1987), Cody (1989), Frenkel, Goldstein, and Masson (1989), Humpage (1990), and the extensive references cited therein, for careful discussions and reviews of the relevant issues.

43. See Heller (1988) for an illuminating discussion of these concepts and Frenkel, Goldstein, and Masson (1989) for an evaluation of the actual options facing policymakers.

44. See Bryant et al. (1989) and Branson et al. (1989) for details.

45. Following a wide-ranging, superb review and evaluation of Federal Reserve policy over the past quarter century, Meltzer's characterization of where the Fed stood at the beginning of the 1990s clearly mirrored Kohn's: "the Federal Reserve was still searching for a reliable method of control that would stabilize the domestic money market without sacrificing longer-term control of the price level" (Meltzer, 1991, p. 49).

REFERENCES

Akhtar, M., and Harris, E. 1987. "Monetary Policy Influence on the Economy: An Empirical Analysis." *Quarterly Review*, Federal Reserve Bank of New York (Winter): 19–34.

Anderson, Robert, and Rasche, Robert. 1982. "What Do Money Market Models Tell Us About How to Implement Monetary Policy?" *Journal of Money, Credit and Banking* 14 (November): 796–828.

Batten, Dallas; Blackwell, Michael; Kim, In-Su; Nocera, Simon; and Ozeki, Yuzuru. 1990. *The Conduct of Monetary Policy in the Major Industrial Countries*. International Monetary Fund, Occasional Paper No. 70.

Blanchard, Olivier. 1984. "The Lucas Critique and the Volcker Deflation." *American Economic Review* 74 (May): 211–15.

Boehne, Edward. 1987. "Is There Consistency in Monetary Policy." *Business Review*, Federal Reserve Bank of Philadelphia (July/August): 3–8.

Bosworth, Barry. 1989. "Institutional Change and the Efficacy of Monetary Policy." *Brookings Papers on Economic Activity* 1: 77–110.

Bouey, G. 1982. "Monetary Policy—Finding a Place to Stand." Per Jacobsson Lecture, International Monetary Fund, Washington, D.C.

Branson, William; Frenkel, Jacob; and Goldstein, Morris, eds. 1989. *Policy Coordination and Exchange Rates*. Chicago: University of Chicago Press.

Brayton, Flint, and Mauskopf, Eileen. 1987. "Structure and Uses of the MPS Quarterly Econometric Model of the United States." *Federal Reserve Bulletin* 73 (February): 93–109.

Brimmer, Andrew. 1989. "Central Banking and Systemic Risks." *Journal of Economic Perspectives* 3 (Spring): 3–16.

Brunner, Karl, and Meltzer, Allan. 1983. "Strategies and Tactics for Monetary Control." In *Carnegie-Rochester Conference Series on Public Policy* 18, edited by K. Brunner and A. Meltzer. Amsterdam: North-Holland.

Bryant, Ralph. 1980. *Money and Monetary Policy in Interdependent Nations*. Washington, D.C.: Brookings Institution.

———. 1983. *Controlling Money: The Federal Reserve and Its Critics*. Washington, D.C.: Brookings Institution.

———. 1989. "Comment on 'Changing Effects of Monetary Policy on Real Economic Activity'." *Monetary Policy Issues in the 1990s*. Federal Reserve Bank of Kansas City, 113–27.

———; Currie, David; Frenkel, Jacob; Masson, Paul; and Portes, Richard, eds. 1989. *Macroeconomic Policies in an Interdependent World*. Washington, D.C.: International Monetary Fund.

Carlson, John. 1988. "Rules Versus Discretion: Making a Monetary Rule Operational." *Economic Review* 3, Federal Reserve Bank of Cleveland: 2–13.

Cody, Brian. 1989. "International Policy Cooperation: Building a Sound Foundation." *Business Review*, Federal Reserve Bank of Philadelphia (March/April): 3–12.

Corrigan, E. Gerald. 1989. "Reflections on the 1980s." *Annual Report*, Federal Reserve Bank of New York, 5–22.

Cukierman, Alex. 1986. "Central Bank Behavior and Credibility: Some Recent

Theoretical Developments." *Review*, Federal Reserve Bank of St. Louis (May): 5–17.

Dotsey, Michael. 1989. "Monetary Control under Alternative Operating Procedures." *Journal of Money, Credit and Banking* (August): 273–90.

Farr, Helen, and Porter, Richard. 1982. "Comment on 'What Do Money Market Models Tell Us about How to Implement Monetary Policy?'" *Journal of Money, Credit and Banking* 14 (November): 857–68.

Fieleke, Norman. 1988. "Economic Interdependence Between Nations: Reason for Policy Coordination?" *New England Economic Review*, Federal Reserve Bank of Boston (May/June): 21–38.

Frenkel, Jacob; Goldstein, Morris; and Masson, Paul. 1989. "International Dimensions of Monetary Policy: Coordination Versus Autonomy." *Monetary Policy Issues in the 1990s*. Federal Reserve Bank of Kansas City, 183–232.

Friedman, Benjamin. 1988. "Lessons on Monetary Policy from the 1980s." *Journal of Economic Perspectives* 2 (Summer): 51–72.

———. 1989. "Changing Effects of Monetary Policy on Real Economic Activity." *Monetary Policy Issues in the 1990s*. Federal Reserve Bank of Kansas City, 55–111.

———. 1990. "Targets and Instruments of Monetary Policy." *Handbook on Monetary Economics*, edited by Benajmin Friedman and Frank Hahn. Amsterdam: North-Holland.

Gilbert, R. Alton. 1985. "Operating Procedures for Monetary Policy." *Review*, Federal Reserve Bank of St. Louis (February): 13–21.

Goldfeld, Stephen, and Sichel, Daniel. 1991. "The Demand for Money." In *Handbook of Monetary Economics*, edited by Benjamin Friedman and Frank Hahn. Amsterdam: North-Holland.

Goodhart, Charles. 1989. "The Conduct of Monetary Policy." *Economic Journal* 99 (June): 293–346.

Gordon, Robert. 1981. "Output Fluctuations and Gradual Price Adjustment." *Journal of Economic Literature* (June): 493–530.

Hallman, Jeffrey; Porter, Richard; and Small, David. 1991. "Is the Price Level Tied to the M2 Monetary Aggregate in the Long Run?" *American Economic Review* (September): 841–58.

Heller, H. Robert. 1988. "Implementing Monetary Policy." *Federal Reserve Bulletin* (July): 419–29.

Hetzel, Robert. 1986. "Monetary Policy in the Early 1980s." *Economic Review*, Federal Reserve Bank of Richmond (March/April).

Hoskins, W. Lee. 1990. "Central Bank Independence." *Annual Report—1989*. Federal Reserve Bank of Cleveland (March), 4–19.

Humpage, Owen. 1990. "A Hitchhiker's Guide to International Macroeconomic Policy Coordination." *Economic Review 1*, Federal Reserve Bank of Cleveland: 2–14.

Jones, David. 1989. *Fed Watching and Interest Rate Projections: A Practical Guide*, New York: Simon & Schuster.

Judd, John; Motley, Brian; and Trehan, Bharat. 1986. "Financial Change and the Design of Monetary Policy: Lessons from the U.S. Experience." Federal Reserve Bank of San Francisco, Working Paper, December.

Kahn, George. 1987. "International Policy Coordination in an Interdependent

World." *Economic Review*, Federal Reserve Bank of Kansas City (March): 14–32.

Karamouzis, Nicholas, and Lombra, Raymond. 1989. "Federal Reserve Policy-making: An Overview and Analysis of the Policy Process." *International Debt, Federal Reserve Operations and Other Essays*. Carnegie-Rochester Conference Series on Public Policy 30, edited by Karl Brunner and Allan Meltzer (Spring): 7–62.

Kohn, Donald. 1989a. "Policy Targets and Operating Procedures in the 1990s." *Monetary Policy Issues in the 1990s*. Federal Reserve Bank of Kansas City, 129–41.

———. 1989b. "Monetary Policy in an Era of Change." *Federal Reserve Bulletin* (February): 53–57.

Laidler, David. 1978. "Money and Money Income: An Essay on the 'Transmission Mechanism'." *Journal of Monetary Economics* 4: 151–91.

Lombra, Raymond. 1988. "Monetary Policy: The Rhetoric Versus the Record." In *Political Business Cycles*, edited by Thomas D. Willett. Durham, N.C.: Duke University Press, 337–65.

Madigan, Brian, and Trepeta, Warren. 1985. "Implementation of U.S. Monetary Policy." Unpublished manuscript, Board of Governors of the Federal Reserve System, November.

Mauskopf, Eileen. 1990. "The Transmission Channels of Monetary Policy: How Have They Changed?" *Federal Reserve Bulletin* (December): 985–1008.

Mayer, Thomas, ed. 1990. *The Political Economy of American Monetary Policy*. New York: Cambridge University Press.

———; Duesenbery, James; and Aliber, Robert. 1990. *Money, Banking, and the Economy*. New York: W. W. Norton.

McCallum, Bennett. 1989. "Targets, Indicators, and Instruments of Monetary Policy." National Bureau of Economic Research, Working Paper No. 3047, Cambridge, Mass., July.

Melton, William. 1985. *Inside the Fed: Making Monetary Policy*. Homewood, Ill.: Dow Jones-Irwin.

Meltzer, Allan. 1991. *Monetary Policy on the 75th Anniversary of the Federal Reserve System*. Norwell, Mass.: Kluwer Academic Publishers, 3–65.

Meulendyke, Ann-Marie. 1988. "A Review of Federal Reserve Policy Targets and Operating Guides in Recent Decades." *Quarterly Review*, Federal Reserve Bank of New York (Autumn): 6–17.

———. 1989. *U.S. Monetary Policy and Financial Markets*. New York: Federal Reserve Bank of New York.

Mishkin, Frederick. 1992. *The Economics of Money, Banking, and Financial Markets*. Glenview, Ill.: Scott, Foresman.

Partlan, John; Hamdani, Kausar; and Camilli, Kathleen. 1986. "Reserves Forecasting for Open Market Operations." *Quarterly Review*, Federal Reserve Bank of New York (Spring): 19–33.

Poole, William. 1970. "Optimal Choice of Monetary Policy Instruments in a Simple Stochastic Macro Model." *Quarterly Journal of Economics* 84 (May): 197–216.

———. 1982. "Federal Reserve Operating Procedures: A Survey and Evaluation of the Historical Record Since October 1979." *Journal of Money, Credit and Banking* (November), Part 2: 575–96.

Romer, David. 1989. "Comment on Bosworth." *Brookings Papers on Economic Activity* 1: 114–19.

Sellon, Gordon, and Teigen, Ronald. 1981. "The Choice of Short-Run Targets for Monetary Policy—Part I: A Theoretical Analysis." *Economic Review*, Federal Reserve Bank of Kansas City, April.

Small, David, and Porter, Richard. 1989. "Understanding the Behavior of M2 and V2." *Federal Reserve Bulletin* (April): 244–54.

Thornton, Daniel. 1988. "The Borrowed Reserves Operating Procedure: Theory and Evidence." *Review*, Federal Reserve Bank of St. Louis (January/February): 30–54.

Tinsley, Peter; Farr, Helen; Fries, G.; Garrett, Bonnie; and Von Zur Muehlen, Peter. 1982. "Policy Robustness: Specification and Simulation of a Monthly Money Market Model." *Journal of Money, Credit and Banking* 14 (November): 829–56.

PART III

MONETARY POLICY IN THE
OTHER G-7 COUNTRIES

9

GERMANY

Manfred J. M. Neumann and Jürgen von Hagen

Germany's monetary constitution divides the responsibility for monetary policy between the Deutsche Bundesbank and the federal government. The Bundesbank has sole responsibility for domestic monetary policy, that is, control of the money supply and the orderly functioning of the internal payments system and of payments with foreign countries. The federal government, on the other hand, has the authority to determine the country's exchange-rate regime, including the fixing of exchange parities, and to regulate financial relations with other nations. Given this external framework, the monetary constitution provides the Bundesbank with a large degree of independence from government, which is unique in the international comparison.

In the last three decades, the Bundesbank has acquired an international reputation for its commitment to price stability. Table 9.1 makes that point by comparing the long-run average inflation rates in the main industrial countries. It shows that the Bundesbank has been more successful in preserving the internal value of its currency than any other central bank. Only more recently, the Bank of Japan and the Swiss National Bank have gained similarly good track records. Thus, the Bundesbank bears out the hypothesis that constitutional central bank independence is an effective institutional mechanism for assuring lasting domestic monetary stability (Neumann, 1991). Price stability is unlikely to prevail, if a country's monetary constitution gives its government the power to use domestic monetary policy to pursue other, short-run oriented, objectives of economic policy, and, therefore, leaves it with the curse of being tempted to do so.[1] In contrast, an independent central bank cannot be forced and has no incen-

Table 9.1
CPI Inflation Rates in the Main Industrialized Countries

Central Bank	1961 – 1989	1979 – 1989
Deutsche Bundesbank	3.5	2.9
Schweizerische Nationalbank	3.9	3.3
Federal Reserve System	5.2	5.5
Bank of Japan	5.6	2.6
Bank of Canada	5.7	6.5
Banque de France	6.9	7.3
Bank of England	8.1	7.4
Banca d'Italia	9.4	11.2

Source: International Monetary Fund (*Yearbook of International Financial Statistics*, 1990).

Note: Geometric averages of annual inflation rates.

tive to subordinate price stability to alternative objectives of monetary policy, such as temporary boosts in employment or the collection of seigniorage. Its independence renders the credibility necessary to convince the private sector of its commitment to price stability and to hold down expectations of long-run inflation.

In this chapter, we describe the institutional framework of German monetary policy and the monetary strategy and operating procedure of the Bundesbank. Section 1 outlines the Bundesbank's constitution and the most important constraints on its policy. Constraints arise from Germany's membership in the European Monetary System (EMS) and its participation in international efforts at economic policy coordination. Section 2 discusses the objectives of German monetary policy and the Bundesbank's approach to monetary targeting. Bundesbank policy can be characterized as monetary targeting oriented toward price stability under external constraints. Excess inflation and undesired exchange-rate developments explain most of the over- or undershooting of the monetary target. Section 3 provides a detailed account of short-run procedures for policy implementation. Section 4 focuses on the Bundesbank's approach to sterilizing interventions in the foreign exchange market. Sterilization is the critical issue in the link between monetary targeting and the external constraints facing the Bundesbank. The more completely interventions are sterilized, the less binding are the external constraints. We show that sterilization is generally complete in the short run. However, interventions do affect monetary growth over a longer time horizon. Section 5 offers some concluding remarks.

1. INSTITUTIONAL FRAMEWORK AND EXTERNAL CONSTRAINTS OF MONETARY POLICY

The monetary constitution of Germany consists essentially of four (simple) laws. The Bundesbank Act (Bundesbankgesetz) of 1957, the Act to Promote Economic Stability and Growth (Stabilitäts- und Wachstumsgesetz) of 1967, and the External Economic Relations Act (Aussenwirtschaftsgesetz) of 1961 regulate the responsibilities of the federal government and the Bundesbank and their relations in monetary affairs. In addition, the Credit Institutions Act (Kreditwesengesetz) of 1961 defines the regulatory function of the Bundesbank in supervising the German banking sector.

The seat of the Bundesbank is Frankfurt (Main). Its supreme policy-making body is the Central Bank Council (Zentralbankrat). The Central Bank Council determines the general course of monetary policy. It formulates guidelines for the business of the Bundesbank, defines the responsibilities of its administrative units in the German states, the eleven Land central banks (Landeszentralbanken), and the Bundesbank Board (Direktorium), and formulates guidelines for their daily business. Under certain circumstances, the Council can give specific instructions to the Board or the Land central banks. The Council meets biweekly under the chairmanship of the president or the vice president of the Bundesbank. Its decisions are taken with simple majorities. Members of the Council are the presidents of the German Land central banks together with the members of the Bundesbank's Board.[2]

The Board consists of the president and the vice president of the Bundesbank and up to eight additional members, all of whom must have special professional qualifications. The number of Board members varies over time. The Board meets under the chairmanship of the president or vice president. Board decisions are taken with simple majorities; in the event of a tie, the chairman casts the vote. The Board directs the execution of the Council's decisions and conducts all daily business of the Bundesbank which is not under the responsibility of the Land central banks. In particular, it has the sole authority to do business with the federal government and to conduct foreign exchange and open market operations. The Land central banks conduct the business with state governments and regional banking institutions.

Institutional Elements of Bundesbank Independence

Following Neumann (1991), central bank independence consists of two elements, the *personal independence* of the Council members and the *institutional independence* of the Council itself. Personal independence relates to the relationship between the government and the Council members as individual persons, in particular to procedures of appointment and compensation of the Council members. Members of the Central Bank Council are appointed by the president of the Federal Republic upon nomination by the federal government or by governments of the federal states (Landesregierungen).[3] The federal government can nominate up to eight Council members; the additional members, who also serve as presidents of the Land central banks, are nominated by state governments.

The governments' right of nomination implies that Council members may be tempted to adopt policies to please their governments and assure reappointment. The incentive for such partisanship remains limited, however. Individual terms of office are eight years, that is, twice as long as a federal government's term and longer than the terms of any federal state government. A second term of equal length is granted almost automatically, unless the incumbent has reached retirement age. Council members have no specific mandate and cannot be released from office except for personal reasons or upon request by the Council. Council members therefore have little reason to fear for their jobs if Bundesbank policies do not conform with the government's political interests. Their personal independence is strengthened further by high salaries in terms of international standards.[4] German central bankers therefore have no reason to lobby for lucrative positions in the financial industry, and Bundesbank positions are not commonly regarded as stepping stones for private sector careers.

Institutional independence relates to the legal arrangements governing the relationships between the central bank and the government. The Bundesbank Act makes the Central Bank Council independent of instructions from government, or any other political authority, with regard to monetary policy. The Council thus holds undivided power over the course of domestic monetary policy under the mandate of the Bundesbank Act. The Bundesbank Act specifies the type of operations the Bank can engage in with the government, domestic commercial banks and private nonbanks, and foreigners, and thereby defines the array of monetary policy instruments available to the Bank. The Bank has no obligation to lend directly to government except for short-term overdraft credit, which is subject to explicit limits and is quantitatively negligible. Thus, its authority over domestic monetary policy instruments is not restricted by a requirement to finance government deficits. As a result, the Bundesbank has full autonomy over the size and composition of its balance sheet within the limits set by the Bundesbank Act. This is a necessary condition for the independent determination of domestic monetary growth. Limitations to its autonomy may arise, however, as a consequence of the federal government's choice of an exchange-rate regime: The obligation to maintain a fixed parity band with another currency means that the Bank may not be free to determine its international assets and liabilities.

Article 3 of the Bundesbank Act assigns the Bundesbank the mandate of "safeguarding the currency." The Bundesbank interprets this legal mandate as an obligation to maintain domestic price stability. This interpretation has become unchallenged general opinion in Germany. Moreover, the Bundesbank argues that domestic price stability carries the external aspect that the international purchasing power of the Deutsche mark (DM) must be preserved as well (Deutsche Bundesbank, 1989, p. 11). This aspect is important, because it implies that exchange-rate developments concerning the DM and other currencies should, in the long run, follow purchasing power parities, that is, incorporate inflation differentials. From this perspective, the Bundesbank's legal mandate provides a justification for asking the federal government for support to obtain timely realignments in the EMS (Deutsche Bundesbank, 1989, p. 13).

The Bundesbank Act does not spell out any other policy objectives. Subject to the principal objective, however, its Article 12 requires the Bundesbank to support the federal government's general economic policies, the broad goals of which are defined by the Act to Promote the Stability and Growth of the Economy: price stability, high employment, external equilibrium, and adequate economic growth. This requirement weakens the Bank's independence by justifying political pressure from the government to adopt more discretionary policies. At times, for example, the federal government on this basis has demanded from the Bank more active policies against the DM's appreciation vis-à-vis the dollar. Yet, there is no obligation to use monetary policy for the purpose of achieving specific employment or output growth targets. Articles 3 and 12 together imply that the Bundesbank cannot place policy objectives other than price stability above the federal government's goals at its own discretion (Deutsche Bundesbank, 1980). In effect, this may serve to reinforce its commitment to price stability as a way to safeguard its independence from government.

Members of the federal government have the right to participate in the meetings of the Central Bank Council. They can propose motions or demand a two-week delay of decisions. However, they cannot vote on or veto any decision.

Exchange-Rate Constraints

The most serious limitation to the Bundesbank's commitment to price stability results from exchange-rate policies. The External Economic Relations Act places all decisions touching Germany's exchange-rate regime with the federal government. Decisions to join or leave international exchange-rate arrangements such as the Bretton Woods system or the EMS must therefore be taken as given by the Bundesbank. Although the federal government generally consults with the Bundesbank on these matters, the historical experience with Germany's entry into the EMS against the strong opposition of the Bundesbank in 1978 and, most recently, with the German

Monetary Union, has long made it clear that general political considerations ultimately have the prerogative over Bundesbank concerns.[5] However, the federal government does not interfere with the Bundesbank's conduct of monetary policy within a given exchange-rate regime or with the Bank's practice of intervention in foreign exchange markets or of sterilizing interventions. Still, the exchange-rate regime is an important limitation of the Bank's independence, since price stability can be impeded if the Bank must maintain fixed parities with inflationary currencies.

In recent history, exchange-rate constraints have arisen from two different grounds. The first, and formal, one is Germany's membership in the EMS. The Exchange Rate Mechanism (ERM), the cornerstone of the EMS, started working in March 1979 as an agreement to keep exchange rates among the eight participating countries—Belgium, Denmark, France, Germany, Ireland, Italy, Luxembourg, and the Netherlands—within margins of ±2.25 percent around fixed but adjustable central rates.[6] In contrast to the Bretton Woods system, the ERM had been envisaged as a "symmetrical" system in which no single country would exert leadership over its partners and assume the role of the *nth currency* determining the rate of monetary expansion for the group. The symmetry of the system would assure that no country had to adopt an inflation rate other than what it deemed optimal for itself and that the burden of adjusting to balance-of-payments disequilibria be shared equally among surplus and deficit countries.[7] To achieve symmetry, the provisions of the ERM stipulate (1) that the central banks conduct unlimited interventions at the margins of the parity bands, (2) that weak-currency central banks have unlimited access to hard-currency reserves from hard-currency central banks through the European Monetary Cooperation Fund, (3) that both hard-currency and weak-currency central banks take appropriate corrective measures of domestic monetary policy, when the *divergence indicator* shows that their currencies diverge too much from the weighted average of the remaining currencies, and (4) that realignments of the central parities be possible only as a result of collective action requiring the consent of all members.[8]

The Bundesbank perceived the original design of the ERM as a threat to its autonomy and ability to preserve domestic price stability. If other members opted for higher permanent rates of inflation than the Bundesbank, as seemed likely, the divergence indicator would designate the DM as the currency in need of corrective, that is, more expansionary, policies. This would force the Bundesbank either to fall in line with the rest of the group or to convince the federal government and the other EMS governments to accept frequent realignments. The historical experience of the Bretton Woods system had shown, however, that governments tend to avoid or postpone realignments because of political repercussions.

As a result, the Bundesbank came to the conclusion that safeguarding domestic price stability within the EMS required taking measures to protect its independence, at least over the longer run. For this purpose, the Bundesbank relied on two strategies. First, before entering the EMS, the Bank obtained a guarantee from the federal government that "in case of fundamental conflict arising for monetary policy as a consequence of the obligation to defend a particular exchange rate, the Bundesbank would have the option to suspend its intervention obligation in the EMS" (Tietmeyer, 1990).

This internal agreement allowed the Bank to have a voice on realignment decisions. In particular, it allowed the Bundesbank, by threatening to suspend interventions in support of the French franc, to enforce the famous March 1983 realignment, which played an important role in the dramatic turnaround of French economic policies, from Keynesian stimulation to stabilization (see OECD, 1988; Wyplosz and Sachs, 1986; and chapter 15 of the present text).

Second, to signal to its EMS partners that domestic price stability had a higher priority than exchange-rate stability, the Bundesbank abstained from intramarginal intervention in the EMS, that is, noncompulsory intervention before exchange rates reach the margins. In contrast, other EMS central banks used intramarginal interventions on a much larger scale than interventions at the margin. Finally, the Bundesbank adjusted its monetary policy instruments to facilitate the sterilization of interventions by offsetting changes in the domestic component of the monetary base.[9]

As a result of these policies, the Bundesbank has attained a special position in the EMS. The DM has been popularly called the nominal anchor of the system. This role combines a relatively large degree of independence in determinating the German long-run rate of monetary expansion and inflation with a leadership function in the daily operation of the system, particularly vis-à-vis the smaller EMS countries neighboring Germany. The long-run independence of the Bundesbank's policy manifests itself in that money growth and interest rates show very little lasting responses to money growth and interest rates in other EMS countries, although they do react significantly in the shorter run (Fratianni and von Hagen, 1990). The Bundesbank's leadership role means that the Bank's reactions to short-run monetary and exchange-rate fluctuations serve as a focal point for the policy responses in other EMS countries. On numerous occasions, other EMS countries simply followed the Bundesbank's reaction to exogenous shocks, instead of determining an autonomous policy response. This pattern of leadership is fostered by the common practice, in all EMS countries, of using short-term money market rates as the principal operating target of monetary policy, since adjusting money market rates assures that the exchange rate remains within the parity bands. During the 1980s monetary policymakers in all EMS countries became increasingly dissatisfied with the results of the traditional, Keynesian, discretionary monetary policies of the 1960s and 1970s. As a result, the Bundesbank's proven commitment to price stability, together with the relative size of the German financial markets in the EMS, made the Bank the natural candidate for such a leadership position. Following its response to shocks in the short run assures the other central banks that they embark on a reaction compatible with long-run price stability.

Some authors have misinterpreted the leadership role of the DM in the EMS, arguing that the DM has acquired the role of the nth currency. In this oversimplifying view, the Bundesbank dominates the EMS in the sense of unilaterally determining the course of monetary policy for the system as a whole (Fischer, 1988b; Giavazzi and Giovannini, 1987, 1989; Gros and Thygesen, 1988). However, empirical research has shown that this conclusion is not warranted (De Grauwe, 1988; Fratianni and von Hagen, 1990; Kirchgässner and Wolters, 1990; von Hagen and Fratianni, 1990). Throughout the 1980s, institutional mechanisms of the EMS, such as realignments and the tolerance of capital and exchange controls, allowed its members to deviate from the Bundesbank's medium and long-run course of monetary policy, even if a short-run leadership relation exists.[10]

The second source of exchange-rate constraints on Bundesbank policies is in the repercussions of the large swings in the international value of the dollar since the 1970s. Given the federal government's decision to let the DM/dollar rate float, the Bundesbank is free, in principle, to engage in interventions in the DM/dollar market and to choose their timing and scale. The Bundesbank has repeatedly stated its intention to smooth fluctuations in the DM/dollar rate over time and has tried to *lean against the wind* of depreciation or appreciation of the DM against the dollar:

The main purpose of intervention in the Deutsche Mark/US dollar spot market has so far been the maintenance of orderly market conditions through short-run official "smoothing" operations and efforts to dampen over- or undershooting of the Deutsche Mark in relation to its warranted long-run trend. . . .

The Bundesbank does not feel that the Deutsche Mark/US dollar rate could or should be "pegged" at unrealistic levels or that exchange market intervention (. . .) can, by itself, be expected to break massive market pressures working in the direction of apparent exchange rate over- or undershooting. Even so, intervention was at times undertaken on a more massive scale in the face of lasting exchange rate aberrations, when such action could be expected to dampen adverse exchange rate movements and, at the same time, was consistent with accompanying efforts of domestic monetary management." (Dudler, 1983 p. 69)

Similarly, "the Bank intervenes [in the DM/US dollar market], in particular, when exchange rate fluctuations are excessively large, happen overly rapidly or begin to assume an erratic character" (Scholl, 1983, p. 121). Such an attitude obviously presupposes that the central bank has superior knowledge about the equilibrium exchange rate truly warranted by market fundamentals and therefore can detect "disorder" and "erratic" behavior in the market. Scholl, then head of the Bundesbank's Foreign Department, quite frankly admits that the Bank does not always have such knowledge: "it may be difficult, however, to distinguish between random and systematic exchange rate movements, and it often can only be said in retrospect with any certainty whether exaggerated movements were happening" (1983, p. 121). However, in the resulting conflict between the desire to smooth exchange-rate fluctuations and the wish to avoid unwarranted manipulation of exchange rates, the former generally seems to dominate.

In addition to this self-imposed constraint, throughout the past decade the federal government has participated in international attempts at co-ordinating economic policies among the main industrial countries. The Bundesbank cannot, in practice, ignore the monetary policy implications of such arrangements. In fact, Bundesbank representatives took part in the negotiations leading to the Plaza and Louvre agreements of 1985 and 1987, respectively.

The United States' abrupt turnaround on exchange-rate matters, from benign neglect of exchange-rate developments under the first Reagan administration to the call for international cooperation to stabilize the dollar under the second Reagan administration, resulted in the Plaza Agreement among the governments of the G-5 group (Britain, Japan, France, Germany, and the United States) in September 1985. The agreement did not speak explicitly of interventions, but it called for "some further orderly appreciation of the main non-dollar currencies" and declared that the G-5 members were ready "to cooperate more closely to encourage this when to do so would be helpful." Although the Bundesbank agreed to cooperate, it refused to commit itself to any specific target exchange rate or a scale of intervention. As Funabashi (1988) points out, the Bundesbank hesitated to endorse "the down-with-the-dollar fanfare" of government officials and preferred a more cautious, stepwise approach promoting a soft landing of the dollar. The Bank's reluctance to participate is documented by its small share in the joint interventions during the six weeks following the agreement, which did not exceed 10 percent of a total of U.S. $10.2 billion. It was justified as a desire to avoid strain in the EMS resulting from an appreciation of the DM against the dollar. To facilitate a balanced appreciation of all EMS currencies against the dollar, the Bundesbank sold dollars to its EMS partners through swap operations.

The French-American strife on policy cooperation and joint exchange-rate management led to the Louvre Accord of the G-7 nations (the G-5 plus Italy and Canada) of February 1987. Again, the Bundesbank participated in the coordination effort but was anxious to avoid a commitment to a specific target zone for the dollar. This time, however, the Bank was pressured to accept a larger burden of monetary adjustment in the agreement "to cooperate closely to foster stability of exchange rates around current levels." Numerical targets were eventually specified in the agreement. As a result of the Louvre Accord and the subsequent interventions to support the dollar particularly in the wake of the October 1987 stock market crash, the Bundesbank allowed money growth to overshoot the upper limit of the monetary target range for 1987 by 2.1 percent.

To summarize, institutional framework of German monetary policy can be characterized as follows: The monetary constitution provides the Bundesbank with a large degree of independence from the federal government. The Bank's authority over domestic monetary policy is limited mainly by its legal mandate to safeguard price stability, and by the federal government's power to engage in international economic policy coordination and to choose Germany's exchange-rate regime.

2. POLICY OBJECTIVES AND MONETARY TARGETING

The breakdown of the Bretton Woods system of fixed exchange rates in 1973 freed the Bundesbank from the obligation to intervene in the DM/dollar market to maintain the fixed parity. Shortly thereafter, the Bundesbank decided to use its newly acquired autonomy over monetary policy to establish a regime of monetary targeting. An annual monetary target was first announced for 1975. Since then, monetary targeting has remained the basic monetary policy regime, modified only occasionally by changes in implementation procedures. Adopting a monetary aggregate as the intermediate target of monetary policy means that, during the course of a year, all monetary policy actions are geared primarily toward reaching the monetary target (Dudler, 1983, p. 41). The basic rationale for monetary targeting is to provide a reference point, both for the government and the private sector, to indicate the course and intentions of monetary policy, to signal clearly the Bundesbank's unwillingness to use monetary policy for short-sighted discretionary policies, and to help avoid the detrimental real effects of inflation expectation errors.[11]

The Bundesbank targets a broad monetary aggregate. The choice of such an aggregate rather than a narrow, more transactions-oriented one, like M1, has been justified on the grounds that broad aggregates internalize short-run portfolio shifts between various types of bank deposits induced by fluctuations in short-term interest rates. Broad aggregates therefore seem more controllable. This argument is in line with von Hagen's (1988) estimates of control error margins for broad and narrow monetary aggregates, which show that the Bank can control broad aggregates with about half the error margin of M1. From 1975 to 1987, the target aggregate was the Central Bank Money Stock (CBM), a weighted sum of currency held by nonbanks, and demand, time, and savings deposits at statutory notice. The weights are equal to one for currency and equal to the required reserve ratios of January 1974 for the remaining components.[12] The use of reserve ratios in computing CBM has caused some confusion in the interpretation of this aggregate and Bundesbank policy. Fischer (1988a), for example, calls CBM a "required monetary base." However, CBM is not a monetary base since it excludes required reserves on foreign deposits and excess reserves and is calculated on the basis of historical reserve ratios. The Bundesbank itself regards CBM as a money stock concept, that is, a non-bank aggregate. Despite recurrent criticism (e.g., Duwendag, 1976; Courakis, 1980; Neumann, 1975), the Bank insisted that the weights reflected fairly accurately the different degrees of liquidity of the components of CBM. Furthermore, the Bundesbank argued that the weighted aggregate was a particularly reliable indicator of monetary conditions in Germany, having a more stable relationship to nominal GNP than other aggregates and being less exposed to interest-rate-induced portfolio shifts between bank deposits of different maturities (Deutsche Bundesbank, 1980, p. 20). In 1988, however, the Bundesbank adopted the simple-sum M3 (consisting of currency held by nonbanks, demand, time, and savings deposits at statutory notice) as its monetary target. This change was motivated by the observation that, in prolonged periods of low-interest rates and appreciation of the DM, the currency component tended to grow faster than other components of M3, so that CBM tended to overstate monetary growth in Germany, the so-called currency bias (Deutsche Bundesbank, *Monthly Report*, March 1988, pp. 18ff.). Empirical research has shown that both CBM and M3, as well as M1, fulfill the basic requirement of a stable money demand function, which, given the targeted money supply, assures a satisfactory degree of predictability and controllability of price-level developments under monetary control.[13]

From 1975 to 1978, monetary targets were expressed as target growth rates either for the year-end or the average annual money stock. Since the Bundesbank did not avoid overshooting the monetary targets, the information value of the target was much in doubt during this period. In 1979 the Bundesbank instead adopted target ranges of 3 percent around a fourth-quarter to fourth-quarter target growth rate. The purpose of the target range is to allow not only for unavoidable control errors, but also for some discretionary activism.[14] The Bundesbank has argued on several occasions that uncertainties about domestic cyclical movements in output and about external monetary developments demanded more flexibility than a simple monetary target could provide. The target range for 1984 was narrowed to 2 percent on the basis of less external uncertainty (Deutsche Bundesbank, *Monthly Report*, December 1983). In 1987 it was again widened to 3 percent in view of the difficulties with the operation of monetary policy caused by the strain in the EMS at the beginning of that year (Deutsche Bundesbank, *Monthly Report*, January 1987). Until 1984, the Bundesbank announced a more precise target following its regular review of the monetary target in the early summer, by stipulating a final range for the end of the year in the upper, middle, or lower part of the initial range. In 1989 the Bank returned to its earlier practice of announcing a single target rate for one year, presumably to convey its commitment to monetary targeting after three years of overshooting the target owing to exchange-rate policies. The monetary target for 1990 was again announced with a corridor of 2 percent.

The derivation of the monetary target is based on three central considerations: the expected growth of potential output, Δy^p, the expected change in the velocity of the target aggregate, Δv^p, and the target inflation rate, π^T.[15] If we apply the quantity theory equation, the monetary target, ΔM^T, is calculated as

(1) $\Delta M^T = \Delta y^p + \pi^T - \Delta v^p.$

The Bundesbank's velocity prediction does not account for short-run changes in actual velocity, but focuses rather on the long-run relationship between the target aggregate and potential output. Its concept of price stability, therefore, does not rule out transitory fluctuations in the price level arising from fluctuations in actual velocity or of output around potential output. In the early 1980s the target inflation rate, then called the unavoidable inflation rate, was chosen each year to undercut somewhat the actual inflation rate of the previous year.[16] In this way, the Bundesbank tried to reduce inflation gradually to avoid the output and employment losses likely to follow from a sharp monetary contraction. Since 1985, when inflation had come down to 2 percent, target inflation has been kept at 2 percent, a number that high officials of the Bank have repeatedly declared to be the empirical equivalent of price stability.

Exchange-rate constraints interfere with monetary targeting in two important ways. As already mentioned, the use of a target range instead of a precise target growth rate is justified mainly with the need for flexibility to respond to exchange-rate movements. As Rieke (1984, p. 55) puts it:

In order to avoid misunderstanding and not to damage the credibility of monetary targeting, the Bundesbank has, since 1979, taken the external constraints of monetary policy into account by adopting conditional monetary targets. By specifying a "target corridor" for the intended growth of the central bank money stock, the Bundesbank shows its readiness a priori to support the goals of exchange rate policy with monetary policy adjustments if necessary, and, furthermore, indicates how much room for manoeuvering is deemed necessary for this purpose.

That is, external constraints reduce the precision of the monetary target. In addition, the Bank has shown its willingness to subordinate the monetary target temporarily to exchange-rate considerations:

Shifts in the orientation of monetary management involved marked departures from the original annual target path for monetary growth only when excessive gyrations in the real Deutsche Mark/US dollar exchange rate throwing the effective rate of the Deutsche Mark off its desired course had to be countered (Dudler, 1988 p. 74).

Whenever excessive appreciation of the Deutsche Mark rate threatened seriously to disturb domestic economic trends—as in 1978 and again in 1986–87—the Bundesbank of necessity tolerated the overshooting of its monetary target in order to mitigate the upward pressure by keeping interest rates down and by buying foreign exchange, and in order to bolster domestic demand. (Deutsche Bundesbank, *Monthly Report*, May 1988, p. 20)

It is interesting to see that the Bank itself is rather critical about the success of such policies. The same quote continues:

However, such deviations from the rule are acceptable only if it is to be expected that a sustained appreciation of the Deutsche Mark will dampen the longer-term growth of domestic costs and prices and steer monetary expansion back on the potential path before exchange rate conditions reverse again. This was not nearly managed in the years following 1978.

Table 9.2 reports the Bundesbank's track record of monetary targeting since 1979. In the ten years from 1979 to 1988, money growth remained within the preannounced target range on five occasions, and it missed the target range as many times. Money growth was below the targeted range in the early 1980s, when the DM was generally weak against the dollar, and it exceeded the target range in the second half of the 1980s, when the DM was generally strong. This is a first reflection of the external constraints. Von Hagen (1989) presents evidence suggesting that, during the 1980s, the Bundesbank deviated from the monetary target in response to external considerations when the mark was either weak or strong against both the dollar and the EMS currencies, but the monetary target dominated in times of different performance of the mark against the dollar and in the EMS.

In general, the Bundesbank may tolerate deviations of money growth from its target during a year in response to undesirable economic conditions affecting other objectives of economic policy, such as inflation exceeding the target inflation rate, cyclical movements in output above or below the growth of potential output, or fluctuations in the external value of the DM. To see that the Bundesbank weighs such objectives against the monetary target, assume the following preference function describing the Bank's valuation of policy outcomes:

(2) $U = -\beta_1(\Delta M - \Delta M^T)^2 - \beta_2(\pi - \pi^T)^2 - \beta_3(\Delta y - \Delta y^P)^2$
$- \beta_4(\Delta q - \Delta q^P)^2,$

where the $\beta_i s$ are the preference weights and $(\Delta q - \Delta q^P)$ denotes the

Table 9.2
Monetary Targets, Inflation, and the External Value of the Deutsche Mark, 1979–89

Year	Target Range (%)	Realized Money Growth (%)	Deviation from Target Mean	Excess Inflation (%)	External Value (change in %)	Actual less potential GNP growth (%)
1979	6 - 9	6.3	-1.2	2.1	0.3	1.4
1980	5 - 8	4.9	-1.6	3.5	-5.5	-1.2
1981	4 - 7	3.5	-2.0	4.3	-9.7	-2.7
1982	4 - 7	6.0	0.5	3.2	1.7	-2.8
1983	4 - 7	7.0	1.5	1.3	0.4	-0.3
1984	4 - 6	4.6	-0.4	0.4	-4.9	1.0
1985	3 - 5	4.5	0.5	0.0	-2.8	0.5
1986	3.5-5.5	7.7	3.2	-2.1	6.1	-0.1
1987	3 - 6	8.1	3.6	-1.8	3.6	-0.7
1988	3 - 6	6.7	2.2	-0.7	-2.8	1.4
1989	5	4.7	-0.3	0.8	-2.5	-0.3

Source: Deutsche Bundesbank, *Monthly Reports.*

Note: The target range, realized money growth, and the deviation from target mean are for the Central Bank Money Stock from 1979 to 1987 and for M3 thereafter. All are fourth-quarter to fourth-quarter growth rates. Excess inflation is the actual cost-of-living rate of inflation less target inflation. The external value change is based on the Bundesbank's weighted index of the real value of the DM against eighteen trading partners of Germany. An increase in the external value indicates a real appeciation of the mark.

unanticipated growth rate of the external value of the DM. The external value of the mark is defined as an average real exchange rate against the currencies of Germany's eighteen most important trade partners. An increase in the external value means a real appreciation of the mark. The last term thus reflects the Bundesbank's tendency to lean against the wind. The relationship between money growth and the remaining variables is described by a reduced-form model linearized around the expected values,

$$(3) \quad \pi - \pi^T = \alpha_1(\Delta M - \Delta M^T) + \epsilon_1,$$
$$\Delta y - \Delta y^p = \alpha_2(\Delta M - \Delta M^T) + \epsilon_2,$$
$$\Delta q - \Delta q^p = -\alpha_3(\Delta M - \Delta M^T) + \epsilon_3,$$

where the $\alpha_i s \geq 0$ are reduced-form coefficients and the $\epsilon_i s$ are random variables. Maximizing the preference function (2) with respect to the Bundesbank's control variable, deviations from the monetary target, yield

$$(4) \quad \Delta M - \Delta M^T = (\beta_1)^{-1}[\alpha_3\beta_4(\Delta q - \Delta q^p) - \alpha_2\beta_3(\Delta y - \Delta y^p)$$
$$- \alpha_1\beta_2(\pi - \pi^T)] + \eta,$$

where η is a random variable. Table 9.2 reports the realizations of the right-hand-side variables of equation (4). Using these data, we regress the deviations from the monetary target, estimated as the difference between the midpoint of the target range and the actual growth of the target aggregate on the three arguments. All variables are corrected for their means and are standardized by sample standard deviations, and Δq^p is measured as the sample average change in the value of the DM. This yields the regression equation

(5) $\Delta M - \Delta M^T = -0.61(\pi - \pi^T) + 0.41(\Delta q - \Delta q^p) + \hat{\eta}$
                  (4.1)   (2.7)
     $R^2 = 0.86, F_{9,2} = 28.3, \rho = 0.20,$

where the nonsignificant term $(\Delta y - \Delta y^p)$ has been omitted. Here, ρ is the estimated first-order autocorrelation coefficient of the errors. It is well below its standard deviation of 0.33, indicating no autocorrelation. $F_{9,2}$ is the F-test for significance of the regression; it is above the 0.005 percent significance level. The numbers in parentheses are absolute t-ratios. Including the cyclical output variable in the regression yields a coefficient estimate of -0.11, which has the anticipated sign, but a nonsignificant t-ratio of 1.25. Thus, the hypothesis that the Bundesbank pays no attention to cyclical output movements during a year, $\beta_3 = 0$, cannot be rejected. In contrast, the results show that deviations of money growth from the target can be explained to a large extent by *excess inflation*, $\pi - \pi^T$, and *leaning against the wind*. The impact of the former on the standardized money growth is 1.5 times the impact of the latter. Note that this ratio reflects the *effective* tradeoff between inflation and changes in the external value of the DM for the Bundesbank, that is, the *preference tradeoff*, β_2/β_4, multiplied by the ratio of the reduced-form parameters, α_1/α_3. Since it is plausible to assume that the ratio of the reduced-form parameters in (3) is less than one, since the price-level effects of a monetary expansion within a year are likely to be smaller than the exchange-rate effects, this implies that the Bundesbank's preference tradeoff between inflation and DM appreciation or depreciation is likely to be even larger than 1.5.

Figure 9.1 illustrates the contributions of excess inflation and changes in the external value of the DM to deviations from the monetary target from 1979 to 1989. Both explanatory variables have been multiplied by their respective coefficients, and the normalization applied for the regression has been reversed. In the early 1980s the real depreciation of the mark led to a more restrictive monetary policy, whereas in 1985 to 1987, the revaluation of the mark induced a more expansionary policy compared with the monetary target. The decline in excess inflation between 1981 and 1985 contributed to the rising deviations from the target, whereas the rise in excess inflation after 1986, which lagged the devaluation of the mark by

Figure 9.1
Contributions of Excess Inflation and Changes in the External Value of the DM to Deviations from the Monetary Target, 1979–89

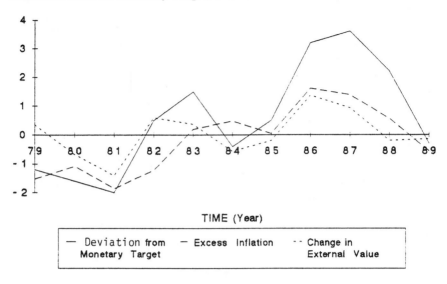

TIME (Year)

— Deviation from   — Excess Inflation   - - Change in
     Monetary Target   External Value

about one year, fostered the return to more restrictive monetary policy in the last years of the 1980s.

The discussion of this section can be summarized as follows: The Bundesbank formulates and pursues monetary targets compatible with price stability. Target ranges are formulated to allow for some discretionary flexibility in the response to domestic economic conditions and, mainly, to exchange-rate developments. Deviations from the monetary target occur in response to excess inflation as well as undesired exchange-rate movements. Thus, the Bundesbank's monetary regime is best characterized as price-stability-oriented monetary targeting under exchange-rate constraints.

3. IMPLEMENTATION OF MONETARY CONTROL

The Bundesbank commands a variety of different policy instruments. The most important ones involve lending to domestic banks. Open market operations in government paper play no significant role in Germany.[17] Changes in international reserves, once the dominant source of central bank money in Germany, lost much of their importance during the 1980s. This change reflects the Bank's efforts, since the late 1970s, to build up a set of sufficiently flexible domestic instruments, thereby offsetting the po-

Table 9.3
Main Sources of Central Bank Money, 1978–89

Year	Base DM bill.	International		Domestic				
		IR$ (%)	IRE (%)	DISC (%)	LOMB (%)	REPO (%)	MOB (%)	SEC (%)
1978	140.7	68.2	----	12.9	4.4	0.0	-3.2	3.0
1979	151.2	46.0	12.8	21.9	2.1	0.0	1.3	1.4
1980	145.0	37.4	6.3	30.1	5.3	4.3	3.1	2.7
1981	142.2	34.3	11.7	35.3	4.2	8.4	2.7	2.6
1982	148.6	33.3	13.2	36.2	8.1	6.1	2.7	3.6
1983	157.4	33.0	9.8	35.6	8.4	10.3	1.5	5.0
1984	163.8	31.8	8.8	38.2	4.9	15.7	1.3	2.6
1985	170.5	28.2	10.1	36.0	1.4	24.4	0.0	2.4
1986	179.6	28.8	9.1	33.9	1.3	18.5	2.2	2.9
1987	196.4	36.2	14.7	27.5	0.4	14.1	1.8	2.3
1988	216.1	21.2	10.0	25.7	5.2	36.1	1.8	2.3
1989	229.0	12.5	7.6	26.8	2.3	47.5	2.0	1.9

Source: Deutsche Bundesbank, *Monthly Reports.*

Notes: End of year figures. Central bank money: currency in circulation plus central bank deposits of domestic commercial banks; IR$: net international monetary reserves less net claims on the European Monetary Cooperation Fund, IRE; DISC: discount window borrowing (domestic and foreign bills); LOMB: Lombard loans to commercial banks; REPO: security repurchase agreements with domestic commercial banks; MOB: net stock of money market paper (Mobilisierungs- und Liquiditätspapiere); SEC: stock of long-term public sector securities.

tential effects of changes in international reserves on monetary base growth arising from its exchange-rate constraints.

Monetary Control Instruments

Table 9.3 provides an overview of the main components of the monetary base. By the end of the 1970s, international reserves accounted for about two thirds of the sources of central bank money. At the end of the 1980s, their share had come down steadily to about 20 percent. During the same period, the share of lending to domestic commercial banks increased from around 20 percent to more than three quarters. The share of the Bundesbank's open market portfolio in the sources of central bank money hovered around 2 percent and, thus, remains negligible. The predominance of lending to banks over open market operations results from the virtual absence of a market for short-term government paper in Germany since World War II.

The Bank's open market portfolio consists entirely of long-term securities issued by the federal government, the state governments, the federal railways, and the federal post office. Operations in *Mobilisierungs- und Liquiditäts* paper (MOB paper) are the only purchases and sales of short-term government bills which the Bundesbank undertakes. The Bank holds a fixed amount of *Mobilisierungspapiere* (DM 8.7 billion) resulting from the currency reform in 1948; it can request the issue of an additional DM 8.0 billion of *Liquiditätspapiere* from the federal government, paper that the Bank can sell to commercial banks to reduce the monetary base. The Bundesbank fixes the rates of return on MOB paper and lets the banking sector determine the quantity purchased. Holding periods typically extend over three days. They are renewable, but the Bundesbank normally does not buy back such paper before maturity. As a result of these practices, the rates on MOB paper are a floor for the German call-money rate. The table demonstrates that these operations were of little importance in the recent past.

Among the loans to domestic commercial banks, discount credit is the most traditional monetary policy instrument. The Bundesbank discounts foreign and domestic commercial bills and prime bankers' acceptances. Discount loans have fixed maturities of up to ninety days and cannot be repaid before maturity. Banks have access to discount credit upon request up to their discount quota, which the Bundesbank extends to banks on the basis of their capital. The discount rate is kept consistently below short-term interest rates, and commercial banks have additional incentives to fully utilize their quota. This practice implies that the Bundesbank can exert tight control over the quantity of discount credit, although the discount rate is fixed for long periods of time. Variations in the discount rate alone have little effect on the money supply.

Lombard credit, in contrast, is freely accessible to banks under normal circumstances. The Lombard rate is consistently kept above short-term interest rates. Lombard credit is collateralized with trade bills, securities, or Treasury bills. The effective maturity is variable, since Lombard loans can be repaid at any time. From the banks' perspective, Lombard credit is therefore the more flexible refinancing instrument. However, the Bundesbank has on occasion introduced Lombard quotas or even suspended Lombard credit altogether and offered *Sonderlombard* (special Lombard) instead.[18] In contrast to discount or Lombard credit, Sonderlombard loans can be canceled on a daily basis by the Bundesbank. Since the late 1970s, the Bundesbank has reduced the role of Lombard credit from its traditional one of being the main instrument for short-run liquidity management to a buffer allowing banks to satisfy unforeseen, transitory peeks in the demand for central bank money (Deutsche Bundesbank, *Monthly Report*, October 1985, p. 19). As a result, the Lombard rate forms a ceiling on the call-money rate.

Since the early 1980s, the Bundesbank has increasingly made use of security repurchase agreements (*REPO*s) as a further and, from its perspective, much more flexible instrument of lending to banks.[19] *REPO*s are loans to banks collateralized by commercial bills or, more commonly, by securities. The main difference with discount and Lombard credit is that the Bundesbank retains the initiative to offer such loans. *REPO*s have fixed maturities of between three and sixty-three days, the majority extending over a month. A new *REPO* is typically offered one day before an existing one expires. The Bundesbank offers *REPO*s either as volume or as interest tenders. Volume tenders, in which the Bank fixes the interest rate at the outset of the transaction, are used when the Bank wants to signal an intended change in short-term interest rates. The total amount of funds provided in volume tenders is generally below 50 percent of the total bids; funds are allocated to banks on the basis of a uniform allocation ratio. Otherwise, interest-rate tenders are used, in which banks are invited to bid for both volume and interest rates. Before September 1988, the Bundesbank quoted a minimum rate for interest-rate tenders and invited banks to submit bids for volume and interest rates. Banks were allowed to submit more than one bid. Funds were allocated uniformly at the rate of the last accepted bid, with all bids above that rate being fully met. As of September 1988, the Bank no longer quotes a minimum rate, and funds are allocated at the individual rates bid by the commercial banks. In both cases, the Bank meets the demand for funds only up to quantitative limits determined a priori. In the early 1980s *REPO*s were used mainly for the short-term control of money market conditions. As a result, the average volume of *REPO*s was quite small. Table 9.3 shows that the share of *REPO*s in the sources of central bank money increased dramatically in the second half of the 1980s, reflecting the Bank's efforts to make *REPO*s the dominant instrument in the control of the monetary base (Deutsche Bundesbank, *Monthly Report*, October 1985, p. 19). Since then, the *REPO* rate has become the main indicator of the Bundesbank's short-run intentions with respect to short-term interest rates.

Foreign exchange swaps and repurchase agreements are foreign exchange operations aimed at controlling the domestic monetary base. They do not affect the Bundesbank's stock of net foreign assets, and, consequently, they have no exchange-rate implications. In a foreign exchange swap, the Bundesbank combines a spot sale of foreign exchange to a commercial bank with a forward repurchase, resulting in a temporary absorption of central bank money. Foreign exchange repurchase agreements are loans to commercial banks collateralized with U.S. dollar-denominated assets.

Another instrument of the Bundesbank is deposit policy. Under this policy, the Bank shifts public sector deposits at the Bundesbank to or from the private banking sector. As a variant of this policy, the Bundesbank at times asks two public banks (Kreditanstalt für Wiederaufbau or Deutsche Verkehrskreditbank) to borrow or lend central bank funds in the interbank market tacitly on its account. These operations serve for very short-term absorption or issue of base money (Deutsche Bundesbank, 1983, pp. 70ff.).

Finally, the Bundesbank can influence the demand for central bank reserves with reserve requirements. Reserve requirements in Germany are a hybrid system of lagged and contemporaneous reserves accounting. Required reserves are calculated on the basis of reservable deposits held between the sixteenth day of a month and the fifteenth day of the following month. Actual reserves counted against the requirement are computed as monthly averages of daily Bundesbank deposits that banks hold between the first and the last day of the second month, so that there is a two-week overlap. This practice allows commercial banks a quite flexible use of normal working balances to fulfill their reserve requirement. Reservable deposits are demand deposits, time deposits, and savings deposits at statutory notice; required reserve ratios are on a progressive scale, with the smallest ratios applying to savings deposits and the largest ones to demand deposits. Banks pay a penalty rate of 3 percent above the prevailing Lombard rate for violating their requirement. As a result, banks tend to meet their requirements very closely, and excess reserves are negligible in Germany.

The Bundesbank has sometimes argued that the reserve requirement impedes tight control of the monetary base in the short run.[20] The argument is that, at a given point of time, the reserve requirement predetermines the banking sector's demand for deposits. Any attempt of the central bank to realize a monetary base target below this predetermined level of demand would lead only to excessive volatility of money market rates. The reserve requirement therefore implies that the central bank must accommodate the banking sector's demand in the short run. Obviously, the flawed logic of this argument rests on the empirical observation that excess reserves are negligible. This, however, is itself only a consequence of the Bundesbank's practice of accommodating banks' demand in the short run, which amounts to relieving banks of the necessity to form expectations about future central bank policy and money market conditions. Von Hagen (1984, 1987) has shown that, if monetary base targets are announced and reliably pursued, lagged reserve requirements do not stand in the way of exercising tight short-run control over the monetary base.

Controlling the Supply Price of Base Money: The Call-Money Rate Regime

As a monopolist in the supply of central bank money, the Bundesbank can choose either to fix the quantity supplied and let the price be determined by the public's and the banking sector's demand, or to set the price and leave the quantity endogenous. The common characteristic of its instruments for monetary control is that, with the exception of deposit policy, they all aim at regulating the supply price of base money, that is, the banks' opportunity cost of holding and borrowing base money. The discount and Lombard rate, and the rates and terms of the *REPO* and swap operations and the money market paper offered to banks, as well as the required reserve ratios, all determine the supply price, whereas quantity decisions are left with banks. This does not imply, of course, that the quantity of base money is uncontrollable in Germany; precise control of the base requires knowledge of the banks' demand function for base money and the flexible use of the pricing instruments.

Given the multiplicity of the Bundesbank's instruments, the supply price of central bank money has many dimensions and is therefore not readily observable. To assess the price effect of a particular policy action, it would be useful to have a scalar measure of the supply price. For this purpose, the Bundesbank uses the call-money rate in the Frankfurt interbank market.[21] The German interbank market consists almost entirely of direct short-term lending and borrowing among banks. The main trading form is overnight loans. The Bundesbank does not directly participate in this market. Trading in the interbank market merely distributes the central bank money available at a given date over the banking sector, without any effects on the total supply. In a macroeconomic sense, therefore, interbank interest rates are irrelevant for monetary policy. From the point of view of an individual bank, however, the interbank market offers alternative opportunities for short-term borrowing or investing central bank money to those offered by the Bundesbank. Therefore, a bank will not borrow money from the Bundesbank, if it can do so more cheaply in the interbank market. Similarly, it will not lend funds to other banks if the Bundesbank offers a more attractive short-term investment. Thus, interbank rates are tied to the Bundesbank's pricing instruments by arbitrage conditions. The relationship between the pricing instruments and the interest rate is strongest for the call-money rate. The call-money rate generally reacts immediately to changes in one of the Bank's instruments. This rate can therefore be regarded as the desired scalar measure of the supply price of central bank money, and the Bundesbank uses it as such.

Given a supply price of base money, the money stock is the result of the private nonbank and bank sectors' equilibrium demand for base money, and numerous portfolio allocation decisions in both sectors which determine the use of central bank money: its allocation between cash and reserves, and the relative quantities of the various types of deposits. Changes in the supply price will, in general, affect both the demand for base money and the portfolio allocations. With this in mind, we can characterize the Bundesbank's approach to monetary control as follows: "The Bundesbank uses its instruments to control the supply price of base money such that the equilibrium quantity, together with the equilibrium portfolio allocations of banks and nonbanks, results in the desired money supply."[22] The Bundesbank calls this approach the control of money market conditions.

The Bank's focus on the call-money rate in the formulation and execution of monetary control must not be mistaken for the Keynesian approach of controlling short-term interest rates to influence the public's demand for money, which is more characteristic, for example, of the U.S. Federal Reserve System. The Keynesian approach neglects the role of the bank sector in determining the money supply and views the money demand function as the important channel of transmission of monetary policy impulses to the economy (Brunner, 1974). In contrast, the Bundesbank's approach recognizes the importance of endogenous bank and nonbank portfolio decisions in the money supply process and the transmission of monetary policy. Any variation of a Bundesbank instrument is based, in this approach, on two assessments: its immediate effect on the supply price of base money as reflected in the call-money rate, and the likely effect of the change in the supply price on the money supply. Controlling a monetary aggregate in this way requires reliable empirical knowledge of the demand for base money and the relevant portfolio processes. In the Bundesbank's practical operations, this knowledge is furnished by its unpublished econometric money market model, supplemented by judgmental experience. Alternatively, von Hagen (1986, 1988) has shown that relatively simple empirical models based on the multiplier approach can be used to implement a reliable control procedure.

The Two-Stage Operating Procedure

The Bundesbank's operating regime for monetary control can be described as a two-stage procedure. It starts from a decomposition of the monetary base, B, into three components: one that is predetermined relative to the control of the money supply, BP; one that is used to set the desired long-run growth path of the monetary base, BL; and one that is used to steer transitory deviations of the monetary base from the trend path, BT. Changes in the monetary base are thus the sum of predetermined, long-run, and transitory changes:[23]

(6) $\Delta B = \Delta BP + \Delta BL + \Delta BT.$

The predetermined component consists mainly of foreign exchange reserves; changes in these reserves reflect both outright transactions of the central bank on behalf of the federal government and foreign exchange market interventions in the dollar market and in the EMS. The remaining elements of BP are public sector deposits, PSD, and central bank float, F.

(7) $\Delta BP = \Delta IR\$ + \Delta IRE + \Delta PSD + \Delta F$.

Here, $IR\$$ denotes changes in the Bundesbank's dollar reserves including gold and SDRs; IRE denotes changes in the Bundesbank's net claims on the European Monetary Cooperation Fund (EMCF), which manages interventions in the EMS. (See Chapter 15.)

The long-run trend growth of the monetary base is controlled using reserve requirements, discount quotas, DQ, purchases and sales of public securities, PB, and, since the second half of the 1980s, $REPO$s in securities.

(8) $\Delta BL = \Delta LR + \Delta DQ + \Delta PB + \Delta REPO_L$,

where LR denotes liberated reserves, and $REPO_L$ the portion of $REPO$s used for long-run control purposes. Finally, the components of the transitory part of the monetary base are the remaining $REPO$s in securities, $REPO_s$, $REPO$s in foreign exchange, $REPO_\$$, foreign exchange swaps, $SWAP$, Lombard credit, $LOMB$, and deposit policy, DP.

(9) $\Delta BT = \Delta REPO_s + \Delta REPO_\$ + \Delta SWAP + \Delta LOMB + \Delta DP$.

Variations in BT are geared primarily at reducing short-run fluctuations in the call-money rate. To underline the transitory nature of such operations, the Bundesbank calls them reversible money market operations. Reversible money market operations have maturities between two and thirty days. Under the current two-stage operating regime, changes in the transitory component of the monetary base are generally reversed after some time, leaving no lasting effect on the total monetary base.

Table 9.4 shows the contributions of the three components of the monetary base to the growth and variability of the base. For lack of more precise data, we subsume the hybrid $REPO$s fully under the transitory component, although in recent years part of it belongs to the long-run component, BL. In the last three years of the 1980s, the growth of the predetermined component, BP, either exceeded or strongly counteracted the growth of the monetary base, almost entirely for changes in international reserves. In 1987 the excess of growth of this component was mainly undone by reductions in liberated reserves and discount quotas. In contrast, in 1988 and 1989 the Bundesbank relied most heavily on $REPO$s to work against the shrinking of international reserves. The table demonstrates that the annual growth in the remaining parts of the transitory component is negligible.

The monthly variability of the predetermined component is generally much larger than the variability of the base. Table 9.4 shows that $REPO$s are the most variable element of the base; the very short-run oriented parts of the transitory component have much lower variability.

Table 9.4
Contributions to Monetary Base Growth and Variability, 1986–89

a) Contributions to Annual Growth

Year	B	IR	BP-IR	LR	DQ	PB	REPO	MOB	DP	SWAP	LOMB
1986	13.1	0.66	0.34	0.56	-0.43	0.11	-0.73	0.05	0.03	0.02	0.05
1987	15.5	2.50	0.02	-0.39	-0.49	-0.08	-0.35	-0.03	-0.10	-0.02	-0.06
1988	18.6	-1.66	-0.31	0.01	0.02	0.05	2.71	0.02	0.00	-0.01	0.12
1989	9.4	-2.14	-0.36	-0.01	0.81	-0.04	2.85	0.00	-0.01	0.03	-0.06

b) Relative Variability of Monthly Change

Year	B	IR	BP-IR	LR	DQ	PB	REPO	MOB	DP	SWAP	LOMB
1986	2.60	1.38	1.87	0.85	0.54	0.13	2.38	0.29	0.61	0.16	0.19
1987	2.88	1.89	1.48	0.57	0.67	0.15	2.32	0.24	0.47	0.06	0.10
1988	3.26	1.49	1.35	0.04	0.66	0.14	2.51	0.19	0.37	0.06	0.33
1989	2.79	0.71	1.24	0.05	0.48	0.11	1.84	0.12	0.10	0.15	0.85

Source: Deutsche Bundesbank, *Monthly Reports*, Table 1.3.

Notes: The upper panel reports the annual change in the monetary base, B, in DM billions, and the annual changes in the components, each divided by the annual change in the base. The lower panel reports the standard deviation of monthly changes in the base in DM billions, and the standard deviations of monthly changes of the components, each divided by the standard deviation of the base.

IR: international reserves at transactions values, BP-IR: public sector and other nonbank deposit flows plus float plus "other factors", LR: liberated reserves, DQ: discount quota, PB: public sector securities plus open market operations with nonbanks, REPO: repurchase agreements with securities, MOB: open market operations in MOB, DP: deposit policy, SWAP: foreign exchange swaps and repurchase agreements, LOMB: Lombard credit.

Under the current operating regime, daily central bank operations use an average operating target for the call-money rate as a yardstick. The operating target reflects the supply price of central bank money believed to be compatible with the monetary target over the time horizon of a month to a quarter. Rates on security *REPO*s are the main instrument to keep the call-money rate on target over this time horizon, whereas the Lombard rate and the selling rates on MOB paper are infrequently adjusted to provide a ceiling and a floor for the call-money rate. Discount quota and minimum reserve ratios are used only infrequently to adjust *BL*. Fine-tuning operations, that is, variations in *BT*, are employed to smooth short-run fluctuations in the call-money rate by accommodating variations in the banking sector's demand for reserves.

To illustrate the working of the regime, consider first a period when money growth is on or close to target. The Bundesbank will usually offer new *REPO*s at rates slightly below the prevailing call-money rate. Fluctuations in the predetermined base component may be accommodated by fine-tuning operations; however, there is no automatic smoothing in general. Fine-tuning operations do play a greater role only toward the end of reserve maintenance periods, especially operations to avoid large-scale uses of Lombard credit, or in the face of larger inflows or outflows of foreign exchange. Typically, in such periods, the call-money rate will be close to the target level and will rarely reach the Lombard or MOB paper rate.

Compare this to a period when the money supply begins growing faster than the target would allow, owing to an increase in the demand for reserves. As long as the Bank believes this situation to be transitory, it will behave in much the same way as above, and not enforce changes in the call-money rate. The rate will, however, move upward, reflecting a higher supply price as banks make heavier use of Lombard credit. If the increase persists, the Bank will eventually revise its operating target upward and start pushing up the *REPO* rate. Depending on how uncertain the Bank is about the appropriate new target level, interest-rate or volume tenders will be applied in this process. Only if the upward revision is sufficiently large, say, 50 basis points, will the Bank adjust the Lombard rate, the MOB paper rate, and the discount rate. With this lagged adjustment, changes in the latter three rates no longer serve to signal the Bundesbank's intention to change its policy stance. Such a signal function can currently be assigned predominantly to the *REPO* rate.

Finally, if the Bank wishes to change *BL* on its own initiative, for example, in response to lasting changes in the predetermined component, the pattern will be very similar to the above. Initial changes in the call-money rate will be induced by adjusting the rate on *REPO*s, first, and other rates later. When the new target level of the call-money rate is reached, the Bank will return to its normal operating procedure.

4. INTERVENTIONS AND STERILIZATION

Interventions and sterilization are the critical links between domestic monetary control and exchange-rate constraints. To accomplish a desired exchange rate, the Bundesbank must buy or sell foreign exchange. Such operations obviously have an impact on the monetary base and, consequently, the money supply, unless they are sterilized, that is, offset by some counteracting operation, usually in one of the domestic components. Thus, the amount of interventions and the degree of sterilization together determine to what extent monetary control is impeded by the exchange-rate constraints.

The Bundesbank, like other central banks, does not publish detailed data on interventions. The amount of interventions can therefore be estimated only indirectly. One way of doing so is to consider changes in the Bank's net foreign assets, which, in addition to interventions, also include foreign exchange market operations related to the Bank's normal business, such as international payments on behalf of the federal government, or interest payments and receipts. Figure 9.2 plots the Bundesbank's net dollar reserves—defined, for simplicity, as net monetary reserves less net claims on the EMCF—together with an index of the external value of the DM against the U.S. dollar since 1979. Net dollar reserves declined dramatically in 1980–81, increased strongly in 1986–87, and fell again in 1988–89. Each of these movements involved changes of 30 to 40 percent of the initial net reserves. The decline in the early 1980s occurred when the dollar was rising, while the increase in the late 1980s came with a declining dollar. Both episodes suggest that the Bundesbank tried to slow down market movements by means of large-scale interventions. Net claims on the EMCF are also plotted in Figure 9.2. The main characteristic here is that the Bank's reserves increased sharply before realignments as a result of interventions in support of other member currencies, and, in most cases, came down again after the realignment. This reflects the practice of the 1980s, to choose the DM new central rate in a realignment so that the market rate will initially be at the lower limit of the exchange-rate band, allowing the Bundesbank to resell previously accumulated reserves. As a result, net EMS reserves do not exhibit the same large and persistent swings as net dollar reserves. The figure illustrates that the international reserve component of the German monetary base was subject to large fluctuations owing to the Bundesbank's exchange-rate policies. A similar message arises from Table 9.3, which demonstrates that the share of the international component in the base gyrated wildly during this period.

Do these fluctuations affect German monetary growth, so that exchange-rate policies are a binding constraint on monetary targeting? The crucial question is, to what extent can the Bundesbank sterilize interventions, that is, neutralize the effect of interventions on the monetary base by an offsetting change in other components of the base? In the context of the Bundesbank's dual exchange-rate constraint from the EMS and from the dollar market, sterilizing operations can occur in two forms: in domestic assets and across foreign exchange markets.

Sterilizing with Domestic Assets: A Two-Stage Procedure

Sterilizing with domestic assets requires the Bundesbank to adjust the domestic component of the monetary base to changes in international reserves so that the growth of the base remains unaffected. Abstracting from other changes in the predetermined component of the monetary base, we can rewrite equation (6) as

Figure 9.2
The Bundesbank's Net Dollar Reserves and Value of DM Against the U.S. Dollar, 1978–89

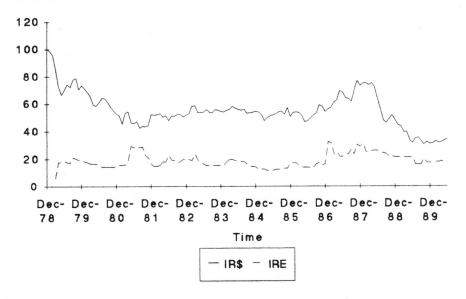

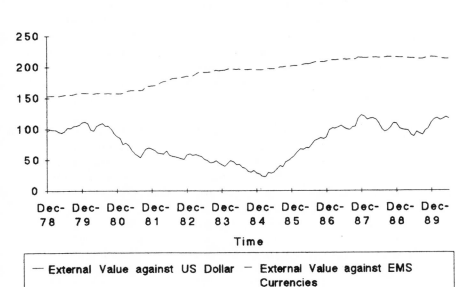

(10) $\Delta B_t = \Delta IR_t + \Delta BL_t + \Delta BT_t,$

saying that the change in net international reserves, IR, during a period t can be offset by variations in the long run and the transitory domestic components. Under the Bank's current operating procedure, changes in the international reserves component, which are not consistent with the Bank's desired base growth rate, are generally offset immediately by a change in the transitory component (Dudler, 1988). However, the very nature of the transitory component means that this immediate reaction, like any other change in this component, must be reversed after some time, say, m periods. Thus, we can describe the Bank's short-run reaction to undesirable changes in the international reserves component by the following reaction function:

(11) $\Delta BT_t = -\alpha\Delta IR_t + \sum_{j=1,m} \beta_j \Delta IR_{t-j} + v_t,$

where v_t stands for all other sources of change in the transitory component. The parameter α indicates the degree of short-run sterilization exercised. It will be between zero and one. Perfect short-run sterilization means that $\alpha = 1$. The reversibility of changes in the transitory component requires that $\sum_{j=1,m} \beta_j = \alpha$.

Two possibilities arise in the process of undoing short-run sterilization of interventions. One is that the fluctuation in the demand for foreign exchange which initially triggered the intervention turns out to be transitory itself. In this case, reserving the intervention together with the sterilizing operation will not affect exchange rates in an undesirable way. That is, if the Bank originally bought foreign reserves, it will now resell them and undo the sterilizing operation at the same time. No lasting effect results on the monetary base. This is the scenario behind the idea of smoothing exchange-rates movements around a given trend, with no lasting purchases or sales of foreign assets.

Alternatively, the shift in the demand for foreign assets may be permanent, so that reversing the initial intervention would result in a violation of the Bank's exchange-rate constraints. In this case, changes in the permanent component, BL, of the base are required to assure that monetary growth remains unaffected as the short-run sterilizing operation is reversed:

If the foreign inflow turns out to be more lasting, the Bundesbank may, at a later stage, replace the reserve absorbing "fine-tuning" operations . . . at least partly by permanent liquidity adjustment measures, for example an increase in minimum reserve ratios or a reduction in banks' rediscount quotas. Such a permanent neutralization of excess reserves is sometimes deemed necessary in order to preserve the Bundesbank's control not only over domestic money market rates, but also over the growth of money and credit aggregates. (Dudler, 1988, p. 73)

Thus, the change in the permanent component is described by

$$(12) \quad \Delta BL_t = \sum_{i=1,n} \delta_i \Delta IR_{t-i} + u_t,$$

where u_t stands for other, exogenous sources of change, n denotes the number of periods over which the Bank's reaction extends, and $\sum_{i=1,n} \delta_i \geq 0$ indicates the Bank's degree of long-run sterilization. The Bundesbank calls this the two-stage sterilization procedure (Dudler, 1988, p. 73). Using equations (11) and (12), we find that the change in the monetary base after n periods is

$$(13) \quad B_{t+n} - B_t = \sum_{i=0,n}(v_{t+i} + u_{t+i}) + (1 - \sum_{i=1,n} \delta_i)\Delta IR_t.$$

Equation (13) demonstrates that the critical issue in the link between monetary targeting and exchange-rate constraints is long-run sterilization. Changes in net international reserves do not affect monetary growth permanently if, and only if, long-run sterilization is perfect, that is, $\sum_{i=1,n}\delta_i = 1$. In contrast, short-run sterilization is irrelevant for the more important policy issues, as monetary base growth over time is independent of the degree of short-run sterilization chosen by the Bundesbank.

Offsetting Interventions

As explained above, the Bundesbank operates under a dual exchange-rate constraint: one in the EMS and one in the DM/dollar market. This dual constraint opens the opportunity for a second type of sterilizing interventions, namely, to offset interventions in one market by counteracting interventions in the other market. Offsetting interventions may occur, for example, if the EMS constraint requires purchases of EMS reserves to hold the mark down, $\Delta IRE > 0$, while the dollar-market constraint requires the sale of dollar reserves to keep the mark up, $\Delta IR\$ < 0$, so that $\Delta IR = \Delta IR\$ + \Delta IRE = 0$. Such offsetting operations across the two markets occurred frequently in the mid-1980s, as reported by the Bundesbank: "The considerable inflows of foreign exchange from the EMS area did not pose any problem for Germany on balance, because the Bundesbank simultaneously sold heavily in the dollar market in the form of smoothing interventions in favor of the Deutsche Mark" (Deutsche Bundesbank, *Monthly Report*, May 1988). In Figure 9.2, such counteracting movements in the two reserve variables are quite visible, especially during 1982. Since mon-

Table 9.5
Estimates of the Bundesbank's Degree of Sterilization

Interventions Across Markets (Periods)	Short-Run Sterilization	Long-Run Sterilization
Offsetting (1979, 1982-84, 1988-89)	perfect	perfect
Non-offsetting (1980-81, 1985-87)	perfect	imperfect

Source: von Hagen (1989).

etary base growth is affected only by changes in the entire international reserves component, no sterilization with domestic assets is required in such periods, and neither exchange-rate constraint is binding.

Empirical Evidence

Several authors have recently studied the issue of sterilization in Germany. Obstfeld (1983), Camen (1986), Mastropasqua et al. (1988), Roubini (1988), and Bofinger (1988) all produce estimates of the Bundesbank's degree of sterilizing foreign exchange interventions. All estimates are close to negative one, suggesting that the Bank's exchange-rate constraints are not binding.[24] Such estimates have been used to support the contention that the EMS has not effectively limited the Bundesbank's independence.

These studies fail, however, to recognize the characteristics of the Bundesbank's operating and sterilizing procedures. The discussion above suggests that an empirical estimate of the degree of sterilization requires a distinction between short-run and long-run sterilization as well as between periods of offsetting and nonoffsetting interventions. In fact, the estimation procedures of these studies focus implicitly on the degree of short-run sterilization, and therefore have no implication for the more important policy issue of whether exchange-rate policies have a lasting effect on monetary growth. In contrast, von Hagen's study (1989) separates periods of offsetting interventions from the remainder of the sample and estimates degrees of both short-run and long-run sterilization. The results of his study are summarized in Table 9.5. Short-run sterilization always appears to be perfect, that is, $\alpha = -1$. In contrast, the degree of long-run sterilization varies according to the possibility of offsetting interventions. If the mark is weak in one market and, at the same time, strong in the other, offsetting interventions occur, and the remaining changes in total net international reserves are perfectly sterilized in the long run. In contrast, if the mark's stance in both markets in the same, long-run sterilization is imperfect. The estimates in von Hagen (1989) suggest that, under such circumstances, about 40 percent of the Bank's dollar market interventions, and about half of its EMS interventions, have a lasting effect on monetary growth.

One interpretation of this result is that the Bundesbank lacks adequate instruments to shield monetary growth from the impact of foreign exchange interventions. This would point to the need for new instruments to control the permanent component of the monetary base. Alternatively, one may argue that, when both exchange-rate constraints are binding, the Bundesbank revises its target path for the monetary base deliberately to allow for more or less monetary expansion than originally intended, when the monetary target was formulated. This view is consistent with the reaction function estimated in section 2, which indicated that the Bundesbank responds to deviations in the external value of the DM from its trend by adjusting the growth rate of the target money stock.

The results of this section can be summarized as follows: The Bundesbank's international reserves exhibit large swings over time, which likely reflect interventions to observe the exchange-rate constraints in the EMS and the DM/dollar market. The Bank's operating procedure and the dual exchange-rate constraints imply that sterilization is different in the short than in the long run, and in periods where the mark performs differently in the two markets. Empirically, the exchange-rate constraints are binding, and interventions have lasting effects on monetary base growth, if both constraints require interventions in the same direction.

CONCLUSIONS

The Deutsche Bundesbank enjoys the international reputation of a central bank firmly committed to domestic price stability. Its reputation has made the Bank more successful than other central banks in containing inflation and has made it an important player in the EMS and in the international arena of monetary policy.

In this chapter, we have pointed to the critical role of the German monetary constitution as a basis for the Bundesbank's successful commitment to price stability. It provides the Bundesbank with an unusual degree of independence from government. Yet, the Bundesbank's authority is limited by the federal government's right to choose Germany's exchange-rate regime. Accordingly, the Bundesbank's policy is best characterized as a policy regime of monetary targeting aiming at price stability under the dual exchange-rate constraints of the EMS and the desire to lean against the wind of swings in the external value of the DM. Although the derivation of the Bundesbank's annual monetary target focuses on domestic price stability, external considerations shape the actual execution. Deviations from the monetary target are strongly correlated with deviations of the real external value of the DM from trend and with excess inflation. In the second half of the 1980s, international agreements to moderate the gyrations of the U.S. dollar contributed to the importance of the exchange-rate constraints, leading to repeated violations of the monetary target and some moderate reflation.

Monetary targeting is implemented in a two-stage operating regime based on the distinction between transitory and permanent changes in the monetary base. Daily operations for monetary control aim at targeting a short-term money market rate viewed as a measure of the supply price of base money. The Bank's approach to sterilizing foreign exchange market interventions is in line with this regime: Interventions are almost automatically fully sterilized on impact. In the medium and long run, however, interventions are allowed to have a significant effect on monetary base growth, if both sides of the dual exchange-rate constraint are binding. In summary, we conclude that the inflation bias embedded in Germany's monetary policy, small as it is in international comparison, stems from the central bank's obligation to honor exchange-rate agreements, inside and outside the EMS, which are imposed by the federal government.

Today, the Bundesbank serves as the institutional model for a future European central bank. In this context, three important lessons can be drawn from the Bundesbank's experience. First, central bank independence from government is an effective institutional arrangement to achieve lasting price stability. Second, central bank lending to the public sector can be strictly limited, as successful monetary control does not require open market operations on a significant scale. Finally, exchange-rate policies pose significant limits to central bank independence and, consequently, price stability. Therefore, neither the European Commission nor the European governments should be given the power to decide on the European Monetary Union's exchange-rate regime, let alone to demand specific interventions.

NOTES

Financial support for this research by the Deutsche Forschungsgemeinschaft, SFB 303 at the University of Bonn is gratefully acknowledged.

1. An alternative institutional tool is a constitutional monetary rule. However, such a rule lacks the flexibility necessary to adjust to changes in the real growth trend of the economy or the velocity of money. See Neumann (1991) for a general discussion.

2. Following Germany's unification in 1990, the five new member states of the Federal Republic did not immediately obtain a vote in the Bundesbank Council.

Currently, proposals for reorganizing the Bundesbank are discussed; the Council favors a solution whereby several states would share a Land central bank.

3. Note that the president of the Federal Republic of Germany is not the head of the federal government but rather performs a representative role separated from government.

4. The average salary of Council members in 1989 has been estimated at DM 450.000.

5. For a recent account of the politics of Germany's entry into the EMS, see Schmidt (1990).

6. For a detailed description, see Chapter 15 of the present volume.

7. See Fratianni and von Hagen (1990) for a discussion.

8. See Chapter 15 for details.

9. See Section 2, below, for details.

10. See Chapter 15 for details.

11. See, for example, Deutsche Bundesbank, *Monthly Report*, February 1974, *Annual Report* for 1975 and Schlesinger (1979), p. 303 and pp. 308ff.

12. Sixteen percent for demand deposits, 12.4 percent for time deposits, and 8.2 percent for savings deposits.

13. For an empirical analysis of German money demand, see Neumann and von Hagen (1987, 1988). The first paper also provides a summary of the relevant literature.

14. Deutche Bundesbank (1980, p. 26); *Annual Report* (1979, p. 15).

15. For a definition of potential output, see Deutsche Bundesbank, *Monthly Report* for October 1981.

16. According to the announcements of the monetary targets, the "unavoidable inflation rates" were 4 percent in 1980, 3.5 to 4 percent in 1981, 3.5 percent in 1982 and 1983, and 3 percent in 1984. In 1979 unavoidable inflation was "moderate" (Deutsche Bundesbank, *Monthly Reports*).

17. We use the term *open market operations* in the traditional sense of buying or selling government securities in the open market. In contrast, the Bundesbank refers to security repurchase agreements with commercial banks as open market operations, although the resulting balance sheet items are correctly reported under loans to domestic banks. Security repurchase agreements are different from traditional open market operations in that the Bundesbank does not acquire ownership of the securities involved and, hence, does not receive interest payments on them. By their economic nature, repurchase agreements are loans collateralized with securities.

18. Lombard quotas were used between 1970 and 1973, in 1977, and in 1980. Lombard credit was suspended from June 1973 to February 1974 and from February 1981 to May 1982. Special Lombard was offered from November 1973 to July 1974 and from February 1981 to May 1982.

19. See Neumann (1990) and Batten et al. (1990) for more details on the following issues.

20. See, for example, Deutsche Bundesbank, *Annual Report* (1983, p. 96); Bockelmann (1984); Dudler (1983, p. 44); and Schlesinger (1979).

21. In the late 1980s, the Bundesbank at times also focused on the money market rate for thirty-day funds.

22. See von Hagen (1986, 1988) for a more detailed discussion. See also Siebke (1972, p. 262) and Duwendag (1978, pp. 60ff.) for similar interpretations.

23. See, for example, Dudler (1983, 1984, 1988) and Neumann (1990).

24. See Neumann (1984) for a test that rejects complete sterilization in the earlier period of March 1974 to December 1981.

REFERENCES

Batten, Dallas S.; Blackwell, Michael P.; Kim, In-Su; Nocera, Simon E.; and Ozeki, Yuzuri. 1990. "The Conduct of Monetary Policy in the Major Industrial Countries: Instruments and Operating Procedures." International Monetary Fund Occasional Paper, Washington D.C., July, 70.

Bockelmann, Horst. 1984. "Orientierungspunkte der Geldpolitik." *Kredit und Kapital* 17: 64–83.

Bofinger, Peter. 1988. "Das Europäische Währungssystem und die geldpolitische Koordination in Europa." *Kredit und Kapital* 21: 317–45.

Brunner, Karl. 1974. "Zwei alternative Theorien des Geldangebotsprozesses: Geldmarkttheorie versus Kreditmarkttheorie." In *Geldtheorie*, edited by Karl Brunner, Manfred J.M. Neumann, and Hans G. Monissen. Cologne: Kiepenheuer & Witsch.

Camen, Ulrich. 1986. "FRG Monetary Policy Under External Constraints, 1979–84." Centre for European Policy Studies, Brussels, Working Paper No. 21.

Courakis, A. S. 1980. "On Unicorns and Other Such Creatures." *Zeitschrift für die gesammte Staatswissenschaft* 136: 28–49.

De Grauwe, Paul, 1988. "Is the European Monetary System a DM-Zone?" Working Paper, Catholic University of Leuven.

Deutsche Bundesbank. *Monatsbericht*. Frankfurt (Main), various editions.

———. *Geschäftsbericht der Deutschen Bundesbank*. Frankfurt (Main), various editions.

———. 1980. *Die währungspolitischen Institutionen und Instrumente in der Bundesrepublik Deutschland*. Sonderdrucke der Deutschen Bundesbank Nr. 1., Frankfurt (Main).

———. 1985. *Die Deutsche Bundesbank. Geldpolitische Aufgaben und Instrumente*. Frankfurt (Main). 3d ed.

———. 1989. *Die Deutsche Bundesbank. Geldpolitische Aufgaben und Instrumente*. Frankfurt (Main). 5th ed.

Dudler, Herrmann J. 1983. "Instrumente und quantitative Hilfsmittel der kurzfristigen Geldmengenkontrolle." In *Geld-und Währungsordnung*, edited by Werner Ehrlicher and Rudolf Richter. Berlin: Duncker & Humblot.

———. 1984. *Geldpolitik und ihre theoretischen Grundlagen*. Frankfurt (Main): Fritz Knapp.

———. 1988. "Monetary Policy and Exchange Market Management in Germany." *Exchange Market Intervention and Monetary Policy*, edited by Bank for International Settlements. Basle.

Duwendag, Dieter. 1976. "Die neue Geldpolitik der Deutschen Bundesbank: Interpretation und kritische Anmerkungen." *Konjunkturpolitik* 22: 265–306.

———. 1978. "Alternative Ansätze der Geldmengensteuerung." In *Probleme der*

Geldmengensteuerung, edited by Alois Oberhauser and Werner Ehrlicher. Berlin: Duncker & Humblot.

Fischer, Stanley. 1988a. "Monetary Policy and Performance in the U.S., Japan, and Europe, 1973–86." *Finanzmarkt und Portfoliomanagement* 4: 8–25.

———. 1988b. "International Policy Coordination." 1988b. In *International Economic Cooperation*, edited by Martin Feldstein. Chicago: University of Chicago Press.

Fratianni, Michele, and von Hagen, Jürgen. 1990. "The European Monetary System Ten Years After." In *Carnegie Rochester Conference Series on Public Policy 32*, edited by Alan H. Meltzer and Charles Plosser. Amsterdam: North-Holland.

Funabashi, Yoishi. 1988. *Managing the Dollar: From the Plaza to the Louvre.* Washington, D.C.: Institute for International Economics.

Giavazzi, Francesco, and Giovannini, Alberto. 1987. "Models of the EMS: Is Europe a Greater Deutschmark Area?" In *Global Macroeconomics*, edited by Ralph C. Bryant and Richard Portes. New York: St. Martin's Press, 237–65.

———. 1989. *Limiting Exchange Rate Variability: The European Monetary System.* Cambridge, Mass.: MIT Press.

Gros, Daniel, and Thygesen, Niels. 1988. "Le SME: Performances et Perspectives." *Observations et Diagnostics Economiques* 24 (July): 55–80.

International Monetary Fund. 1990. *Yearbook of International Financial Statistics*.

Kirchgässner, Gebhard, and Wolters, Jürgen. 1990. "Interest Rate Linkages in Europe Before and After the Introduction of the EMS." Working Paper, Konstanz Seminar on Monetary Theory and Policy.

Mastropasqua, Cristina; Micossi, Stefano; and Rinaldi, Roberto. 1988. "Interventions, Sterilization, and Monetary Policy in the European Monetary System Countries." In *The European Monetary System*, edited by Franceso Giavazzi, Stefano Micossi, and Marcu Miller. Cambridge, England: Cambridge University Press.

Neumann, Manfred J.M. 1975. "Konstrukte der Zentralbankgeldmenge." *Kredit und Kapital* 8: 317–45.

———. 1984. "Intervention in the DM/Dollar Market: The Authorities' Reaction Function." *Journal of International Money and Finance* 3: 223–39.

———. 1990. "Implementing Monetary Policy in Germany." In *Financial Sectors in Open Economies: Empirical Analysis and Policy Issues*, edited by Peter Hooper et al. Washington, D.C.: Board of Governors of the Federal Reserve System, 499–528.

———. 1991. "Precommitment to Stability by Central Bank Independence." *Open Economies Review* 3: 100–18.

———, and von Hagen, Jürgen. 1987. "Theoretische und empirische Grundlagen der Geldmengensteuerung." In *Geldpolitische Regelbindung*, edited by Armin Gutowski. Berlin: Duncker & Humblot.

———. 1988. "Instability Versus Dynamics: A Study in West German Demand for Money." *Journal of Macroeconomics* 10: 327–49.

Obstfeld, Maurice. 1983. "Exchange Rates, Inflation, and the Sterilization Problem: Germany, 1975–81." *European Economic Review* 21: 161–89.

Organization for Economic Cooperation and Development (OECD). 1988. *Why Economic Policies Turn Around*. Paris: OECD.

Rieke, Wolfgang. 1984. "Die Rolle von Interventionen als Bestimmungsfaktor der Wechselkurse beim 'Floating.' " In *Devisenmarktinterventionen der Zentralbanken*, edited by Werner Ehrlicher and Rudolf Richter. Berlin: Duncker & Humblot.

Roubini, Nouriel. 1988. "Sterilization Policies, Offsetting Capital Movements, and Exchange Rate Intervention Policies in the EMS." Harvard University, Ph.D. diss. Chap. 4.

Schlesinger, Helmut. 1979. "Recent Experiences with Monetary Policy in the Federal Republic of Germany." In *Inflation, Unemployment, and Monetary Control*, edited by Karl Brunner and Manfred J.M. Neumann. Berlin: Duncker & Humblot.

———. 1983. "The Setting of Monetary Objectives in Germany." In *Central Bank Views on Monetary Targeting*, edited by Paul Meek. New York: Federal Reserve Bank of New York.

———. 1988. "Das Konzept der Deutschen Bundesbank." In *Wandlungen der geldpolitischen Instrumentariums der Deutschen Bundesbank*, edited by Werner Ehrlicher and Diethard B. Simmert. Berlin: Duncker & Humblot.

Schmidt, Helmut. 1990. *Die Deutschen und ihre Nachbarn*. Frankfurt: Siedler.

Scholl, Franz. 1983. "Implications of Monetary Targeting for Exchange-Rate Policy." In *Central Bank Views on Monetary Targeting*, edited by Paul Meek. New York: Federal Reserve Bank of New York.

Siebke, Jürgen. 1972. "An Analysis of the German Money Supply Process: The Multiplier Approach." In *Proceedings of the First Konstanz Seminar on Monetary Theory and Policy*, edited by Karl Brunner. Supplement Vol. 1 to *Kredit und Kapital*. Berlin: Duncker & Humblot.

Tietmeyer, Hans. 1989. "Anmerkungen zu den neuen internationalen Kooperationsbemühungen seit der Plaza-Vereinbarung 1985." In *Geldwertsicherung und Wirtschaftsstabilität*. Festschrift für Helmut Schlesinger zum 65, Geburtstag.

———. 1990. "The Role of an Independent Central Bank in Europe." Deutsche Bundesbank. *Auszüge aus Presseartikeln* 89 (November): 2–6.

von Hagen, Jürgen. 1984. "Mindestreservesystem und kurzfristige Geldbasissteuerung," In *Geld, Banken und Versicherungen*, Vol. 1, edited by H. Göppel and R. Henn. Karlsruhe: VVW, 251–66.

———. 1986. *Strategien kurzfristiger Geldmengensteuerung*. Hamburg: Weltarchiv.

———. 1988. "Alternative Operating Procedures for Money Stock Control in West Germany—An Empirical Evaluation." *Weltwirtschaftliches Archiv* 124: 89–109.

———. 1989. "Monetary Targeting with Exchange Rate Constraints: The Bundesbank in the 1980s." *Federal Reserve Bank of St. Louis Review* 71, no. 5 (October): 53–69.

———, and Fratianni, Michele. 1990. "German Dominance in the European Monetary System: Evidence from Interest Rates." *Journal of International Money and Finance* 9: 358–75.

Wyplosz, Charles, and Sachs, Jeffrey. 1986. "The Economic Consequences of President Mitterand." *Economic Policy* 2: 261–313.

10

FRANCE

Jacques Mélitz

INTRODUCTION

Monetary policy in France is now evolving in a rapidly changing environment. As recently as 1983, the country was under tight capital controls, faced a wide range of administered and cartelized interest rates, possessed a relative sparsity of financial instruments, and had its banks strapped in a credit "corset" known as the *encadrement du crédit*. Today capital controls are totally gone, the only administered interest rates that remain concern bank deposits, a host of new financial instruments has emerged, and there is no *encadrement*. The essential instrument of monetary policy is the short-term interest rate. Furthermore, the French monetary authorities are working toward irrevocably fixed exchange rates in the European Monetary System and look forward to ultimate monetary unification in the System. Further radical changes—of a kind that would render the present account obsolete—therefore may very well be in store.

In these circumstances, the evolution of the monetary environment is an inevitable concern. The discussion here will accordingly be devoted largely to monetary policy prior to the recent reforms and will try to track the fundamental changes up to the present, starting with the postwar situation and ending with the reforms that brought the current system into being. A separate section will deal with the current framework for policy. This next section will be organized more along analytical lines but will also treat the recent policy record.

1. THE PRECEDING MONETARY SYSTEM AND
ITS EVOLUTION

The Early System of Administered Money and Credit: 1945–66

After World War II, France decided to turn to a highly administered system of money and credit in order to cope with the problems of postwar reconstruction. The government set the entire structure of interest rates and assured the allocation of credit in accordance with social priorities through the use of selective credit controls. The government also funneled private saving directly to preferred uses by disposing of resources that it acquired at a deposit network of its own. The financial environment remained fairly elementary under these conditions. No commercial paper of any sort emerged. The private corporate firm could only borrow at home— except for trade credit—by issuing bonds or obtaining a bank loan. There were no secondary markets in which nonfinancial firms and households could trade any domestic financial assets except equities and securities of over seven years to maturity at the time of issue (hereafter named bonds). All shorter term issues, bills (*bons*), needed to be held to maturity or else renegotiated with the issuer. In addition, bills—that is, ordinary securities of less than seven years to maturity at origin—could only be issued by government and financial institutions. Only once the recent program of reform began did it become fully apparent how much of this system still survived at this time and remained to be cleared away.

Immediately after the end of World War II, the banks outside the direct control of the Treasury—the so-called listed banks, subject to regulation by the Bank of France—accounted for 56 percent of all deposits. These included the four private banks that were nationalized in 1945 and that subsequently became three through a merger in 1966. By 1966, however, these banks' share of deposits had shrunk to 37 percent through the deliberate promotion of the banks in the competing Treasury network. This had been done through preferential tax treatment of the interest payments that these other banks paid. The reason for favoring these other banks (henceforth the Treasury circuit) was to cope with the problems of the successive wars in Indochina and Algeria, as well as post–World War II reconstruction.

The Treasury circuit comprised the savings banks, a few federated and confederated systems of cooperative banks, the National Bank for Foreign Commerce or BFCE (the Banque Française du Commerce Extérieur), and the postal checking system. It also included a nonnegligible volume of deposits held with local tax officials (composing around 10 percent of total deposits in 1966). The deposits collected by the savings banks came under the management of the Bank of Deposits and Consignations or CDC (Caisse des Dépôts et Consignations), which acted under Treasury orders.

The deposits collected by the various systems of cooperative banks and the BFCE were channeled directly into high-priority areas by the relevant managements: agriculture in one case, small-artisan trade in another, local government in a third, and exports in a fourth. The collection by these banks over and above what they required for their work was turned over to the Treasury. This amount was then added to the rich harvest at the post office, the savings banks, and the local tax bureaus, to be used in financing high-priority activities, both private and public, as well as government deficits. A host of institutions in the Treasury circuit specialized in distributing this credit to particular uses: low-cost housing in one case, nationalized firms in another, local government projects in a third, and so on.

A simple analytical description of the system will be useful. Let the basic balance sheet of the monetary sector be

$$F + T + C_g + C_p = N + D = M,$$

where N is currency, D deposits, M money, F official reserves (the foreign source component of the reserve base), T outstanding central bank direct loans to the Treasury (the Treasury source component of the reserve base), C_g the outstanding credit distributed by the banks (including those in the Treasury circuit) to the Treasury, and C_p the outstanding credit distributed by the banks (all of them) to the economy. The reserve base consists entirely of N because legal reserve requirements are absent. (They only appeared in 1967.) The bond issues and capital accounts of banks are ignored, as are excess legal reserves. C_g and over one half of C_p represent subsidized credit to the economy. Some of this credit is eligible for discount at the Bank of France, and a part of $C_g + C_p$ therefore is on the Bank's books.

Let us begin the analysis by taking $T + C_g$ as exogenously determined by the government (in the case of C_g partly through required holdings of Treasury paper, known as *planchers d'effets publics*). Next we may focus, in succession, on the determination of each of the other elements of the balance sheet.

Households and firms decide $N + D$, or M, by choosing how much money to hold at any given price level. The right measure of the opportunity cost of holding money does not meet the eye, for the domestic interest rates accessible to private savers were kept low and largely out of touch with the rate of inflation, while severe capital controls made foreign interest rates inadequate measures of the opportunity cost of holding money as well. The best alternatives to holding money at the time were most likely real assets. It has indeed been shown that the anticipated rate of inflation is a superior measure of the opportunity cost of holding money in this period than any interest rate, at least if we trust the evidence after 1958 when the required time series begins (Mélitz, 1973, 1976).

Regarding the determination of C_p, the best starting point is the bond market. The basic alternative to bank borrowing for the corporate firm, apart from trade credit, as we have noted, was to issue securities of at least seven years' duration. In fact, the government maintained an administered queue on the bond market in which the Treasury was first in line. Next on the queue were a variety of public and semipublic organizations, including the nationalized firms and the specialized financial intermediaries in the Treasury circuit. There followed the "listed" banks. Finally came the ordinary private corporation. Since, in addition, interest rates on the bond market were kept low, the market was fairly thin. Thus, the private corporation was largely rationed out. This yielded unusually large demand for bank credit by corporations, the price of which varied widely depending on the ability of a firm to enter into the privileged circuit. For those who were able to enter there, either directly or because their promissory notes could be automatically discounted later at the Bank of France, credit was no problem. For those whose promissory notes were merely eligible for discounting at the Bank of France, the situation differed depending on current monetary policy. For the rest, the interest rate was always high and nonprice rationing was generally a problem. How monetary policy determined the price of credit for nonpriority uses in this setting is important.

In the first place, the Bank of France maintained quotas on the amount of eligible paper it would accept for discount from the individual listed bank. Above those quotas, the Bank charged penal interest rates. At a mature stage of the system in the 1950s, these rates rose in two successive steps: "hell" and "superhell." In addition, at two particular points—the first in 1958—the authorities resorted to the famous *encadrements* (of which more will be said later), though only as temporary tools. Through this panoply of measures, as well as through direct contacts with the listed banks, the authorities effectively determined the marginal cost of unsubsidized credit and the intensity of nonprice rationing. They could do so all the better because the banks then formed a legal cartel. Under these price and nonprice conditions at the margin, the private sector decided C_p. F was then residually determined.

This last statement means that the monetary approach to the balance of payments applied. Given the level of economic activity and the degree of pressure on domestic prices coming from wage settlements at home and prices of imports from abroad, the private sector decided how much real money balances to hold. With prices and real money balances thus determined, money followed. Government deficits, official monetary actions, and private demand for credit together determined the domestic source component of total money, $C_g + C_p$. There was then no other possible adjustment except through changes in *F*, official reserves, or through the balance of payments. Of course, this supposes a fixed exchange rate. The period was Bretton Woods. In the event of a devaluation—or, hypothetically, a revaluation—official reserves could stay constant while prices and wages adjusted, thereby necessitating a change in the demand for money and the demand for bank credit. But given the exchange rate, while a tightening or loosening of capital controls might temporarily head off reserve movements, the balance of payments was the only genuine safety valve.

Contemporary accounts of the situation do not go exactly this way. But then again the monetary approach to the balance of payments was only clearly formulated shortly afterward.[1] Indeed, the detailed contemporary accounts of the postwar situation in France that proceed chronologically step by step—like André de Lattre's excellent *Politique économique de la France depuis 1945* (1963)—read well from this perspective.

The Liberalization of 1966–76

Two essential changes took place in 1966–67, both of them involving some liberalization. The first was more flexible use of interest-rate intervention by the Bank of France; the second was the injection of an element of bank competition. Underlying the reforms were a couple of basic changes in the environment. Once the problem of repatriating the French Algerians had been settled in 1963–64, shortly after the Algerian War, the country entered into a period of balanced budgets. This lasted a decade, or until the first oil shock, except for an interruption of a year or so after the May-June 1968 labor disturbances. By 1966–67, therefore, the need to finance government deficits through the banking system had disappeared. The mid-1960s also saw large reserve flows into the country, which evidently made less administrative regulation of credit and money easier to contemplate. Indeed, a substantial experiment with freedom of capital movements took place in the mid-1960s. It ended abruptly when pressures against the franc resumed following the wage agreements of June 1968, not to return again for another twenty years. But the advance toward greater interest-rate flexibility continued unabated.

Regarding the more flexible use of the interest rate, moving the official rate more frequently posed a certain problem because changes in the discount rate automatically altered the entire structure of administered interest rates and were interpreted as a signal of a shift in basic policy. In order to circumvent the difficulty, in 1966 the authorities began to intervene at a second discount window, termed the open market, where the price could change without similar repercussions. Within a few years the interest rate at the open market reflected the true marginal cost of central bank credit while the interest rate at the official discount desk concerned only highly subsidized operations. By 1971 the Bank's open market portfolio exceeded rediscounts, and the whole system of discount quotas, "hell" and "superhell," could be scrapped.[2]

The promotion of competition in banking took place by permitting the banks to remunerate their time deposits freely under certain conditions. Beginning in June 1967, banks were allowed to offer any interest they wished on time deposits of sufficient size or of a long enough term—at first one year. Already in March 1966, the legal cartel on lending rates had been ended. But while this reform, in fact, made little difference for price setting, the defreezing of deposit rates did. Once the listed banks became able to bid for deposits, their share of the market rose, going from 37 to 40 percent in eight years. Their share probably would have risen much more had not the cooperative banks benefited more from the changes than these other banks did. In the new environment, the cooperative banks could continue to perform the subsidizing operations that had been assigned to them (and whose cost, in terms of foregone interest, was borne by the Treasury), while they could branch out into ordinary banking activities since the Treasury no longer solicited them nearly as much for their extra resources. In addition, a new profitable avenue of investment became available to these banks when they gained access to the money market in 1967 in the course of a general reorganization of this market.[3] The cooperatives could therefore now begin to lend to the listed banks on the money market. As a result of these changes, the cooperatives' share of deposits went up from 13.5 to 18 percent in the 1966–75 interval. Because of similar (or greater) tax privileges than those of the cooperatives, the savings banks continued to do fine as well. The big losers in relative position were the Treasury and the postal checking system. But such was the fall in the relative significance of subsidized credit and the general needs of the Treasury in the period that the CDC found nothing better to do with a large part of the funds it collected through the savings banks than to funnel these resources back to the nonsubsidized sector through investments in bonds, stocks, and the money market. The CDC became the largest supplier of funds on the money market besides the Bank of France. It had already been the biggest holder on the Paris bourse beforehand.[4]

The years 1966–67 therefore ushered in a context of bank dynamism in the analysis of credit and money. The scarcity of financial instruments stayed much the same; the selectivity of credit allocation remained; interest rates continued to be highly administered (if a bit less), and except for improvements in the money market, the segmentation of financial markets remained as rigid as before. But bank profitability became a fundamental consideration in determining credit and money.

The breakdown of Bretton Woods in 1971 marks another watershed in the 1966–76 interval. With the end of fixed exchange rates, the monetary authorities acquired a new latitude in adjusting to foreign influences. Ironically, just as the monetary approach to the balance of payments was clearly formulated, it was to lose its applicability as the new rules permitted the exchange rate to adapt continuously while official reserves stayed the same. Judging French monetary policy from this perspective, the policy looks basically accommodating in the 1971–76 period. France was induced to leave the European "snake" twice after joining at the beginning of the system in March 1972: once in January 1974, and a second time—following brief reentry in July 1975—in March 1976. The *encadrement*, which had been temporarily restored in 1968–70, became a permanent fixture in 1972. The resort to the measure itself is easily interpreted as a manifestation of official unwillingness to keep the franc from sliding through high enough interest rates or tight enough monetary policy.

In sum, 1971–76 was a time when monetary equilibrium was assured largely by exchange-rate adjustment. Since exchange-rate developments obviously feed directly into wages and prices, while monetary policy acquired more discretion in the period and internal problems of an emergency nature disappeared, it is difficult to avoid the judgment that monetary policy, together with the banks' new active role in the supply of credit and money, had a part in explaining the inflationary performance of the economy (see Table 10.1).

The Barre Years, 1976–81

Double-digit inflation went on for two years after the first oil shock in 1974 until the Barre plan of price stabilization in September 1976 brought temporarily administered rises in prices and wages. The franc firmed right away; inflation came down enough in the last quarter of 1976 to permit inflation for the year as a whole to go below 10 percent; and a couple of years later when the European Monetary System was established, France was able to join at the outset (March 1979), never to leave. Furthermore, the only depreciation of the parity of the franc relative to the mark during Barre's tenure as prime minister came in the course of a 2 percent revaluation of the mark in late 1979 in an incident surrounding the Danish kroner.

During this time, Barre introduced a target rate of growth of money in the sense of M2—a measure of money inclusive of all deposits but those at the savings banks. The practice under Barre was to keep the monetary targets below the predicted growth rates of nominal output. Money-growth rates decelerated well below 1973–75 levels (see Table 10.1).

Another fundamental part of the Barre stabilization program was the effort to curtail the government deficits that had resumed in 1975. This battle was hampered by the second oil shock of 1978–79. However, the government made a concerted and generally successful attempt to assure that those deficits that did arise would be financed outside of the monetary

Table 10.1
Basic French Statistics

Year	M2 Growth	M Target M2	M Target M3	GDP Growth Predicted	GDP Growth Realized	Franc/Mark Realignment in EMS (%)	Government saving)/GDP	Inflation France	Inflation West Germany
1971	18						0.6	5.5	5.1
1972	18.8						0.6	6.2	5.4
1973	14.6						0.6	7.2	7
1974	15.6						0.3	13.8	7
1975	18						- 2.4	11.8	5.9
1976	12.4						- 0.7	9.7	4.4
1977	13.9	12.5		13.2	12.3		- 0.8	9.3	3.6
1978	12.2	12		12.6	13.6		- 2.1	9.1	2.7
1979	14.4	11		13	14.1	- 2(9/24)+	- 0.8	10.8	4.1
1980	9.8	11		11.9	13.4		0	13.5	5.4
1981	11.4	10		12.3	12.3	-8.5(10/5)+	- 1.9	13.4	6.4
1982	11.5	12.5/13.5		17	14.7	- 10(6/14)+	- 2.8	11.8	5.2
1983	10.2	9		11.2	10.3	-8(3/22)+	- 3.2	9.6	3.2
1984	7.6	5.5/6.5		7.7	8.8		- 2.8	7.4	2.5
1985	6.9	4/6		7.5	7.1		- 2.9	5.8	2.1
1986	6.5*	----	3/5(4.5)**	6.1	7.2	- 6(4/7)+	- 2.7	2.7	- 0.1
1987	4.2*	4/6	3/5(9.2)**	4.5	5	- 3(1/12)+	- 1.9	3.1	0.2
1988	4 *	4/6		4.8	6.7		- 1.8	2.7	1.2
1989	4.6*	4/6		5.1	7		- 1.4	3.6	2.7

Sources: CNC *Rapport annuel*, various years ; INSEE, *Rapport sur les comptes de la nation* (1989) as regards last three columns. For M2 growth 1971–76, Patat and Lutfalla (1986) served to assure homogeneity with the subsequent 1977–85 series.

*New M₂ series as of 1986 (see text).

**Realized growth in M3 in parentheses.

+ Calendar date of realignment in parentheses.

sector in order to help attain the money targets. There were several important offshoots. The effort to stir demand for government bonds brought a wider attempt to arouse interest in the dormant French capital market. The most notable move in this connection, initiated by Barre's new finance minister, Monory, in 1978, was to offer an income tax deduction for limited investment in French equities and bonds. Small savers responded en masse to the measure. This, in turn, furthered the development of the mutual funds, which had been fairly stagnant since becoming noticeable in 1963. A number of other Monory actions in favor of the capital market concerned structural features, like the design of mutual funds based on the principle of coproprietorship (the *fonds communs de placement*) and the introduction of preferred stock certificates modeled after the U.S. example. The financial scenery in France became more foliated at last. These steps on behalf of the capital market may have something to do with the rapid climb of the Paris stock market, which took place at an annual clip of 27 percent beginning in 1978 and lasting two years after four years of continuous decline.

But even though monetary policy can no longer be described as accommodating under Barre, it could hardly be viewed as tight either. The M2 targets were overshot two times out of four, once seriously, in 1979. More significantly perhaps, the inflation differential between France and Germany never came down from the 1976 level of 5 percent. It even widened during Barre's last two years in office or in the EMS period, reaching 8 percent in 1980. The surprise therefore is that the franc did not weaken more in the EMS. One reason may be the fact that the currency entered the System on the low side in 1979. Another contributing factor, often mentioned, is that the weak currencies in the EMS were probably protected in the early years of the System by the strength of the dollar relative to the mark. Nonetheless some of the mystery remains.[5]

This leaves us with the issue of the *encadrement*. The tool had come into steady operation in 1972, though it was not always important. With the introduction of the monetary targets, however, the *encadrement* assumed a prominent role in the effort to keep a continuous lid on the growth of money. Moreover, this role became even more important once France joined the EMS, since the interest-rate instrument could then no longer help to control money growth but needed to be assigned primarily to the defense of the franc. Furthermore, any move away from the monetary target at this point would have weakened market confidence in France's resolve to stay in the System. We will come back to this latter importance of the monetary target. For the moment, let us focus on the administration of the *encadrement*.

Under the best of circumstances, the *encadrement* is a difficult tool to operate since the ceilings on credit growth must be defined individually for each bank; therefore, whenever the instrument bites, it tends to preserve the same relative asset positions of individual banks. But in France these difficulties were aggravated by a desire not to interfere with the growth of privileged credits. The chosen method of doing so was to exonerate the privileged credits from the ceilings on credit growth. This compounded the problem of the freezing of the relative asset positions of banks by superimposing additional distortions resulting from the disadvantage of those banks without access to the supply of the privileged credits relative to the rest. In order to alleviate these last difficulties and all the others, as early as 1979 banks were allowed to evade the credit-growth ceilings by financing themselves on the capital market. Thus, the unaided banks were allowed to continue growing without endangering the M2 targets. But the exonerated credits consequently expanded so quickly that the administration was led to enclose a fraction of them within the *encadrement*. By the time Barre left office, one half of the privileged credits had been made subject to the possible application of the regulation, and the fraction of these credits to which the regulation was actually applied had risen to one half.

The problem of administering the *encadrement* could have been managed differently. One fundamental fact about the privileged credits in France in this period is that the institutions bearing the essential responsibility for supplying them collected far more resources than was necessary to finance *all* of them and that they continued doing so when Barre left office in 1981. Starting from the 1973–75 levels of around 41 percent, the privileged credits rose to 44 percent of total bank credits in 1979–81. But in 1981 the institutions responsible for supplying those credits—or those in the Treasury circuit plus the cooperative banks (which had largely shaken loose from the circuit)—still collected around 60 percent of deposits. In terms of francs, the collection of deposits by these institutions totaled around 1,300 billion francs, while the privileged credits were only around 1,100 billion francs (see, *inter alia*, Penaud and Gaudichet, 1985, and Thomas-Roubine, 1986). It would have been possible, therefore, to impose the same credit-growth norms on these financial institutions as all the rest without impeding the growth of privileged credits in the least. The only trick would have been to define the norms as inclusive of interbank lending. In this case, the growth ceilings would have required the cooperative banks and the CDC continually to supply less credit to the other banks on the money market in order to keep their privileged credits growing. The other banks, on the other hand, would have been able to deduct their borrowing from the preceding institutions from the total to which their credit ceiling applied. Since the lending and borrowing on the money market nets out, the aggregate ceilings would have been unaffected. The objections to this solution, which has been proposed earlier (Mélitz, 1980), would probably not have been nearly as serious as those to the measures that were actually undertaken. In any case, the solution was never envisaged. And the difficulties engendered by the *encadrement*—and aggravated by the exonerations—contributed heavily to the radical cures that were eventually adopted.

The Muddled Years, 1981–84

The election of the Socialists in May 1981 ushered in a period of considerable upheaval and contradiction. Three successive devaluations of the franc followed in 1981–83, along with an experiment in expansionary fiscal policy. During this time interest rates were also not allowed to rise sufficiently or long enough to prop up the franc. Instead, the defense of the franc took place largely through capital controls. By late 1983 these controls had become sizable. Foreign equities and bonds could only be traded by the French among themselves on a separate market. Importers had little ability left to cover their foreign exchange contracts, while exporters were forced to repatriate their foreign currency earnings almost at once. French tourists were rationed for foreign exchange and deprived of the use of their credit cards abroad. At least three-quarters of any direct foreign investment had to be financed by borrowing in foreign currency. In addition, as usual, franc loans could only be made to foreigners if they held matching deposits in francs, and French nationals could only keep a foreign deposit while they resided abroad.

The sizable nationalization program that was announced at the start of the Socialist administration also went into effect in 1982. In the field of finance, this program covered all banks with over 1 billion francs in deposits. It meant the nationalization of thirty-six banks in 1982, leaving only 10 percent of deposits in privately owned banks—as much as 10 percent only because of the foreign banks in the country to which the nationalization program did not apply (see Penaud, 1985, pp. 96–102). Admittedly, the nationalization program had little effect on bank behavior. But taken together with the concurrent nationalization actions in industry, the program produced a pall on the stock market. The Paris bourse fell for two consecutive years and only recovered its 1981 level in 1984.

The confusion goes further since the government also wanted to stimulate the capital market in order to finance the resurging fiscal deficits without money creation. The retention of the M2 targets attending the decision to stay in the EMS played a highly significant role in this regard. Furthermore, the M2 targets were kept as low as before in relation to predicted GNP. Thus, the Socialist government extended the Monory program of rewarding households with income tax concessions in return for investing on the capital market; and the government continued to encourage banks to get around the *encadrement* by financing their credit expansion on the capital market. In view of the nationalization actions, these measures could hardly be expected to promote equity financing. But bond issues shot up by 50 percent in 1982 following annual rates of growth of only around 3 percent, and they grew by another 25 percent in 1983. After stagnating in 1982, equity financing also picked up in 1983 when it climbed by 11 percent. As an outstanding feature of the times, the banks sponsored their own mutual funds in which they could place their own bond issues while making available to their customers well-diversified, high-yielding liquid assets that received favorable tax treatment.

The way in which the 10 percent growth target of M2 was satisfied in 1981 is rather telling. Following the victory of the left in May, the Bank of France raised its rate of intervention on the money market to historic levels of over 20 percent for more than a month. Yet the Ministry of Finance would not allow bond rates to increase in pace. Consequently, the banks paid interest rates on deposits in excess of bond rates to their best corporate clients. Correspondingly, M2 grew at an annual clip of 16.5 percent for the first eight months. The official response was to raise the minimum conditions for freely deciding interest rates on deposits. The minimum-size deposit went up from 100,000F to 500,000F, and the minimum holding period rose from one to six months. Faced with potentially heavy drains of funds, the banks, in turn, invited their corporate clients to shift their deposits into the banks' own mutual funds, some of which were especially created for the occasion.[6] This solution received the official blessing—without which it could never have gone very far—after the banks promised to abide by a "code of good conduct," whose essential feature was a pledge to hold virtually only domestic assets (see Bruneel, 1986, p. 22). By year's end, M2 growth was only 11.4 percent, respectably close to target. But the mutual funds were soaring. They went on growing by over 40 percent a year for the next six consecutive years.

This was by no means a stable situation. There was serious question as to how long France could persist in the EMS with regular realignments, capital controls, and a monetary policy neither fish nor fowl, neither easy nor tight. But equally unsustainable, though less conspicuously so, was the *encadrement*.

Because the exonerated credits continued growing much faster than the others, the credit norms relating to ordinary credits needed to be kept exceedingly low. This caused the banks to resort heavily to bond financing. By 1984 the more efficient, unaided part of the system was paying bond rate on marginal funds. From 1978 to 1984, bond debt grew from 6.5 to 11 percent of total deposits for the banks as a whole and must have risen more in the efficient section of banking. At the same time, the inefficient part of the system was able to keep from falling behind very quickly by simply selling its right to lend up to the credit norms (in a special market that had arisen for this purpose) and by lending at attractive rates on the money market. Furthermore, the institutions with privileged access to the issue of the socially expensive, subsidized credits were absolutely thriving. This was the time when the National Agricultural Bank (the largest of the cooperatives) drew ahead of all the rest to become the largest commercial bank in France and when the BFCE came out of nowhere to appear on the list of the world's few hundred largest banks. To add insult to injury, the administrative complexities of reconciling the money-growth targets with the subsidized credits never ceased mounting. Growth norms eventually needed to be introduced for all formerly exonerated forms of credit except for loans of foreign exchange. But new distinctions and exceptions kept cropping up. Therefore, it is not surprising that reform came; the only surprise is that the reform went so far.[7]

The Post–1985 Liberalization

In the fall of 1984, the Socialist government of Fabius unexpectedly announced a substantial overhaul of the system. The *encadrement du crédit* was to be completely scrapped, and the monetary authorities were to rely more heavily on interest-rate changes. A program of financial deregulation was to take effect; the liberalization of capital movements that had started earlier in the year was to continue; and France was to go on disinflating in pursuit of a stronger franc. These changes in policy, whose announcement and implementation notably preceded the European Commission's White Paper on European financial integration of June 1985, have persisted without interruption ever since, despite two intervening changes in government, one from left to right, and the next one back from right to left. The only notable difference that took place during the intervening period of right-wing control of the economy, 1986–88—the time of the so-called cohabitation with Mitterrand still president—was a major program of privatization affecting banking (see Durupty, 1988). The Socialists arrested this program when they regained control of the legislature, but they never reversed it.

The elimination of the *encadrement* took place gradually, with legal reserve requirements serving to smooth the transition. The requirements had been used before, not only in the ordinary way, but also severely to punish transgressions of the *encadrement*. In 1985 the authorities simply lowered the schedule of penalties for exceeding the credit-growth norms and invited the banks to exceed the norms as they wished. After two years, in January 1987, the credit-growth norms could be removed altogether. At this point, however, the authorities decided not only to keep the reserve requirements against deposits, but actually to reinforce them so as to maintain total required reserves about the same or even push them up a bit higher. Furthermore, the extension of the system of required reserves was broadened to cover the cooperatives, the CDC, and the BFCE. The only remaining exceptions were the postal service system, the deposits at the Treasury, and finally those deposits at the savings banks that bore nontaxable interest (or the ones below a certain individual limit). The Banking

Act of January 1984, which replaced earlier 1945 legislation, may have helped to pave the way for these changes by putting all banks on a more equal footing.[8]

Another set of changes connected with the abandonment of the credit ceilings concerned the preparation for greater reliance on the interest-rate instrument. The basic problem in this respect was to widen the secondary markets in financial assets in order to avoid excessive interest-rate volatility. When the question of broadening the money market had first arisen in the mid–1960s, it had been handled by admitting new participants in the interbank market, some of which were not banks. This was the time when all the specialized institutions in the Treasury circuit and most types of financial firms were allowed to enter. But now that the problem was that of carrying the process further and opening up the money market to the ordinary nonfinancial firm, it was deemed necessary to set apart a genuine interbank market, reserved exclusively for banks. The broadening of the money market and the creation of a distinct interbank market posed separate problems.

Limiting the interbank market to banks meant chasing out the nonbank institutions from the previous money market—in particular, the insurance companies, the mutual funds, and the stock brokerage houses. However, the exclusion of these firms had the further effect of withdrawing their privilege of holding interest-bearing checking accounts. Once outside, they became de facto subject to the general law applicable to the ordinary bank client forbidding any remuneration of demand deposits and requiring deposits to be frozen at least three months in order to be freely remunerated.[9] A solution was found: namely, to allow the banks to sell interest-earning assets to these firms along with an option to repurchase the assets—an option that, in practice, would always be exercised. The corresponding assets (*rémérés*) immediately became large, and since it was decided also to consider the ousted firms as ordinary money-holders, the assets began to be treated as a separate class of term deposits in the wide definition M3.[10] This last money measure therefore bore an incidence. The definition of M2 was also adapted to the new circumstances. The old definition had been largely geared to the *encadrement*, as it embraced all the deposits of the institutions subject to the regulation (including high-interest-yielding ones) but excluded all the deposits of the savings banks. Now M2 was brought into greater conformity with basic economic principles by making it encompass all savings deposits bearing low and legally fixed interest rates, regardless of where the deposits were held (1986).[11]

Opening up the new money market to everyone raised a different set of issues: it meant creating financial instruments hitherto unavailable. If the banks were to be able to borrow from anyone, including nonfinancial firms, on the new market, they needed to be allowed to issue certificates of deposits there. The nonfinancial firms, in turn, required the right to issue commercial bills on the new money market in order to borrow there. Indeed, even the trading of Treasury bills on this new market represented a considerable novelty, since only financial institutions had been able to obtain these instruments in the past.

The bond market also underwent major reform with the inauguration of the so-called *petit marché* (small market), where modest bond issues could be floated without waiting one's turn on the administered queue. This happened quite early, in November 1984. The *petit marché* has since become available for issues many times the initial size. Thus, quantity rationing on the bond market is essentially a thing of the past.

Last but not least, foreign capital movements have been completely liberalized. The last vestige of capital controls disappeared in France with the lifting of the ban on holdings of foreign deposits by nationals in January 1990, six months before the EC deadline for the elimination of all capital controls.[12]

A few general observations may be added in order to round out the picture. One problem still facing the country is what to do about the specialized institutions in the Treasury circuit which do not belong in the new liberal financial environment and the others which do but need to be converted into competitively viable firms. It is impossible to do justice to this large topic here. Let us simply say that the savings banks are the main trouble spot at the moment. These institutions still account for 33 percent of total deposits, while they remain heavily reliant on the favorable tax treatment of the interest they pay. These banks were not able to acquire much experience in asset management under the previous system, whereas the EC rules will not permit them to continue receiving special tax advantages.

Another important question is whether the appropriate conditions for extensive use of ordinary open market operations have finally arrived. Are the secondary markets in debt now broad enough? It is difficult to say, but to all appearances, if the answer is not yes already, it is about to be. The rise in trading in outstanding bills and bonds during recent years has been remarkable. Average daily transactions in Treasury bills on the secondary market doubled in 1989 to attain a level of 15 billion francs. Similar transactions in seven- to ten-year government bonds were around 4 billion francs, while total turnover in all bonds, both public and private, stood nearly three times higher. As a basis of comparison, average daily movement in the reserve needs of banks (to meet legal requirements and outflows) hovers around 1 to 1.5 billion francs. In some respects, the higher volume of turnover in bills than in bonds is deceptive, since the spectrum of agents participating on the bonds market is much broader.[13] Yet the authorities remain loath to use the government bond market for open market operations for special reasons. We will need to return to this important subject later on.

As a final topic of interest, there has been a lot of reference in France to financial disintermediation since the wave of financial liberalization began. An official measure of bank intermediation (consisting of the ratio of additional bank credit to the sum of new funds raised by corporations and new borrowing by households, government, and the foreign sector) fell from 68 percent in 1983 to 34 percent in 1986.[14] In part, the fall reflects the efforts of government to finance the sizable fiscal deficits that arose in the 1980s (2–3 percent of GNP) out of saving rather than through the financial system (see Table 10.1 and CNC, 1989, p. 160). In part, it reflects increased financing of the economy by the mutual funds—a breed of organization that is largely controlled and promoted by the banks themselves (see Blanchon and Ferrandier, 1988). If we take these two factors into account, there is little, if any, disintermediation left to explain.

In general, France has witnessed no substantial invasion of traditional bank territory by competing types of financial intermediaries. Furthermore, as investment picked up in the last three years (2 percent more relative to total value added by firms), corporate demand for bank credit has shot back up, thus indicating that there was never any general disaffection of business for bank borrowing. In the process, the official financial intermediation ratio has recently risen again, going up from 34 percent in 1986 to 54 percent in 1989.

Rather than any fundamental problem of disintermediation, what seems to typify the banking situation in France is a greater fluidity in lender-borrower relations. There are wider options both for the banks and their customers. The banks are no longer captives of the state in respect to the financing of public deficits; and however much the government may have wished to finance itself outside the banks in recent years, nothing could have prevented the banks from mopping up government paper on the secondary market, if that is what they had really wished. Similarly, a few years ago (around 1985–86), when corporations seemed to be deserting the banks in favor of the alternatives, the banks succeeded in finding an unusual amount of new household business. When the corporate clientele came back, the increase in household borrowing receded. Based on this evidence, it looks suspiciously as if banks have a certain influence on how much lending they do and to whom.

Along with the new fluidity in the banking relationships, one important change that does appear to be persistent concerns the sources of bank income. Since the reforms of 1985, income from commissions has risen sharply relative to interest income in banking, going up from 29 to 48 percent of total income (INSEE, 1989, p. 233). As a basic concomitant, banks now concede interest rates on business loans that are lower and closer to those on the money market. In 1985 around 97 percent of the interest rates on new bank loans to firms were still indexed onto the oligopolistically determined prime rate—a sluggish rate that tends to follow

bond rates. Now only four years later, a stunning 64 percent of these rates
to firms are linked instead to some money market rate (CNC, 1989, p. 169).
The movement toward securitization promises to extend this process. These
are the changes that really typify the situation in France, much more so
than any permanent bank losses of market shares or permanent movements
in the composition of the bank clientele.

2. THE NEW FRAMEWORK FOR MONETARY POLICY

Having carried the story up to the present, we will now turn to current
monetary policy in France in the context of the new monetary framework.
The order of topics will be the instruments of policy, the mechanism of
transmission, the targets of policy, and the policy record.

The Instruments of Policy

The major policy tool at present is the interest rate and, more specifically,
the interest rate in the interbank market rather than the money market.
In terms of standard textbook treatment, this means that the basic tool of
policy is the discount rate. In simple expositions of the monetary policy
process, which tend to be modeled after the United States, it is often
supposed that the discount rate is subordinate to open market operations.
But the opposite is true in France, and this makes a lot of difference. In
fact, the Bank of France directly supplies the banks the bulk of the reserves
they need in order to finance reserve outflows and to meet legal reserve
requirements. The Bank regularly quotes two interest rates to the banks:
one that it decides following a weekly call for closed bids, and the other
that it announces on a continuous basis. The rate on the closed bids, relating
to loans of over ten days, usually three weeks, is always 50 to 75 basis
points below the continuously quoted rate, relating to five- to ten-day loans
on repurchase agreement ("en pension"). The Bank also rations the quantity at the lower rate. It supplies all banks a set percentage of their bids,
calculating this percentage so as to assure that some unsatisfied demand is
left over to be satisfied differently, possibly at the higher official rate. The
interest rates on interbank loans naturally tend to settle between the two
central bank rates, but occasionally they stray either below or above—
below because of easier conditions than were expected by the banks when
they made their bids, above because the banks sometimes prefer overnight
money at a higher interest rate than they can get for a minimum of five
days. In addition, the two central bank rates tend to stay the same for
weeks on end and to move by small, discrete steps, whereas the interbank
rates vary continually, even within the day. To some extent, the central
bank also buys or sells like other operators on the interbank market,
deciding when it does whether to call attention to itself (or to signal). In

addition, the Bank sometimes trades a bit on the money market in Treasury bills. But these last two types of operations remain minor.[15]

The authorities employ the legal reserve requirement as well. Thus far, the required ratios have stayed low relative to the U.S. or German examples: since October 1990, they have been 5.5 percent on demand deposits, 2 percent on low-yielding savings deposits, and 0.5 percent on high-yielding deposits. But, of course, we should keep in mind that some countries in the EC, like the United Kingdom and the Benelux, have no (or virtually no) legal reserve requirement. There is also some speculation that financial integration in the European Community in connection with the program of 1992 will require the harmonization of legal reserve requirements, in which case the harmonization will almost surely take place toward the bottom. It is important to note, in this regard, that despite the recent lowering of the requirements, the Bank of France continues to speak favorably of the instrument.[16]

Although the Bank's arguments on behalf of reserve requirements vary widely, perhaps the official attitude is best understood in terms of the continued reluctance to make regular use of open market operations. Until recently, required reserves accounted for 40 to 50 percent of the total additional reserves that the banks need to meet legal requirements and net reserve outflows (mostly in the form of currency). The recent lowering of the reserve requirements will cut these percentages down by about a third, but the requirements will still significantly reduce the occasions when the banks need to turn to the central bank for any extra central bank money at all. The foreign and Treasury source components of the monetary base often rise—at times they are on a long-run upward trend—and even currency sometimes flows in rather than out and does so regularly at certain calendar dates. Thus, if it were not for the reserve requirements, the central bank might need to sell outside the interbank market quite often in order to keep the banks constantly on a leash. As long as such sales are not envisaged on the necessary scale, the Bank of France's attachment to legal reserve requirements may seem reasonable. Yet, having said so, one has second thoughts, remembering that some central banks do without the requirements. In any event, the fundamental question is why open market operations are still so little used in France.

As mentioned earlier, the market for government bonds is already possibly thick enough to permit interventions on the necessary scale to create a bank shortage of reserves at all times, quite apart from any legal reserve requirement. Yet the authorities are not fully persuaded of this, and it might be presumptuous to question them on the point. Another element of the situation appears to be the sense of the Bank of France that its interventions should be limited to the short end of the market. This view seems to rest on the belief that the market should be left alone to fix the term structure of interest rates by itself. As far as we know from international experience, however, open market operations in all maturities pose no particular problem and, in particular, do not imply any effort to dictate the term structure of interest rates. The French authorities evidently could buy or sell government bonds at interest rates that fluctuated from day to day along with market conditions, while continuing to behave just as they do on the interbank market. In this case, they would act differently on the bond market than they do on the interbank one, where they call out set prices for weeks. Perhaps the Bank of France would then also modify the term structure of interest rates. That is an empirical question. But it is not clear what harm would come. The term structure would still depend on the rest of the market as well, and the individual operator would not be assured of earning profits on any time horizon but would be forced to take a position on the term structure of interest rates at his or her own risk. Any basic objection to such action, it would seem, must hinge on the earlier problem of possible thinness of the market for government bonds, and therefore excessive price volatility and risk.

The Transmission Mechanism

Our discussion of the transmission mechanism will be more theoretical than any previous part of this chapter. We will center on the impact of the monetary instruments on the stock of money and short-term interest rates. Thus, we will leave aside all questions of repercussions on official reserves and the foreign exchange rate, returning to these matters later, when we deal with the objectives of monetary policy. In effect, therefore, we will proceed for the moment as if all foreign variables were exogenous.

The discussion will necessarily suppose that banks matter. This is important since in simplified macroeconomic modeling, it is often supposed that the monetary branch of the government directly sets the aggregate stock of money, while the rest of the economy consists only of nonfinancial firms, households, and a foreign sector. Obviously, if so, the link between the monetary policy instruments and the quantity of money is simply taken for granted. But it is in this link that the banking system necessarily plays a role.

We must also be careful to avoid a frequent modeling of the transmission mechanism, which consists simply of splitting up money M into a monetary base B and a money multiplier ($M = Bm$). In this case, it is supposed that the authorities determine the base B, the banks affect the multiplier m, the private sector decides the demand for money, and M and the nominal interest rate i follow. But this is clearly not the correct approach for France, where the banks do not face any quantitative limit on the amount of central bank money they can get; correspondingly, the authorities do not try to control B separately. As we will see, under the French conditions, some familiar things appear differently: notably, the impact of open market

operations, that of the legal reserve requirement, and the significance of
the so-called multiplier or the ratio of M to B.

A simple yet adequate interpretation of the monetary mechanism in
France goes as follows. The signs above the variables indicate the direction
of the influences, and the exogenous variables are shown after the equations:[17]   .

(1) $B = B(\overset{-}{i_{cb}}, \overset{+}{i}, \overset{+}{T + F + OM}, \overset{+}{rr})$ The demand for central bank
money by the banks

(2) $B = T + F + OM + RD$ The central bank balance sheet

(3) $\pi = \pi \, (\overset{+}{i}, \overset{-}{i_{cb}}, \overset{+}{T + F} + OM, \overset{-}{rr})$ The rate of profit in banking

(4) $M = m \, (\overset{-}{rr}, \overset{+}{\pi}) \, B$ The desired ratio of money to
central bank money

(5) $M = M \, (\overset{-}{i}, \overset{+}{\pi}, \overset{+}{Y})P$ The demand for money

where

π = rate of profit in banking

i_{cb} = central bank lending rate

i = bill rate; the short-term interest rate on the money market (i.e., the
open market)

T = Treasury source component of B, the reserve base (exogenous)

F = foreign source component of B, the reserve base (exogenous)

OM = open market account of the central bank, consisting strictly of short-
term paper (possibly exogenous)

RD = rediscounts or the borrowed reserve base

rr = legal reserve requirement (exogenous)

Y = real income (exogenous)

P = price level (exogenous)

This model admits only three domestic asset markets: an interbank market
where central bank money is traded, a money market, and a bills market.
Implicitly, commercial bank earning assets consist strictly of bills. There
are therefore no commercial bank loans and no form of credit that only
the commercial banks supply. The main reason for this simplifying assumption is to abstract from all matters relating to the term structure of
interest rates, such as some that we have already encountered in discussing
the policy instruments. It also follows from the assumption, as is close to
the facts, that all central bank open market operations are in bills. The
interest rate on the interbank market, i_{cb}, should be viewed as the true
marginal cost of credit to the banks. That is, this rate should be associated
with the rate on five- to ten-day paper, at which the banks can get all the

central bank money they like (and not the lower interest rate on closed bids, where they are rationed). i_{cb} is also to be understood as always lower than the rate on bills. Otherwise, we would not be sure of the profitability of banking.

Equation (1) is interpreted as a demand for central bank money, B, by the banks, even though B comprises currency outside the banks. This poses no problem since any change in currency must flow in or out of the public's hands through the banking system, and consequently, the demand for B truly represents a cumulative sum of past and present flow demands for central bank money by the banks. The $F + T + OM$ term in the equation reflects the impact of any assets that the central bank purchases outside the interbank market (thus raising F, T, or OM) on the cumulative flow demand for central bank money by the banks. $F + T + OM$ is more commonly known as unborrowed reserves. The signs of the three other influences in equation (1) are obvious. The price of central bank money, i_{cb}, reduces the banks' demand for central bank money; the return on commercial bank earning asset, i, raises it; and the legal reserve requirement, rr, raises it too.

This first equation will assume a more familiar form in many eyes if we simply deduct $F + T + OM$ from B on the left-hand side without changing anything on the right. Consequently, the equation presents itself as a demand for borrowed reserves, RD. The influences of i_{cb}, i, and rr remain basically the same. But the coefficient of $F + T + OM$ drops markedly and necessarily becomes negative. This negative sign is simply an expression of the familiar substitution between borrowed and unborrowed reserves: an extra franc of unborrowed reserves, $F + T + OM$, reduces the desire for the more expensive borrowed reserves. In a system like the French where the banks can get all the central bank money they want at i_{cb}, this last substitution is known to be large. It follows that an extra franc of unborrowed reserves increases total central bank assets by a fraction of a franc, and the positive coefficient of $F + T + OM$ in equation (1) as it stands is far less than one.

Anything that affects demand for central bank money by banks must affect bank profitability and conversely. Thus, all the variables in equation (1) are also necessarily present in equation (3), for the rate of profit in banking. Note, however, the opposite signs of rr in these two equations. These opposite signs reflect the fact that the extra desired central bank money resulting from the legal reserve requirement represents a tax and therefore constitutes a drain on bank profitability.

According to equation (4), if banks become more profitable, they attract more deposits relative to central bank money. The banks are able to do this in a way that is not made explicit in the model but that must involve the provision of extra services to bank depositors, both pecuniary and nonpecuniary. The variable rr is separately present in equation (4), apart from the influence of *rr* on π, because even if public preferences for bank deposits relative to currency stay the same when the legal reserve requirement rises (and thus the fall in π has no effect on M/B), money must go down relative to central bank money on account of the banks' demand for extra reserves. The demand for money, equation (5), is quite conventional. The positive effect of π in this equation refers to the ability of banks to raise the attractiveness of their deposits relative to bills (rather than currency in this case).

In this system, the authorities have a choice between controlling *OM* or the short-term interest rate *i*. The other two official instruments are the lending rate i_{cb} and the legal reserve requirement *rr*. If the authorities decide to control *OM*, i_{cb} and *rr*, then given $T + F$, Y and P, based on equations (1), (3), (4) and (5), B, π, i and M follow. If instead they decide to control *i*, i_{cb} and *rr*, the same four equations yield B, π, *OM* and M. In either case, the identity (2) determines the borrowed reserve base *RD*. The value of commercial bank credit, or the bills held by the banks, always derives from the difference between money M and central bank money B.

Graphically, the system presents itself as follows:

Figure 10.1
The Transmission Mechanism

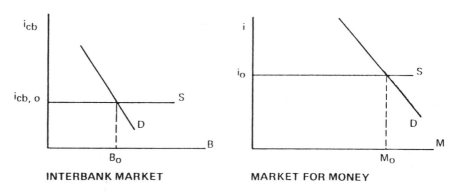

INTERBANK MARKET   MARKET FOR MONEY

The supply of base money on the left-hand side of Figure 10.1 is infinitely elastic at the central bank lending rate $i_{cb,o}$. The demand for money on the right is shown as fully satisfied at the interest rate i_o. This can be correct only if the authorities set i_o. If they determine *OM* instead, the supply of money must be upward sloping since any rise in the demand for money brings upward pressure to bear on the short-term interest rate.

Suppose the authorities raise i_{cb}. Then B falls on the left-hand side. The desired ratio of money to central bank money decreases as well because of the fall in bank profitability π (equation 3). Consequently, even if we suppose i_o stays the same, the demand for money on the right drops and does so proportionately more than B on the left. Of course, if the authorities permit i to rise along with i_{cb}, the fall in money will be even greater. Should the authorities act differently and increase i while keeping i_{cb} the same, the negative effect on money would come essentially from the reduction in the demand for money on the right. The ratio of money to base money in this case could move either way. The rise in i would pull it up by raising π, but the fall in OM would pull it down by lowering π. The reason for this latter fall in OM is that the authorities would need to sell bills in order to meet the higher demand for them that would be associated with the fall in the demand for money at the higher i. The same ambiguity of sign that affects the ratio M/B also surrounds B, the monetary base: the rise in i increases the base while the fall in OM does the opposite (see equation 1).

The relative weakness of open market operations and the legal reserve requirement is very important; in fact, it may be considered the key to understanding the entire system. This weakness comes from the ability of the banks to satisfy their whole demand for central bank money at the rate i_{cb}. Consider first an open market sale by the Bank of France. If the banks so desired, they could substitute borrowed reserves entirely for the fall in OM. Money would then be unaffected. The positive coefficient of OM in equation (1) says that they will not do so. But that can only be because if they substituted borrowed for unborrowed reserves to such an extent, they would reduce their profitability too much. Profitability thus underlies the fall in money. This links up with the earlier stress on the possible moderation of the coefficient of OM in equation (1). But it also sheds light on the earlier emphasis on open market operations as a means of assuring that banks demand borrowed reserves at all times. As follows, only limited importance can be ascribed to heavier reliance on open market operations in the French system as it stands. The instrument would only come into its own if the Bank of France progressively withdrew from the interbank market.

Consider next the consequences of a rise in the legal reserve requirement. Going back to Figure 10.1, the demand for central bank money increases on the left-hand side. However, as the base rises accordingly, why does anything happen on the right? If only the interest rate i stays constant as on the diagram, the answer depends entirely on the term π in the demand for money (equation 5).[18] According to the system, the rise in rr, by reducing π (equation 3), induces the banks to offer less attractive terms to their depositors. If the link between π and the aggregate demand for money was broken, then (in case of a constant i) even if π was still present in equation (4), the rise in B and the fall in M/B would be exactly matching, and there would be no impact on money. Since the effect on money thus depends entirely on the reduced incentive of banks to promote demand for their deposits relative to bills, the effect could obviously be moderate.

There is indeed some international evidence that in systems like the French, higher legal reserve requirements induce banks to offer less attractive terms to depositors (see Bordes, 1990). Nevertheless, the monetary effects are likely to be modest as compared with those in standard expositions of the monetary mechanism where the reserve base is exogenous.

We can therefore see that the turn in France toward full reliance on asset prices in regulating the stock of money has not meant the adoption of the sort of textbook model of monetary control which is typically applied to the United States—far from it. Profitability in banking remains the pivotal factor on the money-supply side rather than any quantitative restriction in reserves or B, as no such quantitative restriction has yet taken place. The whole notion of the ratio M/B as a "multiplier" is therefore misleading in the case of France. M and B are clearly simultaneously determined, and the ratio of M to B can only properly be seen as pertaining to the respective market shares of the government and the banks in the issue of money. The ratio concerns the amount of central bank money the market is willing to hold relative to total money, and nothing else. There is no causality from B to M or from M to B.

If we look back on the earlier *encadrement* now and ask what sort of representation of the monetary system would best apply in these earlier conditions, we can see that the most important modification is a blunted influence of bank profitability, π, in all the equations, at least when π rises. Otherwise, the differences are smaller since the banks could still get all the central bank money they wanted in the earlier arrangement. Still other differences exist. No distinction could be drawn earlier between OM and RD in the central bank balance sheet: RD was the only relevant category. Therefore, the distinction between i_{cb} and i, as drawn here, was essentially absent. In addition, since the rate on bonds arguably represented the shadow marginal cost of central bank money (being that the banks routinely obtained reserves outside of the central bank at this higher rate) and money holders had no access to bills, it can also be asked whether the bond rate did not really belong at the heart of the analysis of the monetary mechanism.[19]

Monetary Policy Objectives

We will now turn to the issue of monetary policy objectives, which will lead us to take into consideration membership in the EMS, exchange rates, and endogenous or induced movements in official reserves.

Since the recent reforms began, French monetary policy objectives have centered on disinflation. The aim has been to get inflation down to the German level, thereby eliminating pressures toward the devaluation of the franc in the EMS. Furthermore, the authorities have looked forward beyond the current EMS to the formation of a unified monetary system with a single currency in the EC. No doubt the adoption of a conservative monetary policy has been meant in part to assure the country a major role in the construction of the new monetary system and the operation of the eventual European central bank.[20]

The implications of these objectives for the exercise of the interest-rate instrument are enormous. Supporting the franc in the EMS clearly requires keeping the short-term interest rates on francs sufficiently high in relation to the German level. In effect, therefore, this objective absorbs most of the freedom the authorities have in setting interest rates—all the more so in the absence of capital controls. To be specific, if the franc weakens, the interest rates in France must go up. The pressures on the currency might possibly be staved off for a while without changing interest rates by selling official reserves. But this can only be temporary if investors view the return on francs as below the one on marks. Rather quickly in this case the interest-rate adjustment must follow. Indeed, if devaluations are to be ruled out entirely, then the adjustment must arrive very early since falling reserves can only reinforce the impression of a coming devaluation.[21]

This brings us to the question of the role of a monetary target. First and foremost in any attempt to explain the significance of such a target are the wider ramifications for other aspects of macroeconomic policy besides monetary policy. The monetary target would be almost impossible to meet in case of large-scale monetary financing of sizable government deficits or if excessive wage settlements took place. Thus, the target imposes limits on fiscal policy and incomes policy. As repeatedly observed in the discussion, the monetary targets have indeed induced successive French governments to try to keep the fiscal deficits down and, more pointedly, to finance those that have arisen out of private saving. The contribution of the monetary targets to wage discipline is more difficult to pin down, especially since the target exchange rate in the EMS works to the same effect. Even so, the monetary targets do provide some extra support for advocating conservative benchmarks for wage increases in labor negotiations and before a wider public.

Interestingly enough, the significance of the monetary targets is especially difficult to exhibit in regard to monetary policy as such. Their significance in this connection obviously depends on some latitude in defending the franc. If any fraction of a decimal change in the short-term interest rate immediately unleashed a speculative attack against the franc or in favor of it, the targets would have little operational meaning for monetary policy. But such is not the case for sundry reasons: the 4.5 percent margins in the EMS, 2.25 percent either way; the aforementioned capacity to gain time by buying or selling foreign reserves; the uncertainty of market forecasts about the extent and timing of realignments; and, finally, the ambiguity of market attitudes toward risk. In addition, in case of a movement in the short-term rate of interest, the associated change in M2 is not rigidly fixed because of some slippage in the relationship between the two. As we saw in our discussion of the monetary mechanism, changes in relative yields on short-term assets (i/i_{cb} in our schematization) and implicit taxes on banking (rr) provide some leeway in the relation between the short-term interest rate and the desired amount of money by the public. Lagged adjustments to influences do the same, as we neglected to mention. These are perhaps not matters of long-run macroeconomic significance and essentially belong in a discussion of short-run monetary management, but they are relevant right here. Within the space for maneuver that the authorities dispose in the EMS, they can pursue an annual target rate of growth of money.

This opens up the subject but does not go far enough. Pursuing the monetary target would still be unwise if the rate of money growth bore no relationship to the ultimate aims of policy. We might have stressed this point earlier in connection with the wider ramifications of the monetary targets for fiscal and incomes policies, but it is particularly apt at this juncture. For central bank pursuit of a monetary target to make sense on a month-to-month basis, the growth rate of money must really say something about the likely satisfaction of the ultimate goals of policy. That is, it must be true that those goals, together with the predicted general performance of the economy, imply a fairly narrow range of money values. But if so, then the official announcement of the pursuit of a target growth rate can be of genuine help. The announcement gives the market some idea of the monetary authorities' intentions and their future behavior. In a word, it promotes what is generally termed credibility about future monetary policy. Of further note, of course, is the fact that the defense of the parity of the franc is never a complete certainty. As far as the monetary authorities have some field for discretionary action, they could stray progressively from a path of monetary growth which is compatible with the current parity, and the monetary targets say that they will not do so.

The targets take on particular meaning when the franc strengthens or weakens in the EMS. Whenever the currency strengthens, a high rate of growth of M2 relative to target argues against relaxing the interest rate. On the assumption of the information value of money, the money data then suggest that the strength of the franc may be transitory. Whenever the franc weakens, a faster rate of growth of money than predicted argues instead in favor of raising interest rates and tightening monetary conditions. But if the growth rate of money is also slow, there is some ambiguity: perhaps the weakness of the currency is fleeting, and raising interest rates would be a bit hasty.

The Recent Record

Table 10.1 contains the record of realignments of the franc in the EMS, the announced monetary targets, the relation of the targets to the predicted

Figure 10.2
Real Interest Rates on Government Bonds

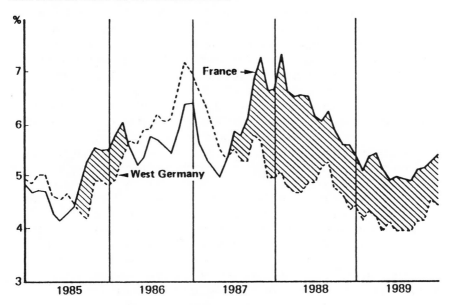

Source: This figure is reproduced from CNC *Annual Report*, 1989.

growth rates of nominal output, and the fulfillment of the targets. The table also compares the French and German inflation rates. From the table, we can detect a marked improvement in the strength of the franc in the EMS since 1983, together with a narrowing of the inflation differential between France and Germany. The only realignments relative to the mark that have come since 1983 were the devaluations of 6 percent in 1986 and 3 percent in January 1987. This last realignment was also well within the 4.5 percent margins of fluctuation both ways and therefore did not even imply any jump in the franc from one market day to the next (as the band was able to shift around the existing price, the franc going from the low part of the old band to the high part of the new one). Since this last adjustment, French attitudes toward avoiding realignments have even hardened. More recently, the French authorities are known to have rejected a German offer of a downward adjustment of the parity at least on one occasion (an offer motivated by the size and persistence of contemporary current account surpluses in Germany).

Interestingly enough, however, since realignments ceased in January 1987, a positive real interest-rate differential in favor of francs has developed. Figure 10.2 traces the differential between the French and German interest rates on government bonds after adjusting for the differential rates of consumer price inflation in the two countries, from 1985 through 1989 inclusively. The picture would be much the same if we looked instead at short-term interest rates. As can be observed, the real interest differential averaged close to zero in 1985–86, but subsequently became appreciably positive in favor of francs—over 1 percent. On the contrary, if we view the same picture for the preceding years 1972–84, we find that the real interest rate was generally far higher in Germany than France, mostly by a couple of percentage points (see, for example, the CNC *Annual Report* for 1983, p. 41). Thus, as long as exchange-rate adjustments took place, the real interest-rate differential between francs and marks never required much of any premium on francs—quite the opposite. But since the currency-price adjustments have ceased, such a premium has been necessary. The conclusion is almost inescapable. Despite the recent narrowing of the inflation differentials between France and Germany to around 1 percent, markets evidently refuse to believe that the franc will not be adjusted downward—or at least markets consider such an event to be a risk.[22] Thus, the decision to pursue a stronger franc has borne costs as well as benefits. But another interesting implication is that France now has more to gain from monetary union than before, since such a union would virtually assure the country a fall in real interest rates relative to the German level, as the nominal interest rate on all outstanding franc and mark debts would necessarily become equivalent for any comparable issuer.

As Table 10.1 shows, the record of satisfaction of monetary targets in France since the beginning in 1977 is good by international standards. Apart from the overshooting in 1979 (over 3 percent) and the aforementioned incident of 1981 when a massive substitution of mutual funds for time deposits was essentially orchestrated, there is hardly any ground for criticism.[23] Nonetheless, the redefinition of M2 in 1986 should be mentioned. While independently motivated, this new measure of money has had the effect of yielding more moderate growth of M2, thereby enhancing the impression of conservative monetary policy. The new measure excludes high-yielding deposits, which, in practice, have been growing rapidly, while incorporating more low-yielding deposits, which have been growing sluggishly. Indeed, the growth rates of M2 have been not only low but recently even lower than those of M1, which is rather inhabitual in France over the last twenty years. Evidently, the savings deposits in M2 are now dominated both by checking accounts on one end, as a means of satisfying demand for transactions services and liquidity, and by high-yielding time deposits on the other end, as a means of satisfying demand for safe investments.[24]

As the impressive record of targeting would indicate, the sharp breaks in demand for money that typified the experience of the United States, Canada, and Great Britain in the 1980s did not occur in France. Fröchen and Voisin (1985) made an interesting attempt to uncover the same sort of instabilities in demand for money in France as those that had been widely established elsewhere. But the effort basically yielded little; that is, the results, covering 1970–84, were consistent with stability of money demand and pretty good on the whole. More recent studies of the French demand for money by Boughton and Tavlas (1989) and Bordes and Strauss-Kahn (1989) have produced more mixed results; nor do they agree entirely. But in both cases, some measure of money has yielded much stability in the demand for money since the late 1970s.

It is interesting to contemplate a recent OECD study from the present perspective. The authors, Blundell-Wignall, Browne, and Manasse (1990), perform a wide variety of tests of change in the effectiveness of monetary policy in the Group of Seven. They consider the usefulness of money as a leading indicator, the controllability of money, and the influence of monetary policy on the economy. In every instance, their results show a considerable decline recently in the effectiveness of monetary policy in Canada, the United States and the United Kingdom, but not especially in France or Italy. The fundamental reason, the authors propose, is the advent of more sweeping financial liberalization in the first three countries than in the latter two. Obviously, however, this proposed explanation is not entirely in line with our discussion of France.

Many low and regulated interest rates on deposits still persist in France, where checking accounts cannot pay any interest as yet. In this respect, Blundell-Wignall, Browne, and Manasse have a point. Nonetheless, high-yielding deposits have also sprouted in the country along with other forms of highly remunerated liquid assets. The transformation of the monetary and financial landscape since 1984 has been awesome. One possible reconciliation with the interpretation of Blundell-Wignall et al. would be the notion that the French liberalization program is still too recent to have borne its full fruit. But other explanations also are possible.

One of these possibilities relates to features of industrial organization: matters such as universal banking, separate or interlocking ownership of competing types of financial intermediaries, and degrees of centralization of regulatory authority. In the Anglo-Saxon countries, there is considerable specialization in finance. Furthermore, the competing types of intermediaries generally lack any tie through management and are subject to different regulatory authorities. On the other hand, universal banking, interlocking ownership, and the coordination of supervisory authority are important features of finance in continental Europe. Competition under the Anglo-Saxon conditions may be fiercer. Moreover, the monetary statistics may be affected, as these seem to be partly drawn everywhere along jurisdictional lines. Thus, various preceding aspects of industrial organization may have a possible bearing on the results of Blundell-Wignall et al. A similar dosage of financial liberalization in the European setting might produce less shifting in relative positions of different *types* of financial

firms—banks as opposed to savings and loan associations or banks as opposed to building societies—with consequences for the statistical relationships.

Another oft-mentioned consideration is the rule of common law in En-
glish-speaking countries and civil law in France and Italy. The following
statement makes the point very clearly:

In the countries of civil law (the cases of Italy and France), contractual liberty is
regulated, and nothing is permitted but what is expressly stated in the law; it is
therefore impossible, contrary to the situation in the Anglo-Saxon countries, to
exploit legal loopholes and to get around the rules in order to develop new financial
instruments. (M. Cavalier, 1989, p. 3 of the section on Italy; my translation)

What this means, to carry the reasoning a step further, is that financial
innovation under Franco-Italian conditions takes place with the continuous
advice and consent of the authorities. This can either hasten or slow down
financial innovation; in any case, it reduces the unforeseen and thereby
may stabilize the statistical relationships.

Finally, membership in the EMS can be a factor. This membership could
stabilize demand for money in two ways. First, insofar as the hypothesis
of currency substitution is correct, membership in the system could reduce
shifts in demand between partner currencies. Second, membership might
increase the predictability of monetary policy.

These are all hypotheses calling for confirmation rather than sure answers. But in any event, the French evidence gives little comfort to the
generalization that extensive financial liberalization yields sharp breaks in
the major financial relationships.

NOTES

In preparing this chapter, I have benefited from valuable written comments by
Yves Barroux of the Bank of France, Dominique Lacoue-Labarthe of the University
of Bordeaux, and Charles Wyplosz of DELTA, Paris. I am also indebted to Christian de Boissieu of the University of Paris I and Michèle Debonneuil and Denis
Richard of the Treasury for suggestions. Last but not least, the editors have been
of enormous help. Except where otherwise indicated, all figures cited in the text
are drawn from the *Annual Reports* of the National Credit Council or the Conseil
national du crédit (CNC).

1. See Johnson (1972, Chap. 9) and Frenkel and Johnson (1976). Even though
the roots of the monetary approach have been traced back to Meade, Alexander,
and others in the 1950s (and way back further to the nineteenth century by Frenkel
and Johnson [1976, Chap. 1], the application to the short-run adjustment process
had not really been clearly spelled out before the 1970s, as Johnson himself recognizes in his 1972 preface (p. 14).

2. The Marjolin-Sadrin-Wormser report played an important role in stimulating this evolution (1969).

3. A good discussion of the reorganization of the money market at this time may be found in Haberer (1973, Chap. 8). See Patat (1987, pp. 58–63) for a useful, brief description of the cooperatives.

4. The single most valuable source for the changes originating in 1966–67 has always been and remains, in my opinion, Fournier (1976). Another important reform in this period was the new ability of banks to open up branches without official approval. Yet the significance of this last reform may have been largely dependent on the other changes mentioned in the text, as requests to open up new branches had been almost routinely accepted before.

5. Perhaps it should also be noted that tests reveal no instability in the demand for money in this period. We will return to this point later, when bibliographical references will be supplied.

6. Within three months, the number of *fonds communs de placement*, which represented the preferred form of mutuals at the time (mostly for tax reasons), leaped up from 375 to 522.

7. One might object here that the development of the bond market and the mutual funds had already weakened the application of the *encadrement* by 1984. Even so, this would be because of bond financing by banks, and the question remains how far bank credit expansion could have continued to be financed this way. It should also be kept in mind that the bond financing itself was largely a response to the *encadrement*.

8. For a good summary of the essential features of the 1984 legislation, see Debonneuil and Ophele (1989, pp. 38–43).

9. The reader will now have noticed that the minimum holding period for a freely determined interest rate on deposits changed repeatedly over the study stretch. As of November 1990 the minimum period was one month.

10. But in October 1990 this decision was reversed as regards the mutual funds. The new series was scheduled to begin in 1991.

11. This last decision went untouched when the money measures were revised once more in October 1990, as mentioned in the preceding note.

12. A host of other reforms in France since 1985 regard finance rather than monetary policy: hedging instruments, futures, options, and the like. The advent of two markets is of particular note in this connection: a futures market in bonds named the MATIF (for "marché international de France"), starting in February 1986; and a market in stock options, the MONEP (for "marché d'options négociables de Paris"), dating from September 1987. Both such events would have been unthinkable seven or eight years ago. See Cavalier (1989) for a good, brief summary of recent financial innovations in France.

13. The recent *Annual Report* of the CNC refers to some remaining difficulty "negotiating large amounts" at any instant on the bills market, though noting improvements (p. 80).

14. These numbers, drawn from the 1989 *Annual Report* of the CNC, are significantly different from those published in the *Annual Reports* of the preceding years, although the general profile of the series remains similar.

15. Finally, there is some subsidized export paper that the Bank of France still discounts automatically—a remnant of the past now slowly fading away. For more

detailed accounts of the Bank's behavior, see Icard (1987), Batten et al. (1989), and Truquet (1986a, 1986b).

16. Thus, in his announcement of the recent drop of requirements (October 16, 1990), the Governor of the Bank, de la Rosière, says: "There is no question of renouncing the use of the reserve tool which remains an essential part of our monetary arsenal" (my translation).

17. Compare the similar recent attempt to model the French monetary system by Artus (1990).

18. The matter looked different in the example of an open market sale in the preceding paragraph because the positive coefficient of *OM* in equation (1) assured a reduction in central bank money and a consequent fall in money. But once we probed more deeply into the matter, we found that the only possible explanation for the positive coefficient of *OM* was the fact that the maintenance of the level of reserves through borrowing would be too costly for the banks. Therefore, the difference is on the surface: bank profitability is just as essential in both cases.

19. For references to the successive efforts to model the earlier French system in the 1976–85 period and analytical discussion, see Lacoue-Labarthe (1980, 1986).

20. On a different register, the switch to conservative monetary policies in France has taken place without any move toward central bank independence but has been based entirely on a consensus of views between the Ministry of the Economy and Finance (most recently under Berogovoy), the Treasury, and the Bank of France. This can be considered surprising since a lot of political analysis treats central bank independence as essential for conservative policies. See the interesting discussion in Goodman (1991), based on comparative evidence from Germany, Italy, and France.

21. If adjustments in official reserves can play only a limited role, the monetary approach to the balance of payments does not help much in interpreting the current French experience, even though the country has largely gone back to fixed exchange rates. However, this must mean that the application of the approach in the 1960s never depended exclusively on fixed exchange rates but always required other factors as well—in particular, factors widening the scope for balance-of-payments adjustments in deficit countries, like capital controls. For similar stress on the constraints implied by the EMS in connection with French monetary policy, see Wyplosz (1988).

22. The Dutch record in the 1980s is remarkably similar. See European Commission (1990, pp. 126–28).

23. Note the move to target M3 in 1986 on Table 10.1 and the error in the prediction of M3 the following year that led to the abandonment of this target.

24. These conclusions are not in any way affected by the changes in the money measures that are about to be introduced in 1991 (see note 10 above). Still, the factors mentioned in the text seem likely to lead to a switch from target M2 to target M3 this next year. For more detailed consideration of French monetary policy, the publications of the CNC and the Bank of France may be consulted, as well as the December issues of the *Lettre mensuelle de conjoncture* of the French Chamber of Commerce, containing a useful annual review of monetary policy by de Boissieu (1989).

REFERENCES

Artus, Patrick. 1990. "La politique monétaire dans les années 1990." Caisse des Dépôts et Consignations *Document de travail*, no. 1990.04/E.

Batten, D.; Blackwell, M.; Kim, I.; Nocera, S.; and Ozeki, Y. 1989. "The Instruments and Operating Procedures for Conducting Monetary Policy in the Group of Five Countries." International Monetary Fund *Working Paper*, July 21.

Blanchon, D.; and Ferrandier, R. 1988. "L'évolution récente du système financier français: les mots et les choses." *Economie et société* 1: 7–30.

Blundell-Wignall, Adrian; Browne, Frank; and Manasse, Paolo. 1990. "Monetary Policy in the Wake of Financial Liberalisation." OECD Department of Economics and Statistics *Working Papers* 77 (April).

de Boissieu, Christian. 1989. "La politique monétaire en perspective." Chambre de Commerce et d'Industrie de Paris, *Lettre mensuelle de conjoncture* (December 1): 21–28.

Bordes, Christian. 1990. "L'objectif de stabilité monétaire et sa mise en oeuvre." Ministère de l'économie et des finances, *Vers l'union économique et monétaire*, actes du colloque du 21 juin, la documentation française, 80–130.

———, and Strauss-Kahn, Marc-Olivier. 1989. "Cointégration et demande de monnaie en France." Banque de France, *Cahiers économiques et monétaires* 34: 161–97.

Boughton, James, and Tavlas, George. 1989. "Modeling the Demand for Money in the Large Industrial Countries: A Comparison of the Buffer Stock and Error Correction Approaches." International Monetary Fund, prepared for conference on "Understanding Velocity: New Approaches and Their Policy Relevance," held at the Federal Reserve Bank of Cleveland, September 25–26.

Bruneel, Didier. 1986. "Recent Evolution of Financial Structures and Monetary Policy in France." Conference on "Domestic and International Aspects of Macroeconomic Policy," sponsored by the University of Illinois, September 12–14.

Cavalier, M. 1989. "Innovations financières dans les grands pays industriels." Banque de France, Service des économies étrangères, October 30.

Conseil National du Crédit. *Rapport annuel*. Various years.

Debonneuil, Xavier, and Ophele, Robert. 1989. *La politique monétaire et son contexte économique*. Paris: la revue Banque. 2d ed.

Durupty, Michel. 1988. *Les privatisations en France*. Notes et études documentaires 4857. Paris: La documentation française.

European Commission. 1990. "One Market, One Money." *European Economy* (October): 44.

Fournier, Henri. 1976. "L'évolution des banques françaises: les réformes de 1966–1972 et leurs conséquences." *Banque* 354: 823–38.

Frenkel, Jacob, and Johnson, Harry. 1976. "The Monetary Approach to the Balance of Payments: Essential Concepts and Historical Origins." In *The Monetary Approach to the Balance of Payments*. edited by Frenkel and Johnson. London: George Allen & Unwin, Chap 1, 21–45.

Fröchen, Patrick, and Voisin, Pascal. 1985. "La stabilité de demande de monnaie: le cas de la France de 1970 à 1984." Banque de France, *Cahiers économiques et monétaires* 21: 5–48.

Goodman, John. 1991. "The Politics of Central Bank Independence." *Comparative Politics* 23, no. 3 (April): 329–49.

Haberer, Jean-Yves. 1973. *La monnaie et la politique monétaire*. Institut d'études politiques de Paris 1973–74. Paris: Les cours de droit.

Icard, André. 1987. "Les instruments de la politique des taux." *Banque* 474 (July-August): 698–702.

INSÉÉ. 1989. *Rapport sur les comptes de la nation*.

Johnson, Harry. 1972. *Further Essays in Monetary Economics*. London: George & Unwin. "Introduction," 11–18; and Chap. 9, "The Monetary Approach to Balance-of-Payments Theory," 229–49.

Lacoue-Labarthe, Dominique. 1980. *Analyse monétaire*. Paris: Bordas.

———. 1986. "Les taux d'intérêt dans les mécanismes d'ajustement et de régulation monétaires en France." Banque de France, *Cahiers économiques et monétaires* 25: 305–40.

de Lattre, André. 1963. *Politique économique de la France depuis 1945*. Institut d'études politiques de Paris. Paris: Les cours de droit.

Marjolin, Robert, Jean Sandrin, and Olivier Wormser. 1969. *Rapport sur le mardé monétaire et les conditions du crédit*. Paris: La documentation Française.

Melitz, Jacques. 1973. "La demande de monnaie en France: tentative d'explication." Ministère de l'économie et des finances, *Statistiques et études financières*. Série orange, 11: 21–48.

———. 1980. "The French Financial System: Mechanisms and Propositions of Reform." INSÉÉ *Document de travail* (July). Revised and abridged version (revised subtitle: "Mechanisms and Questions of Reform"). *Annales de l'INSÉÉ*, (July-December): 47–48, 359–87. Also reprinted in Mélitz and Charles Wyplosz, eds. *The French Economy: Theory and Policy*. Boulder, Colo.: Westview Press, 359–87.

———. 1976. "Inflationary Expectations and the Demand for Money." *Manchester School* (March): 17–41.

Patat, Jean-Pierre. 1987. *Monnaie, institutions financières et politique monétaire*. Paris: Economica. 4th ed.

———, and Lutfalla, Michel. 1976. *Histoire monétaire de la France au XXème siècle*. Paris: Economica.

Penaud, Raymond. 1985. *Les institutions financières françaises*. Paris: La revue Banque. 2d ed.

———, and Gaudichet, François. 1985. *Sélectivité du crédit, financement, politique monétaire*. Paris: Economica.

Thomas-Roubine, Sophie. 1986. "Crédits privilégiés et régulation par les taux d'intérêt." Banque de France, *Cahiers économiques et monétaires* 25: 283–94.

Truquet, Jean. 1986a. "Le développement des interventions de la Banque de France, les changements intervenus dans les instruments et les techniques depuis 1972." Banque de France, *Cahiers économiques et monétaires* 25: 295–304.

———. 1986b. "The Development of Central Bank Intervention on the Money

Market in France." In Bank of International Settlements, *Changes in Money-Market Instruments and Procedures: Objectives and Implications*, March, 41–52.

Wyplosz, Charles. 1988. "Monetary Policy in France: Monetarism or Darwinism." *Finanzmarkt und Portfolio Management* 2 (January): 56–67.

11

ITALY

Franco Spinelli and Patrizio Tirelli

INTRODUCTION

This chapter deals with the evolution of monetary policy in postwar Italy. We are concerned with the final objectives, the intermediate targets, and the techniques of monetary policy.

Throughout the entire period studied, rapid growth in output was one of the Bank of Italy's top priorities. In the 1950s this goal was achieved in combination with trade and capital liberalization, without loss of price stability. During the two following decades, increasing government deficits caused a progressive loss of control over the money stock. Inflation was on an upward trend, and, after the collapse of the Bretton Woods regime, the lira kept depreciating in the exchange market. In this period, the main concern of the authorities was simply to maintain balance-of-payments equilibrium. This goal was achieved through short-lived monetary squeezes during the 1960s and a heavy battery of capital controls during the 1970s. Eventually, in the 1980s, the Bank returned to its goals of price and exchange-rate stability and international integration of the domestic money and financial markets.

The evolution of the techniques of monetary control mirrored these changes. That is, during the 1950s the monetary base was fairly closely controlled, mainly through moral suasion. Then the 1960s and 1970s witnessed a progressive shift toward control of credit through a progressively more systematic use of administrative measures. Finally, in the 1980s emphasis shifted back to the control of the monetary base, this time relying on market incentives.

The rest of the chapter is laid out as follows. Section 1 shows the evolution of the key macroeconomic variables. Section 2 describes some of the basic features of the financial sector and of fiscal policy. It also highlights their implications for the behavior of the monetary authorities. Sections 3 through 5 discuss how monetary policy was actually implemented in the subperiods 1950–69, 1970–79, and 1980–89. Section 6 reviews the evolution of both the Bank's philosophy and its techniques of monetary control. The final section summarizes our main findings.

1. A REVIEW OF THE FACTS

In this section we present a broad-brush description of the evolution of the main macroeconomic variables over the period 1950–89. We focus on real GDP growth, inflation, unemployment, money supply, nominal and real exchange rates, government deficit and debt, and nominal and real interest rates.

Real GDP Growth and Inflation

As Figure 11.1 shows, Italy grew rapidly in the years under consideration, but its output growth gradually declined over time.

The business cycle was dampened in the 1950s. Afterward, the rate of output expansion became more volatile; fluctuations were particularly wide in the 1970s and up to 1983. Over the latter part of the 1980s, steady growth was restored.[1]

Inflation, which was steady and moderate in the 1950s, showed evident cycles afterward. In the 1970s prices grew at an accelerating rate until the peak was reached in 1980. Limited disinflation was not achieved until the end of the 1980s. Relative to the other major industrial countries, inflation in Italy has persistently been above average during the last two decades.

Wages and Unemployment

From Figure 11.2, we notice that the correlation between unemployment and wages became, if anything, positive when inflation was on an upward trend during the 1970s. In the 1980s disinflation was accompanied by a further and sizable increase in the unemployment rate.

The Money Supply

Figure 11.3 shows that the growth rate of high-powered money declined until 1957; became more erratic in the 1960s; showed a strong upward trend in the 1970s, reaching its peak in 1978; and finally fell substantially in the 1980s.

The broader monetary aggregate—M3—followed a similar pattern.

Figure 11.1
Output Growth and Inflation

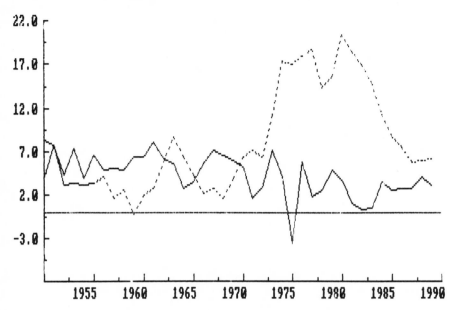

Sources: 1950–80, Spinelli and Fratianni (1991); 1980–89, ISTAT, *Annuario di Contabilita'*
 Nazionale.

Output growth = ———————
Inflation = — — — — —

Nominal and Real Exchange Rates

The nominal exchange rate vis-à-vis the U.S. dollar was fixed until the
collapse of the Bretton Woods regime. In the 1970s its behavior essentially
mirrored that of the (positive) inflation differential, as shown in Figure
11.4. After Italy joined the European Monetary System in 1979, the exchange rate showed greater stability, at least relative to the European
currencies. Several devaluations did occur, especially during the first half
of the 1980s, but they did not fully match the cumulated inflation differentials. Hence, as we can see from Figure 11.5, the real exchange rate
appreciated steadily.

Fiscal Policy, Seigniorage, and Public Debt

Relative to gross domestic product (GDP), government deficits declined
until the mid–1960s, then greatly increased in the 1970s, and remained
very high in the 1980s (Figure 11.6).

Figure 11.2
Wage Inflation and Unemployment

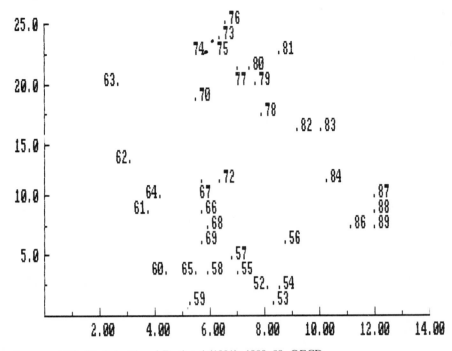

Sources: 1950–80, Spinelli and Fratianni (1991); 1980–89, OECD.
Wage inflation = vertical axis.
Unemployment rate = horizontal axis.

Seigniorage (Figure 11.7) was abnormally high up to the latter part of the 1970s. Subsequently, the decline in the monetization of government deficits led to a dramatic increase in the nominal stock of government debt (Figure 11.8).

Nominal and Real Interest Rates

Nominal rates fluctuated around 5–7 percent until 1969 and showed a strong upward trend throughout the subsequent decade. In the 1980s they remained high.

Ex-post real rates were systematically negative from 1972 and up to 1981. Subsequently, the persistently high nominal rates and the gradual fall in inflation led to a substantial recovery of real yields (Figure 11.9).

Figure 11.3
Monetary Base and the Money Supply (growth rates)

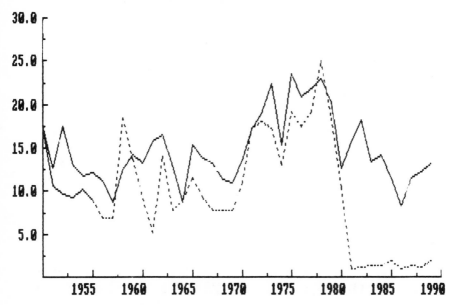

Sources: 1950–80, Spinelli and Fratianni (1991); 1980–89, Bank of Italy.
Money supply = ――――――
Monetary base = – – – – –

The Subperiods

From the analysis above, we can conclude that a first major break in the pattern of the key macroeconomic variables occurred toward the end of the 1960s and the early 1970s. Basically, Italy began to experience high public deficits, high rates of monetary creation, negative real interest rates, stagflation, and depreciations in the lira. The change in regime was made more visible by the total collapse of industrial relations.[2]

Although unemployment and fiscal deficits remained high throughout the 1980s, a second important break occurred in the late 1970s and early 1980s. The authorities favored disinflation, and this meant lower rates of monetary creation, high real interest rates, fast-growing government debt, and a real appreciation of the lira in the exchange market. The 1970s also brought about important changes in the degrees of freedom enjoyed by the national authorities. Specifically, we are referring to the collapse of the Bretton Woods regime in 1971, which was followed by a generalized float, the creation of the European Monetary System in 1979, and the return (at least in principle) to fixed exchange rates.

Figure 11.4
Nominal Exchange Rate Vis-à-Vis the U.S. Dollar, 1970–79

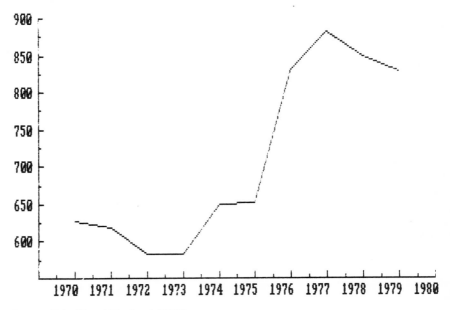

Source: Spinelli and Fratianni (1991).

All considered, it seems appropriate to focus separately on three distinct subperiods: 1950 to 1969, the 1970s, and the 1980s. But before commenting on the monetary developments of each subperiod, we will review some of the key features of both the financial institutions and markets and of fiscal policy. The relative underdevelopment of the financial markets and the trend in fiscal policy turn out to have affected the evolution of both targets and instruments of monetary policy.

2. FINANCIAL INSTITUTIONS, MARKETS, AND FISCAL POLICY AND THEIR IMPLICATIONS FOR THE CENTRAL BANK

Italy's major financial institutions fall into two categories: commercial banks, which supply short-term credit, and the so-called Special Credit Institutions (SCIs), which supply medium- and long-term credit.[3]

The first category includes the six public banks; the three so-called banks of national interest; and a large number of local banks. SCIs can be divided into three groups: those that deal with mortgage credit and those that deal with credit to industry and agriculture, respectively. Through the SCI the

Figure 11.5
Nominal and Real Effective Exchange Rates, 1980–89

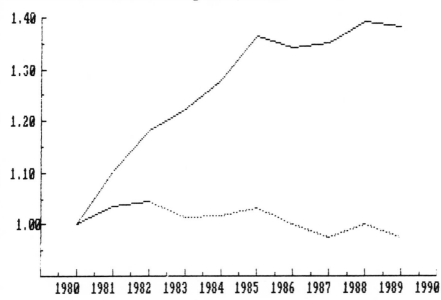

Source: Bank of Italy.

Nominal effective exchange rate = --------

Real effective exchange rate = – – – – –

Italian government has channeled subsidized funds to the productive sector, mainly industry. Fixed-interest finance has always played a key role in the funding of Italian firms since the market for risk capital began to develop only recently. The alleged great vulnerability of industry to interest-rate changes explains, at least in part, why at some stage monetary policy came to rely heavily on nonprice credit rationing.

Traditionally, the money market has been very thin and dominated by transactions in short-term government securities. The narrowness of the money market has limited the extent to which short-term interest rate swings could cushion the domestic bond market from international pressures. As a result, the domestic monetary authorities have often been left with the alternative of either destabilizing bond prices or imposing administrative controls on capital movements.[4]

By and large, because of the structural rigidities on both the revenue and expenditure sides of the budget, throughout the entire postwar period fiscal policy has not played any significant role in demand management.[5] Therefore, the whole burden of short-term stabilization has systematically

Figure 11.6
Public Deficits (ratio to nominal GDP)

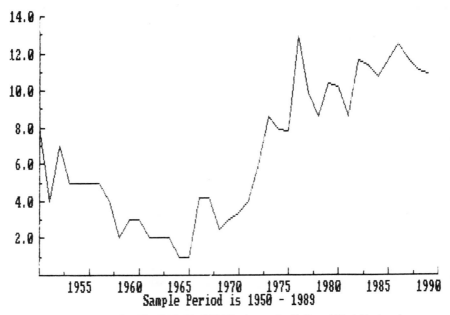

Sources: 1950–66, Fua (1965); 1966–89, ISTAT, *Annuario di Contabilita' Nazionale.*

fallen on monetary policy. Furthermore, as we have seen in Figure 11.7, huge public deficits have been a persistent feature of the last twenty years. Partly because of the institutional weakness of the Bank vis-à-vis the Treasury, their financing has greatly complicated the task of the monetary authorities and substantially limited their independence.[6]

3. MONETARY POLICY IN PRACTICE: 1950–69

We turn now to the monetary developments during the first of the three main subperiods.

High Growth and the External Constraint

Over these years, the country experienced a very rapid rate of growth. According to Maddison (1982), this was a "golden age" of capitalist development, but in Italy economic expansion was particularly rapid, especially between 1958 and 1963.

The main determinants of this favorable outcome were the following:

Figure 11.7
Seigniorage

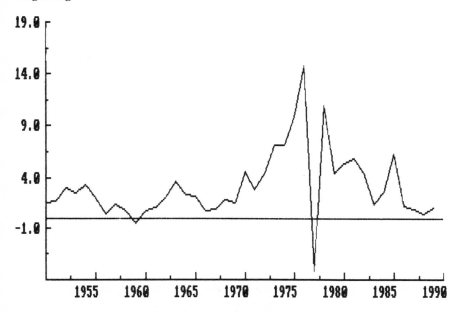

Sources: 1950–80, Spinelli and Fratianni (1991); 1980–89, Bank of Italy.

1. slack labor market conditions and, at least in the early stages, weak trade unions;[7]
2. export competitiveness:[8] Italy was then at the forefront of the process of international trade liberalization and took full advantage of favorable international demand conditions;[9] and
3. high rates of investment. Over the whole period investment averaged about 20 percent of GDP.[10]

Italy adhered to the Bretton Woods regime.[11] Hence, monetary policy was systematically implemented under the constraint of a fixed exchange rate. Table 11.1 shows that the balance of payments was in surplus for fourteen out of twenty years.

Demand Management and Monetary Policy Abroad

As Thygesen (1984) points out, for all the major industrial countries a distinction may be drawn between the 1950s and the 1960s. He defines the first decade as "an extended period of monetary accommodation with no ambition of controlling short-run economic fluctuations," whereas the

Figure 11.8
Public Debt, 1970–89 (ratio to nominal GDP)

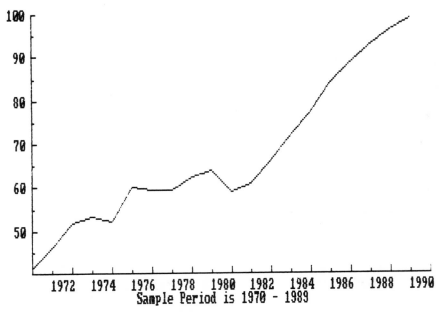

Sample Period is 1970 – 1989

Source: Bank of Italy.

1960s should be regarded as "a period of relative optimism that the proper role of monetary policy had become sufficiently well understood to permit short-run activism."[12] Furthermore, emphasis shifted from one single indicator of the monetary stance—typically, the money supply—to broader concepts, such as the state of liquidity of the economy.[13] An important implication of this new attitude was the increasing reliance on administrative controls, such as credit ceilings.

Monetary Policy in Italy: The 1950s

Broadly speaking, the conduct of Italian monetary policy mirrors this evolution of the international consensus. In the 1950s the commitment to free trade led to the abolition of the two-tier exchange-rate system, which was initially meant to stimulate exports, and to the adoption of a process of progressive liberalization of capital movements.[14] The Bank relied on control of the monetary base, keeping its rate of growth in line with the expansion of output. This task was made easier by the systematically moderate size of government deficits. Also because fast output growth was

Figure 11.9
Nominal and Real Interest Rates

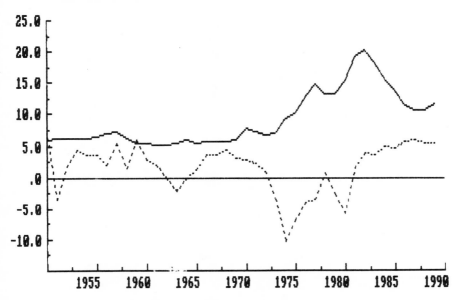

Sources: 1950–80, Spinelli and Fratianni (1991); 1980–89, Bank of Italy.

achieved with substantial price stability and without major balance-of-payments crises, the decade did not present problems of short-term stabilization. In any case, several developments of the period showed that the authorities were concerned mainly with medium-term stability as opposed to short-term fine tuning. For instance, in 1952–53 the balance of trade and the balance of payments turned into a deficit. This was largely due to a resumption of protectionism in some European countries and to the worsening of terms of trade caused by the Korean War. Had this deficit arisen during the following decade it would have probably called for strong deflationary measures. Instead, at the time the Bank kept the growth of the money supply on a steady path.

The story repeated itself between 1955 and 1957 when a monetary squeeze was implemented in many countries, but not in Italy despite the current-account deficit. Again, although in 1958 a downturn in economic activity led to a generalized loosening of the monetary stance, in Italy the Bank decided to cut the discount rate by a mere 0.5 percent.[15]

To some extent the authorities violated the rules of the game of the fixed exchange-rate regime. In fact, for the period a negative correlation exists between domestic credit expansion and foreign reserves flows.[16] When faced with an external surplus, the authorities did not allow for its full

Table 11.1
The Balance of Payments 1950–69 (millions of dollars)

Year	Current Account	Capital Account	Basic Balance
1950	+178	-168	-40
1951	+55	+33	+122
1952	-343	+197	-134
1953	-217	+123	-79
1954	-76	+107	-7
1955	-76	+167	+72
1956	-95	+223	+86
1957	+36	+216	+206
1958	+955	+170	+793
1959	+759	+199	+850
1960	+283	+76	+438
1961	+474	-170	+574
1962	+235	-309	-50
1963	-745	-485	-1.252
1964	+620	+110	+774
1965	+2.209	-455	+1.594
1966	+2.217	-1.277	+696
1967	+1.599	-1.023	+324
1968	+2.644	-1.691	+627
1969	+2.340	-3.624	-1.391

Source: Annual Reports of the Bank of Italy.

conversion into domestic currency and directed commercial banks to reduce (or at least not to increase) their foreign indebtedness. In the opposite case of an external deficit, the authorities lifted the restrictions on foreign borrowing and raised the share of foreign reserves convertible into domestic currency.

The 1960s

In this period the monetary authorities began to aim at the maximum rate of output growth consistent with a short-run balance-of-payments equilibrium. Hence, the procedure of granting or denying permission to the banking sector to borrow and lend abroad became the centerpiece of monetary policy.[17] Output growth was somewhat slower and certainly less stable than in the 1950s (see Figure 11.1).

On the whole, the emphasis of monetary policy unambiguously shifted toward a more interventionist attitude. The time horizon of the authorities became substantially shorter, and nonprice rationing—direct credit controls—replaced the former strategy of monetary base control. As a result, both the mean and the variance of the annual inflation rate increased.[18] Balance-of-payments data show that two crises occurred, the first in 1963 and the second in 1969, with severe repercussions on the real sector.[19]

The 1963 Balance-of-Payments Crisis

After 1958 the Italian economy entered a phase of spectacular export-led expansion. By the end of 1961 the rate of wage inflation had already reached an unprecedented level, and the degree of capacity utilization approached 95 percent. In January 1962, despite these unambiguous signs of impending overheating, mandatory reserve requirements were reduced (Fazio, 1979). Furthermore, nine months later commercial banks were freed from restrictions on foreign borrowing, and the banks' foreign reserves became almost fully convertible. In 1963 capacity utilization rose well above 95 percent and inflation peaked. It was only in the autumn of 1963 that the authorities, facing a massive increase of imports and slower growth in exports, reversed the policy by halting new foreign borrowing and withholding permission to renew foreign loans. Coming at a time of high inflation, this decision, together with the destruction of the monetary base as a result of the balance-of-payments deficit, led to a severe credit squeeze.[20] Industrial production came to an abrupt halt, and capacity utilization fell below 85 percent by mid–1965. Consumer price inflation, which had reached a peak of 7.8 percent in 1963 (third quarter), fell to 5.8 in 1964 (fourth quarter). Between 1963 (third quarter) and 1964 (second quarter), long-term interest rates rose by nearly 2 percentage points. Finally, the external imbalance was quickly reversed.

Return to an Expansionary Monetary Policy, Interest Rate Controls, and a New Balance-of-Payments Crisis

In 1965 monetary policy once again became expansionary.[21] During the following three years the authorities were concerned mainly with two objectives. The first was the sterilization of balance-of-payments surpluses, to be attained by encouraging commercial banks to extinguish their foreign debt and become net creditors on the Eurodollar market. The second was the stabilization of long-term interest rates. The rationale for pegging interest rates was that economic agents would be willing to trade lower yields for a lower risk. This, in turn, would stimulate industrial investment and limit the cost of public debt.[22]

It is well known that, in a small open economy, such policy is bound to create problems as soon as domestic and foreign interest rates begin to diverge, especially if an underdeveloped money market cannot insulate the domestic bond market from international pressures. Starting in 1967, as foreign rates began to rise, the capital outflow widened. By May 1969 it had become clear that a domestic interest rate rise could no longer be avoided.[23]

The subsequent decision to give up interest-rate pegging and to allow long-term interest rates to move up was motivated largely by the need to correct the loss of foreign reserves. Once again, this goal was soon achieved; in 1970 the balance of payments returned to a surplus. On the other hand, industry was badly hit by both the rise in interest rates and labor unrest and wage inflation.[24] As a result, capacity utilization abruptly fell by 15 percent.

Summary

Over the subperiod 1950–69 monetary policy aimed at attaining the highest rate of economic growth, consistent with balance-of-payments equilibrium. But there is a fundamental difference between the 1950s and 1960s. In the 1950s monetary policy had relied mainly on the control of the monetary base and was very concerned with medium and long-term balance-of-payments equilibria. By the early 1960s the sustained output growth had brought the economy close to full employment. Far from recognizing the danger of inflation, the central bank selected more ambitious targets and, at the same time, shifted emphasis to the short run. More rapid output growth was temporarily achieved at the cost of subsequent deep recessions brought about by the need to deal very rapidly with severe balance-of-payments crises.

In the 1960s monetary policy never anticipated events. The Bank often reacted too late and, as a result, with strong doses of medicine.[25] In conclusion, one can say that monetary policy actually exacerbated the cycle it was meant to dampen.

4. 1970–79

Externally, this subperiod witnessed two oil shocks, a generalized exchange-rate float, and stagflation. Domestically, as a consequence of institutional reforms on both sides of the budget, government deficits exploded (Giavazzi and Spaventa, 1989). So did the growth rate of the money supply and inflation. Real interest rates were persistently negative, and seigniorage became a very important source of revenue for the government. Unemployment also rose. Relative to the first subperiod, output growth halved and became more volatile (Spinelli and Fratianni, 1991).

The lira exchange rate showed a marked tendency to depreciate. This was the result of the need to preserve external competitiveness in the presence of a large and negative inflation differential vis-à-vis the major trading partners. The monetary authorities tried to finance the huge budget deficits while holding down interest rates. In order to limit the inevitable capital outflows, the Bank opted for the progressive and almost complete isolation of the domestic monetary and financial sector from international markets.

Table 11.2
The Balance of Payments, 1970–80 (billions of lire)

Year	Current Account	Capital Account	Basic Balance
1970	+476	-148	+222
1971	+981	-374	+491
1972	+1.169	-1.571	-748
1973	-1.473	+1.737	-206
1974	-5.212	+1.559	-3.715
1975	-337	-527	-1.439
1976	-2.343	+1.484	-1.531
1977	+2.175	-54	+1.730
1978	+5.261	+1.319	+6.996
1979	+4.553	-2.404	+1.824
1980	-8.532	+2.749	-6.258

Source: Annual Reports of the Bank of Italy.

A New Currency Crisis

After the 1969 balance-of-payments crisis, monetary policy soon turned expansionary. Interest rates fell and settled well below international levels (Spinelli and Fratianni, 1991). This caused a progressive deterioration of the capital account balance. In the spring of 1972 Italy joined with several European countries in an agreement to limit currency fluctuations within a ± 2.25 percent band, but the Bank overlooked the consequent need for a consistent interest-rate policy (cf. Chapter 15 of the present volume). The negative interest-rate differentials grew wider; in 1973 the gap vis-à-vis Germany was about 7 percentage points (Spinelli and Fratianni, 1991). The top priority was clearly assigned to the reduction of the domestic unemployment rate (Fazio, 1979). The authorities tried to insulate the domestic economy from the loss of foreign reserves. Thus, after nearly twenty years, they reintroduced a two-tier exchange-rate system and accepted a 6 percent devaluation of the financial lira.[26] But after a rapid deterioration of the current account—see Table 11.2—the commercial lira had to be devalued, too. To prevent an interest-rate rise as a consequence of the growing government deficits, a minimum quota was set for bank holdings of government bonds.

In 1973 output accelerated sharply, but so did prices. As a consequence, the first oil shock hit the Italian economy right at the peak of an inflationary cycle similar to those experienced in the 1960s, but made more difficult to handle by the increased turbulence in the labor market and by the concurrent, large currency depreciation. The higher cost of oil fueled domestic inflation and precipitated a new, dramatic balance-of-payments crisis. In 1974 official loans were sought from the European Community and the International Monetary Fund. In the negotiations with the Fund, one of the main conditions accepted by the domestic authorities was the official endorsement of an intermediate target, albeit atypical, called Total Domestic Credit Expansion (TDCE).[27]

The Bank set strict limits on the expansion of commercial credit[28] and "encouraged" commercial banks and even state enterprises to borrow abroad in order to finance the large current-account deficit.

Back to Expansion; Toward a New Currency Crisis

Actual TDCE fell below target, and in 1975 Italy entered a sharp recession.[29] The policy stance was quickly reversed once again. Credit ceilings were removed, export credit was automatically rediscounted, reserve requirements ratios were substantially reduced, and the discount rate was rapidly brought down from 15 to 8 percent.

In 1976 production reacted positively to these policy actions, but the external balance worsened dramatically as a result of both a substantial capital outflow and a strong demand for imports. The foreign exchange market had to be shut down twice,[30] and new foreign loans were negotiated with the Bundesbank, the Federal Reserve Bank, and the European Community. By the end of the year, the discount rate was brought back to 15 percent and credit ceilings were reinstated.

Toward Yet Another Crisis

In 1977 output growth halved and, for the first time since 1971 the balance of payments turned into a surplus. In 1978 the current account benefited from past depreciations in the lira. Because unemployment was on the rise, monetary policy became expansionary, in contrast with what was happening abroad. The interest-rate differential gradually worsened and caused increasing capital outflows. Domestic inflation soared above 20 percent, and a new currency crisis occurred in the spring of 1980, when the second oil shock completely absorbed the previous current-account surplus.

First Signs of a Turning Point

This extremely rapid and chaotic succession of events highlights the unpredictability and the very short-term horizon of the monetary policy of the 1970s. The authorities were consistently aiming at the maximum attainable rate of real growth, acknowledging as their only constraint the external deficit or, better, the periodic occurrence of currency crises.

As a consequence of government budget deficits which grew beyond control, TDCE targets were systematically overshot from 1975 to 1978 (see Table 11.3).[31] Because of the commitment to finance the Treasury, the

Table 11.3
Total Domestic Credit Expansion, 1974–80 (annual percentage changes)

Year	Target	Actual
1974	18.6	16.6
1975	17.6	25.4
1976	17.5	20.2
1977	15.1	17.6
1978	12.9	20.6
1979	18.4	18.5
1980	17.4	18.5

Source: Caranza and Fazio (1985).

Bank found itself in the policy dilemma of either severely squeezing commercial credit or giving up control of both TDCE and the monetary base.

As a matter of fact, the Bank decided to totally accommodate the Treasury demand for funds, give up TDCE as the intermediate target, and switch control of domestic credit to the nonstate sector. Thus, given the flexible exchange rate, the monetary system was left with no nominal anchor.[32]

The years 1976–79 also saw some innovations whose far-reaching implications would become visible in the following decade.

First, a whole range of new financial assets was introduced in an attempt to regain a medium-term control over both the monetary base financing of the Treasury and a monetary aggregate.[33] As a store of value, these assets quickly began to replace bank deposits in private portfolios. This paved the way for the 1981 "divorce" between the Bank of Italy and the Treasury.

Second, the authorities became increasingly convinced that (1) there was a need to forsake the cumbersome apparatus of administrative controls and turn to market mechanisms (Spinelli and Fratianni, 1991) and (2) in a small open economy a high degree of wage indexation nullifies any attempt to preserve external competitiveness and growth by means of repeated devaluations.

5. 1979–89: THE NEW MONETARY REGIME

Despite continuing, huge public deficits and thanks to innovations such as the split between the Bank and the Treasury and the willingness of the monetary authorities to bring the monetary aggregates under control, the 1980s experienced a much slower growth of the monetary base and a contraction of seigniorage as a source of revenues. A growing share of government deficits was financed by issuing government bonds. As a result, by 1989 the domestic creation of the monetary base was smaller than the

Figure 11.10
Domestic and Foreign Creation of the Monetary Base, 1980–89

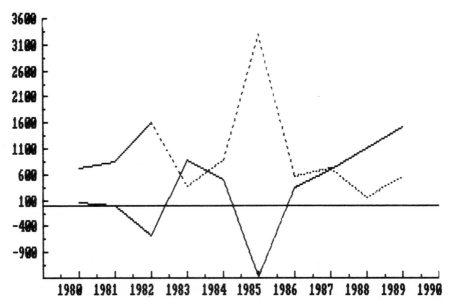

Source: Bank of Italy.

foreign creation (see Figure 11.10) and the ratio of outstanding public debt to GDP climbed to the unprecedented level of 1.0.[34]

Inflation was gradually reduced. Within the European Monetary System, the devaluation of the lira continued. But realignments became far less frequent during the second half of the decade when the inflation differential vis-à-vis the trading partners narrowed considerably and the authorities turned to the goal of real exchange-rate appreciation as a supplementary way to fight inflation (see Figure 11.5 and Chapter 15).

The new commitment of monetary policy to inflation control and to the creation of a stable and market-oriented financial environment took time before it could effectively come into play.[35] To some extent, such slow change in strategy was inevitable, since the relative underdevelopment of the domestic financial sector made it more difficult to rely on market incentives in the conduct of monetary policy. But it was also the result of a sort of "learning by doing" by the authorities, who switched to new monetary targets and techniques of monetary control once the old ones proved unreliable.

The Transition to the New Regime

Some monetary developments of the years 1979–83 are crucial to the understanding of why and how the authorities adopted a new strategy. We have already pointed out that, until 1979, the top priority had been assigned to output growth, followed by the short-term equilibrium of the balance of payments.

The formal commitment to a stable nominal exchange rate—which was implicit in the 1979 joining of the EMS—should not be regarded as a clear abandonment of the former policies. It simply mirrored the increasing skepticism of the Bank about the effectiveness of nominal devaluations in a small, open, and indexed economy. At the time, the causal link from money to domestic inflation was still in doubt, and a lot more emphasis was put on the role of nominal devaluations.

Hence, it should not come as a surprise that in 1979, when inflation was still rising and the twin deficits were widening, the Bank did not show great concern for the rapid growth of the monetary base until speculative pressures mounted against the lira. Domestic nominal interest rates eventually rose,[36] as the Bank tried to cut down on the supply of the monetary base. Commercial banks reacted to the squeeze by borrowing abroad. By so doing, they financed the current-account deficit and contributed to the stabilization of the exchange rate.

By 1981, however, it had become clear that such policies would simply postpone the unavoidable adjustment of domestic demand. Therefore, the ultimate goal of the new monetary contraction, which on all previous occasions had simply been the financing of the current-account deficit, became the control of domestic demand and absorption. This was pursued through a combination of old and new instruments, that is, through administrative credit ceilings and interest-rate changes.

At first, credit ceilings were imposed only on commercial banks, which reacted by expanding the credit instruments that were outside the control scheme. The SCI raised its share of domestic credit, too. Faced with these loopholes, the Bank extended the coverage of ceilings, but in the end it was forced to rely increasingly on increases in interest rates. Real rates became positive around mid-1981.

The switch from credit ceilings to real interest-rate policies did not depend solely on the increasing possibility that the market could bypass regulations and on the fact that, at any given TDCE target, the systematic inability of the government to keep its deficits in line with the preannounced targets did not leave any meaningful room for credit to the private sector. It was also becoming more evident that an entire decade of negative real interest rates had dramatically shifted the market's preferences away from financial assets and toward goods and this, in turn, systematically fueled inflation.[37]

Two years later, credit ceilings were definitively phased out, the current-account balance was back in surplus, inflation had decelerated from 21 to 13 percent, and economic activity was recovering.

At the beginning, the Bank did not follow the new rules of the game in a coherent manner. In fact, the former strategy of aiming at an interest-rate target that was inconsistent with medium-term exchange-rate stability was not abandoned for some time. As a consequence—and, of course, also because of the slow reduction of the inflation differential—in 1981 the lira underwent two devaluations within six months. The authorities were still reacting, with a lag, to the consequences of their incoherent actions.[38] By March 1983 two more realignments had occurred.

Despite the initial shortcomings, it is out of question that in the early 1980s the foundations were laid for a thorough reshaping of monetary policy. Several innovations signaled that the authorities were regaining control over the monetary base. The most important step was the ending, in 1981, of the Bank's obligation to serve as a residual buyer of Treasury bills. The removal of such formal commitment—which had caused the loss of grip on the money supply in the 1970s—enabled the Bank gradually to bring the interest rates to levels consistent with its monetary targets.

Other reforms sought to strengthen control over the monetary base and to increase the flexibility as well as the speed of reaction of interest rates to the impulses coming from the authorities. So, in 1983 mandatory reserve requirements were raised and extended to a wider set of financial assets; in 1985 the Bank obtained more discretion in granting credit to commercial banks.

The Beginning of the New Regime

Perhaps the year 1984 marked the beginning of a new regime. In fact, for the first time the authorities officially stated an M2 monetary target. However, even this fundamental step was marked by substantial ambiguities. First, broader aggregates such as TDCE and credit to the nonstate sector were not officially discarded (see Table 11.4). Second, there was no clear statement about the final policy targets. Third, the adoption of monetary targets, which signaled the decision to pursue an independent monetary policy, led to a conflict with the exchange-rate target; such conflict was settled with the imposition of capital controls.

Obstacles to Monetary Policy Effectiveness and Progress

During the second half of the 1980s several factors kept impairing the effectiveness of monetary policy. The first and foremost was the persistence of large public deficits, which clashed with the decision not to monetize them. This meant that a strong upward pressure was put on domestic real

Table 11.4
Credit and Monetary Aggregates, 1984–89 (annual percentage changes)

Year	Domestic Credit		Private Sector Credit		M2	
	Target	Actual	Target	Actual	Target	Actual
1984	17.4	19.7	12.3	15.6	11	13
1985	16.2	18.1	12	12.9	10	11.2
1986	13.2	15.1	9	11.4	7–11	10.5
1987	11.1	13.1	7	10.3	6–9	8.3
1988	10.4	14.9	6–10	15.7	6–9	7.8
1989	11.0	15.1	7–10	18.4	6–9	11.2

Source: CER (1989).

Table 11.5
The Balance of Payments, 1980–89 (billions of lira)

Year	Current Account	Capital Account (1)	Change of Reserves (2)
1980	-8.532	+9.434	-685
1981	-10.301	+9.704	-12
1982	-8.432	+1.872	+51.583
1983	+2.323	+6.609	-81.787
1984	-4.314	+5.201	-51.195
1985	-7.102	+893	+13.651
1986	+3.802	+2.239	-3.489
1987	-1.940	+12.103	-6.775
1988	-7.819	+21.637	-10.906
1989	-14.452	+35.317	-15.386

Source: Annual Reports of the Bank of Italy.

(1) Unlike Tables 11.1 and 11.2, capital account data include changes in commercial banks' net foreign indebtedness.

(2) The minus sign means an increase in foreign reserves.

interest rates. As a consequence, on several occasions (and especially toward the end of the decade), major capital inflows occurred, swelling foreign reserves and domestic credit (see Figure 11.10 and Table 11.5). By and large, the Bank managed to achieve its monetary target[39] but lost control over other aggregates, such as credit to the nonstate sector.[40]

The second factor that impaired the effectiveness of monetary policy was the larger proportion of financial assets, mainly short-term government securities that ended up in household portfolios. This weakened the impact of short-term interest rates as a regulatory instrument, since the contractionary wealth effect of an interest-rate increase was partly offset by an expansionary income effect.[41]

The third factor was the long lag in the financial markets' responses to monetary impulses. In particular, commercial banks systematically adjusted their interest rates too slowly and only partially.[42] However, the same years witnessed a continuous progress toward a more coherent and consistent policy framework.

The shift in ultimate target from output to inflation became apparent as the authorities increasingly stressed their commitment to exchange-rate stability. Once more, this innovation occurred gradually. The lira was devalued substantially in the EMS in 1985; two more realignments did occur in 1986 and 1987 but fell short of the cumulated inflation differentials.[43]

Restrictions on international capital movements were gradually lifted, with their removal complete by mid–1990. The way the later stages of the liberalization were accomplished clearly indicates how the domestic financial environment had been reshaped and the Bank's attitude had changed during the 1980s. Since the mid–1960s the restrictions on international capital movements had been a constant feature of monetary policy. Hence, there was great uncertainty about the extent to which domestic residents would take advantage of the new investment opportunities provided by the liberalization. Not surprisingly, many were concerned about the sustainability of adverse capital flows, but the Bank managed to ensure the necessary conditions to prevent destabilizing consequences. First, the commitment to a stable financial environment had gained credibility since pressures to devalue the currency had been resisted for more than two years. Second, the growth of foreign reserves had been impressive. Third, domestic interest rates made lira-denominated financial assets very attractive. As a matter of fact, the liberalization coincided with the formation of favorable expectations, which led to an impressive surplus of the capital account balance.[44]

The 1990 innovations—that is, the complete liberalization of capital movements and the enforcement of the narrow band for the lira—together with the formal decision to press for a rapid implementation of the European Monetary Union have stressed the commitment to further narrowing the inflation differential vis-à-vis the major European countries. In the latter part of 1990, the authorities resisted yet another round of devaluation pressures and showed no concern for a continuous appreciation of the real exchange rate. The authorities are now trying to bring about a substantial shift in expectations by convincing the markets that monetary policy has definitively changed, and they are steering inflation down to German levels, even at the cost of sizable output losses. But the persistence of huge public deficits looms ahead and might well undermine this strategy.

6. THE EVOLUTION OF MONETARY TARGETS AND TECHNIQUES OF MONETARY CONTROL

There are obvious and strong links between the global strategy pursued by a central bank and its targets, on the one hand, and between targets and instruments, on the other. In this section, we will therefore concentrate on how the successive changes in the monetary regimes affected the choice of targets and instruments.

The 1950s

In the 1950s monetary policy simply accommodated the sustained output growth that occurred in a noninflationary environment. The Bank tried to preserve the medium-term stability of the financial system and did not set short-run objectives that were inconsistent with its strategy.

The policy relied primarily on control of the supply of the monetary base. The task was complicated by the fact that the two main sources of monetary base fell outside the direct control of the Bank: the balance of payments, which was almost continuously in surplus, and the Treasury, which in principle could obtain unlimited financing from the Bank.

To keep the money supply on a sustainable and noninflationary path, the Bank relied mainly on offsetting changes of its advances to commercial banks. The underdevelopment of the short-term money market prevented a systematic reliance on changes of the re-discount rate and restricted the scope for open market operations.[45] Furthermore, since commercial banks did not have automatic access to the discount window, the Bank exercised its strong discretionary power to curtail banks' borrowing from the Bank. This explains why the Bank, throughout the entire decade, never altered reserve requirements ratios.[46]

The 1960s

In the 1960s monetary policy became more ambitious in the sense that the authorities made repeated attempts to fine-tune the economy and stimulate output growth. To gain better and quicker control over domestic credit flows, the Bank encouraged commercial banks to operate on the Eurodollar market (Allen and Stevenson, 1974, p. 167). The aim of this strategy was twofold. On the one hand, an enlarged access to the international financial markets would make the balance-of-payments constraint less binding; on the other, whenever the need for monetary restraint were to arise, it could be implemented easily and rapidly by withholding permission to borrow abroad. As a matter of fact, controlling the commercial banks' net foreign indebtedness became the main policy tool. Reliance on the other instruments was occasional; for instance, reserve requirements were altered only in 1962.[47]

From the mid–1960s onward, the growing government deficits were financed by selling bonds to the commercial banks, as bank deposits remained the households' preferred financial assets. The Bank engaged in more frequent open market operations aimed at stabilizing interest rates.

But such policy obviously implied that control of the monetary base had to be forsaken. Therefore, by the end of the decade, the Bank's technique of monetary control was totally different from that of the 1950s. In retrospect, such change hardly looks surprising: it was the obvious consequence of the new policy objectives.

The 1970s

Although the absolute interest-rate peg had to be given up in 1969, neither the policy objectives nor the control techniques were altered. After the 1970–71 slump, the authorities still tried to keep domestic interest rates at levels that were inconsistent with balance-of-payments equilibria and exchange-rate stability. The collapse of the Bretton Woods regime had simply given the Bank more room to pursue an independent monetary policy. But the gap between domestic and foreign monetary conditions was wide and would mean currency depreciations that the authorities were not willing to accept. Thus, severe restrictions on capital movements were introduced. In this phase, which culminated with the 1974 crisis, the role of monetary policy was simply to accommodate inflationary growth, and the Bank was concerned mainly with protecting foreign reserves.

In 1974, for the first time, the Bank adopted the TDCE intermediate *financial* target. Calls for the adoption of a *monetary* target were rejected for at least two reasons (Caranza and Fazio, 1985). First, it was believed that the effective availability of credit was more important than its cost. This belief was based on the collusive behavior of the Italian banking system, which limited the central bank's ability to affect the cost of credit. Second, the Bank argued that money stock changes and, more generally, substitution effects were not effective because bank deposits paid a market interest rate; changes in their supply would be absorbed primarily through the adjustment of their own rate of return and would not affect the yields of other assets. All in all, banks were seen as being potentially able to offset a monetary base squeeze through an increase in the yield of deposits.

The TDCE Model

The analytical scheme used by the Bank of Italy was an adaptation of the IMF approach which could be directly derived from the consolidated flow-of-funds accounts. TDCE is defined as follows[48]:

(1) $TDCE = dBMTES + dCRB + dBNB,$

where d is the difference operator, $BMTES$ is the credit extended to the Treasury by the Bank, CRB is the commercial banks' credit to the state and nonstate sectors, and BNB are domestic bonds holdings (including government securities) of the domestic nonbank sector.[49]

The link between the balance of payments[50] (BP) and $TDCE$ is:

(2) $BP = dAFI - TDCE,$

where AFI is the stock of domestic financial assets.

Assuming a stable demand function for AFI (AFI^d), it is possible to affect BP directly by setting $TDCE$:[51]

(3) $BP = dAFI^d - TDCE.$

This system does not allow for the control of domestic absorption and the current account (CA) because

(4) $CA = dAFI^d - (TDCE + CF),$

where CF is the capital account balance. To achieve complete control over domestic demand, it would be necessary for the authorities also to control capital flows (credit from abroad).

The underlying theoretical framework implied that any excess supply of financial assets obtained through an increase in ($TDCE + CF$) would increase expenditure relative to disposable income and therefore worsen the current account.[52] A reduction in total supply of financial assets would achieve the opposite result.

Substitution effects between money and other assets were dismissed as empirically negligible. This claim proved to be ill founded because a close positive correlation soon emerged between current-account and real interest-rate changes (Penati and Tullio, 1983). By neglecting the role of the money supply, proponents of the model also overlooked the influence of inflation expectations on the demand for financial assets.[53]

TDCE: Fiscal Dominance and the Noncontrollability of Credit Flows

The endorsement of $TDCE$ targets amounted to stating that the way budget deficits were financed did not matter and, perhaps more important, that the Bank was not entitled to set any ceiling on $dBMTES$.[54] Therefore, it is quite correct to stress that, under the conditions of the time, "the government budget deficit was an engine for inflationary expansion of the money supply and the supply of financial assets" (Hodgman and Resek, 1989, p. 73).

The theoretical impossibility and practical unwillingness to set a ceiling on either government deficit or *dBMTES* impaired the Bank's ability to target *TDCE*. On several occasions this would have caused an unbearable credit squeeze on the private sector (Caranza and Fazio, 1983). As we have recalled, at some stage the Bank was forced to forsake *TDCE* targets and turn to the less ambitious goal of controlling the flow of credit to the nonstate sector.

In the crises of 1974 and 1975–76 the authorities relied heavily on non-price credit rationing.[55] According to Caranza and Fazio (1985, p. 161), "[the adoption of credit ceilings . . .] was possible for three reasons: a) the share of TDC allocated to the private sector was sufficiently large; b) this credit was mostly intermediated by the banking system . . . ; c) ceilings applied for the first time in 1973 proved quite effective in curbing the volume of bank lending." But as time passed, the share of bank credit decreased, because both financial intermediaries and firms were discovering alternative sources of finance, either in the domestic market or abroad. Thus, ceilings had to be extended to foreign credits, to domestic imports, to bankers' acceptances, and so on.[56]

The 1980s: The Switch to Control over the Monetary Base

Between 1979 and 1982 the effectiveness of administrative controls was quickly fading away despite repeated attempts by the authorities to extend the coverage of controls. Eventually, the Bank was forced to resume direct control over the monetary base.[57]

At first, the Bank simply aimed at achieving an overall balance-of-payments target, so as to stabilize the exchange rate. Hence, the policy was cast in the framework of equation (3) above.[58] Subsequently, by keeping tight control over the domestic creation of the monetary base, the authorities began to force commercial banks to borrow abroad.

By mid-1981, to improve the current account the policy turned to direct control of domestic absorption. Thus, equation (4) above became relevant. At this stage, however, strict credit ceilings were supplemented by rising real interest rates, for it was now acknowledged that these rates could decisively stimulate the demand for financial assets.

The theoretical and practical switch of emphasis away from rationing and toward the cost of credit was undoubtedly made possible by the divorce between the Bank and the Treasury. However, another crucial factor favored this fundamental innovation—that is, the development of the domestic financial sector.

First, banks had experienced a great deal of disintermediation, and substitution effects could no longer be dismissed as negligible. Second, firms had built up a sizable portfolio of short-term assets, which made credit rationing less effective and, again, enhanced the role of interest-rates changes (Vaciago, 1984). Third, a larger share of government deficits could be financed through the sales of short-term Treasury bills to households. In other words, there was a viable alternative to the uncontrolled creation of monetary base.

Since 1983 the Bank has controlled the creation of the monetary base. To enhance the effectiveness of this policy, repeated attempts have been made to increase the financial markets' responsiveness to the impulses coming from the Bank. For instance, the authorities have favored the growth of both the interbank deposits market and the markets for Repurchase Agreements and Certificates of Deposit.

Over time the intermediate target *TDCE* had gradually lost relevance. From 1984 onward, a new M2 money supply target[59] and new methods of monetary control (open market operations and refinancing to commercial banks) came into play. Undoubtedly, this mirrored the switch of emphasis toward market incentives.

By contrast, the final policy targets remained ambiguous.[60] Basically, the markets were left without firm indication of the extent to which the Bank was prepared to trade off output growth for price stability. This led to (and was reflected in) the recurring episodes of mounting speculative pressures against the lira.[61]

SUMMARY

During the postwar period monetary policy in Italy has undergone sweeping changes that reflect the changing external environment, the evolution of the central bank's philosophy, and the gradual development of the domestic financial sector.

The 1950s witnessed a policy aimed at noninflationary growth and international financial integration.

In the 1960s the authorities attempted to achieve more ambitious targets in a short-run perspective. This policy had adverse effects and exacerbated the business cycle.

In the 1970s unchecked monetary financing of government deficits brought inflation to unprecedented levels: seigniorage became a fundamental source of government revenues. Because monetary policy was inconsistent with the central bank's exchange-rate targets, the domestic financial sector had to be almost completely isolated from the international market. Even so, two major currency crises did occur.

In the 1980s the Bank gradually built a credible commitment to curb inflation and developed a stable and viable financial environment. This commitment shows up in the complete liberalization of international capital flows as well as in the narrowing of the exchange-rate fluctuation band vis-à-vis the Deutsche mark.

Over time, the choice of alternative instruments of monetary control has mirrored these changes. In the 1950s the Bank relied primarily on control over the monetary base through moral suasion.

In the 1960s emphasis shifted toward foreign credit and administrative measures. In the 1970s as *TDCE* became *the* intermediate target and as the importance of the monetary base control totally faded out, credit ceilings were widely used. In the second half of the 1980s, as monetary targeting returned, the Bank began to closely monitor the (domestic) monetary base growth through interest-rate changes.

NOTES

We thank Michele Fratianni, Antonio Guccione, and Dominick Salvatore for helpful comments on an earlier draft.

1. By and large, both the gradual slowing down of the growth process and the pattern of its variability have mirrored the evolution of the major industrial economies.

2. The fall of 1969—the so-called hot autumn—was characterized by an unprecedented period of industrial conflict.

3. The banking system is essentially oligopolistic and characterized by a dominant public ownership.

4. Over the last few years, this picture has changed substantially. New financial institutions and instruments have come into play, partly as a result of the need to ease the financing of government deficits and partly as a consequence of the worldwide trend toward more diversified and complex financial structures. In the process, the traditional banking system has lost ground, but it has also gained in competitiveness. New financial intermediaries, such as leasing and factoring firms, investment funds, and portfolio management companies, are taking larger and larger shares of the market. Furthermore, the stock market has shown signs of new life.

5. The process of fiscal decision making in the Italian Parliament is traditionally slow and cumbersome, tax evasion is widespread, and the timely implementation of spending decisions is impossible.

6. Only in 1981 was the Bank formally granted the right to refuse direct financing of the Treasury. More on this below.

7. Initially, sustained output expansion coincided with the absorption of a large amount of unemployed or underemployed labor resources. Later, it was made possible by a large-scale transfer of labor from agriculture to industry. See, among others, Fuà (1965), Kindleberger (1967), and Sylos Labini (1970).

8. See Fuà (1965), Graziani (1969), and Sylos Labini (1970).

9. Tariff barriers within member countries were totally dismantled by 1958.

10. A number of studies have related the strength of investment to the relatively high share of profits in income distribution.

11. Only rarely did it experience some pressure to appreciate or to devalue its currency.

12. Thygesen (1984), p. 335.

13. See the Radcliffe Report (1959).

14. In that year, domestic firms were allowed to buy foreign securities issued by firms operating in the same sector, and commercial banks were allowed to hold foreign currencies. However, the governor of the Bank of Italy ruled out the full deregulation of international capital movements; see Bank of Italy (1959).

15. For a detailed discussion, see Spinelli and Fratianni (1991).

16. See Spinelli and Fratianni (1991).

17. Furthermore, the banks' participation in the developing Eurodollar market was encouraged, in order to make administrative controls on foreign borrowing a more powerful tool.

18. Between 1960 and 1965 wage inflation rose and fell very sharply. However, the consequences of this on the employment levels were not sizable (see Figure 11.2). After 1965 the increase in inflation did not affect the unemployment rate at all. Thus, the 1960s were very different from the earlier decade, when the unemployment rate kept falling at a relatively stable rate of inflation.

Notice that from 1960 onward the unemployment rate was always at least one percentage point below the minimum level reached in the 1950s. Thus, it should be obvious that in the 1960s the economy hit a full employment ceiling, and this certainly complicated the conduct of monetary policy. But there is no evidence of central bank awareness that labor market conditions were now profoundly different from those of the former decade.

19. As a matter of fact, it has been argued that the central bank's behavior made things worse. See Salvati (1968), Allen and Stevenson (1974), and Spinelli and Fratianni (1991).

20. Foreign debt was halved by the end of 1964.

21. The level of economic activity remained low, and the available credit was not taken up by industry.

22. Other European central banks shared this view.

23. In the first quarter of 1969 the central bank had already tried to stop the loss of foreign reserves by penalizing the banks that were exporting capital.

24. The rate of growth of nominal wages rose from 8 percent in 1969 to nearly 20 percent in 1970.

25. In fact, the commitment to create a stable financial environment was abandoned in favor of highly discretionary and unpredictable policies. From this point of view, the experiment of pegging long-term interest rates was no exception, since it was pursued until it became clearly unsustainable.

26. Between 1970 and 1973 exports of capital were severely restricted through a number of administrative controls which went as far as limiting tourism abroad. For a detailed analysis, see Spinelli and Fratianni (1991). A two-tier exchange market is characterized by a separation between exchange transactions originating from goods and capital movements.

27. It included central bank credit to the Treasury and to other final users, commercial bank loans and bond holdings, and domestic bonds held by households and other financial institutions. The rationale for, and the implications of, adopting *TDCE* are discussed in the next section.

28. Fifteen percent on a year-to-year base, which was a rate well below the current inflation rate.

29. But this happened in the rest of Europe too.

30. Beyond these factors, the currency crisis was almost certainly the result of adverse expectations, fueled by the political situation.

31. Between 1971 and 1976 no less than 76 percent of budget deficits was monetized.

32. The unprecedented inflation rates that emerged as a result of this policy never became a real issue.

33. Some of those assets had indexed rates of return.

34. The debt-to-GDP ratio of 1.0 refers to the new national income accounts. To the extent that these revisions have occurred in some countries and not in others, the Italian situation is comparatively worse and close to the interwar event when the ratio reached the value of 1.3.

35. This also shows up in the absence of any abrupt change in the rate of inflation.

36. But real rates were still negative.

37. The link between negative real interest rates, inflation, and current-account deficits is clearly shown in Penati and Tullio (1983).

38. In any case, at that stage Italy was still considering the European Monetary System as more of a crawling peg than a quasi-fixed exchange-rate regime. Inflation targets were not stated clearly, and the recurrent devaluations suggest that great importance was still assigned to short-run output growth. Ex-post, this might be regarded as part of a sensible strategy aimed at bringing about a gradual unwinding of inflationary expectations in the labor market without going through a deep recession. In our view, this could be attained through the preannouncement of intermediate targets.

39. A substantial deviation from the target occurred in 1989.

40. Throughout the decade the foreign supply of monetary base was systematically sterilized (see Bank of Italy, 1988b, Chap. 6); the negative correlation between domestic and foreign creation of high-powered money is shown in Figure 11.10.

41. The income effect relates to the payment of the coupon.

42. At the end of the decade, the bank introduced several reforms that sought to improve the efficiency of the financial sector and to strengthen the effectiveness of interest-rate changes on the money supply. These reforms will be discussed in greater detail in the next section.

43. On several other occasions demands for devaluations were successfully resisted. Finally, the 1990 general EMS realignment did not involve a devaluation of the lira. In fact, the revision of the central parity coincided with the adoption of a narrower fluctuation band, whose upper bound was made to coincide with that of the former, wider band. As a consequence, the maximum devaluation range for the lira has remained constant since the 1987 realignment. Indeed, by the end of the decade the increased exchange-rate stability had greatly enhanced the Bank's reputation as an institution committed to curb inflation.

44. The global coherency of this strategy is striking, especially if one considers that, at least until 1981, the Bank had often failed to take into account the importance of setting consistent internal and external targets.

45. These never played any significant role.

46. The Bank made use of this instrument only in 1958, when it was lowered by half a percentage point.

47. The reserve ratio was lowered by 2 percent.

48. Our discussion relies heavily on, among others, Caranza and Fazio (1985), Vaciago (1984), Hodgman and Resek (1989), and Spinelli and Fratianni (1991).

49. The omission of the stock market credit is not consequential.

50. By balance of payments we mean the sum of the current and capital accounts.

51. Caranza and Fazio (1985) point out that the main policy concern in 1974, when *TDCE* was first endorsed, was financing the *BP*.

52. Assuming exports are constant.

53. This point was raised by Penati and Tullio (1983) who wrote: "In anticipation of a future monetary expansion inflationary expectations will increase. As a result, ... consumers will shift out of financial assets into real goods...Ex-post, the observed income velocity of [*TDC*] will exceed the level which was expected" (p. 44). This probably reflected the Bank's skepticism about the causal link from money to inflation. Instead, the Bank stressed the role of cost-push factors, that is, exchange-rate devaluations and wages indexation.

54. We will also recall that the growth of this variable was rather unpredictable as a result of systematic excesses of actual budget deficits over previous government forecasts.

55. This point was raised by Hodgman and Resek (1989).

56. For a more detailed description of the evolution of administrative controls, see Caranza and Fazio (1985).

57. Once more, then, the adoption of new instruments reflected both a modification of the Bank's philosophy and an endorsement of new targets.

58. See Vaciago (1984). In the very short run, the stability of the exchange rate was obtained through intervention in the foreign exchange market.

59. In fact, the Bank pursued a policy of "twin announcements" (Angeloni and Passacantando, 1990), that is, announcements for M2 and Private Sector Domestic Credit (*PSDC*). However, the systematic *PSDC* overshooting greatly limited its relevance.

60. See CER (1989), p. 26.

61. On the whole, the exchange-rate policy unambiguously proves the systematic attempts on the part of the authorities to enhance the credibility of their commitment to curb inflation. However, it has been noticed that on a few occasions realignments did not bring about an immediate jump of the actual rate; see Avesani and Gallo (1990). This could mean that the former parities were still thought to be credible and that realignments were used as an instrument to preserve competitiveness. By contrast, there is some evidence that at some stage the Bank began to keep the exchange rate within a narrow band for some time before actually undertaking an official commitment to it. In our view, this suggests that the Bank is increasingly prepared to accept the monetary discipline imposed by exchange-rate stability. The complete liberalization of capital movements which has recently been achieved stresses this conclusion.

REFERENCES

Allen, Kevin, and Stevenson, Andrew. 1974. *An Introduction to the Italian Economy*. London: Martin Robertson.

Angeloni, Igazio, and Passacantando, Franco. 1990. "Monetary Policy in Italy. Institutional and Economic Aspects." Banca d'Italia. Mimeo.

Avesani, Renzo, and Gallo, Giampiero. 1990. "Jumping in the Band, Undeclared Intervention Thresholds in a Target Zone." University of Trento. Mimeo.

Bank of Italy. *Relazione Annuale del Governatore*. Rome: Banca d'Italia, various years.

———. 1988a. *Modello Mensile del Mercato Monetario*. Rome: Banca d'Italia.

———. 1988b. *La Mobilizzazione della Riserva Obbligatoria*. Rome: Banca d'Italia.

Caranza, Cesare, and Fazio, Antonio. 1985. "Methods of Monetary Control in Italy: 1974–1983." In *The Political Economy of Monetary Policy: National and International Aspects*, edited by Donald Hodgman. Federal Reserve Bank of Boston, Conference Series No. 26, Boston, pp. 65–88.

CER (Centro Europa Ricerche). 1989. *Rapporto I/89*. Rome.

Fazio, Antonio. 1979. "La Politica Monetaria in Italia dal 1947 al 1978." *Moneta e Credito* 32, no. 127: 269–320.

Fuà, Giorgio. 1965. *Notes on Italian Economic Growth 1861–1964*. Milan: Giuffré.

Giavazzi, Francesco, and Spaventa, Luigi. 1989. "Italy, the Real Effects of Inflation and Disinflation." *Economic Policy* 8 (April): 133–71.

Graziani, Augusto. 1969. *Lo Sviluppo dell'economia italiana come sviluppo di un'economia aperta*. Turin: Einaudi.

Hodgman, Donald, and Resek, Robert. 1989. "Italian Monetary and Foreign Exchange Policy." *Macroeconomic Policy and Economic Interdependence*, edited by Donald Hodgman and Geoffrey Wood. London: Macmillan, 1989.

ISTAT. *Annuario di Contabilita' Nazionale*, Rome.

Kindleberger, Charles. 1967. *Europe's Postwar Growth, the Role of Labor Supply*. Cambridge, Mass.: Harvard University Press.

Maddison, Angus. 1982. *Phases of Capitalist Development*. Oxford: Oxford University Press.

Mastropasqua, Cristina; Micossi, Stefano; and Rinaldi, Roberto. 1988. "Interventions, Sterilization and Monetary Policy in EMS Countries." In *The European Monetary System*, edited by Francesco Giavazzi et al. Cambridge, England: Cambridge University Press, 252–88.

Penati, Alessandro, and Spinelli, Franco. 1986. "I progressi e i nodi irrisolti della politica monetaria italiana dei primi anni Ottanta." *Note Economiche* 1, no. 2: 35–71.

———, and Tullio, Giuseppe. 1983. "Total Domestic Credit as an Intermediate Target of Monetary Policy in Italy." In *Monetary Policy, Fiscal Policy and Economic Activity*, edited by Franco Spinelli and Giuseppe Tullio. Aldershot: Gower.

Pin, Antonio. 1986. "La Riserva Obbligatoria in Italia." *Note Economiche* 3, no. 4 (1986): 320–43.

Radcliffe Committee (Committee on the Working Monetary System). 1959. *Report*. London: HMSO.

Salvati, Michele. 1968. "Distribuzione del reddito, livello dei prezzi e livello d'attività nelle Relazioni della Banca d'Italia." *Rassegna Economica* 32, no. 3: 525–58.

Spinelli, Franco, and Fratianni, Michele. 1991. *Storia Monetaria d'Italia*. Milan: Mondadori.

Sylos Labini, Paolo. 1970. *Problemi dello Sviluppo Economico*. Bari: Laterza.

Thygesen, Niels. 1984. "Monetary Policy." In *The European Economy: Growth and Crisis*, edited by A. Boltho. Oxford: Oxford University Press.

Vaciago, Giacomo. 1984. "Money, Debt and Financial Assets: The Role of Alternative Intermediate Targets (Italy, 1979–1983)." Paper presented at the Conference on Money, Credit and Economic Activity in Italy, Brasenose College, Oxford.

12

THE UNITED KINGDOM

Patrick Minford

Monetary policy in Britain since 1979 has been continuously styled by the government of Margaret Thatcher and her successor, John Major, as monetarist. Yet it differs from textbook monetarism in many ways. Some have even claimed that, in its willingness to use the exchange rate as an indicator, recent British monetary policy has ceased to be monetarist at all; however, this is a misunderstanding.

To understand a policy, it is necessary to know the implicit model politicians and officials use. The model that has dominated official thinking during recent years is the rational expectations model in which the government is playing a repeated game with a watchful public. As everyone now knows, in such a game it pays the government to bind itself to precommitments that prevent "reflation," that is, the use of monetary and fiscal instruments to stimulate the economy. These precommitments create credibility and thereby give greater effectiveness to counterinflationary policy.

A similar implicit model has become influential on the continent as well, especially among central bankers. In Switzerland and Germany it has strengthened the tradition of constitutional restraint on monetary policy through an independent central bank. In France, Italy, and the Benelux countries it has prompted the switch to an increasingly hard exchange-rate link to the Deutsche mark, intended to exploit the Bundesbank's independence.

In Britain, however, this European Monetary System (EMS) approach was, at least throughout the 1980s, rejected in favor of domestic sources of credibility. The reasons for this rejection will be discussed below. The search for domestic discipline was the origin of the Medium-Term Financial Strategy (MTFS), to which we now turn.

Figure 12.1
RPI Inflation, All Items (percentage increase on a year earlier)

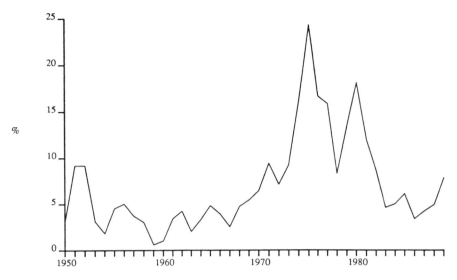

Source: Central Statistical Office (CSO).

THE MEDIUM-TERM FINANCIAL STRATEGY

In 1979 Mrs. Thatcher inherited a monetary mess. Inflation was rising rapidly from an initial rate of over 10 percent (Figure 12.1). The policy of wage controls that had been used to hold it down in 1978 had crumbled in the "winter of discontent" of that year when graves went undug and rubbish piled up in the streets. Large public sector pay increases were promised by a commission under Professor Hugh Clegg which had been set up by the previous government. The budget was in crisis; the deficit was already up to 5 percent of GDP (Figure 12.2), and it would clearly rise sharply with these pay awards on top of the usual spending pressures.

Milton Friedman (1980) advised a gradual reduction in the money supply growth rate and a cut in taxes in order to stimulate output. The first part was accepted, but the second was not because the deficit was seen to be important in conditioning financial confidence. Until the deficit could be reduced by other means, tax rates would have to stay up and perhaps even go higher. This was the view not merely of the Treasury, but also of the financial markets. At Liverpool University it was seen as a rational expectations effect, given the growing pressures for monetary financing of long-lasting budget deficits.

This was the background to the policies pursued. As we will see, little

Figure 12.2
PSBR/Nominal GDP

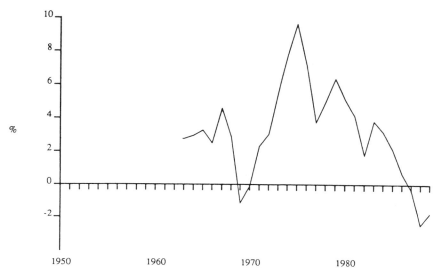

Source: CSO.

importance was attached to the operating method used by the central bank, whether monetary base control or interest-rate setting in pursuit of monetary targets. As a result of this situation and the emphasis on fiscal policy support, the debate on monetary policy in Britain took a very different form from that in the United States, for example, although it perhaps had a rather European character.

THE THATCHER GOVERNMENT'S MONETARY PLAN

Britain's key problem was seen to be the lack of long-term credibility in counterinflation policy. The previous government had instituted monetary targets, starting in 1976, in conjunction with the International Monetary Fund (IMF) support arrangement. It had also managed a substantial reduction in the budget deficit; the Public Sector Borrowing Requirement (PSBR), the usual measure of deficit in the United Kingdom, including government net lending to the private sector, was reduced from 10 percent of GDP in 1975 to below 4 percent in 1977. Nevertheless, the policies lacked long-term durability. Incomes policy that had been emphasized as the key bulwark against inflation crumbled as it was widely predicted it must in a free economy. The money supply target for £M3, a wide aggregate, was generally "achieved" by using a tax on high-interest deposits, the "corset"; excess money showed elsewhere, notably in rising M0 growth. Budgetary discipline was based on cuts without any long-term strategy for reducing the size of the public sector and so were seen as a temporary pain that would be reversed once the pressure (e.g., of the IMF) was off.

Thus, the problem of a credibly durable monetary restraint on prices was one of fundamental political economy, and not merely a technical matter of the central bank fixing appropriate targets. If the central bank had been constitutionally independent or even fiercely committed to price stability in practice with a high-profile governor respected for monetary probity, matters could have been different. For this reason, analysis of Switzerland or the United States or the Federal Republic of Germany, for example, would focus mainly on the central bank. But the Bank of England commanded no such position; formally an executive arm of the Treasury, it was staffed by Keynesians and had as governor a lawyer (now Lord, Gordon Richardson) whose main personal interest was regulation and who had no intuitive grasp of monetary theory.

To achieve durability (and it was hoped that the people would rapidly be convinced of that prospective durability), policy was cast in the form of a Medium-Term Financial Strategy (MTFS). This strategy consisted first of a commitment to a five-year rolling target for gradually decelerating £M3. Second, controls were removed, including the "corset" (a special reserve ratio on excessive growth in interest-yielding deposits), exchange controls, and incomes policy. Third, the monetary commitment was backed up by parallel reduction of the PSBR/GDP ratio. The original plans are shown in Figures 12.3 and 12.4, together with eventual outcomes. Announced in the 1980 budget, the MTFS carried the full authority of the prime minister and notionally of the cabinet, so that future deviations should be seen as a seriously embarrassing breach of promise to the electorate. On the optimistic view that it would be totally credible, market expectations of both short- and long-term inflation should drop, interest rates should fall rapidly, and any recession should be short-lived and possibly nonexistent: the falling money growth should be offset by falling inflation, so keeping up real money balances and consumer purchasing power.

The basic analysis could not be faulted; it rested on the logic of (1) the government's intertemporal budget constraint, whereby deficits today must be paid for by taxes, money expansion, or economies tomorrow and (2) the political pressure for money creation to relieve a rising debt/GDP ratio, with its consequence in rising interest rates and future tax burdens. Later, Thomas Sargent and Neil Wallace widely disseminated this analysis in their well-known paper, "Some Unpleasant Monetarist Arithmetic" (1981). It was applied in the less obvious U.S. context, assuming a constitutionally independent central bank and no rise in interest rates because of Ricardian equivalence (whereby future taxes are perfectly anticipated and offset by

Figure 12.3
The Medium-Term Finanical Strategy and Sterling M3 (percent P.A.)

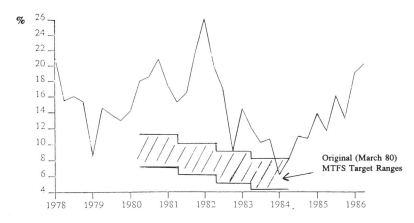

higher current savings). The point is that if one assumes any reasonable termination of the rising debt/GDP ratio, whether because of a limit on distortionary taxes or on available savings, then money financing is eventually required in the absence of quite implausibly severe cuts in public expenditure.

MONETARY POLICY IN PRACTICE

Logic was not enough; the MTFS failed not only to command credibility, but also to be carried out in its own literal terms. Yet policy turned out to be more fiercely contractionary than gradualism had intended; it was closer to shock tactics than gradualism. Here was a paradox indeed: tougher yet less credible, apparently the worst of both worlds.

Trouble came from two directions: technical design and politics. Technically, the choice of £M3 was an error because after deregulating the banks (including offshore banks with no exchange controls) high-interest deposits became the major weapon in the banks' battle for market share. As the banks' fortunes ebbed and flowed, so did £M3. In 1980–81 it overshot its targets massively (see Figure 12.3). Yet money growth (M0)—the most narrow monetary aggregate, consisting of currency in circulation and bank reserves—was unaffected by deregulation and told quite a different story: one of sharply tightening monetary conditions (Figure 12.6). Its growth rate was halved in the twelve months to mid–1980 and

Figure 12.4
The Medium-Term Financial Strategy and the PSBR (4 quarter moving average, percent of GDP)

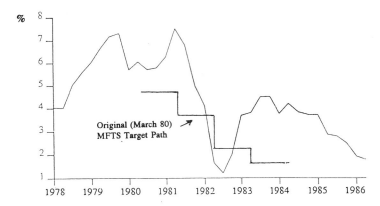

Original (March 80)
MFTS Target Path

Figure 12.5
M4 Growth (seasonally adjusted)

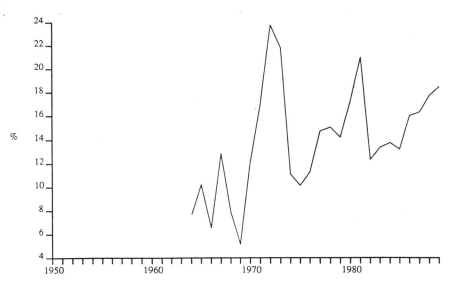

Source: CSO.

Figure 12.6
M0 Growth

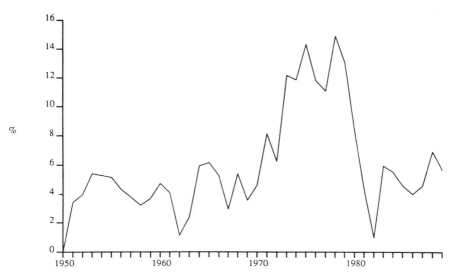

Sources: Bank of England Quarterly Bulletin (March 1981); CSO.

halved again in the next twelve. It is obvious from data on the economy which story is the true one; the sharp recession in 1980–81 (Figure 12.7), the rapid fall in inflation (Figure 12.1), and the strong exchange rate (Figure 12.15) all confirm M0 as the accurate indicator. M4, a broader aggregate than £M3, including building society (equivalent to U.S. savings and loan institutions) deposits, also supports M0 for this period when the main intermediary competition was between the banks and the building societies (Figure 12.5).

Politically, the pain of recession, especially in the manufacturing sector, undermined the already insecure position of the monetarists in the Conservative party, and Mrs. Thatcher faced substantial internal opposition. The days of the MTFS, and perhaps even of Mrs. Thatcher herself, seemed numbered.

So the MTFS was widely written off at this time as a failure because its targets had not been achieved and as a temporary interlude before traditional politics returned. Meanwhile, the chancellor of the Exchequer, Sir Geoffrey Howe, doggedly persevered through 1980 with the attempt to keep the MTFS on course. Short-term interest rates (Figure 12.8) were kept up to reduce the money overshoot, and the PSBR was brought down on its track, even though swollen by recession.

In early 1981, too, the technical problems were appreciated, with the

Figure 12.7
Real GDP Growth (average estimate, at factor cost)

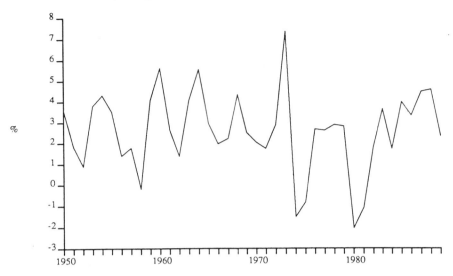

Source: CSO.

arrival of Sir Alan Walters and his circulation of an influential paper by Professor Jurg Niehans of Bern University (Niehans, 1981). The decision was taken to loosen monetary policy in order to weaken the exchange rate, to stabilize M0 at a growth rate around 5 percent, and to permit output to recover. To enhance credibility, the budget of 1981 increased taxes by 2 percent of GDP to cut the PSBR, even though the recession still had not ended. This cut was crucial in finally creating market confidence in the policies' durability. Long-term interest rates which had fluctuated around 14 percent for two years at last began to fall during 1981 (Figure 12.9). Output also started to recover in the spring of 1981. The policy emphasis thus switched toward fiscal, and away from monetary, tightness. Overall, however, policy remained extremely tight throughout.

Policies close to shock tactics were implemented by these means, perhaps mainly by accident but to some degree by intuitive survival instinct. That is, given that recession was connected in popular debate with the monetarist policies, it was vital to get results on inflation in short order as justification— to be hung for a sheep as a lamb, and better still to be applauded for the sheep of much lower inflation. Whatever the reasons, the rapid fall in inflation—down to 5 percent by the end of 1982—restored the fortunes of Mrs. Thatcher and her supporters.

This episode was the furnace in which the current monetary policy of

Figure 12.8
NRS, Treasury Bill Rate

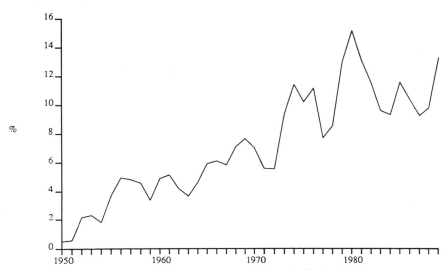

Source: International Financial Statistics, IMF.

the United Kingdom was forged. Those now running that policy have fashioned it with that experience in mind. The key elements are as follows:

1. The PSBR must be kept down to sustain market confidence.
2. M0 is a reliable indicator of monetary conditions.
3. Rapid movements in the exchange rate may contain monetary signals and will in general not be permitted, unless M0 confirms systematically after the event that they should.
4. In controlling monetary conditions, what matters is that interest rates be moved symmetrically as dictated by targets (without political intervention, for example, to hold interest rates down) and that market participants understand the system's signals in forming their expectations. Monetary base control—a method according to which M0 should be kept rigorously to a fixed path—was rejected in favor of a system that used M0 as the key monetary indicator to guide interest-rate changes. This was an extension of familiar methods.

Although much ink has been spilled on such monetary control methods per se (Goodhart, 1989, p. 493, has a useful account), from the modern perspective of rational expectations these key features of symmetry and efficient signaling attach to a wide variety of short-term control methods; and there is no reason in principle to prefer base control over the method

Figure 12.9
NRL, Long-Term Government Bond Yield

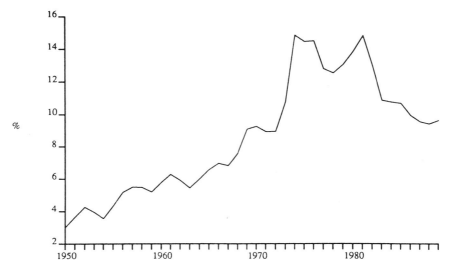

Source: International Financial Statistics, IMF.

currently used. The current method consists of setting the interest rates at which the Bank will lend to the money market on short-term instruments; these interest rates then trigger immediate changes in the commercial banks' base rate (the equivalent of the U.S. prime rate). Difficulties arise under the current method only when ambiguities creep into the practice, as has occurred recently with uncertainty about EMS and the exact status of exchange-rate targets. These problems also arise in base control systems, as the Swiss experience shows.

Since 1982, these principles have been pursued with the objective of keeping inflation below 5 percent. No strong efforts have been made to drive it to zero, because of fears that these might destabilize a smooth recovery and falling unemployment. The emphasis in policy innovation switched to the supply-side deregulation, union laws, privatization, and tax cuts. Nevertheless, even the process of keeping inflation down has implied occasional deflation. Over the whole period from 1979 to 1986 Matthews and Minford (1987) have estimated that the cumulative effect of tight monetary and accompanying fiscal policy on unemployment was no less than 1 million, just over 4 percent of the labor force.

WAS THERE AN ALTERNATIVE?

Clearly, then, the counterinflation policies were far from costless in conventional terms. With hindsight it is natural to ask whether an alternative strategy could have conquered inflation at less cost. Some argued for incomes policy; however, past experience of such a strategy in the United Kingdom is hardly encouraging. As argued earlier, in a free economy (and as shown by Bean et al., 1987, Britain is low in corporatist features) such a policy can only be a temporary expedient. Apart from the costs it imposes in distorting markets while in force, it cannot therefore provide a durable mechanism either for controlling inflation or for reducing its unemployment cost. Hence, policy credibility would not have been enhanced, and so long-term interest rates would not have come down. As for inflation, although it might have been held down in the short term by incomes policy, thereby limiting the contractionary effect of monetary tightening, as the incomes policy crumbled inflation would have been higher than otherwise. Thus, the contractionary effect would merely have been displaced in time.

A more interesting possibility than incomes policy is the shock therapy advocated by Hayek and the new classical economists (e.g., Sargent, 1986). In a recent paper Minford and Rastogi (1989) took the calculations of Matthews and Minford (1987) for the effects of the policies actually pursued and recomputed them assuming a shock strategy.

As we have seen, credibility was only established as the PSBR/GDP ratio actually fell. The rules which the markets, on the basis of available information, believed to be governing the authorities' actions were that this ratio would be kept constant at its current level and that M0 growth would be set to keep the government debt/GDP ratio constant at its current level. The Liverpool model gave a good fit to this period assuming these rules, which represents some evidence that the markets did indeed believe these rules to be in operation. If so, then, to change expectations once-for-all policies should cut the PSBR/GDP ratio immediately to its zero-inflation value and cut M0 growth in line. Although this would represent a big shock to expectations, the economy could recover with no interruption from that point on.

The simulations we carried out assumed that from the beginning of 1980 public expenditure was cut and taxes were raised sharply in order to bring the PSBR down at once to approximately 0.5 percent of GDP on a cyclically adjusted basis. (Since inflation is also planned in this exercise to fall to zero in short order, inflation adjustment is irrelevant.) M0 is cut in parallel. This implies a steady growth of around 1 percent p.a. for stable prices, with temporary exceptions designed to prevent excessively violent changes in monetary conditions in any one year.

Figure 12.10
Shock Tactics Simulation: Inflation

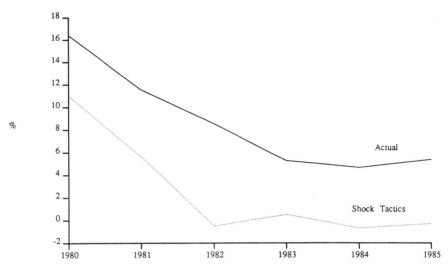

Since 1981 fiscal and monetary policy has been sustained in this mode. Whereas in 1980, of course, the policy was a shock, on a major scale, from 1981 it was fully anticipated for the reasons discussed above.

The story of this alternative strategy is clearly told in Figures 12.10 to 12.12, which compare the model's prediction of what would have happened under shock tactics with what actually happened.

The basic picture is clear. There would have been a deeper recession in 1980–81 and a quicker increase in unemployment, reaching 3 million by 1981. However, because there were no further negative fiscal/monetary shocks after 1980, unemployment started to fall sooner and by 1984 it was falling decisively away from the 3 million mark.

The inflation rate fell more rapidly and settled at zero after 1982. It did not drop at once to zero in 1980 because the world recession and other negative shocks on the supply side reduced money demand in 1980–81 and caused "defensive" price rises. The real exchange rate similarly rose more sharply in 1980, but thereafter it dropped back more quickly, for there were no more negative fiscal/monetary shocks.

We have found, rather in line with the new classical advice, that the short, sharp shock that cannot be reversed and so bypasses issues of credibility can be said to give better results than gradualism. The question that remains is whether the treatment would have been too brutal to be practical even in the honeymoon period of the first six to twelve months of the Thatcher administration.

The scale of the cuts needed would have been of the order of 10 percent

Figure 12.11
Shock Tactics Simulation: GDP Growth

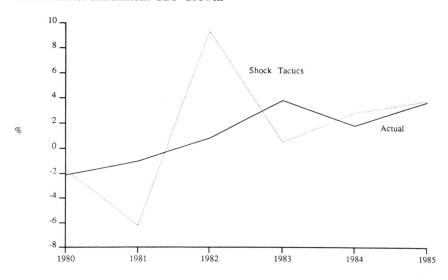

Figure 12.12
Shock Tactics Simulation: Unemployment (millions)

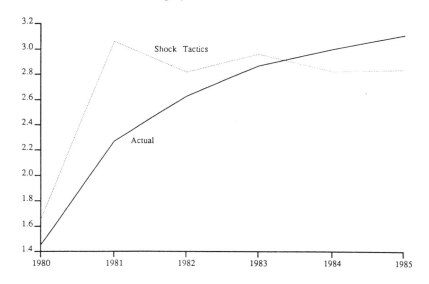

of total government expenditure and 4 percent of GDP. By contrast, even with the Clegg awards (public sector pay increases recommended by the government commission under Professor Clegg in 1978 and implemented by the incoming Thatcher government in 1979–80) actual government spending in 1980 remained roughly constant in real terms (i.e., deflated by the GDP deflator). It is not that difficult to imagine a crisis package that could have been politically viable: withdrawal of Clegg awards, freezing of all benefits in money terms, general 10 percent program cuts, raising of the discount factor on capital projects, and bringing forward the tax rises of the 1981 budget (a total package worth 4 percent of GDP). In fact, the program here assumed that government expenditure would have followed roughly its actual path and that tax rates would have been raised by 4 percent of GDP from 1980 and would have remained at this level throughout.

Judgment of political viability would require an extended discussion that would take us too far afield. But when an opposition has itself been practicing or advocating cuts, experience shows it can be done; witness the mid-1980s policies of Haughey in Eire and Lange in New Zealand in just such circumstances.

In summary, the policies here would have caused substantial dislocation during 1980–81, with the real exchange rate appreciating about twice as much as it actually did and GDP falling 7 percent, also about twice as much. But the recovery would have been faster and inflation eliminated. By 1985, GDP would have been nearly 5 percent higher. Would such a cure have been so much more painful than what actually happened, that its speed and long-term gain would still not have seemed attractive? It hardly seems so. But we say that with the benefit of hindsight, and one can sympathize with the ex-ante reluctance of politicians faced with such uncertainties.

Rules and Discretion

The previous discussion makes it clear that Mrs. Thatcher's government deliberately sought to tie its hands through the Medium-Term Financial Strategy. In this sense it sought to eschew discretion in favor of policy rules. Nevertheless, it was willing to override the MTFS rules when the economy was under severe stress. For example, both the PSBR and the M3 targets were overshot in 1980–81. In the discussion over the Exchange Rate Mechanism (ERM) and the European Monetary Union (EMU) reviewed below, the government has emphasized the desire to control its own policy responses to events, and in this way maintain the potential for discretion, at least relative to the rules of these systems.

This combination of enthusiasm for rules and reluctance to abandon discretionary response may seem paradoxical. Yet it is not really surprising.

The idea of tying one's hands will in general not appeal to governments: they have been attracted to it solely by the evidence that failure to do so in monetary and fiscal policy, at least within certain bounds that rule out the accommodation of inflation, carries large costs. (Minford, 1989, suggests an order of magnitude for the United Kingdom.) Similar evidence is certainly not available for other instruments of policy, such as the exchange rate, tax rates, or public expenditure programs. The Kydland and Prescott (1977) time-inconsistency rationale for monetary and fiscal rules is, as Hillier and Malcomson (1984) have pointed out, something of a special case. It is removed if the natural rate of unemployment is undistorted, and therefore it is also the social/government objective.

Monetary Policy Prior to Margaret Thatcher

Margaret Thatcher was in power from 1979 to 1990 and has conditioned the modern policy debate in Britain to such an extent that even if a Labour government gains power, it is likely to pursue monetary policies in the same mold. Even on the issue of the ERM, there would only be a difference of emphasis, Labour being willing to enter the system and play by its present rules, but not to move any further toward EMU. The main difference with Labour would be quantitative: it would undoubtedly borrow more and be compelled to print more money by its large ambitions for public spending.

Nevertheless, the monetarist policies pursued by Mrs. Thatcher had their antecedents in those pursued by the Labour chancellor, Denis Healey, from 1976 to 1979. It is also important to understand the evolution of monetary thinking in the postwar period because Thatcher's program was not merely a piece of modern conservative theorizing, but was far more a reaction against the overt practical failures of premonetarist policy. In fact, there is not a great deal to say about premonetarist policy, since basically it consisted in an absence of monetary policy. The postwar policy framework until the advent of floating in 1972 was Bretton Woods. Under fixed rates the money supply adjusts to demand via the balance of payments.

In the immediate postwar period with limited convertibility and tight exchange controls, the adjustment was slow and allowed substantial short-run monetary independence. Nevertheless, the British government gave monetary policy a limited role, using fiscal policy and occasional devaluation as its principal instruments for controlling demand and the balance of payments. This subordinacy of monetary policy was given the academic imprimatur of the Radcliffe Committee in 1959 (Radcliffe Report, 1959). It and its principal author, Professor R. S. Sayers of the London School of Economics, argued that money could not be usefully defined because of the many assets that closely substituted in providing "money services" and that instead "liquidity" should be controlled in a discretionary way by interest rates and credit restrictions. In practice, this meant that from time

Figure 12.13
Excess Money Supply Growth (money supply growth less GDP growth)

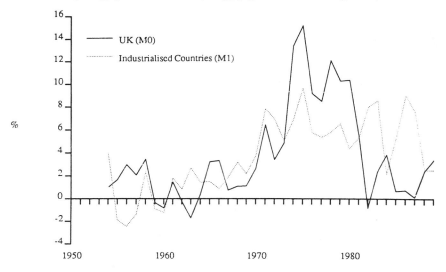

Sources: International Financial Statistics, IMF; Bank of England; CSO.

to time a credit squeeze (using both credit controls and higher interest rates) was implemented to help finance a current-account deficit or as an emergency means of slowing demand when fiscal policy was not working fast enough.

Unfortunately, such a hands-off approach to money creates problems when short-run monetary independence is as great as it was until the world capital market integration of the 1970s. Excessive money supply growth, even with the exchange rate fixed, will drive up domestic prices. The correction from falling reserves will occur only gradually, as the current balance goes into deficit with reduced competitiveness and capital flows respond little, if at all. At this time Britain had a large, though declining, share in many overseas markets for manufactured goods, so that the response to higher prices was slow in coming.

Eventually, the economy is forced either to reverse policies ("stop-go") in an attempt to force relative prices back down or to devalue, validating the previous price shift. There was an enormous devaluation in 1949 (30 percent), and it was probably not eroded until the mid–1960s. During most of this period, 1949–67, the growth of the money supply was excessive (Figure 12.13) and prices rose faster than those of competitors (Figure 12.14). By 1967, when the cumulative price shift had pushed the current account into permanent deficit at normal employment levels, the case for another devaluation appeared overwhelming (Figure 12.15 shows how the

Figure 12.14
Inflation of the United Kingdom and Industrialized Countries

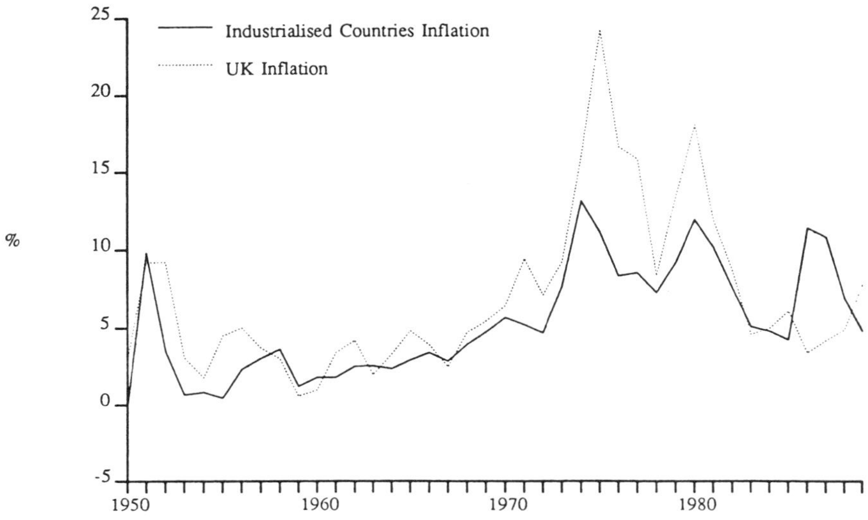

Source: International Financial Statistics, IMF; CSO.

real exchange rate had risen), given the difficulty of driving wages and prices down.

The devaluation of 1967 marked a change in attitudes toward money. The stabilization of sterling with the help of the IMF shifted the emphasis on the control of Domestic Credit Expansion (DCE). DCE is the analogue of money supply control when the exchange rate is fixed: the change in the money supply equals DCE plus the change in foreign reserves, by the banking system's balance sheet identity. At this time, the money supply was defined to include all the commercial banks' deposits, or M3. Using the monetary approach to the balance of payments, some analysts argued that if DCE was controlled to what was dictated by a stable demand for money, the change in reserves (the total balance of payments) would be controlled by implication.

This was probably the first time during the postwar period that the British government took monetary factors seriously. It was not, of course, monetarism, being merely a formalized monetary prop to the fixed exchange rate. But it created an effective control on the domestic creation of money, and it was backed up by the most stringent fiscal policy since the war. By 1970 the budget deficit had been eliminated, DCE growth had been cut back to below 5 percent, and the balance of payments was in substantial surplus (Figure 12.16).

Figure 12.15
Real Exchange Rate (1980 = 0.00)

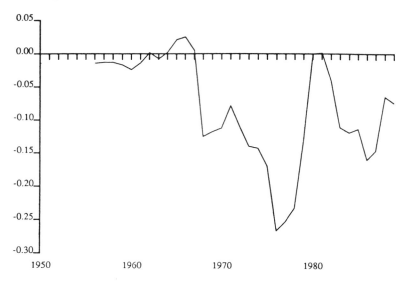

If these attitudes had persisted, the United Kingdom would have gone over to monetarist control when the world went onto floating rates in the early 1970s. However, the monetary approach went only skin deep in government circles. For a long time there had been a belief in incomes policies as the way to control inflation. These policies had been used intermittently from 1960. When the IMF's DCE approach was adopted, it was combined with a tough incomes policy from 1968—the "belt and braces" combination.

Once the balance-of-payments position was under control and the IMF had returned to Washington, the government returned to its incomes policy approach. In 1971 the prime minister, Edward Heath, who had campaigned on a free-market platform, abandoned it in the face of rising unemployment and inflationary pressure to pursue, on the one hand, a highly expansionary Keynesian policy of rising budget deficits, falling interest rates, and a depreciating pound (Britain floated formally in the spring of 1972) and, on the other hand, a highly restrictive incomes policy. The absence of monetary control ensured that the incomes policy broke down by 1974 (with the miners' strike in the aftermath of the oil crisis) and that inflation surged in 1974–75 to rates of 25 percent and up to 50 percent annualized. Such rates were unheard of in the United Kingdom, which had never experienced the hyperinflation of the continent.

As policy veered around into fiscal contraction and credit squeeze, as

Figure 12.16
Domestic Credit Expansion

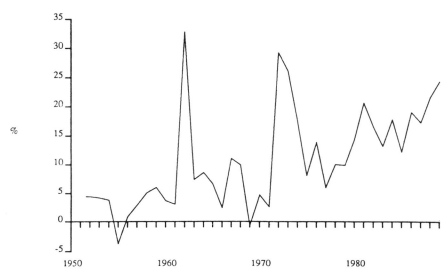

Source: International Financial Statistics, IMF.

well as further incomes restraint, the popular mood was ripe for monetarism. Inflation was the major concern, and as it failed to be reduced in
any permanent way over the succeeding years to 1979, especially after the
breakdown of yet another incomes policy in 1978 in the "winter of discontent," people were ready to try a totally different counterinflationary
policy.

In 1976 the Labour chancellor, Denis Healey, did adopt monetary targets, again under pressure from the IMF, which was called in to help
stabilize the balance of payments. However, again the main burden of
policy was placed on incomes restraint, as the braces, with the monetary
control belt being mainly cosmetic. Indeed, control was achieved mainly
through a tax on the banks' interest-earning deposits, the "corset" that did
no more than divert such deposits into nonbank intermediaries acting in
close competition. Samuel Brittan of the *Financial Times* dubbed this "un-
believing monetarism" (Brittan, 1977, p. 89).

By 1979, the whole framework was unraveling and inflation was rising
to 13 percent; it would ultimately reach 18 percent, with 23 percent wage
settlements before it peaked. The public was eager to try Margaret Thatcher's monetarist experiment.

FUTURE DIRECTIONS: MONETARY POLICY EVOLUTION WITHIN THE EXCHANGE RATE MECHANISM OF EMS?

We have argued that British monetary policy in its efforts to bring inflation under control has taken a form adapted to the institutions and political economy of Britain. It has emphasized the fiscal support needed, has put M0 in the role of key indicator with the exchange rate in a supplementary role, and has used a traditional indicator intervention system. The policy evolved out of the experience of the 1979–82 inflation battle.

We have also argued that immediacy or cold turkey would have given better results, especially for unemployment, than the combination of announced gradualism and near-immediacy in practice.

What lies ahead? The case for Britain joining the Exchange Rate Mechanism of the EMS was urged on the continent and by those in Britain anxious for faster progress toward monetary and political union. It was resisted until 1990 on the grounds that "the time was not ripe," although in principle the case for joining eventually was not questioned. An attempt to delineate the precise conditions of ripeness was made at the Madrid Summit in the autumn of 1989. These conditions were that EC exchange controls should be abolished, that the 1992 program of liberalization should be operative for capital markets, and that the United Kingdom's inflation rate should be close to the German rate. On the face of it, these conditions ruled out any early entry of the United Kingdom into the ERM, but by August 1990 there were strong rumors that for political reasons (the divisiveness of the issue both within the Tory party and the EC) Mrs. Thatcher would soon be willing to treat them as met in the near future and join on wide margins, thus preserving some of the flexibility of floating.

Even though the United Kingdom joined the ERM, it has remained strongly opposed to a rigid link with the DM and to the EMU as proposed by the Delors Committee (Delors, 1989). This is the position of both the Tory and Labour parties. Since the ERM is evolving rapidly toward a fixed-link system with close monetary collaboration, the United Kingdom's opposition will continue to be a bone of contention within the EC.

Hughes-Hallett, Minford, and Rastogi (1990) have evaluated the various design possibilities for the ERM and have concluded that such an evolution was necessary to avoid the severe potential instability implied by adjustable parity systems. As such, the ERM is similar to the later stages of Bretton Woods and is liable to repeated currency crises. To be controllable, monetary policy must veer sharply as a crisis occurs, and probably exchange controls must be in place when currencies are devaluing. Furthermore, the intervals between devaluation produce overvaluation for these currencies. In the face of repeated shocks, our work finds that these economic costs are high. By close monetary cooperation, however, implying the need to change parities only rarely, the ERM can achieve reasonable stability. Hence, there has been rapid progress toward the Delors second stage in which there is virtually no resort to parity change; EMU, the third stage, is thereby brought closer.

The United Kingdom faces two sets of difficulties in joining this ERM system. The first are transitional. Even maintaining wide margins and national control over future parity change, the United Kingdom must reconcile appropriate domestic monetary control, as explained above, with the demands of the ERM. The resulting conflict, given initial inflation, can undermine the current monetary disinflation by putting downward pressure on interest rates (because uncovered interest parity reduces interest differentials when there is a short-term exchange-rate guarantee), while failing to increase long-term monetary credibility because of the lack of parity commitment. This point has been made forcefully by Alan Walters (1990), and it was exemplified by British experience in "shadowing the EMS" in early 1988 when interest rates fell precipitously to prevent the appreciation of sterling. Coming soon after the loosening of money, in reaction to the October 1987 share price crash, this led to a serious resurgence of inflation. This resurgence can therefore be directly ascribed to a temporary lapse in the pursuit of the monetarist approach.

The Walters Critique has been widely accepted among European economists following the experiences of both Spain and Italy. Its force can be limited by accepting greater rigidity in the ERM; both countries have moved in this direction, in keeping with the general trend of the ERM's evolution.

For the United Kingdom, however, such a move raises the second set of difficulties: that a rigid, cooperative ERM leading quickly to EMU is incompatible with the United Kingdom's monetary sovereignty, an all-party requirement. This requirement stems mainly from a political desire for control over the monetary instrument and associated instruments of policy whose operation might be limited by outside monetary control. The surrender of monetary sovereignty usually accompanies the formation of a new state embracing the currency union, as, for example, with German reunification. The reason is that a state giving up the power over its currency is compensated within a unitary state by transfers. However, the United Kingdom totally rejects the idea of a unitary European state on political grounds.

Economically, a strong case can be made against a uniform currency. The attractions of a common currency are obvious enough. It permits the elimination of foreign exchange costs, including those of dealing with exchange-rate uncertainties (e.g., by covering forward) whatever these costs may be (and we have no good estimates). The disadvantages are also well understood. It takes away the power to use independent monetary and exchange-rate policy: this power both yields seigniorage (including potentially large indirect seigniorage on long-maturity public debt) and may be useful for economic adjustment.

Such adjustment could be crucial for the United Kingdom's economy, because its average productivity level is well below that of its continental neighbors. Moreover, its general economic structure is quite different from that of the rest of Europe, as are its rate and direction of supply-side reform. In other words, sharp changes may be needed in the United Kingdom's real exchange rate in the 1990s, which would be more efficiently brought about by the global exchange-rate instrument than by the decentralized wage-price movement. In the new continental fashion for arrangements that deliver credibility in the absence of strong domestic leadership, a fashion inspired ironically by the decidedly noncontinental new classical economics, this old-fashioned power over the currency has been widely overlooked. Recently, Hughes-Hallett, Minford, and Rastogi, in extending their work referred to above (1990), have found that, for this very reason, EMU exhibits markedly less stability than floating in dealing with the typical postwar stochastic environment.

Finally, a surrender of independent monetary policy would inevitably involve constraints on other policies, including taxes and regulations. These are all matters of great concern to a British government pursuing a program of supply-side reform at odds with the prevailing corporatism of the continent. One way or another, the issue of monetary union is clearly destined to create considerable tension between the United Kingdom and at least some other EC members.

OTHER ISSUES

Indexation

Mrs. Thatcher's government was the first and only one, in both the United Kingdom and the major industrial countries, to issue indexed bonds. From a rational expectations viewpoint, it is not clear why their issue should make any difference to any real or nominal interest rates as it does not, for example, in Lucas's cash-in-advance sharecropping economy (Lucas, 1980). The reason is that it does not alter the expected present value of the government's future tax revenue or its distribution between ordinary and inflation tax. It merely adds an extra financial instrument and does not change the distributions of economic outcomes.

Of course, it does enable the government to borrow at a real instead of a nominal interest rate, but each rate reflects the risks on that particular instrument. Why should the government regard issuing this instrument as beneficial now when it did not in the preceding centuries?

Some commentators argue that their issue would reduce one obstacle to counterinflation policy: the windfall gain to holders of long-dated nominal government bonds as inflation, and so interest rates would come down. This gain is made at the expense of taxpayers, and because taxes are distortionary, it is preferable to bring them down rather than hand out this gain to bondholders. According to this argument, a complete replacement of nominal bonds by indexed bonds would be desirable for a government contemplating anti-inflationary monetary policy.

The flaw in this argument is obvious. If a government issues indexed bonds with the intention of curbing inflation less expensively, this intention will thereby be signaled to bondholders, even supposing it could have been kept secret without the issue. The result would be that the existing stock of nominal bonds being replaced would rise to a premium, reflecting the better real prospective returns on their nominal income stream. The bondholders would then reap at once the capital gain they would have reaped when the policy for reduced inflation would have otherwise been revealed. Similarly, the issue of indexed bonds would fail to eliminate the transfer to bondholders.

In the event, modest amounts of indexed bonds were issued in an experimental spirit. Apart from acting as a useful measuring rod for economists wanting to know the real rate of interest and encouraging private insurance and pension companies to offer indexed policies backed by indexed bonds, there is no evidence that they changed the behavior of the economy.

Deregulation and the Rise of the Cashless Economy

In the late 1980s there was a revival of concern about the rapid growth of credit and the broad money supply measures. This feeling has been reinforced by the sharp increase in the current-account deficit on the balance of payments and by other signs of overheating—tighter capacity, skilled labor shortages, and rapidly rising housing costs.

In a freely competitive banking and financial system, however, banks will drive the interest rate on their savings and current-account (sight) deposits up to the rate at which they can lend minus the cost of intermediation. (This cost is small in the United Kingdom, where there are virtually no formal reserve requirements.) Devices like forgoing bank charges on current accounts in credit are equivalent to paying interest on them. As competition between the High Street banks and building societies intensifies, they will probably largely give way to explicit interest payment.

Once interest is paid on these deposits, they cease to be money in a strict sense, and their demand is governed by their relative yield as discussed later in this chapter. But first consider currency. Because it pays no interest, it will only be held for carrying out transactions (such as small-scale purchases) that cannot be paid for by clearing arrangements like credit cards or checks. The advantage of these forms of payment is that one can buy goods without surrendering interest on one's assets until the settlement date. But currency has to be used for certain purchases and its demand is determinate.

As long as no interest rate is payable on current-account deposits, they are like currency; they are held only for transactions that require payment by check (rather than credit card, which ties up no investible funds) and with a determinate demand affected by interest rates and the volume of these transactions.

Compare people's attitudes to deposits with full interest payable. Now they will be indifferent between holding these and some other deposit, say, in a unit trust, or indeed holding a share claim on a company. All these assets are priced so that they yield an equivalent return to the holder, after allowing for their riskiness. They are a part of the greater market for savings. Their use in transactions (for "credit goods") will be paid for directly by the transactor (e.g., in the percentage commission charge for a Visa purchase or the item charge on a current account). The demand for any one of these assets is indeterminate in that there is an infinite number of asset-liability combinations in which the private sector can hold its savings. Each is as good as the other from its viewpoint, though implying a different level of "broad money" in the reshuffling of balance sheets.

The demand for any one of these assets is indeterminate, for there is an infinite number of asset-liability combinations in which the private sector can hold its savings. Each is as good as the other from its viewpoint, although a different level of "broad money" is implied in the reshuffling of balance sheets.

The structure of balance sheets is determined from the supply side by such things as the costs of different sorts of intermediation and the ability of different intermediaries to improve risk-return combinations faced by savers, because they can deal in economic quantities of stock, for example. The structure continues changing until no new intermediary opportunity is available. But the point is that all this reshuffling makes no difference to the overall return available in the market. Fama (1980 and 1983) discusses the behavior of such a world.

If as is surely the case, the "high street" banks are being driven by competition to make themselves more efficient, it is hardly surprising that they seek to expand their operations sharply, raising their interest rates to consumers and improving their loan services to firms. This shift in bank technology is just the sort of thing to cause an expansion on both sides of the balance sheet.

Therefore, financial competition implies that money changes its form, and in particular the only money left is currency. Hence, the government decided to target M0 in the MTFS and abandoned the wider measures, described briefly in an earlier section. With regard to the credit explosion school of though, it is clearly wide of the mark, using concepts appropriate to a financial environment that has passed away.

The question that arises is whether currency itself will not ultimately be displaced by interest-bearing means of payment. In answering this question, one is driven to the microfoundations of money demand; yet these are not helpful in telling us just which transactions will continue to be governed by cash-in-advance technology. It is presumably a matter of cost in interest foregone versus that of using computer technology (switch cards, etc.). Yet the cost of currency technology remains negligible for small transactions. It is crime-free, it requires no equipment, and it is costless to print. Only for large transactions do costs rise: because of physical transportation and the risk of robbery. This suggests that, provided inflation is low, currency will continue to dominate small transactions. If inflation became negative, as in Friedman's (1969) proposal for the optimum quantity of money, then the use of currency could even revive for larger transactions. Negative inflation is not, in fact, far-fetched: stability of measured prices implies falling prices after quality change.

Mechanisms of Control

Is there some new framework that could be set in place to institutionalize the experience set out here? In Britain, oral tradition has generally been preferred, as in any case a sovereign Parliament can always nullify any rule. But any future chancellor will inherit the framework of the MTFS: a balanced budget in normal times, and an M0 target range to be kept inside through interest-rate movements. This is a simple and ancient recipe, revived and adapted for our times, and it is a departure from the pure oral tradition. Even though it can be overthrown at any stage by ministers and Parliament, such an overthrow would bring a serious loss of prestige to Mrs. Thatcher's government, precisely because of the political capital invested in it. It seems doubtful that anything much more binding could be achieved by more formal commitments than now exist (such as the Gramm-Rudman-Hollings amendment on the budget in the United States).

Such commitments would apply strictly if Britain were outside the ERM. However, even within it, as argued above, there is no willingness to abandon in any essential way the independent use of monetary policy and exchange-rate adjustment. Therefore, the ERM British-style would not offer any constitutional override of parliamentary sovereignty.

There has also been discussion of a monetary base control system that would strengthen the commitment to monetary stability and avoid a repeat of recent ambiguities. This was considered in 1982 and rejected in the light of strong opposition from the Bank of England. As argued above, the issue of base control should not be central in a rational expectations world. The key element is to act regularly on interest rates to achieve a Medium-Term

Money Supply growth rate; short-run fluctuations within a narrow range are of little significance. In addition, shifting to a new mode of monetary policy execution is never convenient because the regime shift upsets for a significant period the usual monetary indicators. Bank reserve behavior in particular is likely to shift. The case for doing it anyway has appeared to weak to overcome such transitional difficulties.

One unusual feature of British monetary regulation has been the absence of reserve ratios; there is merely a requirement to hold 0.5 percent of eligible liabilities (essentially sterling deposits) on deposit with the Bank of England. There have also been recent calls for moving toward a system of reserve ratios. However, these have been resisted on the grounds that they merely act as distortionary taxes on the banking system and are unnecessary for the control of bank reserve holdings, which will be dictated by commercial prudence.

CONCLUSION

The 1980s have witnessed a prolonged experiment in monetarist policy for the control of inflation, after three decades culminating in high and persistent inflation in which monetary policy played at most a supporting role, whether to a fixed exchange rate, fiscal policy, or incomes and price controls. Out of that experiment has emerged a strategy for setting long-term targets for money (M0 has come to be seen as the only reliable indicator) backed up by PSBR targets: the implementation of monetary policy has been through interest-rate changes rather than through monetary base control, but, given rational expectations, this tactical issue is of little importance. The result of these policies was the reduction of inflation to around 5 percent from 1983 to 1987. The rise in inflation since 1987 reflects a loosening of monetary policy connected with the October 1987 crash and the shadowing of the EMS. Looking to the future, some argue that Britain should permanently abandon domestic monetarism in favor of the ERM/EMU link to the DM or a common European currency. The ERM is in any case evolving rapidly among an inner core of countries toward a type of EMU. Although this would deliver low inflation under certain EMU arrangements, it would also remove a key policy instrument from British hands, besides implying greater political union than is accepted in Britain. The alternative is to continue with current policies and a loose currency relationship with the EC (perhaps the ERM with wide bands and a crawling peg): the 1980s experience suggests that such policies can control inflation without interfering with a vigorous supply-side reform program.

REFERENCES

Bean, C.; Layard, R; and Nickell, S. 1987. "The Rise in Unemployment: A Multi-country Study." In *The Rise in Unemployment*, edited by Bean, Layard, and Nickell. London: Basil Blackwell, 1–22.

Brittan, S. 1977. *The Economic Consequences of Democracy*. London: Temple Smith.

Delors, J. 1989. "Delors Committee for the Study of Economic and Monetary Union, Report on Economic and Monetary Union in the European Community." Office for Official Publications of the EC, Luxembourg.

Fama, E. 1980. "Banking in the Theory of Finance." *Journal of Monetary Economics* 6: 39–57.

———. 1983. "Financial Intermediation and Price Level Control." *Journal of Monetary Economics* 12: 7–28.

Friedman, M. 1969. *The Optimum Quantity of Money and Other Essays*. Aldine.

———. 1980. "Memorandum on Monetary Policy." House of Commons Treasury and Civil Service Committee. *Memoranda on Monetary Policy*, HMSO, 55–68.

Goodhart, C.A.E. 1989. *Money, Information and Uncertainty*. 2d ed. New York: Macmillan, 493.

Hillier, B., and Malcomson, J. M. 1984. "Dynamic Inconsistency, Rational Expectations and Optimal Government Policy." *Econometrica* 52: 1437–51.

Hughes-Hallett, A.; Minford, P.; and Rastogi A. 1990. "The European Monetary System: Achievements and Survival." Working Paper No. 90/04. Department of Economics and Accounting, Liverpool University, forthcoming in Brookings volume on International Monetary Regimes.

Kydland, F. E., and Prescott, E. C. 1977. "Rules Rather Than Discretion: The Inconsistency of Optimal Plans." *Journal of Political Economy* 85: 473–91.

Lucas, R. 1980. "Equilibrium in a Pure Currency Economy." *Economic Enquiry* 18: 203–20.

Matthews, K., and Minford, P. 1987. "Mrs. Thatcher's Economic Policies, 1979–87." *Economic Policy* 5: 57–101.

Minford, P. 1989. "Ulysses and the Sirens: A Political Model of Credibility in an Open Economy." *Greek Economic Review* 11: 1–18.

———, and Rastogi, A. 1989. "A New Classical Policy Programme." In *Policymaking with Macroeconomic Models*, edited by A. Britton. London: Gower, 83–97.

Niehans, J. 1981. "The Appreciation of Sterling—Causes, Effects and Policies." ESRC Money Study Group Discussion Paper, ESRC, London.

Radcliffe Report. 1959. The Committee on the Working of the Monetary System: Report. Cmnd. 827. London: HMSO.

Sargent, T. 1986. "Stopping Moderate Inflations: The Methods of Poincare and Thatcher." Chap. 4 of *Rational Expectations and Inflation*. New York: Harper & Row. An earlier version appeared as "The Ends of Four Big Inflations," in *Inflation*, edited by R. E. Hall. Chicago: Chicago University Press, 1982.

———, and Wallace, N. 1981. "Some Unpleasant Monetarist Arithmetic." *Quarterly Review*, Federal Reserve Bank of Minneapolis (Fall): 1–17.

Walters, A. A. 1990. *Sterling in Danger: The Economic Consequences of Pegged Exchange Rates*. London: Collins (Fontana) with the Institute of Economic Affairs.

13

JAPAN

Shinichi Ichimura

This chapter deals with the evolution of the Japanese financial markets and the conduct of monetary policy in the postwar period. One of the central themes is that Japan has undergone a deep transformation in the last fifteen years, from a heavily regulated financial environment to one where market forces are increasingly important. In addition to deregulation, Japan has internationalized, thus adding additional competitive pressure to its domestic markets. Monetary policy has mirrored these broad developments. The Bank of Japan has come to influence money market interest rates rather than rely on the old quantitative restraints to achieve the desired value of the money supply. Price stability has the largest weight in the preference function of the authorities, although exchange-rate stability, external balance, and economic growth often come into play. The chapter is organized as follows. Section 1 discusses Japanese postwar economic development; section 2 describes the characteristics of the financial markets and its evolution; section 3 briefly reviews saving and investment patterns; and section 4 is devoted to the conduct and effectiveness of monetary policy.

1. POSTWAR DEVELOPMENTS

Five Stages of Postwar Japanese Economic Development

The most telling statistic of the rapid pace of Japanese economic development is the increase of per capita real GNP in terms of the current value of the yen/dollar exchange rate. The Japanese per capita real GNP in 1948 (in 1988 prices) converted by the current yen/dollars exchange rate was not much above $300, whereas that in 1988 was about $23,000; the average annual rate of growth over the forty years has been 11.3 percent. The exchange rate was 360 yen to the dollar until 1971, when it began to fall (i.e., the yen appreciated) down to today's level of 140. During the last seventeen years, the growth rate attributable to the yen appreciation was about 5.5 percent a year. Therefore, net of exchange-rate movements, we can say that the annual growth rate of Japanese per capita GNP was about 11 percent between 1948 and 1971 and 5.5 percent between 1972 and 1988. The last calculation is, however, bound to underestimate Japanese economic growth because the yen appreciation reflects productivity increase and improved terms of trade and, hence, a better standard of living.

The process of this rapid development may be understood more clearly by dividing the postwar period into six stages: occupation, 1945–52, reconstruction, 1952–60, rapid growth, 1960–70, shocks, 1970–80, internationalization, 1980–90, and the prospective period from 1990 to the year 2000, which will be called the political economy period. The fundamental conditions were very different from one period to another, and financial markets had to evolve in light of these changes.

The occupation period was essentially a continuation of the war, guided by the so-called three D's policies: demilitarization, democratization, and demonopolization. Nevertheless, the base for postwar recovery and reconstruction was laid during this period. The Fundamental Labor Law was passed to liberalize labor unions; a land reform was enacted; and so was an Anti-Monopoly Law to dissolve *Zaibatsu* and make the Japanese markets much more competitive than in the prewar era. Particularly with the outbreak of the Korean War, the Japanese people successfully struggled for survival with the generous help of foodstuffs provided by the United States and the policy guidance embedded in the Dodge Plan for fiscal and monetary policies.

During *the reconstruction period* the greatest concern of the Japanese nation was to regain the highest prewar standards of living and normal international relations. The *Jimmu* boom in 1957 brought Japanese businessmen the exciting dawn of the new postwar era,[1] and the admission of Japan into the United Nations made the Japanese people feel that they had ended their isolation and begun to be emancipated from the fetters of the occupation policies. There were two remaining issues on which the people and politicians were divided: the Japanese Constitution and the Mutual Security Agreement between the United States and Japan. This period ended in 1960 with the successful revision of the Mutual Security Agreement between the United States and Japan. This Security Agreement is still effective today.

The rapid growth period began with the Ikeda cabinet, which shifted the political emphasis on economic matters and concentrated on catching up with the West, particularly the United States. A political season was over, and an economic season had begun. A symbol of this era was the Ikeda Income Doubling Plan, which aimed at doubling national output in ten years. At the end of the decade, Japan's real GNP had actually quadrupled, putting the annual rate of real GNP at above 10 percent. In this decade the disputes between Japanese and U.S. industries began to emerge.

The 1970s may be characterized as *the shocks period*: the Nixon shocks—the yen revaluation, the soybean embargo, the U.S.-China rapprochement with no consultation with the Japanese government—and two oil shocks. These shocks gave the Japanese economy not only difficult problems but also great opportunities to gain a competitive edge in international trade. Japan was very successful in overcoming the oil price jump by introducing energy-saving technologies sooner than any other industrialized economies. In the 1970s the Japanese economy dramatically evolved from a capital-poor to a capital-abundant economy. Domestic savings exceeded domestic investments; exports began to exceed imports; and net capital flow began to move outward rather than inward. The dramatic change in the nature of Japanese financial markets took place in the mid-1970s.

The decade of the 1980s was *the internationalization period*. The word "internationalization" in Japanese became a key word, characterizing the period and offering a guideline in everything from economic to social and cultural. It was inevitable given the rising weight of the Japanese economy in the world. The outside pressure mounted especially from the United States when Japanese businessmen and politicians kept following old practices under the influence of past inertia and hesitated to change the Japanese system, including the financial system, to make it consistent with a globally important Japanese economy. The first requirement was trade liberalization; the next was capital movement liberalization; and the third was liberalization and deregulation of all kinds of restrictions bearing on domestic customs and the practices of Japanese business and government. The Japanese financial markets were no exceptions to the winds of change, as we will see later in this chapter.

The decade of the 1990s promises to be *the political economy period*, because in this decade Japan is likely to be asked to play not only an economic role but also a more active political role in the world. In turn, this is also likely to affect Japan's place in the field of international finance.

Four Types of Japanese Economic Policies

The success of Japan's postwar economic development undoubtedly owes much to the appropriate economic policies of Japanese government and good relations between government and business and between management and labor. The main features of postwar Japanese economic policies and the underlying philosophy need to be spelled out, because they are different from both the standard (American) Keynesian and the neoliberalist approach. The war-devastated economy needed not only demand management policies, but also policies aimed at reconstructing and developing new, promising industries. From the very beginning of the postwar era, the Japanese government was guided by supply-side economics, in a broader sense than the term would later be used in the Reagan administration. That is, *industrial policy* would supplement *macroeconomic policies*, although the macroeconomic policies also played a significant role in controlling the postwar inflation and regulating the aggregate demand.

Two other types of policies of the Japanese government have been important in shaping the development path of Japanese economy for almost half a century: *regional development policy* and *manpower and education policy*. These four types of policies were undertaken by different ministries, respectively, as shown in the accompanying table.

Types of Policy	Main Contents	Ministries in Charge
Macroeconomic policy	Fiscal and monetary policies	Ministry of Finance Economic Planning Agency Bank of Japan
Industrial policy	Promoting promising industries and protecting declining industries and small enterprises	Ministry of International Trade and Industry
Regional development policy	Policies for land-use and industrial location	National Land Agency Ministry of Construction
Manpower and education policy	Human development policies	Ministries of Labor, Welfare, and Education

Japanese economic policies have paid sufficient attention to changes in industrial composition, particularly the needs for promising export industries, but they were too slow in readjusting the institutions and regulations to be consistent with those of trading partners.

2. JAPANESE FINANCIAL STRUCTURE AND LIBERALIZATION PROGRAM

Financial Institutions

Figure 13.1 describes the Japanese financial system and its relative importance in the financial flow of funds. The structure is that which prevailed

Figure 13.1
The Japanese Financial System

Central Bank: .... Bank of Japan

Organizational structure:

Deposit Banks (Private Financial Intermediaries):
- (common b.) — City Banks
- (Commercial b.) — Foreign Exchange Bank / Regional Banks / Foreign Banks
- (Long-term b.) — Long-Term Credit Banks / Trust Banks
- Mutual Banks
- National Federation of Shinkin Banks
- Shinkin Banks*
- National Federation of Credit Cooperatives
- (financial inst. for small bus.) — Credit Cooperatives
- National Federation of Labor Credit Associations
- Labor Credit Associations
- The Head Bank for Commerce and Industry
- (agr.forestry & fishery finance funds) —
  - The Head Bank for Agriculture and Forestry
  - Credit Federations of Agricultural Cooperatives
  - Agricultural Cooperatives
  - Credit Federations of Fishery Cooperatives
  - Fishery Cooperatives

Private Financial Organizations (Nondeposit Banks):
- (insurance) —
  - Security Investment Credit Trust Co.
  - Life Insurance Co.
  - Damage Insurance Co.
  - Other Mutual Insurance Cooperatives (mutual agricultural cooperatives ass..etc.)
- (other) —
  - Housing Finance Co.
  - Consumers Credit Finance Corp.
  - Venture Capital Corp.
  - Securities Finance Corp.

Other Private Fin. Intermed.:
- Securities Co.
- Short-Term Capital Co.

Institution	No.	No. of branches [a]	capital	outstanding deposits & bonds	outstanding loans [b]	outstanding securities [c]
City Banks	13	3,059	12,091	1,282.185d	1,234.712d	221,017d
Foreign Exchange Bank / Regional Banks	64	6,907	6,885	907,333d	708.535d	194,058d
Foreign Banks	77	114	-	17,116	48.883	5,158
Long-Term Credit Banks	3	64	2,821	345,015	285.248	85,557
Trust Banks	7e	363	2,467	666,857f	370,726f	324,909f
Mutual Banks	69	4,279	1,900	375,486g	305.887k	60,363
National Federation of Shinkin Banks	1	17	200	57,573	17,546	28,700
Shinkin Banks*	456	7,090	2,679	501,844	365,419	83,300
National Federation of Credit Cooperatives	1	12	41	14,819	8,003	7,375
Credit Cooperatives	448	2,835	1,429	125,764	95,692	13,256
National Federation of Labor Credit Associations	1	1	150	11,123	559	8,702
Labor Credit Associations	47	600	531	49,082	25,244	11,670
The Head Bank for Commerce and Industry	1	95	1,913	89,611	80.307	12,802
The Head Bank for Agriculture and Forestry	1	38	450	187,374	97,261	92,391
Credit Federations of Agricultural Cooperatives	47	240	2,010	290,134	38,860	101,323
Agricultural Cooperatives	4,286	15,491	9,117	397,221	125,383	20,414
Credit Federations of Fishery Cooperatives	35	124	204	15,474	8,204	459
Fishery Cooperatives	1,753	2,125	1,456	15,528	10,896	289
Security Investment Credit Trust Co.	11	11	47	199,722h	242,123	160,775
Life Insurance Co.	23i	16,652	143	504,885i	24,009	52,781
Damage Insurance Co.	23k	3,896	3,081	102,422i	27,714	57,640
Other Mutual Insurance Cooperatives	481	48	422	101,986j	-	-
Housing Finance Co.	8	148	122	-	50,431	-
Consumers Credit Finance Corp.	na	na	na	-	265.159m	na
Venture Capital Corp.	3n	3	177	-	387o	-
Securities Finance Corp.	3	9	63	-	12,377	73
Securities Co.	212p	2,281	4,574	189,748	29.495q	3,840
Short-Term Capital Co.	6r	12	14	-	193.039s	186

Figure 13.1 (continued)

Public Financial Organizations

Category	Institution	(1)	(2)	(3)	(4)	(5)	(6)
(Postal System)	Postal Savings Special Accounts	1	23,654	-	987,467	4,728	†571,359
	Trust Funds Bureau	3				1,304,037	
	Postal Insurance & Annuity Funds						
	Industrial Investment Special Accounts						
(Banks)	Japan Development Bank	1	10	2,339	67,122†	76,092	240
	Japan Export Import Bank	1	2	9,673	46,618†	57,467	658
	Overseas Economic Cooperation Funds	1	1	16,092	18,055†	32,915	
(Public Corp.)	People's Finance Corporations	1	152	260	51,085†	51,124	1
	Small Business Finance Corp.	1	59	312	50,661†	53,862	333
	Small Business Credit Insurance Corp.	1	1			3,165	
	Environmental & Sanitation Business Finance Corp.	1	1	3,918	6,669†	6,582	229
	Agriculture, Fishery, & Forestry Finance Corp.	1	22	10	50,733†	51,466	1,189
	Housing Loan Corp.	1	14	1,682	244,610†	245,752	47
	Japan Finance Corp. for Municipal Enterprise	1	1	972	95,145†	93,540	1,283
	Hokkaido & Tohoku Development Corp.	1	1	124	8,354†	8,683	155
	Okinawa Development Corp.	1	4	330		7,764	86
	Government-related Finance Corp.	13	6	275	7,356†	81,122	

Source: BOJ, *Economic Statistics Annual,* quoted here from BOJ Institute for Financial Research, *Japan's Financial System* (1986), p. 234.

*"Shinkin" banks mean literally "credit chest" banks and are the local banks of size smaller than mutual banks.

[a] Includes the sum of head and branch offices but not overseas offices or shops for depository machines or subsidiary offices.

[b] Does not include call loans and purchased bills.

[c] Does not include commodity securities.

[d] The sum of banks' a/c.

[e] Does not include the foreign trust banks.

[f] The sum of trust banks' bank a/c and the trust a/c of all banks.

[g] Includes the annuity payments.

[h] Net amount of assets.

[i] Working assets.

[j] Does not include foreign life insurance companies.

[k] Does not include foreign damage insurance companies.

[l] The sum of national association of cooperation and 47 prefectural cooperatives.

[m] An estimate by Japan credit industry association for 1984.

[n] The data for Investment Promotion for Small Business Corp.

[o] Outstanding investment amount.

[p] Does not include the branches of foreign security companies in Japan and "saitori" companies.

[q] Loans for credit transactions.

[r] Does not include the intermediaries for loans in foreign currencies.

[s] The sum of call loans and purchased bills.

[t] The sum of borrowings and bonds including foreign bonds.

at the end of 1985 and provides the most elaborate stage before the liberalization process in recent years. Since 1985, however, some changes have taken place in the functions of various financial institutions indicated in the figure. In the financial system before 1985, many types of financial institutions had more specialized functions than they do now; that is,

1. commercial banks mainly for the short-term financing;
2. long-term credit banks mainly for helping develop manufactures;
3. a special foreign exchange and trade finance bank (the Bank of Tokyo);
4. banks for supporting small and medium-size enterprises;
5. banks for supporting agriculture, forestry, and fishery;
6. security companies dealing with bonds and stocks; and
7. government financial intermediaries for specific public purposes.

Among the above, one can distinguish *financial intermediaries* in the narrow sense and *financial organizations*, which consist of securities companies and short-term credit companies that are supposed to serve as intermediators between the final borrowers and primary purchasers of the primary securities. Financial intermediaries can be divided into deposit banks and nondeposit banks. Among deposit banks, common banks (city and regional banks) are the most important banks. They were created primarily as commercial banks for short-term banking, but in fact they issue two-year time deposits and extend medium- and long-term loans. Moreover, one bank (Daiwa Bank) has trust accounts. In essence, the common banks are more "mixed" banks than commercial banks in the strict sense. On the other hand, nondeposit banks, which specialize in the long-term side of the markets, are permitted to issue demand deposits and hence are part of the credit-creating mechanism.

As shown in Figure 13.1 and as is often pointed out, Japanese financial institutions are segmented or specialized by functions, namely,

1. separation of long-term and short-term finance;
2. separation of commercial banks and trust banks;
3. specialization in specific financing like that for small business;
4. separation of banking and security companies; and
5. government-related financial organizations playing significant roles

But such distinctions are by no means clear-cut. Particularly in recent years, the diversification of bank activities has significantly proceeded along with internationalization and computerization of financial activities, so that the distinctions mentioned above have now become blurred. For example, the distinction between common banks and mutual banks was abolished in 1990, and many banks that used to be called mutual banks are now simply called banks. Today almost all the banks (247 domestic banks plus 77 foreign banks at the end of March 1986) are permitted more or less to deal with foreign exchange and other international transactions. Computerization has proceeded so rapidly that a person can make deposits and withdrawals in any bank using the machines of any given bank in the system.

Moreover, nondeposit financial organizations and other private financial organizations are also extending their financial activities beyond the conventional barriers. They raise funds by devising new financial instruments, such as combining insurance policies and cumulative annuities or extending their loans to consumers by dealing with certificates of deposit or issuing their own credit cards with discount privileges. Another feature of the recent financial innovations is that some financial institutions are cooperating with one another in creating new financial instruments such as the combination of ordinary deposits and medium-term government bonds devised by security companies and credit organizations or the combination of time deposit and old-age insurance policies devised by banks and life insurance companies. Although there are still a number of restrictions on these new financial innovations, the need to reconsider the borderlines between banks and security companies is more pressing.

The role played by government-related financial intermediaries is very significant. The most important one is the postal savings system, which collects the deposits through the nationwide network of post offices. A small part of the deposits is used to extend loans, the largest part going to the Trust Funds Bureau of the Ministry of Finance, which also receives funds from the surplus of the National Annuities or Welfare Annuities Special Accounts. The Bureau grants loans mainly to government-related financial institutions, public enterprises, public establishments, or local governments.

Other government financial intermediaries include those that are completely owned by the government. They are established primarily to supplement the private financial intermediaries or, more to the point, to subsidize industrial activities specified by the policy objectives of the government. Often the enterprises are chosen as the objects according to the industrial policy in each stage of development.[2] Government-owned financial intermediaries were established specifically for long-term financing such as industrial development, export promotion, housing construction, support to small businesses, or overseas economic cooperation, but after 1975 they began competing with private financial institutions. In the late 1980s they held approximately a 30 percent share of total bank loans, compared to about 20 percent in the 1960s. Such an excessive presence of government-related financial intermediaries in the private sector has become controversial and seems to require reconsideration.

Regulated Financial Markets Before 1975

Japanese financial markets were strictly regulated before 1975, but since then, they have been gradually liberalized. The present financial markets in Japan are still in the transition phase, albeit at a regrettably low pace.

One type of regulation pertained to the rates of interest. Short-term (less than one year) money market rates (call market, bill market, Tokyo dollar call market) and the government and corporate bonds rates were market determined; rates on bank deposits, prime rates on loans, as well as the conditions for issuing the corporate bonds were regulated by laws and the negotiations between the authorities and the parties involved.

A second type of regulation had to do with foreign exchange controls. The first pieces of legislation in this area were the Prevention of Capital Flight Law in 1932 and the Foreign Exchange Control Law in 1933. After World War II, a Foreign Exchange and Trade Control Law was enacted (in 1949). After joining the International Monetary Fund in 1964, some foreign exchange controls were relaxed. Liberalization of domestic foreign direct investment began in 1966. However, a temporary strengthening of the restrictions occurred after the Nixon shocks. Additional liberalization has been achieved in recent years. The purpose of these restrictions was to segment domestic from overseas financial markets.

A third type of regulation is sometimes called principles of requiring collateral. The use of collateral has been legally required for the issuance of corporate bonds, bank loans, interbank call dealings, and impact loan dealings, a feature probably unique to Japan. The regulations were issued after some banks went bankrupt in the Great Depression of the 1930s.

Internationalization and Liberalization

As noted in Section 1, the Japanese economy evolved from a capital-poor to a capital-abundant economy in the 1970s and has become a leading world economy. The integration of the Japanese economy with the world has raised the welfare of both Japan and the rest of the world. It has become increasingly clear that expansion of world trade and increasing interdependence among major trading partners necessitated a global integration of financial markets as well as the goods' markets.

The internationalization of the Japanese financial markets has the following four aspects. First, there has been a rise in capital flows in and out of Japan. Tables 13.1 and 13.2 show a dramatic increase in Japanese overseas investment in the 1980s. Although nonresident investments in Japan have increased approximately 50 percent, Japanese overseas investments have increased fifteen times over the span of eight years.

Second, the rising international status of the yen is highlighted by the

Table 13.1
Japan's Long-Term Capital Account (million $)

	1988	1989
Direct Investment	34,210	44,130
Trade Credit	6,939	4,002
Loans	15,211	22,495
Securities	86,949	113,178
Other	6,574	8,313
Assets (A)	149,883	192,118
Direct Investment	- 485	- 1,054
Trade Credit	- 18	- 9
Loans	- 82	17,813
Securities	20,298	85,144
Other	- 760	978
Liabilities (B)	18,953	102,872
Balance (A - B)	130,930	89,246

Source: BOJ, *Balance of Payments Monthly*, April 1990.

relative importance of the dollar-yen markets in London, New York, and Tokyo in Table 13.3A. Table 13.3B underscores the internationalization of the Japanese stock market as well as its size in relation to those of the United States and the United Kingdom.

Third, Japanese banks have branches all over the world now. In 1970 they had only 56 branches, but in 1987 they had established 227 branches and 205 subsidiaries. If one counts offices, the number totals 837. Security companies are also extending their branches abroad; the number of branches at the end of 1987 was 166. Table 13.4 shows the asset holdings of banks from different countries. Since assets are stated in U.S. dollars that are U.S. domestic currencies and in light of the depreciation of this currency, the assets held by U.S. banks are understated. Nevertheless, it seems clear that Japanese banks are leading in international banking activities. It is not surprising that Japanese financial institutions are tapping foreign capital markets by issuing Eurobonds where the interest rates are relatively low and the procedures are relatively simple. Securitization and globalization of finance are progressing rapidly in Europe, and many kinds of hybrid commodities and services are being developed; Japanese banks and enterprises are clearly trying to establish a presence in these markets.

Table 13.2
Net External Assets or Liabilities (billion $)

	1980	1985	1987	1989
Japan	11.5	129.8	240.7	293.2
the United States	106.3	-110.7	-368.2	-663.7
West Germany	33.1	51.5	167.6	206.2*
United Kingdom	40.6	116.0	167.5	180.6
France		-1.7	29.3	-65.3
Italy		-8.7	-10.8	-12.2*

Source: BOJ, *International Comparative Financial Statistics Annals.*

Note: Methods to estimate foreign direct investment are not the same for all the countries, so that strict international comparison is not possible. But Japanese net assets must be number 1 after 1988.

*German and Italian figures in 1989 are those in 1988.

Finally, the rising importance of the yen as an international currency (see Table 13.5) can be gleaned from the fact that the share of Euro-yen deposits in the Euro-deposit market rose from 1.8 percent in the early 1980s to 5.5 percent in 1989 (Tavlas, 1991, p. 32).

Internationalization gave rise to liberalization and deregulation in the mid-1970s. First, in 1974 interest rates on bank deposits were deregulated and certificates of deposit (CDs) were introduced. Flexible-rate deposits (MMC) appeared in 1985. Interest rates on time deposits were gradually liberalized. A remaining problem is liberalization of interest rates on small deposits. Postal savings accounts have not yet been touched by the liberalization process. Since they are an important source of government funds for public investment and loans, the government—the Ministry of Postal Communications—will not easily give up the monopoly practice of fixing the rates.

Second, the specialization nature of financial institutions has become blurred and less relevant as deregulations and liberalization proceeded. Revision of Bank Law and Security Dealing Law in 1976 opened the way to admit the banks to deal with government bonds, and by 1984 all kinds of government bonds could be purchased at major banks. Banks soon began to package a new instrument combining government bonds and time deposits promising a higher rate of return than small time deposits. For their part, security companies joined forces with credit corporations and responded to the challenge with a new product: namely, medium-term government bond funds were tied to ordinary deposits, making bonds very liquid. In 1984 security companies were permitted to give loans with the

Table 13.3A
Major Markets of Foreign Exchange (percent)

	London	New York	Tokyo
$ /¥	14	23	82
DM/$	28	34	8
L /$	30	19	-
SF/$	9	10	-
Other	10	14	10
Total (bill.$)	90.0	50.0	48.0

Table 13.3B
Market Size of the World Stock Exchanges, 1988

		Tokyo	New York	UK
No. of	Domestic	1,576	2,152	1,989
Listed stocks	Foreign	112	82	732
Issues bonds	Domestic	1,197	2,893	2,491
	Foreign	174	213	1,933
Total Market Value ($ billion)	stocks	3,789.0	2,457.5	711.5
	bonds	1,135.8	1,561.0	558.4
Trading Value ($ billion)	stocks	2,234.2	1,356.1	361.0
	bonds	699.7	7.7	525.1
No of Member Firms		114	555	389[a]

Source: Tokyo Stock Exchange.
Note: March 31, 1989.

Table 13.4
Assets of Financial Intermediaries, 1987–end

	million $	(%)
Japan	1,552.1	(35.4)
the United States	647.6	(14.8)
West Germany	347.9	(7.9)
United Kingdom	253.9	(5.8)
Switzerland	196.1	(4.5)
France	375.5	(8.6)
Italy	185.0	(4.2)
other	823.2	(18.8)
Total	4,381.3	(100.0)

Source: BIS, *International Banking Statistics.*

Table 13.5
Foreign Currencies in Official Reserves (percent)

	1975	1980	1987
Japanese Yen	0.5	4.3	7.0
US Dollars	79.4	68.6	67.1
D-Mark	6.3	14.9	14.7
Swiss Francs	1.6	3.2	1.6
UK Pound	3.9	2.9	2.6
French Francs	1.2	1.7	1.2
Others	7.1	4.4	5.8

Source: IMF, *Annual Report.*

Note: The figures in 1975 and later years are not strictly comparable.

government bonds as collateral. The separation of trust banks from commercial banks is also under challenge by banks that want to enter the promising field of annuities. These pressures are getting stronger because of the opportunities available through the overseas markets.

Third, deregulation of foreign exchange control began to be considered when the shift to flexible exchange rates increased the pressure to free international capital transactions. The revision of the Foreign Exchange

Law in 1980 made it virtually free to deal with capital in the international markets. The U.S.-Japan Yen-Dollar Committee Report of 1984 announced a wide range of liberalizations in the field of capital flows, including dealings in the Euro-yen markets. In 1984 the restrictions on the exchange of yen with foreign currencies were abolished, so that commercial banks were able to obtain long-term deposits through long-term foreign currency deposits.

Fourth, in 1984 restrictions on issuing bonds without collateral were relaxed, and in 1985 short-term credit corporations began acting as brokers of call money dealing without collateral. The liberalization of interest rates for large-size deposits opened the way to the liberalization of interest rates for interbank time deposits and interbank transactions without collateral. This has increased the risk and cost for safety in financial transactions and poses new challenges to Japanese financial institutions.

The internationalization and liberalization of Japanese financial markets certainly have modified the behavior of Japanese households, firms, banks, and other financial organizations and changed the way monetary policy transmits its impulses to the economy. It therefore behooves us to look briefly at the structure of the Japanese loanable funds before getting into a discussion of monetary policy.

3. SAVING, INVESTMENT, AND FINANCIAL INTERMEDIATION

Savings and Investment Balance

Savings and investment, as well as the excess or shortage of flow of loanable funds, have undergone a dramatic shift in the 1970s. This can be seen from Figure 13.2, which shows the excess of investment over savings as a percentage of nominal GNP of the corporate sector, the "individual" sector, the public sector, the financial sector, and the foreign sector. It may be noted here that in financial statistics the "individual" sector includes mainly households but also individual proprietors.

The individual sector has always been the surplus sector with about 10 percent of GNP. Households' savings ratios have ranged from 16 to 19 percent of GNP, but about 6 to 9 percent has gone for the purchase of housing and other household investments. *The corporation sector* shows a dramatic change in the use of capital around 1974. Throughout the rapid growth period the excess of investment over saving amounted to about 7 percent of GNP, but after the oil shocks the propensity to invest fell sharply. Indeed, in 1978 the saving deficit was almost nil. Soon, however, it recovered somewhat but not to the levels reached previously. *The public sector*, on the other hand, showed a very small deficit up to 1974; thereafter it jumped to reach about 7 percent of GNP, where it has stabilized. Only

Figure 13.2
Sectoral Excess or Shortage of Funds (percent of GNP)

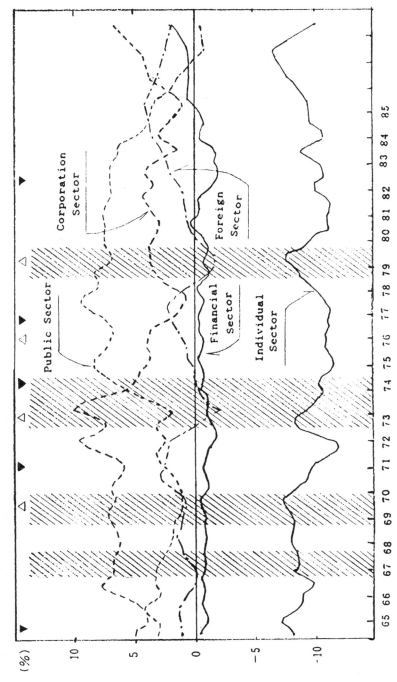

Table 13.6
Financial Assets by Three Economic Sectors (billion ¥)

	65-69	70-74	75-79	80-84
Corporations S.	2,629	7,018	8,003	13,303
Individuals S.	6,434	16,880	30,532	39,768
Public Sector	927	2,367	5,371	4,867
Currency	2,101	5,798	6,170	3,672
- Demand Deposit	1,675	4,722	5,033	2,800
Time Deposit*	4,631	11,768	20,838	25,253
- postal sav.a/c	817	2,623	6,496	8,425
Trust Funds	550	1,315	2,588	3,996
Insurance	940	2,235	4,353	7,831
Securities	808	2,491	5,521	8,161
- bonds	586	1,355	3,847	5,099
Credit abroad	199	652	703	3,322
Total	9,989	26,265	43,905	57,937

Source: BOJ, *Flow of Funds Accounts*; EPA, *National Income Accounts*.

Notes: ‡ Time deposit includes CD and postal savings accounts.

in very recent years after 1985 has it begun to show some decline. *The foreign sector*'s saving deficit is the reverse side of the Japanese current-account balance. With the exceptions of 1973–74 and 1977–78, Japan has been exporting net capital abroad; hence, this sector has been a saving deficit of about 3 percent of GNP or more since 1983.

Table 13.6 reports the financial assets of the corporate, individual (mainly household), and public sectors. The total amount increased very rapidly from 10 trillion yen in the early 1960s to 32 trillion yen in 1972 and 67 trillion yen in 1984 and 163 trillion yen in 1989. This demonstrates an enormous increase in financial transactions, partly reflecting the inflation in asset values. As to the composition of financial assets, nearly half has been in time deposits but shifting from the banks' time deposits to postal savings accounts. A significant change has taken place in the reduction of cash and demand deposits from 16–18 percent to 6 percent and in the increase of insurance, trust, and securities as well as investment abroad. This is one of the effects of having liberalized rates of interest. Assests with higher returns have been the beneficiary of this process.

During the 1960s there had been a predominance of indirect finance: that is, financing through banks and trust funds rather than investment in bonds and stocks; heavy reliance on bank borrowing instead of rasing capital from

Table 13.7
Transition of Government Bonds Issued (trillion ¥)

	1970	1975	1980	1985	1989
stock of gov. bonds	2.8	15.0	70.5	134.4	160.9
as percent of GNP	3.7	9.8	28.8	42.0	39.6
budget dependence on bonds	4.2	25.3	32.6	23.4	10.7

Source: BOJ, *Economic Statistics Annual, 1990.*

Note: Budget dependence is a percentage of the amount of bonds issued to the general account budget in each year.

the security markets; and a propensity of the banking system to extend loans in excess of bank deposits by borrowing from the Bank of Japan. These characteristics were the outcome of the underdevelopment of the long-term banks and the implication of the low-interest rate policy that required rationing of the available loanable funds through the "window guidance" of the Bank of Japan. In the 1970s the major borrower in the financial markets was no longer the corporate sector but the government. The government issued enormous amounts of government bonds, as can be seen from Table 13.7.

The increase in government bonds, in turn, opened up opportunities for open market operations which were not possible before. In the mid-1970s individuals began being very active in government securities markets. The individual sector's holdings of government bonds in 1965 were only 70.5 billion yen; in 1975 they became 910.8 billion yen; in 1985 they jumped to 6.4 trillion yen; and in 1989 to 10.7 trillion yen. As mentioned earlier, this was an innovation that market participants became much more conscious of the rates of return on various financial assets.

4. MONETARY POLICY IN AN ENVIRONMENT OF RAPID ECONOMIC GROWTH

Objectives and Instruments

The objectives of monetary policies have long been recognized as attaining price stability, economic growth or employment, an adequate balance of payments, and exchange-rate stability. Until 1968 there was a consensus in Japan that the primary objective of monetary policies had to be price stability. Price stability was considered a precondition for other objectives as well. But in 1969, with an external surplus and a positive inflation trend, a serious tradeoff problem emerged among the policy objectives for the first time. The Bank of Japan chose price stability as the primary objective and tightened the money supply. As a result, economic growth slowed down, the external surplus grew further, and the yen was revalued. During the regime of flexible exchange rates, the Bank of Japan (BOJ) has emphasized price and exchange-rate stability over other objectives (Batten et al., 1990, p. 16).

The BOJ relies on a variety of policy instruments: instruments that affect bank lending, open market operations, reserve requirement ratios, and "window guidance" or moral suasion. Bank lending instruments include the official rate of discount, the unofficial rate of discount,[3] loan attitudes, and ceilings on bank lending. The last instrument manifests itself in the fact that the official discount rate is below money market rates like the call and bill discount rates. Open market operations consist of transactions in bonds and bills. The reserve requirement applies to commercial banks, long-term banks, and foreign exchange bank and credit corporations whose deposits exceed 20 billion yen. The reserve requirement ratio is higher for demand deposits (2.5 percent) than time deposits (1.75 percent). Reserve deposits with the BOJ pay no interest. Through *window guidance*—also named regulation on the increase in loans or position guidance—the BOJ exercises discretion on the size of the banks' bank credit, in a way that is reminiscent of the Banque de France's old technique of the *encadrement du crédit*. The degree of this discretion changes in relation to how tight monetary policy is at the moment. As the liberalization of Japanese financial markets proceeds, the effectiveness of this practice will decrease in favor of other more market-oriented instruments.

Intermediate Targets and Operating Procedures

The BOJ, like other central banks, has an operating procedure that implements a specific monetary policy strategy and relies on intermediate targets to verify the degree of tightness of monetary policy. The use of an intermediate target is justified by the fact that monetary policy actions take time before their effects are felt on final objectives.

Traditionally, the BOJ paid attention to so-called market conditions and more recently to monetary aggregates. Until the 1960s the BOJ took as the intermediate target variables the interbank market rates like the *call rate* or the *bill discount rate*, which was the only free rate, and the annual increase of loans from city banks. The loan increase was an effective leading indicator of excess-borrowing and excess-loan[4] conditions discussed above. During the 1970s the money supply (M2 and M2 + CD later) became the preferred intermediate variable.[5] Indeed, the BOJ began to announce the quarterly forecast of the growth of the monetary aggregates over the value one year earlier and has had a great deal of success in hitting these forecasts. This fact confirms that the Bank used the monetary aggregate as an intermediate target.

There are several reasons for the shift in intermediate targets. First, interpreting a rise in interest rates as an indicator of money tightness is problematic when several factors contribute to the rise, such as an oil crisis, inflation, a business boom, and prevailing optimism. Second, increases of more than 30 percent a year for both M1 and M2 in the 1971–72 period created a situation of excessive liquidity that subsequently led to the abnormal double-digit inflation of 1973–75. Finally, the banks' purchase of a large sum of government bonds increased the supply of money that was kept in the deposit money holdings in the Corporations Sector and offered the cushion to the loanable funds available in the markets. For these reasons the BOJ decided to shift its target variables.

The BOJ, like other central banks, relies on money market interest rates to achieve its intermediate target. The Bank influences the interbank rate by regulating the supply of bank reserves through its discount window and open market operations. The BOJ always monitors the average amount of each bank's required deposits with the BOJ from the sixteenth day of the month to the fifteenth day of the next month. The calculation is known as the reserve progress ratio, defined as the ratio of the reserve deposits accumulated up to a given moment to the total required reserves of the month before. The BOJ adjusts this ratio as a signal mechanism of where policy is to be directed. If banks fall short of this ratio, they must raise funds, often through the interbank market. The call market rate of interest, therefore, fluctuates, reflecting such market conditions (Batten et al., 1990, p. 18).

The interbank rate of interest influences the supply of money through three channels: effects on banks' and households' portfolio, financial disintermediations, and effects on investment expenditure. The loan rates have always been unregulated, but they have remained relatively stable and low because the restrictions on deposit rates kept the cost of loanable funds low. Prime loan rates change when the official discount rate changes. Banks tend to please established customers and, hence, are unwilling to alter the loan rates suddenly. Thus, when the interbank rates go up, bank loans are curtailed and instead funds are supplied in the call or return call money market. The consequence is a reduction in bank credit and money supply. The deposit rates, as we have seen, have ceilings set by the government. So, when interbank rates go up, households shift into higher yielding assets; consequently there is a reduction of bank credit and money supply. Finally, the rise in the interbank rates sooner or later affects other interest rates and the demand for investment. This adverse effect on economic activity will have a negative feedback on bank credit and the money stock. The more flexible are the market rates of interest, the weaker is the first effect and the stronger are the second and the third effects. Thus, in recent years, the BOJ has more effectively exercised its control of the money supply through its influence on the interbank rates of interest.

Success and Failure of Japanese Monetary Policies

The use of the money supply (M2 + CD) as the main variable for intermediate targets after 1975 has been remarkably successful in helping Japan achieve the objectives of monetary policies, as shown in Figure 13.3. This is all the more surprising because, since 1975, the Japanese economy has stabilized the exchange rate and confronted the worldwide inflation and recessions consequent on the oil crises. On the other hand, price stability should not be measured only in terms of changes in the Consumer Price Index; asset prices, particularly those of land and houses, jumped in the 1980s. The same is true for Japanese stock prices. The GNP deflator used in the figure above excludes, of course, asset price inflation. In sum, if we take into consideration asset price inflation, the assessment of Japanese monetary policy is less sanguine than if we concentrate on the GNP deflator or the Consumer Price Index.

Financial Liberalization and Monetary Policies

Financial liberalization has been accompanied by an increase in government bonds and the emergence of new financial instruments. The first phenomenon has generated a lot of worries about the possible inflation consequences. Many authorities, including the BOJ, published the pessimistic assessment that deficit financing by government bonds would have increased the interest payments and thereby the probability of more deficit financing in the future, created the shortage of loanable funds for the private sector and the inflationary excess demands in the financial markets, transferred the burden of debt to the future generations, and reduced the strict discipline to balance budgets among policymakers.

It is well known that whether deficit financing raises the inflation trend depends on the way it is financed, that is, on the BOJ's monetary policy. When the Japanese government issued the large amount of bonds in the mid-1970s, they were purchased mainly by the financial intermediaries. Nevertheless, the ratio of the money stock to GNP actually fell, an outcome attributable to the BOJ's deliberate policy not to increase the monetary base (defined as currency *plus* reserve deposits with BOJ). Squeezed in their reserve positions, private banks and other financial institutions sold government bonds and restrained loans to the private sector, in essence forcing a decline in bank credit. The critical element for the success of monetary policy was the liberalization of the sales of government bonds by city banks in April 1977, which made it easier for the BOJ to control

Figure 13.3
Money Supply and GNP

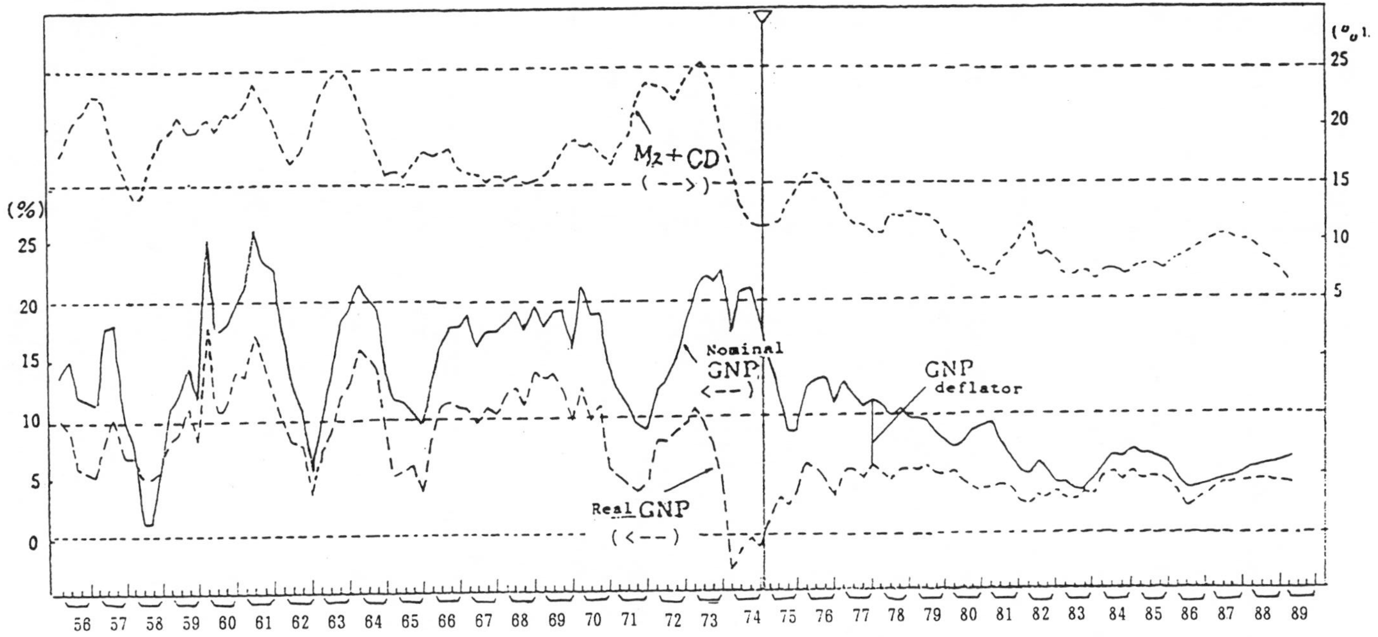

the supply of money without having to worry about the reserve position of private banks.

The second factor, financial innovation, has two aspects. One is that many devices were introduced to save the need for cash and demand deposits, such as cash machines, automatic teller machines (ATMs), and ordinary deposit accounts combined with time deposit accounts. Another aspect is the creation of new financial instruments bearing yields—CDs, MMCs, medium-term government bonds funds, government bonds-time deposit funds, and so on—and giving rise to financial disintermediation.

Effectiveness of Monetary Policy in a Liberal Environment

The effects of liberalization in introducing new financial commodities may go beyond those mentioned above. In the longer run, M1 is likely to lose importance relative to M2 or M3 because of portfolio selection considerations. Furthermore, the broader monetary aggregates may track better than the narrower aggregate business indicators like GNP. Money and near-money may become less elastic with respect to the opportunity cost rate of interest, so that the monetary policy actions such as a change in the official rate of discount may have less impact on the money supply, though retaining the effects on the demand side. The stability of financial variables, such as the market rates of interest and the exchange rate, are regarded as crucial for the success of monetary policy even under liberalized financial markets.

Earlier in this section we mentioned three channels through which monetary policy exerts its influences on economic activity: banks' response, substitution effects, and households' response to changes in the market rates of interest. Market liberalization will lower the first two and raise the third. Both enterprises and households will behave more freely, seeking better ways of managing the financial assets and liabilities. Recent empirical studies of the behavior of Japanese financial institutions as well as business and households have shown that their expenditures for investment are rather elastic with respect to the real rate of interest. Thus, it seems more and more important to be able to find the effective means to influence the short-term interest rates other than the interbank rate in order to foster the development of the Treasury and federal bond markets and short-lived government securities.

Globalization of Financial Markets and Monetary Policy

Capital movements were almost completely liberalized by the revision of the Foreign Exchange Law of December 1980, and restrictions on foreign exchange transactions were abolished in June 1984. The free flow of capital has not affected the Japanese money supply in any significant way, unless the BOJ intervenes in the foreign exchange market. The same holds for Euro-yen transactions because they must be supported by reserves with the domestic banks. Since the payment of reserves always occurs in Japan, the accounts of Euro-yen banks can be controlled through the supply of the yen in Japan. Hence, the rate of interest in the domestic reserve money market closely determines the interest rates of Euro-yen deposits through arbitrage. Despite the difference in location, the relations between Euro-yen market rates and other financial markets like the Gensaki market (bond trading with repurchase agreement) or certificate of deposit rates do not seem to differ a great deal. But owing, among other factors, to the difference in the size of markets, the interest-rate differentials between Japanese and Euro-yen markets may become larger than among the domestic markets. To cope with this situation, one needs to develop the open market operations in the short-term government securities. In fact, the difference between the Gensaki rate and the Euro-yen rate narrowed considerably after 1979 and even more after 1984.

There are, however, a number of problems especially related to the controllability of money supply. The first is associated with the difference in reserve requirements between Euro-yen deposits and domestic deposits. In Japan the reserve ratio for Euro-yen deposits is 0.25 percent, whereas that on domestic deposits (time deposits and certificates of deposit exceeding 3.3 trillion yen) is 1.625 percent. Under these conditions, the shift of deposits from domestic to Euro-yen accounts liberates reserves at home. Banks in Japan are likely to extend more loans on this basis, and the supply of money in terms of yen combining both domestic banks and banks abroad will rise. To avoid this kind of arbitrary creation of money supply, the same percentage requirement of reserve both at home and abroad is necessary. The BOJ can easily resolve this problem by placing the same ratios as in the United States. At the moment Euro-yen balances by Japanese financial intermediaries are tightly controlled, and the amount does not seem to be very significant. Should private residents be allowed to make Euro-yen deposits, these would have to be included in the money stock definition that the BOJ would want to control.

An even more serious control problem arises when Eurobanks extend loans to Japanese businesses on the basis of Euro-yen deposits without holding reserves in Japan. In this case Euro-yen credit and deposits are created. To bring this supply under control requires that reserve ratios be imposed directly on deposits at Eurobanks and, consequently, international cooperation among the relevant governments.

The last problem stems from the fact that the Euro-yen or Eurodollar markets are less regulated than the Japanese financial markets. Many regulations in Japan could become ineffective if Japanese banks were to act more vigorously through their associated Eurobanks. The same would hold if international transactions with forward market dealings become more active at home. The lack of information about Japanese overseas banking activities will make it more difficult for the BOJ to formulate an adequate monetary policy. Hence, it will be increasingly important to monitor the international transactions of Japanese associated banks overseas as well as the international transactions of Japanese banks at home.

Flexible Rates and Monetary Policy

The promise that flexible exchange rates could facilitate the attainment of balance-of-payments equilibrium, while monetary policies could concentrate on the domestic price stability, has not materialized. Flexible exchange rates do not seem to quickly adjust to the level at which the basic balance of payments is obtained because of inelastic responses of exports and imports to the exchange-rate movements. The divergence of the exchange rate from the purchasing parity rate has persisted and has led to protectionism in many industrialized economies. Such a divergence may have been caused by the persistent differentials in real interest rates resulting from different policy mixes across countries. It may also have been influenced by the delayed and reduced effect of the exchange rate to recover the equilibrium of the balance of current payments. The liberalized capital transactions and increased degree of substitutability among various financial assets in any currency denomination must have decreased the need for quickly adjusting the trade gaps through trade or capital movement so as to cause an exchange-rate adjustment. The ordinary ranges of change in exchange rates alone among major currencies do not seem to have sufficient power to keep the current balance of payments among the major economies within reasonable limits. Hence, the BOJ, as well as central banks in major industrialized economies, cannot concentrate on domestic growth or full employment and price stability alone. It has to pay attention to the international financial conditions in which the maintenance of an adequate exchange rate is of a critical nature and can be realized only in close cooperation with G-5 partners in the world financial markets.

NOTES

1. Jimmu is the name of the first emperor in Japanese history; thus, the Jimmu boom meant that the boom was unprecedented.

2. The reserves of special postal insurance special accounts and postal annuities are not included in the funds of the Trust Funds Bureau but are treated in the same way as the government's *Investment and Loan Budget* (Zaisei Toyushi Keikaku).

3. The unofficial discount rate is the rate at which the loans of the Bank of Japan can be extended in emergency cases. This special rate, admitted in March 1981 to be different from the official discount rate, has not been utilized yet.

4. It is called "over-loan"—a Japanese-English expression coined by the Japanese.

5. This was also true in the United States and in Europe.

REFERENCES

Bank of Japan, Finance Research Institute. 1986. *Wagakuni-no Kinyu Seido* (Japan's Financial System). Tokyo: Bank of Japan Finance Research Institute.

Batten, Dallas; Blackwell, Michael; Kim, In-su; Nocera, Simon E.; and Ozeki, Yuzuru. 1990. "The Conduct of Monetary Policy in the Major Industrial Countries: Instruments and Operating Procedures." IMF Occasional Papers no. 70, July, IMF, Washington, D.C.

Elton, Edwin J., and Gruber, Martin J. 1990. *Japanese Capital Markets—Analysis and Characteristics of Equity, Debt, and Financial Futures Markets*. New York: Harper & Row.

Furukawa, Akira, ed. 1983. *Nihon-no Kinyushijo to Seisaku* (Japan's Financial Markets and Policies). Tokyo: Showado.

Horiuchi, Akiyoshi. 1980. *Nippon-no Kinyu Seisaku* (Japanese Financial Policy). Tokyo: Toyokeizai-shimpo.

Ichimura, Shinichi. 1988. *Nippon Keizai-no Sinro-wo Motomete* (Searching For Japanese Economy's Steerage). Tokyo: Sobunsha.

———. 1990. "The Role of Japan in Asia and Contributions of Private Enterprises." IIR Working Papers No. 4, Osaka International University.

Iwata, Kikuo, and Akiyoshi, Horiuchi. 1989. *Kinyu* (Finance), Tokyo: Toyokeizai-shimpo.

Japan Securities Research Institute. 1990. *Securities Markets in Japan*. Tokyo: Japan Securities Research Institute.

Royama, Masamichi. 1982. *Nippon-no Kinyu sisutemu* (Japanese Financial System). Tokyo: Toyokeizai-shimpo.

———, ed. 1988. *Shoken • Kinyu • Finance* (Securities, Banking, Finance). Tokyo: Toyokeizai-shimpo.

———. 1989. *Kinyu Jiyuka-no Keizaigaku* (Economics of Financial Liberalization). Tokyo: Nihonkeizai Shinbunsha.

Suzuki, Yoshio, ed. 1989. *Nippon-no Kinyu to Ginko* (Japan's Finance and Banking). Tokyo: Toyokeizai-shimpo.

Tatsumi, Kenichi. 1986. *Nippon-no Ginkogyo to Shokengyo* (Japanese Banks and Security Companies). Tokyo: Toyokeizai-shimpo.

———. 1989. *Nihon-no Kinyu • Shihon Shijo* (Japan's Financial and Capital Markets). Tokyo: Toyokeizai-shimpo.

Tavlas, George S. 1991. "On the International Use of Currencies: The Case of the Deutsche Mark." *Essays in International Finance* No. 181. Princeton, N.J.: Princeton University.

Tsujimura, Wasuke. 1989. *Nippon-no Kinyu Shoken Kawase Shijo* (Japanese Financial, Securities, and Foreign Exchange Markets). Tokyo: Toyokeizai-shimpo.

van Horne, James. 1985. *Japan's Financial Markets—Conflict and Consensus in Policy Making*. Sydney-London-Boston: George Allen & Unwin.

Viner, Aron. 1987. *Inside Japan's Financial Markets*. Tokyo: The Japan Times.

14

CANADA

Peter W. Howitt

This chapter studies the formation and conduct of monetary policy in
Canada since the creation of the Bank of Canada in 1934, with special
emphasis on the 1980s. The purpose of the chapter is twofold: to describe
how the conduct of policy has evolved up to the present, and to assess
which of the various competing positive theories of monetary policy best
fits the Canadian context.

The chapter is organized as follows. Section 1 examines the institutional
context in which monetary policy is conducted, with particular emphasis
on the relationship between the Bank of Canada and the government of
Canada. This examination addresses the question of whose interests are
likely to have the greatest influence on the conduct of policy. Section 2
looks at the Bank of Canada's operating procedures. These procedures
are interesting partly for the light they shed on the Bank's objectives, since
different objectives are best pursued using different procedures. They are
also interesting partly because of the central role played by the allocation
of government demand deposits between the central bank and private
intermediaries, a role that is unique to Canada. Section 3 describes how
the conduct of monetary policy has evolved in Canada and discusses some
of the policy issues that have arisen in recent years. Section 4 offers some
conclusions.

1. THE INSTITUTIONAL SETTING OF CANADIAN MONETARY POLICY

One of the key issues in assessing positive theories of monetary policy
in a particular country is the institutional setting that governs the incentives

faced by those in control of the central bank's operations. Of particular importance is the degree of independence of the central bank. Models that emphasize the role of electoral competition in shaping monetary policy, such as the political business cycle models of William Nordhaus (1975) and the more recent game-theoretic electoral models of Alberto Alesina (1987) and Kenneth Rogoff (1990), presume a central bank with no independence from the government of the day, or at least with not enough independence to resist the pressure to serve the government's partisan interests.

Similarly, models that emphasize seigniorage as a dominant factor motivating the conduct of monetary policy typically presume that the central bank is subservient to overall government fiscal policy. An independent central bank would have no obvious interest in employing monetary policy in such a way as to maximize seigniorage, as in the model of Leonardo Auernheimer (1974). Even theories like those of Gregory Mankiw (1987), which model monetary policy as choosing the level of the inflation tax as part of an optimal mix of tax instruments, presume that there is some mechanism in place whereby the central bank can be made to act, in effect, as a branch of the government's Department of Finance.

Models that emphasize the role of monetary policy in the government's budget constraint, such as the theory of Thomas Sargent and Neil Wallace (1981), also presume a subservient central bank. The time paths of government expenditures and of nonseigniorage taxes are either exogenous or determined by given functions of aggregate variables, and monetary policy is determined as the residual in the budget constraint. Of course, this begs the question of why fiscal policy would not be forced to fall into line with monetary policy when the two conflict, rather than the other way around. The question is which authority, the government or the central bank, plays the dominant role, or, more realistically in most cases, what is the division of power between the two authorities. There is no reason to think that the answer to this question will be the same in all cases.

By the same token, theories such as those of Finn Kydland and Edward Prescott (1977) and Robert Barro and David Gordon (1983), which argue that in the absence of a binding rule the central bank would use its discretion in an attempt to maximize social welfare, are presuming either that there is a political mechanism that would make social welfare maximization politically opportune, together with a mechanism for imposing this political pressure on a subservient central bank, or that the independent central bank is staffed by publicly spirited individuals who, in contradiction of the rest of economic theory, ignore their self-interest in carrying out their operations.

Accordingly, the present section examines the institutional setting of Canadian monetary policy, in an attempt to shed light on the issue of what influences are most likely to be represented by the conduct of policy, and in particular to shed light on the degree of independence of the Bank of

Canada. The results of the investigation can be stated in advance. The Bank of Canada appears to have a very high degree of independence from the government. Furthermore, the governor of the Bank personally has a high degree of control over the conduct of policy. The influences most likely to be felt are those of the governor's views concerning the desirability and feasibility of various objectives and strategies, as well as the economic interests of the financial community whose confidence in monetary policy is crucial to the power and independence of the Bank and its governor. As a corollary, it seems unlikely that any of the above-mentioned theories applies to the Canadian case.

The Act, the Minister, His Bank, and Its Governor

The Bank of Canada was created in 1934, following the recommendation of a 1933 Royal Commission (Canada, 1933) chaired by Lord Macmillan. The Bank of Canada Act spells out the specific powers and functions of the Bank, but it does not specify any objective or mandate for the Bank, beyond the vague statement in the Preamble to the effect that the Bank was created

to regulate credit and currency in the best interests of the economic life of the nation, to control and protect the external value of the national monetary unit and to mitigate by its influence fluctuations in the general level of production, trade, prices and employment, so far as may be possible within the scope of monetary action, and generally to promote the economic and financial welfare of Canada.

Thus, monetary policy in Canada is conducted under discretion rather than rules, although in the 1930s and 1940s, and again from October 1962 until May 1970, it was subject to a fixed exchange rate. But the question remains: whose discretion, the Bank's, as exercised by its governor, or that of the government which is responsible for the Bank's policies to Parliament, through the minister of finance?

On the surface, the Bank appears to be a mere appendage of the government. Although the Bank of Canada was set up originally as a private corporation, it was nationalized by 1938 and now takes the form of a Crown Corporation whose sole shareholder is the minister of finance. Furthermore, the government has nominal control over who shall operate and direct the Bank. Specifically, the Bank has a Board of Directors, consisting of the governor, the senior deputy governor,[1] the deputy minister of finance,[2] and twelve part-time directors appointed by the government for renewable terms of three years each. There is also an Executive Committee, consisting of the governor and senior deputy governor, the deputy minister of finance, and between two and four other directors. The governor and senior deputy governor are appointed by the Board, for an indefinitely renewable seven-year term, but subject to approval by the government.

In addition, various provisions of the Bank of Canada Act specify decisions of the Bank's Board of Directors that require specific government approval, in the form of an order-in-council. Specifically, Section 6 requires government approval for changes in the governor's salary, and Section 35 requires government approval for changes in the Bank's by-laws concerning any of five specific areas.

The Act also makes it clear that in exercising many of its powers the Bank is subordinate to the government. Section 24 requires the Bank to act without charge as the government's fiscal agent, which the Bank does in managing the government debt and the government's deposits with chartered banks, and intervening in the foreign exchange market through the Exchange Fund Account. Section 30 requires the governor to submit an annual report to the minister of finance, to be published and tabled in Parliament. Section 14 instructs the governor to "consult regularly" with the minister of finance "on monetary policy and on its relation to general economic policy," and states that in the event that this consultative process does not result in agreement the government may issue a written directive, with which "the Bank shall comply."

While these provisions of the Bank of Canada Act make it clear that monetary policy is the ultimate responsibility of the government, the fact remains that the Bank, and in particular its governor, is in a position to exert considerable independent influence over policy.[3] As we have seen, the Act stipulates that monetary policy is to be formulated through consultation between the governor and the minister of finance. Thus, in the normal course of events the government's control over monetary policy is limited by the amount of bargaining power it can exert in these consultations. Although it is impossible for an outsider to know what goes on in these consultations, the application of elementary bargaining theory to the situation implies that the Bank probably has the upper hand.

More specifically,[4] the outcome of a bargain should be biased in favor of the side that stands to do the best in the event that negotiations break down. If one side could inflict enormous damage on the other in the event of disagreement, that other side would normally accede unless it could cause a proportionate amount of damage in return. In the present case it appears that the failure of consultations to result in agreement would inflict enormous harm on the minister of finance and government, with relatively little harm to the governor or the Bank.

In the event of such failure, the governor would have the option of continuing to implement the Bank's preferred policy in the absence of any further direct action on the part of the government designed to thwart the Bank. Furthermore, any such action would almost certainly have to be carried out in public and would embroil the government in unwanted and embarrassing controversy, especially if the government were perceived to be taking its stand against the Bank for reasons of partisan electoral politics.

For example, one option for the government would be to issue a directive, in accordance with Section 14 of the Bank of Canada Act. Although the Act requires the Bank to comply, it also stipulates that the directive must be "in specific terms, and applicable for a specified period," and also that it be published in the *Canada Gazette* and tabled in Parliament within fifteen sitting days after it is issued. Furthermore, the directive would almost surely result in the governor's resignation.[5]

Given that the governor is normally chosen as someone with credibility in financial circles, his resignation would severely damage the government's credibility in those same circles. If the governor believed that he was being asked to place the political objectives of the party in power ahead of the economic welfare of the country, he would undoubtedly make his views public, and the resulting scandal could very probably lose the government more political advantage than it could gain from having its way with monetary policy.

The damage that such a forced resignation would inflict on the governor and the Bank would depend largely on the nature of the disagreement. But assuming, as is likely, that the governor was taking the more financially conservative side of the debate with the minister of finance, the reputation of the Bank and its governor for "protecting the external value of the national monetary unit" would be unlikely to be impaired. Furthermore, the personal fortunes of the governor would probably not be jeopardized; it seems likely that a competent governor could at least match his salary in the private sector.[6]

It seems, therefore, that the most obvious tool by which the minister of finance could command the Bank to follow the government's wishes is one that could be used only under extraordinary circumstances, in which the Bank was behaving in a way that was regarded, by both the electorate at large and the financial community in particular, as sufficiently misguided that the governor should be fired. Otherwise the weapon would almost surely backfire, and the government would suffer either electoral or financial losses, without having much effect on the Bank or its governor. This consideration probably accounts for the fact that since provision for issuing a directive was introduced in the 1967 revision of the Bank of Canada Act it has never been exercised.[7]

Another option for the government would be simply to fire the governor. This option, however, would also be quite costly to the government. According to the Bank of Canada Act, the governor holds office "during good behaviour." This puts him in a privileged position quite different from that of the head of other Crown Corporations who hold office "during pleasure." In effect, it grants tenure to the governor at least for the duration of his term. The only way to remove a public official holding office during good behavior is to have both houses of Parliament pass a bill declaring the official's position vacant, a bill that would almost amount to an act of attainder and that would have to be justified by demonstrating misconduct on the official's part.

The government might try to minimize the damage inflicted on itself from employing any of these options by means of a campaign to persuade the public and the financial community that its policies are preferable to those being pursued by the Bank. Such a campaign would be difficult to mount, however, partly because, as is now well established, the government has responsibility for monetary policy. Therefore, the dilemma facing a government attempting such a campaign would be how to avoid being hoist with its own petard. Somewhat paradoxically, perhaps, the fact that the government bears responsibility for the Bank's policies enhances the Bank's freedom from the kind of criticism that the executive branch of the U.S. government sometimes directs at the Federal Reserve Board.

Even if the government could somehow dissociate itself from the Bank, it would find it difficult to mount a more effective publicity campaign than the Bank. The Bank has a large, competent research staff with a strong esprit de corps and a reputation for conducting the best macroeconomic research within the government. It has direct access to considerable information, being the agent responsible for collecting and publishing many official statistics. It has excellent channels of communication through which to make its case. In particular, the governor, unlike other senior civil servants, is free to make public speeches on his own behalf, with no presumption that his words are those of his minister's, and these speeches receive wide press coverage. In addition, the Bank has its own publishing department, which it uses regularly to publish and distribute not only its monthly review, which contains speeches by the governor and other Bank officials, and its weekly statistical report, but also a steady stream of research papers.

The large size and excellent quality of the Bank's resources, both human and nonhuman, are at least in part attributable to two advantages that the Bank has over government departments. The first is that, like other central banks, it has access to an enormous independent source of income, in the form of seigniorage. The second is that, being a Crown Corporation, it is free from the constraints of the Civil Service Commission that would apply if it were a government department, with respect to hiring, promotion, and remuneration of personnel. As well as making it difficult for the government to make a credible argument against the Bank's policies, these advantages also make it difficult for the government to exert pressure on the Bank by threatening to cut its budget, to raid its staff, or to block its hiring.

Another strategy that might be employed by the government is that of lobbying the Bank's Board of Directors to censure the governor, to direct him to follow a different course, or to propose someone else for the job when the governor's term is up for renewal. It is not clear, however, how effective such lobbying would be. Since it would constitute indirect criticism of the governor, it would embroil the government in as much controversy as would direct criticism if it were to become public.

Even if lobbying were kept quiet it is not clear how successful it would be. The directors would not have a big incentive to do the government's bidding. Being a director of the Bank is not a full-time job.[8] Nor are the director fees very large.[9] So the threat of nonrenewal of the appointment would not carry much force in most cases. Of course, if the government were able to stack the Board with directors with strong views on monetary policy that coincided with the government's, or with people who are dependent on the party in power for favors other than their director fees and the small prestige that goes with the position, the Board could be used as a lever against the governor. But it would take considerable time before such stacking were to succeed, since the government-appointed directors sit with overlapping three-year terms. With every change of government the process would have to start anew. The only director who could be counted on to follow government policy is the deputy minister of finance, who is a nonvoting member, however.

Not only do the directors have little incentive to do the government's bidding, but they also have little means to do so. They have no research or other support staff that they could command independently of the governor. Furthermore, the governor acts as chairman of the Board, as well as chairman of the Executive Committee and chief executive officer. He is thus in a position to control the agenda of the Board and the Executive Committee, to curry their favor on a regular basis, and to put his case to them in a forceful way that makes it hard for them to resist.

Nor is there a great deal of expertise on the Board. In fact, section 10 of the Bank of Canada Act expressly forbids bankers or those associated with other private financial institutions from sitting on the Board. The same section also states that the directors shall be chosen from "diversified occupations," thereby effectively preventing the Board from having a large number of economists or others with expertise in the area of monetary policy.

Since 1987, extracts of the minutes from Board meetings have been published in the *Bank of Canada Review*. These extracts do not contradict the view that one would take on the basis of the above considerations, namely, that the Board acts as a rubber stamp with no influence whatsoever on monetary policy. According to the extracts, senior bank officials attend the meetings and brief the directors on economic conditions in Canada and abroad, on Bank actions and policies, and on financial developments, following notes that are published as part of the extracts. The governor delivers some remarks on the same subjects, following which the directors "report on conditions in their regions." There is no record of the directors having questioned or challenged the governor or officials on a policy matter, or of their having made independent policy proposals.

This is not to say that the Board of Directors plays no role in the governance of the Bank. In particular, section 5 of the Act assigns to the Board rather than to the government the responsibility of managing the Bank. In this way, the Board provides a buffer between the Bank and the government, which helps to maintain the Bank's independence from detailed control by the government.

Perhaps the safest weapon with which the government could threaten a recalcitrant governor would be that of nonrenewal of the governor's term. This might have some effect on a governor whose term is almost finished and who values highly the prestige and authority conferred by the position. But even this weapon is not without its dangers to the user. For the job of appointing or reappointing the governor belongs to the Board of Directors, not to the government. In order for the government not to renew it would have to lobby the directors, which as we have seen is not without its dangers and difficulties to the government, or veto the Board's choice, which would require an order-in-council that would become part of the public record.

This is not to say that the government does not have ultimate control over monetary policy. It has the option, for example, of introducing into Parliament amendments to the Bank of Canada Act, which could include a specific mandate that was binding on the Bank. It could also tie the Bank's hands by choosing to fix the exchange rate, thereby forcing monetary policy to be dictated by the need to maintain the external value of the currency. These means whereby the government might exert its ultimate control over monetary policy are, however, not the sort that could easily be used to exploit a short-run unemployment tradeoff, to manipulate monetary policy for electoral purposes, or to make monetary policy subordinate to the government's fiscal needs, because any such action would be open to public scrutiny and debate, and the confidence of the financial community would soon be lost if they were seen to be used in a way that risked inflation. Instead, they are the sort of ultimate checks necessary to make an independent central bank compatible with the principles of responsible government.

The Coyne Affair

This discussion of threats and counterthreats may seem far removed from the actual conduct of monetary policy, which almost always takes place in a context not of open hostility but of consultation and negotiations behind closed doors, with all participants maintaining a common front. It is worth stressing, therefore, that threats and counterthreats that could potentially be carried out in the event that hostilities broke out into the open can have a crucial impact on the outcome of negotiations, even if they are never carried out and even if relations between the two bureaucracies remain cordial and cooperative. In fact, Nash Bargaining theory predicts that in the case of perfect information the ultimate threats that govern negotiations will never be carried out as long as positive gains from trade remain.

Furthermore, it must be remembered that in judging the relative influence of the government and the Bank in the formulation of monetary policy we do not have extensive empirical evidence of a direct sort, in the form of a public record of consultations between the parties involved. The best we can do is to infer the relative influence of each side by indirect means such as available evidence on the nature of the threats that could ultimately be carried out.

This is not to say, however, that open hostilities never break out between the government and the Bank, or that there is no direct evidence whatsoever concerning the relationship between the government and the Bank. Fortunately for us (if not for the Canadian economy at the time), there was an incident of open hostility in the late 1950s and early 1960s, one that provided a great deal of controversy at the time and that has provided some direct evidence of the ability of each side to survive an open conflict and to inflict damage on the other. This was the famous Coyne affair.[10]

James Coyne was governor of the Bank from January 1955 to July 1961. His views on monetary policy were at odds with the Keynesian views that had become well established not only in the economics profession at large but also in the federal civil service. In particular, Coyne believed that the overriding objective of monetary policy should be that of maintaining a low rate of inflation, and that it was useless to rely on countercyclical monetary policy to stabilize unemployment.[11] These views were not only controversial but also, especially during the last two years of his tenure, very unpopular with the government of the day. His willingness to see interest rates rise rather than allow rapid monetary growth to persist in 1959 conflicted with the prairie populism of the Conservatives under Prime Minister John Diefenbaker.

The government, increasingly annoyed not only by the Bank's monetary policy but also by Coyne's public statements on broad aspects of economic policy, tried a series of measures to get rid of him quietly. In mid-March 1961 the minister of finance, Donald Fleming, told him that his speeches were interfering with government policy objectives and asked him to stop making them, which he agreed to do. The two met again on May 30, when the minister told Coyne that the government thought he should resign. According to both Coyne and Fleming, there were two reasons for urging the resignation. First, the government was concerned that there may have been some impropriety associated with the pension increase that the Bank's

Board of Directors had granted Coyne a year earlier. Second, the budget which the minister was preparing contained plans with which he was sure Coyne would not be in agreement.

This attempt having failed, the government then lobbied the Bank's Board of Directors to censure the governor and ask him to resign, which they did on June 13 by a vote of 9 to 1. Even this maneuver failed to induce Coyne to resign. It did result, however, in the battle becoming public, when opposition member Paul Martin rose in the House of Commons the next day and asked the minister of finance if it was true that the Bank's Board had asked Coyne to resign. The minister, visibly embarrassed by the question, responded that Coyne had obstructed government economic policies with his actions and speeches and also mentioned that there had been some concerns raised about the propriety of the pension arrangements that Coyne had won from the Board. The immediate result of this exposure was to bring the government under widespread public criticism for the disarray of its economic policies. Meanwhile, Coyne remained in office.

The government's next move was to introduce a bill into the House of Commons to declare the governor's position vacant. The bill did not specify any reason for the dismissal. Furthermore, the government tried to avoid prolonged debate on the issue of its policy differences with Coyne by not referring the bill to a House committee. At this time Coyne was releasing a series of statements, documents, and correspondence, all of which were intended to make the point that the government was trying to change monetary policy without taking responsibility for it. In particular, he charged that the minister of finance had at no time expressed a desire for the Bank to be following any particular course other than the one he had in fact been following.

The bill passed the House of Commons and then went to the Senate. Normally, the Senate, being a nonelected upper house along the lines of the British House of Lords, passes all bills received from the lower house. However, it has an independent set of committees. Furthermore, the majority in the Senate at the time belonged to the opposition Liberal party, whose members decided to refer the bill to the Senate Committee of Banking and Finance, in order to give Coyne a forum for defending himself and, they hoped, for further embarrassing the government.

On July 12 Coyne made an emotionally charged statement to the Senate Committee in which he defended his economic policies, repeated his charge that the government had not exercised its responsibilities by urging on him any specific monetary policy, and defended himself against all insinuations of impropriety concerning his pension arrangements. He told the senators that it had now become impossible for him to conduct his job effectively and in good conscience, and that whatever the decision of the Senate he was going to resign as governor. But he pleaded that his honor was at stake. Given the charges of impropriety that had been made against him, and given that he was holding his office "during good behaviour," a recommendation that the Senate vote for this bill would shame him forever, whereas a recommendation to reject the bill would allow him to resign with honor.

The next day the Committee passed a motion that the bill should not be proceeded and that the governor had not misconducted himself. Later that day the whole Senate accepted the Committee's report. Coyne resigned immediately and the bill died. No impropriety was ever shown with respect to Coyne's pension, which went into effect shortly after his resignation.

Who Runs the Bank?

It is hazardous to draw firm conclusions concerning the relationship between the Bank and the government from a single case involving highly idiosyncratic individuals under institutional arrangements that prevailed more than thirty years ago. Nevertheless, several points are worth noting for the light they shed on the relationship between the Bank of Canada, its governor, and the federal government.

First, the Coyne affair and its aftermath established once and for all that the government bears ultimate responsibility for monetary policy. Coyne's successor, Louis Rasminsky, made it one of his first priorities to clarify this point. His first Annual Report (Bank of Canada, 1961, p. 3) stated that the Bank and the government share a dual responsibility for monetary policy, that the Bank is mainly responsible for day-to-day operations, whereas the government is responsible for the overall direction of policy. Rasminsky also made it clear that a governor who disagreed with the direction of policy should resign, after taking steps to inform the public of his reasons. He later presented these views[12] to the 1964 Royal Commission on Banking and Finance, on whose recommendations the current section 14, including provision for the directive, was inserted in the 1967 revision of the Bank of Canada Act.

Coyne's open arguments against the government, in the form of documents and statements released to the press, the fact that the June 13 vote of the Board of Directors meeting became public, the willingness of the Senate to give him a public hearing, and the widespread press coverage of the affair all show how difficult it would be to force a governor to leave quietly. The inclusion of section 14 has made it even more difficult, for it states that any directive must be "in specific terms and applicable for a specific period," and that it be made public. Thus, a mechanism that at first glance seems to strengthen the government's hand in dealing with the Bank actually weakens it by making it less likely that a reluctant governor could be forced to comply or resign quietly in the event of irreconcilable differences.[13]

The affair also illustrates the damage that such open conflict with the central bank can inflict on the government. The Canadian dollar fell sharply during the affair. Shortly after Rasminsky assumed the governorship, there was a foreign exchange crisis that resulted in the Canadian dollar finally being pegged at U.S. $0.925, after having been as high as U.S. $1.01 at the start of 1961. The Conservative government that had finally succeeded in removing Coyne soon developed a reputation for ineptitude, especially with respect to matters of economic policy. Although it had been elected in 1958 with an unprecedented majority in the House of Commons, it lost its majority in the next election, and it was not until 1979 that the Conservative party was again to form a majority government.

As David Laidler (1991) has spelled out, much of the independent power over monetary policy resides not just in the institution of the Bank of Canada but in the office of the governor. The weakness of his Board of Directors, already apparent from the above discussion, was nicely illustrated by the fact that Coyne was able to ignore the Board's vote of censure against him. The governor is chairman of the Board, chairman of the Executive Committee that is supposed to implement the Board's policies, and chief executive officer of the Bank. Furthermore, the Executive Committee is quorate with only two members present.

On the basis of these considerations, then, it seems that to a large extent the governor of the Bank of Canada determines Canadian monetary policy. If this tentative conclusion is accepted, then it follows that policy will be influenced by the governor's beliefs concerning what policy objectives are desirable and feasible, and what specific operating procedures can best carry out those policies. To date there have been only five governors:

Graham Towers	1935–54
James Coyne	1955–61
Louis Rasminsky	1961–73
Gerald Bouey	1973–87
John Crow	1987–

It also follows from the above considerations that monetary policy in Canada is influenced by the pressures that are brought to bear on the governor by bureaucratic forces, public opinion, and pressure groups. The role of bureaucratic forces seems fairly straightforward. For the reasons described above, the Bank of Canada is almost completely independent of the rest of the government bureaucracy for acquiring material and personnel resources, for publicizing its views, for acquiring information, and for carrying out its operations. Thus, it seems safe to say that to the extent that bureaucratic forces influence the conduct of Canadian monetary policy, they are the forces that work within the Bank of Canada rather than forces that relate the Bank to the rest of the government bureaucracy.

More specifically, the governor's ability to function effectively is dependent on his control over the bureaucracy of the Bank. Although the Bank of Canada Act places the governor nominally at the head of this bureaucracy, it is clear that, if he were unable to secure the cooperation of his fellow officers and staff, he would be in a much weaker position with respect to the government in framing the overall course of monetary policy, because he relies on the bureaucracy to keep him well informed, to help in drafting reports and speeches, to develop cogent arguments, and to maintain a common front. Thus, it seems reasonable to expect that the views of the bureaucracy as to what constitute desirable and feasible objectives, and what operating procedures are best suited for the purpose of carrying out those objectives, will also play some role in the conduct of policy.

In addition, the need to secure the cooperation of his own bureaucracy gives the governor a strong incentive to defend the institution of the Bank. In effect, the governor and his bureaucracy are in a situation where they can engage in mutually beneficial exchange.[14] The bureaucracy can offer support to the governor and his policies. In exchange, the governor can offer defense against external threats to the bureaucracy by adjusting his policies in response to those threats. Thus, monetary policy will be biased at least to some extent in the direction of serving the interests of those who are in the position to do the greatest damage to the Bank.

In summary, it seems that the principal influences on monetary policy will be threefold. First, there are the views of the governor and his staff as to what constitute desirable and feasible means and ends of policy. This influence will be seen to operate in Canada, where each governor has managed to impart his personal influence on the conduct of policy, and where developments in economic theory and international fashions of central bank thinking have had their influence on Canadian policy.

The second principal influence will be the interests of the financial community on whose confidence much of the Bank's power rests. This influence can be seen in the weight given by policy to the objective of preserving "orderly financial markets," an objective that few outside of financial circles see as important, especially in comparison to the more obvious goals of price stability and stability of overall economic activity. As we will see, the weight given to orderly markets has varied over the course of Canadian monetary history, but it has always played an important role.

The third principal influence is that of public opinion. A Bank whose policies were much less popular than those of the federal government in general would not be in a position to impose electoral losses on the government, and hence would be in a weakened position. Thus, even though the Bank of Canada is independent of the government of the day it is not independent of public opinion. Furthermore, there are several channels through which the Bank can be held accountable to the public for its policies, including the recently instituted annual appearances of the governor in front of the House Standing Committee of Finance, where he has often faced hostile questioning.[15]

2. OPERATING PROCEDURES OF THE BANK OF CANADA

Although the overall strategy of Canadian monetary policy has changed over the years, the basic operating procedures of the Bank of Canada have remained more or less the same. These procedures have been outlined recently by Kevin Clinton (1991), whose description differs from that given by the Bank of Canada (1975a) only insofar as financial markets and institutions have evolved over the intervening period.[16] This section summarizes the procedures outlined by Clinton and comments on their significance for the broader issues of responsibility for, and conduct of, Canadian monetary policy.

The Procedures

The Bank of Canada's daily aim is to bring about a given change in the level of short-term interest rates. Although it employs a variety of operations from time to time to affect interest rates, the primary operation used each day is the injection of cash into the economy, or withdrawal of cash from the economy, by means of the transfer of federal government demand deposits between the government's account with the Bank of Canada and the government's accounts with various banks and nonbank financial intermediaries.

The Bank of Canada is in a position to make these transfers because of its position as the federal government's fiscal agent, because chartered banks hold some of their primary reserves in deposits with the Bank of Canada, and because banks and other financial intermediaries hold deposits with the Bank of Canada for use as clearing balances under the Canadian Payments Association (CPA). By law, all financial institutions that issue demand deposits must belong to the CPA. An institution that generates at least one half of 1 percent of the total volume of clearings is eligible to be a directly clearing member, or a "direct clearer." As such, it holds a clearing account with the Bank of Canada and is eligible for Bank of Canada advances. Other institutions must engage direct clearers to act on their behalf. At present the direct clearers consist of eight chartered banks and five nonbanks. Some idea of the relative order of magnitude of their deposits with the Bank of Canada can be gleaned from the balance sheet reproduced in Table 14.1.

The federal government holds its demand deposits with direct clearers as well as with the Bank of Canada. The Bank exercises discretion on a

Table 14.1
Bank of Canada Balance Sheet as of December 31, 1989 (millions of dollars)

ASSETS		LIABILITIES	
Foreign Currency Deposits	370	Notes in Circulation	22,093
Advances to Members of the Canadian Payments Association	312	Deposits	
		Government of Canada	21
Treasury Bills	10,816	Chartered Banks	1,787
Other Government Securities maturing within three years	3,425	Other Members of the Canadian Payments Association	230
		Other Deposits	397
Other Government Securities not maturing within three years	6,585	Foreign Currency Liabilities to Government of Canada	209
Other Investments	2,765	Others	43
Miscellaneous	507		
	24,780		24,780

Source: Annual Report of the Governor, Bank of Canada, 1989.

daily basis as to the size of total deposits with direct clearers; the allocation of deposits between direct clearers is done according to ratios that are fixed in twice-monthly auctions.

In practice, transfers of government deposits between the books of the Bank and those of the direct clearers are routinely accompanied by foreign currency swaps between the Bank of Canada and the government's Exchange Fund Account, and they show up on the Bank of Canada's balance sheet not as offsetting movements in the accounts of the government and the direct clearers but as offsetting movements between the Bank's holdings of foreign currency and the accounts of the direct clearers. So, for example, in order to inject $100 million of cash into the economy, the Bank will arrange a swap with the Exchange Fund Account that adds $100 million worth of foreign currency to the Bank's assets and $100 million to the government's deposits with the Bank of Canada. It will then immediately withdraw the $100 million from the government's deposits and add it to the deposits of the direct clearers, according to the ratios determined in the most recent auction. At the same time, the direct clearers will credit the deposit accounts of the federal government by an amount totaling $100 million. Similarly, a withdrawal of $100 million of cash from the economy would show up as a transfer of $100 million worth of foreign currency from the Bank to the Exchange Fund Account and a total reduction of $100 million in the direct clearers' deposits with the Bank of Canada.

Although the transfers show up as changes in the Bank of Canada's net holding of foreign currency assets, it is important to realize that these operations have no direct implications for Canada's net foreign asset position, since they are exactly offset by movements in the Exchange Fund Account. No change occurs in the consolidated foreign asset position of the Canadian government sector. Table 14.1 shows that as of the end of 1989 Bank of Canada operations had resulted in $209 million being owed to the government in foreign pay.

From the point of view of the consolidated private sector, this kind of operation works roughly the same way as an open market operation. For example, in the case of a "redeposit" operation by the Bank of Canada, the impact effect on the private sector's asset position is to make high-powered money rise by the increase in chartered bank deposits with the Bank of Canada, and to make net bond holdings go down by an equal amount, by the increase in the government's deposits with the chartered banks. The only difference between this and an open market purchase of Treasury bills by the Bank of Canada is that the decrease in net bond holdings of the private sector shows up as an increase in private liabilities to the government rather than a decrease in private holdings of government securities.

The Bank's net transfer each day is the sum of two components, the neutralization component and the monetary policy component. The neutralization component consists of the amount which the Bank estimates is necessary to offset various predetermined transactions affecting the total supply of clearing balances. The Bank forms this estimate at the close of each business day. Pressure will be exerted on interest rates when the monetary policy component is different from the change in clearing balances that the direct clearers had targeted for that day.

The proximate objective of these operations is to influence the overnight rate of interest. For example, if the monetary policy component is negative, the direct clearers will experience a shortfall of clearing balances. If there has been a sufficiently large net reduction in clearing balances, the accounts of some direct clearers with the Bank of Canada will be overdrawn, and this will trigger an advance to that clearer from the Bank of Canada. In any case, all direct clearers will want to restore their clearing balances to targeted levels. They will attempt to do this first by borrowing on a very short-term basis (or by calling very short-term loans). These efforts will result in a higher short-term interest rate than would otherwise have been the case. A chain of substitution from the overnight rate to longer rates will then influence the overall level of interest rates. Open market operations, Special Purchase and Resale Agreements (*REPOS*), and Sale and Repurchase Agreements (reverse *REPOS*)[17] are also used from time to time when this chain of substitution seems too weak to bring about the desired result.

The effectiveness of this method for controlling interest rates depends on the existence of a determinate demand for clearing balances. If direct clearers were indifferent as to the level of their balances, they would allow a negative monetary policy component to deplete them without responding, and hence without affecting interest rates. In fact, chartered banks will demand clearing balances for two reasons: to satisfy primary reserve requirements and to satisfy a precautionary motive. Other direct clearers have only a precautionary motive.

The precautionary motive is easy to understand. Clearing balances pay no interest. But advances from the Bank of Canada are made at a positive rate of interest that depends on the Bank rate and that can rise sharply if the same clearer requires repeated advances.[18] (In addition, there is a strong motive to avoid having such advances on their balance sheets in their annual reports.) Thus, the usual theory of the precautionary demand for excess reserves ought to apply to this motive of the demand for clearing balances.

The need for chartered banks to hold primary reserves adds a speculative motive. The requirement is that each bank hold sufficient primary reserves not each day, but as a daily average that must be satisfied during each "averaging period," which lasts two weeks. During the averaging period a bank's required reserves depend on the amount of deposits of various kinds[19] held on average on the four Wednesdays ending with the second Wednesday of the previous month. The amount of vault cash held on average over the same four Wednesdays counts toward satisfying the requirements for the current averaging period. The remainder must be made up by the daily average[20] of deposits with the Bank of Canada over the averaging period.

Thus, on any day a bank will know exactly how much must be held on average over the current averaging period in order to satisfy its primary reserve requirements, but except for the last day of the averaging period it has the choice of substituting more or less primary reserves this day for less or more in the near future. Hence, the speculative motive. When very short-term rates are expected to rise in the near future, banks will hold more primary reserves than otherwise, thus freeing themselves in the near future to invest more than otherwise in short-term interest-bearing assets.

A careful empirical analysis of the demand for reserves on the part of Canadian chartered banks is presented by J. F. Dingle, G. R. Sparks, and M. A. Walker (1972).

The Bank's operating procedures require it to be able accurately to predict both the correct neutralization component and the direct clearers' demands for clearing balances. Otherwise its operations would result in large random movements in interest rates as a result of changes in either actual or desired clearing balances which the Bank had been unable to anticipate. Because settlement is retroactive and because the Bank processes government payment flows as they enter the clearing system, it is able to calculate the appropriate neutralization component with great precision. The Bank is also in daily contact with the large banks to assess the overall level of demand. Thus, on most days the Bank needs no other form of operation in order to achieve its short-term interest-rate objectives.[21]

Strategic Implications

In principle, this operating procedure could be used for a variety of different monetary strategies. For example, it was used under monetary gradualism (see below) after 1975 in an attempt to contain M1 within target bands. The Bank would estimate a monthly M1 demand equation. Preliminary estimates of the current price level and national income were inserted, and the equation was inverted in order to derive an estimate of that value of a short-term rate of interest at which the demand for money would equal some target amount. Then the above-described operating procedures were used to establish that rate of interest.

Note also that this technique could in principle be used in order to control a broader monetary aggregate (with much smaller interest elasticity of demand) or credit aggregate, if the credit hypothesis[22] of money supply were correct. That is, when the Bank wanted to reduce the rate of monetary growth, it could use the technique to engineer a steady rise in interest rates until the demand for credit slowed to the point where the money growth began to slow as desired.

Furthermore, the technique does not require the existence of reserve requirements in order to work. In fact, reserve requirements complicate the procedure by introducing a hard-to-estimate speculative component into the demand for clearing balances, as indicated above. The federal government is currently planning to abolish all primary reserve requirements in the upcoming revision of the Bank Act. Even after this goes into effect, it will still be true that the effect of a negative net transfer of government deposits will be to create a latent excess demand for overnight funds on the part of clearers wanting to restore their clearing balances.

Although the technique could thus be used for implementing a strategy that focused on some monetary or credit aggregate as an intermediate target, it is better designed for implementing a strategy that focused on stabilizing interest rates. Given the Bank's claims that this technique is remarkably effective in creating the level of interest rates that it wants, it should be remarkably effective in reducing the short-term variability of interest rates if the Bank wished to use it in this way.

Indeed, even during the period of monetary gradualism, when the Bank was committed to controlling M1, it also attempted to use this procedure to stabilize short-term interest-rate fluctuations. The argument at the time was that in the very short term there were large random fluctuations in the demand for M1 arising from the vagaries of the transaction process.[23] The standard IS-LM analysis of Poole (1970) implies that such shifts ideally ought to be accommodated by sympathetic shifts in the supply of M1, with no change in interest rates. Under this operating procedure, such sympathetic shifts in supply would in fact occur.

More specifically, suppose there were an exogenous downward shift in the demand for M1, whereby people wanted to reduce their holdings of M1 and to increase their holdings of Treasury bills. The impact of this shift would be to create a latent excess demand for short-term interest-bearing securities, putting downward pressure on the rate of interest. But then the Bank would presumably step in to engineer a negative net transfer of government securities, resulting in a decrease in high-powered money and offsetting the downward pressure on interest rates. Unless the Bank wished to see a change in interest rates, the resulting overall change in private portfolios would be a decline in M1 and an increase in short-term securities (indirectly in the form of a reduction of chartered bank short-term liabilities to the government) in the same magnitudes as those dictated by the original shift in portfolio preferences.

If the shift turned out to be temporary, then when preferences shifted back again the above mechanism would work in reverse. Again there would be no change in the rate of interest, and the quantity of M1 would go back to its initial value. If, on the other hand, the shift turned out to be permanent, then again there would be no necessary change in the rate of interest, and M1 would remain permanently lower. Eventually, an averaging period would be reached in which required reserves were lower as a result of the initial fall in M1, and this would reduce the demand for clearing balances. This change in reserve requirements need not, however, have any effects on interest rates, because the Bank could calculate accurately the resulting reduction in demand for clearing balances and include that in the "monetary policy component" of the net transfer at the start of the averaging period, thereby impounding any latent excess reserves. If, after this downward shift had been observed for long enough, the Bank decided that it did not want to accommodate it after all, it could always reverse the initial neutralization operation.

In effect, the procedure amounts to using the level of short-term rates of interest as the proximate instrument of monetary policy. What distinguishes it from the techniques used in other countries is that it does not require the central bank to intervene directly in any particular financial market and does not involve it pegging any particular short-term rate. Instead, the Bank of Canada's handle on this instrument comes about through manipulating the reserves of financial intermediaries, not through intervening in markets. What allows it to use a quantitative method for handling an interest-rate instrument is the highly concentrated nature of the financial intermediation industry in Canada. The method would be cumbersome and impractical if there were thousands of banks over which to distribute the daily redeposits and drawdowns of government deposits.

The impression that the Bank of Canada has used this procedure rather than some alternative because of a desire to stabilize interest rates is confirmed by other observations. The article by White (1979, p. 595) defending the Bank's choice of instruments explicitly refers to the avoidance of "disorder" in financial markets as an "important short-run objective." Charles Freedman's (1983a) arguments against base control invoked the dangers of "instrument instability," a danger that Timothy Lane (1983) showed is not likely to persist under rational expectations but that is commonly invoked by those concerned directly with smoothing interest rates rather than activity levels. However, the empirical arguments of Clinton and Lynch (1979) added the further justification for using interest control rather than base control, namely, that the instability of the money multiplier in Canada induced by lagged and differential reserve requirements raises the danger that base control would destabilize not only interest rates but also monetary expansion.

The problem with the operating procedure is the problem common to all techniques that use some interest rate as the instrument. Unless the central bank is willing to move the instrument vigorously in response to variations in money or credit aggregates, it will tend to exacerbate spending shocks. When spending intentions rise exogenously, so usually will the demand for bank loans to finance some of that increased spending. Under current operating procedures, the Bank of Canada will accommodate that desired increase in credit by allowing the supply of bank loans to expand without any immediate increase in interest rates, at least until it has seen a definite enough indication of an increase in spending to make it want to raise its instrument settings.

3. THE EVOLUTION OF CANADIAN MONETARY POLICY

The stability over time of the Bank of Canada's operating procedures has not been matched by any corresponding stability of overall strategy. The strategic focus of policy has tended to swing between the two poles of controlling the rate of monetary expansion and preserving orderly financial markets—that is, dampening or smoothing fluctuations in interest rates and the exchange rate, over periods longer than a few days. The chronology presented in this section describes how the pendulum of Bank policy has been kept in motion by the preferences and beliefs of its successive governors, which in turn have been influenced by changes in economic theory and by the lessons of monetary experience.

Orderly Markets

Under its first governor, Graham Towers, the Bank of Canada was occupied largely in building up its bureaucracy, carrying out its fiscal duties to the government, providing financial advice to the government, helping to organize a Canadian money market, and conducting a comprehensive examination of the financial structure of dominion-provincial relations. Towers was very much a team player who preferred to operate behind the scenes.[24] He saw it as his job to help govern the country and to preserve orderly financial markets. Thus, for example, when testifying to a House of Commons Committee on the subject of postwar monetary policy he indicated that immediately after the war the Bank had "felt it necessary to give a firm indication that chaotic conditions [in the bond market] would not be allowed to develop" and that throughout the late 1940s, "Concern with reasonable stability of bond prices and interest rates tended to have priority" over the objective of "keeping chartered bank cash reserves from rising and restraining the use of bank credit" (Towers 1964, pp. 266–67).

Both the wish to preserve orderly financial markets and the wish to have influence in the broader aspects of government policy made monetary policy take a largely accommodative stand with respect to fiscal policy. This accommodative attitude implied that for most of Towers' tenure monetary policy was not used to stabilize the business cycle. Indeed, the first active attempt to use monetary policy for stabilization purposes was made in 1951, when monetary restriction was deliberately employed to cope with the perceived threat of inflation arising from the Korean War.[25] Thus, Canada was among the many countries in which monetary policy was revived in 1951, the year of the Federal Reserve Treasury Accord in the United States and of the end of "cheap money" in England.

The policies of the next governor, James Coyne, were much less accommodative. As can be seen from Figures 14.1–14.3, rising interest rates and a low rate of monetary expansion started at about the same time that he assumed office, in 1955. Currency appreciation started a year later. There was one episode of rapid monetary growth during his term of office, in 1958, but it did not signal a permanent loosening of policy.

The 1958 burst of rapid monetary growth was associated with the war-conversion loan of that year, which the Bank played a large part in organizing and promoting, and in which almost $6 billion of short-term federal

Figure 14.1
90 Days Treasury Bill Rate, 1954–62

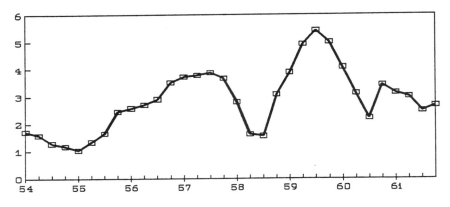

Figure 14.2
Exchange Rate (U.S. Cents/Canadian Dollar), 1954–62

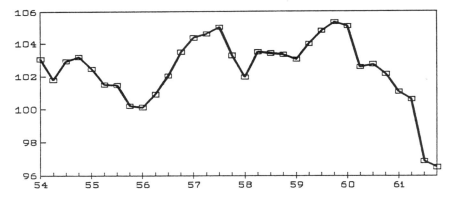

government debt was refinanced by selling long-term bonds. Monetary growth provided the substitutes for short-term debt that the public required in order to be willing to add a substantial amount of long-term debt to their portfolios without a large increase in interest rates. Once the conversion was over, however, monetary policy became sharply more contractionary. Interest rates rose in the first half of 1959, and the rate of monetary expansion became negative. The capital losses that this turnaround in monetary policy inflicted on those who had been persuaded by the Bank to buy the newly issued long-term government debt earned Coyne the enmity of Canadian savers. This episode, together with the effects of continued monetary restriction and some ill-conceived attempts on the part

Figure 14.3
Percentage Change in M1 from Four Quarters Earlier, 1954–62

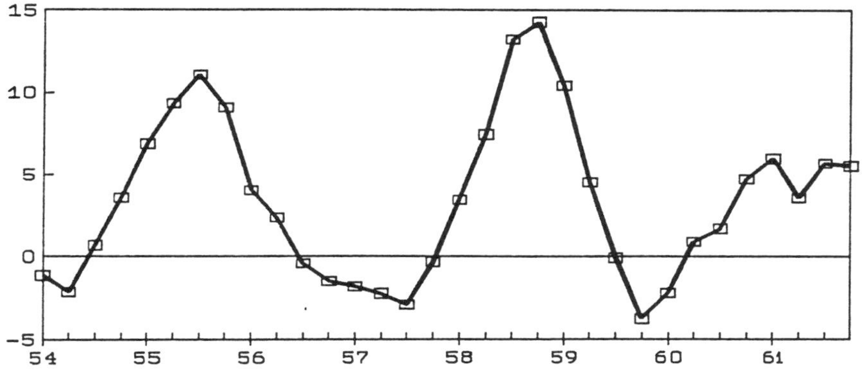

of the governor to misuse statistics in his Annual Report to the minister of finance, were important factors eventually leading to Coyne's forced departure.[26]

Coyne's successor, Louis Rasminsky, brought a return to the accommodative policies of Towers. Like Towers, Rasminsky viewed his role as that of assisting the government and preserving orderly financial markets, and he attached relatively little significance to the rate of monetary expansion per se. A full statement of his views can be found in Bank of Canada (1962). He saw monetary policy as working mainly through the lending activities of the chartered banks, rather than through the supply of their liabilities. He also tended to see the important indicators of monetary policy as being financial prices and liquidity ratios rather than quantitative magnitudes. Thus, in contrast to the later credit-oriented theories of monetary policy associated with Benjamin Friedman (1983), Rasminsky did not attach primary importance to the quantity of credit outstanding or to its rate of growth as an indicator of policy.

Rasminsky's focus on orderly financial markets implied that, like Towers, he was inclined to let monetary policy accommodate fiscal policy and the financial needs of the government. But unlike Towers, Rasminsky was also willing to let monetary policy play an active role in the attempt to stabilize the business cycle. To a large extent this change in attitude reflected the changing times. Both Towers and Rasminsky saw themselves as part of the government's team. The difference was that by the 1960s, under the growing influence of Keynesian ideas, the team had become much more confident in its ability to stabilize the business cycle than it had been in the 1930s. The influence of the times can also be detected in Rasminsky's emphasis on both the "terms and availability" of credit, an emphasis very much consonant with the view of monetary policy expressed in the famous

Radcliffe report (Committee on the Workings of the Monetary System, 1959).

The Radcliffian view of monetary policy dictates an instrument of monetary policy that would operate directly on the willingness of banks to grant loans. The 1967 revision of the Bank Act gave the Bank such an instrument, in the form of a secondary reserve requirement. Primary reserves consist of vault cash and deposits with the Bank of Canada. Secondary reserves consist of excess (above the required minimum) primary reserves, holdings of federal government Treasury bills, and day-to-day loans. Since 1967, chartered banks have been required to hold secondary reserves in at least some required ratio to total Canadian-dollar-denominated deposits. The Bank of Canada is free to vary that ratio as it sees fit, anywhere between zero and 0.12.

This revision of the Bank Act formalized a procedure that had already been instituted on an informal basis, through moral suasion. That is, since 1956 the chartered banks had agreed to maintain a secondary reserve ratio of at least 7 percent, even though there was no legal requirement to do so. The formalization of the requirement gave the Bank the authority to use the secondary reserve ratio as an active instrument of policy. The theory underlying the use of this instrument was that an increase in the ratio would impound liquidity and thus make banks less willing and able to expand their loan portfolios. Banks would therefore be led to tighten up the terms and availability of credit on personal and commercial loans.

The Radcliffian view also dictates the use of some measure of loan availability as an indicator of monetary policy. Accordingly, the Bank under Rasminsky repeatedly defined the stance of monetary policy in terms of two main instruments: the level of nominal interest rates and the Canadian liquid asset ratio (CLAR) of the chartered banks. CLAR measures the sum of reserves, day-to-day loans, loans to brokers and investment dealers, and government securities, expressed as a ratio to total Canadian-dollar-denominated assets. The idea underlying the use of CLAR as an indicator of monetary policy was that an increase in the ratio would indicate that banks were in a position to be lending more liberally than they had been and would be likely to do so until the CLAR fell to a level more in line with what the banks would prefer in the long run.

After the 1967 revision of the Bank Act, it was recognized that increases in the CLAR which were mere responses to increases in the required secondary reserve ratio could not be interpreted as an indication of an easing of monetary policy. Accordingly, the Bank began increasingly to focus on the free liquid asset ratio (FLAR), which differed from the CLAR only in that its numerator was that of the CLAR minus required primary and secondary reserves. In this focus the Bank was following the lead of the Federal Reserve System, which for many years had used free reserves, albeit primary reserves, as the main indicator of the stance of policy.[27]

Figure 14.4
Percentage Change in Money from Four Quarters Earlier, 1961–75

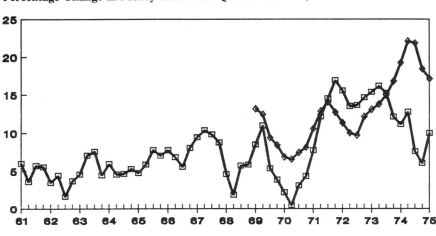

From a monetarist perspective, both the instruments and indicators used by the Bank under Rasminsky were deficient.[28] The required secondary reserve ratio could be raised without any significant effect on the underlying rate of monetary expansion, although it might result in a larger fraction of new credit being allocated on a short-term basis, and to borrowers with sources of credit other than chartered banks. Similarly, an increase in the demand for credit, caused, for example, by an increase in the marginal efficiency of capital, could easily induce the chartered banks to want to reduce their CLAR in order to take advantage of new income-earning opportunities in the field of commercial loans. The Bank of Canada, taking this reduction in CLAR as an indication of a tightening of credit market conditions, would be induced to reinforce the resulting expansion of the banking system.

In fact, this is what critics of the Bank argue happened in the period from 1965 to 1975. As Figure 14.4 shows, monetary growth continued on an upward trend from the early 1960s until 1975, attaining rates that were not consistent with a sustained single-digit rate of inflation. But the Bank, taking nominal interest rates and CLAR (or FLAR) as its primary indicators, was slow to realize that it was allowing inflationary pressures to mount. The Treasury bill rate, for example, rose from an annual average of 3.99 in 1965 to 7.40 in 1975, as shown in Figure 14.5.

During the second half of the 1960s, the fact that Canada was on a fixed exchange rate with respect to the U.S. dollar at a time when inflationary pressure was starting to build in the United States presented an increasingly

Figure 14.5
90 Days Treasury Bill Rate, 1961–75

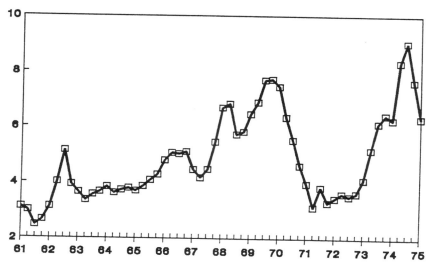

difficult constraint on Canadian attempts to keep inflation under control. Canada's ability to sterilize its balance-of-payments surplus was limited by an agreement that it had undertaken with the United States. Specifically, in exchange for exemption from provisions of the U.S. interest-equalization tax, Canada agreed not to allow its official reserves to rise above U.S. $2.6 billion.

In December 1968 the ceiling on official reserves was lifted, on the condition that Canada invest all reserves in excess of working balances in nonliquid U.S. government bonds. Canadian reserves soon rose above the previous limit, as the Bank of Canada was now able to pursue a tighter monetary policy. The rate of monetary expansion fell sharply in 1969 (Figure 14.4). But the inflow of foreign capital continued, and in order better to be able to fight the continuing inflationary pressures, the government abandoned the fixed exchange rate on May 31, 1970.

What followed illustrates a recurrent dilemma of Canadian monetary policy. Although it was now free from the constraints of a formal commitment to a fixed exchange rate, the Bank's ability to fight inflation was still hampered by strong pressure from the Canadian export lobby, and especially from primary products producers, to resist appreciation of the Canadian dollar. In effect, the Bank followed a compromise policy of allowing the Canadian dollar to appreciate but not by enough to avoid an intensification of inflationary pressure. Although the Canadian dollar appreciated starting in 1970 (Figure 14.6), nevertheless the rate of growth of M2 remained high. In fact, it was greater than 10 percent per annum in

Figure 14.6
Exchange Rate (U.S. Cents/Canadian Dollar), 1961–75

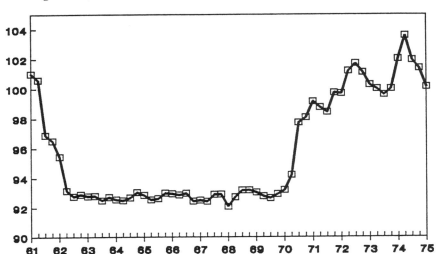

each quarter from 1971 through 1975 (see Figure 14.4 above). Not surprisingly, inflation continued to rise (Figure 14.7), until by 1975 it was well into the double-digit range.

Monetary Gradualism: A Regime of Monetary Targeting

In the fall of 1975, the federal government announced two programs designed to fight inflation. The first was a program of wage and price controls, administered by the Anti-Inflation Board. The second was a program of monetary targeting, known as monetary gradualism. The program was announced by Governor Gerald Bouey in an appearance before a House of Commons Committee on November 6.[29] (Bouey had succeeded Rasminsky in February 1973.) It was aimed at controlling the rate of growth of M1. A target band was introduced immediately, setting the limits on annual growth of M1 between 10 and 15 percent. This band would gradually be brought down to a level consistent with the elimination of inflation, although no fixed schedule was set.

Monetary policy was not going to keep the rate of growth of M1 within the target band on a month-to-month basis, but "over periods long enough for the behaviour of the economy to be significantly affected by the trend of the money supply" (Bank of Canada, 1975c, p. 7). This loose application of monetary targets was designed to leave room for the Bank to react to perceived temporary money-demand shocks, or to intervene during foreign exchange crises, or even to direct monetary policy over short periods to-

Figure 14.7
CPI/Inflation Rate (Percentage), 1961–75

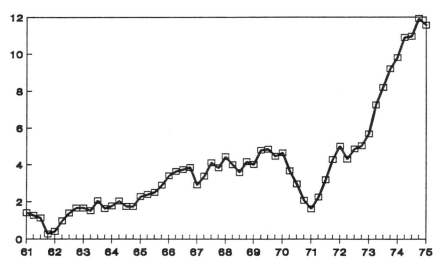

ward macroeconomic stabilization in the face of aggregate-demand shocks. But it put limits on these other applications of monetary policy, and in the long run it made them subservient to the objective of reducing inflation. Governor Bouey's emphasis on the rate of monetary expansion, and particularly his recognition that "it is simply not possible for the Bank of Canada to control the rate of monetary expansion while at the same time trying to hold interest rates to some fixed level" (Bank of Canada, 1975b, p. 24), indicated a drastic shift from the views of his predecessor. Rasminsky had argued that he saw no important role for the concept of the money supply in the operation of monetary policy. Similarly, the willingness to commit to a very specific policy, defined in terms of a particular definition of money, showed an openness and a willingness to expose the Bank to public accountability that had been unheard of under previous governors. In short, the philosophy of the Bank of Canada had moved all the way from post-Keynesianism to monetarism. In fact, Milton Friedman (1975), commenting shortly after a speech in which Bouey had outlined the reasons for focusing on M1, referred to it as "the best speech I have ever heard a central banker give."

For the next five years the Bank of Canada carried out this program of monetary gradualism more or less as announced. By 1980 the target range had been reduced to between 4 and 8 percent. As Figure 14.8 shows, the actual rate of expansion of M1 fell even further than this target range. The method by which the Bank exercised control over M1 was a version of interest control. The Bank estimated a monthly M1 demand equation. By

Figure 14.8
Percentage Change in Money from Four Quarters Earlier, 1975–90

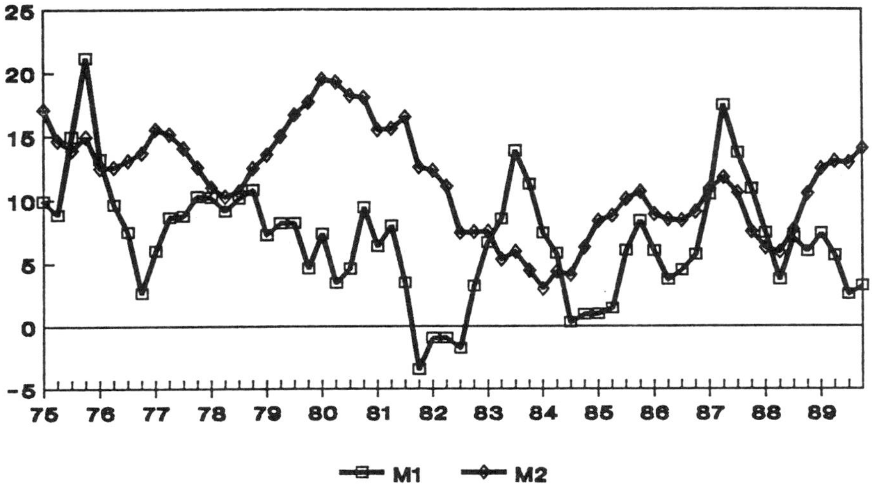

substituting forecasts for the price level and national income in this equation, it could calculate what level of short-term interest rates would be consistent with a given target level of the money supply in the current month, on the assumption that the supply of money would adjust automatically to meet the demand at that rate of interest and that the error term in the equation would be zero.

The Bank ruled out base control on the grounds that the money multiplier was unstable as a result of lagged reserve accounting and differential reserve requirements (see Clinton and Lynch, 1979). But as we have seen (Section 2 above), the rejection of base control in favor of interest control also reflected a residual concern for orderly markets and stable interest rates that persisted despite the overall movement toward monetarism. Governor Bouey expressed this residual concern in his speech announcing monetary gradualism when he said that "if the Bank of Canada reacted sharply to every temporary spurt or pause in the growth of currency and demand deposits, its actions would necessarily involve much larger, more frequent and more disruptive changes in interest rates than would serve any useful economic purpose" (Bank of Canada, 1975c, p. 7).

A residual concern for orderly markets was also reflected in the Bank's choice of M1 as the aggregate to be targeted. Because of its higher interest elasticity of demand, short-term fluctuations in M1 could be controlled with smaller changes in interest rates than would be the case with broader aggregates such as M2. The Bank responded to critics who argued that M1 was a small and shrinking part of the monetary system by saying that the

Figure 14.9
CPI/Inflation Rate (Percentage), 1975–90

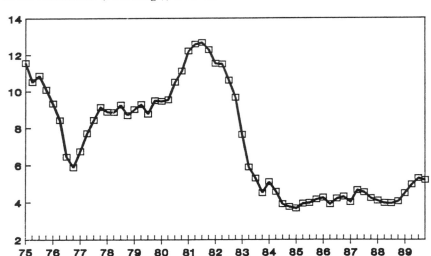

attempt to control M2 would require unacceptably large variations in interest rates.[30]

Although monetary gradualism succeeded in reducing the rate of growth of M1, it did not succeed in its ultimate objective of reducing the rate of inflation. As Figure 14.9 reveals, the rate of inflation did come down somewhat during the first three years of the program, but then it began to rise again. By 1980 it was as high as it had been at the outset of the program. The GDP deflator showed 10.6 percent inflation in 1980 compared with 10.8 in 1975; the Consumer Price Index showed 10.0 percent inflation in both years. By 1981 both measures showed even higher inflation than at the outset of the program.

Some of the details of what happened to inflation from 1976 through 1980 can undoubtedly be explained by two special factors: the Anti-Inflation Board (AIB) wage-price controls and the approximately 20 percent depreciation of the Canadian dollar that occurred during 1977 and 1978 (Figure 14.10). Controls may help to explain why inflation fell at first. Empirical assessments of the effects of the AIB are somewhat mixed, but the consensus seems to be that it had at least a temporary effect of reducing inflation.[31] The depreciation probably contributed to the resurgence of inflation in 1977, which was given added impetus by the expiration of controls in 1978.

Nevertheless, these special factors cannot explain the overall failure of inflation to come down more than temporarily, despite the reduction in the rate of monetary expansion. The burst of inflation following the ex-

Figure 14.10
Canadian Dollar Index Against G10 Currencies, 1975–90

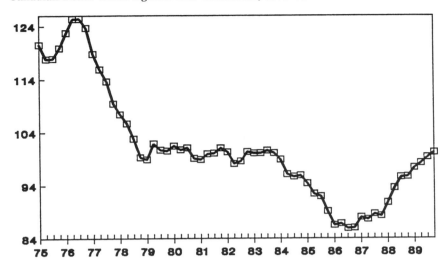

piration of AIB controls should have ended as soon as prices registered the inflationary pressures that had previously been suppressed by controls. As for the substantial depreciation, it is hard to see this as an independent factor causing inflation. To the extent that nonmonetary factors caused a real depreciation, this should have produced at most a once-over effect on the level of prices.

It seems more likely that the failure of monetary gradualism was attributable to special factors having to do with the choice of M1 as the aggregate to be targeted. As Figure 14.8 shows, the broader aggregate M2 continued to grow at double-digit annual rates throughout the period 1975 to 1980, with no discernible downward trend. The same pattern is displayed by M3 and all other available broader aggregates. (See Peter Howitt, 1986, pp. 42–43.)

Two special features of M1 are particularly noteworthy in this regard. The first is its much higher interest elasticity of demand compared with the broader aggregates, most probably attributable to the fact that the components of M1 are largely noninterest-bearing. Nominal interest rates rose in Canada, as in the rest of the world, in the second half of the 1970s. As a result, some reduction in the rate of growth of M1 over this period would have been compatible with a maintenance of a constant rate of inflation. More specifically, based on annual averages the ninety-day Treasury bill rate rose from 7.4 to 12.8 over the period 1975 to 1980. (See Figure 14.11.) Assuming an interest elasticity of 0.3,[32] this increase implies that

Figure 14.11
90 Days Treasury Bill Rate, 1975–90

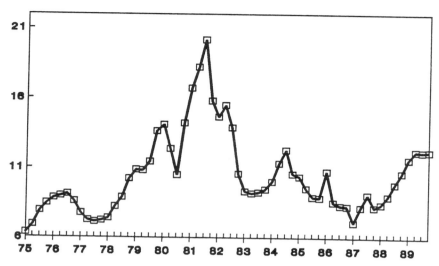

M1 could have fallen by a cumulative amount equal to 22 percent of its starting value over the same interval with no effect on inflation.

The other special feature of M1 is that over the second half of the 1970s the demand for M1 was destabilized by a series of shocks. According to the estimates of Stephen Poloz (1984), the demand for M1 shifted down by 5 to 8 percent in 1976, immediately after the start of monetary gradualism. By 1981 the cumulative downward shift amounted to at least 28 percent.

It is an open question to what extent the destabilization of the demand for M1 under monetary gradualism is attributable to exogenous factors and to what extent it is simply a manifestation of the Lucas Critique, or, more specifically, Goodhart's Law. Evidence in favor of the exogenous shift explanation is that the shifts in M1 demand took place at roughly the same time as technological innovations were facilitating the introduction of new accounts and services by chartered banks which clearly had the effect of reducing the demand for M1.

More specifically, in 1976 the chartered banks began offering cash-management packages to their largest corporate customers. These packages included *concentration accounts*, which allowed the corporation to consolidate many accounts across the country into a single account that could be used to pool the random variations in cash flow across the individual accounts, and *sweep accounts*, which provided for overnight investment of cash from noninterest-bearing current accounts. The packages also included various techniques for more efficient collection of payments and disbursement of funds. In 1981 the packages were offered to medium-sized corporate customers. On the household side, the introduction of daily-interest savings accounts in 1979 and daily-interest chequable accounts in 1980 encouraged a drastic reduction in the demand for the traditional demand deposits included in M1.[33]

Many of these financial innovations were clearly dependent on the computer technology that banks were just starting to put on line at the time. Although in the case of household accounts the banks were largely forced to offer daily-interest accounts by competition from trust companies that had already begun to do so, there is reason to think that the shifts in demand for M1 associated with financial innovations in this period were not entirely exogenous with respect to monetary policy. In particular, Courchene (1981, pp. 69ff.) has suggested that the program of monetary gradualism gave the chartered banks an incentive to encourage their customers to shift out of accounts included in M1 so that they could continue to expand faster than the Bank of Canada's target growth rates. This incentive would not have been as strong had the Bank chosen a broader monetary aggregate as its target, because, for example, having customers switch into daily-interest accounts may have helped to reduce the growth rate of M1, but it would not have helped the banks avoid limits on M2 growth because daily-interest accounts are included in M2. Note that this particular version of Goodhart's Law is more likely to apply to the Canadian case than it would in many other countries because of the high degree of concentration of the Canadian banking industry.[34] In a more atomistic system, no individual bank would see its own actions as being important enough to cause a relaxation of monetary policy.

Exchange-Rate Stabilization: Disengaging from Monetary Targets

Whatever the cause of the shifts in M1 demand in Canada, the Bank of Canada clearly began to worry about the efficacy of its targeting program as early as the spring of 1978, at which time it began a gradual disengagement from what had seemed to be a firm commitment to monetarist principles. A key turning point was the press release of April 3, 1978, announcing an increase in the Bank rate.[35] This announcement cited currency depreciation, not monetary growth, as the reason for the increase. From then on the Bank began to pay more attention to the Canadian exchange rate in justifying its policy actions and correspondingly less attention to the rate of monetary expansion.

The problem facing the Bank in the foreign exchange market over the next few years was that foreign interest rates, and especially U.S. interest rates, began to rise, in real as well as nominal terms, and to become more variable than they had previously been. The Bank had to decide whether or not to allow Canadian monetary expansion to stay on course in the face of such changes. It feared that sticking to a fixed monetary target in the face of a large increase in U.S. interest rates would put the ultimate inflation target in jeopardy. Specifically, the Canadian dollar would have to be allowed to fall, and this would put upward pressure on Canadian prices both directly through the Canadian price of imported goods and indirectly through various channels, including the cost increases that would arise from the increase in the Canadian price of imported raw materials and the increased demand that would result for Canadian-produced import-competing goods. (See, for example, Thiessen, 1982.)

The Bank was worried that the depreciation would feed through to higher wage increases, both because of the reduction in unemployment that would come from having a higher demand for Canadian produced goods and also because of the increase in the cost of living. Furthermore, it worried that allowing the depreciation to take place would raise expected inflation through either extrapolative expectations of inflation and depreciation or loss of credibility of monetary policy. In short, the Bank was concerned that currency depreciation would initiate an inflationary spiral that would be hard to reverse.

Even though Bank officials recognized that the effects on inflation of a once-over depreciation would be strictly temporary if monetary growth were held on target, they argued that this would involve a costly overshoot. (See, for example, Freedman, 1983c.) That is, the once-over rise in the price level that would suffice to reestablish the initial real situation with the money supply held on course would be exceeded because of the momentum of the inflationary spiral. Eventually, according to the Bank's reasoning, the price level would rise so far relative to the unchanged path of the money supply that domestic interest rates would rise, and this increase in domestic interest rates would cause enough slack in the domestic economy to bring the price level back into line. Since this meant that domestic interest rates would eventually have to rise anyway, the Bank argued that it was better to raise rates right away rather than go through a costly cycle of inflation and recession. This would not necessarily require domestic rates to rise by enough to keep the exchange rate fixed, but it would require them to rise by enough to make monetary expansion fall below target, at least temporarily.

This policy with respect to foreign interest shocks resulted in the Canadian dollar following an intermediate course between the U.S. dollar and European currencies. That is, over the first part of the 1980s the European currencies fell a lot with respect to the U.S. dollar, and the Bank's policy made the Canadian dollar fall a little with respect to the U.S. dollar. As Figure 14.10 shows, Canada's G-10 exchange rate, which gives a weight of 82 percent to the U.S. dollar,[36] stayed virtually constant for the six and a half year period from fourth-quarter 1978 through first-quarter 1984.

Thus, Canada was on a de facto fixed exchange rate for the six and a half year period. Yet the Bank was also able to keep the growth of M1 from falling more or less as scheduled, at least through 1980. The targets were maintained officially until Governor Bouey finally announced their cancellation in November 1982 (Bank of Canada, 1982a).

The incompatibility between Canada's de facto fixed exchange rate and its program of monetary targeting finally forced the Bank to choose between the two policies in 1981, when the Bank's response to the rise in U.S. interest rates combined with the continuing shift in the demand for M1 to create a negative growth rate for the calendar year, even though the target range was between 4 and 8 percent.

Canada's attempt to cope with the continued rise of the U.S. dollar throughout the period until early 1984 kept the rate of M1 growth low. In 1981 growth in the broader aggregates also started slowing. Figure 14.8 shows a fall in the growth rate of M2 between 1981 and 1984. A similar pattern is shown by all the other broader aggregates on which the Bank of Canada collects data. (See Howitt, 1986, 42–43.) The dramatic reduction in broad monetary growth, coming after ten years of uninterrupted double-digit growth, helped to make the 1981–82 recession more severe, by almost any measure, than recessions in any other OECD country. Canada's GNP fell by 6 percent from first-quarter 1981 through second-quarter 1982, whereas the Canadian unemployment rate rose from 7.3 to 12.8 percent of the labor force.

This collapse of monetary expansion continued until the de facto fixed exchange rate was abandoned in the second quarter of 1984. At that time, the G-10 exchange rate fell below the narrow band in which it had been contained for six and a half years, and the growth rate of M2 finally stopped its downward movement. Monetary policy was then in a state of transition. Recovery from the 1981–82 recession, which had been relatively weak in 1983, was facilitated in 1984 and 1985 by the revival of monetary expansion, and by the willingness of the authorities to allow the Canadian dollar to continue to decline. Although the Bank of Canada continued throughout the mid–1980s to emphasize both the importance of fighting inflation and the necessity of avoiding sudden movements in the exchange rate, no clear strategy for monetary policy was evident.

Price Stability

A new direction for monetary policy was signaled in January 1988, when a speech by the new governor, John Crow (1988), outlined his approach to the subject. The speech was notable for its renewed emphasis on monetary aggregates, a subject to which we will return below. It was also notable for stressing that the main objective of monetary policy was the pursuit of "price stability." This was the most forthright and unequivocal statement yet that the elimination of inflation was the overriding objective of Canadian monetary policy. It soon embroiled the Bank in considerable controversy.

As in much of the rest of the OECD, the 1981–82 recession in Canada had been followed by a sharp decline in inflation. Figure 14.9 shows a sharp fall in CPI inflation. Other measures of inflation show a similar fall. (See Howitt, 1986, p. 64.) However, the decline in inflation ended once recovery began. The annual rate of increase in the CPI lingered around 4 percent for the next five years, and in 1989 it edged up to 5 percent. Crow's 1988 speech indicated the Bank's belief that 4 percent was not good enough, that the fight against inflation would continue until price stability had been achieved.

The ensuing controversy focused on the meaning of price stability, whether it was worth pursuing, and if so how fast. Pierre Fortin (1989) argued that the CPI was the best available measure of the price level and that given the bias attributable to failure to account fully for substitution, quality changes, and the introduction of new goods, price stability should be defined as corresponding to a rate of CPI inflation between 0.5 and 1 percent per annum.

Howitt's (1989) argument in favor of zero inflation as a long-run goal was presented in terms of the pervasiveness of money in its role as unit of account and standard of deferred payment as well as medium of exchange. A large number of financial and accounting practices and conventions presume that money is an unvarying measure of value. Critics such as Robert F. Lucas (1990) and William Scarth (1990) emphasized the costs of disinflation, especially in view of the possibility of hysteresis in unemployment.

Other critics of the Bank argued that, although zero inflation might be a sensible goal for the very long run, the recent signing of the Canada-United States Free Trade Agreement made this a particularly inopportune time to be pursuing an anti-inflationary policy that would involve a high value of the Canadian dollar in terms of the U.S. dollar, and high Canadian interest rates. Many industries would be rationalizing, closing small operations in some locations and enlarging in others to take advantage of the increased scope for economies of scale. It would not be to Canada's advantage if these temporary effects of monetary stringency induced a lot of firms to locate in the United States instead of Canada. They also argued that disinflation would exacerbate regional differences in unemployment.

In February 1991 the Bank went further in specifying its goal of price stability by publishing a target path for inflation. The goal is to achieve a rate of CPI inflation of 2 percent by 1995 and to move to price stability thereafter.[37] Operationally, however, the Bank uses a modified version of the CPI from which the volatile food and energy components have been removed. The Bank will also accommodate one-time price-level effects on the CPI as a result of indirect tax increases. Of particular importance is the Goods and Service Tax, introduced on January 1, 1991, which the Bank estimates will have an impact effect of 1.25 percent on the CPI.[38]

Another significant feature of the announcement of inflation targets is that it was made jointly and simultaneously by the Bank and the minister of finance, on the occasion of the presentation in the House of Commons of the government's annual budget. This close cooperation between the Bank and the government is intended to add credibility to the pursuit of price stability. Whether and to what extent it will reduce the independence of the Bank is a subject likely to receive a good deal of academic attention in the near future.

The other noteworthy feature of the governor's January 1988 speech was its renewed emphasis on monetary aggregates. He was careful to point out that in the Bank's judgment there was still no single monetary aggregate sufficiently reliable to bear the weight of being a formal target as M1 had been under monetary gradualism. But he did say that particular attention was being paid to the Bank's preferred aggregate, M2, which was being used as a "guide" to monetary policy. The willingness to pay close attention to a broad monetary aggregate like M2, even if not to the point of targeting it, was unprecedented for the Bank of Canada. As we have seen, the period of monetary gradualism was one of sustained double-digit growth in the broad aggregates. And suggestions that the Bank attempt to control M2 had been met in the past with the argument that its interest elasticity was so weak that the attempt to control it would involve unacceptably large interest-rate fluctuations.

The renewed concern for monetary aggregates implies a renewed turning away from concern for preserving orderly financial markets, both bond markets and foreign exchange markets. With respect to the foreign exchange markets, Crow stated that "it is vital to avoid treating short-run market stability as more important than the underlying policy changes that are essential for economic balance and market stability in the medium term. In particular, the pursuit of short-term exchange rate stability cannot be pushed so far that it jeopardizes the good domestic price performance that is the key objective of monetary policy" (Crow, 1988, p. 14). This statement marks a definite change from the attitude that Crow's predecessor had formed toward the exchange rate as he was disengaging from the targets of monetary gradualism, an attitude summed up by his statement that "To have such an important price swinging around widely would be about as disruptive an influence on the evolution of Canadian economic affairs as one could imagine" (Bank of Canada, 1982b, p. 9).

The argument for putting more emphasis on controlling monetary ag-

Table 14.2
Correlation Between Cyclical Movements in Real GNP in Quarter *t* and M2 in Quarter *t + k*, over the Period 1968:II to 1990:III

k	Coefficient of Correlation
-4	0.04216
-3	0.13035
-2	0.22741
-1	0.35690
0	0.35748
1	0.31183
2	0.33182
3	0.33596
4	0.32256

gregates can be supported by several kinds of empirical evidence. Within the Bank of Canada there has been a series of papers[39] emphasizing the informational content of monetary and credit aggregates. These papers have shown that, given the past history of GNP, and given the past history of other variables, including specifically the rate of interest, there is predictive content in broad monetary and credit aggregates. Furthermore, the results show a positive effect of money on GNP. Similar results are found whether real or nominal GNP is used, or the GNP deflator, although different money and credit aggregates correlate best with different target aggregates.

The empirical work of David Laidler and William Robson (1990) has also shown that increases in money, either M1 or M2, when averaged over several years, are very highly, positively correlated with subsequent movements in inflation. Similarly, the correlations reported in Table 14.2 show a procyclical pattern of fluctuations in M2. In this table, cyclical movements in both M2 and real GNP are constructed by use of the Hodrick-Prescott filter to remove a variable trend.[40]

All the evidence cited in the two preceding paragraphs suggests that monetary policy has in the past tended to amplify the business cycle rather than to counteract it and that therefore the Bank should pay more attention to controlling fluctuations in monetary expansion. Furthermore, the results of Laidler and Robson using M1, together with the finding by Doug Hostland, Stephen Poloz, and Paul Storer (1987) to the effect that M1 is the most informative variable in predicting movements in real output, suggest that the Bank should not neglect the behavior of M1 despite the instability of demand that led to its failure as a target under monetary gradualism.

Finally, the demand functions for M2 estimated by Francesco Cara-mazza, Doug Hostland, and Stephen Poloz (1990) show a significant in-terest elasticity (see their Table 3), indicating that the attempt to control this broad aggregate would not necessarily involve instrument instability or the wild interest-rate variability that the Bank has warned against in the past.

The Bank's emphasis on controlling M2 is still, however, far from what a monetarist would consider satisfactory. In particular, the Bank has not abandoned its concern for orderly markets. Crow's 1988 speech dwelt on the difficulties posed by exchange-rate volatility, particularly the possibility that attempts to ease monetary conditions might be frustrated by a spec-ulative run on the currency that would result perversely in a rise in interest rates.

From a monetarist perspective, this possibility is simply a manifestation of the fact that the extent to which an expansionary monetary policy works through interest rates rather than through the exchange rate depends in a subtle and complicated way on expectations about future policy develop-ments. It is not clear why short-run speculative movements in exchange rates should be prevented from being the proximate channel through which policy impinges on the real economy. Nor is there any good reason to believe that these movements will be a destabilizing influence in the absence of destabilizing movements in the rate of monetary expansion. If exchange rates tend to overshoot, it is because they are among the important relative prices with sufficient flexibility to act as automatic stabilizers in the econ-omy. Controlling their fluctuations prevents them from doing their job.

Furthermore, the Bank is concerned about the stability of the demand for M2.[41] There are two main aspects of this concern. The first arises from a particular Canadian government scheme for borrowing from small savers, the Canada Savings Bond (CSB). These bonds are issued in small denom-inations during a marketing campaign in the autumn of every year. Al-though they are of long duration, they are extremely liquid, since the government guarantees redemption at face value, virtually on demand. They are, therefore, highly substitutable for the personal saving and term deposits included in M2.

CSBs have constituted as much as 30 percent of the federal government's debt in the 1980s, although their share has been falling in recent years and was less than 11 percent at the end of 1990. Large increases in interest rates tend to induce large-scale encashments of CSBs. This induces a pro-cess of reintermediation, whereby people switch their funds into savings and term deposits and the government is forced to borrow the money back by means of Treasury bills and conventional debt instruments, many of which are bought by the banks that have received the proceeds of CSB encashments. The resulting increase in M2 clearly cannot be taken as an indication of monetary expansion.

This problem is compounded by the way CSBs are marketed. At the beginning of the sales campaign each fall, the government announces the interest rate that will apply to the new issue. The campaign then goes on typically for several weeks, as people invest savings and sign onto payroll deduction programs. The size of each campaign then becomes a random variable influenced largely by unanticipated movements in market interest rates during the campaign. If interest rates rise unexpectedly, the campaign will be small and M2 will be swollen artificially. If interest rates fall unexpectedly, the reverse may happen, although in this case the government may limit the effect by closing the campaign early.

Some adjustment must be made, therefore, to account for CSBs in the demand function for M2. The results of Caramazza, Hostland, and Poloz (1990) indicate that this can be done. They find a highly significant and stable coefficient of changes in CSBs outstanding in an equation predicting the change in M2. The subsequent results of Francesco Caramazza, Kim McPhail, and Doug Hostland (1990) indicate that CSB sales have a different effect than CSB redemptions, suggesting that there may still be some problems in interpreting movements in M2. These problems, however, will soon disappear if the proportion of federal debt in the form of CSBs continues to shrink at the same rate as in recent years.

The other aspect of the Bank's concern for the stability of M2 demand is the possibility that there have been large permanent shifts unconnected with CSBs. Caramazza, Hostland, and Poloz (1990) find evidence of a near-unit root in the demand for M2. Furthermore, there was a positive shift in M2 velocity in 1983–84 that the Bank interpreted as a reason for continuing the monetary deceleration shown in Figure 14.8 into the first quarter of 1984 (see Bank of Canada, 1986, p. 14). Specifically, the Bank interpreted this shift as coming from a balance-sheet consolidation on the part of the household sector. According to this theory, people's attitudes toward debt, particularly mortgage debt, had been changed by the experience of the 1981–82 recession, and they had decided to use their savings accounts to pay down existing debt. What was involved, according to this story, was simply a decline in demand for M2 with no necessary implications for the strength of aggregate demand for goods and services.

Critics of the Bank argue that unexpected movements in M2 should not generally be interpreted as simply shifts in money demand which monetary policy should accommodate. Authors such as Brunner and Meltzer (1976) and Laidler (1984), for example, have argued that random fluctuations in money are frequently attributable to shifts in the demand for credit that induce banks to expand their balance sheets, which will be permitted by a central bank concerned with orderly financial markets. Elsewhere (Howitt, 1986) the 1983–84 velocity shift has been interpreted as the result of increased caution on the part of financial institutions that had been burned by the experience of the 1981–82 recession and the onset of the global debt crisis, a shift that the Bank should not have accommodated but did. More generally, the fact that the Bank's own studies (for example, Muller, 1990) show a positive effect on output and prices of unanticipated movements in money, given the history of output, suggests that whatever the source of unexpected changes in money the Bank would have been better to resist rather than accommodate them.

This qualified but, for Canada, unprecedented movement toward monetarist doctrine on the part of the Bank has been apparent in its actions as well as its words. It seems, for example, that the Bank has allowed interest rates to fluctuate more widely than they would have in the past. During the period from 1987 through 1989, when the Canadian economy was growing more rapidly than the U.S. economy, the Bank allowed a large increase in domestic interest rates and in the value of the Canadian dollar (see Figures 14.10 and 14.11). The interest differential vis-à-vis the United States, measured by ninety-day corporate paper rates, was allowed to rise above 500 basis points.

This willingness to allow interest rates and the exchange rate to rise contrasts sharply with what happened in the early 1970s, when, as we have seen, the Bank allowed monetary expansion to rise into the double digits in an effort to prevent what was seen as an unacceptable degree of appreciation of the Canadian dollar. However, as Figure 14.8 above makes clear, the Bank is still unwilling to allow the amount of flexibility in interest rates and the exchange rate that it would take in order to prevent monetary expansion from being procyclical. Over the 1987–89 period when domestic interest rates were allowed to rise much more than their U.S. counterparts, the rate of growth of M2 averaged 10.3 percent per year, after having been below 10 percent for five years in a row. By calendar year 1989, the rate of M2 expansion had risen to 13.1 percent.

CONCLUSION

We conclude with some brief remarks summarizing the implications of the above concerning what kind of positive theory of monetary policy is likely to best describe the Canadian case. Section 1 argued that the Bank of Canada, and in particular its governor, are too independent from the government of the day for political business-cycle theories or seigniorage-based theories to apply. The chronicle given in section 3 confirms this point, in the sense that different episodes of monetary policy can be associated with changes in the governorship of the Bank. Towers' accommodative policies were changed very quickly when James Coyne became governor in 1955 and were restored just as quickly when Rasminsky succeeded him. The targeting policy of monetary gradualism was instituted two years after the appointment of Gerald Bouey, whose monetarist theories were radically different from those of Rasminsky. The revival of attention to monetary aggregates, as well as the explicit elevation of price stability to the status of primary goal, took place within one year after the appointment of Bouey's successor, John Crow.

These changes of policy orientation did not just reflect the personalities and beliefs of the particular men who have run the Bank of Canada. They also reflected the prevailing wisdom of the times. As we have seen, the activation of monetary policy in 1951 coincided with similar developments in the United States and England. Rasminsky's views on the importance of credit were similar to the Radcliffe post-Keynesianism of his time. Bouey's rationalization of monetary targeting was in line with the monetarist thinking that had then reached its height of popularity. (The Bank of Canada was certainly not the only central bank to have been persuaded by this thinking to implement targets.) Similarly, John Crow's emphasis on price stability as the primary goal can be seen as reflecting a philosophy that is becoming increasingly prevalent in central banks elsewhere and that has many advocates in the United States.

These examples of Canadian monetary policy having followed international trends have implications for the central issue of whether monetary policy is influenced by ideas or by vested interests. The question is how the Bank of Canada uses its independence from the government: to implement its theories as to what would be best for the country, or to cater to pressure groups. Stigler's Law would suggest the latter, but the above examples suggest that ideas do matter. A straightforward explanation of these examples is that the governor and his senior bureaucrats are influenced by the lessons of monetary experience, as embodied in currently popular theories. It is hard to believe that such a correlation between Canadian policy and internationally fashionable thinking could be accounted for by special-interest theory.

There is evidence, however, that special interests also influence the Bank of Canada. This influence is manifest in the importance that the Bank of Canada has always given to the objective of preserving orderly financial markets. This objective exemplifies the tendency that Milton Friedman (1962) pointed out, for independent central bankers to view the world from a banker's point of view, according to which economic stability is sometimes seen as being the same as financial stability. The analysis of Section 1 above suggests one reason why the Bank of Canada might be sympathetic to such a point of view, namely, that the support of the financial community is crucial to the Bank's independence.

We have seen that the objective of preserving orderly markets has always had at least some influence on policy. For example, the operating procedures outlined in Section 2 above, which are best suited to controlling interest-rate fluctuations, have been in effect for over twenty years now. The extent of this influence has depended on the extent to which it conflicted with the overall philosophy of the governor of the day. Under Towers and Rasminsky there was little conflict, and an orderly market was the primary goal. Bouey started monetary gradualism with a recognition that interest rates and exchange rates had to be allowed to fluctuate to control monetary growth. But even then the choice of monetary target, which was eventually to undermine the policy, was motivated to a large extent by the desire to avoid large interest-rate fluctuations. John Crow has been most explicit about having to make orderly markets subservient to the primary goal of price stability, and he has allowed interest rates and the exchange rate to vary far more freely than his predecessors. But the vestiges of concern for orderly markets can still be detected in Crow's unwillingness to allow interest rates and the exchange rate to rise enough to prevent an inflationary rise in monetary growth in 1987–89.

Despite this concern for orderly markets, the influence of special interests over Canadian monetary policy is not nearly as great as is pictured by most positive theories of monetary policy. For although the concern reflects the particular viewpoint of the financial community, it does not necessarily reflect the narrow self-interest of those in the financial community, who actually stand to gain from market volatility because of their superior ability to anticipate price movements. Instead, the concern reflects a particular view of the overall interest which is conditioned by the personal experiences common to those in the financial community.

Furthermore, concern for orderly markets has tended to diminish over the years and has now almost disappeared. The gradual disappearance of the concern reflects an important implication of the role of ideas in monetary policy, an implication that is missed by most positive theories of monetary policy—namely, that monetary policy can benefit from experience. The Bank of Canada has shown a commendable willingness to learn from past mistakes, as when it undertook monetary targeting in 1975, again when it abandoned the aggregate M1 whose demand function had become unstable under that program, and yet again more recently when it finally indicated a willingness to tolerate as much interest-rate and exchange-rate volatity as it would take to control broad monetary aggregates.

NOTES

For useful comments on an earlier draft, the author thanks Joel Fried, Paul Jenkins, David Laidler, and the editors of the handbook, none of whom is responsible for the views expressed in the chapter. Jien Chien provided useful technical assistance.

1. The Bank of Canada Act refers to this Board member as deputy governor.

However, the practice has been established of having several deputy governors of the Bank; at present there are five.

2. That is, the chief civil servant in the Department of Finance.

3. This conclusion appears to be the consensus view of those scholars who have investigated the subject. The following analysis was especially influenced by Scott Gordon (1961a) and David Laidler (1991).

4. The seminal work on which most bargaining theory is now based is John Nash (1950). For modern developments in bargaining theory, see, for example, Alvin Roth (1985).

5. The provision for a directive was recommended by the Porter Commission (Canada, 1964), after strong urging from the Bank's Governor Louis Rasminsky. Rasminsky stated in his 1966 Per Jacobsson Memorial Lecture that "if the Governor were directed to carry out a policy which, in good conscience, he could not regard as being in the national interest, he would, after taking steps to ensure that the issues involved were placed clearly before the public, resign" (quoted from Cairns, Binhammer, and Boadway, 1972, p. 178). In its memorandum (reprinted, Bank of Canada 1978, p. 11) to the 1978 Royal Commission on Financial Management and Accountability, the Bank again stated that the governor would very likely resign in the event a directive was issued.

6. The exact salary of the governor is not known, but according to order-in-council PC 1991–337 it is between Can.$ 168,800 and 253,200.

7. An interesting consequence of these considerations is that the larger the outstanding stock of government debt, and hence the more the government has to lose from losing credibility in financial markets, the more power the Bank has in formulating monetary policy.

8. According to the Bank of Canada (1978), there are normally only seven meetings of the full board each year (p. 17), and since the directors other than the governor and deputy governor "are expected to devote only a small part of their time to the affairs of the Bank . . . it would not, as a practical matter, be reasonable to look to them to formulate monetary policy" (p. 13).

9. Bylaw number 6 (as of May 16, 1987) reads: "Pursuant to the provisions of Section 11 of the Bank of Canada Act, the fee to be paid a director shall be $3,000 per annum plus $300 for each meeting of the Board which he or she attends and the fee to be paid the directors who are members of the Executive Committee shall in addition be $3,000 per annum plus $300 for each meeting of the Executive Committee which they attend. In addition each director shall be paid $200 for each day in excess of one day for which he or she needs to be absent from his or her place of residence in order to attend a meeting."

10. The following narrative draws heavily on the detailed historical account of Jack Granatstein (1986, Chap. 4).

11. For a sample of Coyne's views, see E. P. Neufeld (1964, pp. 308–17).

12. See note 5 above.

13. Bade and Parkin (1987) have a contrary interpretation of the introduction of the directive mechanism in 1967, namely, that it weakened the Bank's independence by giving the government explicit responsibility for and authority over monetary policy. The question at issue is whether the directive constitutes an effective means for exercising that authority.

14. For a systematic analysis of the role of exchange within a bureaucracy in shaping its collective outcomes, see Breton and Wintrobe (1982).

15. An example of how public opinion can be brought to bear on the Bank through the governor's appearance in front of this committee occurred in March 1991, when the committee's questioning focused on salary increases within the Bank, alleging that these were above the guidelines established for the civil service. The Bank's Board responded with a rare public announcement that it intended to ask management to revise its salary policy. Although this pressure does not bear directly on the conduct of monetary policy, it does strike at one of the important sources of Bank independence, namely, its freedom from normal civil service constraints on personnel policy.

16. The central role of the allocation of federal government deposits in the operation of monetary policy dates back even further than the 1970s, as can be seen from Bank of Canada (1962).

17. Designated money market dealers ("jobbers") are eligible for short-term borrowing from the Bank of Canada, up to prespecified limits, in the form of Purchase and Resale Agreements, which they may undertake at their own initiative. Special Purchase and Resale Agreements and Sale and Repurchase Agreements, on the other hand, are made at the intitiative of the Bank of Canada to investment dealer jobbers and direct-clearing chartered banks.

18. The Bank of Canada will make advances at Bank rate to a chartered bank once per two-week averaging period (see next paragraph) and to other direct clearers twice per month. The rate on advances beyond these limits can be set at the discretion of the Bank of Canada. According to Clinton (1991, p. 16), advances have sometimes been made at rates higher than twice the Bank rate.

19. Since 1984, the required rates have been: 10 percent on demand deposits, 2 percent on notice deposits less than $500 million, 3 percent on notice deposits more than $500 million, and 3 percent on Canadian residents' foreign currency deposits.

20. The daily average is weighted, with deposits held at the close of business on a Friday preceding a normal two-day weekend, for example, receiving a weight of three times that of a typical Thursday, to reflect the extra interest-opportunity cost of reserves held over the weekend.

21. Clinton (1991, p. 18).

22. This is the hypothesis that short-term fluctuations in the supply of money under a regime of interest control are attributable to exogenous shocks in the demand for credit, not for money. The hypothesis is associated with the buffer-stock theory of money. For references relevant to the Canadian context, see Howitt (1986, pp. 58ff).

23. See, for example, William White (1979).

24. This impression is confirmed by Douglas Fullerton's (1986) biography of Towers.

25. This turning point in Canadian monetary policy is described in detail by George Watts (1974).

26. Scott Gordon (1961b) describes all three of these factors in detail.

27. For a description and analysis of the use of free reserves by the Federal Reserve System, see Meigs (1962).

28. The monetarist critique was made forcefully by Courchene (1971, 1976), on which the following analysis is based.

29. No specific target range was specified in the published version of Bouey's remarks on that occasion (Bank of Canada, 1975c). It was specified, however, in the published version of a speech made by Bouey a few weeks later (Bank of Canada, 1975d).

30. See, for example, White (1979).

31. See Christofides, Swidinsky, and Wilton (1979) and Reid (1979).

32. The demand function estimated by Boothe and Poloz (1988) implies a steady-state elasticity of just over 0.31.

33. For more details of these financial innovations, see Freedman (1983b).

34. In December 1990, for example, the six largest banks owned 89 percent of total assets in the industry (Canada, 1990).

35. A detailed discussion of this shift in monetary policy can be found in Courchene (1981, pp. 102ff.).

36. See Bank of Canada (1984) for details on the construction of this exchange rate.

37. The inflation targets and details concerning their use are described by Bank of Canada (1991a, pp. 61–62; 1991b).

38. One of its rationalizations for the persistence of tight monetary policies through the end of 1990 was the need to maintain enough slack in the economy to prevent the goods and services tax from starting an inflationary spiral.

39. See Muller (1990) for a summary of this work.

40. See Prescott (1986) for a precise description of the Hodrick-Prescott filter.

41. The Bank's views on the demand for M2 are summarized by Caramazza (1989).

REFERENCES

Alesina, Alberto. 1987. "Macroeconomic Policy in a Two-Party System as a Repeated Game." *Quarterly Journal of Economics* 102 (August): 651–78.

Auernheimer, Leonardo. 1974. "The Honest Government's Guide to the Revenue from the Creation of Money." *Journal of Political Economy* 82 (May/June): 598–606.

Bade, Robin, and Parkin, Michael. 1987. "Central Bank Laws and Monetary Policy." Unpublished, University of Western Ontario, June.

Bank of Canada. 1961. *Annual Report of the Governor to the Minister of Finance.* Ottawa: The Bank.

———. 1962. *Submission to the Royal Commission on Banking and Finance.* Ottawa.

———. 1975a. "Cash Reserve Management." *Bank of Canada Review* (June): 3–12.

———. 1975b. "Remarks by Gerald K. Bouey, Governor of the Bank of Canada." *Bank of Canada Review* (October): 23–30.

———. 1975c. "Statement by Governor Gerald K. Bouey before the House of Commons Committee on Finance, Trade, and Economic Affairs, November 6, 1975." *Bank of Canada Review* (November): 3–7.

———. 1975d. "Remarks by Gerald K. Bouey, Governor of the Bank of Canada:

To the Saint John Board of Trade Seminar, Saint John, N.B., 26 November, 1975." *Bank of Canada Review* (December): 3–10.

———. 1978. "Bank of Canada: Management and Accountability." *Bank of Canada Review* (June): 9–21.

———. 1982a. "Recovering from Inflation: A Speech by Gerald K. Bouey, Governor of the Bank of Canada." *Bank of Canada Review* (December): 3–9.

———. 1982b. *Annual Report of the Governor to the Minister of Finance.* Ottawa: The Bank.

———. 1984. "Technical Note: A Weighted-Average Exchange Rate Index for the Canadian Dollar." *Bank of Canada Review* (September): 119–24.

———. 1986. "Monetary Aggregates: Some Recent Developments." *Bank of Canada Review* (December): 3–21.

———. 1991a. *Annual Report of the Governor to the Minister of Finance.* Ottawa: The Bank.

———. 1991b. "Targets for Reducing Inflation." *Bank of Canada Review* (March): 3–21.

Barro, Robert, and Gordon, David. 1983. "A Positive Theory of Monetary Policy in a Natural Rate Model." *Journal of Political Economy* 91 (August): 589–610.

Boothe, Paul, and Poloz, Stephen. 1988. "Unstable Money Demand and the Monetary Model of the Exchange Rate." *Canadian Journal of Economics* 21 (November): 785–98.

Breton, Albert, and Wintrobe, Ronald. 1982. *The Logic of Bureaucratic Control.* Cambridge, England: Cambridge University Press.

Brunner, Karl, and Meltzer, Allan. 1976. "An Aggregative Theory for a Closed Economy." and "Reply—Monetarism: The Principal Issues, Areas of Agreement and the Work Remaining." In *Monetarism*, edited by Jerome L. Stein. New York: North-Holland.

Cairns, James; Binhammer, H. H.; and Boadway, Robin. 1972. *Canadian Banking and Monetary Policy.* 2d ed. Toronto: McGraw–Hill Ryerson.

Canada. 1933. *Report of the Royal Commission on Banking and Currency.* Ottawa: The King's Printer.

———. 1964. *Report of the Royal Commission on Banking and Finance.* Ottawa: The Queen's Printer.

———. 1990. *Canada Gazette, I.* December 22.

Caramazza, Francesco. 1989. "Technical Note: The Demand for M2 and M2+ in Canada." *Bank of Canada Review* (December): 3–20.

———; Hostland, Doug; and Poloz, Stephen. 1990. "The Demand for Money and the Monetary Policy Process in Canada." *Working Paper 90–5.* Bank of Canada, May.

———; McPhail, Kim; and Hostland, Doug. 1990. "Studies on the Demand for M2 and M2+ in Canada." Bank of Canada, April. Mimeo.

Christofides, Louis; Swidinsky, Robert; and Wilton, David. 1979. "The Impact of the Anti-Inflation Board on Negotiated Wage Settlements." *Canadian Journal of Economics* 12 (May): 195–213.

Clinton, Kevin. 1991. "Bank of Canada Cash Management: The Main Technique for Implementing Monetary Policy." *Bank of Canada Review* (January): 3–25.

————, and Lynch, Kevin. 1979. "Monetary Base and Money Stock in Canada." Bank of Canada Technical Report No. 16.

Committee on the Workings of the Monetary System. 1959. *Report*. London: HMSO.

Courchene, Thomas J. 1971. "Recent Canadian Monetary Policy." *Journal of Money, Credit and Banking* 3 (February): 35–56.

————. 1976. *Money, Inflation, and the Bank of Canada: An Analysis of Canadian Monetary Policy from 1970 to Early 1975*. Montreal: C. D. Howe Research Institute.

————. 1981. *Money, Inflation, and the Bank of Canada II: An Analysis of Monetary Gradualism, 1975–80*. Toronto: C. D. Howe Research Institute.

Crow, John. 1988. "The Work of Canadian Monetary Policy." *Bank of Canada Review* (February): 3–17.

Dingle, J. F.; Sparks, G. R.; and Walker, M. A., 1972. "Monetary Policy and the Adjustment of Chartered Bank Assets." *Canadian Journal of Economics* 5 (November): 494–514.

Fortin, Pierre. 1989. "Do We Measure Inflation Correctly?" In *Zero Inflation: The Goal of Price Stability*, edited by Richard G. Lipsey. Toronto: C. D. Howe Institute.

Freedman, Charles. 1983a. "Some Theoretical Aspects of Base Control." In *The Canadian Balance of Payments: Perspectives and Policy Issues*, edited by Douglas D. Purvis. Montreal: Institute for Research on Public Policy.

————. 1983b. "Financial Innovation in Canada: Causes and Consequences." *American Economic Review Proceedings* 73 (May): 101–6.

————. 1983c. "The Effect of U.S. Policies on Foreign Countries: The Case of Canada." In *Monetary Policy Issues of the 1980s*. Kansas City: Federal Reserve Bank of Kansas City.

Friedman, Benjamin M. 1983. "Monetary Policy with a Credit Aggregate Target." *Carnegie-Rochester Conference Series on Public Policy* 18 (1983): 117–47.

Friedman, Milton. 1962. "The Case for an Independent Central Bank." In *In Search of a Monetary Consititution*, edited by Leland B. Yeager. Cambridge, Mass.: Harvard University Press.

————. 1975. "Remarks at the Milton Friedman Seminar, Montreal, October 2, 1975." Montreal: C. D. Hodgson.

Fullerton, Douglas. 1986. *Graham Towers and His Times*. Toronto: McClelland & Stewart.

Gordon, H. Scott. 1961a. "The Bank of Canada in a System of Responsible Government." *Canadian Journal of Economics and Political Science* 27 (February): 1–22.

————. 1961b. *The Economists Versus the Bank of Canada*. Toronto: Ryerson Press.

Granatstein, Jack. 1986. *Canada 1957–1967: The Years of Uncertainty and Innovation*. Toronto: McClelland & Stewart.

Hostland, Doug; Poloz, Stephen; and Storer, Paul. 1987. "An Analysis of the Information Content of Alternative Monetary Aggregates." *Technical Report No. 48*. Bank of Canada.

Howitt, Peter. 1986. *Monetary Policy in Transition: A Study of Bank of Canada Policy, 1982–85*. Toronto: C. D. Howe Research Institute.

————. 1989. "Zero Inflation as a Long-Term Target for Monetary Policy." In

Zero Inflation: The Goal of Price Stability, edited by Richard G. Lipsey. Toronto: C. D. Howe Institute.

Kydland, Finn, and Prescott, Edward. 1977. "Rules Rather Than Discretion: The Inconsistency of Optimal Plans." *Journal of Political Economy* 85 (June): 473–92.

Laidler, David. 1984. "The Buffer Stock Notion in Monetary Economics." *Economic Journal* 94 (Supplement): 17–34.

———. 1991. *How Shall We Govern the Governor?: A Critique of the Governance of the Bank of Canada.* Toronto: C. D. Howe Institute.

———. and Robson, William. 1990. "Mainly Money: The Cause of Canadian Inflation." *Inflation Monitor No. 4.* Toronto: C. D. Howe Institute.

Lane, Timothy. 1983. "Essays on Monetary Control." Ph.D. Thesis, University of Western Ontario.

Lucas, Robert F. 1990. "The Case for Stable, But not Zero, Inflation." In *Taking Aim: The Debate on Zero Inflation*, edited by Robert C. York. Toronto: C. D. Howe Institute.

Mankiw, Gregory. 1987. "The Optimal Collection of Seigniorage: Theory and Evidence." *Journal of Monetary Economics* 20 (September): 327–41.

Meigs, A. J. 1962. *Free Reserves and the Money Supply.* Chicago: University of Chicago Press.

Muller, Patrice. 1990. "The Information Content of Financial Aggregates During the 1980s." Bank of Canada, April. Mimeo.

Nash, John. 1950. "The Bargaining Problem." *Econometrica* 18 (April): 155–62.

Neufeld, E. P. 1964. *Money and Banking in Canada.* Toronto: McClelland & Stewart.

Nordhaus, William. 1975. "The Political Business Cycle." *Review of Economic Studies* 42 (April): 169–90.

Poloz, Stephen J. 1984. "Unstable Velocity and the Monetary Approach to Exchange Rate Determination." Paper prepared for the Economic Research Institute, Economic Planning Agency, Tokyo, December.

Poole, William. 1970. "Optimal Choice of Policy Instruments in a Simple Stochastic Macro Model." *Quarterly Journal of Economics* 84 (May): 197–216.

Prescott, Edward. 1986. "Theory Ahead of Business Cycle Measurement." *Carnegie Rochester Conference Series on Public Policy* 25: 11–66.

Reid, Frank. 1979. "The Effect of Controls on the Rate of Wage Change in Canada." *Canadian Journal of Economics* 12 (May): 214–27.

Rogoff, Kenneth. 1990. "Equilibrium Political Business Cycles." *American Economic Review* 80 (March): 21–36.

Roth, Alvin, ed. 1985. *Game-Theoretic Models of Bargaining.* Cambridge, England: Cambridge University Press.

Sargent, Thomas, and Wallace, Neil. 1981. "Some Unpleasant Monetarist Arithmetic." *Federal Reserve Bank of Minneapolis Quarterly Review* (Fall): 1–17.

Scarth, William. 1990. "Fighting Inflation: Are the Costs of Getting to Zero Too High?" In *Taking Aim: The Debate on Zero Inflation*, edited by Robert C. York. Toronto: C. D. Howe Institute.

Thiessen, Gordon. 1982. "The Canadian Experience with Monetary Targeting."

In *Central Bank Views on Monetary Targeting*. New York: Federal Reserve Bank of New York.

Towers, Graham. 1964. Testimony to House of Commons Standing Committee on Banking and Commerce, March 18, 1954. Excerpted in *Money and Banking in Canada*, edited by E. P. Neufeld. Toronto: McClelland & Stewart.

Watts, George S. 1974. "The Bank of Canada from 1948 to 1952: The Pivotal Years." *Bank of Canada Review* (November): 3–17.

White, William. 1979. "Alternative Monetary Targets and Control Instruments in Canada: Criteria for Choice." *Canadian Journal of Economics* 12 (November): 590–604.

15

MONETARY POLICY COORDINATION IN THE EUROPEAN MONETARY SYSTEM

Jürgen von Hagen

INTRODUCTION

When the international monetary system of Bretton Woods broke down in the early 1970s, many economists expected that flexible exchange rates would insulate the national economies from monetary and business conditions in other countries. Domestic monetary policy would gain its full autonomy and independence from other countries and could pursue its own goals. Yet, it soon turned out that the new exchange-rate regime did not eliminate the correlation of monetary fluctuations and business cycles across countries. On the contrary, the free floating of exchange rates has often been regarded as a genuine source of instability in the world economy since then. Numerous attempts have been made to coordinate monetary policies internationally to prevent ostensibly pernicious exchange-rate swings and to improve the performance of the international monetary system.

Based on their already long tradition of cooperation in other areas of economic policies, the countries of the European Community (EC) have made the strongest efforts and have achieved the most in international monetary policy coordination. Since 1978, the European Monetary System (EMS) has become the formal framework for this purpose. Its cornerstone is the Exchange Rate Mechanism (ERM), the agreement to limit bilateral exchange-rate fluctuations among the participating currencies. The EMS has placed policy coordination in the EC on the basis of exchange-rate management. Today, the EMS is generally regarded as a success. It has remained the only functioning arrangement for multilateral policy coordination and exchange-rate management among industrial countries. What is more, the EC is now about to use the EMS as the launching pad for a future monetary union in Europe.

Despite the general acclaim of its success, there is little agreement on the nature of its achievements. The literature has developed two alternative, though not mutually exclusive, interpretations of the EMS. One views the EMS as a cooperative device: Exchange-rate management serves to improve response to aggregate economic fluctuations. The other interprets the EMS as a disciplinary device that allows traditional high-inflation central banks a credible commitment to price stability.

This chapter presents an overview of policy coordination in the EMS. Section 1 describes the history of the system, its main institutions, and its basic economic performance. Section 2 discusses the two interpretations of the EMS and reviews empirical evidence for their relevance. Section 3 looks at the question of strategic asymmetries in the EMS. Section 4 summarizes conclusions relating to the future of a European Monetary Union.

MONETARY POLICY COORDINATION IN THE EUROPEAN COMMUNITY

Integration, Policy Coordination, and Exchange-Rate Stability

Since the foundation of the EC in 1958, the Community has developed numerous proposals regarding monetary policy coordination.[1] In fact, the idea of a European Monetary Union (EMU) is almost as old as the EC itself.[2] This endeavor rests on two foundations. One is the view that economic integration and the completion of the customs union in the EC require and promote the coordination of monetary policies, though not necessarily fixed exchange rates. The other is the high value the EC places on exchange-rate stability.

Tsoukalis (1977) and van Ypersele and Koeune (1985) explain the relation between economic integration and monetary policy coordination by the "cumulative logic of economic integration": Dismantling regional barriers to trade and factor mobility, and the resulting integration of national goods and factor markets increase the degree of interdependence in other fields of policymaking, particularly the monetary field. Triffin (1960, p. 131), for example, argues that the customs union forces the members to give up commercial policies as an independent tool of economic policy, which otherwise could be used to preserve a country's external balance. Monetary (and fiscal) policies must therefore be coordinated to avoid balance-of-payments problems and large swings in exchange rates which would jeopardize the working of the customs union. Moreover, the liberalization of international financial markets raises the speed and size of exchange-rate fluctuations and capital flows reacting to monetary policy changes at home and elsewhere in the Community, which increases the importance of international transmission of monetary policies and expands the scope for policy coordination (von Hagen and Fratianni, 1990 a,b). On the other hand, van Ypersele and Koeune (1985) and Fratianni and von Hagen (1990c) argue that increasing economic integration likely reduces the efficiency of national economic policies to pursue domestic policy objectives. Domestic demand stimuli lose effectiveness as more and more of the additional demand they create dissipates externally. Coordinating national policies provides a way to restore their effectiveness over the integrated area. Finally, economic integration creates solidarity among countries, which is reflected in the fact that agreements for policy coordination often include provisions for mutual financial assistance to cope with external imbalances and adjustment problems. Agreements to coordinate national policies in the EC, or even delegate policy authority to Community institutions, can therefore widen and improve the opportunity set of national policymakers (Triffin, 1960, p. 133).

In sum, economic integration makes monetary policy coordination more beneficial and desirable. The Delors Report (Commission, 1989), the EC's most recent blueprint for an EMU, calls this the principle of parallelism: Economic and monetary integration are two aspects of the same process and have to be pursued simultaneously to maximize the benefits of either one.

By itself, the desire for policy coordination does not imply a desire for fixed exchange rates. On the contrary, the loss of policy degrees of freedom in the customs union should increase the value of exchange-rate flexibility to allow the economies to adjust to idiosyncratic shocks (Dornbusch, 1980, p. 67). The EC's interest in exchange-rate stability derives from the close connection between exchange-rate and commercial policies. Given that goods prices adjust slowly relative to exchange rates, exchange-rate fluctuations can distort relative prices across countries, resulting in comparative disadvantages for national industries which are unjustified by "real" factors, such as relative productivities.[3] Governments then come under political pressures to reintroduce protective measures of commercial policy. Furthermore, they may be tempted to use exchange-rate policies to pursue trade interests and thereby undermine the customs union. The Treaty of Rome recognized this connection between exchange-rate and commercial policies authorizing retaliation against exchange-rate policies that distort competition (Art. 107). In contrast, exchange-rate stability creates a favorable climate for the progress and stability of the customs union by avoiding such pressures and temptations.

Since the mid-1960s, the EC's Common Agricultural Policy (CAP) has added another strong motivation for stable exchange rates (Giavazzi and Giovannini, 1989, p. 12ff.; van Ypersele and Koeune, 1985, p. 36). The cornerstone of CAP is the agreement to fix agricultural prices on a Community-wide basis in terms of the European Unit of Account.[4] Since the common price must be translated into national currency prices, all exchange-rate changes with the common numeraire result in national price changes of agricultural products and produce undesirable distortions of farm price relations and trade patterns in the EC. The immediate impact on farm incomes changes production incentives in the EC.[5] Exchange-rate changes are therefore likely to meet political opposition from the well-organized farm sectors in the EC.

In conclusion, the common desire for monetary policy coordination and exchange-rate stability has led the EC to approach policy coordination strategically through exchange-rate management. Since the late 1960s, the debate over how to achieve this goal has involved monetarists and economists (e.g., Tsoukalis, 1977). The monetarists, mostly French and Belgian, regarded exchange-rate fixity as a vehicle for policy coordination. Imposing fixed exchange rates forces the authorities to adjust their policies and results in an increasing degree of international conformity and compatibility of monetary policies. This process itself creates a force strengthening the economic and political unification in the EC. The economists, mainly Dutch and German, argued that convergence and compatibility of national policies have to be achieved first. A fixed exchange rate can then be introduced as the result of policy coordination. The real difference between the two positions is in the incidence of the burden of adjustment to a common monetary policy (Tsoukalis, 1977). The economist solution presumes that high-inflation countries change their policies to achieve a greater price stability before the introduction of fixed exchange rates with the low-inflation currencies. The monetarist solution instead leaves open the question of who adjusts to whom. In particular, it does not exclude the adjustment of the low-inflation countries to a higher common inflation rate, or permanent inflation differentials with the result of lasting balance-of-payments deficits of the high-inflation countries financed by their low-inflation partners.

The EC's monetary policy coordination efforts had to seek a compromise between these two positions. This compromise is reflected in the two principles on which policy coordination in the EMS was to be built: flexibility and symmetry (e.g., van Ypersele, 1979). Flexibility means that an arrangement for policy coordination must be able to support lasting divergences in price-level developments. Symmetry dictates that no participating country would be forced to adopt an inflation rate different from its own, most preferred one, and that all members would share the burden of adjustment to balance-of-payments disequilibria.

The Road to the EMS: A Brief Review

The Treaty of Rome, which established the EC among Belgium, France, Germany, Luxembourg, Italy, and the Netherlands in 1958, lays down the foundations for macroeconomic policy coordination among the member countries, though only in rather general terms. Article 103 declares the members' stabilization policies a "matter of common concern" and requires mutual information about such policies. Article 104 defines external equilibrium, full employment, price stability, and (indirectly) stability of currencies as the common general objectives of economic policy.[6] Article 105 calls on the members to coordinate their economic and monetary policies and to facilitate cooperation among the relevant national authorities. Article 107 requires that exchange-rate policies be treated as a "matter of common concern." Article 108 calls for mutual assistance in balance-of-payments crises. The Monetary Committee (1958) and the Short-term Policy Committee (1960) were created to institutionalize policy coordination.

During the following decade, attempts to coordinate monetary policies in the EC did not go much further. In fact, there was little perceived need to do so. All six countries were members of the Bretton Woods system, which provided the EC with monetary and exchange-rate stability under the leadership of the United States. The joint peg of the dollar implicitly limited exchange-rate fluctuations among the EC currencies. The European Monetary Agreement of 1958 reduced their bilateral margins of fluctuation to 3 percent. This external constraint was tightened in the aftermath of the 1961 revaluations of the DM and the Dutch guilder by the commitment (in 1964) to consult their EC partners before a country would change its central parities against the dollar. Several more policy committees were created in 1964 to strengthen policy coordination. In view of this and the motivation CAP added to its environment, it became popular during the mid–1960s in the Community to speak of a "de-facto monetary union" in the EC (Tsoukalis, 1977). With the benefit of hindsight, Tsoukalis calls this "agricultural mythology."

The 1960s witnessed the gradual erosion of the Bretton Woods system, as U.S. monetary policy became less committed to its role of providing international price stability. By the end of the 1960s, the EC had to face the loss of its external source of monetary and exchange-rate stability and its own inability to deal with the new situation.[7] In 1969 speculation against the French franc and in favor of the DM led to a devaluation of the franc in August and to a revaluation of the DM after a short period of floating. Both decisions were taken unilaterally. To avoid the repercussions in the agricultural sector, the French government, soon imitated by the German government, introduced the system of monetary compensation amounts, which effectively separated market exchange rates from the parities applicable to agricultural products. This violation of the agreements was widely regarded as a death-blow to CAP (Tsoukalis, 1977).

Much political turmoil shook the EC in connection with these events. Against this background, Germany's Chancellor Willy Brandt took the lead at the EC Summit of the Hague in early December 1969 and proposed to create a monetary union in the EC. His proposal was favorably received by the French government (Tsoukalis, 1977). For the first time, the EC formally adopted the goal of an EMU. The Werner Committee was formed, whose report (Council of the European Communities, 1970) presented a strategy for monetary union and a number of steps to strengthen monetary policy coordination in the Community. Although the EC Council approved the Werner Plan in 1971, its implementation did not go very far. The international monetary crisis of 1971 instead revealed that the EC was as yet unable to agree on a common monetary policy. France and Italy rejected the proposal of a joint float against the dollar, and the DM and the guilder eventually began to float freely. Belgium, Luxembourg, and the Netherlands finally adopted a joint float in August 1971, and the DM and the lira floated freely, while the French government stiffened foreign exchange controls and maintained a fixed dollar parity.

The Smithsonian Agreement of December 1971 temporarily restored the Bretton Woods system. It allowed for a maximum range of fluctuation of 9 percent among the nondollar currencies. The Community decided to narrow this range in its first European exchange-rate arrangement, the "Snake," in 1972. The Snake limited bilateral exchange-rate fluctuations to ±2.25 percent. Interventions to maintain these limits were compulsory and were generally to be executed in member currencies rather than U.S. dollars to avoid the accumulation of large dollar balances. To facilitate interventions, the new European Monetary Cooperation Fund (EMCF) would consolidate bilateral claims among the participating central banks. But the Snake lacked stability: The United Kingdom and Ireland left as early as June 1972, Italy in 1973, and Denmark and France left and reentered, France only to leave again in 1976. The Snake's central parities were changed in ten realignments between 1972 and 1978. By then, it had essentially become a DM-block, grouping the Northern EC members—Belgium, Denmark, Luxembourg, and the Netherlands—around the leadership of Germany.

The process of European monetary unification did not regain political momentum until the late 1970s. In 1977 the president of the EC Commission Roy Jenkins advocated a big leap toward an EMU as a way to push the process of economic unification (Jenkins, 1978). The European Council reaffirmed the objective of EMU in December 1977. In 1978 the French President Giscard d'Estaing and the German Chancellor Helmut Schmidt launched a tour de force leading to the creation of the European Monetary System (EMS) by the end of that year. Schmidt's (1990) own reflections on his and d'Estaing's initiative leave no doubt that their motivations were as much based on economic as on general political considerations. Closer coordination and, eventually, monetary unification in Europe were part of a larger strategy aiming at the political unification of Europe, increasing Europe's clout in world affairs, and assuring Germany's firm integration into the Western alliance. All EC members joined the EMS. The documents establishing it state that the stability of prices and exchange rates, the narrowing of inflation differentials, and the harmonization of economic policies in the Community were the main goals of the new system (Commission, 1979, p. 94; Emerson, 1979, p. 34ff.; Ungerer et al., 1983, p. 10; van Ypersele, 1979, p. 8ff.).

Among economists, the EMS was widely received with skepticism.[8] For some, it was a mere continuation of the Snake, a product of political opportunism (Vaubel, 1980). In view of the marked differences in the members' economic performance during the 1970s, many predicted its early failure. In contrast, the proponents praised the EMS as a new kind of exchange-rate arrangement. Based on its principles of flexibility and symmetry, the EMS would prove capable of surviving the tensions caused by the economic divergencies.

The European Monetary System

The EMS consists of four main institutional elements (Commission, 1979): the ERM, the ECU (European Currency Unit—a basket currency), credit facilities among the participants, and the EMCF. The ERM is the most important and visible of these four. We will therefore follow common practice and treat EMS and ERM as synonyms. The ERM became effective on March 13, 1979. Greece and Portugal chose not to participate in the ERM; Spain joined it in July 1989; and the United Kingdom joined it only in October 1990. The ERM limits bilateral exchange-rate fluctuations to margins of ±2.25 percent around predetermined central parities. Italy obtained a margin of ±6 percent for the lira, which was reduced to the narrow band in January 1990; Spain and the United Kingdom also entered the ERM with a margin of ±6 percent.

The ECU is a basket of all EMS currencies, including sterling and the Greek drachma. It contains fixed quantities of each currency reflecting the relative importance of the individual economies. The fixed quantities imply that the relative weight of each currency in the value of the ECU varies over time. The basket quantities are revised periodically to ensure that the value of the ECU will not be dominated by a single member currency.[9] The ECU serves as a denominator for the determination of central rates and for transactions in the EMS intervention and credit mechanisms. The EMCF pools international reserve assets of the EMS members. Within the fund, an initial supply of ECU for intervention was created against the deposit of 20 percent of the members' gold and dollar reserves in three-month revolving swap operations.[10]

To facilitate interventions, weak-currency central banks can borrow unlimited amounts of reserves from their hard-currency partners under the Very Short Term Facility (VSTF) of the EMCF. VSTF credits are denominated and can be repaid in ECU. Members are required to grant such credits upon request. The credits are due forty-five days after the end of the month in which the intervention occurred. Repayment of up to 100 percent of the debtor's VSTF quota can be delayed for an additional thirty days unilaterally by the borrower; the Nyborg Agreement extended this possibility to two months and increased the eligible amount to 200 percent of the debtor's quota. Beyond that, the lender's consent is required. In 1985 the possibility of obtaining intervention currencies was increased by allowing the temporary drawing of dollars or member currencies from the EMCF for up to about 60 percent of a member's ECU quota.

In practice, weak-currency central banks obtain base money denominated in hard currency for compulsory interventions by drawing on the VSTF. The EMCF receives the necessary funds simultaneously from the hard-currency central bank. This results in an additional liability in the weak-currency central bank's balance sheet and an additional asset in the hard-currency central bank's balance sheet. The monetary base of the weak-currency central bank automatically declines, while the monetary base of the hard-currency central bank rises. Conversely, if the hard-currency central bank intervenes, it sells its own currency against base money denominated in the weak currency. The funds thus acquired are transferred to the EMCF, which credits them to the hard-currency central bank's account and debits them to the weak-currency central bank's account. Again, the monetary base of the latter falls, while the monetary base of the former rises. Thus, the operating procedures of the EMCF assure that the immediate liquidity effects of compulsory interventions in the ERM are perfectly symmetric among the countries involved. It is therefore irrelevant which central bank engages in the intervention (Bofinger, 1988a).

The assured symmetry of the immediate liquidity effects of compulsory interventions does not imply, however, that the final liquidity effects will be symmetric, too. Central banks can sterilize foreign exchange interventions, that is, undo their impact on the monetary base by offsetting operations in domestic components of the base. In the EMS, central banks are free to sterilize the liquidity effects of interventions. They have used this possibility in the past to reduce their consequences for domestic monetary growth (Mastropasqua et al., 1988; Roubini, 1988; von Hagen, 1989). This lack of rules for the sterilization means that there are no clearly specified provisions for the final incidence of the liquidity effects resulting from interventions.

Apart from intervening at the margins, central banks in the EMS may engage in intramarginal interventions before the exchange rates reach their limits. Such interventions serve to suppress exchange-rate movements before they cause tensions in the ERM. Under the original rules of the EMS, intramarginal interventions in member currencies required the consent of the central bank issuing the intervention currency. The Bundesbank had insisted on this requirement to prevent other EMS central banks from accumulating large DM balances, because it feared they would impair the conduct of German monetary policy. As a consequence, intramarginal interventions were mostly executed in dollars and did not have symmetric immediate liquidity effects in the weak and strong-currency country. Later, the Bundesbank loosened its strict opposition and at times even encouraged partner central banks to build up sizable DM balances (Ungerer, 1990, p. 16ff.). The Nyborg Agreement of September 1987 allowed EMCF financing of intramarginal interventions for up to 200 percent of the members' VSTF quotas. As a result, a sizable part of intramarginal interventions now have symmetric liquidity effects similar to obligatory interventions. The agreement stipulated the presumption that intramarginal interventions financed in this way meet the consent of the central bank issuing the intervention currency. In practice, intramarginal interventions have become much more important than interventions at the margins. The latter amount to only 10 to 15 percent of total gross intervention. Between 1979 and 1985, between 60 and 80 percent of gross intramarginal interventions were executed in U.S. dollars, compared to about one third in 1986 and 1987. The Bundesbank did not participate in intramarginal interventions in DM, but conducted most dollar interventions before 1985 (Giavazzi and Giovannini, 1987, p. 239; Mastropasqua et al., 1988).

EMS members can obtain loans to finance transitory balance-of-payments deficits under the Short-Term Monetary Support. Such loans are usually denominated in the creditor's currency and are granted for three months, with a possible extension of six months. Under the Medium-Term Financial Assistance, credits can be granted to help finance the adjustment to persistent balance-of-payments deficits. Loans under this facility are denominated in ECU and have maturities of two to five years; they can be made conditional on economic and monetary policy changes.

From the beginning, there was a common understanding that the central parities in the ERM would be adjusted to changes in economic conditions and relative performance if necessary to avoid persistent external imbalances. Early proponents of the EMS even stressed the point that the frequency of realignments should not be taken as a criterion of success (Commission, 1979, p. 78; van Ypersele, 1979, p. 9). In contrast to the practice of the Bretton Woods system, where changes in central rates were decided unilaterally, realignments in the EMS should be the outcome of collective decision making by all members (Council of the European Communities, 1985, para. 3.2). So far, there have been twelve realignments in the EMS.[11] The possibility of realignments assures that individual members can chose their own long-run course of monetary policy independently, even though exchange rates are stabilized. To preserve additional policy autonomy in the short run, EMS members have relied on capital and exchange controls, which drive a wedge between domestic and international interest rates and financial markets and permit the central bank to use its domestic and international assets as two fairly independent instruments, one to pursue domestic policy goals and the other for exchange-rate management (Wyplosz, 1988a). Capital and exchange controls have also been necessary in the ERM to avoid speculative attacks on the system when markets anticipated a realignment.[12]

In summary, the EMS seems best characterized as a framework for optional, rather than automatic or required, policy coordination, leaving its members considerable room for independent policymaking. The indeterminacy of its rules became the subject of much criticism of the EMS early on. It is still the source of controversy over the appropriate interpretation of EMS policy coordination and its economic consequences.

Basic Economic Performance of the EMS

Table 15.1 reports annual CPI inflation rates for the EMS from 1977 to 1989. On average, inflation peaked a year after the EMS started, a year also after the second oil price shock. The peak occurred in the same year in all member countries, except Belgium and Ireland. Between 1980 and 1986, EMS inflation rates declined steadily, but they started rising again in 1987. The average inflation reduction from peak to trough was 9.4 percent; Ireland and Italy experienced the largest individual reductions. The standard deviation of inflation rates in the system also peaked in 1980 at 6.2 percent and declined steadily to 1.4 percent in 1989. In this sense, EMS inflation rates converged during the 1980s.

In the lower part of Table 15.1, we compare the EMS record to the performance of a group of non-EMS countries. These countries had similar average inflation rates and standard deviations during the 1970s. Since EMS membership was the main difference between the monetary policy arrangements of these two groups in the 1980s, the merits of the EMS in the European disinflation would be most obvious, if the performance of the EMS countries was much better in this decade. Table 15.1 shows, however, that the two groups behaved very similarly. Average inflation in the non-EMS group fell by 10.1 percent from the 1980 peak to the trough in 1986. The largest reductions occurred in Greece (69.7 percent) and the United Kingdom (14.6 percent). The standard deviation of inflation fell from 5.1 percent in 1980 to 1.6 percent in 1989. Neither disinflation nor convergence is peculiar to the EMS.

Tables 15.2 and 15.3 show that the disinflation was generally associated with slow real growth and high unemployment. Between 1977 and 1980, average output growth rates were 2.9 percent in the EMS and 3.7 percent

Table 15.1
CPI Inflation Rates, EMS and Non-EMS Countries (percent)

EMS	1977	1978	1979	1980	1981	1982	1983	1984	1985	1986	1987	1988	1989
Belgium	7.1	4.5	4.5	6.6	7.6	8.7	7.7	6.3	4.9	1.3	1.6	1.2	3.1
Denmark	11.1	10.1	9.6	12.3	11.7	10.1	6.9	6.3	4.7	3.7	4.0	4.6	4.8
France	9.4	9.1	10.7	13.8	13.4	11.8	9.6	7.4	5.8	2.5	3.3	2.7	3.5
Germany	3.7	2.7	4.1	5.4	6.3	5.3	3.3	2.4	2.2	-0.1	0.2	1.3	2.8
Ireland	13.6	7.6	13.2	18.2	20.4	17.1	10.5	8.6	5.4	3.8	3.1	2.2	4.0
Italy	17.0	12.1	14.8	21.2	17.8	16.5	14.7	10.8	9.2	5.9	4.7	5.0	6.2
NL	6.5	4.2	4.2	6.5	6.7	5.9	2.8	3.3	2.2	0.3	-0.1	1.5	3.4
Average	8.8	5.9	8.5	11.6	11.2	10.0	7.9	6.0	4.9	2.2	2.3	2.6	3.8
St.D.	4.9	5.3	4.4	6.2	4.6	4.4	4.4	3.2	2.7	2.3	1.9	1.5	1.4

Non-EMS	1977	1978	1979	1980	1981	1982	1983	1984	1985	1986	1987	1988	1989
Australia	12.3	7.9	9.1	10.1	9.7	11.1	10.1	4.5	6.7	9.1	8.5	7.2	7.6
Austria	5.5	3.6	3.7	6.4	6.8	5.4	3.3	5.7	3.2	1.7	1.4	1.9	1.6
Canada	8.0	9.0	9.1	10.2	12.4	10.8	5.8	4.3	4.0	4.2	4.4	4.0	5.0
Finland	12.7	7.8	7.5	11.6	12.0	9.3	8.4	7.1	5.9	2.9	4.1	5.1	6.6
Greece	12.2	12.5	19.0	24.9	24.5	21.0	20.2	18.4	19.3	23.0	16.4	13.5	13.7
Japan	8.0	3.8	3.6	8.0	4.9	2.6	1.8	2.3	2.0	0.6	0.0	0.7	2.3
CH	1.3	1.1	3.6	4.0	6.5	5.7	3.0	2.9	3.4	0.8	1.4	1.9	5.2
U.K.	15.8	8.3	13.4	18.0	11.9	8.6	4.6	5.0	6.1	3.4	4.1	4.9	7.8
U.S.	6.5	7.6	11.3	13.5	10.4	6.2	3.2	4.3	3.6	1.9	3.7	4.0	4.8
Average	7.7	7.0	9.6	12.4	9.7	6.4	3.9	4.2	3.8	2.3	3.2	3.5	4.7
St.D.	4.1	3.7	4.7	5.1	4.1	4.2	7.2	2.3	2.7	2.3	2.1	1.9	1.6

Source: International Financial Statistics, IMF.

Note: Averages and standard deviations (ST.D.) are computed with the following 1982 real GNP-based weights (percents): EMS: Belgium 4.55, Denmark 2.97, France 28.84, Germany 34.42, Ireland 0.99, Italy 21.07, Netherlands (NL) 7.22. Non-EMS: Australia 3.08, Austria 1.23, Canada 5.61, Finland 0.94, Greece 0.71, Japan 20.03, Switzerland (CH) 1.79, U.K. 8.98, U.S. 57.63.

Table 15.2
Growth Rates of Real GDP (percent)

EMS	1977	1978	1979	1980	1981	1982	1983	1984	1985	1986	1987	1988	1989
Belgium[1]	0.3	3.0	1.6	3.4	-1.5	1.2	0.2	2.3	1.4	2.1	2.2	4.2	4.2
Denmark	1.6	1.5	3.5	-0.4	-0.9	3.0	2.5	4.4	4.2	3.6	-0.6	-0.2	1.3
France	3.0	3.8	3.3	1.0	0.5	2.5	0.7	1.3	1.7	2.5	2.2	3.8	3.6
Germany[1]	2.7	3.3	4.0	1.5	0.0	-0.9	1.9	3.3	2.0	2.3	1.7	3.6	4.0
Ireland	8.2	7.2	3.1	3.1	2.6	2.3	-1.1	3.8	1.1	-0.3	4.9	3.7	4.0
Italy	1.9	2.7	4.9	3.9	0.2	2.4	1.0	3.2	2.8	2.6	3.0	4.2	3.2
NL[1]	2.3	2.1	2.5	0.8	-0.7	-1.5	1.7	2.9	2.8	1.5	1.0	2.2	4.3
Average	2.5	3.2	3.7	1.9	0.1	1.0	1.3	2.7	2.2	2.4	2.0	3.6	3.7
Non-EMS													
Australia	2.6	3.5	3.5	1.9	3.6	3.0	0.4	6.7	5.5	2.0	4.2	3.8	4.8
Austria	4.4	0.5	4.7	3.0	-0.1	1.1	2.2	1.4	2.8	1.1	2.0	4.2	3.8
Canada	2.0	3.6	3.2	1.1	3.3	-3.2	3.2	6.3	4.6	3.2	4.0	4.5	3.0
Finland	0.2	2.6	7.4	5.6	1.8	3.6	3.0	3.3	3.5	2.5	3.8	5.2	5.4
Greece	3.4	6.7	3.7	1.7	-0.3	0.4	0.4	2.7	3.1	1.4	-0.5	3.7	3.1
Japan[1]	5.3	5.1	5.2	4.8	4.0	3.1	3.2	5.1	4.7	2.5	4.6	5.7	4.9
CH	2.4	0.4	2.5	4.6	1.5	-1.1	0.6	2.0	3.8	2.9	2.0	2.9	3.5
U.K.	1.0	3.8	2.2	-2.3	-1.2	1.1	3.5	2.1	3.9	3.6	4.8	4.2	2.1
U.S.[1]	5.5	5.0	2.8	-0.3	2.5	-2.5	3.6	6.4	2.7	2.8	3.4	4.4	3.4
Average	4.6	4.6	3.6	0.9	2.5	-0.7	3.3	5.6	3.4	2.8	3.7	4.6	3.1

Source: See table 15.1.

Note: Averages are weighted.

[1]Real GNP after 1982.

Table 15.3
Unemployment Rates (percent)

EMS	1977	1978	1979	1980	1981	1982	1983	1983	1985	1986	1987	1988	1989
Belgium	9.8	10.5	10.9	11.8	14.2	16.6	18.4	18.6	17.3	16.1	15.9	14.5	13.1
Denmark	7.7	7.4	6.0	7.0	9.2	9.8	10.7	10.2	9.3	8.0	8.0	8.8	9.4
France	4.9	5.3	6.0	6.4	7.5	8.3	8.5	9.9	10.2	10.4	10.5	9.9	9.4
Germany	4.5	4.3	3.8	3.8	5.5	7.5	9.1	9.1	9.3	9.0	8.9	8.7	7.9
Ireland	11.9	10.7	9.3	10.3	13.5	16.5	20.9	16.4	17.7	18.1	18.8	18.4	17.8
Italy	7.2	7.2	7.7	7.6	8.4	9.0	9.9	10.1	10.1	11.1	12.0	12.0	12.0
NL	3.4	3.4	3.5	4.1	6.3	8.8	11.2	11.2	10.1	9.2	8.6	8.3	7.4
Average	5.5	5.5	5.6	5.9	7.3	8.7	9.9	10.3	10.2	10.2	10.4	10.3	9.5

Non-EMS	1977	1978	1979	1980	1981	1982	1983	1983	1985	1986	1987	1988	1989
Australia	5.6	6.3	6.2	6.1	5.8	7.2	10.0	9.0	8.2	8.1	8.1	7.2	6.2
Austria	1.8	2.1	2.0	1.9	2.4	3.7	4.5	4.5	4.8	5.2	5.6	5.4	4.4
Canada	8.1	8.4	7.5	7.5	7.6	11.0	11.9	11.3	10.5	9.6	8.9	7.8	7.5
Finland	6.1	7.5	6.2	4.7	5.1	5.9	6.1	5.2	5.0	5.4	5.1	4.6	3.5
Japan	2.0	2.2	2.1	2.0	2.2	2.4	2.7	2.7	2.6	2.8	2.8	2.5	2.3
CH	0.4	0.3	0.3	0.3	0.2	0.4	0.9	1.1	1.0	0.8	0.8	0.7	0.6
U.K.	5.8	5.7	5.4	6.4	9.9	11.5	12.3	11.1	11.3	11.4	10.2	8.1	6.3
U.S.	7.1	6.0	5.8	7.1	7.6	9.7	9.6	7.5	7.2	7.0	6.2	5.5	5.3
Average	5.7	5.2	4.9	5.7	6.4	8.1	8.3	6.9	6.7	6.5	5.9	5.2	4.8

Source: See Table 15.1.

Note: Averages are weighted.

521

in the control group; between 1981 and 1984 they dropped to 1.3 percent and 2.9 percent; they rebounded to 2.4 percent and 3.6 percent between 1985 and 1987. Both groups had similar average rates of unemployment around 5.5 percent between 1977 and 1980. In the early 1980s the EMS average rose to 9.4 percent and then to 10.7 percent (1985–87). The non-EMS average rose to 7.4 percent (1981–84), followed by a decline to 6.4 percent (1985–87). Thus, the growth and employment record was worse in the EMS during the 1980s.[13] A noticeable difference between the two groups of countries is the much lower speed of disinflation in the EMS. Disinflation outside the EMS was a shock therapy, causing relatively deep but short recessions. In contrast, disinflation in the EMS was a gradual process, stretching the economic cost over a much larger time period (De Grauwe, 1990).

Table 15.4 shows that the EMS has not prevented sizable long-run changes of nominal and real exchange rates. Since 1979, all EMS currencies have depreciated in nominal terms against the DM, but almost all appreciated in real terms. Non-EMS currencies first appreciated and then depreciated against the DM, both in nominal terms; they appreciated steadily in real terms. Absolute DM exchange-rate changes were even larger on average inside than outside the EMS. The dispersion of nominal exchange-rate trends, measured by the standard deviations of changes in each group, declined in the EMS. In the non-EMS group, the dispersion of DM rates declined in the early 1980s, then increased and finally declined again. Throughout the 1980s, the dispersion was much smaller in the EMS than outside. The dispersion of real DM exchange-rate changes in the EMS increased sharply in the early 1980s, to return to pre-EMS levels thereafter. For non-EMS members, real exchange-rate dispersion changed in line with nominal exchange-rate dispersion.

To summarize, the EMS combined a smaller average reduction in inflation rates with an inferior performance of the real economy during the 1980s. From a long-run perspective, the main difference in exchange-rate developments between EMS and non-EMS currencies has been the greater conformity of exchange-rate changes in the EMS.

ALTERNATIVE INTERPRETATIONS OF POLICY COORDINATION IN THE EMS

A Model of Monetary Policymaking in the EMS

In this section, we develop a model of monetary policymaking in the EMS to discuss the alternative interpretations of the system. Our model is taken from Canzoneri and Henderson (1988) and Fratianni and von Hagen (1990a). It is deliberately simplified, aiming at characterizing the strategic aspects of policymaking rather than at a realistic description of

Table 15.4
Average DM—Exchange Rate Changes (percent)

	1975–78		1979–83		1984–86		1987–89	
	N	R	N	R	N	R	N	R
EMS								
Belgium	0.8	-4.2	7.0	4.4	0.8	-1.9	0.6	0.0
Denmark	-3.2	-3.9	7.7	0.7	1.2	-2.2	1.3	-1.8
France	4.0	-3.1	8.4	-1.2	2.0	-1.7	1.9	0.1
Ireland	11.0	-3.1	5.3	-10.2	2.7	-1.7	2.7	-1.2
Italy	13.2	-2.2	10.4	-8.0	4.4	-2.7	1.8	-2.1
NL	0.7	-3.2	1.0	0.5	0.3	-0.2	0.0	-0.2
Average	6.4	-2.9	8.1	-2.9	2.5	-1.9	1.6	-0.8
St.D.	4.9	0.8	2.6	4.0	1.4	0.7	0.6	0.7
Non-EMS								
Australia	12.0	1.8	-0.1	7.0	16.5	11.2	-0.6	-7.0
Austria	0.0	-2.4	-0.7	-1.0	0.0	-2.0	0.0	-0.5
Canada	9.8	4.1	-3.8	-10.1	8.2	5.5	-0.4	-3.9
Finland	7.9	-3.6	1.6	-4.8	2.0	-1.8	-0.6	-4.5
Greece	11.2	0.1	22.5	-6.0	18.5	-8.6	9.8	-3.3
Japan	-1.4	-6.3	-2.8	-2.0	-4.7	-4.8	-1.5	-1.1
CH	-4.4	-2.8	-2.0	-1.5	0.2	-0.5	1.6	0.8
U.K.	11.0	-5.0	-0.1	-8.7	6.1	2.8	1.0	-3.2
Average	4.0	-3.6	-1.0	-4.9	1.7	-0.4	-0.4	-1.0
St.D.	6.2	4.3	3.6	3.5	7.0	4.9	1.7	2.8

Notes: N = nominal exchange rate; R = real exchange rate; real exchange rate changes are calculated with CPI inflation differentials. A positive sign indicates a devaluation of the currency of the country named in left column against the DM. Averages and standard deviations are weighted with GNP weights.

Table 15.5
A Model of Policymaking in the EMS

(1) aggregate supply: $y = y^n + (1-\alpha)n + \xi$; $y^* = y^n + (1-\alpha)n^* + \xi$

(2) demand for labor: $w-p = -\alpha n + \xi$; $w^*-p^* = -\alpha n^* + \xi$

(3) aggregate demand: $y^d = \delta^{-1}r + \beta y^* + (1-\beta)y - \delta^{-1}\eta$

$\qquad\qquad\qquad\qquad y^{*d} = -\delta^{-1}r + \beta y + (1-\beta)y^* + \delta^{-1}\eta$

(4) money market equilibrium: $m - p = y - y^n$; $m^* - p^* = y^* - y^n$

(5) consumer price levels: $q = \alpha m + \epsilon(m - m^*) + \xi + \beta\eta$

$\qquad\qquad\qquad\qquad q^* = \alpha m^* + \epsilon(m^* - m) + \xi - \beta\eta$

(6) preference functions: $2U = -\sigma(n - N)^2 - q^2$;

$\qquad\qquad\qquad\qquad 2U^* = -\sigma(n^* - N^*)^2 - (q^*)^2$

$0 < \beta < 0.5$; $\epsilon = \beta^2\delta(1-\alpha)$; $y^n = -\ln(1-\alpha)$

the economies. The model is displayed in Table 15.5. There are two countries, Germany and France. All variables are defined in logarithms, and all French variables are denoted with a "*." Each country produces an output good y (y^*) according to the production functions (1), where n (n^*) is employment and ξ is a supply shock with expectation zero and variance $\sigma\xi^2$ common to both countries. Assuming profit maximization yields the labor demand functions (2), where w (w^*) is the nominal wage and p (p^*) is the output price. Let s be the nominal DM/FF exchange rate and define the real exchange rate as $r = s + p^* - p$. Aggregate demand is given by the demand functions (3), where η is a relative demand shock with expectation zero and variance σ_η^2. The consumer price levels are defined as $q = (1-\beta)p + \beta(s+p^*) = p + \beta r$, and $q^* = p^* - \beta r$, where β is the marginal propensity to import. Normalizing past prices and the past exchange rate to zero, we find that the current values of q and q^* are equivalent to current consumer price inflation rates. Money is the only asset in these economies. It is held for transactions purposes with a constant velocity (equation 4). Equation (5) gives the solution for the equilibrium price levels.

In the private sector, nominal wages are contracted at the beginning of each period, prior to the realization of all shocks. Wage-earners aim at a constant expected real wage, which implies that $w = m^e$ and $w^* = (m^*)^e$, where the superscript e denotes a rational expectation. During the period, labor supply is perfectly elastic at the fixed nominal wage, which implies $n = m - m^e$ and $n^* = m^* - (m^*)^e$. In contrast, monetary policymakers choose the current money supply after the realization of all shocks has been observed. The policymakers' preference functions (6) express their distaste for price-level and employment fluctuations. Policymakers have employment targets N and N^* different from the natural levels of employment, which are normalized to zero. Presently, we assume that $N = N^* = 0$.

Cooperative Interpretations of the EMS

Cooperative interpretations of the EMS rest on the observation that, even in a world with flexible exchange rates, monetary policy has international spillover effects. Policy actions in one country affect the outcomes in other economies and, therefore, create externalities between the authorities. Standard economic theory entails that independent decision making leads to inefficient outcomes under such circumstances.

Consider the example of a negative supply shock, $\xi < 0$, such as an oil price shock, hitting both countries. The shock leads to an increase in the output price levels driving down the real wage. But with its preference for price stability, a central bank reacts with a restrictive monetary policy to stabilize the price level at the cost of some reduction in employment. The domestic monetary contraction leads to an appreciation of the domestic currency, which, in turn, affects the foreign price level positively and works against the foreign central bank's attempt to contain inflation. By assumption, the foreign central bank faces the same policy problem and acts in the same way, so that its efforts work toward more inflation in the first country and a greater monetary contraction by its central bank. With independent monetary policies, the two central banks ignore this interdependence. In the resulting equilibrium, their policies offset each other, and neither currency appreciates. The two central banks react "too much" to the original shock in the sense that they could achieve the same degree of price stability at a lower employment cost.

In contrast to this competitive appreciation (or devaluation in the case of a positive supply shock), a different spillover arises from a relative demand shock, $\eta > 0$. Such a shock raises the demand for German output and lowers the demand for French output. The German central bank reacts with a monetary contraction, which causes the mark to appreciate. At the same time, the French central bank reacts with a monetary expansion, causing the franc to depreciate. In this scenario, the actions of the two central banks work to each other's benefit; with independent monetary policies, however, they do not realize this mutual benefit, and they react "too little" to the relative shock. With coordination, they could reach the same degree of price stability with less variation in employment.

In the absence of an agreement to coordinate their monetary policies, each central bank sets its money supply to maximize its preference functions

(6) given the policy of the other central bank. The resulting Nash equilibrium is

(7) $m = (\alpha + \epsilon)(k_n\xi - h_n\beta\eta)$ $m^* = (\alpha + \epsilon)(k_n\xi + h_n\beta\eta)$
     $q = -\sigma(k_n\xi - h_n\beta\eta)$ $q^* = -\sigma(k_n\xi + h_n\beta\eta)$,

where $k_n = 1/(\sigma + \alpha(\alpha + \epsilon))$, and $h_n = 1/(\sigma + (\alpha + 2\epsilon)(\alpha + \epsilon))$.

There are two ways to evaluate this equilibrium, corresponding to alternative interpretations of the policy problem. One is to assume that the *policy regime* has to be chosen in advance, before the actual shocks are realized. Policy regimes are then evaluated in terms of the expected utility they yield. This is appropriate if the regime changes involve significant transaction cost and hence occur infrequently. The other is to assume that a policy regime can be adopted after the realization of the shocks, so that alternative regimes are evaluated in terms of the actual shocks. Here, we follow the first one. The Nash equilibrium yields the expected utilities

(8) $E2U_n = -(\sigma + (\alpha + \epsilon)^2)\sigma(k_n^2\sigma_\xi^2 - 2\beta k_n h_n \sigma_{\xi\eta} + h_n^2\beta^2\sigma_\eta^2)$
     $E2U_n^* = -(\sigma + (\alpha + \epsilon)^2)\sigma(k_n^2\sigma_\xi^2 + 2\beta k_n h_n \sigma_{\xi\eta} + h_n^2\beta^2\sigma_\eta^2)$,

where $\sigma_{\xi\eta}$ is the covariance of the two shocks. In contrast, in a cooperative equilibrium the central banks maximize the joint preference function $U + U^*$:[14]

(9) $m = \alpha k_c\xi - (\alpha + 2\epsilon)h_c\beta\eta$; $m^* = \alpha k_c\xi + (\alpha + 2\epsilon)\beta\eta$
     $q = -\sigma(k_c\xi - h_c\beta\eta)$; $q^* = -\sigma(k_c\xi + h_c\beta\eta)$,

where $k_c = 1/(\sigma + \alpha^2) < k_n$ and $h_c = 1/(\sigma + (\alpha + 2\epsilon)^2) > k_n$, with expected utilities

(10) $E2U_c = -\sigma\{k_c\sigma_\xi^2 - 2(\sigma + \alpha(2\epsilon + \alpha))k_c h_c\beta\sigma_{\xi\eta} + h_c\beta^2\sigma_\eta^2\}$
      $E2U_c^* = -\sigma\{k_c\sigma_\xi^2 + 2(\sigma + \alpha(2\epsilon + \alpha))k_c h_c\beta\sigma_{\xi\eta} + h_c\beta^2\sigma_\eta^2\}$.

Both central banks unambiguously gain from cooperation, as long as either the common supply shock or the relative demand shock is the only source of the stabilization problem, or the two shocks are uncorrelated ($\sigma_{\xi\eta} = 0$). The same would be true for a common, symmetric demand shock and a relative supply shock. The result is more complicated, if the common supply shock and the relative demand shock are correlated ($\sigma_{\xi\eta} \neq 0$). Equations (8) and (10) indicate that the expected utility levels depend critically on the sign of their covariance. Equations (7) and (9) show why this is so. With a negative covariance, France expects that its reactions to common supply shocks and relative demand shocks offset each other, requiring less monetary variance and, consequently, less variation in employment. In contrast, Germany expects that its reactions to these shocks reenforce each other. Under the plausible condition that $(\alpha + \epsilon) < 2$, France unambiguously gains from cooperation, if the covariance is negative, while Germany may be worse off than in the Nash equilibrium (8). The situation is reversed when the covariance is positive. The correlation between the common supply shock and the relative demand shock thus creates a distribution problem for the two countries: Cooperation may result in a utility loss relative to the Nash equilibrium for one country, although the two together benefit from it. Under such circumstances, cooperation is not acceptable unless some form of compensation is made for the partner who loses.

A second problem with cooperation is that it is not individually incentive compatible. To see this, consider the marginal loss from a German monetary expansion, given that France plays the cooperative strategy, assuming $\eta = 0$ for simplicity:

$$(11) \qquad \left. \frac{U}{m} \right|_{m=m^* = \alpha k_c \xi} = -\sigma \epsilon k_c \xi.$$

Equation (11) implies that, in the presence of a nonzero supply shock, the German authorities can improve their outcome by deviating from the joint strategy. There is a conflict between the individual and the common interest, a problem familiar from cartel theory. This makes the cooperative solution nonviable, unless policy actions can be monitored closely and the agreement can be enforced. Canzoneri and Gray (1985) argue that "cheating" is relatively easy in the international context, given the complexity of the national policy processes and the ambiguity of the definition of variables such as money.

The cooperative interpretation of the EMS says that, by pegging the exchange rate at a predetermined level, the two countries together may improve over the Nash solution and reap at least some of the benefits from cooperation.[15] Fixing the exchange rate then is a surrogate for cooperation. Since exchange rates are easy to monitor, cheating would be immediately discovered. Therefore, fixing the exchange rate is a viable strategy. To illustrate the point, assume that France pegs the DM/FF rate. Germany chooses the money supply given this constraint. The resulting equilibrium has

$$(12) \qquad m = \alpha k_c (\xi - (1-\epsilon\theta)\beta\eta); \qquad m^* = m + \theta\beta\eta;$$
$$q = -\sigma k_c (\xi - (1-\epsilon\theta)\beta\eta)_j \qquad q^* = q + (1-\epsilon\theta)(1-2\beta)\eta,$$

$$(13) \qquad E2U_e = -\sigma k_c (\sigma_\xi^2 - 2(1-\epsilon\theta)\beta\sigma_{\xi\eta} + (1-\epsilon\theta)^2\beta^2\sigma_\eta^2)$$
$$E2U_e^* = -\sigma k_c \sigma_\xi^2 + 2\sigma\alpha k_c (2\zeta - \beta^2\theta)\sigma_{\xi\eta} - (\sigma\zeta^2 + \alpha^2(\zeta - \beta^2\theta)^2\sigma_\eta^2,$$

where $\zeta = \beta\theta(1-\alpha^2 k_c B)$ and $\theta = 1/(\epsilon+\alpha\beta)$. Comparing (13) with (8) reveals that the fixed-rate arrangement can be preferable to the Nash solution for both countries. In fact, it is identical to the cooperative equilibrium if the relative shock plays no role $(\sigma_\eta^2=0)$.[16] More generally, the improvement of the fixed-rate solution over the Nash solution is the greater, the less important relative shocks are comparing to common shocks. The distribution of the gains from the arrangement again depends critically on the covariance of the two types of shocks. If it is positive, Germany is likely to fare even better than with full coordination. The reason is that fixing the exchange rate forces France to respond to a positive η with a larger monetary expansion than otherwise, and thus to take a larger share in the adjustment to this shock. A large positive covariance will make the fixed-rate arrangement unacceptable for France. The situation is reversed if the covariance is negative. This implies that the distribution of the gains is not automatically in favor of the "dominant" country, which determines money growth in the arrangement.[17]

Given the empirical covariance structure of common and relative shocks, there are two fundamental ways to devise a distribution of welfare gains from fixed exchange rates. Ex ante, the distribution depends critically on the assignment of the responsibility to peg the exchange rate. Rules for sharing foreign exchange market interventions and for sterilization generate distributions of the welfare gains. We have seen in Section 1 above that the provisions of the EMS only determine the immediate impacts of compulsory interventions. Because the members of the EMS did not specify explicit rules for sterilization, the final distribution of the intervention effects and, consequently, of the welfare gains was left indeterminate ex ante. The recent emphasis on intramarginal interventions, and their inclusion in VSTF financing, can be regarded as one attempt to alter the ex-ante distribution of gains in favor of the weak-currency members of the EMS.

In contrast, the EMS has two basic instruments to deal with the distributional problems ex post, that is, after the realization of shocks. One is the institution of transfer payments among the participants, which facilitates compensation of those who lose by those who benefit from the arrangement. The various credit mechanisms discussed above are important in this respect. The other is the provision of realignments. A realignment temporarily restores the lost degrees of freedom in the response to an exogenous shock. Since all members are involved in the realignment decision, realignments do not necessarily mark a return to noncooperative behavior. Instead, a realignment facilitates the cooperative use of all degrees of freedom when the distributional problems become too large because of large asymmetric shocks.

Begg and Wyplosz (1987) and Hughes-Hallett and Minford (1989, 1990) assume that policymakers choose policy regimes such as the EMS after the exogenous shocks have been realized. In this view, important exogenous shocks occur infrequently compared to the adjustment of monetary policy arrangements. The initial conditions leading to the EMS are characterized by high inflation, low employment, and sluggish output growth. Policy-makers have a fixed time horizon for improving economic performance and compare alternative regimes in terms of the actual shocks instead of their expected stochastic properties. Realignments and capital controls are important policy instruments that will generally be used in optimal strat-egies, a result that confirms the practical experience of the EMS. Despite these differences in the approach of these studies and our analysis, the main message remains the same: The EMS is a surrogate for policy co-ordination yielding welfare gains unless relative shocks are too large.

The discussion so far has assumed that the monetary authorities have perfect information about all relevant variables, whereas the private sectors have no current information at all. In reality, central banks cannot observe all shocks immediately and directly. Instead, they observe goods and asset prices that convey imperfect information. In the case of economies of similar size, imperfect information has additional, strategic aspects.[18] Here, we illustrate its role with an example of asymmetric information.

Central banks do not generally have access to the information systems of foreign central banks. Therefore, it is plausible to assume that central banks have "private" information about their domestic economies. To model this asymmetry, we rewrite the aggregate demand functions

(14) $y^d = \delta^{-1}r + \beta y^* + (1-\beta)y - \delta^{-1}\eta_1$
          $y^{d*} = -\delta^{-1}r + \beta y + (1-\beta)y^* + \delta^{-1}\eta_2,$

with $E\eta_1\eta_2 = 0$.[19] We assume that the German central bank knows η_1 but has no information about η_2. For the French central bank, the situation is reversed. Both central banks know the value of the common shock ξ but cannot observe the foreign central bank's current money supply. For sim-plicity, we let $\xi = 0$. The first-order conditions for the present policy game are

(15) $m = h_c(\alpha+\epsilon)(\epsilon E^G m^* - \beta\eta_1/2); \quad m^* = h_c(\alpha+\epsilon)(\epsilon E^F m - \beta\eta_2/2),$

where E^G and E^F denote the German and French central banks' expec-tations. Since $E^G\eta_2 = E^F\eta_1 = 0$, and the expected French policy can only be a reaction to $E^F\eta_1$ or η_2, $E^G m^* = 0$. This yields the optimal policy $m = -(\alpha+\epsilon)\beta h_c\eta_1/2$. The French optimal policy can be found accordingly. The new Nash equilibrium has

(16) $E2U_a = -\sigma h_c\beta^2\sigma_{\eta 1}^2/4 - (\sigma+\alpha(\alpha+\epsilon))^2 h_c^2\beta^2\sigma_{\eta 2}^2/4 < EU_n$
          $E2U_a^* = -\sigma h_c\beta^2\sigma_{\eta 2}^2/4 - (\sigma+\alpha(\alpha+\epsilon))^2 h_c^2\beta^2\sigma_{\eta 1}^2/4 < EU_n^*.$

Asymmetric information worsens the outcome for both central banks. Thus, there is a potential gain for both from exchanging information. This is the basis for a popular view of arrangements for international policy coordination, which holds that such arrangements serve the main purpose to facilitate the exchange of "private" information among policymakers. However, a simple exchange of information does not work. From above, we know that the realizations of η_1 and η_2 determine the distribution of the utility levels. Therefore, both central banks have an incentive to overstate the true size of their domestic shocks, because doing so would increase the foreign central bank's part of the adjustment to the shock. Consequently, central bank officials would rationally perceive the information obtained from other central banks as not credible.[20]

Pegging the exchange rate now becomes a mechanism to transmit information indirectly. If, as above, the French central bank commits to fixing the DM/FF rate, the German optimal policy is $m = -\alpha(1-\epsilon\theta)\beta\eta_1/2(\sigma+\alpha^2)$, whereas the French policy remains $m^* = m + \theta\beta(\eta_1+\eta_2)$. The exchange-rate peg allows the French authorities to react to η_1, which they are unable to do otherwise, and it prevents their Nash reaction to η_2, which is unknown to the German authorities. The resulting equilibrium has

$$(17) \quad E2U_E = -\sigma k_c(1-\epsilon\theta)^2\beta^2\sigma_{\eta_1}^2/4 - (1-\epsilon\theta)^2\beta^2\sigma_{\eta_2}^2/4 > U_a$$

$$E2U_E^* = -\{\sigma(\theta-(\alpha+\epsilon)h_c)^2 + \alpha^2(\theta(1-\beta)-(\alpha+\epsilon)h_c)^2\}\beta^2\theta_{\eta_1}^2/4$$
$$- \{\sigma+\alpha^2(1-\beta)^2\}\beta^2\theta^2\sigma_{\eta_2}^2/4.$$

The fixed-rate equilibrium unambiguously yields an improvement for Germany. The outcome for France is less clearcut. If the variance of the French demand shock is large relative to the variance of the German shock and the parameter ϵ is large relative to the parameters α and σ, the French central bank finds the EMS preferable. As before, the distribution of gains depends on the rules for intervention and sterilization.[21]

Policy Coordination in the EMS: Empirical Evidence

Padoa-Schioppa (1985, p. 94ff.) and Ungerer (1990) argue that realignments have become the most important aspect of practical policy coordination in the EMS. The EMS has gradually developed a process of bargaining and joint decision making over realignments, in which no single country can be sure to obtain the changes it prefers most. More often than not, realignments have been combined with changes in other significant fields of economic policy (cf. Ungerer et al., 1986, Tables 6 and 10). However, realignments can at best achieve ex-post coordination, that is, a coordinated solution to policy incongruences committed in the past. During the second half of the 1980s, realignments have become much less frequent. Giavazzi and Spaventa (1990), among others, interpret this as evidence of closer ex-ante policy coordination in the EMS.

The literature has proposed to measure coordination in terms of the convergence and correlation of EMS central bank operating targets, such as money growth and money market interest rates, and in terms of exchange-rate stability. Rogoff (1985b) and Ungerer et al. (1986) were skeptical about policy coordination in the EMS because money-growth rates in the participating countries showed little convergence in the first half of the 1980s and have remained low since then (Russo and Tullio, 1988). But this evidence is hard to interpret because coordination may well require divergent monetary developments depending on the symmetry of the underlying shocks. Weber (1990) reports that monetary shocks have become more symmetric in the EMS, which is consistent with closer coordination of monetary expansions.

The evidence on EMS interest-rate co-movements speaks more in favor of policy coordination in the EMS. Ungerer et al. (1986) report that the correlation of money market rates between Germany and the smaller EMS countries increased between 1979 and 1985. Russo and Tullio (1988) use principal components analysis to show that interest-rate movements in the EMS countries increasingly depend on a common factor explaining more than 75 percent of the cumulative variance. Kirchgässner and Wolters (1990) show that EMS interest rates became more interactive in the 1980s and followed a common stochastic trend in the 1980s. Weber (1990, p. 17) separates symmetric from asymmetric interest-rate movements in the EMS and shows that the symmetric component dominated in the 1980s.

There is a general agreement in the literature that the EMS has produced significantly lower exchange-rate variability in the sense of variations around long-run trends. This has been shown for both nominal and real exchange rates (Artis and Taylor, 1988; Fratianni and von Hagen, 1990a; Giavazzi and Giovannini, 1989; Meltzer, 1990; Weber, 1990). Artis and Taylor find no evidence that reduced exchange-rate variability has been traded for greater variance of interest rates, as some critics suggest (Hughes-Hallett and Minford, 1990). Fratianni and von Hagen (1990a) present evidence suggesting that stabilization of intra-EMS exchange rates has been achieved at the cost of destabilizing EMS exchange rates with outside currencies, most notably the U.S. dollar.

Other authors have looked at fiscal policy coordination in the EMS countries. Ungerer et al. (1986) and Russo and Tullio (1988) do not find greater convergence or increasing correlation of fiscal policy instruments among the EMS countries. This is generally interpreted as indicating a need for more fiscal coordination in the EMS. However, perfect coordination of monetary policies may well require divergent fiscal policies to deal with asymmetric shocks to the participating economies. The model above demonstrates the point. If the aggregate demand functions included independent fiscal policy instruments, the optimal use of these instruments would be to counteract the relative demand shock η, while monetary policy absorbs the common shock ξ. That is, monetary policy coordination results in a solution of the assignment problem which ascribes fiscal policy the role of dealing with country-specific shocks (Branson, 1990; von Hagen and Fratianni, 1990c).

Fratianni and von Hagen (1990a) evaluate the EMS by looking at inflation uncertainty, that is, the conditional variance of inflation surprises. They find significant reductions of inflation uncertainty in Denmark, Germany, Italy, and the Netherlands during the EMS period. Similar reductions are also observed in Japan, the United Kingdom, and Canada, however. The specific contribution of the EMS therefore remains unclear. Furthermore, the conditional covariances among EMS inflation rates have increased, meaning that inflation shocks spread out more evenly among the participants of the EMS. This result is consistent with Weber's (1990) finding that inflation shocks became more symmetric in the EMS during the 1980s, and with Russo and Tullio's (1988) result that EMS inflation rates depended more strongly on a common factor in the 1980s than in the 1970s. Finally, Fratianni and von Hagen (1990a) show that the conditional covariance of EMS and non-EMS inflation rates decreased significantly in the 1980s. Without, of course, proving that the EMS has induced welfare-improving policy coordination, these changes in the covariance patterns of inflation rates are consistent with several conjectures: Policy coordination in the EMS has reduced the burden of common external shocks borne by the EMS countries relative to that borne by non-EMS countries; the EMS has reduced the inflation impact of shocks originating outside the EMS and has equalized their distribution among the EMS members; finally, EMS policy coordination has reduced the variance of member-country-specific shocks.

Hughes-Hallett and Minford (1990) use simulation exercises to demonstrate the impact of EMS policy coordination on economic performance in the participating countries. They compare alternative policy paths to reduce inflation and stimulate output growth over a fixed time horizon. Hughes-Hallett and Minford (1989) and Minford (1988) present simulations of two-year, independent monetary expansions in individual EMS countries. They model the EMS as an arrangement allowing Germany to determine money growth unilaterally for all participants. EMS exchange rates are allowed to fluctuate within margins of ± 3 percent, and realignments occur in fixed time intervals. In their simulations, the EMS produces welfare gains that are small and badly distributed among the participants. The distribution of gains can be improved by transforming the EMS into an "equal shares" coalition or one that yields at least the same welfare as uncoordinated policies for all members. Both alternatives require a weakening of Germany's assumed dominant position. The authors conclude that

EMS policy coordination achieves little and is difficult to sustain, since the gains are easily wiped out by additional adverse shocks.

It remains unclear, however, how much their results depend on the peculiar specification of the EMS. Apart from treating the United Kingdom as a member of the ERM, their treatment of realignments is unrealistic. The fixed periodicity of realignments clearly contradicts the historical record and is inconsistent with Begg and Wyplosz's (1987) result that the timing of realignments is an important strategic variable in the policy problems under consideration. In their model, the anticipation of a realignment triggers a rise in contract wages and prices that lead to a real appreciation of the currency and a loss of competitiveness, hence output and employment. A monetary expansion in EMS countries other than Germany increases real interest rates and real exchange rates and depresses real output.

Hughes-Hallett and Minford (1989) use their model to evaluate how the EMS copes with country-specific shocks to the real exchange rate or the demand for money or a common oil price shock. Again, the results are quite deceptive for the EMS. The country-specific shocks in these simulations can be regarded as examples for significant asymmetric shocks to the EMS countries. The results therefore confirm the theoretical result derived above, that the quality of exchange-rate management as a surrogate for cooperation depends crucially on the importance of asymmetric or relative shocks.

The result that the equivalence of cooperation and exchange-rate fixity theoretically depends on the symmetry of the economies naturally leads to two questions: How important are asymmetric shocks empirically, and how robust are the welfare gains from fixed exchange rates to asymmetries in the exogenous shocks and the economic structures of the participating countries. Weber (1990) gives a partial answer to the first question. He shows that the co-movements of simple measures of aggregate supply and demand and of real wages in the EMS became increasingly dominated by symmetric shocks during the 1980s. Yet, the standard deviation of asymmetric shocks was at least half as large as the standard deviation of symmetric shocks in almost all cases, indicating that asymmetric shocks still remain significant.

Von Hagen and Fratianni (1990c) use simulations to evaluate the robustness of welfare gains from the EMS. In their model of the EMS, exchange rates are completely fixed, and money growth is determined either unilaterally by Germany or cooperatively. The question is, how large can structural and stochastic asymmetries be without making the EMS unsustainable? The EMS is sustainable if membership yields at least the same utility levels as uncoordinated policies.[22] Von Hagen and Fratianni find that policy coordination in the EMS is quite frail. To hold the system together, asymmetric shocks must be small relative to symmetric shocks, particularly if structural heterogeneities among the EMS participants are significant. Hughes-Hallett and Minford's (1989) results indicate that the robustness of welfare gains can be moderately strengthened by allowing for margins of fluctuation of exchange rates. Von Hagen and Fratianni show that improving the distribution of gains directly by transfer payments among the members does little to increase the robustness. This suggests that the role of institutions facilitating transfer payments, such as the medium- and long-term credit mechanisms of the EMS, is likely overstated. Finally, closer economic and financial markets integration and deregulation in their simulations tend to improve the robustness of the welfare gains from policy coordination in the EMS. This corroborates the "cumulative logic of integration": The completion of the "internal market" in Europe promises to improve the scope for welfare-improving monetary policy coordination.

The EMS as a Disciplinary Device

The disciplinary interpretation of the EMS has emerged from the discussion of central bank credibility. It is based on the idea that central banks with a historical record of high inflation and low credibility of price-stability-oriented policies can "borrow" credibility from the Bundesbank by joining the EMS and tying their monetary policies to the policy of the Bundesbank through the fixed DM exchange rate. The Bundesbank has superior credibility based on its long record of low-inflation policies and its large degree of political independence. We call this the credibility hypothesis of the EMS.

Suppose that the monetary authorities have employment targets $N^* > N > 0$, which reflect perceived differences between the socially optimal levels of employment and the levels mostly preferred by their private sectors (Barro and Gordon, 1983). Let $\xi = \eta = 0$ for analytical convenience. The employment targets create incentives to use monetary policy to raise employment, once private sector expectations and nominal wages have been set. Since a formal precommitment by the central banks to a low-inflation monetary target is impossible owing to the lack of credible punishment for reneging on it, a central bank will always succumb to the temptation of deviating from prior announcements if doing so contributes to maximizing its preference function. The private sector sees through this incentive structure and does not consider the announcement of a monetary target credible unless there is no incentive left for the central bank to renege. In a subgame perfect equilibrium, therefore, the incentive for monetary surprises vanishes. The subgame perfect Nash equilibrium with independent monetary policies is

$$(18) \quad m = m = \sigma N/(\alpha + \epsilon) = q; m^* = q^* = \sigma N^*/(\alpha + \epsilon)$$
$$n = n^* = 0,$$

(19) $2U_n = -\sigma N[1 + \sigma/(\alpha + \epsilon)]$; $2U_n^* = -\sigma[(N^*)(1 + \sigma/(\alpha + \epsilon))]$.

Equilibrium inflation is positive but yields no employment benefit. The fact that the authorities aim at employment levels different from the natural ones and cannot precommit to a policy compatible with price stability leads to an inefficiency. Both authorities would be better off if they could credibly pursue noninflationary policies. France has a higher equilibrium inflation rate because of its larger employment target.

Giavazzi and Giovannini (1987, 1989), and Giavazzi and Pagano (1988), among others, contend that France can improve on equation (19) by fixing its DM exchange rate. This conjecture rests on the observation that fixing the exchange rate requires France to adopt the same monetary policy as Germany, $m^* = m$, which would allow France to achieve a lower inflation rate. However, it follows from equation (5) that the fixed exchange rate changes the Bundesbank's policy constraint by eliminating the term $m - m^*$. The intuition is that the Bundesbank need no longer take into account the adverse exchange-rate effects of a monetary expansion. Instead, part of its inflation consequences are "exported" to France. As a result, the Bundesbank's employment-inflation tradeoff (dn/dq) increases from $1/(\alpha + \epsilon)$ to $1/\alpha$. The incentive for inflation surprises grows, and the previously tight German policy is no longer optimal or credible. The new EMS equilibrium has a higher German inflation rate:[23]

(20) $m = q = m^* = q^* = \sigma N/\alpha > \sigma N/(\alpha + \epsilon)$; $n = n^* = 0$

(21) $2U_e = -\sigma N^2(1 + \sigma/\alpha^2) < U_n$ $2U_e^* = -\sigma(N^{*2} + \sigma N^2/\alpha^2)$.

Equation (20) demonstrates that Germany loses from the EMS if $N > 0$. That is, credibility cannot be transferred freely among central banks, and the credibility hypothesis cannot explain German membership in the EMS. The literature has proposed various explanations of German membership. One is that the Bundesbank has no employment target different from natural employment ($N=0$), which makes the equilibria (18) and (20) equivalent for Germany. The Bundesbank would then be indifferent about the EMS, which is inconsistent with the Bundesbank's strong opposition against the EMS in the late 1970s. Alternatively, the Bundesbank may indeed lose in the EMS, but one may argue that the German government imposed membership on it (Fratianni, 1988). According to German law, the federal government made the decision to join the EMS. Indeed, Helmut Schmidt's recent memoirs (Schmidt, 1990) relate how he and Giscard d'Estaing tried to work around the Bundesbank in setting up the EMS in 1978. Vaubel (1980) argues that EMS membership was forced on the Bundesbank as a way of weakening its political independence.

Giavazzi and Pagano (1988) and Mélitz (1988a) assume that monetary authorities, including the Bundesbank, are inclined to use exchange-rate policies to favor domestic export industries. This additional policy goal would make the German authorities willing to accept more inflation and less monetary discipline in the EMS in return for a real depreciation of the DM. The problem with such mercantilistic explanations for Germany's EMS membership is that no country can expect permanent competitive advantages in the EMS. The resulting trade imbalances would make the EMS unsustainable in the long run. As markets realized this, speculative attacks on the EMS parities would follow and precipitate the breakdown of the system (Wyplosz, 1986). A more plausible explanation of German membership comes from the observation that Germany has historically borne the brunt of speculative capital flows originating from the U.S. dollar market. By increasing the substitutability between the DM and other EMS currencies, the EMS produces a more even distribution of speculative capital flows.[24]

According to equation (21), France will gain from the EMS, $U_e^* > U_n^*$, if $N^*/(\alpha + \epsilon) > N/\alpha$. This condition is more likely to hold the larger the relative difference in the employment targets, the smaller the import elasticity of demand, the larger the relative price elasticity of demand, and the larger the marginal product of labor. Even if this condition is fulfilled, however, it is not clear that the fixed exchange rate is a credible strategy for the French central bank. The crucial question is, what makes the private sector believe in its commitment to a low-inflation exchange-rate target when the commitment to a low-inflation monetary target is not credible by assumption? Formally, consider the French marginal utility of a monetary surprise, once private sector expectations and wages have been set according to the EMS equilibrium (20):

$$(22) \quad dU^*/dm^* \bigg|_{m^* = m^{*e} = \sigma N/\alpha} = \sigma(N^* - (\alpha + \epsilon)N/\alpha).$$

The marginal utility is positive under the same condition, assuring a welfare gain from the EMS. Given EMS expectations, the French central bank has an incentive to abandon the exchange-rate target and choose a more inflationary policy. Thus, the EMS is not a subgame perfect strategy for France, that is, membership cannot prevail in equilibrium.

The way to overturn this negative conclusion is to assume that, once the EMS has been put into place, there is an additional cost of breaking the arrangement. Let P^* be a utility loss accruing to the French central bank for reneging on its EMS commitment. The new marginal utility of a monetary surprise now becomes $dU^*/dm^* - P^*$. To make the EMS credible, the additional cost must be large enough to balance the incentive for a monetary surprise:

$$(23) \quad P^* = P^*(\sigma, \epsilon/\alpha, N^*/N) \geq \sigma [N^* - (\alpha + \epsilon)N/\alpha].$$
$$+ \quad - \quad +$$

The larger the weight of the employment target and the larger the difference in the pre-EMS inflation biases, the larger the French cost of reneging on the exchange-rate target must be. The superiority of EMS membership as a French monetary strategy thus hinges entirely on the assumption that, by creating new threats to the policymaker, the EMS can alleviate the institutional deficiency behind the inflation bias.

To explain the nature of the additional cost, Mélitz (1988a) argues that devaluations in a fixed exchange-rate system cost electoral support. In an EMS-like arrangement, voters regard exchange-rate changes as political events rather than market outcomes and punish policymakers for loss of national reputation resulting from a devaluation. The empirical strength of this suggestion remains unclear, however. Hughes-Hallett and Minford (1989) and De Grauwe (1990) propose that the perverse effects of monetary policy in EMS countries other than Germany raise the economic cost of independent monetary expansions. The disciplinary effect of the EMS would thus arise from the reduced attractiveness of using monetary policy for domestic employment goals. Still, since the perverse effects prevail only as long as realignments are not used strategically, this explanation ignores the fact that the EMS was devised so that realignments could be an integral part of policy coordination.

The Credibility Hypothesis: Empirical Evidence

We have noted earlier that the disinflation and convergence of inflation rates of the 1980s do not distinguish the EMS from other countries. Consequently, the empirical strength of the credibility hypothesis cannot be judged simply in terms of the inflation performance of the EMS. Instead, empirical evidence of its effect on central bank credibility is necessary.

The end of the French "Mitterrand experiment" (1981–83) with expansive demand management in a recessionary international environment is one episode in the history of the EMS which is often considered a prime example of the credibility hypothesis (e.g., Giavazzi and Giovannini, 1989). In their account of the events, Sachs and Wyplosz (1986) contend that EMS membership was the critical fact convincing the French government to revert to a more restrictive stance in 1983. The political threat of having to leave the EMS otherwise—and other forms of European cooperation with it—forced the government to adopt policies consistent with greater price stability.

Yet, at a closer look, the example is quite ambiguous. Sachs and Wyplosz explain that the Mitterrand experiment resulted in unsustainable external imbalances that demanded correction. By late 1982 the French government had realized that a more restrictive policy was unavoidable and pondered the alternative options for reversing the trends of high inflation and devaluation of the franc (Eggerstädt and Sinn, 1987). Thus, the relevant political question was not whether or not a correction should take place at all, but whether or not it should occur inside or outside the EMS. A review of the case in OECD (1988) argues that, based on the French experience in the 1970s, the authorities expected adjustment under a flexible exchange rate to be even more harmful than adjustment within the EMS. Furthermore, the EMS offered recourse to financial assistance: The French stabilization program was supported by an ECU 4 billion loan under the medium-term facility in May 1983 (Ungerer et al., 1986, p. 6). Thus, remaining in the EMS could be regarded as the lesser evil in the unavoidable policy adjustment. Such a view, however, contradicts the very essence of the credibility hypothesis. If EMS membership reduces the prospective economic cost of correcting inflationary demand policies, it can only diminish central bank credibility.

The history of the Italian disinflation is equally ambiguous with respect to the credibility hypothesis. In the 1970s the Italian Treasury could automatically expand the monetary base through an overdraft facility and through reliance on the central bank as a residual buyer of government debt at Treasury auctions. The absence of a secondary market for government debt prevented the Bank of Italy from neutralizing these "automatic" sources of monetary base creation. After the Treasury had begun to offer securities to the public in 1976, the possibility of open market operations gave the central bank some monetary independence. It was strengthened further when the government freed the Bank from being the residual buyer of government debt at Treasury auctions in 1981. According to Tabellini (1988, p. 77), the purpose of this "divorce" was to enforce greater fiscal discipline on the Italian government and had little to do with the EMS.

In 1984 the Italian opposition, together with militant labor unions, called for a national referendum against the government's attempts to limit wage indexation. Giavazzi and Spaventa (1989) regard the government's firm stand in this affair and the eventual defeat of the referendum as the critical event that lowered inflation expectations. Gressani et al. (1988) find the empirical impact of this event on inflation expectations much larger than Italy's EMS membership. The government had to prove its willingness first to bear the cost of unpopular domestic policies before wage and price setters became convinced that the commitment to the new monetary regime was lasting. Giavazzi and Spaventa speculate that EMS membership provided Italian politicians with a justification for unpopular policies and thus made it politically easier to implement a disinflation program. But such a scapegoat role of the EMS only contradicts the essence of the credibility hypothesis. It would reduce the threat of political unpopularity when embarking on a program that seeks to correct the inflation consequences of previous discretionary monetary policy. In this way, EMS membership would lower the expected political cost of discretionary policy and thereby undermine the credibility of domestic policymakers.

Dornbusch (1989) reviews the Irish experience of the 1980s. He argues that the main element in the disinflation process was the restoration of government budget balance. Starting in early 1982, the long-term interest-rate differential with Germany began to fall, an indication of the increasing credibility of the Irish stabilization program. Dornbusch suggests that the Irish decision not to seek a devaluation in the 1982 realignments contributed somewhat to this credibility gain. But, he argues, the fact that the stabilization program was carried by a broad domestic political consensus, and that this consensus became very visible when, in March 1982, the new Irish government submitted essentially the same tight budget over which its predecessor had fallen, was much more influential in shaping inflation expectations. Again, a clear demonstration of policymakers' willingness to bear the political cost of unpopular policies seems to have been much more important than EMS membership to establish the credibility of the new policy.

The well-known Lucas Critique suggests that changes in policy regimes which induce changes in private sector expectation formation cause parameter instabilities in reduced-form econometric models (Lucas, 1976). Giavazzi and Giovannini (1988) and Kremers (1990) follow this suggestion and use regression analysis to explore the impact of the EMS on inflation expectations. Giavazzi and Giovannini present vector autoregressions of real output, wages, and inflation in the EMS. Although they do not find structural breaks in the model coefficients, simulations of inflation and output growth in the 1980s based on parameter estimations using data up to 1979 tend to overpredict inflation in France, Italy, and Denmark, underpredict inflation in Germany and real growth in Denmark, and overpredict real growth in Germany. This is consistent with a reduction of inflation expectations in France, Italy, and Denmark, and a rise in Germany, as suggested by the credibility hypothesis. Unfortunately, their results lack statistical testability. Kremers (1990) estimates a rational expectations model of inflation expectations in Ireland. He finds a significant break in the model structure between 1979 and 1982. The impact of the United Kingdom's inflation on Irish inflation expectations vanishes and is replaced by average EMS inflation. At the same time, the effect of lagged real exchange rates, a measure of competitiveness, rises.[25] Kremers interprets these findings as indications of credibility gains.

According to one interpretation of the credibility hypothesis, the welfare benefit from borrowing credibility from the Bundesbank is a lower real cost of disinflation in the other EMS countries, because EMS membership helps to avoid large negative inflation expectation errors. Several authors have proposed to test the credibility hypothesis on this basis. Giavazzi and Spaventa (1989) and Dornbusch (1989) compare sacrifice ratios inside and outside the EMS. The sacrifice ratio is the ratio of cumulated unemployment above a base-year level to the total reduction in inflation. The authors do not find that sacrifice ratios are lower in the EMS. De Grauwe (1990) uses the misery index to measure the cost of disinflation. The index is a weighted sum of unemployment and inflation rates, the weights reflecting the relative importance of the two variables in the central bank's preference function. The EMS had a higher average misery index than the non-EMS OECD countries both before and after 1979. More importantly, the EMS index rose during the 1980s, whereas the index of the other countries fell. De Grauwe compares indexes computed on the basis of various hypothetical central bank preference structures. The result is that EMS membership yields a higher misery index unless one is willing to assume that EMS governments care much more about inflation than about unemployment. Referring to the lower speed of disinflation in the EMS, which we noted in Section 2, De Grauwe concludes that a lower total cost of disinflation over the entire period under consideration can be derived only if EMS governments have relatively large time preferences.

In conclusion, the empirical evidence gives little support to the credibility hypothesis or the view of the EMS as a disciplinary device. The general disinflation of the 1980s inside and outside the EMS was most likely the result of an increasing awareness and consensus among policymakers to reduce inflation from the high levels of the 1970s and their willingness to bear the political cost (Chouraqui and Price, 1984). For the EMS countries, the Bundesbank's strong commitment to price stability has likely strengthened this consensus and favored their choice of low-inflation strategies. With its reliable orientation at containing inflation, Bundesbank policy may have served as a focal point for monetary policy in other EMS countries as they strove for greater price stability. But this is a much weaker role than the coercive one claimed by the credibility hypothesis.

4. ASYMMETRIES IN THE EMS

We have noted that the proponents of the EMS stressed the intended symmetry of the system as one of its most innovative features. Today, there is a widespread belief that the EMS exhibits a strong asymmetry in the sense that monetary policymaking in the EMS stands under the leadership of the Bundesbank, to which the other central banks have surrendered (part of) their policy autonomy (Fischer, 1988; Giavazzi and Giovannini, 1987, p. 237; Gros and Thygesen, 1988, p. 62; Katseli, 1987; Russo and Tullio, 1988, p. 332; Sarcinelli, 1986, pp. 58–59). We call this the German dominance hypothesis (GDH).

The German Dominance Hypothesis

GDH can be interpreted in two ways. In the relative size version, the argument simply states the obvious, namely, that the EMS combines countries of different economic size. With the relatively large German financial markets, German interest-rate movements and, hence, monetary policy have had a larger impact than those of other countries in the system. The more interesting and relevant policy is the strategic version of GDH. The essence here is that the EMS has become strongly hierarchical and allows the Bundesbank alone to pursue its own, domestic policy goals independently. The remaining central banks have no freedom to pursue independent goals; the ERM forces them to adopt the Bundesbank's policy stance, even if it goes against their own interest.

There are several explanations as to why the EMS might have developed in this way. Triffin (1960) and Wyplosz (1988b) argue that all fixed exchange-rate systems have a natural tendency to be dominated by the lowest inflation central bank. Suppose that both a high-inflation and a low-inflation central bank are forced to intervene in the foreign exchange market. Both central banks can attempt to sterilize their interventions by counteracting domestic credit operations. However, the high-inflation central bank now must continuously sell foreign exchange reserves, whereas the low-inflation central bank buys foreign reserves. The high-inflation central bank therefore faces a more binding constraint than its low-inflation counterpart because at some point it will run out of reserves. Knowing this, the high-inflation central bank should rationally abandon its policy even before interventions become necessary to avoid the unnecessary loss of reserves.

In the EMS, the argument needs some qualifications. Its credit mechanisms give high-inflation central banks "unlimited" access to low-inflation currency reserves. This reduces the threat of being without reserves and raises the danger that the low-inflation central bank will have to squeeze domestic credit in order to maintain its policy stance. Furthermore, high-inflation central banks can demand a realignment to relieve the obligation to intervene without adopting the low-inflation policies. Even before realignments take place, capital controls help to reduce the pressure for intervention. This suggests that the importance of low-inflation Germany should have increased in the late 1980s, when capital controls were removed and realignments became rarer in the EMS. This is consistent with the observation that the complaints about alleged German dominance have become louder and more numerous in recent years, together with claims and attempts to strengthen the symmetry of the EMS, such as the Nyborg Agreement.[26]

Giavazzi and Giovannini (1987) and Giovannini (1989) regard German dominance in the EMS as a consequence of the attempts of other central banks to borrow credibility from the Bundesbank. In this interpretation, GDH is a version of Kindleberger's hegemonic stability theorem, which holds that international financial arrangements need a hegemon providing (price) stability as a public good to the remainder of the system. German dominance would then have positive welfare implications. From this perspective, testing GDH empirically yields another way to test the credibility hypothesis. Wyplosz (1988b) points out that an asymmetric EMS may have lost its raison d'être in the 1990s, given the general achievement of dis-inflation in the EC.

Empirical Evidence of German Dominance

One class of empirical tests for GDH builds on the premise that German dominance has testable implications for the correlation structure of EMS central bank operating targets such as money-market interest rates or mon-etary-base growth rates. Let Y be a 7×1 vector of operating targets of EMS central banks, X a matrix of domestic target variables, and W a 7×1 vector representing monetary policy actions in the rest of the world, outside the EMS. Consider the following system of linear dynamic equa-tions:

$$(24) \quad A(L)DY_t = b + B(L)DX_t + C(L)DW_t + e_t,$$

where $A(L)$, $B(L)$, and $C(L)$ are polynomial matrices in the lag operator L; $D = 1 - L$ is the difference operator; b is a fixed intercept vector; and e_t is a vector of residuals with $E(e_i) = 0$. The leading coefficient of $a_{ii}(L)$ is normalized to one. System (24) yields a dynamic representation of monetary policy interaction in the EMS. After imposing appropriate restrictions, tests of GDH focus mainly on the properties of the matrix $A(L)$.[27]

Fratianni and von Hagen (1990a,b) distinguish four separate hypotheses, which together establish German dominance. First, GDH requires that EMS countries other than Germany not react *directly* to monetary policies outside the EMS. The world at large influences these countries only through Germany's monetary policy. Defining country 1 as Germany, we find that this yields[28]:

H1: World insularity $c_i = 0, i = 2, \ldots, 7.$

Rejecting H1 means that monetary policies in other EMS countries react independently to what goes on outside the EMS, over and beyond what is implied by the German rule. Second, German dominance implies that each EMS country reacts only to Germany and not to other members' policies:

H2: EMS insularity $a_{ij} = 0, i,j = 2, \ldots, 7.$

Rejecting H2 signifies that EMS countries interact independently with one another, which is inconsistent with their joint adherence to the path set by the Bundesbank. Third, German dominance implies that monetary policy in a member country depends on German policy and the rejection of

H3: Independence from Germany $a_{i1} = 0, i = 2, \ldots, 7$.

Fourth, a coercive role of Germany in the EMS requires that Germany itself is independent of the policy actions of other members:

H4: German policy independence $a_{1i} = 0, i = 2, \ldots, 7$.

In this formulation, German dominance does not allow any short-run deviation of the other members' policies from the path prescribed by the Bundesbank. We call this the strong form of the hypothesis. A less restrictive, and more realistic, view of German dominance is to allow short-run deviations from the Bundesbank rule but not long-run deviations. This weak form of German dominance can be formulated by imposing the restrictions of H1 to H4 on the sum of the coefficients of each lag polynomial, instead of all individual coefficients.[29]

Fratianni and von Hagen present two versions of their tests for GDH, one implemented with monthly (onshore) money market rates and the other with quarterly monetary base growth rates as operating targets. Since central banks in the EMS commonly express and assess their short-run actions in terms of the resulting changes in domestic money market interest rates, modeling monetary policy actions and interactions on the basis of money market interest rates produces a picture of the policy game in the EMS in the short run that comes closest to how policymakers perceive it. The use of monetary base growth rates as a summary of the money supply effects of central bank actions, in comparison, seems more appropriate to develop a longer run perspective of the game. The model using money market rates has different parameterizations for the subperiods 1979 to 1983 and 1983 to 1988 that allow us to consider changes in the structure of the EMS.

The test results reported in Fratianni and von Hagen (1990a, b) and von Hagen and Fratianni (1990d) reject the strong form of GDH for both policy variables. Germany certainly is a significant player in the EMS, but so are other central banks in the system, particularly the French and the Italian. German interest rates and monetary base growth rates respond significantly to monetary policy actions in other EMS countries, and other countries interact and react to the rest of the world independently. From these results, the EMS appears interactive and not hierarchical.

The results for the weak form of German dominance are more instructive. They are summarized in Table 15.6. Here, an *n* indicates that the test result is not consistent with GDH, and a *y* indicates that it is. The overall result is, again, to reject GDH. But the table reveals several characteristics

Table 15.6
Results of German Dominance Tests

	Belgium	Denmark	France	Germany	Ireland	Italy	N'lands	EMS
	A: Base Money Growth Rates, Sample 1979 - 1988							
H1	y	y	n	--	n	n	n	n
H2	n	y	y	--	y	n	n	n
H3	n	n	n	--	y	y	n	n
H4	--	--	--	y	--	--	--	
	B: Money Market Interest Rates, Sample 1979 - 1983							
H1	y	n	y	--	y	y	n	n
H2	y	n	y	--	n	n	y	n
H3	n	n	y	--	y	n	y	n
H4	--	--	--	n	--	--	--	
	Money Market Interest Rates, Sample 1983 - 1988							
H1	y	y	y	--	y	n	y	y
H2	y	n	y	--	n	y	n	n
H3	y	n	y	--	n	n	y	n
H4	--	--	--	n	--	--	--	--

Sources: Fratianni and von Hagen (1990a, b); von Hagen and Fratianni (1990b).

Notes: H1: World insularity, H2: EMS insularity, rejection of H3: independence from German policy, and H4: German policy independence together constitute German dominance in the EMS. *Y* and *n* indicate a test result consistent and inconsistent with GDH, respectively. Results under EMS relate to tests of restrictions imposed on all countries simultaneously, and results under country headings to tests of restrictions on individual countries only.

of the structure of the EMS. First consider the interest-rate version. EMS reaction to the outside world shows a large degree of conformity in the second EMS period, when world insularity is accepted for all countries except Italy and for the system as a whole. In this limited respect, the evidence could be interpreted as indicating that German leadership prevents other countries from reacting independently to interest-rate movements outside the EMS.

Furthermore, the results point to a striking difference between the French and the Italian position in the EMS. French interest-rate responses accord well with all three restrictions posed by the German dominance hypothesis, whereas the Italian responses do not. French interest rates are much more closely bound to German interest rates than are the Italian rates.

Next, consider the more long-run-oriented results based on monetary base growth rates. A first important finding is that in the long run German money growth does not respond to policies in other EMS countries. This is consistent with the view that the Bundesbank pursues an independent policy in the EMS. In a system with truly fixed exchange rates and perfect capital mobility, this finding would imply German dominance because, under such circumstances, only one central bank can act independently. But the empirical evidence shows that, in the EMS, German policy independence does not prevent the other countries from reacting to one another and to the rest of the world independently. The solution to this apparent puzzle lies in the institutional design of the EMS: Realignments and capital controls assure us that German policy independence is not the same as German dominance.

Both Italy and France show significant long-run reactions to the rest of the world; Italy also reacts significantly to other EMS countries. The more striking difference between the French and the Italian position in the system is that Italy's long-run monetary growth path depends significantly on Germany's, whereas the French does not. France and Denmark appear to be the least influenced by the EMS. Thus, there is an apparent contradiction between the interest rate and the base money-growth rate results for France and Italy. According to the former, France seems to be more strongly linked to the EMS than Italy. The opposite seems to be true according to the latter results. This contrast is resolved by the fact that France has used realignments more often and more effectively than other countries to set its own monetary trend. Italy, on the other hand, was granted more short-run flexibility than France by its wider exchange-rate band. Consequently, in the short run Italy has less need to align with other EMS countries.

Fratianni and von Hagen (1990b) aggregate the base money-growth rates of Belgium, Denmark, Germany, and the Netherlands. Replacing the German growth rate by this average in their tests, they find that "world insularity," "independence of the core group" from the rest of the system, and "EMS insularity" of the smaller countries in the average with respect to France, Italy, and Ireland are all compatible with the data. This suggests the existence of a core group in the EMS consisting of Germany and its smaller neighbors, more closely tied together among themselves than to the other two larger EMS countries. This core group itself is not dominated by Germany, nor does the core group dominate the system, but French and Italian reactions to policies in the rest of the world appear to have run largely in accordance with the reaction of the core group.

Cohen and Wyplosz (1989) test "German policy independence" and "independence from German policy" of GDH for a subgroup of EMS countries, using bivariate vector autoregressions of domestic interest rates and monetary base growth rates. They find that German interest rates and base growth have significant impacts on the same variables in other EMS countries, but the opposite is also true. Mastropasqua et al. (1988) report a similar outcome for base growth. Weber (1990) tests "German policy independence," "EMS insularity," and "independence from German policy" in bilateral causality tests using three-month money market rates and call-money rates. Again, Germany is characterized as an important player, but GDH fails the empirical test. Koedijk and Kool (1991) use a dynamic version of principal components analysis to investigate GDH with monthly money market interest rates. They conclude that GDH must be rejected both for the entire EMS period and the period after 1983. Finally, Kirch-gässner and Wolters (1990) take a more long-run-oriented view and test GDH on the basis of co-integration of EMS interest rates. They, too, reject the hypothesis of German dominance.

Bofinger (1988a), Camen (1986), Mastropasqua et al. (1988), and Roubini (1988) test "German policy independence" by looking at central bank interventions in the EMS. The common result is that the Bundesbank sterilizes almost all interventions within the quarter of their occurrence. This suggests that the Bundesbank can pursue its own policy objectives independently of the EMS. However, this conclusion fails to account for important institutional characteristics of Bundesbank monetary policy. The design of the Bundesbank's operating procedure requires a distinction between short-run sterilization, which is automatic and complete, and long-run sterilization, which is not. On the basis of this distinction, von Hagen (1989) shows that interventions have at times had significant long-run effects on German monetary base growth.

A third class of test starts from the presumption that, in an asymmetric EMS, expected exchange-rate changes and reserve flows should affect short-term interest rates only in the dominated countries. Giovannini (1989) finds this pattern confirmed for France, Italy, and Germany. De Grauwe (1988b) observes that the German interest rate does not respond to expected devaluations of the Belgian and French franc and the Italian lira. However, interest rates in these three countries do not fully adjust either. This indicates that capital controls and dual exchange-rate systems isolated their money markets from international forces. De Grauwe finds that interest-rate adjustments are shared between Germany and the Netherlands, which had no capital controls. He concludes that his findings provide no support for GDH.

A final argument comes from the observation that, in a fixed exchange-rate system, only one country can independently choose the exchange rate with an outside currency. German dominance could, therefore, consist of the imposition of a dollar policy on the EMS by the Bundesbank (Sarcinelli, 1986). Evidence of the Bundesbank's engagement in the G-5 policy co-ordination efforts since the 1985 Plaza Agreement (Dominguez, 1990; von Hagen, 1989) could then be interpreted as evidence of German dominance. The crucial question here is, How independent of EMS considerations was Germany's role in the G-5 coordination process? Funabashi's (1988) detailed account of the G-5 process stresses three points. First, the Bundesbank was very reluctant to participate in coordinated intervention to stabilize the dollar and was skeptical about its success. Second, the German reservations were predominantly due to EMS considerations, the fear that manipulating the dollar would create tensions within the EMS. Finally, the Bundesbank and the Bank of France—also a member of G-5—consulted and informed other EMS central banks during the process. Thus, the historical events give no reason to believe that the Bundesbank enforced a dollar policy on the EMS.

Asymmetries in the EMS: Another Look

Von Hagen and Fratianni (1990d) use the parameter estimates of the interest-rate version system (24) to develop simple, descriptive measures of interest-rate interaction in the EMS and explore asymmetries.[30] Table 15.7 reports their estimated responses of other members' interest rates to an increase in the German rate, and the German response to an innovation in other members' rates. Responses to a German innovation generally increase over the six-month time horizon. During the first EMS period, French and Italian interest rates adjust fully to the German rate within six months; in the other countries, the adjustment remains incomplete even after six months. In contrast, the German response to other countries is constant or declines with increasing lag length. The only exception is the response to a Dutch interest-rate innovation. The German response to an Italian interest-rate innovation vanishes after six months. This picture changes in the second EMS period. Germany's impact on French and Italian interest rates falls. The reaction to French interest-rate innovations continues to decline with increasing lag length, but the reaction to Belgium, Italy, and the Netherlands increases.[31]

Using the currency weights of the ECU, von Hagen and Fratianni con-

Table 15.7
Responses to Unit Interest-Rate Innovations, 1979–83

	Lag 0		Lag 1		Lag 6	
	H_{1j}	H_{j1}	H_{1j}	H_{j1}	H_{1j}	H_{j1}
France	0.29	0.36	0.56	0.30	1.06	0.38
Italy	0.28	0.39	0.57	0.02	1.11	0.00
Belgium	0.09	0.16	0.16	0.12	0.34	0.20
Netherlands	0.26	0.30	0.28	0.21	0.56	0.41
Ireland	0.31	0.03	0.27	0.03	0.25	0.05
Denmark	0.03	0.09	0.09	0.06	0.27	0.10

1983.4 − 1988.4

	Lag 0		Lag 1		Lag 6	
	H_{1j}	H_{j1}	H_{1j}	H_{j1}	H_{1j}	H_{j1}
France	0.28	0.36	0.58	0.17	0.75	0.08
Italy	0.29	0.39	0.43	0.70	0.23	0.51
Belgium	0.09	0.16	0.75	0.22	0.68	0.21
Netherlands	0.26	0.30	0.22	0.40	0.53	0.55
Ireland	0.30	0.03	0.18	0.04	0.23	0.07
Denmark	0.03	0.09	0.35	0.11	0.36	0.09

Source: von Hagen and Fratianni (1990d).

Note: H_{1j} denotes the response to a German innovation in country j, H_{j1} denotes the German response to an innovation in country j.

struct an average money market rate for the EMS.[32] The relative contribution of an innovation in an individual country's money market rate to a change in the average EMS rate yields a proximate measure of this country's relative importance in the EMS. Empirical estimates of this measure, reported in the upper part of Table 15.7, show that Germany's relative contribution is clearly the largest in the EMS. During the first period, the French and Italian contributions at lag six are similar to their relative weights in the ECU. In contrast, the French contribution in the second period is much smaller than the French weight would lead us to expect, whereas the Italian and the Dutch contributions are larger.

The relative importance of the EMS for an individual country can be measured by the relative contribution of interest-rate innovations in all other EMS countries to changes in this country's rate. These measures are reported in Table 15.8. They increase with increasing lag length in Belgium, Denmark, France, Italy, and the Netherlands. In contrast, the German measure decreases or remains the same. Before 1983, Germany's measure is the smallest of all EMS countries at lag six, indicating that the Bundesbank, more than any other EMS central bank, was able to pursue a relatively independent policy. After 1983, Germany's measure is more in line with the other countries.

These interest-rate responses suggest a characterization of the EMS. First, Germany is a nondominated player in the sense that other countries react more strongly to its policy than vice versa (Weber, 1990). But this relative strength cannot be equated with the strict hierarchy postulated by GDH. Second, France and Italy appear to be relatively weak players who adjust more completely to German policies than other EMS members and who have little influence on the rest of the EMS. In the later EMS period, the French position continues to be relatively weak; the Italian position, in contrast, improves. In this period, the Bundesbank seems to have lost some of its relative independence. These characterizations provide a suggestive explanation for the dissatisfaction French and Italian officials have expressed about Germany's role in the EMS.

In conclusion, the empirical evidence refutes the hierarchical structure of the EMS claimed by GDH. Many casual observers of the EMS seem to have mistaken the combination of an undominated German position and the relatively weak French and Italian positions with German dominance. Again, the evidence does not support the credibility hypothesis of the EMS.

CONCLUSIONS: FROM THE EMS TO EUROPEAN MONETARY UNION

Together with the EC's program to complete the internal market, the idea of European monetary unification underwent a strong revival in the late 1980s. In 1989 the EC Council reaffirmed the Community's desire for EMU and adopted the Delors Report as its official program for the achievement of this goal. Like its predecessor, the Werner Report, the Delors Report proposes to build an EMU in three stages, the first of which will be the enlargement of the EMS to include all members of the EC and the strengthening of policy coordination in the EMS.[33]

What has the EMS achieved to deserve this central role? Clearly, it has brought a reduction of nominal and real exchange-rate variability, and in that way it has helped to stabilize trade and agricultural integration in the EC. There is little empirical evidence of a significant contribution of the EMS to the European disinflation in the 1980s. EMS countries were no more successful in fighting inflation than other coun-

Table 15.8
Decomposition of Interest-Rate Changes

a) Relative Contribution of Domestic Rate to Changes in EMS Average Rate

b) Relative Contribution of EMS Rates to Changes in Domestic Rate

1979.3 – 1983.3

Lag	G	F	I	B	NL	Ire	Dk	G	F	I	B	NL	Ire	Dk
0	0.31	0.21	0.18	0.10	0.16	0.02	0.04	0.53	0.32	0.46	0.35	0.35	0.60	0.17
1	0.35	0.25	0.10	0.09	0.15	0.02	0.04	0.40	0.40	0.57	0.45	0.33	0.38	0.58
6	0.41	0.20	0.08	0.09	0.17	0.02	0.04	0.40	0.56	0.64	0.58	0.53	0.58	0.68

1983.4 – 1988.4

Lag	G	F	I	B	NL	Ire	Dk	G	F	I	B	NL	Ire	Dk
0	0.31	0.21	0.18	0.10	0.16	0.02	0.04	0.53	0.32	0.46	0.35	0.35	0.60	0.17
1	0.28	0.17	0.24	0.10	0.16	0.02	0.04	0.57	0.47	0.49	0.68	0.31	0.58	0.71
6	0.32	0.10	0.20	0.09	0.23	0.03	0.03	0.56	0.61	0.51	0.70	0.47	0.53	0.64

Source: von Hagen and Fratianni (1990d).

Note: G = Germany, F = France, I = Italy, B = Belgium, NL = Netherlands, Ire = Ireland, and Dk = Denmark.

tries, nor was the real cost of disinflating lower than elsewhere. Policy-makers in the EMS may have found it easier to implement a stabilization program simply by pegging the relatively stable Deutsche mark, making the Bundesbank the focal point of policymaking in the region. But the role of EMS membership in establishing the credibility of the new policy orientation has been largely overstated. On the other hand, there is some suggestive evidence of the merits of strategic policy coordination in the EMS. But the gains appear to be badly distributed and to lack robustness to asymmetries in economic structures and fluctuations. Therefore, a monetary union in Europe will likely be difficult to sustain, especially in a period of structural adjustments following the completion of the internal market.

Under the new conditions of integrated European capital markets, capital and exchange controls will no longer be available to shield individual money markets from international capital flows and will facilitate some degree of domestic monetary autonomy even with fixed exchange rates. Realignments will become rather unwieldy instruments as speculative attacks in the anticipation of a realignment become more likely. Monetary independence therefore stands increasingly in contrast to the goal of exchange-rate stability in the EC. In this sense, given the European desire for exchange-rate stability, the completion of the internal market requires a larger degree of monetary policy coordination and, ultimately, favors EMU. This and the economic benefits of monetary integration will help sustain the monetary union to some extent. Ultimately, however, Triffin's (1960) judgment still holds: The decision for an EMU is first of all a political one. The history of the EMS has shown that progress with monetary cooperation required strong political impulses to forge greater union in the EC. Europe's monetary unification is an important element of the efforts to achieve political unification; therefore, its prospects ultimately rest on the strength of the quest for political union in Europe.

The analysis of central bank credibility teaches us that the absence of institutions that facilitate commitment to stability-oriented policies results in inefficient and undesirable outcomes. The important lesson for the EMS and EMU is that policy coordination in the EMS needs an institutional framework that provides credible commitment. The strategic implication is that the Delors Committee's proposal of a lengthy and ambiguous transition and training period from national policymaking to a common policy in the EMU must be rejected. To gain credibility, the EMU needs policy institutions with clear responsibilities and operating principles and the authority over a common monetary policy. The institutional implication is that the EMU requires an independent central bank.[34] This would transform the EMS from a framework for optional coordination into an EMU committed to price stability.

NOTES

Financial support by the Deutsche Forschungsgemeinschaft, SFB 303 at the University of Bonn, is gratefully acknowledged. This chapter has benefited extensively from joint work with Michele Fratianni. I wish to thank him and Manfred J. M. Neumann for their many valuable comments and suggestions.

1. For a history of monetary integration in Europe, see Tsoukalis (1977) or van Ypersele and Koeune (1985).

2. As early as January 1959, the Economic and Financial Commission of the European Parliament called for the long-term development of a European central bank along the lines of the U.S. Federal Reserve System.

3. Williamson (1983) calls this the "misalignment problem"; see, for example, De Grauwe (1988) and Bini Smaghi (1990) for a discussion.

4. In the EMS, the European Unit of Account was replaced by the European Currency Unit (ECU).

5. Note, however, that the reverse may also be true: Maintaining fixed nominal exchange rates in the presence of persistent international inflation differentials equally results in relative price distortions, a point often neglected in the debate over CAP (e.g., Giavazzi and Giovannini, 1989; van Ypersele and Koeune, 1985).

6. The Treaty speaks of maintaining the confidence in member currencies.

7. As early as 1964, Italy turned to the United States and the IMF instead of its European partners for help in a balance-of-payments crisis.

8. See Fratianni and von Hagen (1990a) for a review.

9. The value of the ECU in terms of a currency i, ECU_i, is $ECU_i = \Sigma_j s_{ij} q_j$, where s_{ij} is the exchange rate between currencies i and j and q_j is the basket quantity of currency j. The relative weight of currency k in the value of the ECU is therefore $w_k = s_{ik} q_k / ECU_i$. Thus, a depreciating currency k (decreasing s_{ik}) has a declining weight. The quantities q were redefined on July 7, 1984, and September 21, 1989, lowering the quantities of the DM and the guilder and increasing the quantities of the lira, the French franc, and the drachma.

10. See, for example, Levich and Sommariva (1987) on the private use of the ECU.

11. The realignment dates are September 24, 1979, November 30, 1979, March 23, 1981, October 5, 1981, February 22, 1982, June 14, 1982, March 21, 1983, July 22, 1985, April 7, 1986, August 4, 1986, January 12, 1987, and January 5, 1990.

12. See, for example, Wyplosz (1986) and von Hagen and Fratianni (1990a) for an empirical analysis of realignment expectations.

13. This observation was first pointed out by de Grauwe (1987).

14. More generally, the cooperative game entails the maximization of the joint preference function $aU + (1-a) U^*$, $0 < a < 1$, where a is determined in a bargaining process.

15. Canzoneri and Gray (1985), Canzoneri and Henderson (1988), Mélitz (1985), Laskar (1986), Collins (1988), Fratianni and von Hagen (1990a). This situation must be distinguished from the case where one country adopts the exchange rate as policy instrument. See Canzoneri and Henderson (1988).

16. This equivalence of cooperation and the fixed exchange rate is a consequence of the contrived symmetry of our model. In fact, the relative demand shock in our

model can be interpreted more generally as a deviation from symmetry which could arise alternatively from differences in the economic structures of the two countries.

Mélitz (1985) argues that if the exchange-rate arrangement is equivalent to cooperation with a flexible rate, it is preferable to choose the fixed rate, because it saves the cost of bargaining over joint policies which might arise otherwise.

17. We have argued above that exchange-rate fixity is valued for its positive effects on the customs union in the EC and therefore constitutes a common good achieved in the ERM. Preserving this common good will induce an EMS central bank to tolerate an outcome otherwise worse than the Nash equilibrium, at least temporarily. For this reason alone, an exchange-rate peg may be more robust to the distributional problems arising from relative shocks than coordination with flexible exchange rates.

18. Recent literature based on the paradigm of a small open economy pegging the exchange rate with the currency of a large country shows how exchange-rate arrangements can be used to cope with problems of imperfect information (e.g., Aizenman and Frenkel, 1985; Boyer, 1978; von Hagen and Neumann, 1990). In these models, the exchange-rate regime determines the LM curve and, consequently, its stabilizing characteristics. Furthermore, exchange-rate policies alter the information content of goods and asset prices and therefore have an impact on the private sector's ability to infer to imperfectly observed shocks.

19. The previous relative demand shock η is now the average of two shocks, one originating in each country, $\eta = (\eta_1 + \eta_2)/2$.

20. Note that in a repeated game context the incentive to overstate the domestic shock is limited only to the extent that the foreign central bank can monitor the true shock ex post.

21. Gros and Lane (1992) analyze the welfare gains and their distribution from exchange-rate pegging in a model where exchange-rate targets are set ex ante (before shocks are realized) and monetary targets ex post. Their model can be interpreted as one where exchange-rate management is used to transmit information.

22. With serially uncorrelated shocks and no dynamics in the model, the issue of strategic realignments does not arise in their analysis.

23. See Canzoneri and Henderson (1988) and Fratianni and von Hagen (1990a). This result is similar in spirit to Rogoff's (1985a) point that cooperation can produce adverse outcomes.

24. See, for example, Giavazzi and Pagano (1988), Giavazzi and Giovannini (1987), and Fratianni (1988). In addition, Giavazzi and Giovannini (1987) argue that intervention practices in the EMS free the Bundesbank from the need to adjust to EMS portfolio shocks, a point, however, that holds strictly only for intramarginal interventions.

25. The pre-EMS role of U.K. inflation results from the Irish peg of the pound sterling since 1926.

26. See Bofinger (1988b) for a review of further reforms in the EMS.

27. A more detailed explanation can be found in Fratianni and von Hagen (1990 a,b) and von Hagen and Fratianni (1990d).

28. We define $c_i = 0$ and $a_{ij} = 0$ to mean $c_i(L) \equiv 0$ and $a_{ij}(L) \equiv 0$.

29. Specifically, define the operator $g(a_{ij})$ and $g(c_i)$ as the sum of the coefficients of the relevant lag polynomial. "Weak" German dominance consists of the hy-

potheses H1W: $g(c_i) = 0$, $i = 2,\ldots,7$; H2W: $g(a_{ij}) = 0$, $i,j = 2,\ldots,7$; H3W: (reject) $g(a_{ii}) = 0$, $i = 2,\ldots,7$; H4W: $g(a_{1i}) = 0$, $i = 2,\ldots,7$.

30. The estimates serve to compute the impulse response functions, $h_{ij}(k)$, which specify the current change in country j's interest rate owing to an autonomous, unit-size innovation in country i's interest-rate k periods ago. The total effect $H_{ij}(k)$ of this innovation on the *level* of country j's interest rate is obtained by cumulating the individual $h_{ij}(n)$ over the $n = 1,\ldots,k$ periods.

31. The result that the German reaction to a Dutch interest-rate innovation is of the same order of magnitude as the Dutch response to a German innovation is consistent with De Grauwe's (1988b) observations of interest-rate links between Germany and the Netherlands.

32. The ECU weights used here are 0.395 for Germany, 0.221 for France, 0.11 for Italy, 0.104 for Belgium, 0.125 for the Netherlands, 0.013 for Ireland, and 0.032 for Denmark. These weights are as of April 1988, excluding the pound sterling and the drachma.

33. See Fratianni and von Hagen (1990c) for a discussion of the Delors strategy.

34. For a discussion of central bank independence and its implications in an EMU, see Neumann (1991) and von Hagen and Fratianni (1991).

REFERENCES

Aizenman, Joshua, and Frenkel, Jacob A. 1985. "Optimal Wage Indexation, Foreign Exchange Intervention, and Monetary Policy." *American Economic Review* 75: 402–23.

Artis, Michael J. 1987. "The European Monetary System: An Evaluation." *Journal of Policy Modeling* 9, no. 1: 175–98.

———, and Taylor, Mark. 1988. "Exchange Rates, Interest Rates, Capital Controls and the European Monetary System: Assessing the Track Record." In *The European Monetary System*, edited by Francesco Giavazzi, Stefano Micossi, and Marcus Miller. Cambridge, England: Cambridge University Press, 185–205.

Barro, Robert J., and Gordon, David B. 1983. "A Positive Theory of Monetary Policy in a Natural Rate Model." *Journal of Political Economy* 91: 589–610.

Begg, David, and Wyplosz, Charles. 1987. "Why the EMS? Dynamic Games and the Equilibrium Policy Regime." In *Global Macroeconomics*, edited by Ralph C. Bryant and Richard Porters. New York: St. Martin's Press.

Bini Smaghi, Lorenzo. 1990. "Progressing Towards European Monetary Unification: Selected Issues and Proposals." Banca d'Italia Temi di Discussione 133, April.

Bofinger, Peter. 1988a. "Das EWS und die geldpolitische Koordination in Europa." *Kredit und Kapital* 21: 317–45.

———. 1988b. "New Rules for the EMS?" *Geld und Währung—Monetary Affairs* 4: 5–22.

Boyer, Russel S. 1978. "Optimal Foreign Exchange Market Intervention." *Journal of Political Economy* 86: 1045–55.

Branson, William. 1990. "Financial Market Integration and Monetary Policy in 1992." Working Paper, Princeton University.

Camen, Ulrich. 1986. "FRG Monetary Policy Under External Constraints, 1979–84." Working Paper 21. Brussels: Center for European Policy Studies.

Canzoneri, Matthew B., and Gray, Jo A. 1985. "Monetary Policy Games and the Consequences of Non-Cooperative Behavior." *International Economic Review* 26: 547–64.

———, and Henderson, Dale W. 1988. "Is Sovereign Policymaking Bad?" In *Stabilization Policies and Labor Markets*, edited by Karl Brunner and Allan H. Meltzer. *Carnegie-Rochester Conference Series on Public Policy* 28. Amsterdam: North-Holland, 193–235, 1988.

Chouraqui, Jean-Claude, and Price, Robert W. R. 1984. "Medium-Term Financial Strategy: The Co-ordination of Fiscal and Monetary Policies." *OECD Economic Studies* No. 2: 7–49.

Cohen, Daniel, and Wyplosz, Charles. 1989. "The EMS: An Agnostic Evaluation." In *Macroeconomic Policies in an Interdependent World*, edited by Ralph C. Bryant et al. Washington, D.C.: International Monetary Fund.

Collins, Susan M. 1988. "Inflation and the EMS." In *The European Monetary System*, edited by Francesco Giavazzi, Stefano Micossi, and Marcus Miller. Cambridge, England: Cambridge University Press.

Commission of the European Communities. 1979. "The European Monetary System." *European Economy* (July).

———. 1989. *Report on Economic and Monetary Union in the European Community* (Delors Report). Luxembourg: Office for Official Publications of the European Communities.

Council of the European Communities. 1970. *Interim Report on the Establishing by Stages of Economic and Monetary Union* (Werner Report). Supplement to Bulletin 11–1970 of the EC. Luxembourg: Office for Official Publications of the European Communities.

———. 1985. Resolution of December 5, 1978. Reprinted in Jacques van Ypersele and Jean-Claude Koeune. *The European Monetary System: Origins, Operation, and Outlook*. Brussels: Commission of the EC.

De Grauwe, Paul. 1987. "Fiscal Policies in the EMS: A Strategic Analysis." Paper presented at the conference on the international monetary system, the EMS, the ECU and plans for world monetary reform, European University Institute, Florence, April.

———. 1988a. "Exchange Rate Variability and the Slowdown in Growth of International Trade." *IMF Staff Papers* 35: 63–84.

———. 1988b. "Is the European Monetary System a DM-Zone?" Working Paper, Catholic University of Leuwen.

———. 1990. "The Cost of Disinflation and the European Monetary System." *Open Economies Review* 1: 147–74.

Deutsche Bundesbank. 1979. "The European Monetary System." *Monthly Report* (March): 31.

Dominguez, Kathryn. 1990. "Market Responses to Coordinated Central Bank Intervention." In *Carnegie-Rochester Conference Series on Public Policy* 32, edited by Allan H. Meltzer. Amsterdam: North-Holland.

Dornbusch, Rudiger. 1980. *Open Economy Macroeconomics*. New York: Basic Books.

―――. 1989. "Credibility, Debt, and Unemployment: Ireland's Failed Stabilization." *Economic Policy* 8 (April): 173–209.

Eggerstädt, Harald, and Sinn, Stefan. 1987. "The EMS 1979–86: The Economics of Muddling Through." *Geld und Währung Monetary Affairs* 3: 5–23.

Emerson, Michael. 1979. "The EMS in the Broader Setting of the Community's Economic and Political Development." In *The European Monetary System: Its Promise and Prospects*, edited by Philip H. Trezise. Washington, D.C.: Brookings Institution.

Fischer, Stanley. 1988. "International Macroeconomic Policy Coordination." In *International Economic Cooperation*, edited by Marten Feldstein. Chicago: University of Chicago Press.

Fratianni, Michele. 1980. "The European Monetary System: A Return to an Adjustable-Peg Arrangement." In *Monetary Institutions and the Policy Process*, edited by Karl Brunner and Allan H. Meltzer. *Carnegie-Rochester Conference Series in Public Policy* 13. Amsterdam: North-Holland, 139–72.

―――. 1988. "The European Monetary System: How Well Has It Worked?" *The Cato Journal* 8: 477–501.

―――, and von Hagen, Jürgen. 1990a. "The European Monetary System Ten Years After." In *Unit Roots, Investment Measures and Other Essays*, edited by Allan H. Meltzer. *Carnegie-Rochester Conference Series in Public Policy* 32. Amsterdam: North-Holland, 173–242.

―――. 1990b. "German Dominance in the EMS: The Empirical Evidence." *Open Economies Review* 1: 68–87.

―――. 1990c. "Public Choice Aspects of the EMS and European Monetary Union." *Cato Journal* 10: 389–411.

Funabashi, Yoichi. 1988. *Managing the Dollar: From the Plaza to the Louvre*. Washington, D.C.: Institute for International Economics.

Giavazzi, Francesco, and Giovannini, Alberto. 1986. "The EMS and the Dollar." *Economic Policy: A European Forum* 1: 455–85.

―――. 1987. "Models of the EMS: Is Europe a Greater Deutschmark Area?" In *Global Macroeconomics*, edited by Ralph C. Bryant and Richard Portes. New York: St. Martin's Press, 237–65.

―――. 1988. "The Role of the Exchange Rate Regime in a Disinflation: Empirical Evidence on the European Monetary System." In *The European Monetary System*, edited by Francesco Giavazzi, Stefano Micossi, and Marcus Miller. Cambridge, England: Cambridge University Press.

―――. 1989. *Limiting Exchange Rate Variability: The European Monetary System*. Cambridge, Mass.: MIT Press.

―――, and Pagano, Marco. 1988. "The Advantage of Tying One's Hands." *European Economic Reveiw* 32: 1055–82.

―――, and Spaventa, Luigi. 1989. "Italy: The Real Effects of Inflation and Disinflation." *Economic Policy* 8 (April): 135–71.

―――. 1990. "The 'New' EMS." In *The European Monetary System in the 1990s*, edited by Paul De Grauwe and Lucas Papademos. London and New York: Longman.

Giovannini, Alberto. 1989. "How Do Fixed Exchange Rate Systems Work? Evidence from the Gold Standard, Bretton Woods, and the EMS." In *Blueprints for Exchange-rate Management*, edited by Marcus Miller, Barry Eichengreen, and Richard Portes. London: Academic Press, 13–42.

Gressani, Daniela; Guiso, Luigi; and Visco, Ignazio. 1988. "Disinflation in Italy: An Analysis with the Econometric Model of the Bank of Italy." *Journal of Policy Modeling* 10: 163–203.

Gros, Daniel, and Lane, Timothy. 1990. "Asymmetry in a Fixed Exchange Rate System: Who Gains from the EMS?" Paper presented at Konstanz Seminar on Monetary Theory and Monetary Policy.

————. 1992. "Monetary Policy Interaction Within or Without an Exchange-Rate Arrangement." *Open Economics Review* 1: 61–82.

————, and Thygesen, Niels. 1988. "Le SME: Performances et Perspectives." *Observations et Diagnostics Economiques* 24 (July): 55–80.

Hughes-Hallett, Andrew, and Minford, Patrick. 1989. "The EMS—Does It Achieve Its Aims?" Paper presented at Konstanz Seminar on Monetary Theory and Policy.

————. 1990. "Target Zones and Exchange Rate Management: A Stability Analysis of the EMS." *Open Economies Review* 1: 175–200.

International Monetary Fund. 1990. *International Financial Statistics*. Washington, D.C.

Jenkins, Roy. 1978. "European Monetary Union." *Lloyd's Bank Review* 127 (January): 1–14.

Katseli, Louka T. 1987. "Macroeconomic Policy Coordination and the Domestic Base of National Economic Policies in Major European Countries." Conference Paper, Andover, November.

Kirchgässner, Gebhard, and Wolters, Jürgen. 1990. "Interest Rate Linkages in Europe Before and After the Introduction of the EMS." Working Paper, Konstanz Seminar on Monetary Theory and Policy.

Koedijk, Kees G., and Kool, Clemens J. M. 1991. "Dominant Interest and Inflation Differentials Within the EMS." Working Paper RM 91.008, Limburg University.

Kremers, J.J.M. 1990. "Gaining Policy Credibility for a Disinflation: Ireland's Experience in the EMS." International Monetary Fund Staff Papers 37: 116–256.

Laskar, Daniel. 1986. "International Cooperation and Exchange Rate Stabilization." *Journal of International Economics* 21, no. 1/2 (August): 151–64.

Levich, Richard M., and Sommariva, Andrea. 1987. *The ECU Market*. Lexington, Mass.: Lexington Books.

Lucas, Robert E., Jr. 1976. "Econometric Policy Evaluation: A Critique." In *The Phillips Curve and Labor Markets*, edited by Karl Brunner and Allan H. Meltzer. *Carnegie-Rochester Conference Series on Public Policy* 1. Amsterdam: North-Holland.

Ludlow, P. 1982. *The Making of the EMS*. London: Butterworth.

Mastropasqua, Cristina; Micossi, Stefano; and Rinaldi, Roberto. 1988. "Interventions, Sterilization and Monetary Policy in the EMS Countries (1979–1987)." In *The European Monetary System*, edited by Francesco Giavazzi, Stefano Micossi and Marcus Miller. Cambridge, England: Cambridge University Press.

Mélitz, Jacques. 1985. "The Welfare Case for the European Monetary System." *Journal of International Money and Finance* 4: 485–506.

———. 1988a. "Monetary Discipline and Cooperation in the EMS: A Synthesis." In *The European Monetary System*, edited by Francesco Giavazzi, Stefano Micossi, and Marcus Miller. Cambridge, England: Cambridge University Press.

———. 1988b. "Monetary Discipline, Germany, and the European Monetary System." *Kredit und Kapital* 21: 481–512.

Meltzer, Allan H. 1990. "Some Empirical Findings on Differences Between EMS and Non-EMS Regimes: Implications for Currency Blocks." *Cato Journal* 10: 455–84.

Micossi, Stefano. 1985. "The Intervention and Financial Mechanisms of the EMS and the Role of the ECU." *Banca Nazionale del Lavoro Quarterly Review*, 327–45.

Minford, Patrick. 1988. "Das EWS—Eine kritische Betrachtung." In *Internationales Währungssystem und weltwirtschaftliche Entwicklung*, edited by Christian Dräger and Lothar Späth. Baden-Baden: Nomos, 313–32.

Neumann, Manfred J. M. 1991. "Precommitment to Stability by Central Bank Independence." *Open Economics Review* 3: 110–118.

OECD. 1988. *Why Economic Policies Change: Eleven Case Studies*. Paris: OECD.

Padoa-Schioppa, Tommaso. 1985. *Wirtschafts- und Währungspolitische Probleme der Europäischen Integration*. Luxembourg: Publications Office of the European Community.

Rieke, Wolfgang. 1984. "Die Rolle von Interventionen als Bestimmungsfaktor der Wechselkurse beim 'Floating,' " In *Devisenmarktinterventionen der Zentralbanken*, edited by Werner Ehrlicher and Rudolf Richter. Berlin: Duncker and Humblot.

Rogoff, Kenneth. 1985a. "Can International Monetary Policy Cooperation Be Counterproductive?" *Journal of International Economics* 8: 199–217.

———. 1985b. "Can Exchange Rate Predictability Be Achieved Without Monetary Convergence?" *European Economic Review* 28: 91–115.

Roubini, Nouriel. 1988. "Sterilization Policies, Capital Movements and Exchange Rate Intervention Policies in the EMS." Harvard University, Ph.D. diss., Chap. 4.

Russo, Massimo, and Tullio, Guiseppe. 1988. "Monetary Policy Coordination Within the EMS: Is There a Rule?" In *Policy Coordination in the European Monetary System*. Occasional Paper No. 61. Washington, D.C.: IMF.

Sachs, Jeffrey, and Wyplosz, Charles. 1986. "The Economic Consequences of President Mitterand." *Economic Policy* 2 (April): 261–305.

Sarcinelli, Mario. 1986. "The EMS and the International Monetary System: Towards Greater Stability." *Banca Nazionale del Lavoro Quarterly Review* (March): 57–83.

Schmidt, Helmut. 1990. "Die Bürokraten ausgetrickst und Kampf gegen die Nationalisten." *Die Zeit*, August 24 and August 31.

Tabellini, Guido. 1988. "Monetary and Fiscal Policy Coordination with a High Public Debt." In *High Public Debt: The Italian Experience*, edited by Francesco Giavazzi and Luigi Spaventa. Cambridge, England: Cambridge University Press.

Tanzi, Vito, and Ter-Minassian, Teresa. 1987. "The European Monetary System and Fiscal Policies." In *Tax Coordination in the EMS*, edited by H. Cnossen. Deventer: Kluwer.

Trezise, Philip H., ed. 1979. *The European Monetary System: Its Promise and Prospects*. Washington, D.C.: Brookings Institution.

Triffin, Robert. 1960. *Gold and the Dollar Crisis*. New Haven, Conn.: Yale University Press.

Tsoukalis, Loukas. 1977. *The Politics and Economics of European Monetary Integration*. London: George Allen & Unwin.

Ungerer, Horst. 1990. "The EMS—The First Ten Years—Policies—Developments—Evolution." *Konjunkturpolitik* 36: 329–62.

———; Evans, Owen; Mayer, Thomas; and Young, Phillip. 1983. "The EMS: The Experience 1979–1982." Occasional Paper No. 19, IMF.

———. 1986. "The EMS: Recent Developments, Occasional Paper 48." Occasional Paper No. 48, IMF.

van Ypersele, Jacques. 1979. "Operating Principles and Procedures of the EMS." In *The EMS: Its Promise and Prospects*, edited by Philip H. Trezise. Washington, D.C.: Brookings Institution.

———, and Koeune, Jean-Claude. 1985. *The European Monetary System: Origins, Operation, and Outlook*. Brussels: Commission of the European Communities.

Vaubel, Roland. 1980. "The Return to the New EMS." In *Monetary Institutions and the Policy Process*, edited by Karl Brunner and Allan H. Meltzer. *Carnegie-Rochester Conference Series on Public Policy* 13. Amsterdam: North- Holland, 173–221.

von Hagen, Jürgen. 1984. "Mindestreservesystem und kurzfristige Geldbasissteuerung." In *Geld, Banken und Versicherungen*, Vol. 1, edited by H. Göppel and R. Henn. Karlsruhe: VVW, 251–66.

———. 1989. "Monetary Targeting with Exchange Rate Constraints: The Bundesbank in the 1980s." Federal Reserve Bank of St. Louis *Review*, October, 71.

———, and Fratianni, Michele. 1990a. "Asymmetries and Realignments in the EMS." In *The European Monetary System in the 1990s*, edited by Paul De Grauwe and Loukas Papademos. London and New York: Longman.

———. 1990b. "Credibility and Asymmetries in the EMS." In *The Choice of an Exchange Rate Regime: The Challenge for the Smaller Industrialized Countries*, edited by Victor Argy and Paul De Grauwe. Washington, D.C.: IMF.

———. 1990c. "Policy Coordination in the EMS with Stochastic and Structural Asymmetries." Working Paper, Indiana University School of Business.

———. 1990d. "German Dominance in the European Monetary System: Evidence from Interest Rates." *Journal of International Money and Finance* 9: 358–75.

———. 1991. "Monetary and Fiscal Policy in a European Monetary Union: Some Public Choice Considerations." In *European Monetary Integration*, edited by Paul J. J. Welfens. Berlin: Springer.

———, and Neumann, Manfred J.M. 1990. "Relative Price Risk in an Open Economy with Flexible and Fixed Exchange Rates." *Open Economies Review* 1, no. 3: 41–61.

Weber, Axel A. 1990. "European Economic and Monetary Union and Asymmetries and Adjustment Problems in the EMS: Some Empirical Evidence." Discussion Paper 9–90, University of Siegen.

Williamson, John. 1983. *The Exchange Rate System*. Washington D.C.: Institute for International Economics, 1983.

Wyplosz, Charles. 1986. "Capital Controls and Balance of Payments Crises." *Journal of International Money and Finance* 5: 167–80.

———. 1988a. "Capital Flow Liberalization and the EMS: A French Perspective." *European Economy* (May): 85–103.

———. 1988b. "Das EWS: Vom Erfolg zum Wandel." In *Internationales Währungssystem und weltwirtschaftliche Entwicklung*, edited by Christian Dräger and Lothar Späth. Baden-Baden: Nomos, 267–81.

SELECTED BIBLIOGRAPHY

Bank of Japan Finance Research Institute. 1986. *Wagakuni-no Kinyu Seido* (Japan's Financial System). Tokyo: Bank of Japan Finance Research Institute.

Barro, Robert, and Gordon, David. 1983. "A Positive Theory of Monetary Policy in a Natural Rate Model." *Journal of Political Economy* 91 (August): 589–610.

Begg, David, and Charles Wyplosz. 1987. "Why the EMS? Dynamic Games and the Equilibrium Policy Regime." In *Global Macroeconomics*, edited by Ralph C. Bryant and Richard Portes. New York: St. Martin's Press.

Blanchard, Oliver. 1984. "The Lucas Critique and the Volcker Deflation." *American Economic Review* 74 (May): 211–15.

Blundell-Wignall, Adrian; Browne, Frank; and Manasse, Paolo. 1990 "Monetary Policy in the Wake of Financial Liberalization." OECD Department of Economics and Statistics Working Papers, No. 77.

Brunner, Karl, and Meltzer, Allan. 1983. "Strategies and Tactics for Monetary Control." *Carnegie-Rochester Conference Series on Public Policy* 18, edited by K. Brunner and A. Meltzer. Amsterdam: North-Holland.

Cairns, James; Binhammer, H. H.; and Boadway, Robin. 1972. *Canadian Banking and Monetary Policy*. 2d ed. Toronto: McGraw–Hill Ryerson.

Crow, John. 1988. "The Work of Canadian Monetary Policy." *Bank of Canada Review* (February): 3–17.

Dornbusch, Rudiger. 1980. *Open Economy Macroeconomics*. New York: Basic Books.

Dudler, Hermann J. 1983. "Instrumente und quantitative Hilfsmittel der kurzfristigen Geldmengerkontroller." In *Geld-und Wahrungsordnung*, edited by Werner Ehrlicher and Rudolf Richter. Berlin: Duncker & Humblot.

Elton, Edwin J., and Gruber, Martin J. 1990. *Japanese Capital Markets–Analysis and Characteristics of Equity, Debt, and Financial Futures Markets*. New York: Harper & Row.

European Commission. 1990. "One Market, One Money." *European Economy*, no. 44 (October).

Fama, E. 1983. "Financial Intermediation and Price Level Control." *Journal of Monetary Economics* 12: 7–28.

Fischer, Stanley. 1988. "International Policy Coordination." In *International Economic Cooperation*, edited by Martin Feldstein. Chicago: University of Chicago Press.

Friedman, Benjamin. 1988. "Lessons on Monetary Policy from the 1980s." *Journal of Economic Perspectives* 2 (Summer) 51–72.

Giavazzi, Francesco, and Pagano, Marco. 1988. "The Advantage of Tying One's Hands." *European Economic Review* 32: 1055–82.

Goodhart, C.A.E. 1989. *Money, Information and Uncertainty*. 2d ed. New York: Macmillan.

Hillier, B., and Malcomson, J. M. 1984. "Dynamic Inconsistency, Rational Expectations, and Optimal Government Policy." *Econometrica* 52: 1437–51.

Hodgmen, D., and Resek, R. 1989. "Italian Monetary and Foreign Exchange Policy." In *Macroeconomic Policy and Economic Interdependence*, edited by D. Hodgman and J. Wood. London: Macmillan.

Kindleberger, C. P. 1967. *Europe's Postwar Growth, the Role of Labor Supply*. Cambridge, Mass.: Harvard University Press.

Kydland, Finn, and Prescott, Edward. 1977. "Rules Rather Than Discretion: The Inconsistency of Optimal Plans." *Journal of Political Economy* 85 (June): 473–92.

Lucas, Robert E., Jr. 1976. "Econometric Policy Evaluation: A Critique." In *The Phillips Curve and Labor Markets*, edited by Karl Brunner and Allan H. Meltzer, *Carnegie-Rochester Conference Series on Public Policy* 1. Amsterdam: North-Holland.

Maddison, A. 1982. *Phases of Capitalist Development*. Oxford: Oxford University Press.

Mastropasqua, C.; Micossi, S.; and Rinaldi, R. 1988. "Interventions, Sterilization, and Monetary Policy in the EMS Countries." In *The European Monetary System*, edited by Francesco Giavazzi et al. Cambridge: Cambridge University Press.

Mayer, Thomas, ed. 1990. *The Political Economy of Monetary Policy*. New York: Cambridge University Press.

Mélitz, Jacques. 1980. "The French Financial System: Mechanisms and Propositions of Reform." INSEE *Document de travail*, July. Revised and abridged version (revised subtitle: "Mechanisms and Questions of Reform"). *Annales de L'Insee*, no. 47–48 (July-December): 359–87. Also reprinted in *The French Economy: Theory and Policy*, edited by Jacques Mélitz and Charles Wyplosz. Boulder, Colo.: Westview Press, 359–87.

Penaud, Raymond, and Gaudichet, François. 1985. "*Selectivite du credit, financement, politique monetaire.*" *Economica*. Paris.

Poole, William. 1970. "Optimal Choice of Monetary Policy Instruments in a Simple Stochastic Macro Model." *Quarterly Journal of Economics* 84 (May): 197–216.

Rogoff, Kenneth. 1990. "Equilibrium Political Business Cycles." *American Economic Review* 80 (March): 21–26.

Royama, Masamichi, ed. 1988. *Shoken, Kinyu, Finance* (Securities, Banking, Finance). Tokyo: Toyokeizai-shimpo.

Scarth, William. 1990. "Fighting Inflation: Are the Costs of Getting to Zero Too High?" In *Taking Aim: The Debate on Zero Inflation*, edited by Robert C. York. Toronto: C. D. Howe Institute.

Tavlas, George S. 1991. "On the International Use of Currencies: The Case of the Deutsche Mark." *Essays in International Finance*, No. 181. Princeton, N.J.: Princeton University.

Trezise, Philip H., ed. 1979. *The European Monetary System: Its Promise and Prospects*. Washington, D.C.: Brookings Institution.

van Horne, James. 1985. *Japan's Financial Markets—Conflict and Consensus in Policy Making*. Sydney-London-Boston: George Allen & Unwin.

von Hagen, Jürgen. 1986. *Strategien Kurzfristiger Geldmengensteuerung*. Hamburg: Weltarchiv.

INDEX

Canada, 459–501
  Bank of Canada Act, 461–66
  Canada Savings Bond (CSB), 497–98
  Coyne Affair, The, 466–69
  demand stability, 497–98
  exchange-rate stabilization, 491–93
  fixed exchange rate, 492
  government influence, 461–66
  inflation, 492–93
  institutional setting, 459–72
  interest elasticity, 495–96
  M1, 489–91
  M2, 495–96
  monetary aggregates, 491, 495–96
  monetary expansion, 491
  monetary gradualism, 485–90
  monetary policy, evolution of, 478–99
  monetary targeting, 485–90
  operating procedures, 472–76
  orderly markets, 479–85
  price stability, 493–99
  short-term interest rates, 477–78
Central Bank/Federal Reserve, 195–286
  borrowed reserves strategy, 202
  conduct, 245–96

  employment/output, measures of, 197–200
  endogenous central bank policy, 68
  history of (1914–1937), 195–240
  interest rate smoothing, 208–17
  model of money stock determination, 255–56
  monetary aggregate strategy, 253–55, 280–82
  open market operations, 203–8
  pre-Great Depression, 200–203
  required reserves, 217–26
Classical quantity theory model, 56–60
  output/employment, 57–59
  policy implications, 60
  transmission mechanism, 59–60

Discount rate, 27–29

Employment, 57–59, 197–200
England, 405–30
  alternative policies, 415–18
  deregulation, 427–29
  Exchange Rate Mechanism of EMS, 424–26
  indexation, 426–27
  mechanisms of control, 429–30
    monetary base control, 429–30

reserve ratios, 430
Medium-Term Financial Strategy,
    406–11
monetarism, 407–8
monetary policy
    credibility, 407
    during 1979, 406–9
    prior to 1979, 419–23
monetary targets, 407–9
rules vs. discretion, 418–19
European Monetary System, 509–51
    asymmetries, 540–49
    basket currency, 515
    capital controls, 541, 547
    cooperative interpretation, 525–30
    coordination in EC, 510–12
    credibility hypothesis, 537–40
    disciplinary device, 534–37
    disinflation, 518–22
    economic integration, 510–11, 551
    Economic Monetary Cooperation
        Fund, 514
    ECU. See European Monetary
        System, basket currency
    exchange controls, 517–18
    exchange-rate stability, 510–12, 513
    externalities, 525
    fixed exchange rates, 511, 533
    flexibility, 511, 512, 515
    German dominance hypothesis, 540–
        47
        empirical evidence, 542–47
    history of, 512–15
    inflation, 512, 518–22
    intramarginal interventions, 516–17,
        528
    monetary compensation amounts,
        513
    Nash equilibrium, 526–29, 534
    nominal exchange rates, 522, 523
    parallelism, 511
    performance of, 518
    policy coordination, 530–34
        empirical evidence, 530–34
    real exchange rates, 522, 523
    realignment, 530–33
    Smithsonian Agreement, 514
    symmetry, 516

    unemployment, 518, 521
    Very Short Term Facility (VSTF),
        515–17
    Werner Committee, 514

Financial structure, 172–74, 183–87
    stability of, 181–87
France, 335–64
    Barre years (1976–81), 341–45
    early system (1945–66), 336–39
    encadrement, 338, 344–5, 346, 347,
        348
    liberalization (1966–76), 339–41
    muddled years (1981–84), 345–47
    new framework for monetary policy,
        351–64
        instruments, 351–53
        objectives, 358–60
        recent record, 360–64
        transmission, 353–58. See also
            France, transmission mechanism
    policy, instruments of, 351–53
        discount rate, 351–53
        interest rate, 351–53
        reserve requirement, 352–53
    post–1985 liberalization, 347–51
    transmission mechanism, 353–58
        monetary mechanism model, 354–
            58
        monetary target, 356–58
        open market operations, 356–58

Germany, 299–330
    Bundesbank independence, 301–3
    call-money rate regime, 316, 318–23
    empirical evidence, 328–29
    external constraints, of monetary
        policy, 303–8
    institutional framework, of
        monetary policy, 301
    intervention/sterilization, 323–28
    monetary control
        implementation, 314–23
        instruments of, 315–18
            discount credit, 316
            Lombard credit, 316
            open market portfolio, 317–18

security repurchase agreements
(REPOs), 317
monetary targeting, 308–14
policy objectives, 308–14

High-powered money, 30–33

Inflation, 93–117
empirical studies, 101–10
excess demand model, 95–99
monetarist model, 99–101
Interest rate
monetarist model, 70–72
smoothing the, 208–17
as a target, 64–66
Italy, 371–98
financial institutions, 376–78
fiscal policy, 373–74, 376–78
history of monetary variables, 372–
76
monetary policy
in 1950–69, 378–84
in 1970–79, 384–87
new regime (1979–89), 387–92
monetary targets, 393–97
in 1950s, 393
in 1960s, 393–94
in 1970s, 394
in 1980s, 396–97
Total Domestic Credit Expansion
(TDCE), 394–96

Japan, 433–56
Bank of Japan, 450–54
bill discount rate, 450
call rate, 450
corporation sector, 446, 448, 449
deregulation, 441–46
economic policies, 435–36
industrial policy, 436
manpower and education policy,
436
regional development policy, 436
supply side economics, 436
Euro-yen transactions, 455
financial structure, 436–46
banks, 439–40
financial institutions, 436–40

financial intermediaries, 439–40
financial organizations, 439
foreign exchange controls, 441,
445
interest rate, 449–52
regulation, 441
role of government, 440
flexible rates, 445–46, 456
foreign sector, 448, 453
indirect finance, 448–49
individual sector, 446
interest rates, 443
internationalization, 441–46
investment, 446–49
liberalization, 441–46
monetary policy, 449–56
effectiveness, 452, 454
instruments, 449–50
intermediate targets, 450–52
monetary aggregates, 454
objectives, 449–50
open market operations, 449
price stability, 452
reserve requirement ratios, 450,
454–55
"window guidance," 450
postwar development, 433–36
exchange rate, 433–34
internationalization period, 435
occupation period, 434
political economy period, 435
rapid growth period, 434–35
reconstruction period, 434
shocks period, 435
principles of requiring collateral, 441
public sector, 446
savings, and investment, 446–49

Keynesian model, 60–69
endogenous money, 68
policy implications, 68–69
real output, 68
transmission mechanism, 64–66

Monetarism/monetarists, 69–74
implications, 73–74
prices/output, 69–70, 72–73
transmission mechanism, 73

Monetary neutrality, 60
Monetary policy
  rules vs. discretion, 68–69, 76–78
  See names of specific countries
Monetary politics, 145–58
  bank regulation, 167–70
  debts, deficits, and democracy, 152–
    53
  international policy coordination,
    153–58, 282–85
  policy bargains, 150–52
  political business cycles, 145–50
  role of the U.S. president, 233–38
Money stock, 26–33
  determination of, 26–29
  relationship with high-powered
    money, 27–33
  total, 26–29
Money supply, 25–47
Multipliers, 30–33
  average, 31
  base money, 32
  marginal, 32

New classical model, 74–78
  policy implications, 76–77
  policy ineffectiveness, 75–76, 77–78
  rational expectations, 75
New Keynesian models, 80–85
  policy implications, 85
  price rigidity, 81–82
  real rigidities, 83–85

Open market operations, 29, 203–8

Policy instruments
  in France, 351–53
  in Germany, 308–14
Price rigidity, 81–82

Rational expectations, the concept of,
  75
Real business cycle theory, 78–80
  policy implications, 80
Repeated policy games, 135–37
Reputation, 125–64
  conservatism, 133–35
  conservatism vs. flexibility, 142–43

information, 137–42, 143–45
  partial commitment, 132–33
  randomization, 140–42
  stabilization, 142–43
Reserves, 33–42
  excess, 33, 37, 38, 41–42
  nonborrowed, 41–42
  required, 33–40, 217–26

Stability, 181–87

Time-series analysis, of the money
  supply process, 43–46
Total money stock, 26–33
Transactions money, 31, 41–42
Transmission, 64–66, 73

United States, 195–286
  Bluebook, 258–62
  borrowed reserves strategy, 203–8
  bureaucratic approach, 226–33
  "Current Economic and Financial
    Conditions." *See* Greenbook in
    this entry
  defensive open market operations,
    201, 271
  discount rate, 205
  dynamic open market operations,
    201, 271
  empirical problems, 197–200
  Federal Open Market Committee
    (FOMC), 247–48
  Federal Reserve Banks, 247
  Greenbook, 257
  implementation of monetary policy,
    267–68
  interest rate operating procedure,
    274–77
  interest rate smoothing, 208–17
  intermediate target approach, 253–
    55
  "Monetary Aggregates and Money
    Market Conditions." *See*
    Bluebook in this entry
  monetary aggregates strategy, 264,
    274–75
  monetary policy, 262–67
  formulation, 248–51

objectives, 248
transmission mechanism, 251–53
monetary policy regimes, 200–201
monetary politics, 145–53
central bank behavior, 145–52
money demand, 258, 259
money stock determination, 206,
279
money supply, 258–59
neutrality, 251
long-run, 251
short-run, 251

nonborrowed reserves operating
procedure, 277–80
open market operations, 268–74
pre-Great Depression, 200–203
"reserve need," 269–71
reserve requirements, 217–26
"reverse-causation," 206
"St. Louis model," 267–68
stability, 248
symmetrical directive, 267

Velocity of money, 110–17

ABOUT THE CONTRIBUTORS

KEITH BLACKBURN is Professor of Economics at the University of Southhampton in England. He was Visiting Professor at the University of Western Ontario in Canada and Research Fellow at the Centre for International Economics at the University of Aarnus in Denmark. His research interests and publications are in the fields of macroeconomic policy design, exchange rate regimes, game theory in macroeconomic policy, business cycles, and growth. He has published many articles in some of the leading economics journals, including *The Economic Journal, Journal of International Money and Finance, Journal of Economic Literature, Manchester School*, and *Journal of Economic Surveys*.

EDUARD J. BOMHOFF has been professor of Economics at Erasmus University Rotterdam (formally, Netherlands School of Economics) since 1981. He is an Associate Editor of the "Journal of Monetary Economics," which has published his work on the money multiplier and on macroeconomic determinants of floating exchange rates. Professor Bomhoff has been a visiting scholar at the Bank of Japan and the International Monetary Fund as well as an advisor to the European Community and several financial institutions. In addition to his research in empirical monetary economics, he has a strong interest in Kalman Filtering and its applications to economic problems.

MICHELE U. FRATIANNI is Professor of Business Economics and Public Policy at the Graduate School of Business of Indiana University. He has also taught at the Catholic University of Louvain, the Università Cattolica of Milan, and the Università Sapienza of Rome; was Economic Adviser to the European Commission in Brussels (1976–79), Senior Staff Economist with the U.S. President's Council of Economic Advisers (1981–82) and an adviser to the Italian Ministry of the Treasury, Italian Ministry of the Budget, the Bank of Italy, and the Confindustria; and in 1991 was elected a director of the International Trade and Financial Association. Fratianni is the managing editor of *Open Economies Review*. He is the author of thirteen books and approximately 100 articles dealing with macroeconomics, monetary economics, international finance, and public choice.

RICHARD T. FROYEN is Professor of Economics at the University of North Carolina at Chapel Hill where he has taught since 1971. He has been a Visiting Economist at the Board of Governors of the Federal Reserve System, a Visiting Professor at the University of Leeds (U.K.), and a Research Fellow at the Brookings Institution. Professor Froyen is the author of *Macroeconomics: Theories and Policies*, 3d ed., and of articles on macroeconomics and monetary policy in various economics journals.

PETER W. HOWITT is Professor of Economics and Bank of Montreal Professor of Money and Finance, University of Western Ontario. He has been a Visiting Professor at Hebrew University of Jerusalem, Université Laval, Massachusetts Institute of Technology, and Université de Paris. Among Professor Howitt's publications are "The Transactions Theory of the Demand for Money: A Reconsideration," *Journal of Political Economy* (1978, with Robert Clower), *Monetary Policy In Transition: A Study of Bank of Canada Policy 1982–85* (1986), and *The Keynesian Recovery and Other Essays* (1990).

SHINICHI ICHIMURA received his B.A. in Economics from Kyoto University in Japan and his Ph.D. in Economics from the Massachusetts Institute of Technology. He was Professor of Economics at Kyoto University from 1966 to 1988. In 1988, Professor Ichimura retired from Kyoto University and helped establish Osaka International University. He has become Vice-Chancellor, Director of the Institute of International Relations, and Professor of Economics at the university. He was Visiting Professor at the universities of Bonn, Johns Hopkins, Columbia, and Pennsylvania. Among his numerous publications are his editorship of *Challenge of Asian Developing Countries* (Tokyo: Asian Productivity Organization) and *Indonesian Economic Development* (Tokyo: Japan International Cooperation Agency).

RAYMOND E. LOMBRA is Professor of Economics at Pennsylvania State University. He formerly served as a Senior Staff Economist at the Board of Governors of the Federal Reserve and has been a Visiting Scholar at the International Monetary Fund. Author of four books and over sixty articles, many of which have appeared in such leading journals as the

Quarterly Review of Economics, Review of Economics and Statistics, Journal of Monetary Economics, and the *Journal of Money, Credit and Banking*, his work has focused on money demand, money supply, interest rates, various facets of the conduct of monetary policy, and, most recently, the effects of financial innovation and deregulation and the underlying determinants of changes in monetary regimes.

JACQUES MÉLITZ is a research economist at INSEE, the French National Statistical Institute in Paris, a CEPR Research Fellow, and Professor of Economics at Hautes Etudes Commerciales and the Institut des Etudes Politiques. He has consulted for the EC, the OECD, and the IMF, is a former managing editor of the *Annales de l'INSEE*, and has written numerous journal articles on money and international macroeconomics, apart from a book on *Primitive and Modern Money* and some jointly edited works, including *The French Economy*.

PATRICK MINFORD has been Edward Gonner Professor of Applied Economics, University of Liverpool since 1976. He was formerly Economic Assistant to Finance Director, Courtaulds Ltd.; Economic Adviser, Ministry of Finance, Malawi; Economic Adviser to HM Treasury's external division, serving with HM Treasury's Delegation, Washington D.C., 1973–74. Among Professor Minford's publications are *Substitution Effects: Speculation and Exchange Rate Stability, Unemployment: Cause and Cure, The Housing Morass*, and a textbook on rational expectations (with David Peel). Professor Minford contributed actively to the macroeconomic policy debate in the UK, including writing a regular column in *The Daily Telegraph*.

MANFRED J. M. NEUMANN is Professor of Economics and Director of the Institute of International Economics at the University of Bonn. He has been an Economist in the Research Department of the Deutsche Bundesbank and a Professor of Economics at the Free University of Berlin. He has published extensively in the field of monetary and international economics and serves on the editorial boards of several international journals. Since 1970 he has organized the annual Konstanz Seminar on Monetary Theory and Monetary Policy. Currently he is a Member of the EC-advising Macroeconomic Policy Group at the Centre for European Policy Studies (CEPS) and of the United States–German Consultative Group on International Monetary and Economic Policy.

ROBERT H. RASCHE is Professor of Economics, Michigan State University. He has been a Visiting Scholar at the Federal Reserve Bank of St. Louis, the Federal Reserve Bank of San Francisco, 1985, and the Institute for Monetary and Economic Studies, Bank of Japan. Among Professor

Rasche's publications are *Controlling the Growth of Monetary Aggregates* (1987), with J. Johannes, "Equilibrium Income and Interest Elasticities of the Demand for M1 in Japan," *Monetary and Economic Studies* (1990), and "Long-Run Income and Interest Elasticities of Money Demand in the United States," *Review of Economics and Statistics* (1991), with D. Hoffman.

DOMINICK SALVATORE is the Director of the Graduate Program and Professor of Economics at Fordham University in New York City. He is Co-Chairman of the New Academy of Sciences, consultant to the United Nations in New York and the Economic Policy Institute in Washington, and the author of the leading *International Economics Text*. Professor Salvatore has written and edited twenty-eight books, including *Protectionism and World Welfare* (1993), the *Handbook of National Economic Policy* (Greenwood Press, 1991) and the *Handbook of National Trade Policies* (Greenwood Press, 1992). Professor Salvatore has published over fifty articles in leading economics journals and presented his research at numerous universities in the United States and abroad. He is the co-editor of *The Journal of Policy Modeling* and *Open Economies Review* and is Associate Editor of the *American Economist*.

ANTHONY M. SANTOMERO is Richard K. Mellon Professor of Finance and Deputy Dean of The Wharton School of the University of Pennsylvania. He serves as Associate Editor of the *Journal of Money, Credit and Banking, Open Economies Review, Journal of Economics and Business*, and *Journal of Banking and Finance*. He has been active in research and publication in the areas of monetary theory, bank capital theory and regulation, bank financial management, financial restructuring, and risk management of financial institutions.

FRANCO SPINELLI is Professor of Economics at the University of Brescia in Italy. He holds degrees from the Catholic University of Milan and the University of Manchester. Professor Spinelli has taught at the Catholic University of Milan, at the University of Trento, and at the University of Western Ontario. He was also Economist in the research department at the International Monetary Fund and Advisor to the Minister of the Budget in Italy. He has written and edited several books, including *Storia Monetaria D'Italia* (1991) and *Macroeconomics and Macroeconomics Policy Issues* (1992). He has also written many articles on monetary policy.

PATRIZIO TIRELLI is Professor of Economics at the Catholic University of Milan. He holds degrees from the Catholic University of Milan and the University of Glasgow. He has published many articles, including "Target Zones and Wealth Effects: Current Account Implications of Alternative

Policy Assignments" in the *Open Economies Review* (no. 1, 1990) and "Simple Rules for Policy Coordination: An Evaluation of Alternative Proposals" in the *Journal of Policy Modeling* (no. 1, 1992).

JÜRGEN VON HAGEN obtained his Ph.D. in economics at the University in Bonn. Having taught at the Indiana University School of Business from 1987 to 1991, he currently holds a chair in economic policy at the University of Mannheim, Germany. Professor von Hagen was a Visiting Scholar at the Federal Reserve Bank of St. Louis, the Federal Reserve Board of Governors in Washington, and the International Monetary Fund. His research covers the areas of monetary policy, international macroeconomics and economic policy, and European economic and monetary integration. Besides two books and contributions to various books, he has published in leading professional journals, such as the *Journal of Public Economics, Public Choice*, the *Carnegie-Rochester Conference Series on Public Policy*, the *Journal of International Money and Finance*, the *European Economic Review*, the *International Economic Review, Open Economies Review*, and others.

ELMUS WICKER is Professor of Economics at Indiana University. He has written three books, including *Federal Reserve Monetary Policy, 1917–1933* (1966). Among his thirty articles are "Leaning Against the Wind: The Behavior of the Money Stock in Recession and Recovery," in *The Political Economy of American Monetary Policy*, edited by Thomas Mayer (1990); "Termination of Hyperinflation in the Dismembered Habsburg Monarchy," *American Economic Review* (1986); and "Colonial Monetary Standards Contrasted: Evidence from the Seven Years' War," *Journal of Economic History* (1985).